More Praise for *Children of the Stone*

"Eye-opening . . . Tolan's exhaustive research and journalistic attention to detail shine through every page of this sweeping chronicle." —*Publishers Weekly*

"A resolute, heart-rending story of real change and possibility in the Palestinian-Israeli impasse." —*Kirkus Reviews*

"Not only about music's ability to change an individual's life, this moving book also shows how it can serve to bridge the gap between two sides that remain at odds." —*Library Journal*, "Best Books of 2015"

"Moving and diligently told . . . Teasing out all the details of this story, from the granular facts of Ramzi's life to the complicated history of the region, Tolan is a scrupulous craftsman . . . careful enough to let us make up our own minds, never making the case for or against either 'side.'" —*Los Angeles Times*

"A complex report on the nuances of the conflict and the possible future of a Palestinian state—as explained through the attempts of Ramzi Aburedwan and others to play music . . . By following Ramzi's journey from stone-throwing child to accomplished musician, Tolan has helped to explain the struggle and pain of being Palestinian." —*St. Louis Dispatch*

"Somewhere amidst the separation barriers and the countless checkpoints, the refugee camps and the demolished homes, the fruitless negotiations and endless conflict, there is a people yearning for a life of dignity and normalcy. You won't see them on TV or in many newspapers. But you will find them in *Children of the Stone*." —Reza Aslan, author of *No God But God* and #1 *New York Times* bestseller *Zealot: The Life and Times of Jesus of Nazareth*

"*Children of the Stone* is alive with compassion, hope, and great inspiration. It is not necessary to believe in music's power to defeat evil in order to be enchanted by this wonderful story." —Tom Segev, Israeli historian and author of *One Palestine, Complete*

"Sandy Tolan's narrative artistry fuses the coming of age of a talented, ambitious, and fiercely dedicated musician with the story of Israel's occupation of the Palestinian territories conquered in 1967. A major contribution to our understanding of who they are and essential to a political resolution of the conflict." —Joel Benin, Donald J. McLachlan Professor of History, Professor of Middle East History, Stanford University

"Sandy Tolan has produced another gem on what is happening under the surface in Palestine. The book contains enthralling biographical trajectories of ordinary people fighting against the odds. Written in the style of investigative journalism, the book is riveting and uplifting, without skirting issues of contestation and controversy." — Salim Tamari, Professor of Sociology, Birzeit University (West Bank) and author of *Year of the Locust*

"A symphony of international locations, big ideas and human dramas . . . Tolan shows a novelist's preoccupation with empathy in portraying two conflicting worlds: music's timeless idealism and occupation's brutal realities. What emerges is a deeply moving parable of struggle and mastery—over an instrument, over painful injustice and ultimately over self." —*Newsweek*

"Tolan never purports to show the parallel narratives of Palestinians and Israelis, nor does he detail the Palestinian provocations that have inflamed the Israeli military. He simply attempts, and succeeds, at humanizing these musicians." —*The Seattle Times*

"Sandy Tolan sympathetically lays bare the stresses behind the monolithic WEDO façade, as musicians whose off-stage lives couldn't be more different—comfortable affluence for the Israelis, poverty and hardship for the Arabs—find themselves in entrenched opposition regarding a stance over the West Bank occupation." —*The Independent*

"Ambitious . . . Tolan excels as a dogged reporter, and his musical descriptions amplify his core themes." —*Truthdig*

"*Children of the Stone* is a nuanced, intelligent, in-depth discussion not only of Aburedwan's life, but of the many complex issues his work raises . . . I would highly recommend to those grappling with the thorny issue of the relationship between art and conflict . . . [It] is a rare, detailed and intimate portrait of a working-class Palestinian from the occupied West Bank, grappling with poverty and class." — *Electronic Intifada*

"Tremendous . . . [Children of the Stone] is clearly a labor of love, and it provides a priceless chronicle of a fascinating slice of Palestinian life through the unique lens of a boy with an uncomplicated love of music—and how such a love can become complicated by politics, personal relationships, and the violent, choking restrictions of occupation . . . One is left astonished that such sparks of creativity and beauty continually pop up like wildflowers against enormous odds. And that in itself feels like cause for some hope." —Mondoweiss

"Tolan's particular gift to his readers is his juxtaposition of the realization of Ramzi's impossible dream with the setbacks and defeats of the Palestinian people. You just never get to a place where you throw up your hands and say, 'All is lost,' because he keeps surprising us with Ramzi's ability to rebound from catastrophe. In this respect, Ramzi's story is both parable and possibility."—*Middle East Report*

CHILDREN OF THE STONE

CHILDREN OF THE STONE

The Power of Music in a Hard Land

SANDY TOLAN

BLOOMSBURY

NEW YORK · LONDON · OXFORD · NEW DELHI · SYDNEY

To Andrea

Bloomsbury USA
An imprint of Bloomsbury Publishing Plc

1385 Broadway
New York
NY 10018
USA

50 Bedford Square
London
WC1B 3DP
UK

www.bloomsbury.com

BLOOMSBURY and the Diana logo are trademarks of Bloomsbury Publishing Plc

First published 2015
This paperback edition published 2016

Lines from poem "Children Bearing Rocks" from *On Entering the Sea: The Erotic and Other Poetry of Nizar Qabbani*, published by Interlink Publishing Group, Inc.
Original Arabic copyright © Nizar Qabbani, 1980, 1986, 1995.
English translation copyright © Salma Jayyusi, 1996, 2013.
Reprinted by permission.

ISBN: HB: 978-1-60819-813-9 / PB: 978-1-63286-341-6
ePub: 978-1-60819-817-7

LIBRARY OF CONGRESS CATALOGING-IN-PUBLICATION DATA

Tolan, Sandy.
Children of the stone : the power of music in a hard land / Sandy Tolan.—
First U.S. edition.
pages cm
Includes bibliographical references and index.
ISBN 978-1-60819-813-9 (hardcover) – ISBN 978-1-63286-341-6 (paperback) –
ISBN 978-1-60819-817-7 (ebook)
1. Aburedwan, Ramzi. 2. Violists—West Bank—Biography. 3. Music—Social aspects—West Bank. 4. Music—Instruction and study—West Bank. 5. Refugees, Palestinian Arab—West Bank—Education. I. Title.
ML418.A287T65 2014
780.95695′309051—dc23
2014032528

2 4 6 8 10 9 7 5 3 1

Typeset by RefineCatch Limited, Bungay, Suffolk
Printed and bound in USA by Berryville Graphics Inc., Berryville, Virginia

To find out more about our authors and books visit www.bloomsbury.com. Here you will find extracts, author interviews, details of forthcoming events and the option to sign up for our newsletters.

Bloomsbury books may be purchased for business or promotional use. For information on bulk purchases please contact Macmillan Corporate and Premium Sales Department

at specialmarkets@macmillan.com.

With mere rocks in their hands,
they stun the world
and come to us like good tidings.
Bursting with love and anger,
they defy, and topple,
while we remain a herd of polar bears
bundled against weather
      —NIZAR QABBANI, "CHILDREN BEARING ROCKS"

CONTENTS

Note to Readers

THIS IS A WORK of nonfiction. As such there are no imagined conversations or composite characters. Everything in this book is the result of interviews, archival research, news accounts, and primary and secondary sources. All facts in the book have been subject to rigorous fact-checking, including verification with the dozens of people interviewed in the course of the reporting.

That said, much of the book relies on the reflections of people who were in places where neither I nor any other journalist was present as witness. Thus, of course, not every detail can be independently verified, in particular old and sometimes selective memories that describe small details, or unrecorded conversations. However, I have made significant efforts to corroborate the stories captured for this book through multiple accounts. This is the case in particular for incidents that may be especially difficult for readers, such as the circumstances surrounding the death of a child in a refugee camp during the first Palestinian intifada. In such cases I relied on a combination of the available record—books, newspaper and magazine articles, scholarly papers, human rights reports, United Nations records, and eyewitness accounts—to build a multiple-sourced narrative.

This book tells the story of Palestinian children learning and playing music in a war zone. It is therefore inherently about one people's tragedies, dreams, artistic triumphs, struggle against a military occupation, and aspirations for freedom, and for an ordinary life. Readers should not expect the traditional journalistic approach—that is, the parallel narratives of Palestinians and Israelis. Rather, the story is told largely through the eyes and experiences of a remarkable group of children and of the visionary

Palestinian musician at the heart of this book. Still, in all of the stories the book conveys, and especially in the sections providing historical context, I have tried my best to apply my own personal and professional journalistic standards of rigor, accuracy, and fair-mindedness.

For the most part the story is told chronologically. In rare cases, for ease of reading, I have juxtaposed events that may not have happened one right after the other. In those instances I have noted this in the source notes.

The bulk of the research and reporting took place from 2009 to 2014 and grew out of a feature story I produced for National Public Radio in 1998. For more details, see the acknowledgments and source notes.

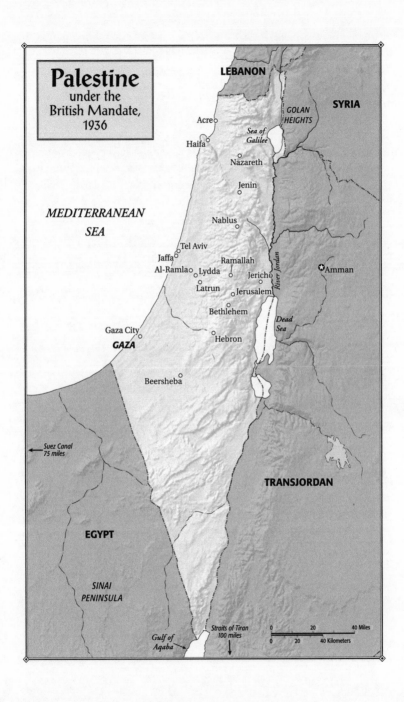

Palestine
under the
British Mandate,
1936

LEBANON

SYRIA

Acre

*GOLAN
HEIGHTS*

Haifa

*Sea of
Galilee*

Nazareth

Jenin

*MEDITERRANEAN
SEA*

Nablus

Tel Aviv

Jaffa

Ramallah

Al-Ramla

Lydda

Jericho

River Jordan

⭑ Amman

Latrun

Jerusalem

Bethlehem

*Dead
Sea*

Gaza City

GAZA

Hebron

Beersheba

*Suez Canal
75 miles*

TRANSJORDAN

EGYPT

*SINAI
PENINSULA*

*Straits of Tiran
100 miles*

| 0 | 20 | 40 Miles |

| 0 | 20 | 40 Kilometers |

*Gulf of
Aqaba*

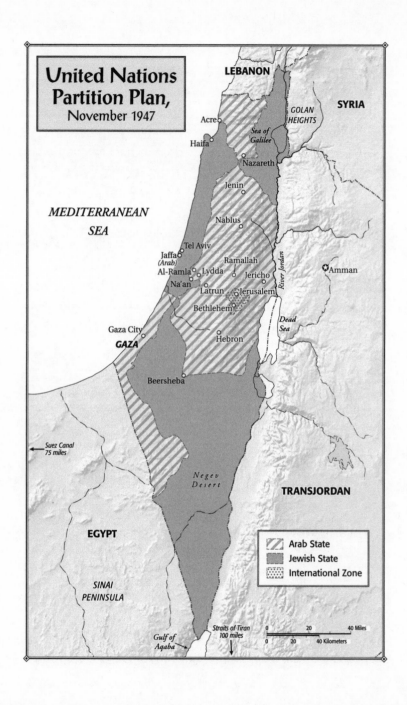

United Nations Partition Plan,
November 1947

LEBANON

SYRIA

Acre

GOLAN HEIGHTS

Haifa

Sea of Galilee

Nazareth

Jenin

MEDITERRANEAN SEA

Nablus

Tel Aviv

Jaffa *(Arab)*

Ramallah

Al-Ramla

Lydda

Jericho

Na'an

Latrun

Jerusalem

River Jordan

Amman

Bethlehem

Dead Sea

Gaza City

Hebron

GAZA

Beersheba

Suez Canal 75 miles

Negev Desert

TRANSJORDAN

EGYPT

SINAI PENINSULA

Arab State

Jewish State

International Zone

Straits of Tiran 100 miles

0   20   40 Miles

0   20   40 Kilometers

Gulf of Aqaba

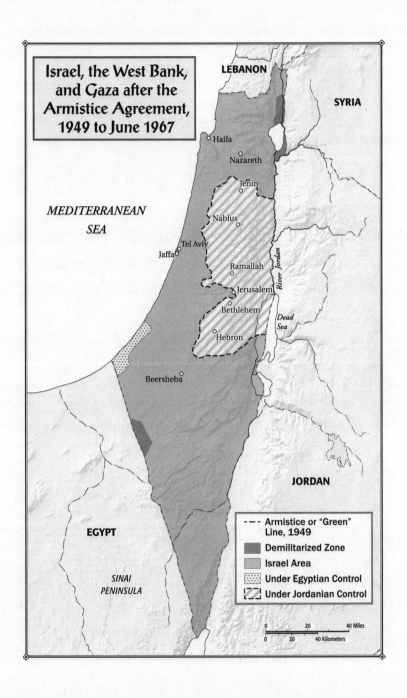

Israel, the West Bank, and Gaza after the Armistice Agreement, 1949 to June 1967

LEBANON

SYRIA

Haifa

Nazareth

MEDITERRANEAN SEA

Jenin

Nablus

Tel Aviv
Jaffa

Ramallah

Jerusalem

River Jordan

Bethlehem

Dead Sea

Hebron

Beersheba

JORDAN

EGYPT

SINAI PENINSULA

- - - Armistice or "Green" Line, 1949
Demilitarized Zone
Israel Area
Under Egyptian Control
Under Jordanian Control

0   20   40 Miles
0   20   40 Kilometers

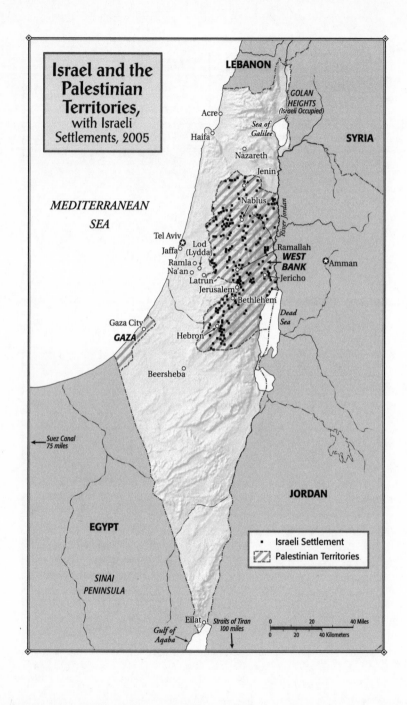

Israel and the Palestinian Territories, with Israeli Settlements, 2005

LEBANON

GOLAN HEIGHTS
(Israeli Occupied)

SYRIA

Acre

Sea of Galilee

Haifa

MEDITERRANEAN SEA

Nazareth

Jenin

Nablus

River Jordan

Tel Aviv

Jaffa
Lod (Lydda)
Ramla
Na'an
Latrun
Jerusalem
Bethlehem

Ramallah
WEST BANK
Jericho

Amman

Gaza City
GAZA

Hebron

Dead Sea

Beersheba

Suez Canal 75 miles

JORDAN

EGYPT

• Israeli Settlement
Palestinian Territories

SINAI PENINSULA

Eilat
Gulf of Aqaba
Straits of Tiran 100 miles

| 0 | 20 | 40 Miles |
| 0 | 20 | 40 Kilometers |

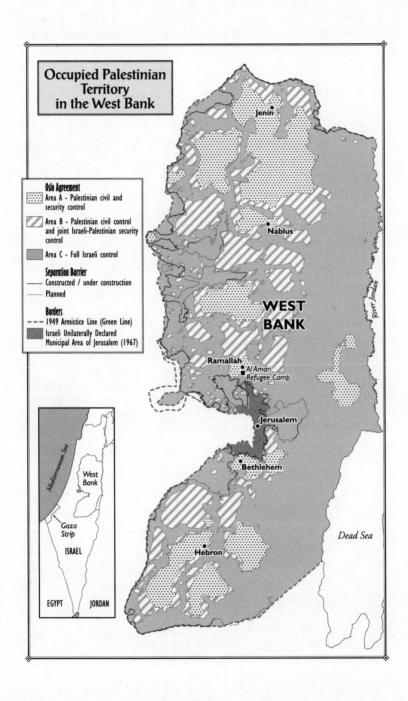

Occupied Palestinian Territory in the West Bank

Oslo Agreement

Area A - Palestinian civil and security control

Area B - Palestinian civil control and joint Israeli-Palestinian security control

Area C - Full Israeli control

Separation Barrier

Constructed / under construction

Planned

Borders

1949 Armistice Line (Green Line)

Israeli Unilaterally Declared Municipal Area of Jerusalem (1967)

Jenin

Nablus

WEST BANK

Ramallah

Al Amari Refugee Camp

Jerusalem

Bethlehem

Dead Sea

Hebron

River Jordan

Mediterranean Sea

West Bank

Gaza Strip

ISRAEL

EGYPT

JORDAN

INTRODUCTION

December 2009
Pronto Italian Restaurant, Ramallah, West Bank

IT WAS A CHANCE encounter, in December 2009, at an Italian restaurant in the West Bank. I was in Ramallah, working on a story on the dim chances for genuine Middle East peace. I was standing with two fellow journalists, looking for an open table, when I heard my name called out from across the restaurant.

"Sandy! Sandy!"

I looked at the bearded young man sitting at a corner table. He was beaming at me. I didn't recognize him. He pointed to himself: "Ramzi!"

I hadn't seen him in nearly a decade. Ramzi Hussein Aburedwan had been a child of war, one of thousands of Palestinian children who threw stones at Israeli forces during the six years of the intifada (1987–93; later known as the First Intifada), the uprising against Israel's occupation of the West Bank and Gaza. At age eight, Ramzi had been immortalized in one of the most iconic images of the era: a shaggy-haired David with fear and resolve in his eyes, unleashing a stone at an unseen Goliath.

By the time I met Ramzi in 1998, the intifada was over. He was a skinny, clean-shaven eighteen-year-old who lived with his grandparents in the Al Amari refugee camp on the outskirts of Ramallah. No longer was he sneaking through the camp, hurling rocks at soldiers and dashing from rooftop to rooftop to escape. Now, still relatively early in the Oslo peace process, Palestinians long in exile were returning to the West Bank to help build a state of their own. New cultural institutions were springing up, and

Ramzi suddenly had a chance to study a long-held passion: music. He had laid down his stones and, with the help of two middle-class Palestinian mentors, picked up a viola.

Within a year, posters around Ramallah showed little Ramzi, throwing the stone, alongside an image of Ramzi as a young man, pulling a bow across his viola strings. The poster announced the arrival of the new National Conservatory of Music. It looked like an advertisement for a newly independent Palestine.

In that winter of early 1998, I sought out Ramzi in the refugee camp where he lived with his family in their modest plaster-and-cinder-block home. I recorded his music and his memories of the intifada. He remained proud of his stone-throwing days, echoing the sentiments of many Palestinians who believed, then, that the stone would lead to their liberation. "I wish I could collect all of the stones I threw and frame them or put them on the wall or put them in my own museum," he told me then. "Because I was only a child. And all I had was a stone."

Ramzi's playing was crude and halting; at eighteen, he'd barely had a year of practice. More vivid were his memories of racing through the warrens of the camp during the intifada as one of the "children of the stones," as Abu Jihad, the assassinated Palestinian revolutionary, called Ramzi's generation. Most striking of all was the teenager's vision to transform the lives of children and show the world what his people could accomplish. "I want to see many conservatories opening up in all of Palestine, so that people can learn to play," Ramzi told me one cold gray afternoon, looking out his window at the narrow alley in the refugee camp. "And I want for children to understand that there's something called a viola and a violin. I want people to see that we Palestinians are capable. We are like everybody else in the world. We can do a lot. I hope one day I'll be a teacher and a professional viola player. I hope we'll have a big orchestra and we'll tour the world in the name of Palestine. I want to show the world that we are here, on the map."

Later that spring of 1998, around the time my story about Ramzi aired on National Public Radio, he landed a coveted scholarship to study the viola at a music conservatory in Angers, France.

We kept in contact for a couple of years. I followed his progress at Angers. I'd heard he'd started a traveling band, playing mostly Arabic music, while he continued to learn classical viola at the French conservatory.

Eventually, we lost touch—until that night at the restaurant in Ramallah. He joined us at the table.

"What are you doing back here, Ramzi? I thought you were still in France."

"No, I'm back."

"So what are you up to?"

"I've been opening up music schools all over Palestine." I got chills. This was precisely what Ramzi had said he wanted to do, twelve years earlier, when he was a teenager.

With the help of musicians and supporters from the United States, England, Germany, France, Italy, and the West Bank, Ramzi had created musical programs in ten locations, including three in refugee camps in Lebanon. He called his school, centered in Ramallah, Al Kamandjati—Arabic for "The Violinist." In five years, his vision of freedom through music had reached thousands of Palestinian kids.

"That was my dream," he told me at dinner. "I wanted to have many schools, everywhere, in all of Palestine. And now," he laughed, "I say, 'Wow, I'm crazy, what have I done?'"

The building of Al Kamandjati is the story of a child from a refugee camp who confronts an occupying army, gets an education, masters an instrument, dreams of something almost surely beyond his reach, and inspires scores of others to work with him to pursue it. Daniel Barenboim, the Israeli musician and director of the Berlin State Opera, was among them. He has performed with Ramzi over the years—at chamber music concerts at Al Kamandjati, and in the West-Eastern Divan Orchestra that Barenboim founded with the late Palestinian intellectual Edward Said. "Ramzi has transformed not only his life, his destiny, but that of many, many, many other people," Barenboim told me. "This is an extraordinary collection of children from all over Palestine that have all been inspired and opened to the beauty of life."

Not only children: An American violist quit the London Symphony Orchestra partly to help Ramzi build his dream. A French violinist took leave from his Spanish orchestra to help bring the music school to the refugee camps. A gifted soprano who trained at the English National Opera put off her career in the United Kingdom to live in Ramallah and give voice lessons to Palestinian children. A score of Palestinian teachers and professionals signed over deeds to properties, raised hundreds of thousands of foundation dollars, donated thousands of hours of labor, and cajoled local civic and religious leaders to make room for a new form of musical education in the villages and camps.

Here, I realized, was a story in sharp contrast to the darkness I'd been encountering that December across the occupied West Bank. In the South Hebron Hills, children told me of settlers who stoned them, or unleashed German shepherds, as the children made their long trek to school. Near Qalqilya, a few miles inland from the Mediterranean coast, I met with local Palestinian leaders whose community was surrounded on three sides by the twenty-five-foot-high separation barrier that Israel had declared necessary to protect Israeli citizens from suicide attacks. Yet the wall sliced deep into the West Bank, seizing nearly 10 percent of the land supposedly set aside for an independent Palestinian state. It cut off access to farmers' olive orchards, and in places, it blocked daylight. At the military check-point at Qalandia, just south of Ramallah, I watched as Palestinians passed beneath soldiers in machine-gun nests and through long corridors of metal bars, carrying precious permits that would allow them a rare trip to the holy city of Jerusalem. On the Palestinian side of the wall, I met with teenagers in the Balata and Qalandia refugee camps who had given up hope of ever living in a free country. Their leaders, they believed, had sold them out, while enriching themselves and fellow elites with funds siphoned off from the international community.

After my fifteen years of traveling to Terra Sancta, these stories underscored the bleak prospects for meaningful peace. But my reconnection with Ramzi sparked something else. Hundreds of young Palestinian musicians, inspired by Beethoven, Mozart, and indigenous Arabic music, were forging their own independent vision. As the military occupation intensified, shrinking the free space around them; as their own leadership failed time and again to deliver on their promise of a "viable and contiguous" state of Palestine, these young musicians kept playing. Through the music, in small but meaningful ways, Ramzi, his teachers, and his students were creating their own freedom. At times it was an interior freedom: In the midst of violence and chaos, music brought inner calm. At times it was external, an assertion of independence in direct resistance to the occupation itself: children standing before stunned soldiers, performing impromptu classical symphonies.

I first learned these details of Al Kamandjati over dinner that night, and then the next night at a Christmastime concert of baroque music in a church north of Ramallah. In the coming summers, on the road in the West Bank; at a Bethlehem music camp with dozens of international musicians; and in a sunny courtyard echoing with the sounds of violin, piano, bassoon, and timpani, I learned a new way to navigate through a landscape of checkpoints, refugee camps, olive groves, military night raids, and endless failed peace talks.

The story of Al Kamandjati is about music, violence, and a dream of liberation. It's about a growing movement of nonviolent resistance, new ways of thinking across the Israeli-Palestinian divide, the challenge of confronting religious extremism, the potential of music to protect and heal traumatized children, the struggle of one young musician to master an instrument, and, above all, the transformative power of music in a land of brutality, beauty, and confinement.

In *Children of the Stone* I hope to show what it's like for ordinary Palestinians to live under a military occupation. Despite the boatloads of ink and forests of newsprint devoted to the "Israeli-Palestinian conflict," precious little has examined day-to-day life under its most enduringly corrosive aspect: Israel's forty-seven-year occupation of the West Bank. To explore this I have focused not on "both sides" of the conflict as I did with my 2006 book, *The Lemon Tree*, but rather on the West Bank, on the "other" side of Israel's separation barrier, through the drama, grace, joy, and hardship of a group of children engaged in learning music.

These children, along with Ramzi and the teachers who work with him, suggest an alternative way of understanding the conflict and its resolution. Edward Said, the late Palestinian intellectual and Columbia University professor, was himself drawn to music as a way of exploring alternative solutions to one of the world's most impossible struggles. The story of his rare friendship with Barenboim, and the orchestra they founded, is told in this book, alongside Ramzi's.

"The role of the intellectual is to ask questions," Said once said. "To disturb people, to stir up reflection, to provoke, you might say, controversy and thought. The role of the intellectual is to challenge power by providing alternative models. And, as important, resources of hope. It's not our destiny to be refugees. It's not our destiny to be prisoners of war. It's not our destiny to be commandos. It's not our destiny to be an army of occupation.

"We have a choice."

*

At the dinner at Pronto, the Italian restaurant, as Ramzi told me the details of what he and his friends had accomplished, I kept grabbing his arm, leaning toward him, and exclaiming, "You *did* it, Ramzi! You did it! You did *exactly* what you said you would do!"

He smiled. "Come tomorrow. You must visit, and learn how we made this happen."

PRELUDE:
OVER THE WALL, TO PLAY
BEETHOVEN

Qalandia military checkpoint, between Ramallah and Jerusalem
Summer 2013

*F*IVE YOUNG MEN *stare through the windows of their bus, stalled at a military checkpoint known as Qalandia. Outside, an exhaust-choked border crossing divides Jerusalem from the West Bank city of Ramallah. Behind it stands a massive gray wall, seemingly impenetrable except by special permission. The men look out as drivers jockey for position, funneling into a single line before submitting for inspection. Vendors, mostly children, weave through the knots of vehicles, amid the plastic litter and chunks of broken concrete, selling kebab, tissue packets, pillows, bottles of water, and verses from the Qur'an.*

Soldiers enter the bus, M-16s on their shoulders. A young woman inspects documents. She orders twenty people off the bus, including the five young men. They will not be allowed to cross the checkpoint in relative dignity, unlike the foreigners who remain on the air-conditioned coach. Instead, they walk through the heat into a trash-strewn terminal and pass down a long narrow corridor framed by silver bars. It looks like a cattle chute on a western American ranch. At the end the men push through two eight-foot-high turnstiles known as iron maidens. A stray cat straddles a wall above them. KEEP THE TERMINAL CLEAN, *a sign instructs.*

The men crowd with dozens of others into a small holding area in front of a third floor-to-ceiling turnstile. Every few minutes a red light turns green, a click sounds, and three or four more people pass through the iron maiden to place their possessions on a conveyor belt. They hold up their permits to a dull green bulletproof window and look through the smoky glass, waiting. On the other side, bored-looking soldiers glance up, inspect the documents, and, one by one, wave the permit-holders through.

All but the five young men. "You do not have proper permits," they are told.

Denied the Holy City, the men click their way backward through the gates, along the metal chute, and into the maze of cars and vendors, uncertain what to do next. It is urgent that they reunite with the others on the bus, so they can all reach Jerusalem.

"Hey, boys," calls an unshaven man sitting on a stool inside a crude metal shed. The man takes a drag of his cigarette. He glances at the glass tumbler in his hand and the dregs of his Turkish coffee. The young men look behind him, toward the twenty-five-foot-high wall. They approach. Two of them carry long felt bags; another holds a blue canvas case.

The unshaven man takes a last drag of his cigarette, flicks it in the dirt, and looks up. "Ya, shabab," he says, exhaling a long column of smoke. He smiles. "You boys need to get to Jerusalem?"

"Yes," says the oldest of the five young men. He appears to be in his thirties: slim, of medium height, with a scraggly beard, a receding line of curly black hair, and bags under his eyes. His eyes are brown and unblinking, narrowed with intent. "It's very important."

The man sets down his glass, stands up, and regards the men in front of him. Except for the older one, they look a little nervous.

"For two hundred fifty shekels, I will get you to the middle of Jerusalem," he boasts. "Fifty shekels each." About fourteen dollars per man.

"Fine," says the oldest of the five, who appears to be their leader. "What do we do?"

The man looks over his shoulder. "Jamal," he says. "Get these guys to Jerusalem."

They climb into a battered white van. The door slides shut and the driver begins working two phones, making arrangements. He drives with his forearms as the van rattles down a potholed access road. He turns to the men in the van: "Give me the money." They haggle over price, finally agreeing on eleven dollars each. "But you have to pay now," the driver says. He gives them his phone number and tells them to call once they reach Jerusalem. Apparently he wants satisfied customers.

A short time later the driver pulls over and steps into a tall garage made of corrugated metal. He returns with a ladder, extends it to its full length, and rests it against the top of the wall. He scales the ladder and sits beside it at the top. "Come," he commands.

The men approach the base of the wall and look up, shifting their burdens from one shoulder to another.

They are classical musicians: a violinist, a violist, a double bass player, and two timpanists. Their felt bags contain sticks for concert timpani. The blue canvas case holds a violin. The rest of their orchestra is on the bus, rolling south toward Jerusalem. In four hours, they are due to play Beethoven's Fourth Symphony in the Old City, at a French church built during Crusader times. Hundreds are expected to attend. If these five players don't make it, the orchestra's leader has warned, they will cancel the concert. It is impossible, after all, to play Beethoven's Fourth without the timpani.

The musicians gaze to the top of the wall, where loops of razor wire present a dangerous obstacle. With a sweep of his arm, the smuggler brushes the loops aside, like a curtain. The wire has already been cut. This is a regular crossing point.

The smuggler pulls a long knotted rope from a plastic bag, loops it around a metal post at the top of the wall, and drops it to the other side.

"Ta'al, ta'al," he repeats. "Come."

The leader, who plays the viola, goes first. He mounts the ladder rapidly, sits atop the wall, pivots his legs, grabs the rope, and slowly slides down. He tries to use the knots as footholds, but they are small and his feet keep slipping off.

A vehicle approaches on the narrow access road. The violist freezes about halfway down the rope.

"Who's in that truck?" he shouts, craning his neck upward. "Are those soldiers?"

If they are, the violist will be arrested or, possibly, shot. It would not only mean he won't get to Jerusalem for the Beethoven concert that evening. It could signal the end of everything he has been building for years.

First Movement:

STONE

One

PUSHCART

January 1985
Ramallah

A LIGHT RAIN FELL as the five-year-old boy looked up from the bottom of his uncle's three-wheeled vegetable cart. From the street, no one could see him. He was hidden, curled in the shape of a U, breathing in the faint smell of cucumber and tomato. In the semidarkness, the shaggy-haired boy gazed down at his hands, then up through the slats of the wooden lid to bands of gray sky. He could hear his uncle's footsteps behind him; he could feel the uneven pavement as the pushcart bumped along. He listened to the whir of the scooters and the sputter of passing trucks as his uncle pushed him through the wet, hissing streets. Neither man nor boy spoke a word.

The boy in the vegetable cart had just left the courtroom, where his mother sat before a judge. His father was in prison, hauled away by the occupation authorities. In a drunken rage, he had beaten the boy's mother and set fire to the home where she slept. The boy remembered waking to the fire, and the sound of his father screaming at his mother in the middle of the night. Two years later, the mother, twenty years old, fearful of her husband's drinking and violence, had come to ask the judge for a divorce.

As a grown man twenty-seven years later, Ramzi Aburedwan did not remember how he had learned about the divorce proceeding that day, nor why he had felt compelled to convince his uncle to take him to the court.

"Do you wish to keep your children?" the little boy had heard the judge ask his mother. She had been married at sixteen; six years later, she was the mother of two boys and two girls. Ramzi was the oldest.

The mother hoped to bring her children to live with her parents. But her father would not allow it.

"No," Ramzi heard his mother say to the judge. "I cannot keep them."

Ramzi's grandfather, the father of Ramzi's father, had pleaded with the mother. "If you stay with them, I will give you half of my salary." The older man lived in a refugee camp and earned his living by sweeping the streets of the municipality. "This way you will have enough to raise up your family. And you will live near us. I will pay for your house."

But for the mother, this seemed impossible. How could she agree to live with her children in such close proximity to her estranged husband? His beatings had sent her to the hospital many times. After a divorce, she feared, he would be more violent.

"God will give me others, *ensh'allah*," she told the judge. God willing.

The mother was heartbroken, but the son did not know this. He only heard her words.

The pushcart rolled on, bouncing through ruts and puddles. The boy looked up into strips of wet sky. His uncle pushed him forward, toward somewhere.

Where are we going? he wondered. *What will happen?*

Two

GRANDFATHER

Summer 1985
Al Amari refugee camp, near Ramallah, West Bank

RAMZI PRETENDED TO sleep as his grandfather lifted the covers and rose from bed. It was five A.M. He lay motionless, slowly opening his eyes. Grandfather stood in the half light, sifting through a mound of discarded clothes. In a corner stood large sacks of donated flour, rice, and sugar, and a giant tin of cooking oil.

Ramzi had been delivered in his uncle's vegetable cart on a rainy day a few months earlier. His younger brother, Rami, and two younger sisters, Rana and Rula, had come the same day. Their arrival nearly doubled the size of the household. Ramzi, by now six years old, shared the bed with his grandfather Mohammad, in the makeshift addition at the top of a winding metal staircase. Uncle Jamal snoozed beside them on a mattress on the floor. The others slept downstairs, three to a room.

Ramzi watched his grandfather pick through the pile of old clothes he'd salvaged from the nearby homes of the better-off. He chose a pair of tan pants and his favorite khaki shirt with the double breast pockets. Sido (pronounced SEE-doe, Arabic for "Grandpa") was squat and broad-shouldered, his hands and face lined with age and browned from working in the sun. He laced his work boots, set his black skullcap on his head, and lumbered down the stairs toward the tiny kitchen. Grandmother Jamila would be there, at the camping stove, preparing Sido's dark tea, extra sweet, and his flatbread with hard yellow cheese.

When Sido slept beside him, Ramzi felt safe and protected: a small crescent curled inside a larger one. When he was alone, memories rushed in.

The six-year-old sat up in bed, alert. He listened for the sound of the latch on the front door. Glancing at his sleeping uncle, he crept from the bed, pulled on his jeans and sneakers, and tiptoed down the stairs. Twice before, Ramzi had tried to follow Sido to work; each time, Grandmother had caught him and hauled him back inside.

As quietly as he could, Ramzi lifted the latch and slipped into the narrow alley of the camp.

In the pale light, the boy looked at the stone bench where Grandfather liked to sit on warm summer nights, telling harvest stories from his family's village on the coastal plain. Decades earlier, they had lived as peasant farmers in Na'ani, near the sea. *Now would be the time for the oranges,* Sido Mohammad would tell Ramzi. *Now, for the* simsim, *the sesame. How soft the earth was, how smooth, like this,* and he'd reach out his flattened palm. *See? Flawless. No matter how far you gazed, you could not lay your eyes on a stone.* All the family's modest wealth was planted there.

At the end of the block Ramzi's grandfather moved steadily away, his long stride marked by a slight limp. Ramzi set off in quiet pursuit. He ran along a line of crudely made row houses, mortar oozing out from their layers like frosting on a hastily made cake. He moved down the uneven concrete path strewn with refuse and broken curbstones and past small groceries battened tight with gray steel shutters. He kept his gaze forward, sure to maintain a safe distance, ready to dart into a doorway should his grandfather turn around.

Ramzi was running through a landscape born in collective trauma and inhabited by exiles who longed to go home. Al Amari refugee camp had been built by the Red Cross as temporary shelter in the aftermath of mass expulsions by the army of Israel during the war of 1948.

The previous year, Britain, which had ruled the Holy Land for nearly three decades, had announced its intention to quit Palestine. Then in November 1947, the newly formed United Nations voted to divide the land into two sovereign states, one for the Arabs and one for the Jews. Jews, mostly recent migrants from Europe, made up one third of Palestine's population and owned about 7 percent of the land, or roughly one-fifth of the cultivable land, but their state was to receive 55 percent of Palestine. The majority of indigenous Arabs rejected the partition plan as unjust and demanded a single state for Arabs and Jews. They did not want to be separated, or to live as a minority in a Jewish state. Yet the Arabs of Palestine were not ready to confront the new state of Israel. Thousands had been killed in an uprising against British rule, and the leadership was deeply divided over how to respond to the large influx of Jews into Palestine from Europe. The U.N. vote prompted attacks, bombings, and reprisals between the Arab and Jewish sides. In April 1948, a massacre by Jewish militias in the Palestinian village of Deir Yassin sent waves of fear throughout Arab Palestine, causing thousands of villagers to flee. By May, when full-scale war broke out, the Arabs of Palestine were weak and unprepared. Neighboring Arab states sent troops, but their numbers were limited, and their commitment to an independent Palestine was questionable at best. By mid-July, the determined army of Israel was on the march in the coastal plain of Palestine, and hundreds of thousands of Palestinian Arabs had fled or been driven out of their homes.

For the victors, it was a war of independence following the murder of six million Jews in the genocide in Europe; they believed they were returning home after two millennia of exile. For the vanquished, it was the Nakba, the Catastrophe, when three quarters of a million Palestinians fled or were driven into their own exile. Of those, one hundred thousand flooded Ramallah, overwhelming the once-sleepy Christian hill town, crowding into schools and gymnasiums or sleeping in olive groves, barnyards, or caves and on the open ground along the roadsides. Two thousand refugees, mostly poor villagers, took shelter in Al Amari, the hastily erected tent city on the outskirts of Ramallah. Many of the wealthier Arabs had managed to escape earlier by car and bus; some would join the global Palestinian diaspora, in Jordan, Egypt, Lebanon, and, later, London and America.

Thirty-seven years later, where the tents had stood, Ramzi secretly followed his grandfather down a narrow warren, past an unbroken row of dwellings made from cinder block, plaster, and corrugated tin. He trotted past his friend Zakaria's house, past the house of his cousin Adli next door, and along a brick wall near where Umm Mohammad (the mother of Ramzi's friend Mohammad) lived. Rusted rebar jutted from unfinished second-floor additions. The United Nations now ran the camp, providing the refugees with food, education, and housing. Since 1948, the camp had doubled in size, to four thousand people on the same twenty-five acres. Yet nothing felt permanent. Like his neighbors in Al Amari, Ramzi, having heard Sido's stories of a lost homeland, dreamed constantly of return—in his case, to a place he had never seen. Nor could he ever see it, at least as it had been. After the Nakba, Na'ani, like more than four hundred other Palestinian villages, had been eliminated by Israel, specifically so that the refugees could not return. Still, Palestinians in camps across the Middle East, and in the global diaspora, waited for their chance to go home.

Half-running, half-walking, Ramzi managed to close the gap. Sido Mohammad cut left, then right; Ramzi shadowed him, moving down alleys so narrow a grown man could touch the plaster walls on either side. Each year, amid the fading prospects of return, families added more rooms; the walls pressed in farther and blocked out more of the sky. In these narrow lanes noontime felt like dusk. Ramzi glanced down, careful to avoid the shallow open trenches carved into the middle of the concrete paths and running with wastewater.

Sido reached the main road to Jerusalem. It was quiet. He walked on, traversing the highway without looking back.

Ramzi waited, standing at the wide road he was forbidden to cross. He looked both ways, then dashed to the other side.

Soon, Sido reached his destination near the city hall of the village of Al Bireh, the town that bordered Ramallah. His grandson peered around the corner of the stone building. From the courtyard, in front of a pair of latched metal doors, Sido rolled out a pushcart. He took a black plastic garbage can and slipped it inside the cart's steel frame. A second can slid in beside the first one. Into the space remaining, Sido stuffed a long push broom, a shorter broom, and a shovel.

Ramzi popped out from behind the wall. "Ya, Sidi!" he announced. "Hello my Grandfather!"

"Ya walad!" came Mohammad's stunned response. "Hey, boy, what are you doing here?"

"I know the way," the six-year-old said brightly. "Don't worry! I want to stay with you."

Sido looked at Ramzi with a mixture of amazement and annoyance. He could not send his grandson back across the main road by himself, and he didn't have time to walk him home. For today only, he would let Ramzi tag along.

As Sido hauled bags of garbage from city hall to dumpster Ramzi took the short broom, sweeping meticulously along a stretch of pavement. He wanted to prove himself.

After a while they switched. Sido pushed his long broom down the sidewalk. Ramzi dragged an empty garbage can behind him up several flights of stairs to the top floor of a city office building. One by one, he raised the wastebaskets above his head and dumped their contents into the big black can. The can was nearly as tall as he was, and it became ever heavier as he thumped it down the steps and back out to the road. Grandfather arrived with the cart, and together they rolled it to the green dumpster on the corner.

"Let me go with you every day," Ramzi urged his grandpa when the work was finished. "*See*-doe. Let me help you." Ramzi smiled. His eyes pleaded. Sido relented.

* * *

"Every day is a new day, a new discovery," Ramzi's grandfather told him one morning as they crossed the Jerusalem road. They moved with purpose. Despite Sido's limp, the result of a broken leg suffered during a rare winter blizzard, the skinny boy had to run to keep up with him. Sido warned Ramzi to watch for the speeding cars. If he wasn't careful, he could be run over.

Ramzi watched his grandfather sweep up plastic bags, paper scraps, and cigarette butts in the path of his broom, leaving clean streets and sidewalks in his wake. The job was in garbage, but Sido took his work seriously, as if it were holy.

As they scoured the streets, Ramzi and his grandfather came across curbside boxes filled with items the wealthy and middle-class Palestinian owners no longer wanted. These families lived behind black wrought-iron gates in houses made of cream-colored stone. Olive trees graced their gardens. They were the old families of Al Bireh and Ramallah, many of them Christian, who had lived here long before the towns were transformed by the tens of thousands of refugees of the Nakba. Some of them looked down on the refugee families, the ex-villagers whose poverty and overwhelming numbers had become a source of resentment.

Ramzi and Sido sifted through each box, carrying home pants, shirts, and coats to wear or to sew and resell in the camp. They collected cups, glasses, and a set of champagne flutes for the cupboard. For the interior walls, they took a framed aerial photo of Mecca during the Hajj pilgrimage, a small painting of the Virgin Mary, and the prayer, "God Bless Our Home," embroidered in English. Sido didn't understand the words; he liked the way it looked.

Once Sido found an abandoned teddy bear. Ramzi pulled the plastic ring on its back and out came the melody from Beethoven's "Ode to Joy," part of the Ninth Symphony. Ramzi carried the stuffed animal upstairs and placed it on a shelf above the bed. At night he would reach for the toy, pulling the string again and again as his grandfather slept. Finally he would grow tired and sleep, but often, at midnight, a neighbor's confused rooster hopped to the wall a few feet away and began crowing. Ramzi would awaken to find Sido sleeping through it all.

In the evenings, at suppertime, Sido turned on the big wooden radio atop the potbellied refrigerator, twisting the large knob past the static of Syrian and Jordanian stations, and the nearer sounds of Hebrew, to Israel's Arabic–language broadcasts of Umm Kulthum. The Egyptian "Star of the East," with her haunting, undulating voice accompanied by a full classical Arab orchestra, was, next to the late Egyptian president Gamal Abdel Nasser, the most beloved figure in the Arab world. Even a decade after her death, Umm Kulthum's music, and the Arabic poetry she sang, could be heard in nearly every Palestinian household.

The Egyptian diva sang of two intoxicated lovers; the orchestra throbbed behind her, playing every note in unison. Grandmother Jamila, in her embroidered Palestinian housedress, spread a cover on the floor and laid out dinner: small plates of hummus, smoked eggplant, *ful mudammas* (warm fava beans), Arabic salad, hard-boiled egg, and sliced liver. The family sat cross-legged, chatting and listening as Umm Kulthum's husky, resonant voice sailed over the orchestra. She sang of shattered euphoria, of dreams of slumber ruined by wakefulness, of wounds replacing other wounds; and of how everything was fated: Misfortune was always delivered by someone else's hand, never by one's own. Ramzi listened to Umm Kulthum's voice booming over the sound of the strings. He scooped up the salads with soft round bread made from dough Grandmother prepared with rationed U.N. flour.

After dinner Ramzi often sought refuge in his grandmother's lap. He closed his eyes as Jamila's warm hands moved through his black curls. She wore a white scarf draped loosely over her long hair, and as she stroked Ramzi's head she and Sido told him stories of Na'ani, the beauty of old Palestine, and the Nakba. Ramzi looked up at the intricate red, green, and yellow stitching on his grandmother's embroidered bodice. In the past the urban elite of Palestine had looked down on this traditional dress as fit only for the *fellahin*, or Palestinian peasants; now, in exile, it was popular across Palestine and the diaspora as a symbol of the homeland, with the village at its center.

*   *   *

In 1948, Ramzi's grandparents had fled the village of Na'ani, on the coastal plain southeast of Jaffa and Tel Aviv, after a trusted Jewish neighbor from a nearby kibbutz rode into the village on horseback, shouting, "The Jewish army is coming! You must leave or you will all be killed!" They knew the man as Khawaja Shlomo (Mr. Foreigner Shlomo); villagers were on friendly terms with him and had little reason to think he was lying. They fled the village. For safekeeping, Sido Mohammad buried boxes of valuables in the ground. They traveled north a few miles to the city of Ramle, taking with them little besides Jamila's gold, mostly in the form of jewelry; they assumed they would be returning within a few days.

Instead, in July 1948, Israeli soldiers conquered Ramle and trucked Mohammad and hundreds of other men to an internment camp. Jamila was bused to the front lines and, with thousands of others, ordered to march into the hills, toward Ramallah, in the one-hundred-degree heat of mid-July. "Yallah Abdullah! Yallah Ramallah!" soldiers shouted in crude Arabic, taunting the refugees with the name of Jordan's king, whose forces were locked in battle with Israel. "Go to Abdullah! Go to Ramallah!"

For miles Jamila and her fellow exiles—fifty thousand of them from Ramle, Lydda, and their surrounding villages—stumbled through rocky terrain in the heat, thirsty and unsure of the way to Ramallah. The sun, Jamila recounted, was burning her baby; she feared that if she didn't find him water, Hasan would die in her arms.

They came upon an abandoned well with a broken rope. Jamila removed her headscarf, lowered it into the black standing water, and squeezed drops of moisture between baby Hasan's lips.

Mother and child managed to reach Ramallah the next day, eventually coming to Al Amari, where they began their life in exile. Jamila was anxious for news of Mohammad, and perhaps of the homecoming to Na'ani. At the end of 1948, United Nations Resolution 194 declared that refugees from the Nakba who were ready to "live at peace with their neighbors" should be allowed to return home. Israel rejected the resolution, and no world power was willing to enforce it—in part because it had been passed by the U.N. General Assembly and not by the Security Council.

In May 1949, Israel and the warring Arab states signed an armistice, marked by a cartographer's pen delineating the new boundaries in green ink. The "Green Line" showed Israel now in control of 78 percent of the territory of old Palestine. Of the 22 percent that remained, Egypt's King Farouq would oversee Gaza, and Jordan's Abdullah the territory on the West Bank of the River Jordan, a kidney-shaped piece of land wedged between Israel and his desert kingdom. The parties were still technically in a state of war, but the fighting, for now, had ended.

After the armistice Mohammad was released from the internment camp. He made his way to Ramallah and then to Al Amari, where, amid the sea of canvas tents, he found his wife and son.

For the refugees, return was all that mattered. As hope faded, over the months and then years, for implementation of the U.N. resolution, they turned to a charismatic new Arab leader, Egypt's Gamel Abdel Nasser, the revolutionary colonel who had toppled King Farouq in July 1952. Reviled in the West and Israel, Nasser was beloved across the Arab world, by far its most popular figure. By the mid-1960s, Mohammad and Jamila believed they would be delivered home to Na'ani on the backs of Nasser's armies. But the Arabs' humiliating defeat in the Six Day War in 1967 instead forced Syria from the Golan Heights, Egypt from Gaza and the Sinai Peninsula, and Jordan from East Jerusalem and the West Bank. Beginning in June 1967, Israel's military forces occupied all those lands, and to the anger of Palestinians and international observers, Israel annexed East Jerusalem, declaring it united with West Jerusalem and part of Israel's "eternal capital." Now refugees from across old Palestine confronted not only the dream of return, but the reality of military occupation.

After the 1967 war, Palestinians believed their only way to reclaim Palestine was to return to "armed struggle" against Israel. This ranged from failed cross-border attacks on Israeli infrastructure, to spectacular and some-times deadly hijackings of commercial airliners in European capitals, to the murder of eleven members of Israel's Olympic team at the 1972 Olympic Games in Munich, to a machine-gun attack on Christian pilgrims in Israel's airport, coordinated with the Japanese Red Army, which killed twenty-five people that same year. The hijackings and attacks against civilians were an attempt by militant factions to capture the world's attention and put the issue of Palestinian freedom on the map. Internally, other factions disagreed with this strategy, believing the only thing Palestinians were winning was a reputation as terrorists. Israel sent teams of spies into neighboring countries, or mailed letter bombs disguised as books and presents, to assassinate suspected Palestinian terrorists. Infantry teams raided Palestinian towns and refugee camps, arresting hundreds of youths and suppressing any efforts to assert Palestinian self-determination. The idea of an independent Palestinian state was seen by Israel as an existential threat.

Sido Mohammad was recruited by a young rebel leader named Yasser Arafat, cofounder of Fatah, one of the factions that formed the Palestine Liberation Organization, for his would-be army of freedom fighters. In late June 1967, under the cover of night, Arafat and a small band of rebels-in-exile crossed the River Jordan and snuck into the occupied West Bank. Kalashnikovs and old rifles slung over their shoulders, their heavy rucksacks stuffed with grenades, land mines, and explosive charges, they crossed beneath the date palms of the Jordan Valley, rode past Bedouin sheep camps on the road to Jerusalem, and continued on into the mountains of the West Bank, dotted with the pale green of terraced olive groves. The young men aimed to spark an armed insurrection against Israel from the Occupied Territories. The future PLO leader slept in caves, one step ahead of Israeli intelligence. To escape capture, he dressed as a shepherd, even as an old woman; once, he crawled through a back window as soldiers stormed the front door. Another time, his pursuers tracked him to a cave, to find only a coffeepot steaming on the fire. To humiliated Palestinians, Arafat's mythical, shadowy presence was electrifying. But weeks of secret meetings in the towns and villages of occupied Palestine did not foment a rebellion against Israel. Eventually Arafat retreated to Jordan, where he repeated his pledge of armed struggle to liberate all of historic Palestine.

For his part, Sido was not captured by the revolutionary fervor. For one thing, he wasn't a warrior. He had lost his own father in the Arab Rebellion of 1936–39 against the British, and he didn't have a taste for fighting. "My aim was terrible," he told Ramzi many years later. To Arafat he had said, "Give me a job other than shooting." Sido's days with the resistance were short-lived. He returned to the refugee camp, his lands occupied and the dream of return ever more distant.

*   *   *

"After stealing our land, they're following us here again," Sido told his grandson angrily as they swept the sidewalk near the municipality. It was 1986. Ramzi had just turned seven. Sido pointed to a hill he knew as Jabal al-Tawil, once a hiking area for summer visitors from the Gulf. There they could see the new houses of a Jewish settlement. Five years earlier, when Ramzi was two years old, Jewish nationalists, backed by Minister of Defense Ariel Sharon, had seized the land, planted it with trailers for temporary housing, and renamed it Psagot. The settlement project was driven increasingly by messianic Jews who believed it was their mission to claim all of the land in Judea and Samaria, as they called the West Bank. Their champion and strategic visionary was Sharon, the political hardliner who had boasted, in the days of the first settlements, that he would turn the West Bank into a "pastrami sandwich."

"We'll insert a strip of Jewish settlement in between the Palestinians," Sharon told a British journalist in 1973. "And then another strip of Jewish settlement, right across the West Bank, so that in twenty-five years' time, neither the United Nations, nor the United States, nobody, will be able to tear it apart." By the mid-1980s, red-roofed buildings towered over Ramallah and Al Bireh from the new settlement, and from Beit El, just north. Outside of Israel settlements were universally considered a violation of international law, in particular Article 49 of the Fourth Geneva Convention, which states, "The Occupying Power shall not deport or transfer parts of its own civilian population into the territory it occupies."

Originally Israeli authorities had declared that their occupation would be benign and "inconspicuous," with few displays of Israeli flags and military patrols. As settlements began springing up, this strategy was abandoned. When Palestinians protested the settlements and demanded self-rule, the occupation grew more violent. The military imposed curfews and closures. When the protests persisted, soldiers fired live ammunition into crowds of demonstrators. And as Jewish settlers continued moving onto Palestinian land in the West Bank, some Palestinians began to fight back. Others, like Ramzi's grandfather, just grew more anxious.

Sido Mohammad, long preoccupied with the dream of return, now worried about holding on to what his family still had. No place, he told Ramzi, was safe from the settlers and the government that backed them.

He refused to invest Jamila's gold, saved since Ottoman times, in land outside the refugee camp. He even worried about expulsion from the camp itself. The Israelis, Sido warned his family, could come at anytime to take their homes again. "The occupation is following us everywhere we go," he told his grandson. As the settlers drove through Ramallah, young men from the refugee camp began pelting their cars with rocks. Such attacks often provoked a more violent response: One afternoon masked settlers opened fire on a crowded bus near Ramallah. Six Palestinians were wounded, and Sido grew more concerned about his family's safety.

Ramzi's father, Hussein Aburedwan, had spent time in jail for beating Ramzi's mother, and for his drunken attempt to set fire to her parents' home, where she and the children had taken refuge one evening. Now he had been released and was back in Al Amari. He moved in with Sido, Jamila, Ramzi, and the family. To make a living, he took on odd jobs. He rode a van to Jerusalem, half an hour south, where he washed dishes at Jewish restaurants and swept the stairwells of the Hebrew University. At night he drank.

In a rare photo from the time, Hussein poses on a stool covered by a sheepskin. He wears tight jeans and a tight Adidas T-shirt. His right arm sports a tattoo; his fist is clenched on his thigh as he plants a clean white sneaker on a red plastic chair. The bangs covering his forehead make him look vaguely like a British rock star of the early 1960s. Behind him, the studio photographer has unfurled an outdoor backdrop, perhaps from a village: Hussein appears to be sitting on a rock outcropping adorned with pink flowers. His thin lips form a tight line. Ramzi's father is unsmiling; his eyes are hard.

Ramzi recalls his father as remote. His sisters, Rana and Rula, two and three years old at the time, could snap him out of his melancholy, but with Ramzi and Rami, Hussein was unable to show his feelings. Ramzi had been born when his father was only nineteen; his little brother had come a year later. Hussein didn't know how to be a father, Ramzi concluded later. In a home dominated by Sido, the younger man's presence seemed tentative. At night Ramzi's father slipped away to unnamed destinations, stumbling back into the house after everyone had gone to sleep. Other times he would bring his bottle of vodka and bag of pistachios into his room, listening to Arab pop stars on his cassette player until he passed out.

Despite the harsh circumstances, the joy of childhood was within reach in the alleys of the refugee camp. Ramzi took on the responsibility of teaching his younger siblings neighborhood games. They played soccer and hide-and-seek, and Ramzi introduced Rami to *shuhaf*, a game played with a ball and seven flat stones they retrieved from a local quarry. They played in the alleys in front of dark and narrow shops whose shelves were stuffed with toiletries, potato chips, small chocolates, and canned vegetables. Outside, men sat on plastic chairs, smoking water pipes; kerchiefed women with open-toed shoes perched on wooden stools, leaning their faces near each other, passing the time. The boys' favorite place was the bakery owned by Abu Darwish. The neighborhood baker received the unbaked loaves from Jamila and her neighbors and finished them in his communal ovens. When cold weather set in, Ramzi and Rami took frequent breaks from their games and huddled behind the ovens. They inhaled the smell of olive-wood smoke, sawdust, and the rising loaves of bread. The mustachioed Abu Darwish, in his blue baker's apron, reminisced with other refugees about the days before the Nakba and gossiped about life in the camp: who had died, who was getting married, who fought with his wife. The baker pulled warm flatbread from his oven and offered pieces to the boys; when he forgot, they helped themselves.

When Ramzi and Rami came home, Aunt Nawal cornered the boys, undressed them, and prepared a large metal basin with hot water from the teapot. Often the brothers escaped, screaming and racing naked through the living room as seventeen-year-old Nawal, who had suffered polio as a child, limped after them.

This ritual ended abruptly the day Sido brought home a small used black-and-white television. Its arrival was greeted with loud cheering, led by Ramzi. But Sido laid down a rule: "No TV," he vowed, "until after your bath."

*   *   *

By the fall of 1986, Ramzi had begun first grade at the U.N. elementary school in Al Amari. It was there he encountered a short, stocky refugee the children knew simply as Teacher Khalidi.

One morning, Teacher Khalidi, in an olive suit and shiny brown shoes, a ring of hair surrounding his bald pate, pulled a jangling set of keys from his pocket and unlocked a large wooden cabinet. The doors swung open, revealing a small treasure of musical instruments in a cardboard box: maracas, a hand drum known as a tambour, and an old violin, or *kamandja*, belonging to Teacher Khalidi himself. He passed the box of instruments around to his students. Ramzi took the maracas.

Teacher Khalidi held his violin high, raised his bow, placed it on the strings, and, beaming, pulled it downward. The children grew silent as an Arabic melody filled the room. To Ramzi, it sounded vaguely like the orchestra that played behind Umm Kulthum every evening on the big radio at home. Yet this music was alive. Ramzi had never watched anyone play a musical instrument—had never even seen one, except on an Arabic cartoon. He looked up at Teacher Khalidi: knees bent, eyes closed, swaying to his own music. The man had transformed himself: Teacher Khalidi was now a *kamandjati*, a violinist.

Ramzi picked up his maracas and began shaking them.

Teacher Khalidi's impromptu concert had a profound effect on Ramzi. Looking back years later, he recalled, it changed his life.

* * *

Money was tight, and Sido, in any case, didn't enjoy sitting around the house, so he began looking for work on Fridays, the Muslim day of rest. He found it in the private gardens and courtyards of well-off Palestinian families. Ramzi insisted on going along to help his grandfather prune and plant. "During this time, we would just eat oranges and bread," Sido would say. The work was another opportunity for Grandfather to conjure up a lost village of melons, sesame, and citrus, and for Ramzi to absorb every detail.

Sido Mohammad was born in 1922, five years after the decline of the Ottoman Empire in Palestine and the arrival of imperial British rule. In the 1917 Balfour Declaration, Britain had agreed to help establish a "national home for the Jewish people" in Palestine. Soon, boatloads of Jews began arriving from Europe, seeking land. In 1930, when Sido was eight, a Zionist youth group established a kibbutz, Na'an, a few miles from his village of Na'ani. Wealthy Arab elites, some of them absentee landlords, were selling plots of land to the Zionists, creating a landless class of indigenous Arab peasants. The amount of land they sold was small, about 6 percent of Palestine, but alarmed Arab nationalists declared that selling land was treason, punishable by execution.

The boats filled with European Jews kept coming, in even greater numbers after the rise of Hitler in 1933. By the time Sido turned fourteen in 1936, the Jewish population had increased sixfold, to 350,000, in the two decades since Britain's arrival. The Palestinian nationalists launched the Arab Rebellion, cutting phone lines, sabotaging water pipelines, derailing trains, and planning attacks from the villages against British forces and Jewish kibbutzim. Sido's father, Hasan Abu Askar, took up arms and was killed by the British; he died when Sido was very young. To suppress the rebellion the British imposed martial law and ordered aerial bombardments, hundreds of executions, and the introduction of a new military tactic: house demolitions of suspected Arab terrorists.

In the years ahead, the fighting between the Arabs, the Zionists, and the British would end in war and would lead to Sido and Jamila's expulsion from Na'ani.

*   *   *

Half a century later, Sido had many hardships to share, but he preferred to recount for Ramzi the happier times in his village, preserved in an idyllic time capsule.

"We did not buy things," Sido told his grandson as they watered and trimmed. "We just ate from what grew on our land." In Na'ani, Sido recalled, Jamila had gathered firewood and placed blackened pots on large rocks, preparing their meals on an open fire and baking bread atop an earthen oven called a *taboun*. As Sido and Ramzi worked across the seasons, the old man recounted which harvest would be ready back home—the figs, the watermelon, or the giant grapefruit known as *bomeli*.

Ramzi saw his grandfather's labor in the private gardens as a product of his work ethic and his restlessness. It was also necessary, because the family was poor. With the arrival of Ramzi and his siblings nearly two years earlier, Sido's income had to stretch nearly twice as far. The family rarely ate meat. In the wintertime, they often could not afford electric heat, and so lit lumps of coal in a metal barbeque container, careful not to inhale the smoke that blackened the interior walls.

In theory, Ramzi's father contributed to the household, but he drank up much of what he earned. At night he caroused with friends, coming home in the wee hours, broke. One night in July 1987, he didn't return. Instead, a neighbor pounded on the door. There had been an accident. The car in which Ramzi's father was riding had swerved off the road and crashed into a tree. The driver had been badly injured, and Hussein had been rushed to Ramallah Hospital, unconscious. Both men had been drinking.

Ramzi's father suffered severe head trauma, according to a doctor's report. He was transferred to a Jerusalem hospital, which offered better care for brain injuries. Hussein Aburedwan spent forty days in the hospital, much of it in a coma.

Finally Ramzi's father came home. Thereafter, he was a vacant presence, sitting in a chair, staring into space. He had no income and no energy for work, Ramzi recalled; Hussein depended on Sido for everything, including his cigarettes and coffee.

Ramzi decided he needed to find work. Into the fall of 1987, many mornings before school, he still helped Sido sweep the streets and empty the garbage. But that didn't augment the family income. Ramzi had begun to see older kids at the newsstand, picking up newspapers to deliver across the city. They were coming back with handfuls of silver coins.

Ramzi approached the kiosk. "You're so little," the man told him. "We'll start you out with twenty papers."

One afternoon, Ramzi came from school to find an old broken bicycle leaning against the exterior wall of the house. Someone had tossed it out as junk, and Sido had salvaged it. The tires were flat, the chain broken, and both wheels and rims were badly bent. Ramzi and his grandfather took it to Abu Sliman, the local bike repairman, whose tiny refugee-camp shop was crammed with disassembled two-wheelers in various states of repair. Tires, inner tubes, and handlebars hung above the entrance. Abu Sliman banged out the wheels, patched the tires, found a new chain, and affixed a bell to the handlebars and a green metal box to the rear bumper. Now Ramzi had a delivery vehicle. Each morning before school, Ramzi sped through streets and alleys on his way to the newsstand, where he picked up one hundred copies of the Jerusalem paper, *Al Quds*, and a few copies of the English-language *Jerusalem Post*. He delivered them all. Each day at the end of his paper route, he gathered all his coins and paper wads of Israeli shekels and took them home. He never counted the money; he just handed it to Sido.

*   *   *

In the smudgy gray light just before dawn, Ramzi liked to stop at the Manara, the roundabout that marked the center of Ramallah. A modest sand-colored obelisk protruded from a stone fountain, inside a circular fence of black wrought iron. At that hour the Manara was empty. He paused, straddling his bicycle seat and feeling the cool air on his face. It was the late fall of 1987. Ramzi was eight years old, about to enter the second grade. He felt as though the whole town belonged to him.

Three

Uprising

December 9, 1987
Al Amari refugee camp

Ramzi and rami were playing in the alley in front of Abu Darwish's bakery, on a cool day after school, when everything changed.

They looked up as neighbor boys streaked past. *"Jeish, jeish!"* the boys yelled. "Army, army!" The brothers paused to listen. Dull pops of gunfire sounded from near the Jerusalem road. Closer, they could hear the crack of metal canisters hitting the pavement on the camp's main street. Moments later, white smoke with an acrid smell drifted toward them. They felt a burning in their eyes, and abandoned their game.

The boys could see a thick column of black smoke rising above the camp near the Jerusalem road. They went to investigate. As they drew closer, they could smell burning tires. At the main street teenagers were dragging concrete blocks and metal debris onto the pavement to block army jeeps. A hundred meters away stood a column of olive-clad Israeli soldiers holding hard plastic riot shields, dispatched to quell the protests. As the soldiers advanced, the youths, or *shabab,* showered them with stones.

Ramzi Aburedwan looked around for something to throw at the soldiers. He was angry at them, he recalled years later, for interrupting his game. He found a stone, picked it up, and hurled it at the advancing line of troops.

A day earlier, on December 8, 1987, in the Gaza Strip, an Israeli truck had veered into a long line of vehicles carrying Palestinian day laborers home from Israel. Four workers were killed. The deaths were tinder for a fire that had been smoldering for years. Protests broke out in Gaza that evening and spread quickly across the West Bank, reaching Al Amari camp the next day.

The protesters sought to avenge the killings of the four Gaza workers. But the outbreak of the Palestinian intifada, or uprising (literally, "shaking off," from the Arabic), sprang from much deeper traumas: the Nakba of 1948, and the two decades of Israeli occupation. Since 1967, when the Six Day War ended and the occupation of the West Bank and Gaza began, Palestinians had been subject to the daily indignities of foreign military rule, which dictated nearly every aspect of public life. Israel controlled West Bank and Gaza borders, streams, and aquifers, levied occupation taxes, imposed its own currency (the shekel), censored Arabic-language media, and issued or denied precious travel permits. Palestinians needed Israeli permission to open a business, drill a well, raise chickens, or plant trees. Occupation authorities issued driver's licenses, birth certificates, and death certificates. Israel ran the military courts where Ramzi's father was tried and the prison where he served his time; it approved and banned the textbooks in Ramzi's classes, closed schools and universities at will, and outlawed flags and all other national symbols of Palestine.

"Occupation," wrote the Palestinian poet Mourid Barghouti, "interferes in every aspect of life and of death; it interferes with longing and anger and desire and walking in the street. It interferes with going anywhere and coming back, with going to market, the emergency hospital, the beach, the bedroom . . ."

In Al Amari and beyond, protesters of these conditions were often expelled to Jordan or Lebanon, and many times Ramzi had watched soldiers arrive to round up his neighbors: young men to be placed in "administrative detention" for weeks or months without charge. Many of these laws were rooted in the British Mandate, when His Majesty's government, during its rule of Palestine from 1917 to 1948, imposed strict punishments for the transgressions of its Arab and Jewish subjects. Under Israeli rule, even speaking of resistance proved dangerous: By 1987 the military had built a vast intelligence network, paying local spies, or issuing them the coveted permits, in exchange for their eyes and ears in the camp.

The intifada, however, was not simply an expression of rage at a foreign power. Behind it were more concrete goals: ending the occupation, and building a sovereign, independent state of Palestine. For Ramzi's family and thousands like them, this meant one secular nation for Palestinians and Israelis in the whole of old Palestine; this would allow them to return to their lands in what was now Israel. Others believed their best chance lay in compromise: a Palestine in the West Bank and Gaza, part of a two-state solution based on United Nations Resolution 242, which had been adopted in November 1967. "Two-four-two," however, did not acknowledge the Palestinian right of return, and many believed it did not go far enough.

These divisions, for a time, would be buried in the struggle to oust Israel from the Occupied Territories. The intifada, in its early days, became a disciplined, well-organized struggle for national liberation, overseen by a secret Unified National Leadership of the Uprising. The Unified Leadership, a coalition of Palestinian resistance factions, would in the coming months coordinate its actions with Yasser Arafat and the PLO in exile. Its first clandestine handbill, which papered the camps and towns one night in January 1988, declared:

> All roads must be closed to the occupation forces . . . its cowardly soldiers must be prevented from entering refugee camps and large population centers by barricades and burning tires . . . Stones must land on the heads of the occupying soldiers and those who collaborate with them . . . We must set the ground burning under the feet of the occupiers. Let the whole world know that the volcanic uprising that has ignited the Palestinian people will not cease until the achievement of independence in a Palestinian state whose capital is Jerusalem!

In the early mornings, when Sido left home to sweep the streets, he found fliers scattered overnight by the Unified Leadership: *demonstration, noon today, at Manara.* Graffiti scrawled on a whitewashed wall greeted Ramzi when he came home from his paper route: *general strike tomorrow, no business may open.*

Women and children formed the neighborhood protection committee. Kids shouted *"jeish!"* at the sight of entering jeeps; their mothers and grandmothers relayed the warnings by banging rocks on resonating electrical poles. Ramzi's aunt Widad ferried secret ballots for the popular committees, the votes hidden in the folds of her clothing. When Israel closed the schools, volunteer teachers, risking deportation or prison, organized secret classes in a musty shack in Al Amari. A pile of old

mattresses served as seats and a green metal door as a blackboard. Ramzi
learned math, Arabic, and Palestinian history from teenaged girls who had
just finished high school. When patrolling soldiers approached, the children stuffed their forbidden notebooks under the mattresses and rushed
outside to play.

Israeli leaders, including the prime minister, Yitzhak Shamir, and the
defense minister, Yitzhak Rabin, dismissed the early protests as local and
insignificant. Within weeks, as clashes persisted across the West Bank,
Gaza, and East Jerusalem, they were proven wrong. So many protests had
erupted that Israel was running out of teargas and had to import more
from abroad. Military leaders were armed with heavy weaponry that was
more suitable to wage war with Syria or Jordan than to chase children
bearing rocks. The Israelis had to revise their strategy. At Al Amari, soldiers
filled fifty-five-gallon drums with cement, piling them high and tight
between narrow walls, sealing off the exits. Occupation forces comman-
deered a four-story stone building with a view of the entire refugee camp.
Military snipers perched on the roof. Each day, jeeps and armored trucks
entered Al Amari; soldiers spilled out for foot patrols through the veins of
the camp. Military authorities imposed periodic curfews; violators could
be shot on sight.

Because of the curfews, food supplies dwindled. Secret networks
became critical for the resistance. At night Aunt Widad met pickup trucks
with their lights cut; from the flatbed, she passed along crucial provisions
in a house-to-house chain. Outside the camp, chicken coops and rabbit
hutches rose up in the courtyards of the wealthy. Dozens of rabbits quickly
became thousands; squash and tomatoes sprouted in forbidden "victory
gardens." Rice, lentils, potatoes, and olive oil were hidden in neighborhood caches, then distributed in the small hours to the doorsteps of needy
families.

Palestinian shopkeepers, en masse, refused to pay taxes to the occupying
authorities. Heeding the call of the Unified National Leadership, they
shuttered their shops in protest, refusing to return even when soldiers
broke the locks and threw open the doors. Ramallah residents recalled that
no one ever stole from the unattended shops. The few shopkeepers who
did not comply with the strikes received visits from the shabab, whose
persuasive powers were formidable. Other shabab scattered nails and oil in
the streets, making them slick and dangerous for the incoming army jeeps.

*   *   *

For Ramzi, at first, it was like a game. Soldiers came; he threw stones at them. They chased him; he escaped. His favorite place to begin the ritual was a yellow stucco wall at a house on the corner of Al Amari's main road, about 150 meters from the four-story stone building and the entrance to the camp. Across the road he could see the white plaster minaret of the camp mosque, where, five times a day, the muezzin made the musical call to prayer. During the chaos of the occupation and the resulting absence of local government, the mosque had become a focal point of community life and a trusted civic institution for the exchange of vital information in the camp. Frequently Al Amari's news was announced over the loudspeaker on the minaret. Next to the mosque stood Kareem's grocery, with the over-stuffed shelves where the brothers got their half-shekel chocolate biscuits.

On a cold morning in early 1988, the older shabab were smashing big rocks and curbstones into smaller pieces, good for throwing. Ramzi watched them wrap their faces in checkered keffiyehs, to guard their identities from the military surveillance crews and the informants, and to protect themselves from teargas. Others deployed fresh-cut onions to dull the effects of the gas.

Ramzi and the other young boys began crumpling newspapers and stuffing them into tires, the better to get them smoking. From his pocket Ramzi pulled out the slingshot he had made from the laces and tongue of an old shoe. He preferred this for long-distance targets. The boys rotated their arms like baseball pitchers warming up in the bullpen. This way, they wouldn't get cramps.

Someone lit a match. From the blazing tires, twisting black columns rose above the camp, signaling the start of another day of battle. At the camp entrance, soldiers formed an unbroken line. Often they kept their distance, firing teargas canisters, rubber-coated metal bullets, and, occasionally, live ammunition to disperse the crowds. Today, however, the line began to move forward.

Ramzi wrapped his right hand around a jagged piece of curbstone. He glanced behind him to the long row of cement-block homes, checking his escape route. On the rooftops, laundry flapped from metal wires suspended between posts. Crooked TV antennas poked toward the sky.

He wore blue jeans and tennis shoes; his red jacket with the faux-sheepskin collar was flying open. In his left hand Ramzi held a rock nearly half the size of his head. His raised right arm was drawn behind him, his hand clutching the piece of curbstone. Ramzi's eyes conveyed a mixture of anger, fear, and resolve. His arched eyebrows seemed to say, *We are here.* His left foot was planted, and he was stepping forward with his right. In one more second, the stone would fly.

In that instant, a photojournalist snapped a picture. It captured a lone boy—one of thousands of the *atfal al hijara*, or children of the stones— confronting an unseen army.

The stone flew and the chase was on. Ramzi turned and ran hard around the corner, past the stucco wall, down the alley toward the bakery. "Stop!" a voice called in accented Arabic just behind him. Elated and terrified, Ramzi zigzagged through the camp, darting left, doubling back through a darkened passage, bursting into a neighbor's house, climbing through an upstairs window, and racing along the rooftops.

Still, he hadn't shaken his pursuer, who ran along below, pointing and shouting.

Ramzi felt his sneakers grabbing the dimples of the tin roof; he saw his limbs pumping in a perfect rhythm with his panting breath. In times like these, in full flight from the soldiers, a strange sense of calm often settled over him. There wasn't time to put words to a prayer, but he put out the energy of a fragmented offering: *God, I love you. I need you. I need to be alive.* There was nothing more in the world that could help him; once, a bullet whizzed past, and he understood his life in terms of centimeters. Oddly, in these moments, Ramzi felt protected: buoyed, lifted, and cared for as he ran and ran, sprinting from rooftop to rooftop, leaping toward an imagined freedom.

Just below the roofline, he braced himself between two facing walls, slithered down, jumped to the ground, and peered out into the alley. It looked safe. Then the soldier peeled around the corner. Ramzi sprinted out of the camp, the heavily burdened soldier steps behind him. He raced through a weedy lot and arrived at the edge of an abandoned building beside a bluff. Twelve feet down was a mound of sand in a clearing. Ramzi had to leap or surrender.

He jumped, landed in the soft pile, began running, turned back, and looked up. The soldier aimed his Galil. He had an unobstructed shot; in the clearing, Ramzi had no cover.

The soldier lowered his rifle. *"Ben zonah!"* he yelled in Hebrew. "Son of a bitch!" He turned and trudged back toward the camp.

*   *   *

The next day the photograph of Ramzi stepping forward to hurl his stone ran in a leftist newspaper in Israel. Soon after, it was published in an underground magazine in the West Bank. A few days later Ramzi was at home, looking out over the camp from his rooftop, when a neighbor boy from a few houses down called over to him. "Hey, I saw your picture!" the boy shouted. "You were throwing a stone."

Within days the iconic image was transmitted to newspapers around the world. Before long, it would be reproduced on posters in Europe, depicting the rage and apparent fearlessness of the children of the stones. Ramzi embodied the legendary status of the shabab, as immortalized by Syrian poet Nizar Qabbani, who wrote of children who shone like lanterns, amazing the world with only stones in their hands.

The photograph would become perhaps the single most recognized image of the Palestinian intifada. Ramzi was destined to be a child legend, and a potent visual symbol of his people's national uprising.

For years, especially in the wake of the 1967 war, Israel had been seen worldwide as the fragile and vulnerable Jewish state in a sea of Arab hostility. Now, as images of children like Ramzi—wily, swift, indomitable—poured out from newsstands and television screens across the world, perceptions were reversed—even, to some extent, within Israel. One Israeli historian called the intifada "the Palestinian war of independence"; another labeled it "an anti-colonial war of liberation."

Israeli officials saw Palestinian liberation as a basic threat to their state's existence. A free Palestine would mean the end of the occupation of the West Bank, which military leaders considered essential to preserve the buffer, or "strategic depth," from Jordan, with which it had just fought a war. Israeli leaders also feared that even if they agreed to a Palestinian state, their long-time adversaries would never be satisfied until all of old Palestine was liberated. Indeed, for many Palestinians, self-determination meant not just the end of occupation, but the right to return to lands from which they had been dispossessed during the creation of Israel. For these reasons, Israeli officials believed, it was better to put down the uprising in order to quell all Palestinian nationalist aspirations.

*   *   *

Ramzi woke up to the sound of armed men pounding on the front door. He looked out his second-floor window. A dozen soldiers, maybe more, surrounded the house. Some were examining fresh graffiti scrawled on a wall in the alley. Others pointed up to a forbidden symbol: the Palestinian flag, green, black, red, and white, flapping from a telephone poll. The Unified National Leadership, in one of its secret handbills, had declared, "Palestinian flags are to be flown from minarets, churches, rooftops, and electricity poles everywhere."

Ramzi's uncle Hasan opened the door. The Israeli commander ordered him to climb the pole and take down the flag. From inside his house, Ramzi watched as Hasan did as he was told. The soldiers went next door and summoned a neighbor outside. The commander ordered him to scrub off the graffiti.

It was a daily ritual. In the evenings, Ramzi's aunt Widad would join other women of Al Amari in secret living room sewing groups, stitching the flags of Palestine. Sometimes they sewed the national colors right into their clothing. The next day, the graffiti and the flags would reappear, and the ritual would begin again.

Another time soldiers in frantic pursuit caught up with Ramzi at home, just after he burst through the door. The family often left the door unlocked and a small kitchen window open in case any of the neighborhood shabab needed an escape route. Other neighbors did the same. But this time, the soldiers came in right behind Ramzi. Nawal was at the stove, cooking. The soldiers announced a search for weapons. They moved roughly through the house, knocking over furniture, flipping mattresses, upending boxes and crates of knickknacks, tools, and food.

"They started dumping all kinds of food," Nawal recounted: rice, vegetables, flour, sugar, tea, and cooking oil. They poured the food in the sink and dumped jars of tea and vegetables on the floor.

"God help us!" Sido cried. "God give us revenge!"

The soldiers left, having found no weapons. As soldiers and stone-throwers alike recall, during the first intifada, there were virtually no arms to be found. They would come later.

Nawal looked at Ramzi. "We have nothing to eat," she said. "What are we going to do?"

Ramzi and Rami climbed to the roof, clutching big plastic bags, and jumped over to the rooftop of their neighbor, Zakaria. He was waiting for them with his own plastic bags. The three boys jumped to the next roof, where Ramzi's cousin, Adli, lived. He, too, was waiting with big bags.

The curfew was in force, and the boys had to be careful not to be seen by the soldiers. In blue jeans, tennis shoes, and winter coats, they dropped to the alley, running quietly along the graffiti-covered walls until they reached the high stack of fifty-five-gallon drums, by now blackened with soot from the burnt tires. The stack was welded together and wedged between the alley's narrow walls. At the bottom of the barrier the boys peered through a small hole, perhaps eighteen inches wide. Using hammers and sharp tools, and working secretly over days, the shabab of the camp had pierced the barrier to create an escape route. Now Ramzi, Rami, and the two other boys would use it for their own mission. They slipped through the hole, then moved quickly, staying close to the walls and overhangs, passing through the gardens of private homes, into ditches and empty lots. Always, they listened for the sound of the army jeeps. Finally they reached the produce market, known as the *hisbeh*.

In the silent market mounds of fruits, vegetables, and mountain herbs lay hidden under lumpy green, blue, and black tarpaulins. Stray cats moved about the vegetable bins. The boys reached beneath the tarps and stuffed their big plastic bags with onions, oranges, carrots, potatoes, cabbages, eggplants, tomatoes, and cucumbers. In a short time each boy had four bulging bags: too bulky and too heavy to carry all at once. They ferried their loads, taking two bags a hundred meters, then racing back for the other two. In this way the boys lunged and stumbled back through the ditches, side streets, and private gardens, and into the camp. The whole trip took nearly five hours, Ramzi recalled, but he was energized by the thought of feeding his family and neighbors in an emergency.

They reached the cousin's house, left most of the bags there, and returned for the rest.

Suddenly a jeep peeled around a corner. "Stop!" a voice called. Two soldiers leaped out and grabbed the boys. They held each boy by the scruff of his neck and led them roughly around the corner to the entrance of the camp, and to the stone building the military had seized. Outside the building, soldiers tied the boys' hands behind their backs with hard plastic handcuffs and commanded them to face the wall, then began punching and kicking them. This was common practice at the time; an estimated ten thousand children suffered broken bones at the hands of Israeli soldiers during the first two years of the intifada. "We just wanted to get some tomatoes," Ramzi shouted in response to the blows. "We are hungry." The soldiers continued to beat the boys, then left them in the cold, cuffed and facing the wall. Jamila came when she heard the news. She screamed and pleaded for the soldiers to let the children go, and finally, they did.

At home Ramzi pledged to never again go out in defiance of the soldiers, but no one in the family believed him.

*   *   *

Yitzhak Rabin, the Israeli defense minister, had miscalculated: The Palestinian resistance had not been broken. On the contrary, it was the Israeli soldiers, facing the unrelenting stream of rocks, stones, and, far less frequently, Molotov cocktails and firebombs, who were coming unglued. Nowhere was this more evident than in Israel's own assessment of its soldiers' behavior in an incident that appeared to have shocked the nation.

After soldiers from an elite unit beat and kicked an unarmed father to death in Gaza, an "appalled" Israeli investigative commission asked: "How did it happen that combat soldiers . . . cast off all the principles that their parents instilled in them and underwent a mental metamorphosis which left them ready and willing to deliver what the pathologist called 'murderous blows' to a person old enough to be their father?"

By the fall of 1988, nearly a year into the intifada, numerous reports documented the frequent Israeli use of live ammunition against demonstrators armed only with stones. Under international pressure, the military changed its policy to make greater use of plastic bullets and issued orders to aim at demonstrators' legs; but the rules of engagement were unclear. Confronted by the Palestinian resistance, soldiers developed "a fierce desire to fight back, including the desire to use firearms," according to an Israeli brigadier general. "The Intifada led to the development of an insensitivity to human life."

*   *   *

On the morning of September 17, 1988, Ramzi woke up to fresh graffiti on the whitewashed wall facing his house. It was the sixth anniversary of the massacres of Palestinians at the refugee camps of Sabra and Shatila, in Lebanon, which claimed at least 700 Palestinian lives and perhaps as many as 2,750, many of them women and children. The massacres were seared into Palestinian memory, including that of young children.

Ramzi pulled on his jeans and laced up his scuffed white tennis shoes. Aunt Widad, now twenty, would go with him. They left the house in the late morning to the sound of chants and the whiff of smoke from burning tires. They reached the yellow stucco wall. The chanting grew louder.

Ramzi and Widad turned the corner onto the camp's main street. Banners implored REMEMBER SABRA/SHATILA and END THE OCCUPA- TION; the boys were hurling rocks with their leather launchers at a distant line of soldiers. "Stop occupation!" Widad yelled. Ramzi grabbed handfuls of rocks and ran forward. At nine, he was no longer the youngest or least experienced of the shabab. Already the back of his head was covered with lumps from the stones of smaller children whose projectiles never got past the front line.

On this day, soldiers answered the stones with teargas, rubber-coated metal bullets, and, suddenly, live fire from a rooftop sniper. Demonstrators scattered. Ramzi and Widad retreated to the yellow wall, out of sight of the snipers. The streets were quiet. Ramzi peered around the corner. No one moved, he would recall many years later, and no one, apart from soldiers, could be seen along the main camp road coming from the Jerusalem highway.

Ramzi and Widad were crouching at the wall when a twelve-year-old neighbor girl came walking toward them from the mosque and Kareem's grocery on the other side of the road. Her name was Nahil Tukhi; she was a schoolmate of Ramzi's. She carried a wooden bread board on her head, and, to Ramzi's alarm, seemed unaware of any danger.

Nahil knew about the clashes that day. Scarcely an hour earlier, her mother had worried about anyone leaving the house. But she needed to send the dough she'd prepared to the baker, Abu Darwish; otherwise, the family wouldn't have bread that day. Nahil had calmly volunteered.

Abu Darwish's ovens, about fifty meters in from the main road, were well out of the line of fire on September 17, 1988. But while the bread was baking, Nahil had crossed the main road toward Kareem's, where she bought chocolate and biscuits. Now she was coming back.

At school, Ramzi had taken note of the older girl. He recalled arriving at her side, eyes alight, hoping she would let him walk her home. She had never paid much attention to Ramzi; he was small and immature. But Ramzi continued to admire her from a distance. She was pretty and regal. To him, Nahil did not walk so much as glide through the refugee camp, somehow both of it and removed from it. Her family came from Na'ani, the village of Ramzi's grandparents. Ramzi had developed a crush on the older girl. "Kids' things," he called it later.

Nahil was crossing the road: a beautiful child, tall and graceful, with long black hair flowing over her shoulders, carrying the wooden slab that, until a few minutes earlier, had held her mother's dough. Soon, she would be out of the road, safely at the bakery.

It didn't occur to Ramzi to warn her.

Nahil hesitated. For a moment, she stopped in the road, about forty meters from Ramzi and Widad. She seemed to be smiling.

A shot echoed in the street. Nahil fell, limp. The bread board clattered on the pavement.

Ramzi and Widad rushed out from their hiding place and directly into the line of fire. Nahil lay motionless, blood spurting from a hole in her forehead. She was still breathing.

Ramzi looked up to see a blue-and-white Volkswagen with the letters *U.N.* on it coming toward them from the side street near the mosque. A neighbor, Abu Freimo, was running in their direction. Widad, Ramzi, and Abu Freimo lifted Nahil and hurried her toward the VW station wagon. The driver jumped from the car and threw open the door to the backseat. They frantically loaded Nahil into the car and slammed the door. The driver raced off, toward Ramallah hospital. Sometime afterward, Nahil was transferred to Makassed Hospital in East Jerusalem, where, seven days later, she died of her wounds.

The shooting of Nahil Tukhi brought the death toll to at least 250 Palestinians in the first nine and a half months of the uprising. Of those on the other side, three had died. During the same period, 5,000 Palestinians were injured, 18,000 were arrested, and 2,500 were taken into administrative detention; freedom of movement was cut off for hundreds of thousands now living under regular curfew.

*   *   *

After Nahil's death, Ramzi left the house nearly every day to join the clashes. "My son, this will not bring anything," Sido pleaded with his grandson one afternoon. He was resting on his stone bench outside the house, spooning sugar into his small glass of Arabic tea. In the alley someone had posted handbills of Yasser Arafat, the revered revolutionary leader of the PLO. Like millions of Palestinians, Arafat had spent much of his life in exile—in Egypt; in Jordan, before King Hussein expelled the PLO in 1970; then in Lebanon, before Israeli military forces drove him to a seaborne exit; now in Tunis, farther still from Palestine. Across the West Bank and Gaza, the illicit handbills of Arafat's visage remained an inspiration. Recently the revolutionary Arafat had softened his political stance. He had given an important speech in Geneva recognizing Israel's right to exist and proposing a free and independent Palestine, but only on part of their historic land—the 22 percent that made up the West Bank and Gaza. Ramzi's family had only heard cryptic bits of news of this on Israel's Arabic-language radio. It wasn't clear; would they have to stay in the camp forever, or after forty years would they finally be allowed to go home? Sido was skeptical. "Why are you trying to fight for this, Ramzi?" he asked. "The rich Arabs live in castles, they sold us out already. Don't give up your life. Be careful. They will shoot you. They will kill you."

"I have seen them killing, Sido," Ramzi replied. "I know."

Conversations like this were taking place in homes all over the West Bank and Gaza, especially in the refugee camps. Children on the front lines of the intifada literally had the future of Palestine in their hands. The pleadings of their parents and grandparents were futile, and the children and teenagers went out as they pleased.

Yet their independence came at a price. As their trauma accumulated, both Ramzi and his little brother began to develop severe stuttering problems, which often took hold, Ramzi found to his horror, at times of greatest danger. "R-r-r-r-r-r-rami!" Ramzi would stutter when he saw a sniper aiming toward them from the camp's entrance. "B-b-b-b-b-e c-c-c-c-careful!"

Ramzi had begun to worry that something terrible could happen to his little brother. Only a year younger, Rami wasn't as clever. His reactions weren't as quick and he wasn't good at calculating danger. Ramzi was far more aware of the risks the boys were taking. He couldn't shake the memory of Rami running at full speed, his mouth open and his hands on the sides of his head, after a bullet had grazed his ear.

Ramzi did not want to brazenly defy his grandfather. He snuck upstairs and stepped through a window, pulling himself up to the roof to stand among the old mattresses, broken plastic chairs, and feral cats. It felt strangely peaceful as he gazed out upon the expanse of Al Amari. Across the camp, rusted rebar poked up through a sea of corrugated tin. Muffled clucking drifted from makeshift chicken coops. *It's time*, he told himself, *for my circus technique.*

Ramzi examined the narrow gap between his house and his neighbor's. He planted a sneaker on each roof, placed his hands just below on the facing walls, slid down, and, like a gymnast on the parallel bars, swung his legs up and down in unison, before dropping to the ground and setting off to join the clashes.

*   *   *

One day, between the curfews, Ramzi took Rami out to explore the open lands on the other side of the hill they knew as Jabal al-Tawil. The hill had been taken over by the Israelis, and from Al Amari, the brothers could look up at red roofs of the settlement of Psagot.

Ramzi led his little brother toward a white brick wall at the northern edge of the camp. They ran through a vacant field and alongside a latticed vineyard. There they veered right, stealing in among the vines. They walked the rows beneath the lattices, laughing and stuffing grapes in their mouths, picking up handfuls of the rotted, fallen fruit and throwing them at each other. Their faces smeared with juice, they ran out of the vineyard with as many bunches as they could carry. They came to the white brick wall, stuffed the grapes in their pants, hoisted themselves to the top, jumped down, and trotted across the Jerusalem road.

On the other side, the boys walked northeast toward Jabal al-Tawil and the base of the hill, beneath the Israeli settlement. There they encountered a wide swath of high, deep green grass. A foul smell wafted out; they looked up, just east, to see raw sewage trickling down the hillside from the settlement. The boys ran on, into the valley below the hill. They found themselves in a wild land, quiet and uncluttered, covered in olive, sage, and *Flora Palaestina*. There in the tall grass, on the sloping land, they spotted rabbits, hedgehogs, even a gazelle—wildlife unlike anything they knew at the refugee camp, where the only animals worthy of mention were cats, dogs, sheep, chickens, and the occasional donkey.

At the far end of the valley they came upon a cave. The boys stood at the entrance, squinting in. They moved on, scrambling halfway up another hill, looking back toward Jabal al-Tawil and the valley in between. "Heyyy!" Ramzi yelled across the valley. "Heyyy!" Rami followed. *Heyyy! Heyyy!* their voices echoed back.

This was the closest the brothers had come to a kind of Palestinian wilderness, a mythical place between the villages of old Palestine, with their houses made of ancient stone. In that place of their collective imagination, the landscape stretched forward, without walls or fences. Without boundaries.

Ramzi and Rami played there for a while, then turned back, walked beneath the settlement, crossed the road to Jerusalem, and went home.

Four

FATHER

Spring 1989
Al Amari camp

B Y MARCH 1989, when Ramzi turned ten, the intifada showed few
signs of letting up. The family heard daily reports on the radio.
Palestinian militants had launched firebombs at Jewish vehicles crossing
from West to East Jerusalem. An Israeli soldier was caught in a lethal
ambush in the old city of Nablus. Shepherds stabbed a Jewish man to
death near the West Bank settlement of Ariel. With each such attack,
the army cracked down harder in the camp and across the Occupied
Territories. Soldiers would pull up at the home of suspected perpetrators,
order everyone out, load it with explosives, and blow it up. Now Ramzi
heard of a new form of collective punishment, called "house sealing,"
directed at the families of stone-throwers. Soldiers arrived with a load
of bricks, cement blocks, and mortar and sealed shut the doors and
windows of the house, making entry impossible. Other families of stone-
throwing children, spared these "house sealings," were subjected instead to
substantial fines.

Often Ramzi broke the curfew to deliver his newspapers. On these
mornings, he left his bicycle at home; he could better dodge the Israeli
patrols on foot. He slipped out of the camp, skirted the obelisk and
wrought-iron gates of the Manara, and hurried down side streets until he
reached the home of the distributor in a run-down part of town known as
Old Ramallah. There the newspapers awaited Ramzi, leaving him to
wonder who else had broken the curfew to bring the news from Jerusalem.

On other mornings, when the closures were lifted, Ramzi pedaled through the center of town and into the produce market, the hisbeh, where, by now, many people recognized him from his photo. Ramzi was becoming well known. Through the famous image, Ramzi, perhaps more than any other child, represented the shabab, the young people, mostly from the refugee camps, who had paid the highest price in the struggle for Palestinian freedom. This was not lost on the professional and middle-class Palestinians who bought newspapers from Ramzi each morning.

One of them was Soraida Hussein, a single woman in her late twenties who worked in public relations for a local university. Soraida had wavy brown hair, which she wore short; her easy smile and soft brown eyes shone with warmth and curiosity. She had seen Ramzi from a distance, sweeping the streets with his grandfather. Until recently, however, she hadn't distinguished him from the many waiflike children of the refugee camps who descended on downtown Ramallah every morning, scouring the streets to sell trinkets, gum, and small packages of tissues. Soraida's sister, a regular on Ramzi's newspaper route, introduced them one morning. Soraida was struck immediately by the smiling, clear-eyed, self-respecting boy "who sold newspapers with dignity." Unlike some of the refugee boys, Ramzi's face was scrubbed and his clothes unfrayed. When Soraida asked for a paper, Ramzi counted her change carefully; when he handed it back, he looked her in the eye.

Compared to Ramzi, Soraida had grown up comfortably. Both her parents came from land-owning peasant families in the West Bank village of Kobar. Unlike Ramzi's family, they had not been expelled during the Nakba; they had kept their land. But eight years later, in 1956, with too few Palestinians living close enough to buy their figs and grapes, they quit Kobar and emigrated to Colombia. Twenty-one years later, as a young adult, Soraida returned to Palestine and took a job at Birzeit University, based in the village of the same name, which meant "well of the olive oil." Like the five other universities, thirteen colleges, five training centers, and nearly twelve hundred schools in Palestine, it had been closed by Israeli military order. Eventually Palestinian kindergartens would also be subject to closures.

One day Soraida saw Ramzi returning from his newspaper rounds. The few remaining papers fanned out under his skinny arms. She greeted him and pressed a coin into his hand. Though their backgrounds were different, Soraida saw them as joined in struggle. The Palestinian uprising was uniting people across religions, class, and gender toward a common purpose: a free and independent Palestine. Soraida was convinced of this outcome. For Ramzi it was simpler: He just wanted the soldiers and the settlers out of his homeland. He wanted to be able to climb Jabal al-Tawil, look out from a summit cleared of machine guns, barbwire, and settlement housing, and see a unified Palestine. He wanted to take Rami with him, so their voices could carry into the valley, all the way to the cave where they had played on that day of exploration.

Soraida wanted to understand the experience of children on the front lines in the refugee camps. She invited Ramzi to lunch in her modest home of Jerusalem stone at 4 Al Ma'amoon Street, where she lived alone. Deep reds of Palestinian embroidery covered the couches and end tables. Books lined the shelves. Over plates of stuffed chicken, rice, and Arabic salads, Soraida explored their common experience. The secret classes she held in her family's ancestral village of Kobar—about the Nakba and the birth of Palestinian resistance—were much like the lessons Ramzi took in the musty shack in Al Amari. With Birzeit University ordered closed, Soraida had time to work for the nationalist cause. She took village children into the hills, where she taught them patriotic songs and quizzed them about different species of trees. Her village stories were a lot like Sido's, except that unlike Na'ani, Kobar still existed. Soraida told Ramzi that, much like in Al Amari, the intifada and the curfews had led to high unemployment in Kobar; to generate income for village women, she helped them jar pickles and make fig and apple jams for the local markets. This would be difficult in Al Amari camp, where there were only a few scattered mulberry and fig trees. Her stories intensified Ramzi's longing to see a real Palestinian village; he had only heard of them.

Soraida was taken by Ramzi's politeness and his table manners. She tried to draw him out: *Does your family worry about you? How many martyrs have you had in the camp? What about you, Ramzi—are you ever afraid?* Ramzi was not accustomed to speaking his mind to older people. He was surprised that any grown-up would seek his opinion. Yet Soraida, just one year older than his mother, seemed genuinely curious. Ramzi told her about Aunt Widad's clandestine work for the resistance, about Aunt Nawal's polio, about watching Nahil fall on the main street of the camp, and about his secret mission to bring food from the produce market. Soraida saw Ramzi as a hero of the uprising. Unlike Sido, she did not spend a lot of time worrying about him. She believed that liberty was coming. This meant that everyone gave everything they had to the struggle. In this she felt a common purpose with the ten-year-old boy at her dining room table.

Ramzi returned Soraida's invitation, in the tradition of Arab hospitality, and soon she paid a visit to Al Amari. Over tea, Sido and Jamila reminisced about Na'ani. Soraida noticed how their eyes glimmered when they shared the memories of their village. She had spent many hours talking with old people who had lost their land in the Nakba, and though it was sad, she found it helped them to relax. It reminded them that they hadn't always been in a refugee camp; that they had had a good life, once upon a time. They had all been landowners. It was there, in their villages, that they felt like themselves, even if it was only through their memories.

Before the Nakba, an educated Arab class fueled a vibrant cultural life in Jerusalem, Jaffa, Haifa, and other cities; but Palestine had been a fundamentally rural place. It was at the village level that traditions among Palestinians had been lived and celebrated. In the struggle to maintain a national memory and evoke the dream of return, it was the displaced villagers whose stories were most often retold. Soraida believed it was good for the old people to remind the younger generation who they were, and where they had come from.

*   *   *

On the evening of March 30, 1989, a few weeks after his tenth birthday, Ramzi huddled around the flames of burning tires, singing liberation songs near the entrance to Al Amari refugee camp. *"Filestin, lazem nehmi haliblad,"* the shabab sang. "Palestine, we must protect this land." The song was one of hundreds in a long tradition of Palestinian protest music dating to 1948, most evoking loss of land and the right to return to old Palestine. Nationalist music was banned by the Israeli authorities, and out of respect for those killed during the intifada, Palestinian musicians themselves performed rarely, even in private. But the burning tires at the front lines represented an exception, and Ramzi sang with the older boys, his high voice joining the chorus.

It was Land Day, another of the many anniversaries marking Palestinian tragedy and dispossession. It commemorated the day in 1976 when six Palestinian citizens of Israel were killed, and more than one hundred wounded, in protests over Israel's appropriation of land near Arab villages in the Galilee, which were seized in order to build Jewish industrial villages. The Land Day remembrance allowed Palestinians in the Occupied Territories to exercise solidarity with their brethren across the Green Line. The day always promised clashes with Israeli troops.

Ramzi fixed his eyes ahead, toward the entrance to the camp and the four-story building the Israeli soldiers had taken. Suddenly he heard a commotion behind him. He turned around to see soldiers quickly approaching from the rear of the camp. They yelled for the shabab to disperse, and began firing teargas and plastic bullets.

Ramzi started to run, then felt a sharp pain in his arm. He was bleeding heavily, just above the elbow. He ran home, alone in the dark.

His family had heard the shots, and as Ramzi turned the corner Aunt Widad awaited him in front of the house. When he saw her he began to cry.

Ramzi needed medical attention, but the camp's main exits were sealed. Uncle Jamal carried him to a ladder in the alley, scaling the wall with his nephew in one arm. On the other side, Jamal flagged down the first car that came by. The Palestinian driver took them to Ramallah Hospital.

Ramzi sat on the hospital bed, under a light so bright he had to shield his eyes. Eventually the light became blurry as Ramzi felt faint. He noticed he was not the only patient in the room. The doctor applied local anesthesia, extracted a plastic bullet, and cleaned out the wound, just above the elbow on the boy's left inner arm. Ramzi asked the doctor if he would lose his arm. No, the doctor said, you will recover. He wrapped Ramzi's arm in heavy bandages and kept him at the hospital for several hours. Ramzi's shooting was not uncommon; he was one of an estimated seventy-five hundred children wounded by Israeli gunfire in the first two years of the intifada.

After midnight, Ramzi returned to Al Amari, his left arm in a sling. But his stone-throwing arm was unhurt. The next day he went back to the front lines. "Where are you going?" Grandmother Jamila asked. "I'm going to p-p-play," Ramzi said. They both knew he was lying. Her pleadings, and Sido's, no longer held sway.

"What the hell are you doing?" asked a woman who had seen Ramzi shot the night before. "You don't learn? You were just injured yesterday. You're crazy."

Ramzi didn't respond. He ran off, carrying stones in his pockets.

*   *   *

Soraida met Ramzi near the camp, in a cluster of pine trees adjacent to the municipality in Al Bireh, where the boy and his grandfather had spent many mornings sweeping the streets. With Soraida were two reporters from the Spanish Basque country. Soraida had worked as a journalist in Colombia, and when foreign reporters visited the West Bank, especially Spanish speakers, she would take them to the camp for the children's perspective. Ramzi had recently healed enough to remove his sling. He spoke dutifully of the struggle, of liberation for his people, and of the homeland for which he was fighting.

The Basque journalists asked Ramzi, "What is your dream?"

Soraida expected more big talk from the boy. He smiled. "I d-d-dream that when I die, and go to heaven, I can meet P-P-Pinocchio."

Soraida choked up, privately celebrating. Underneath the political bravado and the slogans in defense of Palestine, Ramzi was still a child, with a child's dreams.

As he would be, still, for a short while longer.

*   *   *

By the beginning of 1990, Israeli soldiers had killed 574 Palestinians, mostly with live ammunition. More than one in five were children sixteen and younger. Children accounted for more than twenty-three thousand injuries during the same period. The deaths and injuries were well documented by numerous human rights groups, which blamed the casualties on "excessive force" on the part of the Israel Defense Forces. Defense Minister Yitzhak Rabin had instituted a policy of "force, might, and beatings," which included orders to soldiers to break the bones of stone-throwers. Rabin believed more force would break the intifada and return a sense of calm to the occupied territories.

Alongside those casualties, however, arose a shocking figure, much less discussed: During the intifada, nearly as many Palestinians died at the hands of other Palestinians as from the bullets of Israeli soldiers. Throughout the camps and villages, Israel's elaborate network of spies and informants led to arrests and detention of suspected organizers and militants. These collaborators were recruited by Israel in exchange for money, travel permits, sexual favors, sidearms, or reduced criminal charges; young women, according to an investigation published by the Israeli human rights group B'Tselem, were sometimes taken into detention and raped, "while another collaborator photograph[ed] the act. The collaborators or the GSS [General Security Service also known as the Shin Bet or Shabak] threaten[ed] to shame the girl publicly if she [did] not cooperate with them." Children were also targets for recruitment, enticed with money or threatened with demolition of the family's home, or with the simple revocation of a father's work permit.

On raids, Palestinian collaborators accompanied Israeli soldiers, black masks pulled over their faces to protect their identities. Suspicions of "collaborators" were everywhere in the camps. To be accused of being one could be the equivalent of a death sentence. There were no independent Palestinian police, detention facilities, or courts, and therefore no trials; suspicion was sometimes the only consideration. Occasionally enforcers gave warnings, along with a chance to repent; other times, not. The knife was frequently the preferred instrument of execution, and occasionally, the hatchet.

*   *   *

Ever since his drunken car accident and the subsequent diagnosis of brain trauma, Hussein Aburedwan, Ramzi's father, had been largely silent, sitting around the house for endless spells. He had stopped drinking, but to Ramzi it was as if the life force had been drained out of him. When he did go out, it was usually to a local coffee shop. His life seemed quiet, his days uneventful.

At four o'clock in the morning on February 19, 1990, a few weeks before Ramzi's eleventh birthday, five shabab, most apparently in their late teens, knocked on the door of Sido's house. Jamila rose from bed and opened the door. "We'd like to talk to Hussein," they told her. Ramzi's father appeared in his underwear. They asked him to go with them. He dressed and went out.

An hour later, when Sido and Ramzi awoke, Hussein had not returned. Jamila told them about the shabab. Sido was angry that Jamila had not sent the boys away, and he was worried that their son had not returned.

A man's voice came over the loudspeaker of the Al Amari mosque. "There is a body at the mosque," said the voice. "Please come to identify it."

Grandfather, grandson, and two of Ramzi's uncles left the house and walked swiftly down the darkened alley, rounding the corner past Abu Darwish's bakery and toward the main road. Ramzi ran ahead, turned around, waited for the men to catch up, raced ahead again, stopped again. He was afraid to get too far in front. Ramzi looked right, toward the Israeli command post, with the camp entrance just beyond. The mosque stood on the other side of the main road.

Ramzi raced across the road, his uncle Hasan right behind him. Now Sido was running, too. Before they could reach the mosque, they saw a dark outline lying still in the alley near Kareem's grocery. As they got closer, they saw it was Hussein. His stomach faced upward, and his head was missing.

Ramzi began shouting uncontrollably. Sido, in shock, went looking for his son's head. A short distance away, he found it and picked it up. It bore the marks of a hatchet.

Ramzi was slapping his head with his open palms, his eyes stricken, his mouth in a wide-open scream.

Sido went inside the mosque to retrieve a coffin. There were no funeral homes in Palestinian society, and so the mosque facilitated the rituals of the deceased. Coffins were available for use. Sido and Ramzi's uncles placed the body of Ramzi's father into one, and next to it, they set his head. They carried the coffin home. Ramzi walked beside them, still smacking his face with his open hands, shouting, "*Baba, baba, baba!*" "Father, father, father!"

Ramzi's father was killed by youths who accused him of collaborating with Israeli security forces. The family was told that these shabab acted on orders from "outside"—apparently a reference to the PLO leadership in exile. Hussein, however, did not appear to have the stature to attract such attention. He was a troubled alcoholic, a small-time laborer who, before his accident, washed dishes, swept stairwells, and hauled heavy bags of cement. Even if his actions had somehow been able to attract the attention of the PLO in Tunis or Algiers, the brain damage from his car accident, which severely limited his activities and even his speech, made him a most unlikely spy. Instead, it appears that Hussein Aburedwan was one of the estimated 60 percent of Palestinians killed by other Palestinians during the intifada who could not be considered guilty of collaborating with Israel. There was simply a lack of evidence.

Nevertheless, a local representative of the Palestinian government in exile went to Sido's house, offering to cleanse the family's image. The man said, "I will give you a certificate that the Aburedwan family is clean"—i.e., not a family of spies—"if you give me a letter saying you disown Hussein."

"This is my son!" Sido shouted. "I am not going to disown him. Get out! Get out! Get out of my house!"

*   *   *

Early on the same morning—February 19, 1990—Sido's house was filled with the sounds of wailing. It was still dark outside, but Sido was determined to act quickly. He believed the family needed to get Hussein's body out of Al Amari immediately. Rumors in the camp held that soon after a killing, Israel would claim the corpse to conduct an autopsy, and that upon the body's return, in many cases, the horrified family would learn that the organs had been removed.

In haste, Sido made plans for burial. Ramzi walked through the dark with his grandfather and uncles, toward the Muslim cemetery. The men carried the coffin out through a side entrance to the camp. They flagged down a VW station wagon and rode in silence to the graveyard. A moment later the imam from the Al Amari mosque arrived on his bicycle. They found an open grave. In the cemetery, there were always open graves.

The imam began to pray as the men of Ramzi's family, according to religious guidelines, removed his father's body from the coffin, slowly lowered Hussein into the earth, and covered him with soil. Without a moment to reflect, they walked back to Al Amari, the sun still not yet risen on the winter's morning.

Five

ACCORD

Spring 1992
Ramallah

R AMZI PLUNGED HIS hands into the dark soil of Palestine. He knelt
in the garden outside Soraida's house, where he regularly pruned and
watered her citrus and almond trees, raking the dirt around them, just as
Sido had taught him.

Two years had passed since the murder of Ramzi's father. Ramzi was
thirteen years old. Since the killing, he had spent even more time out of
the house, earning money for the family and confronting soldiers and
settlers. Often Ramzi and his cousin would sneak out of the camp to the
Jerusalem road, where they waited for settlers' cars and pelted them with
rocks. Once, working together, faces strained and knees buckling, they
heaved a boulder through the windshield of an approaching minibus filled
with Israeli soldiers. The vehicle screeched to a halt, and they could hear
shouting behind them; it wasn't clear if anyone was hurt. The boys escaped
through a rusted metal fence, racing behind a pirate videocassette store
and down a narrow lane they liked to call Palestine Street. They tore around
a corner, deciding to split up. Ramzi's cousin went one way, Ramzi the
other, straight into the arms of a soldier. Ramzi had seen him before. He
had blond hair and blue eyes and wore a red beret; he was tall, perhaps six
foot six. Ramzi called him the Russian.

The Russian grabbed Ramzi by his collar and looked him sternly in the
eye. He was not aware of what the boys had just done, but at the time,
Ramzi didn't know that. Suddenly Ramzi felt a warm liquid trickling down

his leg. His jeans turned a darker blue. The soldier flagged down a military jeep, and other soldiers came to take Ramzi away. They held him for an hour, then released him.

Ramzi and Rami liked to scour the fields and ditches just beyond the camp, looking for bits of copper or strips of aluminum, which they sold at the junkyard run by Abu Tabsha, a scary-looking man with a bulging eye, a permanent scowl, and rust on his pants from his endless work with scrap metal. He never spoke to the boys, only grunted, jerking his thumb toward the scale. After selling him the scrap, they would sneak back into the yard, steal the same metal, wait a few days, and sell it to him a second time. They were always searching for ways to bring home money, and they delighted in cheating Abu Tabsha.

Ramzi didn't work much with Sido anymore. He was too busy with school and his three jobs. He still delivered newspapers, and recently he had taken on work unloading the trucks that rumbled into the hisbeh from across the homeland, overburdened with mud-crusted fruits, vegetables, and herbs from nearby farms. This was the same place from which the brothers had once stolen vegetables during a curfew. The labor was taxing— some of the boxes Ramzi carried weighed nearly half as much as he did—and his bosses were often hard, explosive men who seemed to enjoy shortchanging him. Others invited him for hummus and clementines.

The work with Soraida was more relaxing. On this afternoon Ramzi had brought her two olive saplings. Together they paced the property, looking for the best place to plant. He dug two foot-deep holes in the dirt flanking the entrance to her front door and eased the saplings into them.

Again Ramzi buried his hands in the dark soil. Kneeling, he looked up toward the soot-streaked stones at the top of the house. On the rooftop a twisted television antenna framed a cold blue sky. Ramzi looked down again and thought of Sido's stories, and of all of the land he had never seen.

Soraida told Ramzi that a man from a village near Jenin had asked for her hand in marriage, and that she had accepted. The wedding was to take place in late summer. "I want you to be the guest of honor, Ramzi," Soraida told him. The ceremony would be held near the home of the bridegroom, but first they would stop in Kobar, where Soraida was born. Finally, Ramzi would see a Palestinian village.

In late August 1992, Ramzi and Soraida rode north out of Ramallah, rolling through the West Bank, past centuries-old terraces planted with olives. They passed the old Christian village of Birzeit, the "well of the olive oil," then turned off the lonely highway and rose along with an old road flanked by fir trees.

They were climbing toward Soraida's village. As Kobar drew near, Ramzi looked out the window at the houses clinging to hillsides; he couldn't understand why they didn't simply fall into the valley.

Fig, almond, plum, and apple orchards surrounded Soraida's family home, which was made of stone from a nearby quarry. Beyond the fruit trees lay yellowing fields of wheat, nearly ready for the harvest. Olive trees crawled up the terraced hills at the edge of the valley. That evening, Ramzi and Soraida watched the sunset, fired with yellows and reds, from the family's rooftop. In the morning, Ramzi woke to the smell of fresh loaves baking in the oven downstairs.

So this, Ramzi now understood, was what a village was like.

The next day they set out for the bridegroom's village, where the wedding was to take place. On an overlook near Nablus, they came upon a spectacular panoramic view of whitewashed Palestinian villages tucked deep into the valleys. A few miles to the west lay the border of Israel, and beyond that, the Mediterranean Sea. On a few of the nearer hilltops, they could see the red rooftops of new Israeli settlements. These were sprouting up across the West Bank with alarming frequency. Recently construction had begun on the "Seven Stars" plan announced by Israel's housing minister, Ariel Sharon. The plan called for a string of Jewish communities along the Green Line on Israel's border, eventually spilling into the West Bank. Sharon envisioned 250,000 Jews in these new settlements, many newly arrived from the former Soviet Union.

Though the presence of occupation was evident, the road was open, and Ramzi and Soraida traveled that day without restrictions. They passed fields of sunflowers and grapes and scattered wildflowers growing from roadside embankments, and came to a junction where they saw a rusted Iraqi tank: a casualty of the 1967 war. From there, they turned north, and rode in anticipation toward the wedding village.

*   *   *

Twenty-two hundred miles to the north in Oslo, Norway, Palestinian and Israeli negotiators were meeting in secret to try to forge a permanent agreement based on U.N. Resolution 242. In essence, "two-four-two" called for Arab recognition of the "sovereignty, territorial integrity and political independence" of Israel and for Israel's withdrawal from territories it occupied after the Six Day War. This, Yasser Arafat believed, would lead to the creation of an independent Palestine alongside Israel. For Arafat this represented a monumental compromise. Instead of a shared secular democratic nation on all of historic Palestine, he now was agreeing to a state on 22 percent of it. After forty years of liberation struggle, the PLO leader was convinced this was the best the Palestinians could do. The Soviet Union, which had backed Palestinian resistance for decades, had collapsed. Arafat, disastrously, had supported Saddam Hussein during the recent Gulf War. At the time his support of Saddam had made sense in the Palestinian political context. Saddam, seen by Palestinians as brave enough to stand up to the West and Israel, had been wildly popular in the West Bank, Gaza, and East Jerusalem. But with Saddam's defeat in the first Gulf War, and the expulsion of two hundred thousand Palestinian wage earners from Kuwait after the war, Arafat's strategy had backfired. The PLO leader was therefore economically and politically weakened. In the wake of the intifada, however, he saw an opening. The long uprising, fought from 1987 to 1993 in the occupied territories while Arafat was in exile, had ironically given him a measure of leverage with Israel.

Israelis, too, were exhausted by the intifada. Though their casualties were only a fraction of those suffered by Palestinians—ninety-four Israeli civilians, compared to nearly eleven hundred Palestinians killed by Israeli security forces—the "stone revolution" had created a deep unease in much of Israeli society. Many Israelis were troubled by the sight of their own young men and women chasing, beating, and sometimes gunning down rock-bearing youths. Growing numbers of Israelis had come to believe that the Palestinian quest for statehood was legitimate, and that the military occupation, the brutalities of which had become familiar to people all over the world, was not. In the end the intifada brought reluctant Israelis to the table. Yitzhak Rabin, formerly the hardline defense minister, had become prime minister, voted in by hopeful Israelis who believed the veteran soldier and his Labor Party coalition could bring a lasting peace.

In September 1993, Yasser Arafat and Yitzhak Rabin shook hands on the White House lawn in front of a smiling President Bill Clinton. Israel and the PLO had just agreed on the Declaration of Principles, which signaled their intent to negotiate a "just, lasting and comprehensive peace settlement" based on "mutual dignity and security." The declaration, forged in Oslo, Norway, without U.S. involvement, called for Palestinian elections and an interim self-government and for Israel's withdrawal from the Gaza Strip and Jericho, the ancient West Bank town in the Jordan Valley. The declaration did not promise a Palestinian state, nor mention it. Rather, it was the beginning of a five-year "interim period" in the "Oslo process," a "preparatory step toward the realization of the legitimate rights of the Palestinian people." The ultimate step, Arafat believed, would be a free and independent state. But the words *independence, sovereignty, freedom*, or *Palestine* were not to be found in the document. (*Security*, however, was mentioned twelve times.) Rather, the declaration referred to "permanent status negotiations" over Jerusalem, refugees, settlements, water, and borders, which were to commence within three years. In the meantime, Israel maintained a strong military presence throughout the West Bank and Gaza, protecting settlers and controlling the movement of Palestinians.

Despite its limited promises, many Palestinians rejoiced in the possibilities the Oslo process seemed to represent. Thousands who had been in exile for a generation, including Arafat, would soon be returning home amid the dreams of liberation and statehood. Yet the accord drove a wedge between Arafat and some of his closest Palestinian allies, who believed the PLO leader had given up far too much. Many still believed in a single, secular, democratic state for all the people "between the river and the sea"—that is, all of Israel, the West Bank, and Gaza. Why, they asked, would any Palestinian leader agree to a state on only 22 percent of historic Palestine? Mahmoud Darwish, the great Palestinian poet, resigned from the PLO executive committee, predicting the Oslo process would lead to more conflict, not less. Others believed Arafat was sacrificing the right of Palestinians to return to their old homelands, and to a single, secular, democratic state for all the people in the West Bank, Gaza, and Israel—Palestinians and Israelis alike. And a new player had emerged: Hamas, founded in Gaza in 1988, was the Islamist rival to the PLO. Its founding documents advocated for an Islamist state in all of old Palestine, accused Jews of aspiring to "rule the world," and declared, "only the jihad can solve the Palestine issue."

Polls within the occupied territories indicated, however, that most Palestinians were willing to give Oslo, Arafat, and the two-state solution a chance.

During that month, for many days in a row, people gathered in joyful celebration. Ramzi, now fourteen years old, made his way to the Manara, the traffic circle that marked the center of Ramallah. Here, six years prior, in the early mornings just before the uprising, Ramzi had straddled his bicycle, taking in the quiet. Now, for days on end, thousands of Palestinians packed the Manara, spilling out of the square, jubilant and delirious.

"*T-t-t-tahrir!*" Ramzi shouted with his fellow Palestinians. "Freedom! Free, free, free Palestine!"

Six

VIOLA

December 1995
Ramallah and Al Amari refugee camp

O<small>N</small> D<small>ECEMBER</small> 27, 1995, after twenty-eight years of military occupation, Israeli troops began pulling out of Ramallah. More than two years had passed since the famous Rabin–Arafat handshake on the White House lawn, and despite agonizing delays, some Palestinians chose to mark the occasion by placing carnations in the gun barrels of the departing soldiers. Others preferred to send them away with a rain of stones, though thrown from such a distance that they fell not on the troops, but on the unfortunate Palestinian revelers.

Three days later, on December 30, tens of thousands of Palestinians greeted the thundering helicopter carrying Yasser Arafat to a euphoric welcome in Ramallah. Phase one of Arafat's return to Palestine had been to establish the semiautonomous Palestinian Authority (PA), the new entity created by the Oslo accord, in Jericho and Gaza. Palestinian flags now flew at border crossings manned by Palestinian police; nearby sat Israeli security officials, invisible behind tinted glass, in full control of approving or denying each entry.

Phase two included Ramallah. "Palestine is for all her sons!" Arafat shouted from the podium at the district headquarters for the PA, wearing his black-and-white checked keffiyeh and looking out through thick glasses. "Today, we are making the history of the independent Palestinian state with holy Jerusalem [Al Quds] as its capital!

"Al Quuuds!" Arafat cried again and again as thousands repeated his jubilant promise. "Al Quuuds!"

The idea of Jerusalem carried great power for every Palestinian. Its sudden loss, when Israel annexed East Jerusalem after the 1967 war and declared the city "united" as the "eternal capital of Israel," was a shock. Military bulldozers razed the Moroccan (or Maghribi) Quarter, a centuries-old neighborhood, evicting more than six hundred Palestinians. This was to facilitate the gathering of thousands of Jewish pilgrims intent on worshipping at the Western (or Wailing) Wall. Before the war, under Jordanian rule, Jews had been prohibited from praying there; after Israel's conquest of East Jerusalem, they rushed to the site. The rubble of the old Moroccan Quarter, built in 1193, had been cleared to create the broad plaza at the Western Wall. According to Jewish tradition, this is the surviving wall of the Second Temple. The platform just above it is known to Jews as the Temple Mount. For Muslims, it is the Haram al-Sharif, or Noble Sanctuary, upon which stand the Al Aqsa Mosque and the gold-encrusted Dome of the Rock; it is the place from which Mohammad made his night ride to heaven on a winged steed. Thus, the same stone is among the holiest places for Muslims and Jews alike.

For Palestinians, however, the loss of Jerusalem also represented something beyond the sacred. "The Jerusalem of houses and cobbled streets and spice markets . . . The oil market and the sellers of antiques and mother-of-pearl and sesame cakes," the poet Mourid Barghouti wrote. "The library, the doctor, the lawyer, the engineer, and the dressers of brides with high dowries. The terminals of the buses that trundle in every morning from all the villages with peasants come to buy and to sell. The Jerusalem of white cheese, of oil and olives and thyme, of baskets of figs and necklaces and leather and Salah al-Din Street. Our neighbor the nun, and her neighbor, the muezzin who was always in a hurry. The palm fronds in all the streets on Palm Sunday, the Jerusalem of houseplants, cobbled alleys, and narrow covered lanes . . . This is the city of our senses, our bodies, and our childhood . . ."

Jerusalem, beyond all other places, captured the Palestinian imagination. Many had returned from exile just to be near it, even if they were not allowed to visit. Arafat's promise of a return—and the establishment of the Palestinian capital in East Jerusalem—tapped his people's deepest aspirations.

Ramzi watched Arafat's Ramallah homecoming on the news that evening. He was confused, and had decided not to go to the celebration. Yes, Arafat was back, and with him, a Palestinian police force, thirty thousand strong, each officer subject to Israel's approval, that would replace the

Israeli soldiers patrolling Ramallah and other Palestinian cities and towns. Yet Ramzi wondered what "peace" meant if it could coexist with the settlements. Israel's flag still flew on the red-roofed hilltop at Psagot, in plain view from Al Amari, signaling that the occupation was nowhere near over. The army's withdrawal from Ramallah consisted of retreating one kilometer, to the hospital near the edge of town. Ramzi, now sixteen years old, wasn't in a mood to celebrate.

Still, there had been big changes. Israel's army had pulled out of Al Amari, abandoning its positions in the four-story stone building at the camp's entrance. Snipers no longer perched on the rooftop. Ramzi's family could leave home without fear of teargas or of jeep or foot patrols. Random night raids had ceased, curfews and general strikes were lifted, and the family enjoyed simple liberties like walking freely, shopping when they wanted to, or seeking regular work: Ramzi's uncles now resumed their travel across the "Green Line," the pre-1967 border between the West Bank and Israel, to wash dishes and clean hotels in West Jerusalem. Schools were no longer subject to closures by occupying authorities, and Ramzi didn't have to sneak into private homes or musty shacks just to get a few hours of instruction.

As part of the Oslo agreements, tens of thousands of Palestinians long exiled by Israel were finally coming home. These included former fighters and other nationalists committed to liberating Palestine and absorbing Israel into a larger, secular state, who had been deemed a security threat by Israeli authorities. As a result, they had been deported to Lebanon and Jordan. Others had fled or been driven out during the Nakba in 1948, or the Six Day War in 1967, and were not allowed to come back. Now, because of the limited amnesty, Palestinians from all over their global diaspora were returning to the West Bank or Gaza.

The exiles returned after decades to a homeland they could barely recognize. High-rise apartments had sprung up in Ramallah. Israeli flags flew at border crossings and from hilltop settlements. Villages from childhood seemed familiar but remote. "Among all the children playing in the streets," lamented the poet Mourid Barghouti, who came back after thirty years, "there were none who knew me."

Among those coming home was Mohammad Fadel, a violinist trained in musical therapy. Mohammad had helped build a classical music conservatory in Amman at the request of Jordan's Queen Noor, and now he was returning to Palestine at the urging of an old friend, Suhail Khoury, to help do the same in Ramallah. Suhail, a clarinetist and teacher, came from the wealthy extended family of Palestinian Christians who had founded Birzeit University, which sponsored the new National Conservatory of Music. Suhail had recently been released from prison after his arrest and subsequent torture by Israeli authorities: He had secretly recorded, mixed, copied, and distributed tens of thousands of cassettes of Palestinian resistance music, known as the "Intifada Tapes."

Mohammad believed he and Suhail could now be part of the cultural renaissance of an independent Palestinian state. And so he crossed the bridge at the River Jordan and into the West Bank, where, like so many others, he emerged from the bus, kissed the ground, and wept.

Mohammad was related by marriage to Soraida, Ramzi's friend. One day shortly after he returned, he went to see Soraida to discuss his plans. During the intifada, Soraida reminded him, with all of the PLO officials and thousands of others like Mohammad in exile, it was the youth of the camps who had sacrificed the most. Wealthy and middle-class Palestinians bringing their riches from exile, Soraida emphasized, could not afford to ignore the shabab. They needed to be accounted for in any new Palestinian society. That included new cultural institutions, like a music conservatory.

The National Conservatory of Music was to be a small but important aspect of emerging Palestinian nationhood through the creation of national and cultural institutions, including new government ministries, tourist offices, and independent Palestinian media. Beachside cafés were under construction in Gaza, and luxury hotels in Ramallah; there were even plans for a locally owned Palestinian brewery. Arafat himself had broken ground at the Gaza International Airport, to be served by the new Palestinian Airlines. A postage stamp now bore the name Palestine. There were plans for a telephone country code, 970, for the country-in-waiting. And now, a music conservatory. Worn down by the toll the six-year intifada had taken, and energized by a chance at peace, many Palestinians allowed themselves to dream not only of a state, but of the normal things, like playing and teaching music, that might accompany the end of violence. The conservatory, cofounder Rima Tarazi believed, could be part of a "musical and cultural awakening in Palestine." It would offer "the younger generations artistic means that would help them express themselves and cope with the challenges" all around them.

*   *   *

Soraida and Mohammad knocked on the door of Sido's house in Al Amari. Jamila, in her Palestinian housedress and loose white scarf, answered and invited them in. Ramzi wasn't home, but Sido was. The house was spotless, Soraida noticed, and smelled of chlorine, as if it had just been cleaned.

Soraida introduced Mohammad as he looked around the room. A framed greeting in English, made of embroidered beads, read GOD BLESS OUR HOME. Alongside that was a depiction of Al Aqsa Mosque in Jerusalem, in yellow, blue, red, and green sequins. In the center of the wall was the poster of eight-year-old Ramzi, holding the pieces of curbstone, under a slogan in Basque: AGORA INTIFADA. Intifada now. Near that, Soraida noticed, was a small framed photograph of Ramzi's father, Hussein.

They chatted about the village of Na'ani, the end of the uprising, Oslo, the music school founded by Queen Noor of Jordan, the new conservatory in Ramallah, and Ramzi's plans. He was still in high school, but only for another year. At school, Ramzi was pounding out a five-beat rhythm, *Bah-bah-bah-BAH-ba, Bah-bah-bah-BAH-ba,* even during class. "Stop it, Ramzi!" the teachers would shout. But it seemed he couldn't. He carried his humming and rhythms home. Ramzi, his family had concluded long ago, was in his own world, and this was just another expression of it.

Soraida hadn't noticed any intrinsic musical talent in Ramzi; rather, she believed that as a child from a refugee camp, Ramzi should have the same opportunity to play music as any other child.

Sido told his visitors that he was sure his grandson would be interested in learning music.

"All right, then," Mohammad said. "Of course we will teach him. Please have him come tomorrow afternoon."

*   *   *

Ramzi climbed the stairs of the new center for music, a short walk from Al Amari camp. When he walked through the door, a few students were sitting in a semicircle as Mohammad Fadel showed them their instruments. Ramzi saw a girl with a cello and a tall, rangy young man with a large bass. On his long face he wore a scruffy goatee and a sad smile. "I'm Ramadan," he said.

"I'm Ramzi."

Mohammad came over and introduced himself. "I met your grandfather yesterday."

"He told me," Ramzi said.

"What would you like to learn to play?" Mohammad asked, leading him to a room filled with stringed instruments.

"I like the violin," Ramzi replied, remembering Teacher Khalidi.

"You have large hands," said Mohammad. "Here, take this one. It's just like a large violin. It's called a viola."

Seven

HARMONY

May 1996
Ramallah

T HE DOUBLE METAL doors of the National Conservatory of Music
swung open and five American chamber musicians ducked under
the transom and stepped into the crowded attic room. Ramzi watched
them shaking hands with Mohammad Fadel and conservatory director
Suhail Khoury. The tallest one, he noticed, carried his instrument in a
black backpack. His name was Peter, and he played the viola.

The chamber musicians had traveled from Jerusalem, seven miles to the
south, through multiple military checkpoints, on a special mission for the
Consulate General of the United States in East Jerusalem. In the wake of
the Oslo peace accords, they had been recruited as cultural ambassadors of
the American government.

Trips like this one were still unusual in the early days of Oslo, so the
security-conscious Americans had sent an advance team to scope out
the conservatory a day earlier, then arranged for a pair of bulletproof
Chevy Suburbans to bring the chamber musicians—pianist, violinist,
violist, cellist, and double bass player—and their entourage from East
Jerusalem to the music school. The irony of such protection was not lost
on the musicians, especially considering they were part of a program called
Playing for Peace, from the Apple Hill Center for Chamber Music in New
Hampshire. But any awkward feelings evaporated as the chamber players
stepped into the room and peered into a sea of smiling, expectant faces,
Ramzi's among them.

In small practice rooms, the American musicians sat in on Arabic music classes—Ramzi was also learning the bouzouk, a kind of cross between a mandolin and a banjo—and they taught workshops in classical Western music. Ramzi had his first lesson with an actual violist. Until now his teacher had been Mohammad, a violinist, who also taught Ramzi's friend Ramadan Khattab, a double bass player. Violist Peter Sulski, working with Ramzi and two others, started with the fundamentals: How to stand, as if your feet had roots, to give you strength and flexibility. How to hold the instrument, resting between the left side of your neck and your left hand, at a forty-five-degree angle to the floor. How to cradle the bow.

"It's like a good handshake, you know?" Peter said hopefully. "It's not a death grip." He looked around the room as Ghadeer, Ramzi's fellow viola student, translated: Not too light, not too aggressive; firm but inviting. He demonstrated proper form: thumb latched underneath, four fingers resting atop the bow. Everyone did the same. And pulled their bows downward.

Peter's goal with every young student was to get them to believe they could play something beautiful from the beginning, even if it was just one note. This would begin to give them the physical confidence to play entire pieces.

Ramzi eagerly awaited his turn. He found it difficult to contain his excitement. His mouth was slightly open, curved into a perpetual smile. Presently Peter looked over at the seventeen-year-old boy. Slowly, deliberately, Ramzi pulled his bow across the second string of his viola. His downbow made a powerful, steady, resonating G, or *sol*. The sound on the open G string was pure and clear—even, Peter thought, beautiful.

There was so much more that Peter wanted to get into. How to discern pitch. How to observe silence. The correct placement of the fingers on the fingerboard. For a brief workshop, however, there wasn't time. At least, Peter thought, in their first lesson together, they had made one beautiful thing.

For Ramzi, it wasn't enough. He was hungry, and wanted more.

Before they left, the visiting chamber musicians put on a concert. Ramzi, Ramadan, and twenty other students sat cross-legged on the floor in front of an upright piano. Teachers leaned back against the walls as the Apple Hill Chamber Players began the first movement of the Brahms Piano Quartet no. 1 in G Minor. The ceilings were so low that Peter, six foot two, could barely stand up straight.

The piece opened serenely, with single lines passing back and forth, from Eric Stumacher's hands on the piano, to Peter's on the viola, then to violinist Movses Pogossian, and finally to cellist Paul Cohen. As the strings carried the melody one way, Eric's hands began to fly across the keyboard, creating what Ramzi heard as a completely different melody. Yet it was one piece of music.

Ramzi leaned forward, eyes wide. He hadn't known that music could sound this way, with everyone playing different notes. In Arabic music, the entire orchestra played the same melody, together. Now Ramzi was hearing four different melodies playing simultaneously, all in the same piece of music. He didn't understand what was happening. This was Ramzi's first experience with harmony.

After the performance, in the cramped upstairs room, the delighted young Palestinians crowded around the Americans, eager for more. Peter recalled being enveloped by the warmth. "P-p-p-lease stay," Ramzi told Peter urgently. "S-s-s-tay."

The musicians were due back in East Jerusalem, however, and soon they were climbing into their Suburbans for the ride back to the American Colony Hotel. Already, Peter was sure of one thing: He was coming back.

*   *   *

By the fall of 1996, three years after the White House celebration of the Oslo agreement, many Palestinians remained hopeful about statehood. But the peace process had been gravely wounded. The previous November, Israeli Prime Minister Yitzhak Rabin had been assassinated at a peace rally of one hundred thousand in Tel Aviv, killed by a religious Jewish extremist who claimed to be acting on orders from God. Rabin had been embraced by the surging Israeli peace movement, which saw Oslo as a solution to decades of violence and misery on both sides.

For Palestinian critics, however, the problems with Oslo had less to do with Rabin's death than with misgivings borne of the agreement itself. Under the "Oslo process," Israel was not restricted from building new West Bank settlements, military bases, and roads for the exclusive use of settlers and "VIPs." Some of the land was seized from Palestinian owners who had been abroad and barred by Israel from returning after the Six Day War; thus Israel considered the land "abandoned" and it therefore "reverted" to their ownership as part of ancient "Judea and Samaria."

The new construction took place on territory the Palestinians considered essential for their own sovereign state. This was part of the 22 percent of historic Palestine that was left for them, and the Palestinian leadership believed it had made a giant concession by agreeing to a state on this fraction of the land. Now even the prospects of a Palestine in the West Bank and Gaza seemed compromised by the increasing Israeli presence. For critics of the peace process, it appeared that the dreams of the PLO—to bring liberation to its people—had shrunk to limited self-government, in Ramallah, Jericho, Gaza City, and other towns, under the new Palestinian Authority. Through its military patrols and tightly monitored borders, Israel remained in control—of border crossings, West Bank and Gaza checkpoints, even access to water resources—and had no apparent plans, and no explicit requirement under Oslo, to relinquish it.

Mourid Barghouti, the poet who had returned from thirty years in exile, was stunned by the change in the PLO's image and duties. "Now here is that same freedom fighter (chained with the conditions of his enemies), exercising his direct authority on the ordinary citizen, on the old men, on the students and the shops and the traffic and the customs and excise and arts and letters, taxes, courts, investments," he wrote. "Israel succeeded in tearing away the sacred aspect of the Palestinian cause, turning it into what it is now—a series of 'procedures' and 'schedules' that are usually respected only by the weaker party in the conflict . . ."

"What Israel has gotten is official Palestinian consent to continue occupation," wrote Edward Said, a Palestinian born in Jerusalem and a professor of comparative literature at Columbia University in New York City. Edward, considered one of the twentieth century's great intellectuals, was author of the masterworks *Orientalism* and *Culture and Imperialism*. He was perhaps best known for his fierce defense of the rights of his people in numerous books and hundreds of essays and articles published worldwide.

Edward considered the Oslo agreement "an instrument of Palestinian surrender." He had declined an invitation to attend the White House ceremony with Arafat and Rabin in September 1993. The agreement, he wrote, represented "a kingdom of illusions, with Israel firmly in command. Clearly the PLO has transformed itself from a national liberation movement into a kind of small-town government." Under the new Palestinian Authority, several security services were responsible for public order, including one charged with keeping Palestinian demonstrators from confronting Israeli troops. The security services were funded in large part by the U.S. government, with training from the CIA.

"Those of us who fought for Palestine before Oslo fought for a cause that we believed would spur the emergence of a just order," Edward wrote. "Never has this ideal been further from realization than today."

The poet Mourid Barghouti put it more simply: "The others," he concluded, "are still masters of the place." The sense of powerlessness was perhaps most deeply felt in East Jerusalem. In September 1996, Israeli archeologists excavated a tunnel underneath Al Aqsa Mosque, uncovering archaeological remains which they said dated back twenty-five hundred years. It was part of Israel's attempts to establish Jewish history at the Temple Mount. The excavations led to violent clashes. Palestinians believed the digging, which Israel's Ministry of Religious Affairs had undertaken periodically for years, could weaken the foundation of Al Aqsa and lead to its collapse; they suspected this was Israel's intent. The Palestinian Islamic Higher Council called the work a "severe aggression against our people's rights in Jerusalem." A short time later Benjamin Netanyahu, the new prime minister, announced construction of Har Homa on a hill above Bethlehem, which was known to Palestinians as Jabal Abu Ghneim, and upon which Palestinian protesters camped out in a peaceful resistance, vowing to block construction of the settlement. Har Homa would nearly complete a circle of Jewish settlements around East Jerusalem. "The battle for Jerusalem has begun," Netanyahu declared.

As he grew more frustrated with Oslo, Edward Said began to seek other ways his people and the Israelis could find a just solution between equal partners. The lifelong quest had taken on greater urgency in recent years as Edward fought for his life: In 1991, he had been diagnosed with leukemia.

Improbably, Edward Said's search would put him on the same path as a seventeen-year-old boy from Al Amari refugee camp who had recently taken up the viola.

*   *   *

One afternoon, Ramzi scaled the steps of the school for his viola lesson with Mohammad Fadel. He was early; he could hear his teacher working with another student. Ramzi sat on a plastic chair, jiggling his leg, tapping out a rhythm on his knee.

The jittery boy had twenty minutes to spare before he demonstrated his repertoire: "Frère Jacques," "Jingle Bells," and the simple but powerful melody of the "Ode to Joy," which he had first heard years earlier from the musical teddy bear Sido had salvaged from the street.

The humble upstairs quarters of the National Conservatory of Music had become the lively musical and social hub for Ramzi and his friends. Here he usually found Ramadan plucking his bass or other friends on the piano or the oud. Today everyone else was out or in practice, however, and Ramzi didn't feel like sitting and waiting. He set down his viola, slipped outside, and trotted back down the steps. He stood near the municipality building, where he had worked many hours with his grandfather. As he watched, passing a quiet moment, a white Subaru approached from the direction of Psagot. From the yellow license plates and the appearance of the passengers, he could tell it was a car filled with Israeli settlers. He stepped into the street, picked up a stone, and hurled it at the approaching car. Ramzi heard the windshield crack. He turned and ran. A moment later he could hear shouting in Hebrew, then the sound of rapid machine-gun fire. *Mini Uzi*, Ramzi thought, without looking back. *Shot into the air.* From the acoustics, and the percussion, he determined the make and the direction of fire.

Ramzi waited for a while, hidden in safety. As long as the settlers remained, he believed, there would be no peace.

Ramzi walked back toward the music conservatory, calmly, as if nothing had happened. He arrived at his viola lesson on time.

*   *   *

Mohammad Fadel understood that Ramzi was struggling to pivot from his past as a child on the front lines to a dedicated music student. The problem wasn't desire. Ramzi practiced plenty, and always showed up for his lessons. The problem, to Mohammad, was how traumatized Ramzi often seemed, how "he had something very bad inside." Mohammad didn't know all of the details, but he was learning what Ramzi's generation had lived through as he and other Palestinians had been in exile.

During the six-year intifada, nearly 1,100 Palestinians had been killed by Israeli soldiers, nearly a quarter of them children. In the same period, 180 Israelis, about half of them soldiers, had been killed by Palestinians.

More than 130,000 Palestinians were injured; 120,000 had been arrested. Twenty-five hundred houses had been demolished, and 184,000 olive trees uprooted, largely in the name of Israeli security in villages near settlements. In addition, at least 750 Palestinians, including Ramzi's father, had died by Palestinian hands: by one estimate, as many as those killed by Israeli troops. This number, often overlooked, revealed a society torn from both outside and in.

It was impossible to measure the exact degree of emotional damage the youth of Ramzi's generation had suffered. Countless international studies examined the victimization of Palestine's children, especially in the refugee camps, citing increased sleep loss, disobedience, unruliness, fear of leaving the house, and other effects of the recurring trauma. But, perhaps unexpectedly, researchers also found a reduction of some pathological symptoms, concluding that the children and youth of the intifada felt empowered by their own courage and leadership. Ramzi saw himself less as a victim of trauma than as a brave boy who had stood up to an occupying army and helped pave the way for his people's independence. He regarded himself as an agent of his own destiny, a young man who was learning to convert his trauma into positive energy in the service of his people. To what extent he could transcend the many losses he had already suffered, and the ones to come, remained to be seen.

Mohammad believed his training in music therapy could help children like Ramzi. He had received his B.A. from the Conservatory of Arabic Music in Cairo, then studied music therapy at George Mason University in Virginia. Mohammad recalled sitting in a practice room with Ramzi, quietly drawing him out through his viola, and through conversation. Mohammed's insights were borne out by studies on music and trauma from other conflict zones, including Bosnia, South Africa, and Northern Ireland, where researchers found that music reduced the recurrence of traumatic memories, raised the threshold for anxiety, and, perhaps more important, created the possibility to "reimagine" one's own life. Playing music, the researchers found—making something new in response to the trauma—not only was a way to move beyond victimhood; it was a path to healing and, eventually, to a complete personal transformation.

"Now you play music," Mohammad recalled saying to Ramzi. "Now, you are another color. You are something else." Step by step, Ramzi "learned to talk through the viola."

Ramzi does not remember any music therapy lessons. He does recall Mohammad's spontaneous energy and his welcoming spirit with the students. "I love him," he said in 1998. "He's like a father to me."

*   *   *

At first, hearing the teasing of other shabab in the camp, Ramzi felt shy about taking his viola home. Once he got over that, and began practicing in an upstairs room at Sido's, he found his viola uncooperative. The proper notes were not coming out. Ramzi found this hard to believe. He had stood up to soldiers and dodged their bullets. Adults considered him a hero. But in front of this instrument, he felt weak. It was as if the instrument had its own will and was refusing to cooperate. "Make the sound happen!" Ramzi declared, glaring at his viola. "*Min shan Allah!*" he fumed. "For God's sake!"

The more he practiced, Ramzi noticed, the more the frustrations evaporated. As the sound from his instrument improved, Ramzi felt the vibrations of the notes penetrating his body, through his chin and neck. The physical and emotional sensation, as he played upstairs at Sido's, alone in a bare, echoey room, was eerie and calming. He was breathing differently now, more slowly, and his stutter had begun to improve. Soon it would disappear completely.

Walking through town, Ramzi no longer felt like just a kid from the refugee camp, selling newspapers to well-off professionals. Now he encountered them as a musician; they had been friendly to him before, but Ramzi sensed they were seeing him differently. He played in auditoriums of buildings he'd had no reason to enter previously—like the Friends Boys' School, where many of the Christian elites sent their children. He saw their parents fill the seats for recitals. At first he wondered how the people knew that studying music was important. Slowly he began to understand what a musical culture was, and why parents believed it important to urge their children to learn an instrument.

*   *   *

In early 1997, Peter Sulski returned to Ramallah. He booked a fifteen-dollar room at a pension across from the bus station, a short walk from the Conservatory. He had come to teach Ramzi and other viola students.

Peter had just turned thirty. Tall, with dark blond hair in a military-style buzz cut, he had grown up in Worcester, Massachusetts, the son of a Polish-American father who taught math at the College of the Holy Cross, and a British stay-at-home mom. He had joined the London Symphony Orchestra at twenty-four, performing in Japan, Korea, China, and across Europe and the United States—including at Carnegie Hall. Yet Peter had doubts about staying in the LSO. His instrument was but one in a section of twelve violas, in an orchestra of a hundred and seven people. There wasn't much chance for individual expression. He wanted to play more chamber music, and he had grown weary of the constant traveling and living in hotels. He longed to be part of a community and to make an impact with his music. He was now on a break from the LSO and soon would have to decide whether or not to make that permanent.

Ramzi had been longing for a true viola teacher like Peter. There was almost no classical musical culture in Palestine upon which he could draw. Nowhere in Ramallah could he buy sheet music by Beethoven, or even strings for his viola. He and his fellow students were all just starting, and they didn't even know how to begin to talk about music.

In Ramzi, Peter saw an uncut diamond, "a seventeen-year-old punk, full of beans," with charisma and desire. And raw: Ramzi had no inner rhythm; he could barely read music; he didn't hold the viola correctly; he was just now learning the difference between whole, half, and quarter notes. "He didn't know shit," Peter laughed years later. Ramzi spoke virtually no English, and Peter, no Arabic. But Ramzi's thirst, and Peter's wish to connect, formed a bridge. They focused on the music.

"An A is an A," Peter told Ramzi one day in a tiny conservatory practice room. "Four hundred forty vibrations per second." Peter tried to explain that on the viola, notes don't just come out, as they do when you put your fingers on the keys of a piano. You have to have the right pitch. You have to know what you want to hear from the viola. And if you have the right repetition—muscle memory—your body will do it for you.

Muscle memory—the body's learned repetition of a pattern of notes— not only accelerated the process of building a repertoire; through its acti- vation of neural networks in the brain, it was also helping to reconfigure Ramzi—to form a new core. To become a string or a horn player or a pianist, musicians themselves reflected, meant to be rewired physically, as a different person. Muscle memory was the path to that transformation. Eventually, it would help Ramzi see his future in a new way.

*   *   *

For the past few summers, on breaks from the LSO, Peter had been teaching and performing with the Apple Hill Chamber Players at their leafy retreat in New Hampshire. A centerpiece of Apple Hill was the Playing for Peace program, where the children of long-time enemies—from Cyprus, Northern Ireland, the Middle East—could see each other as equals while making music together. Peter wanted to get the unpolished, undertrained Ramzi ready for the summer camp.

The two worked long hours on Mozart's "La Marche Turque," a relatively slow and simple piece for a beginner. At home in Al Amari, Ramzi practiced late into the evenings, sometimes on the rooftop, the sound of his instrument drifting over the camp.

In the spring of 1997, pianist Eric Stumacher, a cofounder of Playing for Peace and director of Apple Hill, returned to Ramallah. Ramzi played the Mozart for him. This was his audition for the summer camp Apple Hill.

Now he waited.

A few days later, Peter and Eric invited Ramzi to a concert of the Apple Hill Chamber Players in East Jerusalem. The performance was scheduled to begin at seven. Ramzi arrived at the Israeli military checkpoint at Beit Hanina, just north of Jerusalem, at six thirty, in plenty of time to make it to the concert.

A soldier accused Ramzi of throwing stones. Many times he had, of course, but not on this day. The soldier instructed Ramzi to put his hands up against the wall and asked him where he was going. Ramzi replied that he was invited to a classical music concert near the Old City of Jerusalem. The soldier didn't believe him. He frisked Ramzi roughly, then left him standing against the wall. Yet Ramzi was unbothered; his mind was occupied by an exotic place called New Hampshire. He sensed an invitation was coming soon to travel to the summer camp there.

Finally the soldier let Ramzi go. He took a shared taxi the last ten minutes to East Jerusalem. Ramzi gazed through the window of the beat-up stretch Mercedes, packed with fellow West Bankers who'd been allowed passage to Jerusalem. In the distance, the golden dome of Al Aqsa

Mosque rose up from the Holy City. He could hear the faint sound of chamber music coming from the concert hall of the East Jerusalem YMCA, two hundred meters north of the walled Old City and next to the American consulate building. The concert hadn't finished yet. Ramzi trotted up the stairs and walked into the hall, to the sound of Mozart's Piano Quartet in G Minor. There on stage were the same four musicians who'd only recently come to the conservatory and introduced Ramzi to the concept of harmony. Peter, swaying with the music, smiled and nodded at his student.

The piece reached its thunderous conclusion, and the room erupted in applause.

As the clapping died down, Eric stood up and stepped to the microphone. He told the audience about the Playing for Peace program in New England, where young Arab, Israeli, and other international musicians would live side by side as equals, and sometimes even as friends. The concept was simple: no elaborate forums or dialogues; they would just play music together.

Now Eric said, "Would Ramzi Hussein Aburedwan please come up to the stage?"

Ramzi bounded up to the podium, and Eric handed him an announcement.

BE IT HEREBY DECLARED ON THIS 6TH OF MAY, 1997

THAT

RAMZI HUSSEIN

OF RAMALLAH

IS THE RECIPIENT OF THE 1997 PLAYING FOR PEACE

PALESTINIAN SCHOLARSHIP

Providing

Full tuition, room, board and transportation expenses for

participation in the 1997

Apple Hill Summer Chamber Music and Festival

East Sullivan, New Hampshire, USA—

July 28 to August 26, 1997

Ramzi looked for something else besides the invitation. He was confused, and struggled to hide his disappointment. This was great news, but something was missing: Where was the airline ticket to America?

That, Eric explained later, would be coming soon.

* * *

In July 1997, Ramzi, now eighteen years old, boarded a flight from Tel Aviv to New York. It was the first time he'd been on a plane; the first time he'd left his homeland; the first time since the day, at age five, when he arrived in his uncle's pushcart, that he'd been apart from Sido, his grandmother, aunts, and siblings, Rami, Rana, and Rula.

From his middle seat in the smoking section, Ramzi gazed down at the distant earth. For long stretches he'd get up from his seat and stand in the back, peering through the small square window on the exit door. How did a plane actually fly, he wondered. Chain-smoking, he squinted down at the lights seven miles below, and later toward a black ocean. He imagined the land he was bound for. The United States, he assumed, would be just as he had seen it on television: At Apple Hill Chamber Music Camp in New Hampshire, he was sure, there would be skyscrapers everywhere.

Eight

MOZART

July 1997
Southern New Hampshire

THE PINE-PLANK BUILDINGS of the Apple Hill Center for
Chamber Music stand at the top of a two-mile rise on a dirt road
flanked by snapdragons, birch trees, and wooden houses half-hidden by
the forest. Once the hub of a musical hippy back-to-the-land movement,
the center was built on one hundred acres, two miles from the nearest
village.

The van carrying Ramzi stopped in front of the weathered Concert
Barn, alongside a farmhouse built in 1780. As he climbed out, he saw that
the lushness of New Hampshire in summer had been completely outside
his imagination.

Wildflowers covered a meadow leading to the edge of the woods. In the
near western distance rose Pinnacle Peak, a bump on a ridge; beyond that,
forty miles away, the deep greens of Mount Snow and Hogback Mountain
in Vermont.

All around Ramzi, other young musicians piled out of family cars:
boys and girls together, in shorts and short sleeves, instrument cases
slung over shoulders, laughing, joking, and embracing like old friends. At
folding tables in front of the barn, counselors checked in new campers,
taking turns leading them past the old gazebo and into the buggy forest
thicket, to the rough-hewn cabins named after famous composers:
Albinoni, Beethoven, Copland, Dvořák, Eccles, Franck. Ramzi's roommates in Glazunov cabin were a Jordanian and two Egyptian brothers,

Mahmoud and Mohamed Saleh. He was thrilled to meet Egyptians, whom he had only seen on TV.

After dinner on the first night, Eric Stumacher, Apple Hill's director, welcomed the campers. He was broad-shouldered, with thick bushy eyebrows and curly hair that fell well below his collar. Apple Hill, and its Playing for Peace program, Eric explained, lived the idea that all people on this earth are of equal value. "You might be a Jordanian, an Israeli, a Palestinian, or Egyptian," Eric said. The basis of Apple Hill was that everyone was an equal member of the community, and they all needed to find a way to get along, to respect and listen to each other. Chamber music was the path for this.

On the first night away from his family, Ramzi slept surrounded by pulsating crickets in the blackest night he had ever experienced. Mahmoud, the Egyptian, woke up in the middle of the night, after an apparent nightmare, thrusting out his arms and yelling, "Crocodile!" Ramzi found the darkness disconcerting in a way the soldiers at the refugee camp never were. He wouldn't admit to fear, not even years later. Still, it was too quiet.

The first morning brought the sound of complaining crows and a breeze in the pine boughs. At breakfast in the concert barn, morning light shone through the ten-foot-high paneled windows, adding sheen to the finish of the 1896 Steinway B concert grand piano. Ramzi grabbed a tray and stood in line. People here didn't have olives with their breakfast, he noticed, and they dunked little bags into hot water to make their tea. The orange juice came from a whirring glass machine that seemed to never go dry.

After breakfast the students stacked the benches and tables in a corner and arranged music stands for the session's first rehearsal. Ramzi noticed instruments he'd never seen: clarinet, bassoon, oboe, French horn. The sheer amount he didn't know, about things others took for granted, was at first overwhelming. Back home, he had assumed that his sheet music was somehow *Arabic* sheet music—that other musicians would be reading the music in their own languages. How, he wondered, would all these young musicians, from so many different places, manage to play together? Ramzi looked over at his neighbor's sheet music. It was the same as his. He stole a look at another music stand; that sheet music was identical, too. Amazingly, there was no difference. Everyone was reading in the same language.

Ramzi said nothing. He kept this revelation to himself.

He looked up; Eric, who was coaching Ramzi's Mozart group, was talking.

"If we can be friends, and if we can play beautiful music together," he was saying, "what else is possible?"

Ramzi's English was bad, but in this case he understood Eric's basic idea. However, he wasn't at all certain that the young Israeli violinist sitting nearby would become his friend. On the other hand, he held nothing personal against twelve-year-old Nati, and he had no problem playing alongside him. In fact, Eric made clear that morning, Ramzi and Nati formed half of the chamber group for the Mozart Piano Quartet in G Minor, to be performed at the culmination of the Apple Hill session.

Ramzi leafed through his sheet music until he came to the Mozart. He was terrified. Instead of half and quarter notes, with rest stops in the expected places, he saw a jumble of notes jammed into a single measure: ascending and descending scales of eighth and sixteenth notes; quarter notes followed by a sixteenth-note rest; full note trills, followed by a sixteenth-note si-do-si, played fortissimo, and suddenly piano. The very speed of the piece, combined with the volume and rhythm changes, were far beyond anything Ramzi had ever attempted. It was going to be a difficult camp.

*   *   *

In the afternoons the musicians played games, mostly volleyball. Ramzi ranged over the entire court, trying to reach every ball. He saw the ball, so he followed it. Teachers watched in amazement, exchanging glances as Ramzi flew around, out of control. On the soccer field, he kicked a ball so hard he knocked the goalie on his rear. On the ricochet, the goalie—a music teacher, perhaps forty years old—scrambled back to his feet. Ramzi smashed the ball into his face, breaking the man's glasses.

Completely rough, Peter, the violist from the London Symphony Orchestra, thought to himself. *Completely untrained. And amazingly alive.*

In the evenings, moonlit swims led to bonfires, singing, and improvisation. Ramzi had brought cassettes of Fairouz, the great Lebanese singer, and Arab pop stars. In the concert barn, Ramzi and fellow campers from Jordan and Egypt showed the others how to dance in the Arabic style, with hips swaying and arms snaking overhead. This, and elaborate hand gestures, helped compensate for his rudimentary English.

Sometimes the players would break into country music, and swing dancing ensued, accompanied by a banjo, another instrument Ramzi had never seen. The energy reminded Ramzi of *Dabkeh*, the dancing he'd seen in Al Amari, where the men crouched low and danced from their knees, as in the Cossack-style squat dancing in Russia. "He was having the time of his life," recalled Nadia Abboushi, a piano teacher from the music conservatory in Ramallah, who visited Apple Hill that summer. "He was a sponge, spending every minute learning, running around, asking everyone: 'How exactly do you play this? How do you reach this note?'" Often Ramzi liked to sit by himself in the old gazebo, strumming his bouzouk after midnight, the sounds drifting over the concert barn and into the woods.

For Eric, an American Jew who believed in Arab-Jewish coexistence, it was emotionally potent to see Ramzi, Nadia, and their fellow Arab musicians playing alongside Israelis in the chamber music setting at Apple Hill. Eric believed the musical interaction could accomplish much more than any series of lectures and debates ever could; hence, none was scheduled. "If these problems were solvable by words they would have been solved long ago," Eric said.

Others found this attitude naive. "To put Palestinians and Israelis together to play music could be a wonderful thing," said Richard "Dobbs" Hartshorne, a burly classical bass player with a full, bushy beard; he taught at Apple Hill for decades and traveled many times to Palestine. "But unfortunately there was no chance to deal with the day-to-day situation, letting the Israelis know what it was like to be a Palestinian in the West Bank."

Ramzi knew he had been chosen in part to literally take the stage of coexistence, to be an example of the possible. He didn't mind this, as long as he was learning to play. He treated relations with Israelis outside the Holy Land less as a political issue than as a human one: judging each person based on whether he felt respected. Still, he was struck that he had had to travel six thousand miles in order to see an Israeli as a human being. And he found it odd to speak about peace when peace had not arrived back home, where he still had to spend hours at checkpoints, humiliated and harassed. It felt strange that a place like Apple Hill would avoid such realities.

Yet Ramzi began to notice subtle changes in his own attitudes, especially toward the idea of teamwork. His fellow campers and musicians relied on each other by working together every day—washing dishes, setting the table, sweeping the floors, stacking the lunch or dinner chairs, and, most of all, playing music. Chamber music relies on body language, on eye contact, and on learning where your partner places his bow, or how she breathes in on the first note. It is a slow and subtle process of getting to know each other, in order to listen, and to play in your own voice, alongside others.

Slowly, Ramzi began to notice a calmer feeling taking hold.

At nights, during the recitals, Ramzi liked to stretch out on a flat, wide beam above the balcony; there he would doze off, listening to the Bach, Brahms, and Beethoven rehearsals drifting up from the stage below, seeping into his dreams.

*   *   *

Mozart's Piano Quartet in G Minor was not only the most complex piece Ramzi had ever looked at; it was so far beyond his level that students and teachers alike wondered if it had been wise to ask him to learn it.

Together, Peter and his fellow Apple Hill viola teacher, Leonard Matczynski, found they could teach Ramzi the viola part of the Mozart Piano Quartet in only one way: painstakingly, excruciatingly, literally one note at a time.

Peter clapped the rhythms to the Mozart. Haltingly, staring nervously at his sheet music, Ramzi followed, hunched over, sliding his bow too quickly from note to note, creating a woozy, gliding effect known as glissando. Peter placed his hands on Ramzi's back and shoulders, straightening him. Ramzi needed to put his whole body into the playing, Peter said, just like when he kicked a soccer ball. He needed to know the precise location of the bow on the string, what string it was on, and what finger placements he would chose for each note. For the six-note phrase that opened the Mozart—think of it as "AN-swer the TEL-e-phone," Peter suggested— Ramzi learned the best fingering: fourth finger, first finger, first finger, second finger, first finger, first finger. *4, 1, 1, 2, 1, 1. DA-da, da-DA-da-dahh! 4, 1, 1, 2, 1, 1. DA-da, da-DA-da-dahh! 4, 1, 1, 2, 1, 1 . . .*

Ramzi's playing remained crude and halting. He had made immense progress since Peter had heard him play that lone beautiful note in the small practice room in Ramallah. Yet he still played at a beginner's level.

Peter worried privately that his student, too far behind his fellow players, could come unraveled onstage during the Mozart performance. He considered a desperate alternative for the night of the concert: to sit beside him and point to the passages as he performed.

And so the work Ramzi needed to do, in order to play Mozart's Piano Quartet with even a minimal level of competence, became the work of all of Apple Hill that session. Fadi, the Jordanian cellist, often sat with Ramzi, playing slowly to help him with the fingering. In the afternoons and evenings their fellow chamber musicians joined them for rehearsal: Bishara, the pianist from Nazareth, and Nati, the violinist from Tel Aviv. This represented Apple Hill's ideal: bringing together people who would ordinarily never meet, in a place where they learned to respect and listen to each other in pursuit of a common goal—in this case, a piece of music by Mozart.

Not all of Ramzi's fellow musicians bought into Apple Hill's vision, however. Eric had to talk to twelve-year-old Nati about being more sensitive to Ramzi's level of playing. Nati "had spent his entire life winning the game the Israelis play, that you're the best and the brightest," Eric said. "He liked to play as fast as possible. I was hammering home the point that this is a special case and an opportunity to do something else other than playing at a CD-recording level. I told him, 'Nati, it's not all about you. If you play your notes in isolation, that doesn't mean anything. You have to buy into the idea that every note and every person is of equal importance.' So the idea of a twelve-year-old learning that his job is not to just play his part, but to listen, and help Ramzi, that's a huge accomplishment."

Yet some of the musicians saw an uncomfortable dynamic developing, whereby the Israeli musicians were experts playing beside struggling Palestinians. Since the only formal "dialogue" was musical, the bass teacher Dobbs reasoned, there was no opportunity to establish equal footing. "The Israelis were always the whiz kids, and the Palestinians beginners. So it reinforced terrible stereotypes. Eric would put them in these groups together and say, if we could do this, we could do anything." But among Palestinians Dobbs spoke with, "there were huge amounts of resentment. The cynic in me would say, this is for fund-raising."

Reconciliation and *coexistence* were watchwords in the Oslo era, and funders looked for evidence of those principles at work. Occasionally, resentments simmering below the surface were therefore subsumed by the sought-after image of togetherness. Palestinian nongovernmental organizations also found they could raise money by promoting the new spirit of harmony. After the famous handshake in Washington, and the Palestinian agreement to a state on 22 percent of its historic land, NGOs adopted new terminology. Language like *justice, resistance, liberation, right of return,* and *anticolonial struggle* gave way to *conciliation, peace, accommodation,* and *compromise.*

*   *   *

Ramzi grew extremely anxious, full of self-doubt. He brooded, alone, considering his options. Never had he been or felt so far from home. He missed his grandfather's deep, raspy voice, his grandmother's roasted eggplant and stuffed grape leaves, the smell from Abu Darwish's ovens, and the daily rhythms, and the noise, of the refugee camp.

Ramzi went to Eric. "This is too hard," he said of the Mozart piece. "I can't do it."

Eric asked Ramzi what he meant by that. "You absolutely can do this," he assured Ramzi. Help was all around, Eric stressed. But not playing the Mozart was not an option.

Peter came, trying to cheer Ramzi up and add his reassurance. "AN-swer the TEL-e-phone!" he sang playfully, evoking the six-note opening to the piece.

Ramzi played late into the evening and early in the morning, sometimes after jamming with his new friends all night and staying up to watch the sunrise. He practiced six or eight hours a day, often alone, staring at the music, closing his eyes, dreaming of the concert performance; dreading it.

*   *   *

On a warm, bug-thick evening in early August in the concert barn, a hundred folding chairs formed a semicircle around three music stands and the black Steinway. Camp counselors, teachers, students, parents, and a few chamber music lovers from the nearby New Hampshire towns began to fill the rows of metal chairs. More young musicians sat in the balcony, legs dangling from the overhang. The resident Apple Hill bat swooped down from the rafters, circling the room; a pair of chipmunks peered out from the dormant summer fireplace and scurried back up the chimney.

The Mozart quartet took the stage, dressed in white shirts and black slacks for the camp's final concert. Faintly, Ramzi could hear the audience's applause as he took his seat in front of the sheet music and gazed once more at the sea of notes that still seemed beyond him.

The quartet paused in the seconds of silence before the music. Ramzi looked at Nati, whose bow hovered above the strings, ready to attack. Nati inhaled quickly, and simultaneously the three string players leaned sharply downward, pulling their downbows, as the musicians say, for the first note. Simultaneously Bishara brought his hands down on the keys. Six notes of the opening motif echoed in the barn—the masculine *AN-swer the TEL-e-phone!*—and Bishara played the answering motif, lilting and feminine. Then the six notes again; Bishara's second interlude; and the chamber musicians were in it.

The piece was taking off, and Ramzi was inside it, no longer consumed by his worries, and beginning to enjoy himself. A musical conversation was bringing the theme together, then breaking it off as each musician imitated the other, repeating above and below his partner. *I can do this better,* the violin seemed to be calling, only to be answered by the viola and cello, and Bishara's right hand waterfalling right and left along the upper registers.

Ramzi felt the music in his body. He experienced a surge of feelings—feelings he hadn't been completely aware of during rehearsal: elation, sadness, a sense of profound relaxation. At one point, the joy came with such intensity that Ramzi didn't know if he could contain it. He had to remind himself to count the beats, to remember when he had to play forte, and when to play piano, and when to put different stress on different strings, with his first, second, and fourth fingers. He had to concentrate on each note on the page, and listen to the players beside him. A passage of sixteenth notes was approaching, and Ramzi didn't have the capacity to play it comfortably; still, he remembered he had to use force, with his up bow. He looked over at Fadi on cello—younger but far more experienced in music—who exaggerated his gestures, trying to show Ramzi what was coming next. Ramzi's eyebrows were arched, his eyes lit up. Sweat was beading on his forehead.

They reached the fourth movement and raced toward the end. Ramzi felt like he was riding on a runaway train, hurtling toward the station. He leaned forward, now aware of his surroundings in the packed barn: of the visitors, of his teachers and fellow students, rapt and apprehensive, rooting for him, wondering if Ramzi was going to make it.

DA-da, da-DA-da-da! the instruments called out. *Da-DA, da-DA-da-da. Da-DA, da-da-da-da-da-da, da, DAH!*

Then, for the briefest moment, silence, as a panting Ramzi looked over at Bishara, Fadi, and Nati. They exchanged astonished glances, as if to say, *What just happened?*

The room burst into applause. Teachers, students, parents, and the visitors from rural New Hampshire sprang to their feet. Ramzi looked at Eric, standing in the back of the room, his face broad and open, his curly black locks flopping over his ears. Tears were streaming down his face. "He was *so* happy," Ramzi reported. "He could *not* contain himself."

*   *   *

For months afterward, Ramzi felt euphoric about what had happened, musically, at Apple Hill; beyond that, he didn't know how much meaning to ascribe to his experience. Playing Mozart beside an Israeli—being part of a triumph onstage—did not make him see peaceful coexistence as suddenly more possible. Still, there was no denying the power of what had happened. "It was like a symbolic gesture, a metaphor for peace," Ramzi said a short time later. "Yes, I did feel there was a chance for coexistence."

But something else had happened to Ramzi at Apple Hill. He'd been given a gift few other Palestinians had experienced. To play before an audience in a concert barn, or alone in an open field; to use his instrument as part of an exploration of what's possible to do in the world; to feel a sense of liberation by strumming his bouzouk in the gazebo at two in the morning; to simply *be*, in a free open space: to swim and dance and sleep among crickets in a cabin in the forest. Ramzi thought, *Why should I be just one of a few who gets to experience that?* "I knew that, because of the way I grew up, this is something that each child misses," he said. "And I thought that the music, it's a beauty that many kids should profit from."

It was at Apple Hill that Ramzi, the eighteen-year-old from Al Amari refugee camp, began to wonder: What if music could be a big part of the new state he still believed was coming? What if, one day, he could start something like Apple Hill in Palestine?

"It would be unfair if I were enjoying this alone," he said. "As we say in Arabic, Paradise would mean nothing without people."

*   *   *

At Tel Aviv airport, after the return flight from Boston, the Israeli border police and intelligence officers had a lot of questions for Ramzi. *Why did you leave? What was the purpose of your trip? Did you have permission to go? What kind of music camp was this? Who else was there? What were their names, and where do they live? How many of them are Arabs? Do you have their contact numbers and addresses?*

The interrogations went on for two hours; one officer would come in and ask a series of questions, then leave, to be replaced by another, who asked the same questions, then a third, who repeated everything again. This was common practice. During the interrogations, officers opened Ramzi's suitcases and took everything out, examining each piece—underwear, comb, toothbrush, socks. They strip-searched Ramzi. "They made me take my shoes off, and they searched my body," he recounted.

During the questioning Ramzi saw Nati, the violinist and his Apple Hill chamber music partner, whisk through security on the way to his reunion with family in Tel Aviv. He didn't seem to notice Ramzi.

"We were in Apple Hill without any discrimination," Ramzi reflected. "Nobody banned me from going anywhere. I didn't need permission to travel or move around. I felt that we were all equal.

"Everything changed the moment we landed at the airport. My happiness was spoiled. That feeling of freedom didn't last."

Nine

SYMBOL

March 1998
Ramallah

B Y THE SPRING OF 1998, six months after his return from Apple Hill, Ramzi had become something of a celebrity around Ramallah. All across town, posters stapled to electrical poles and taped to store windows showed the famous photo of the scruffy eight-year-old Ramzi about to hurl the stone. Alongside this image was another one: eighteen-year-old Ramzi, in a plaid shirt and brown leather vest, playing the viola.

The poster celebrated the National Conservatory of Music (known as the Ma'had, from the Arabic), and it spoke to the hope many still held: that an independent state of Palestine, free of war and occupation, was imminent. Ramzi's story illustrated what the life of a Palestinian free of occupation might look like. It didn't hurt that "Ramzi," in Arabic, means "symbolic"; for Palestinians and outsiders alike he seemed to represent possibility.

Ramzi turned nineteen in March 1998. He was in his last year of high school, living at Sido's and practicing his Mozart. He began a new piece, "Flight of the Bumblebee" by Rimsky-Korsakov, and continued his lessons on the bouzouk. Ramzi liked to play his viola on the rooftop, but often the neighbors complained, so more often he played indoors, in the echoey second-floor addition the family had recently built. In the evenings from seven to midnight he worked at a local fitness club frequented by wealthy Palestinians, including many recently returned from exile. There he wiped down the exercise machines and prepared and cleaned the saunas, earning three hundred dollars a month. In the time remaining he played music. In Arabic ensembles and chamber music groups, he played with Ramadan, the aspiring bass player and percussionist. Ramzi told his friend about Apple Hill and urged him to apply the next year. The two young musicians were alert for new opportunities, and soon they heard that two *professeurs* from a French conservatory would pay a visit to Palestine. They would hold auditions for a scholarship program in a city called Angers.

*   *   *

By now, as few of the promised freedoms materialized, more Palestinians had begun to question whether the "peace process," as designed, was ever going to lead to freedom. The Israeli army frequently imposed severe restrictions on freedom of movement for Palestinians trying to get from town to town. East Jerusalem, and all of Israeli territory, remained closed to West Bank and Gaza Palestinians without a permit. For many Palestinians, this effectively sealed off the Holy City they considered the capital of their future state. Safe passage between Gaza and the West Bank, which Israel had promised as part of the Oslo agreement, remained unimplemented. "As a result, these areas are almost totally severed from each other," declared B'Tselem, the Israeli human rights group.

Most alarming to Palestinians, 52,000 new Jewish settlers had arrived on the West Bank since the signing of the Oslo accords less than five years earlier—an increase of almost half, to more than 163,000. Many of these new settlers looked down from their hilltops in Psagot and Beit El, toward Ramallah and Al Amari refugee camp.

"They still are confiscating land, pushing people out of their homes," Ramzi said at the time. "It makes me feel like I'm about to explode. I'm here, I'm a Palestinian, and the Israelis bring in immigrants from abroad, build new settlements for them, and I'm just watching. They have already taken my land. And I feel that it's just being repeated again and again, and I cannot do anything about it."

For growing numbers of Palestinians, the Oslo process seemed designed to implement a permanent order of occupier and occupied, with "limited autonomy" the maximum reality for Palestine. "The United States–supported peace process is a process with no real and lasting peace," wrote Edward Said. It "neither provide[s] for real Palestinian sovereignty in Gaza and the West Bank nor allow[s] for peace and reconciliation between Jews and Arabs . . . In its present form, it will not stand the test of time: I am convinced it must be completely rethought and put on a more promising course."

Edward's search for an "alternative way of making peace" intensified in the spring of 1998, when he traveled across Israel and Palestine for an autobiographical film produced by the BBC. The film would mark the fiftieth anniversary of the creation of Israel and the Palestinian Nakba. One day he went to a rubble-strewn field where, hours earlier, a Palestinian home had been demolished by Israeli bulldozers. "Every day, every hour, every minute for fifty years, and it's continuing," a visibly anguished Edward told the film crew. Behind him, an old man in a checkered keffi-yeh knelt beside the fallen stones outside his former home, praying to Mecca. "Look, the little bits of plastic, the little logs, the bit of railing here, a tin can crushed here," Edward said. "These are the atoms out of which the tragedy of Palestine is constructed." Edward paused repeatedly, short of breath, holding back tears. "It's very, very hard for me to stand here talking about it . . . when I see my own people going through this . . . without any relief, without any sympathy or support from the so-called civilized world. And we hear about the peace process, but who is protecting, who is giving these people peace?"

Encounters like this drove Edward Said deeper into the search for new ideas. He remained convinced that one day Palestinian independence was inevitable—just not through Oslo. "Palestine and Palestinians remain, despite Israel's concerted efforts," he wrote. "As an idea, a memory, and as an often buried or invisible reality, Palestine and its people have simply not disappeared." As he traveled across the West Bank, Gaza, and Israel that spring, Edward encountered Palestinian and Israeli artists, politicians, and intellectuals who shared his views, and who were willing to try different approaches. This new thinking, he believed, should focus not on the details of a flawed agreement, but on bringing the two peoples together on an equal footing.

In his search for alternatives based on equality, Edward had found a kindred spirit in Daniel Barenboim, the Argentine-born Israeli conductor and pianist, whom he had met by chance in 1993 at the check-in desk of the Hyde Park Hotel in London. Daniel, once the husband of the late cello virtuoso Jacqueline du Pré, was director of the Berlin State Opera, a former conductor of the Paris and Chicago symphony orchestras, a virtuoso pianist, and one of the most sought-after musicians in the world. Once a child prodigy, he had performed on stages in Vienna and Rome as a ten-year-old. Now in his mid-fifties, Daniel's rail-thin, angular frame had grown rounder, his thinning hair had turned white, and his broad, expressive face reflected playfulness, curiosity, and occasional flashes of anger. Daniel considered himself a political progressive and strong advocate of reconciliation between Israel and the Palestinians.

Since their chance encounter in the London hotel lobby, Edward and Daniel had spoken nearly every day. Daniel considered Edward his intellectual and artistic "soul mate"; Edward, himself a talented amateur pianist and a music critic for the *Nation* magazine, took increasing solace in music, and in the creative brilliance of his new best friend. Edward was tall and lean, and fancied well-cut suits; he was considered charming, dignified, even gallant, by his wide circle of friends. He lived in a world of ideas, and relished debate; like his friend Barenboim, he didn't suffer fools, and he too was given to occasional sharp bursts of anger.

"We must do something for our people," Daniel told Edward repeatedly. The two had begun to consider a musical enterprise based on listening and common ground—much like Ramzi had experienced at Apple Hill, but on a grander scale.

*   *   *

Edward was in East Jerusalem, at the American Colony Hotel, eager to share his thinking, and his friendship with Daniel, with his friends in Palestine. There was also the matter of a highly unusual invitation—one that would have been unheard of just a few years earlier. Edward picked up the phone and called Tania Nasir, with whom he shared a deep love of classical music.

Tania and Hanna Nasir were old friends of Edward and his wife, Mariam. Edward and Hanna both had lived in West Jerusalem as children in the 1940s, before Palestinians fled or were driven out during and after the war of 1948. Later, the two couples met in Jordan, where Hanna, the president of Birzeit University in the West Bank, lived in exile for nineteen years after his deportation by Israel. He'd been charged with "security violations" following university protests against Israeli rule. In the early days of Oslo, as a high-profile gesture of reconciliation, Israel had allowed Hanna to return. From New York, Edward and Mariam watched the historic event on television. Afterward, they called their old friends in celebration.

Now Tania and Hanna were back in the home they had shared with their children before his exile.

"Tania," Edward said from his room at the American Colony, sounding urgent. "I am here with my close friend Daniel Barenboim. He is a wonderful man, a great human being." Tania knew of Daniel's reputation as an advocate for the Palestinian cause. Trained as a soprano, she had long been familiar with his music. Edward and Daniel's friendship, Tania recalled, "was part of the general atmosphere of people seeking rapprochement. It was all part of our inner dialogue: to where will this lead us? Edward was hungry. He wanted to know what could change."

"Daniel is giving a concert this weekend in West Jerusalem," Edward told Tania. "You're invited, Tania. We want you to come."

Tania paused, unsure of how to respond. Attending a concert in West Jerusalem would be a huge leap. She'd been born there nearly fifty-seven years earlier, in 1941, but hadn't been back in decades. She was not allowed to go by the authorities.

Tania believed the arts could be a vehicle for understanding. But she did not feel comfortable traveling to West Jerusalem, now part of another country, when that country still held her people under occupation. The situation was not normal and she did not want to suggest by going to Israel that it was. Still: Why should she decline to attend a piano recital in West Jerusalem by one of the world's great musicians—and a defender of her people's rights—on the invitation of her dear friend, Edward Said? What purpose would that serve?

She promised Edward she would think about it. Soon she called him back, and found herself not only accepting the invitation to the concert, but inviting Edward and Daniel to dinner the next night at the family home in Birzeit.

The guests arrived in the early evening, walking into a family room of twelve-foot cross-vault ceilings and foot-thick plaster walls draped with Palestinian embroidery, and framing an upright piano, above which hung Nasir family photos dating to the 1930s. Persian carpets covered the red-tiled floors. In this house, in the 1920s, Hanna's Christian family had established the Birzeit Higher School, which later became Birzeit University, eventually under Hanna's leadership.

Daniel, Edward, and their hosts settled into couches, sipping arak, the popular anise-based spirit, and snacking from plates of grape leaves and candied almonds. Daniel asked about Hanna's experience of deportation and exile. In November 1974, the university president explained, following the demonstrations of his students, he was arrested, handcuffed, blindfolded, placed in a van with other deportees, and "driven for seven hours towards an unknown destiny." Soldiers removed the blindfold and told Hanna he was in Lebanon. From there, he went to Jordan.

Tania was struck by Daniel's concern and his respectful questions. She told him about the years of shuttling their children between Birzeit and Amman. They needed travel permits, which required multiple stamps of approval from various occupation authorities. "From the municipality, the police station, the ministry of education, the tax center, whatever," Tania said. "You'd have such long lines, and all this waiting. There would be a soldier there, and if someone was out of line, he would start scolding us like children, and kick us all out. 'We're finished now. Come tomorrow.' That's when you really feel occupied. And there was a fear inside you, that he would never stamp your permit, so you would shut up. And I would burn inside, because I had to get to Amman, to my husband, to the children, who had to go back to school."

At the Allenby Bridge at the River Jordan, the dividing line between the West Bank and the kingdom of Jordan, "we would wait for eight hours, the children would have no food, no water, no diapers, no changing. I would be terrified if they would find a piece of paper in the children's clothes, like a chocolate wrapper or something. And then they would send you all the way back to the end of the line. They knew it was chocolate, but it was an excuse: 'You never know what's on that piece of paper.'"

When Oslo arrived, Hanna said, Israel allowed him to return home. Tania went to Amman to accompany him. Hanna pledged never to cry and kiss the ground upon his return, like so many of the more sentimental refugees had done. The moment they crossed the Jordan and reached Palestinian soil, however, Hanna leapt from the bus in tears, kneeling down and kissing the earth. "Right on the bridge!" Tania laughed. "He was the first to go down from the bus!"

In nearby Jericho, throngs of jubilant Birzeit students cheered their president's triumphant return. She and Hanna had come back, Tania said, in a "genuine spirit of hope and reconciliation. We shared a sense of cautious joy."

Five years later, the hope was dimming, she said, amid an "avalanche of militancy and violence," and the ever-expanding settlements. She pointed through the living room's twin arched windows. Daniel looked to the southeast, beyond the darkened palm and cypress trees, to the bright yellow lights of a hilltop Jewish settlement a mile away.

*   *   *

Throughout the cocktail hour, and over a dinner of stuffed chicken and red wine, Tania sensed Edward's pleasure at being with friends from both sides of the divide. He listened intently; he knew all these stories, but his friend Daniel did not. "This was the first time I was confronted with people who had lived such a destiny," Daniel said years later. "I was very, very moved by that."

Politics dominated the evening, but music was never far away. Hanna's sister, Rima, a pianist, was a cofounder of the National Conservatory (the Ma'had), where Ramzi was studying; his nephew, Suhail Khoury, was the Ma'had's director. Together the Nasirs and the Khourys were among the most prominent Christian families in Palestine, and were connected through both Birzeit and now the Ma'had. Though they didn't know it at the time, soon they would make arrangements for Daniel to play recitals there.

Edward and Daniel were in the nascent stages of a grand project rooted in their friendship. It would originate in Europe and recruit musicians from both sides of the Arab-Israeli conflict, in a way that could help break the impasse and demonstrate a new way of thinking. The project still hadn't taken shape. But soon, Daniel would be considering an invitation by the city of Weimar, Germany, which was to be the cultural capital of Europe in 1999. That year also marked the two hundred fiftieth birthday celebration of Goethe, a son of Weimar. Goethe sparked Edward's sense of the possible. Unlike the "Orientalists" he regularly skewered as agents of Western imperial domination, Edward saw Goethe as the epitome of a Westerner reaching out to understand the "other." Goethe had begun his inquiry into Islam and the Arab world after receiving a torn page of the Qur'an from a German soldier in the early nineteenth century.

Such an inquiry, Edward believed, represented what could be possible, two centuries later, as a kind of parallel alternative to what he saw as a collapsing peace process. No place would be more appropriate for this than Weimar, where the currents of high culture and terrible history swirled together. It had been home to Bach, Liszt, Wagner, Nietzsche, and the death camp at Buchenwald. The Weimar invitation excited the two friends, and soon they would add another component: bringing together young musicians from across the Middle East, to create a youth orchestra.

It was close to midnight by the time Edward and Daniel rose to leave and summoned their driver for the ride back to Jerusalem. Again, Daniel extended his invitation to Tania to attend the concert the next night in West Jerusalem. Tania assured him she would be there. There was risk involved, everyone knew: If caught trying to enter Israel without a permit Tania could be arrested. It was too late to apply for a permit, but in any case Tania would have been reluctant to do so; she didn't want to ask permission to travel to a place she considered her own homeland.

Late the next afternoon Tania climbed into the backseat of a taxi, alone, heading for the first time in decades to the city of her birth. Hanna had also lived in Jerusalem as a child, and as she rode, Tania recalled his old haunts: the Cinema Rex, the coffee shops, the YMCA, where he had played tennis and studied Arabic typing, where his family had attended concerts by the Palestine Symphony, and where the Palestinian musician Salvador Arnita had given his organ recitals. Now, without a permit, Tania recalled, "I had to come to Jerusalem in secrecy. I had to infiltrate it like an outlaw."

Alone at the piano in the West Jerusalem concert hall, Daniel played the first notes of Tchaikovsky's Sixth Symphony in B Minor, the *Pathétique*. Tania began to weep. She longed to disappear into the music, and for moments, she would, only to be gripped by doubts over whether she should have agreed to come.

An hour later, after Daniel had played the last notes of Liszt's Sonata in B Minor, the audience rose in a standing ovation. Tania and Edward rose, too. Daniel walked forward, closer to the audience, spoke briefly in Hebrew, then switched to English.

"Last night I was in the West Bank, at the home of a Palestinian academic, who has recently returned from an unjust twenty-year deportation by the Israeli government," Daniel said. "He and his family received me not just as a friend, but more as a member of the family."

Tania was astounded. She and Edward looked at each other. In the silent auditorium, Daniel stood in the small pool of light. He spoke into the darkened hall, calling for peace, justice, and an end to the suffering on both sides. Suddenly Tania heard him say: "I am happy to have my Palestinian hostess of last night with us here this evening. She has accepted my invitation to come to Jerusalem, despite prohibitions and many reservations. To thank her, I would like to dedicate my encore to her."

Edward embraced Tania. "Only Daniel can do it," he said. "Only he has the guts." Tania was overcome with emotion, which grew deeper as Daniel sat down at the piano to play a Chopin nocturne. Daniel didn't know it, but this was the music Tania loved the most. As a child in Ramallah, Tania had danced to the nocturnes.

*   *   *

François Hetsch, Juilliard-trained violist and conservatory *professeur*, stood in a windowless room at Tel Aviv's airport, stripped to his underwear. He was of medium height and build, with short brown hair thinning on top. It was the spring of 1997. François had just arrived from France with his colleague Richard Lowry, the British-born director of the Conservatoire d'Angers in the Loire Valley. Inspired by the Oslo peace process, they came on a mission from the French government to assess the quality of classical music education in Palestine and to recruit young musicians to study abroad. Their destination was Ramallah, and the National Conservatory of Music, the Ma'had, where they would hear Ramzi, Ramadan, and other students audition for musical scholarships in France.

François did not understand why he'd been forced to remove his clothes or why his mission seemed so suspect. Who do you know there? the officer asked François repeatedly. And why are you going there? What relationships do you have with them? Where are the papers authorizing this trip? And for how long have you known Richard Lowry? Twelve years? He says thirteen—someone is lying.

Oh my goodness, the normally easygoing Frenchman thought. *Where have I come to?* His round face and heavy eyelids ordinarily conveyed a gentle, bemused expression; now they reflected fear. In a nearby room, Richard was undergoing similar questioning.

"I was quite suspect, because I'm British originally. On a French passport," he remembered. "With an introductory letter from the French foreign affairs. They just didn't understand. I was terrified."

Three successive officers questioned him, for half an hour each. "Aren't we good enough?" one officer asked Richard.

"I know you've got good musicians," he responded. "I know some of your good musicians. They don't need any help. They've got talent, they've got jobs, they've got money." Where his mission was taking him, Richard said, in terms of classical music, the people "have got nothing. And we would like to help them. That's why I'm here."

After two hours the authorities allowed Richard and François to enter Israel. They immediately set out for the occupied territories.

François and Richard peered through the windows of the car heading northeast, toward Ramallah. Teenaged soldiers with machine guns kept watch from lookout towers surrounded by barbwire. Finally the visitors from France crossed a boundary and into occupied territory. It felt and looked like another country. The driver navigated huge potholes, dodging rocks and chickens in the road. Garbage overflowed from dumpsters, amid broken chunks of concrete with rusted rebar protruding—remnants of broken buildings. Incessant honking rang in their ears along the choked roads. François would remember thinking of the Middle Ages, of "another civilization."

Farther on, sweetshops abounded. Racks of clothes fluttered in the sunshine. Old men smoked water pipes, sitting idly in roadside cafés. "You can really feel a certain misery," François said. "Their faces are so tired with the weight of life." *What do they do in life?* Richard wondered. He was in his late forties, a chain-smoker with a wavy shock of salt-and-pepper hair and bags under his eyes. *Do they have jobs? Do they have a family? How do they manage to survive?*

At the hotel in Ramallah, the receptionist welcomed the men warmly and led them upstairs. Each room, François noticed, had bullet holes. *Oh my goodness*, François thought again to himself. *I know we're in Palestine for sure.*

At the Ma'had, Suhail Khoury and his colleagues had prepared nearly two dozen pupils for auditions. Richard was taken aback. Windows were open and soundproofing nonexistent. The strains of piano, strings, horns, and Arabic tablas and ouds drifted out of tiny practice rooms. "It was all mixed up with the minarets calling for the prayer and all that," Richard recalled. "It was just a hell of a noise. You wondered how on Earth they could do anything and produce any real results."

Ramzi paced back and forth in front of an upright piano and a framed print of Renoir's 1892 painting *Jeunes filles au piano*. He had practiced hard at Sido's, sharpening his notes on Rimsky-Korsakov's "Flight of the Bumblebee." Months earlier Peter had played it a Ramallah recital. Ramzi was dumbfounded by its speed and by Peter's bow movements. When he closed his eyes, he swore there were three instruments playing, not one. The frantic pace reminded Ramzi of escaping from the clumsy soldiers down the narrow alleys of Al Amari camp. Immediately he wanted to learn the piece.

Richard and François entered the room and shook Ramzi's hand. Ramzi handed the sheet music to Richard, who immediately sat down at the piano, ready to play accompaniment. Ramzi was amazed that Richard didn't need to warm up first. Apparently, some musicians could play like this.

They began. Ramzi launched into Rimsky-Korsakov's undulating phrases of sixteenth notes. The speed was no longer beyond him. Again he was transported to the refugee camp during the intifada. Each measure sounded like a sprint down a narrow alley, a cut through a row house, a dash through a neighbor's front door, a dive through an open window, a frantic climb to the rooftop. Ramzi felt the piece, so it came out naturally.

The viola fell silent. Ramzi stood, nervous, alert, smiling, and a little out of breath, in front of the two French visitors. *Rough*, thought François of the young Palestinian string player. *Very rough. But hungry.* And for someone who had only started playing, and whose main teacher was a violinist, Ramzi showed promise.

The same day the two *professeurs* auditioned Ramadan, the bass player who, like Ramzi, had only recently started playing music. He, too, took his lessons from a violinist. At twenty-four, Ramadan seemed to possess a maturity and a humility borne of his years working in his father's tire shop. This, thought the two Frenchmen, would suit him well for living in a foreign culture.

For these reasons, Richard Lowry and François Hetsch, under the auspices of the French Cultural Attaché to Palestine, invited Ramzi and Ramadan to study at the Conservatoire d'Angers in France's Loire Valley, beginning in the fall of 1998.

*　　*　　*

A few months before their departure for France, Ramzi and Ramadan, with some friends from the Ma'had, went to hear a special concert given by two visiting French musicians, a violinist and a flutist.

The duo played in an unheated auditorium at the Latin Church in Ramallah. Ramzi, Ramadan, and their friends huddled together in the balcony. Ramadan left briefly and came back with falafel sandwiches and Cokes for everyone. The friends jostled and whispered, their breath rising over the balcony; then they grew silent, transfixed by the music.

Ramzi shivered, looking down at the French duo, wrapped in their coats and scarves and playing Rimsky-Korsakov's symphonic poem, *Scheherazade*—inspired by the tale from *The Thousand and One Nights*—in a small circle of light. He thought of himself on some future day, after he had returned from France; after Palestine had been established as a member of the international community, and he and Ramadan were playing in its national symphony orchestra.

Before, it had been the war of the stone, Ramzi liked to say. Now it was the war of the viola.

END OF FIRST MOVEMENT

INTERLUDE I

*A*s the violist *dangles from the rope beside the concrete wall, squint-ing into the distance, the truck comes closer on the road below. He tries to determine its color and markings.*

"Is that the army?" he shouts again, looking up to the smuggler standing atop the wall, beside the looping razor wire.

He begins to imagine his arrest and incarceration. "What are you here for?" his fellow prisoners would ask. "For trying to play Beethoven," he would respond. At his trial, he would ask the judge, "Why am I guilty? The only thing that I am doing is trying to make music for people in Jerusalem."

A voice from above yanks him back to the present.

"Don't worry," the smuggler shouts. "It's just a local vehicle."

The truck passes below without incident. The musician struggles for a better foothold on the small knots, then slides down the final ten feet with his hands, feeling the heat of the rope in his palms.

He lands hard and looks up. Four musicians remain on the wall, staring back down. They must move quickly in order to make the connection with the others on the bus. "Saed," he calls to the violinist. "Toss me your instrument!"

"Ready?" the violinist shouts.

"Ready!"

The violin floats downward in its soft blue case. The violist plants his legs, bends his knees, and reaches out his arms.

Second Movement:

INSTRUMENT

Ten

CONSERVATOIRE

Fall 1998
Loire Valley, France

RICHARD LOWRY, DIRECTOR of the Conservatoire d'Angers, turned off the two-lane road and bumped slowly up a long dirt driveway. Ramzi sat beside him, gazing out at the French countryside, a twenty-minute drive from the Conservatoire, where he and Ramadan had recently enrolled. Laurel trees, creeper vines, and late-season red, white, and purple roses colored the fringes of the lane. At the end of the driveway, beside an abandoned well and a massive apple tree, stood a stone farmhouse covered in ivy. The house, built in 1810 on a land grant for one of Napoleon's soldiers, was set back about three hundred meters and perched on a bluff above the Loire River, in the Savennières district where the chenin grapes produced dry white wine.

Richard had approached his old friend John Cassini about hosting Ramzi Aburedwan. John, a political science professor, and his wife, Francine, a piano teacher, had come to France from Cincinnati in the early 1980s. Their three teenaged children were aspiring musicians. Richard had brought along the famous poster—little Ramzi with the stone, older Ramzi with the viola—and told John his story. Ramzi and Ramadan would be in Angers for a minimum of two years until they received sufficient training to go back and teach Palestinian children, and to perform, for the conservatory in Ramallah. The family had agreed to host Ramzi.

John and Francine led Ramzi and Richard through the front door, past the doorbell of an angel blowing a trumpet and the clapper bell with its muffled ring of G-sharp. Exposed beams and a black cast-iron chandelier hung from eight-foot ceilings. Scattered rugs partially covered terra-cotta floors. Beyond the small farm kitchen was Ramzi's room: a one-time stable converted to living quarters long ago, with a Dutch door formerly attended by horses and cows. Ramzi's bunk bed stood in the corner.

They gathered at the entrance to Ramzi's new room, smiling and managing small talk. Ramzi felt like he was in a cartoon—"Belle the Dog and His Friend the Boy," from his childhood, in which a family lived in a crooked house in the forest, smoke curling from the chimney. All this newness in an unfamiliar terrain, and the promise of so many things to come, made it hard for Ramzi to contain his excitement.

*   *   *

Ramzi's new viola teacher was François Hetsch, the thirty-year-old Frenchman who had gone to Ramallah with Richard Lowry for the auditions. François had joined the Conservatoire after earning his degree at Juilliard, where he had studied under the renowned conductors Simon Rattle, James DePreist, and Seiji Ozawa, then conductor of the Boston Symphony Orchestra, and where he had met his future wife, Julia.

On the day of Ramzi's first lesson, student and teacher stood in Salle 312, François's small practice room at the Conservatoire. Through the window Ramzi could look down onto the Parc Bellefontaine, where children scooted down slides, old men on benches leaned on their canes, and couples strolled arm-in-arm between well-trimmed hedges flanked by red and yellow violets.

François asked Ramzi to play something, then, after hearing a few bars, promptly declared, "Let's start from zero." First, Ramzi would need a proper viola. Whatever he had brought with him, François concluded, it wasn't an instrument. "Just a nightmare," François remembered. "It was a piece of wood, with four strings. I don't know if I can call them strings, they were so old. He made noise for me, more than sound."

Ramzi had thought that he and his instrument were doing fine, but in the presence of his new teacher he quickly concluded otherwise. He needed to learn how to breathe; how to stand as if a string from the crown of his head was pulling him toward the ceiling; how to hold his bow; how to curl his fingers around the fingerboard, for sufficient vibrato; how to quit moving so much. "Stop it, Ramzi!" François said, laughing, as the young violist's shoulders lurched and he swayed back and forth in front of the music stand. "You're giving me a headache!"

François led Ramzi through exercises for proper breathing and finger movements in order to sharpen his reflexes and improve his tone. Often Ramzi didn't understand François, but he didn't need a common language to know he was far behind his fellow students: His classmates in the solfège (theory) course on the ground floor were mostly between seven and twelve years old. *I need to improve,* Ramzi told himself constantly. *I need rigor, discipline. Loving something is not enough.* At night, Francine Cassini would drive Ramzi back to the house, listening to his deep sighs, glancing over to see him brooding silently. Yet these moods, she noticed, never seemed to last long.

The Western concept of time posed another challenge for Ramzi. François lived in Paris with Julia, a pianist, and their three-year-old son and traveled to Angers twice a week by bullet train. The lesson was for two in the afternoon; in the early months, Ramzi often arrived, smiling and ready to play, at three-thirty. "What's going on, Ramzi?" François asked. "Maybe in your country you have a different way of living with time. And two can be one or three, it doesn't matter. But here in France, two is two."

Yet François found it impossible to stay annoyed with Ramzi. His charm was immediate and unambiguous, and his enthusiasm to learn was unencumbered by any notion of European cool. In Ramzi, François encountered a perpetually smiling man-child from a faraway land: "a boy who came from another planet." For François, Ramzi brought an abundance of sunlight; a capacity for "eating life." François was amazed by Ramzi's hunger to learn. "He was always in a hurry, Ramzi. Always, always. For everything."

At first Ramzi's French was terrible, and sometimes it got him in trouble. On the street he would wave and smilingly exclaim, "*Salope!*" (slut!) when he meant to say *salut* (hi). Slowly, through daily conversation and twice-weekly French lessons, he grew more comfortable.

For Ramzi, coming into the Conservatoire was like walking into a big factory of music. He entered programs for orchestra, chamber music, choir, and piano, in addition to his classes in viola, theory, and harmony.

By the late fall, Ramzi's playing had improved—aided, perhaps, by his previous lessons in Ramallah. He had surpassed the single open-string exercises François had prescribed, with no fingering, to playing Bach's Cello Suites arranged for viola, which relied on playing two or three strings simultaneously—double and triple stops—with multiple fingerings and dozens of possibilities.

Through François, Ramzi understood that his bow was the breath, the voice of the viola. It contained thousands of microscopic barbs of horsehair that, when drawn against the metal strings, forced them to vibrate into the instrument's cavity and out the F holes. This creates the tone that chamber musicians recognize as the "inner voice" between the violin and the cello in tone, and the closest to a human voice. "You have to breathe with your bow, Ramzi," François said. "When you play with your bow, that's your breath." François insisted that Ramzi practice for hours each day. Through the monotony of endless repetition—a melody, repeated thousands of times—he would develop muscle memory. It was only after such labor that Ramzi could have an aha moment—recognizing how, through tiny increments, his ability to play a particular piece of music had grown profoundly. Ironically, the monotony freed Ramzi to feel the music more deeply.

As Ramzi's musicianship—and his French—improved, François could began to teach him about colors in music—not just volumes like piano and forte, but a more subtle understanding that invoked feeling. This was a new concept for Ramzi, yet he quickly grasped the idea that emotions could be expressed through musical colors. Dark could be powerful, yet soft. Sometimes darkness required a light touch of the bow upon the strings—so light that his hand would start to tremble. Ramzi now understood that power in music was not related to physical strength. This, too, was a new concept. "A child from Palestine has a different perception of power than a European kid," Ramzi said. "Power for a kid in Europe could be to do a beautiful painting. Power for him could be to do a beautiful chord. It's the perception of power that's different."

Slowly, François noticed, Ramzi was earning a reputation as a player who felt the music deeply.

* * *

Near the end of 1998, in Berlin, Edward Said, Daniel Barenboim, and the cellist Yo-Yo Ma were making plans for a grand experiment in Weimar,

Germany, during the following summer. Yo-Yo, when he learned of the idea from Daniel, asked, "Why does it have to be limited to Israelis and Palestinians? Can I come too?"

"We would be honored," Daniel responded.

The three men met in Daniel's office at the Berlin State Opera to discuss a bold and possibly controversial idea: an orchestral workshop made up of Arabs and Jews, living in the same region but separated by barriers few had ever had right or reason to cross.

The genesis of the idea, Daniel believed, was the current situation in the Middle East. It could not remain as it was. It had to either get better or worse. He was counting on improvement, and he continued to dream of a warm coexistence between peoples who had been, technically or literally, in a state of war for decades. "Music would serve as a wonderful way to bring people together," Daniel declared, "because you cannot be a lukewarm musician: Music requires passionate involvement and effort."

For Daniel, the faltering peace process still offered hope, and perhaps could be prodded, however slightly, through this musical effort. Edward, who had long ago given up on Oslo, saw their effort as an alternative to the status quo. For him the intention, discussed at length in Berlin, was to see what would happen if Arabs and Israelis came together with Germans in one of the most culturally potent and historically terrible places on earth: Weimar. "Nobody could fully comprehend," Edward said, "the proximity of such sublimity to such horror."

It was Goethe, considered the greatest of all German writers, who most fascinated Edward, the literary scholar, for having reached out to "the other" through his "fantastic collection of poems based on his enthusiasm for Islam." The collection, published in 1827 and called the West-Eastern Divan was, Edward believed, "unique in the history of European culture." It provided the inspiration for their new project's name—the West-Eastern Divan Orchestra—and, with the help of Yo-Yo, they made plans to recruit young musicians.

Edward returned home, and soon after, his leukemia resurfaced. At one thirty each afternoon, Mariam would drive him to Long Island Jewish Hospital. The treatments each took three hours, and afterward he would feel awful until he went to sleep. Daniel and Yo-Yo, meanwhile, began to recruit and audition young musicians from across the Middle East. They received more than three hundred applications for auditions.

In the mail one afternoon, at his apartment on Riverside Drive near Columbia University in Manhattan, Edward received a handwritten note from Yo-Yo:

Dear Edward,
It's been over six months since we met in Berlin, but the glow is still there. I hope the treatment was not as traumatic as feared but more import-antly its benefits are long-lasting. I would love to have a chance to visit with you. Until then I'm sending some CDs that may be of some interest. It looks like Weimar is happening and kids are applying and the quality is not half bad!

*   *   *

One day in the spring of 1999, near the end of his first year at Angers, Ramzi walked into Salle 312 and handed François a fax. The viola teacher read it, stunned.

The message was from Edward Said and Daniel Barenboim, inviting Ramzi to audition for a new orchestral workshop to be convened that summer in Germany. The details weren't clear. Ramzi certainly knew of Edward Said, but he hadn't heard of this Barenboim fellow.

"*You?* Invited by *Barenboim?*" François asked. He thought the notion of Ramzi playing with an international orchestra, at this point, was ludicrous. "What's this business? Ramzi, you still have everything to learn. Why would you do this? Don't make politics before study."

François believed that musically, Ramzi wasn't ready. He consulted with Richard Lowry, the Conservatoire's director.

"Ramzi was a light-year away from being able to make a significant contribution," Richard recalled. "He hadn't yet acquired any sort of means that were necessary to fulfill his role in an orchestra. There were still times he stopped playing and looked around because he didn't know what was going on." Richard and François didn't know what level of playing the other musicians would be bringing to Weimar. "But when we heard there were people being recruited from Egypt, Jordan, Israel, other countries, we thought, *Christ, he'll go down just like the* Titanic."

François told Ramzi he had not been invited because he was a musician; the invitation had come because Ramzi was Palestinian. This was not the first time opportunity had stemmed from Ramzi's identity. The idea made him uncomfortable; he wanted to be recruited because of his talent and promise.

François was right, Ramzi concluded. It wasn't time to join an international orchestra. Ramzi called Daniel's manager. "I'm sorry, I can't come," he told the man. "I'm busy."

The decision would forestall Ramzi's inevitable connection with the musical experiment about to get under way in Weimar. And it would mean that, despite the intentions of mutual friends who wanted to connect Edward and Ramzi, the young Palestinian violist would not be destined to meet the great scholar, intellectual, and fierce advocate of their people.

*   *   *

The first rehearsal of the Weimar workshop began with a long note from an oboe that marked the beginning of Beethoven's Seventh Symphony. It was August 1, 1999. Maestro Daniel Barenboim focused on that note for a long time.

"Legato, legato," Daniel told the young Egyptian oboist, Mohamed Saleh, stepping toward him in the orchestra pit. "Softer."

"We kept repeating it, repeating it, forever," remembered Mohamed, who had roomed with Ramzi two years earlier at Apple Hill in New Hampshire. "It was quite powerful for me. He was just basically building everything from scratch. He really wanted to make something." Just as Ramzi had started with a single note—in his case, the open G—so would the Divan. The maestro explained that the note, which begins at C-sharp, flowing to F-sharp, was an example of legato, from the Italian, "tied together," and its soft migration was essential for creating the sound that Beethoven had envisioned. "Everybody was watching," recalled Mina Zikri, a violinist from Egypt. "We played a chord, and the line was in the oboe. He wanted a unified sound. We were scared, because he spent twenty minutes on the third and fourth notes of the symphony. Oh my God, we have a whole symphony to learn! Basically, we understood that it's not going to be easy."

Laborious as it was, Daniel's selection of Beethoven's Seventh as the orchestra's first piece was significant for a gathering of traditional enemies. The symphony begins with a surge of optimism, as if throwing open the

shutters on a sunny day, and proceeds into a joyful, allegro dance of celebration. It would have been impossible for any of the young musicians that
day to not feel Beethoven's message of humanity. All this was unspoken,
however; the maestro focused on the musicianship. By the time the orchestra reached the third movement of the Seventh, Daniel's face was bathed in
sweat. "He was really, really working, moving, trying to get the kind of
sound that he wants for the orchestra," Mina remembered.

Edward watched from a corner of the room. The latest round of leukemia treatments had worked; he was feeling stronger and healthier. He
had noticed the tentative atmosphere as the players settled into their chairs,
regarding each other warily as Daniel prepared to direct rehearsals and
Yo-Yo organized the string sectionals. "I'm here to play music," one cellist
proclaimed at an early workshop. He was a soldier and a Jew, and he told
Edward, Daniel, Yo-Yo, and his fellow musicians that he was only interested in the music. "I feel very uncomfortable," he said in Hebrew,
"because, who knows, I might be sent to Lebanon and I'll have to fight
some of these people."

"If you feel that uncomfortable," Daniel replied, "why don't you leave?
Nobody's forcing you to stay."

The young man grew quiet and remained seated.

For Edward, the possibility in the room went well beyond music; the
gathering represented a counterpoint to the deeply flawed Oslo process. In
his view, the PLO, a national liberation movement, had given way to the
Palestinian Authority, a subservient government of "collaborators with the
military occupation." The musical experiment at Weimar stood for what
Edward liked to call a third way:

> The third way avoids both the bankruptcy of Oslo and the retrograde
> policies of total boycotts. It must begin in terms of the idea of citizen-
> ship, not nationalism, since the notion of separation (Oslo) and of
> triumphalist unilateral theocratic nationalism whether Jewish or Muslim
> simply does not deal with the realities before us. Therefore, a concept of
> citizenship whereby every individual has the same citizen's rights, based
> not on race or religion, but on equal justice for each person guaranteed
> by a constitution, must replace all our outmoded notions of how
> Palestine will be cleansed of the others' enemies. Ethnic cleansing is
> ethnic cleansing whether it is done by Serbians, Zionists, or Hamas.

*   *   *

In the evenings at Weimar Edward led the youth orchestra in discussions on culture, music, and politics. Musicians debated who had the right to play music: Could a Jew play Arabic music? No, a Lebanese violinist told Edward. "Well," Edward responded, "What gives you the right to play Beethoven? You're not German." Ten days later, Edward said, "the same kid who claimed that only Arabs could play Arabic music was teaching Yo-Yo Ma how to tune his cello to the Arabic scale. So obviously he thought Chinese people could play Arabic music.

"Gradually the circle extended," Edward recalled, "and they were all playing the Beethoven Seventh. It was remarkable to witness the group, despite the tensions of the first week or ten days, turn themselves into a real orchestra. One set of identities was superseded by another set. All of them suddenly became cellists and violinists playing the same piece in the same orchestra under the same conductor."

"They were trying to play the same note, to play with the same dynamic, with the same stroke of the bow, with the same sound, with the same expression," Daniel echoed. "They were trying to do something together. It's as simple as that. If we foster this kind of contact, it can only help people feel nearer to each other."

Slowly, the members of the orchestra began to understand what Daniel meant.

*   *   *

Edward Said believed that any reconciliation between Israel and the Palestinians would require his people come to terms with the horror of the Holocaust. For Edward, it was an essential part of mutual witness: Each side had to understand the experience and history of the other. For this reason Edward and Daniel had decided from the start that the musicians should visit Buchenwald.

Edward sat at a table beside Daniel and Yo-Yo, facing the one hundred Arab, Israeli, and German musicians sitting on maple bleachers in the Weimar rehearsal room. He looked vibrant. "Tomorrow we have a trip planned to the ex-concentration camp of Buchenwald," Edward began. "You can see the tower from the road as you're going into town toward Weimar."

Edward spoke of Goethe's Faust and the evil that is in everyone. "I think we all are privileged by being here and privileged to have such extraordinary musicians and teachers as Yo-Yo and Daniel," he said. "But I think that experience would be incomplete without recognizing the trail of hatred and hostility, which a place like Buchenwald, next to Weimar, has produced. The kind of energy which sometimes goes into the producing of a driven symphony like the Seventh Symphony can also produce the kind of energy that goes into genocide and ethnic cleansing, and systematic cruelty of the kind that produces a Faust, whose pact with the devil gives him a certain kind of fantastic power." This fervent power, Edward said, could be employed in the service of the sublime or the horrific. He described the human ability to dehumanize and thereby justify "sordid and appalling cruelty": slavery for tens of millions of Africans, extermination for native peoples in North America and Australia, massacres in Guatemala and Chile. "Whether it is war, whether it is injustice, ethnic cleansing, apartheid: All of those things have to be understood as coming from the same place that Buchenwald came from, and that place is also in the human heart, if you allow a romantic expression for it. It coexists with and is part of the same impulse that can produce a Michelangelo or a Beethoven or a Picasso."

As for Buchenwald, and the cold, murderous efficiency of the Nazis, Edward said: "If you just go to this and see it as part of the Jewish experience, it's wrong, because it's part of the human experience, which we as human beings have to understand. In other words, universalize it and understand it as a horror that afflicts all of humanity."

All but one of the musicians agreed to go. Still, some of the Arabs, whose English was limited, did not understand what was in store.

▦▦▦▦ ▦▦▦ ▦▦▦ ▦, read the words forged on the metal gate at the camp's entrance, which, loosely translated, means "Everyone gets what he deserves."

The musicians walked through a vast open landscape, flat and barren, coming eventually upon the "Little Camp," where stables built for fifty horses instead housed up to two thousand people, and where death came from disease, the cold, and starvation. They trudged to the museum, where combs, buttons, and broken soles of shoes marked lives lived, and to the corpse cellar, where hundreds of Jews, gypsies, homosexuals, and political prisoners were strangled to death, their bodies hung on meat hooks before being fed to the ovens.

Edward stood in the courtyard of the crematorium. Suddenly he felt "fantastically tired," unable to take in any more. For a time he couldn't walk. Nearby, Yo-Yo had sat down, alone, overwhelmed and trying to collect himself. Edward's nephew, ten-year-old Karim Said, stood beside Daniel. "Mr. Barenboim sat me down on his knee and said, 'Do you know why you're here?'" Karim recalled. "You're quite young and you probably shouldn't have come, but do you know why you're here? You're here because it's important for this to never happen again, and young people should see this, too."

After Buchenwald, Edward reconvened the group in the Weimar practice room. He was careful not to equate the atrocities of the Holocaust with the dispossession of his own people. Still, he said, "suffering is the monopoly of no one." Edward had long insisted that Palestinian recognition of the Holocaust would be "a sign of our humanity, our ability to understand history, our requirement that our suffering be mutually acknowledged." Edward had been forcefully asserting this for years, to the discomfort of some Palestinian activists and scholars. But he also had written that the Holocaust could not be used as a justification for continued victimization of the Palestinians. "How long can the history of anti-Semitism and the Holocaust be used as a fence to exempt Israel from arguments and sanctions against it for its behavior towards the Palestinians?" he wrote in *The Politics of Dispossession*. "How long are we going to deny that the cries of the people of Gaza . . . are directly connected to the policies of the Israeli government and not to the cries of the victims of Nazism?"

Edward looked over at Daniel. "He's an Israeli and I'm a Palestinian. One of the reasons for our friendship, one of the rare things about him is that he's a person who can understand and experience the suffering of others. And is willing to make the effort to do that. It's very, very hard to do. Especially if you feel, as so many of us do, vulnerable, defensive. And say, 'What about my suffering? I mean, who's looking after me?'" Edward paused, placing the tips of his fingers on his chest, looking out at the young musicians. "What I think is possible for each of us is to understand that we can do something about suffering. By understanding and acknowledging that it took place. And by our capacity as citizens, as musicians, as people who think, to make sure that it's lessened. That there's less of it."

*   *   *

Ramzi stood on a bluff above the Loire behind the Cassinis' house, smoking a Gauloises. He liked to come here to look out at the broad, slow-moving channel below. Beside the river lay the railroad tracks: eastbound to Paris; west, to Nantes and the mouth of the river, flowing to the Atlantic Ocean. At times, it still seemed to Ramzi that he was living inside a childhood cartoon.

The pace of his life didn't often allow for reflection, and for Ramzi, that was probably good. Like Sido, he preferred to stride forward without looking back. He didn't dwell on loss, despite its accumulation; still, at times, it came back: the death of his friends, the murder of his father, the ride in the pushcart on the day his mother abandoned him.

Since Apple Hill, Ramzi had been thinking about what he could do with his musical education. Even before he left Palestine, he had told people of his dream to make something musical for Palestinian children. He had begun thinking about the childhood trauma carried by his generation, and the kids coming up now. He didn't believe music could magically purge the trauma. But the presence of music in a child's life could provide a means of therapy and protection. It could point the way, Ramzi believed, to a more normal life. This is what he wanted to share.

"He likes very much the pleasure of Angers," François recalled years later. "He always tells me he wants a house near the Loire. But I knew from the beginning that his life was there, in Palestine."

Ramzi gazed down at the wide river plain. It was tempting to think of a life as an itinerant Arab musician, perhaps in Paris, playing his viola and his bouzouk for money. But he also knew his destiny would unfold with the children of Palestine. Even, or especially, when war came again.

Eleven

ADAPTATION

September 2000
Angers and Jerusalem

A T SEVEN O'CLOCK ON a Thursday morning, September 28, 2000, Ramzi was asleep in his new apartment, a short walk from the Conservatoire, when the spark for the second Palestinian uprising was lit.

Eighteen hundred miles to the southeast, in the Old City of Jerusalem, retired Israeli general Ariel Sharon marched onto the most contested piece of ground in the entire Holy Land, accompanied by fifteen hundred soldiers. The site was known to Muslims as the Haram al-Sharif, or Noble Sanctuary, and it contained Al Aqsa Mosque and the Dome of the Rock. To Jews it was the Temple Mount, and on the same ground, just adjacent to the mosque, stood the Western Wall, which Israel had reclaimed after the 1967 war. The same ground, the very same stone, was sacred to both faiths. Sharon's strategy on that September morning, it seemed, was to publicly, and with a massive show of force, assert Jewish sovereignty over the third holiest site in Islam.

Ariel Sharon had recently returned from Israel's political wilderness. In 1983, an Israeli investigative commission had found him indirectly responsible for the massacres of hundreds of Palestinians at the Sabra and Shatila refugee camps in Lebanon the previous year. Now Sharon, in a political battle with Benjamin Netanyahu, sought to claim the leadership of the Likud party.

Sharon was exploiting weaknesses in the troubled Oslo peace process. In late July, American-backed peace talks at Camp David had collapsed, in large part because of the very holy ground Sharon was walking through. Muslims worldwide considered Arabs to be the stewards of Haram al-Sharif. At Camp David, Yasser Arafat had refused the American and Israeli proposal to give Palestinians only limited and symbolic autonomy over the site. This would have included a "sovereign presidential compound," which Arafat derided as "a small island surrounded by Israeli soldiers who control the entrances." The Palestinian capital itself would not be in East Jerusalem—a core of the Palestinian demands for state-hood—but in Abu Dis, a village east of the city, toward the Jordan Valley. Arafat told President Bill Clinton that he would not go down as the Palestinian leader who gave up Jerusalem. "Mr. President," he asked Clinton at Camp David, "do you want to come to my funeral? I would rather die than agree to Israeli sovereignty to Haram Al Sharif." A furious Bill Clinton responded: "Failure will mean the end of the peace process. You won't have a Palestinian state and you won't have friendships with anyone. Let's let hell break loose and live with the consequences."

Two months later, by approaching the holy sites with hundreds of Israeli soldiers, the provocation by Sharon, Arafat's longtime nemesis, would help ignite the bloodiest fighting between Israel and the Palestinians in decades.

On Friday morning, September 29, in Angers, Ramzi turned on French television to see the images of young men pouring out of Al Aqsa after Friday prayer and pelting soldiers with rocks. None of the demonstrators that day fired weapons. Nevertheless, Israeli soldiers responded with live bullets from their M-16s, killing four Palestinians. The Second Intifada was born.

Ramzi filled his phone card and reached his family at Al Amari. Rami told him demonstrators were confronting Israeli soldiers at the Best Eastern Hotel in Ramallah, near the entrance to the Jewish settlement of Beit El, not far from where he and Sido had swept the streets. The scenes were reminiscent of the days many had hoped and believed were long past: In East Jerusalem, across the West Bank, and even in Nazareth and other parts of Israel, Palestinian youths, the shabab, were back in the streets, their faces wrapped in keffiyehs. Lines of soldiers stood in full riot gear, raising plastic shields against the torrents of stones.

Ehud Barak, the Israeli prime minister, accused Arafat of engineering the intifada in a "grand plan" of terror out of frustration with the failure at

Camp David. Yet in the first eight weeks of clashes, few Palestinians were armed; during that time, 264 Palestinians in the occupied territories died, compared to 29 Israelis. The Israeli deaths would soon rise sharply, as Palestinian militant groups changed their tactics.

The uprising was not simply a protest against Israeli rule and the continuing occupation seven years after the Oslo accords. Hundreds of checkpoints and other barriers remained in place across the occupied territories, and Israel remained in full military control of 60 percent of the West Bank. Yet some saw the new uprising as a protest against a peace process that had not delivered freedom, and of the weak, compliant government it had spawned: the Palestinian Authority.

"What of the much-vaunted peace process itself?" wrote Edward Said in an essay published in December 2000 in the *London Review of Books*. "What have been its accomplishments, and why, if indeed it was a peace process, has the loss and miserable condition of Palestinian life become so much greater than before the Oslo accords were signed in September 1993? And what does it mean to speak of peace if Israeli troops and settlements still exist in such large numbers?"

Edward continued to teach and write even as he underwent his regular leukemia treatments. Late in the day he would tire, but the next morning he was back at his desk, writing and preparing his lectures. "We must press on," he told Mariam repeatedly.

*   *   *

During an especially bad bout of Edward's leukemia, Daniel Barenboim rerouted his trip from Germany to stop in New York. "I cannot tell you how overjoyed I am that you are making this detour to see me tomorrow," Edward wrote in a fax to his friend in Berlin. "It means a great deal to me."

They sat in the living room of Edward and Mariam's sprawling twelfth-floor apartment on Riverside Drive, overlooking the Hudson River and the George Washington Bridge. For years the two friends had been recording a series of conversations covering music, culture, and the role of the artist and the intellectual in wartime, to be published as *Parallels and Paradoxes*. Much of their conversation had focused on the 1999 orchestral workshop at Weimar. After the success of that first gathering, they decided that the West-Eastern Divan Orchestra should continue, again in Weimar for the summer of 2000.

By the late fall of 2000, Edward was also fighting off accusations that he advocated terrorism. The previous June, he and Mariam, originally from Lebanon, had traveled there with their grown children, daughter Najla and son Wadie, and Wadie's fiancée, Jennifer. Israel had recently withdrawn from southern Lebanon, ending its long occupation. Near the Israeli border, Edward and Wadie had engaged in a stone-throwing competition; their target was an abandoned Israeli guard station. For supporters of the Palestinian cause, Edward was showing his solidarity with the historic resistance of stone-throwers. He later called it a "symbolic gesture of joy that the occupation had ended," adding: "One stone tossed into an empty place scarcely warrants a second thought." But for Edward's many critics, both in Israel and among American Jewish organizations, the Columbia professor was advocating violence. Critics on the right had labeled Edward a "professor of terror." The Zionist Organization of America called on Columbia to discipline him. The university declined.

*   *   *

In Angers, during his winter holiday break at the end of 2000, Ramzi was following the news from his homeland on a nearly hourly basis. On January 1, 2001, bombs exploded three cars in Netanya, near Tel Aviv, sending glass, shards of metal, and people flying through the air. More than thirty Israelis were injured. It was the fourth such attack in a period of six weeks, and it signaled a change in the strategy of Palestinian militant groups, which, prior to the current wave of bombings, had carried out only four similar attacks in the previous two years. After weeks of relative restraint following the outbreak of the Second Intifada, the militant Islamic groups Hamas and Islamic Jihad, and the Al Aqsa Martyrs Brigade, a military wing of the PLO, unleashed what some called the "weapon of the weak": the suicide bomber. The coming year would see three dozen more such attacks, most directed at civilians, which would claim at least ninety-five lives and injure more than one thousand Israelis. The New Year's Day explosions were linked to Hamas, though some in the Israeli government blamed Yasser Arafat and called for suspension of the last-ditch peace talks taking place in Taba, Egypt, during the waning days of the Clinton administration. As the talks collapsed and the Clinton presidency gave way to that of George W. Bush, Ariel Sharon was elected Israeli prime minister in a landslide. He stepped up incursions into Palestinian territory.

Ramzi called home nearly every day. Israel's army had returned to Al Amari, this time accompanied by tanks and, on occasion, American-made Apache helicopter gunships, neither of which had been factors during the First Intifada. Sometimes Ramzi could hear them through the phone line. The entire family was having trouble sleeping, Rami reported, and with Israeli tanks at the entrance of the camp, and soldiers again undertaking house-to-house searches, Sido was worried about a random raid at any time. The army had retaken the four-story stone building at the camp's entrance and placed snipers on its roof. Rami reported the deaths of young men from the camp. A neighbor had taken up arms and been gunned down by soldiers, and a local produce merchant had been shot and killed by a sniper as he arranged his fruit.

Soldiers themselves recounted stories of driving into family homes with bulldozers, beating children as young as eight years old, shackling teenagers for hours until their hands turned blue, and provoking worshippers by throwing teargas canisters into mosques. Some of this was instigated by terrified, angry soldiers seeking a measure of revenge after waves of suicide bombings, or rattled by constant stoning from village youth and children. Yet much of it, soldiers acknowledged, was done under orders to intimidate the local population—in military parlance, a "demonstration of presence" defined as "shooting in the air, throwing sound bombs, shooting off flares or teargas, conducting random home invasions and takeovers, and interrogating passersby," according to a report of soldiers' eyewitness accounts. "A significant portion of the IDF [Israel Defense Forces]'s offensive actions are not intended to prevent a specific act of terrorism, but rather to punish, deter, or tighten control over the Palestinian population."

"Snipers are everywhere, shooting anything that moves," Rami told his brother. He had taken over Ramzi's job wiping down the exercise machines at the fitness center, but lately it was difficult to reach work. To Ramzi it was little relief to be in a safe place, far from the front lines. Whenever he hung up the phone, he felt a wave of regret that he wasn't at home. To feel more connected, he tacked newspaper clippings or Internet images of the *shuhada*, or martyrs, on his walls, and joined regular demonstrations sponsored by local pro-Palestinian solidarity groups.

*   *   *

In the fall of 2000, Ramzi and Ramadan entered their third year at the Conservatoire. Living so far away, they worried about the safety of their families and friends in Palestine. Out of homesickness, and in solidarity, they began to play Arabic music in the courtyard of the Conservatoire. They wanted to represent their culture, Ramzi recalled, to "give an impression of who we were." Students gathered around, asking questions, pointing to Ramzi's bouzouk and to Ramadan's *darbuka*, a goblet-shaped drum with a crisp, distinctive Middle Eastern sound. Soon a clarinet player, Matthieu, joined them. Two teenaged sisters, Sophie and Sarah, French Jews who wore Star of David necklaces, brought their violin and cello. One of the sisters, Ramzi thought, had a crush on Ramadan. The sisters invited Ramzi and Ramadan to a Lebanese restaurant, to help them feel at home in France. Together they founded a small ensemble and played Arabic classical music in recitals at the Conservatoire. With Ramzi on bouzouk, Ramadan on percussion, and their friend Sedi on viola, they introduced the girls to music inspired by *The Thousand and One Nights*.

That fall Ramzi and Ramadan's scholarships dried up, which meant a monthly loss of about six hundred euros each (at the time, about six hundred dollars). Ramadan took a job washing dishes. Ramzi taught percussion to twenty students, ate on credit at the Lebanese restaurant, and ran a monthly tab at the Bar du Centre, where he would take his demitasse coffees and smoke his Gauloises. To supplement their incomes, the two friends began playing in the clubs of Angers. At night they joined a Moroccan friend and other African drummers in free percussion jams. They'd start at ten P.M., pounding out Oriental and African rhythms on the darbuka and *dom dom*, a big African bass drum, watching the crowd swilling *combas*, a bright green African drink made of rum, lime, and mint: a kind of African mojito, only stronger. "If the drumming was good, the girls started to dance," Ramadan remembered. "Girls sweating, you continue to play for two, three hours." The music, the pulsating rhythms, and the social interaction helped Ramzi and Ramadan's French develop faster. At dawn they slept, then stumbled into the Conservatoire.

*   *   *

One day a sixteen-year-old singer and student of early classical music came to the courtyard to watch the two Palestinians and their friends jamming with their exotic instruments. Ramzi recognized Jessie Nguenang from the choir, where her soaring and powerful soprano stood out among the students at the Conservatoire. "Do you want learn how to sing Arabic music?" Ramzi asked Jessie during a break.

"Why not?" Jessie responded. The daughter of African immigrants, Jessie wore her hair in tight black curls that fell to her shoulders; her beauty was enhanced by her broad smile and warm demeanor. She was open and inquisitive. Jessie was learning her own exotic instruments—the lute, recorder, and Renaissance flutes from early period music—and recalled how Ramzi once stopped her to ask about each instrument. "Show me everything," Ramzi had said eagerly. "Tell me about the music. Tell me about the instruments."

Jessie and Ramzi began rehearsing on the courtyard steps.

"El-bint el shalabiya," Ramzi sang, again and again, softly strumming his bouzouk as Jessie echoed the words and scribbled in her notebook. The words were from Arabic folklore, from a song made famous by the legendary Lebanese singer Fairouz. It told a love story about a beautiful girl with eyes in the shape of almonds.

Ramzi had a strategy: Jessie, who'd never spoken a word of Arabic, would learn the Fairouz well enough to perform with Dalouna, the new Arabic-French band he'd been putting together with Ramadan. Jessie was French, with roots in Cameroon, and she could see that Ramzi liked the idea of mixing music, culture, and language—what she called "that melting pot of ethnicity." She knew Ramzi could have found singers from the Arab community in Angers, but it was unlikely they could have matched Jessie's operatic power.

In the coming months, Jessie devised her own special phonetic code to remember the lyrics, transposing them from the Arabic in her ear to the French on the page, and back to the Arabic that she sang. Ramzi and Ramadan, meanwhile, were assembling the rest of Dalouna: Ramzi on bouzouk, Ramadan on darbuka, Matthieu on clarinet, and a fellow student, Carla, on violin. Later, Ramzi recruited a local street musician, Julien Leray, whose repertoire included the American blues and jazz singers Robert Johnson, Nina Simone, Ray Charles, and the Mills Brothers. Finally Ramzi decided Jessie was ready, at least for the French-speaking public. Fifty or sixty people packed into a local club called L'Étincelle.

On the small stage, Jessie stepped into a spotlight and up to the microphone. *"El-bint el shalabiya,"* she sang in her French-tinged Arabic, channeling Fairouz and transporting herself into another world. Thus Jessie christened the first performance of the full Dalouna ensemble.

Soon, Ramzi would book appearances for Dalouna across France. As he spoke onstage, he laid out his vision to bring music to the children of Palestine. At first the idea was vague; it was more about the music and performances. But as his audiences responded enthusiastically, Ramzi began to see his music school as something real.

*   *   *

On March 5, 2002, amid another wave of Palestinian suicide bombings, Israeli prime minister Ariel Sharon announced a new military offensive in the West Bank. "We are in a difficult war facing a cruel and bloodthirsty enemy," Sharon declared. He called Yasser Arafat a "patriarch of terror" and ordered missile strikes on Arafat's Palestinian Authority compound in Ramallah. Sharon linked Israel's predicament to the global war on terror in the wake of the September 11 attacks in New York and Washington. "The Palestinians must be hit and it must be very painful," Sharon declared. "We must cause them losses, victims, so that they feel the heavy price."

The comments drew a rare rebuke from Washington, where Secretary of State Colin Powell was trying to keep prospects for a peace deal alive. "If you declare war against the Palestinians and think you can solve the problem by seeing how many Palestinians can be killed—I don't know if that leads you anywhere," Powell told a committee of the U.S. House of Representatives. Sharon "has to take a hard look at his policies."

Three weeks after Sharon's speech, Hamas dispatched a twenty-five-year-old Palestinian man, Abd Al-Baset Odeh, who, disguised as a woman, walked past security in a Netanya hotel and blew himself up. Thirty people died, most in the midst of a Passover seder. Some of the victims were Holocaust survivors. "As long as there is occupation, there will be resistance," declared a Hamas spokesman. He denied that the bombing was an attempt to undermine a new peace proposal recently launched by Saudi Arabia.

Two days after the Passover bombing, the IDF called up thirty thousand reserve troops. Tanks, armored bulldozers, and American-made attack helicopters surrounded Palestinian cities and towns, now deemed "closed military areas." Commanders issued orders for round-the-clock curfews; violators would be shot on sight. Soldiers conducted house-to-house searches, using loudspeakers to summon males between the ages of fifteen and forty-five. In five weeks, seven thousand Palestinians were arrested, many under Military Order 1500, which allowed incarceration without access to a lawyer, judicial review, or family. Authorities barred the movements of journalists and international aid workers, hampering medical assistance and making it impossible to assess the precise level of loss. In April, missiles fired from Apache helicopters leveled hundreds of Palestinian buildings, including government offices, schools, and private homes. In a two-month period nearly 500 Palestinians were killed, more than 1,400 injured, and some 875 homes demolished or destroyed, leaving 17,000 Palestinians homeless.

The stated aim of Operation Defensive Shield, Sharon announced to the Israeli Knesset (the country's parliament), was to "catch and arrest terrorists," to "confiscate weapons," and to "target and paralyze anyone who takes up weapons." The degree of destruction, however, suggested that Sharon was intent not only on rooting out militants, but on destroying any emergence of a free Palestinian society.

At his desk in New York, Edward Said wrote: "What antiterrorist purpose is served by destroying the building and then removing the records of the Ministry of Education, the Ramallah Municipality, the Central Bureau of Statistics, various institutes specializing in civil rights, health, and economic development, hospitals, and radio and television stations? Isn't it clear that Sharon is bent not only on 'breaking' the Palestinians but on trying to eliminate them as a people with national institutions?"

In early April 2002, Israeli troops, backed by aerial bombardment, tanks, and armored bulldozers, laid siege to Jenin refugee camp, declaring it a center of planning and operations for suicide attacks. The soldiers, many of them temporary reservists called up after the Passover bombing, encountered stiff and unexpected resistance from fighters who lay in waiting in narrow alleys, or from a maze of trip wires rigged to explosives. On April 9, Israeli soldiers walked into an ambush, then encountered a suicide bomber. Thirteen soldiers died. "This group of suicide bombers has refused to surrender," said General Yitzhak Eitan, the IDF's West Bank commander. "We will continue to make this camp submit." Armored Caterpillar D9 bulldozers crushed rows of Palestinian houses, burying alive fighters and civilians unable to leave their homes in time. In all, an estimated fifty-two Palestinians were killed in the Battle of Jenin.

For several days afterward, IDF authorities refused to allow ambulances or medical personnel to enter the camp, despite reports of rotting bodies and fears of spreading disease, and despite repeated pleas from the United Nations. Meanwhile, the military authorities cut off power to the hospital in Jenin. Days later, Israel refused to cooperate with a U.N. investigation into what happened at Jenin. Citing that refusal, the United Nations called off the investigation.

*   *   *

As Israeli military operations were reducing large parts of Palestine to rubble, Ramzi and Ramadan were taking Dalouna on the road across France. Weekends they would play in Angers, Paris, Toulouse, or Le Mans, performing the mélange of French-infused Arabic music for benefit concerts, often in collaboration with activist groups. Ramzi called ahead to local newspapers and sympathetic musicians; word of mouth spread. Ramzi and Ramadan produced the first Dalouna CD without any money. Ramzi had managed to convince the studio to wait for payment until the CDs were pressed and could be sold, after concerts. This strategy also fueled production for a second CD.

Onstage, Ramzi talked about his idea of a music school for the vulnerable children of Palestine, in the villages and refugee camps. "I want to show these children that there is something else beside war and occupation," he said. For emphasis he projected his famous image as a child throwing the stone.

Yet it was clear that Ramadan, who had no such picture to circulate, and who was not convinced of the need to open a second music school in Palestine, was growing uncomfortable. Strains between the two old friends had started to surface. They had cofounded Dalouna, but for the most part Ramzi hired the musicians, chose the music, booked the gigs, and arranged publicity. After concerts, Ramzi moved quickly from one conversation to another, shaking hands and scribbling down names and phone numbers that could one day prove useful. He grew annoyed when he spotted the goateed, pony-tailed Ramadan chatting and laughing with fellow musicians. "There is public relations to do, Ramadan," Ramzi said sharply.

"And I'm doing all of it." Through Ramzi's efforts, the bookings began to expand, across the borders of France to Brussels, London, Geneva, and other parts of the European Union.

As the two old friends traveled across Europe, their bandmates noticed an increasing distance between them. They talked less, and they no longer planned and strategized as they had at Dalouna's founding. The band, Ramadan believed, had not been established to help Ramzi build his dream; Ramadan, his friends would say, felt Ramzi had co-opted Dalouna.

Ramzi's emergence as the de facto leader of Dalouna also took a personal toll. Managing all the logistics was stressful; it consumed Ramzi at times, and his fellow musicians considered him more and more the opposite of the bohemian, salt-of-the-earth Ramadan, who seemed to live by the old Arabic saying, "Let me live today; you can kill me tomorrow." Ramzi, juggling his identities as musician, producer, tour manager, publicist, and an exile from a Palestine at war, grew increasingly remote from his fellow musicians. "He was upset, stressed, always thinking," remembered his bandmate Julien Leray. But for Julien, even those factors did not fully explain why Ramzi distanced himself. "Other musicians came from the same place," he said, "and they were not in this state of mind. But Ramzi, I didn't know him very well. I never really had a deep discussion with him about life. It's very hard to know him deeply."

*   *   *

François Hetsch was losing patience with Ramzi. He saw the effects of the outside gigs on his student, and he wanted Ramzi to show more commitment to his classical practice, and to the meticulous repetition in front of a metronome, that would take him to the next level. "You're always making shortcuts," François scolded Ramzi one day in Salle 312, as he slid his fingers down the fingerboard. "You feel like you know the piece, but you don't really know it. You have to go into it more deeply." François believed that Ramzi had remarkable instinctual gifts as a musician, but that without six or seven hours a day of rigorous practice, his student would never be the violist he could be. "You need to practice moderation, Ramzi," François said. "Try to get enough sleep. You need to be strict with yourself."

François, however, believed that something deeper was holding Ramzi back. It wasn't just the lack of sleep and the outside gigs. Ramzi had a tendency "to take all that could hurt him, all that could affect him, anything that would make him feel bad, and push it away." For François, this helped explain Ramzi's shortcuts and poor practice habits. François knew that in order to play well, a musician had to give without reservation or self-protection. Ramzi, he believed, was part charmer, part "hurt little boy," always coming up with excuses for not spending sufficient time with his viola: "I am Palestinian; you're going too fast; I'm not used to all this practice. I'm thinking about my grandfather; I'm worried; I need to go back to Palestine." These were deflections, François believed, from something deeper inside Ramzi: a fear of being vulnerable.

Yet certain music, mostly in minor keys, reached Ramzi emotionally and brought out his talent. With those pieces—the Brahms Piano Quartet no. 1 in G Minor, Schubert's Trout Quintet, Tchaikovsky's Fourth Symphony—his protective layer fell away.

One afternoon in the spring of 2002, near the end of his fourth year at the Conservatoire, Ramzi stood with François in the practice room overlooking Parc Bellefontaine, playing from the mournful first movement of the Sonata in G Minor by Henry Eccles. Ramzi now understood that a piece of music was like a story, and that playing it with sensitivity could convey the sense of a journey. Ramzi felt he was channeling Eccles's intentions, singing with his viola. He played with tears in his eyes.

In moments like these, François noticed, Ramzi was playing, listening to himself play, and feeling the music, all at the same time. For François, time stopped. There was a silence in the room. Ramzi was open. It was as though all he had lived through in Palestine—abandonment, occupation, brutality, loss—was coming through in his playing. Ramzi's vulnerability was there for François to feel, finally, in his viola.

"Okay, Ramzi," François said when Ramzi stopped playing. "This is your sound."

François was convinced Ramzi could reach this level much more consistently. Despite his built-in disadvantage—Ramzi had first touched a viola only six years earlier, when he was seventeen—François believed that if he worked hard enough, Ramzi could build a career as a classical violist in Europe. Gradually, however, François came to understand that this did not interest Ramzi. "He knew very early that he wouldn't make a career with this," François said. "Of that I'm absolutely sure."

*   *   *

Ramzi returned home in June 2002, flying from Paris to Amman, then traveling overland to the Jordan Valley, where he crossed into Israeli-occupied Palestine. The Second Intifada had not abated. Palestinian families still suffered the effects of Israel's Operation Defensive Shield, which had killed several hundred; Israelis were reeling from a new suicide bombing that had taken sixteen lives in May. Hamas had claimed responsibility. Israel was preparing to announce the construction of a vast barrier, which they would call a security fence.

Ramzi didn't know what to expect when he arrived in Al Amari. Despite the dangers, he was coming back determined to test his dream of building a music school in a war zone. Once through Israeli security, he caught a collective taxi and rode northwest, out of the flattening heat, into the mountains of Palestine, and past Qalandia checkpoint, which was eerily silent due to the curfew imposed by Israel's army. The road along the last few miles to Ramallah, normally packed with cars, pedestrians, vendors, and bustling shops for furniture, clothing, and sweets, was nearly empty. At the center of Ramallah, in the nearly vacant Manara, he met Rami and a cousin. They grabbed Ramzi's bags as he looked around. Cars had been flattened by tanks. Nearly every building was pockmarked from fifty-millimeter shells. Broken glass was everywhere. At Sido's, Ramzi saw evidence of another house invasion by the soldiers: The glass of the framed Basque poster of Ramzi, with the slogan AGORA INTIFADA, had been shattered. The family had hidden it behind some chairs, hoping somehow that Ramzi wouldn't notice its absence.

The Palestine National Conservatory of Music, Ramzi learned, had not escaped the army's incursions. During Operation Defensive Shield, Israeli soldiers had blown off the door of the Ma'had. In the aftermath, Nadia Abboushi, the Ma'had piano teacher who had been with Ramzi at Apple Hill five years earlier, had made her way around tipped-over file cabinets and shards of broken glass, and into her practice room. There she had found a large Star of David spray-painted on the wall. Her framed print of Renoir's 1892 painting *Jeunes filles au piano* lay smashed on the floor.

Israeli curfews imposed severe restrictions on Palestinian movement, making it more difficult for Ramzi to test his idea. Most days, he couldn't even leave the camp. After discussing his dilemma with Rami, however, he realized he could investigate the prospects of his music school without leaving Al Amari.

A few days after his arrival from France, Ramzi sat in a chair at the front of a classroom at the Center for Rehabilitation, a small school where handicapped and able-bodied children learned together. He smiled at the children, his bouzouk in his lap. In the same refugee camp seventeen years earlier, he had watched Teacher Khalidi open the magical cabinet full of musical instruments.

Ramzi looked around the room at the artwork taped onto the walls. In front of him was a large scroll of butcher paper, partly unrolled across a ten-foot patch of floor, revealing the children's artwork. Between the images of birds and trees, orange fire exploded from tank barrels. Soldiers confronted mothers and children at checkpoints. Houses burned. Ramzi had visited classrooms in France, too, and there the children just drew houses, sun, and trees. Children are children, the same everywhere, he believed. They draw what they see.

Ramzi began to strum his bouzouk, playing a soft instrumental version of "El Hilwadi," "The Beautiful Girl." He played folk and revolutionary songs for thirty minutes, then went home, looking up at the red roofs of Psagot, the Israeli settlement on the old hill of Jabal al-Tawil. Recently, at the height of the Second Intifada, the settlement had begun marketing "Cave à vins Psagot" to Jews in Israel and beyond. A web site boasted of a Cabernet Sauvignon "aged in a special cave containing winemaking implements that date to at least the time of the Second Temple."

A few days after his first visit, Ramzi returned to the school for rehabilitation. This time, the children surrounded him, wide-eyed, touching the bouzouk. One by one, Ramzi would play a note, then reach out for a child's hand, placing his or her finger on the fingerboard. In this way, the children could hear the change in pitch. "Hey, this is magic!" someone shouted. This was the same feeling Ramzi had experienced as a boy, staring open-mouthed as Teacher Khalidi transformed himself into a kamandjati—a violinist.

Before he left, Ramzi looked out onto the scroll of butcher paper, where days earlier he had seen images of rockets, tanks, and mothers in distress; now he watched children trying to draw musical instruments: violin, bouzouk, and oud. In the moment, Ramzi had a simple epiphany, tied to his history and his music: "I thought, it would be more useful for your country if you're still alive. You know? Than if you die, killed by a soldier in the beginning of your life." Now, he thought, his idea—which he dreamed of calling Al Kamandjati (The Violinist)—could actually work. Previously, the school had existed in the abstract. Now, with children in a war zone drawing musical instruments after hearing Ramzi play for only half an hour, he saw that music could help safeguard his people's children.

Next year, he said to himself, *I will come back. And I will do the work.*

Twelve

BROTHER

October 2002
Angers, France

THE FIRST MEETING OF the Al Kamandjati Association (L'association
Al Kamandjâti) took place in a tiny one-room apartment in Angers,
just down the pedestrian walkway from Ramzi's favorite hangout, the Bar
du Centre, where he took his daily coffee. Five French citizens and Ramzi
sipped juice in the sparsely furnished room, sharing glasses since there
weren't enough to go around. Ramzi was entering his fifth year at the
conservatory, which had certified his visa extensions in order for him to
pursue a Diplôme d'Etudes Musicales, the highest degree offered at the
Conservatoire.

At the meeting everyone donated ten euros in order to open a bank
account and register the association with the French government, in
accordance with French law. They drew up articles of incorporation and
elected officers. Ramzi would be president; Karim Rissouli, a French-
Moroccan law student, vice president; and Marie Albert, an international
business student, vice secretary. Karim and Yamna Amraoui, another board
member, had just returned from Palestine, where they had joined the
Association of French-Palestinian Solidarity (Association France Palestine
Solidarité), serving as "human shields" to protect Palestinians in the line
of Israeli fire. They were part of a wave of hundreds of international activists from the International Solidarity Movement, Christian Peacemaker
Teams, and other groups that had flooded the West Bank and Gaza to
conduct direct nonviolent intervention during the Second Intifada. The

movement's most visible symbol was Rachel Corrie, a twenty-three-year-old American peace activist who was crushed and killed by an Israeli military bulldozer while trying to prevent the demolition of a home in Gaza.

While in Ramallah Karim and Yamna had visited Ramzi's family in Al Amari, spending time with Rami, who, they reported, was still working at the fitness center despite the Israeli siege of the West Bank. He had also begun playing the bass. Ramadan, on his visits home, had been giving him lessons.

Ramadan was noticeably absent from the Al Kamandjati Association's inaugural meeting. He was not interested in attending, Ramzi said, though Ramadan did not recall any invitation.

The Al Kamandjati Association of France would start, Ramzi proposed, by soliciting donations of instruments. Dalouna audiences would be asked to find old violins, trumpets, piccolos, or flutes, and bring them for donation. Eventually Al Kamandjati would approach French music schools, orchestras, and instrument makers for more donations. Once the instruments arrived, Ramzi promised, they would build a school.

Some on the board were skeptical of such ambition. They assumed they were simply getting some instruments to music-starved Palestinian children. "In the end, you will see," Ramzi vowed. "We can have more than one thousand students."

Soon Ramzi embarked for Palestine to begin planning. There, he met with Rima Tarazi, the cofounder and chair of the board of the Ma'had, where he had first learned viola under Mohammad Fadel. They sat beside Rima's black Bechstein grand piano as Ramzi described his vision for a new music program focused on the refugee camps and villages in Palestine. It was a good idea, Rima agreed, but not a good fit for the Ma'had: It would require layers of approval and wouldn't fit well into their existing structure. She urged Ramzi to start Al Kamandjati on his own.

Ramzi took this advice as rejection. He felt slighted, and he suspected that the bad fit had more to do with the contrast in their backgrounds. The Ma'had founders were part of Palestinian aristocracy, unlike Ramzi's humble background. Perhaps they thought he wasn't up to the task; but Ramzi was determined to prove them wrong. A kid from a refugee camp could bring a music school to life, even if his grandfather swept the streets.

*   *   *

In October 2002, as Ramzi began to organize the Al Kamandjati Association in France, Edward Said and Daniel Barenboim arrived in Oviedo, in northern Spain, to receive one of the highest honors in Europe: the Prince of Asturias Concord Prize "for understanding between peoples." Their work together on the West-Eastern Divan Orchestra was cited for its contributions "in a generous and exemplary way to international understanding and peace."

The Divan, in its fourth year, had been performing across Europe, and in Chicago, with new concerts planned for Morocco, Mexico, and South America. The orchestra was now based in Pilas, a village outside of Seville in the southern Spanish province of Andalucía, the government of which provided financial support. Edward loved the idea of basing the Divan in *Al Andalus*. Before the Spanish Inquisition and the expulsion of Jews and Muslims, Andalucía had provided a rare moment of fellowship among the three Abrahamic faiths. In the present, as the Second Intifada had grown more violent, fellowship was hard to find.

Edward had traveled through Andalucía many times over several decades, often on vacation with Mariam, drawn by its history as "a magnet for talent in many arenas: music, philosophy, mysticism, literature, architecture, virtually all of the sciences, jurisprudence, religion." Cities like Granada, Seville, and Córdoba (once three times the size of Paris), Edward wrote, had been home to an astonishing variety of poets, mystics, and troubadours.

That summer, Edward and Mariam had not been able to join the orchestra in southern Spain. Edward's cancer had resurfaced; his white blood cell count had plummeted, and with it his immunity. He had spent ten days in quarantine; Mariam, Wadie, and Najla had been able to enter only with masks and sanitized hands and stand far from Edward.

Now, three months later, Daniel and a revived Edward walked side by side across a courtyard of gray stones and into the Teatro Campoamor, an opera house built in the nineteenth century, where they would receive their prize from the Spanish royalty. Edward, gaunt and smiling, with a mostly white beard, was introduced alongside Daniel. The *excelentísimo señor,* whose twenty-four books explored literature, colonial power, classical music, the question of Palestine, and the responsibility of the intellectual in a free society, strode to the podium. He looked out at the hall, packed to the farthest row of the second balcony, with an expression of peaceful resolve. He spoke of his history as an intellectual and an Arab, examining and experiencing the "battling identities and nationalisms," some fueled by "imperial partition such as took place in India and Palestine," and which "aggravated communal tensions . . . and seemed to have settled nothing," but rather nursed "a sense of sustained injustice."

Then Edward turned to the theme of the Spanish prize:

Spain's Islamic, Judaic, and Christian histories together provide a model for the coexistence of traditions and beliefs. What might have been unending civil war has resulted instead in the recognition of a pluri-cultural past, a source of hope and inspiration, rather than of factionalism and dissension. As a Palestinian born in Jerusalem my national history and society of my forebears was shattered in 1948 when Israel was established. Since that time—the better part of my own life—I have participated in the struggle not just to bring justice and restitution to my people, but also to keep the hope for self-determination alive. I have always believed in the primacy not of armed struggle but of rational argument, openness, and honesty, all deployed in the interests not of exclusion but of inclusion. How to reconcile the reality of an oppressed people, much abused and ignored as having no political and human rights, with the reality of another people, whose history of persecution and genocide unjustly, in my opinion, overrode the presence of an indigenous people in the march toward self-determination? . . .

It has been a hard fight, and we are far from nearing its end. Daily sacrifices are made by courageous Palestinian men and women who go on with their lives despite curfews, house demolitions, killings, mass detentions, and land expropriation . . . We need to show those who believe Palestine/Israel is the land of only one people that it is [instead] a land for two peoples who can neither exterminate nor expel each other, but must somehow approach each other as equals with equal rights to live in peace and security, together. It is therefore crucial for me to recognize the energy and dedication of those Israeli and non-Israeli Jews who have crossed the line of convention, conformity, and assertive identity and acknowledged their moral involvement in a cause that in so many ways is also their cause.

I should like to pay tribute to Daniel Barenboim, whose great musicianship has been offered as a gesture of the highest form of human solidarity to Palestinians and other Arabs . . . Literature and music open up such a space because they are essentially arts not of antagonism principally but of collaboration, receptivity, re-creation, and collective interpretation. My friend Daniel Barenboim and I have chosen this course for humanistic rather than political reasons, on the assumption that ignorance and repeated self-assertion are not strategies for sustainable survival. Discipline and dedication have provided us with the motor to bring our communities together in concert, without illusion and without abandoning our principles. What is so heartening is how many young people have responded, and how, even in this most difficult time, young Palestinians have chosen to study music, learn an instrument, practice their art.

Who knows how far we will go, and whose minds we might change?

*   *   *

In December 2002, as the siege of Palestinian towns and cities by the Israeli army continued, Prime Minister Ariel Sharon declared that Israel was prepared to "allow" a Palestinian state on less than half of the West Bank and 70 percent of Gaza, with borders, water resources, and airspace controlled by Israel, and with one further proviso: Yasser Arafat would not be allowed to continue as the Palestinian leader. Unsurprisingly, Arafat, confined to a virtual bunker in what was left of his bombed-out government headquarters in Ramallah, rejected Sharon's proposal. He believed that in signing the Oslo accords he had already agreed to a monumental compromise for a state on 22 percent of historic Palestine. Now, Sharon was offering half of that land, and none of the sovereignty.

Palestinians and their supporters saw Sharon's proposal as a blueprint for permanent Bantustans cut off from each other in an emasculated state still under the control of an occupying power. Increasingly, they were using the term "apartheid" to describe their fractured territory and the statelet that Sharon was proposing. South African archbishop Desmond Tutu, recipient of the 1984 Nobel Peace Prize, had made the comparison himself in a 2002 speech. "I've been very deeply distressed in my visit to the Holy Land," Tutu declared. "It reminded me so much of what happened to us black people in South Africa. I have seen the humiliation of the Palestinians at checkpoints and roadblocks, suffering like us when young white police officers prevented us from moving about."

Such arguments held little sway in the administration of George W. Bush, wherein Palestinian leaders searched in vain for some form of influence. With the U.S. buildup to an invasion of Iraq in the "global war on terror," which Sharon had embraced, the American alliance with Israel appeared stronger than ever. In February 2003, a few weeks before the invasion, the emboldened Sharon rejected any proposal to share Jerusalem or allow a single Palestinian refugee to return home. Moreover, he demanded that the Americans make more than one hundred changes to their new peace initiative, which Bush was calling the Road Map for Peace.

*　　*　　*

In the summer of 2003 Edward's health was deteriorating rapidly. In early July, eight months after the award ceremony in Spain, Edward and Mariam were on vacation on the Amalfi Coast in the south of Italy, where, Mariam recalled, "he was not himself at all." They stayed at Positano, at a hotel on the beach, but Edward "had no energy. He did not want to go in the sea. He would say, 'You go, go, go.'" When friends invited them for dinner, Edward would eat very little; it was too painful. His appetite had disappeared since May, when X-rays showed a growing cancerous node lodged between his liver and his heart, in a place where it would be very difficult to operate. But he had managed to travel to Beirut in June, where he received an honorary degree from the American University. After the Amalfi Coast, Edward and Mariam returned to New York, where Edward received more treatments. In mid-August they traveled to Spain for the Divan orchestral workshop in Edward's beloved Andalucía. "He was fairly okay there," Mariam recalled. But each day, Edward grew weaker.

On July 10, 2003, Ramzi and the Al Kamandjati Association of France, along with fifteen French musicians, held a press conference announcing a new musical initiative in the Holy Land. This would be the first sustained test of Ramzi's idea. The musicians would tour the occupied West Bank and Gaza, visiting villages and refugee camps and putting on concerts and workshops with an aim of building a permanent school in the near future.

After the press conference Ramzi sat with his coffee at the Bar du Centre, mapping out plans. In less than a month he would be hosting fifteen musicians, none of whom spoke Arabic or had ever traveled to Palestine. They had little notion of what awaited them. Tanks still blocked the entrances to some of the camps, nightly raids still terrorized camp residents, and Yasser Arafat's government compound had been reduced to a single besieged building, surrounded by rubble, with a tattered Palestinian flag fluttering on the roof.

For his French-Palestinian musical experiment, Ramzi had strategic and logistical help. Karim Rissouli and Marie Albert, Al Kamandjati board members who spoke decent Arabic, would accompany the group from France. More importantly, Rami had agreed to escort the French musicians and schedule appearances in the camps and other venues. His flat in Ramallah would be the landing site for the entourage. Together, the brothers were designing a way to make a musical tour in the middle of a war zone.

Ramzi gazed idly at his espresso, musing on the details. Suddenly, without any apparent provocation, the coffee jumped out of his cup. *How strange,* Ramzi thought. But his mind quickly traveled elsewhere.

*   *   *

Two days later, on a Saturday evening, Ramzi flew to Amman. By Sunday afternoon, after a hassle over paperwork with the Jordanian authorities, which led to an overnight on a bench at the Amman airport, he was in the West Bank and on his way to Ramallah.

Ramzi arrived at Al Amari in the late afternoon. Immediately he sensed something was wrong. Everyone was there but Rami. "Where is my brother?" Ramzi asked his grandfather. "We haven't seen him in four days," Sido replied. Rami had disappeared on July 10, the day of the press conference in Angers. Aunt Nawal had been trying to call Rami, but he wasn't picking up. She had decided not to call Ramzi while he was still in France; the family didn't want him to worry.

Ramzi went out immediately to search the area, asking everyone what they'd heard. He enlisted several friends, but some of their questions only made his unease deepen: *What was he wearing?* And then: *Did he have a medallion on his keychain?* An acquaintance who worked in the Palestinian Authority seemed to know something, but he acted strangely vague and elusive. Rami had been seen entering his flat with two unknown men. A six-year-old boy had seen them and remembered the model of the car, and the faces of the men who had accompanied Rami.

The siege of his homeland was complicating Ramzi's search. Israel's complete reoccupation of the West Bank had badly weakened the Palestinian Authority's security apparatus. In one case, Israel surrounded the PA's Preventive Security Services headquarters, accusing it of hiding "wanted terrorists" in its ranks. Israeli troops brought nearly two hundred Palestinians, many of whom had previously been responsible for maintaining public order, into custody.

By the time Ramzi went looking for his little brother, internecine violence and lawlessness had spread throughout the occupied territories. Palestinians were taking the law into their own hands. Suspected Palestinian collaborators with the Israeli army were murdered; others took advantage of the crumbling order by forming gangs to traffic contraband and steal cars. As he made his way through the camp and the streets of Ramallah, Ramzi grew increasingly uneasy that his little brother's disappearance could be somehow linked to the growing anarchy. That night Ramzi slept badly. He dreamed that he was dreaming, asleep in Angers, in the hope that he would awake to know that the bad feeling was all in his head. "I am in France, sleeping," the dream told him. "I wish that there were no day coming."

Ramzi awoke to the screams of Nawal. While he slept, his friends had arrived and told his uncle, "There is a body in the morgue, and the body is Rami's."

Rami Aburedwan, Ramzi's younger brother, had been murdered by Palestinian criminals who had lured him into a trap. Ramzi would learn that Rami had gathered four thousand dollars in cash to purchase a car from two men Rami knew and considered friends. The criminals had brandished knives and bludgeoned Rami to death.

Sido's modest cinder-block home at Al Amari refugee camp was filled with mourners, spilling out of the door and into the narrow alley where Ramzi had taught his little brother how to play soccer and Seven Stones, and how to escape from soldiers chasing them down the camp's narrow alleys.

The family rented a hundred plastic chairs, placing them in the alley outside the house where men sat, drinking unsweetened coffee in small plastic cups and reciting the Qur'an. Inside, the women gathered, wailing loudly. Neighbors brought hummus, labneh, salads, and warm dishes, but Ramzi ate none of it; he fasted for days.

Ramadan, home from Angers for the summer, came to pay his respects, despite the growing tensions over Dalouna. "Everybody was crying," recalled Ramzi's old friend. He found Ramzi and wrapped his long arms around the younger man. "I couldn't imagine such a catastrophe," he told Ramzi. Neither man cried; to Ramadan it was as if they were frozen, in a silent film, completely unreal. "It was such a shock that you cannot accept it, so you do not cry," Ramadan remembered. "I loved Rami like a brother."

Before laying Rami to rest, Ramzi and his grandfather went to the bombed-out remnants of Yasser Arafat's government compound, known locally as the Muqata. Grandfather and grandson demanded the killers be found and brought to justice. They wanted the death penalty. Eventually a woman came forward after finding blood smeared on the interior walls of her home. Her husband was linked to the murder. The Palestinian Authority issued a declaration that, because the murderer was a suspected collaborator with Israel, Rami had therefore died a martyr. Later, through an intermediary, the family of the murderer offered one hundred thousand dollars for forgiveness. How they raised such a sum was unknown. The cash, the family hoped, would spare the murderer's life. "We refused," Ramzi said. In a land with little justice, they wanted promises from the weak and battered Palestinian Authority that some small measure of fair play still existed in their occupied land.

Yasser Arafat agreed to see them; Grandfather Mohammad was a well-known fixture around town, and Rami, through his work at the gym, had come to be well liked by many of the Palestinian elite and others who worked out there. The Palestinian president took them into his inner offices. Grandfather was weeping. When Arafat kissed his cheeks, the old man began sobbing.

"I offer you my condolences," said the Palestinian president. Sido told Arafat that his family wanted the death penalty. "We'll do what needs to be done," Arafat promised. "I promise you that we will make the law function."

Before sunrise the next morning, the family went to Rami's gravesite in the Muslim cemetery. There they again recited the Qur'an and offered supplications for Rami, seeking their own forgiveness through their prayers for Rami's soul. Sido, Jamila, and Nawal reported being visited by Rami in their dreams, before he passed on to paradise.

They removed Rami's body from the coffin and lowered him directly into the earth. According to belief, the angels visited Rami's soul in the grave, asking him about his faith, about God and the prophet: a test, so that the angels would know Rami Aburedwan was on the right path.

*   *   *

In two weeks, fifteen French musicians were due to arrive for the first summer music tour and workshop, a test run for Al Kamandjati.

Ramzi felt broken and unable to proceed with the tour. He planned to contact his friends in France and call everything off. My brother is dead, he would tell them, and so is Al Kamandjati. Cancel your tickets.

But as the day grew closer, Ramzi kept putting off the call. He had been brooding over what Rami would want, and he had finally concluded that Rami would not like to see him doing nothing. He believed that Rami's life energy still existed, and that he could somehow use it for the better. He thought, *If I get his energy, plus my energy, I will do something good for him.*

No one in France yet knew of the tragedy. Ramzi decided to keep the news of Rami's murder from them, for now. When they arrived in the last week of July, Ramzi would be ready.

Thirteen

TROUBADOURS

Late July 2003
Ramallah

THE STREETS WERE nearly empty and the light still pale. At six in the morning the French entourage—fifteen musicians, two documentary filmmakers on hand to chronicle the building of the music school, and several other members of Al Kamandjati's French board of directors—sprawled bleary-eyed in folding chairs outside a Ramallah café.

The visitors had just arrived from Angers by way of Paris and the airport at Tel Aviv. They told the authorities they were on a religious pilgrimage with intentions to travel only to the holy sites in Jerusalem. Travelers who announced plans to visit the occupied territories, Ramzi had warned, could be barred by Israel.

The Palestinian proprietor offered Turkish coffee to the visitors, and there they waited for Ramzi, who hadn't shown up and wasn't answering his phone. Karim watched warily as a taxi swooshed past. The last time he had been in Ramallah, at the height of the Israeli military operations in the West Bank, he and Yamna had acted as "human shields," escorting children safely back and forth between home and school. They'd seen buildings crumble beneath the force of Israeli rockets and tank shells. Now it seemed quiet, but Karim didn't trust the calm.

With a rhythmic clatter a shop owner raised his metal shutters. A man shaved the fat from a fresh round of beef shawarma spinning slowly on a spit beside a gas flame. The musicians looked around anxiously, blowing into their demitasse cups, wondering what was next.

Julien Leray, the street musician from Angers, snapped open his instrument case, pulled out his guitar, and began singing a World War II–era song about a worker in occupied France. It seemed appropriate for the occasion.

A kerchiefed old woman began screaming. "Who are these people and what are they doing?" she yelled as she walked past the café. She had confused Julien's French for Hebrew and therefore thought the guests were a musical accompaniment to the occupying army. "Are they Israelis?" she demanded of the shopkeeper, adjusting her kerchief.

"They are French," replied the shopkeeper.

"I don't believe you!"

Julien paused, looked around, and took a drag from his cigarette. He seemed unsure whether to keep playing. The old woman was still shouting. "Calm down, Grandma," the shopkeeper said gently.

"Why would I?" came her angry reply. "The Israelis are bombing! They are bombing! They are bombing!" She walked away, muttering to herself. Julien resumed singing.

Karim redialed and again got a recording on Ramzi's line. He watched the impromptu concert from the perimeter. *Those musicians are crazy*, he said to himself. On their first hour of their first day in a war zone, they were behaving like troubadours in Paris.

"Welcome to Palestine!" Ramzi exclaimed half an hour later as he stepped out of a car and the musicians crowded around him. "I am happy you are here." Two weeks before, he had buried his brother. Since then he hadn't shaved, and his beard was growing scraggly.

Karim watched Ramzi embrace and kiss the cheeks of his visitors. Despite the welcomes, he looked exhausted and worried. In a private moment in the car, after they had dropped off the musicians at Rami's flat and were riding toward Al Amari, Karim learned why.

They rode in silence to the camp. The house was quiet; Grandfather was at work. Grandmother Jamila awoke. She and Aunt Nawal served tea, accepting Karim's stunned condolences.

Ramzi and Karim left the house to buy groceries for the French entourage and took the food to Rami's flat. One by one, Karim told them the news.

*   *   *

By the summer of 2003, the George W. Bush administration had unveiled the final draft of the Road Map for Peace, which called for Palestinians to hold elections and end suicide attacks. The plan required Israel to partially withdraw from the Palestinian towns it had reoccupied during the Second Intifada, and to freeze the expansion of settlements. This last requirement, Prime Minister Ariel Sharon bluntly told U.S. secretary of state Colin Powell, would be impossible to grant. "Our finest youth live there," Sharon told Powell, a fellow former general. "They are already the third generation, contributing to the state and serving in elite army units. They return home and get married, so then they can't build a house and have children? What do you want, for a pregnant woman to have an abortion just because she is a settler?" Sharon repeated his insistence that any Palestinian state would have to exist alongside the settlements. For years Israel had encouraged families to move to the settlements with generous subsidies for housing, education, business development, and income tax relief, making it far less expensive to be a settler than a city-dweller.

The Palestinian leadership agreed to American and Israeli preconditions for peace talks. Arafat had handed the reins of power to his second in command, Mahmoud Abbas, fulfilling a demand Sharon had been pressing for months. In midsummer, several Palestinian factions declared a *hudna*, or truce, pledging to end suicide attacks. By late summer, after a spate of attacks and reprisals, the number of suicide bombings began to decline dramatically. Palestinian analysts declared this was because of the hudna. Israelis insisted the sharp drop in casualties was due to the twenty-five-foot-high concrete wall and electrified fence they were building along and inside the boundary of the West Bank. The planned barrier was to be 439 miles long. Six thousand workers would pour more than fifty million tons of concrete and install nine million yards of barbwire and twenty-five thousand electronic detector posts. The barrier—partly a wall and partly a series of ditches, trenches, electronic fencing, monitors, cameras, and multiple layers of razor wire—would snake back and forth across the old Green Line that once separated Israel from the West Bank. On its way it would incorporate sixty Jewish settlements on the "Israeli" side. In the process Israel would effectively annex more than 130,000 acres, or nearly 10 percent of West Bank land, over the protests of local farmers and the Palestinian Authority.

*   *   *

On the other side of the barrier, the visitors from France were testing Ramzi's idea that music could make a difference in the middle of a military occupation. Above all, they contended with physical obstacles. In the summer of 2003, 757 checkpoints, roadblocks, ditches, concrete-block barriers, rammed-earth blockades, and other physical obstacles impeded passage across the West Bank and Gaza—an area slightly larger than the American state of Connecticut. Most ubiquitous were the army checkpoints, where soldiers in canvas-draped kiosks, flanked with sandbags and Israeli flags, summoned drivers forward, one car at a time, as fellow soldiers pointed automatic rifles from their lookout posts.

What the hell is this? thought Jessie Nguenang, the Dalouna vocalist who had taught herself to sing in Arabic. After years of performances in France she had finally come to Palestine, only to spend hours with her fellow musicians idling in the long lines of vehicles. There they waited, watching through the windows of the van, as pedestrians crowded beneath sweltering roofs of corrugated tin. *Why are all these people waiting with the babies and the little kids in the sun?* Jessie mused. Soon these scenes began to feel normal: the van, inching forward toward the kiosk; the Palestinians on foot, squeezed into a narrow passage behind a long row of vertical bars; the musicians, flashing their French passports, then sailing through—sometimes with Ramzi, sometimes without. Frequently soldiers would summon Ramzi from the van and refuse to let him pass. From the checkpoint he would board a collective taxi and navigate a series of back roads, around the barriers, sometimes arriving at a workshop several hours after the rest of the group.

As they rode across the occupied territories, stopping in villages and refugee camps for concerts and workshops, the musicians sought ways to insert their music within the physical space of the occupation. At the old city in Hebron, the most surreal tableau in the entire Israeli-Palestinian tragedy, some six hundred Israeli settlers lived protected by soldiers amid thirty-five thousand Palestinians in the immediate surroundings—an area referred to as H-2. The fifteen hundred soldiers, more than twice the number of settlers they were sent to protect, spent much of their time escorting their charges from one part of Hebron to another. The musicians were stunned, as most visitors are, to learn that Palestinians were barred from many of their own streets, now "sterile zones" cleared to allow for the settlers' free passage; it was not uncommon to see a bearded settler pushing a baby stroller down an empty street, an M-16 slung over his shoulder. The entrances to many Palestinian homes and businesses, meanwhile, had been welded shut by the army. To get home, some had to cross a neighbor's rooftop; others cut holes in their walls, or even scaled their buildings with a rope. Unlike other West Bank settlements, where Israelis seized hilltops before building new homes, settlers in downtown Hebron occupied buildings amid a sea of Palestinians. Wire screens spread over the old Arab casbah to catch the debris—stones, bricks, crowbars, bags of human feces—these settlers hurled down from the upper floors toward the Palestinians. The enmity went back decades, but the current arrangement was sanctioned by an agreement between Israel and the Palestinian Authority, encouraged by the United States, as part of the Oslo peace process.

A few hundred meters away, the gray steel of a military checkpoint blocked the entrance to the Ibrahimi Mosque and the Tomb of the Patriarchs. Inside the mosque in 1994, a settler from Brooklyn, Baruch Goldstein, had gunned town twenty-nine Palestinian worshippers. Now at the checkpoint outside the mosque, the musicians from France tried in vain to play. "You don't have the right to play here," bearded settler-soldiers told the group.

Twenty miles north, at the military checkpoint at Qalandia, which divided Ramallah from Jerusalem, the musicians tried again, gathering near the soldiers' kiosk to play a Vivaldi concerto adapted for baroque flute. Again, they were ordered to stop. "It's not a gun," a Frenchman objected, holding out his clarinet. They continued the Vivaldi for as long as they could before soldiers pushed them from the checkpoint. "All of Palestine is a military camp!" a musician protested. Later they came to the separation wall itself, a vast, sprawling stretch of concrete driven into the soil of the West Bank. There, amid a landscape strewn with broken blocks of concrete, where graffiti promised liberation, a lone French cellist in a white embroidered blouse, blonde hair curling over her collar, played the prelude to the Bach Cello Suite no. 1.

At times the physical space seemed to overwhelm the possibility of music. At the village of Azzoun, about seven miles east of the Mediterranean, the concrete barrier rose twenty-five feet on three sides, twice as high as the Berlin Wall, dividing the community from itself, separating farmers from their orchards and fields, and cutting off light. MORTAL DANGER-MILITARY ZONE, read signs posted along the barrier. ANYONE WHO PASSES OR DAMAGES THE FENCE ENDANGERS HIS LIFE.

"Against this, what can music do?" one musician lamented.

"Nothing," came the answer.

By the time the musicians reached Gaza to conduct a series of work-shops, the French visitors were openly debating the purpose of their mission. "With blood in the streets, do you think children would come to play bass or would they still think about the previous day?" asked Fred, a violist from Paris. They were in Gaza City, sitting in the back room of a community center.

"Is it better that they keep in mind the previous day and stay at home crying?" Karim responded. "Don't you trust them when they say it's important for them?"

"Of course I do, but they tell me they are hiding under the table when it's not calm," Fred replied. "So what can we do? Not much. Try to think as a six-year-old child. If I were six, always seeing helicopters, blood, my parents being dead, I would not feel like playing bass."

"Then what *would* you feel like doing?" Karim asked. "Would you take a Kalashnikov and go and shoot a soldier?"

"Possibly."

"At the age of six? Most six-year-old children have a child's mind. Soldiers are stealing their childhood. So let us try to give them what they deserve to have."

Despite the disagreements, it was hard to miss the fact that, at a minimum, the presence of music was bringing much-needed diversion to children across occupied Palestine. At the Red Crescent headquarters in Gaza, in a refugee camp near Hebron and another near Jerusalem, in a broad courtyard at Jenin camp, at a school in Al Amari: Children crowded around an oud or a guitar, giggling and flashing victory signs, touching flutes and clarinets, taking their turns on baby violins. Old people who had lived through multiple wars quietly approached Ramzi, thanking him for bringing a moment's joy and laughter to their grandchildren. To Yamna, the Al Kamandjati board member, the concerts and workshops represented "an escape, a way for the children to get out of what is going on in Palestine. The children, for this short instant, will think of something else. The music makes us think of something else." Yamna, thin-faced and striking, with dark eyes and long black hair, was Moroccan by heritage, and she saw herself in the children. "They are always smiling. In France we are always complaining. They have nothing, and you bring them a little violin and they are so happy."

For Ramzi, these encounters reinforced his belief in bringing music to children during a time of violence and reprisals, rather than waiting for calm to return. "People discover you during the difficulties, not during the normal days," he said.

Ramzi was spending his days organizing the workshops in the camps, calling ahead to confirm venues and double-check sleeping arrangements, and plotting the most direct routes with the fewest checkpoints. Rami had begun this work, but now Ramzi immersed himself in it, along with all of its complicated logistics. This allowed him to think of something other than his brother's murder.

"He worked so hard not to think about Rami's death," Yamna recalled. "He never sat down. He ran all over." Even when Ramzi did sit, he nervously jiggled his right leg, as if he needed to jump up and run some more. He was smoking two packs of cigarettes a day and drinking well into the early mornings.

But if all this was an effort to escape his grief, it failed. At Al Amari there were constant reminders of Rami: in the alleys, near the bakery, on the rooftops, and upstairs in Sido's room, where the brothers had often slept on opposite sides of their grandfather, touching hands across the old man's sleeping bulk. Ramzi brooded constantly over Rami's dreams of finding a wife, filling his flat with furniture, and making it into a home where he could raise his family.

Ramzi tried not to show this grief to his visiting colleagues. He believed his strength resided in his ability not to reveal his vulnerable side. That would be a sign of weakness, and he feared he could lose the respect of people around him. He did, however, allow Yamna to see some of his pain. In recent months, the two had grown closer. Publicly, they wouldn't speak of a relationship; despite secular, international roots both in the Palestinian liberation struggle and the global Palestinian diaspora, the society in Palestine itself was conservative. Both Ramzi and Yamna wanted to keep their personal lives private. That summer, even some of the French musicians were unaware of how close Ramzi and Yamna had become.

"Why us?" Ramzi asked Yamna late one evening in Sido's house in Al Amari. "Why my family? Why ever more disappointments?" He felt not only the of loss of Rami; it was the accumulation of losses, going back to his early childhood. Later, as she lay alone in the dark, Yamna could hear Ramzi in the next room, crying softly.

But that was the only time. Yamna felt unable to help Ramzi, and she came to believe he would never let her grow too close. "He protects himself because he is scared. He's afraid to disappoint. It comes from his life. He lacked the affection of his mom.

"He has a hole," Yamna said. "An emptiness."

*   *   *

My heart is full of sorrow, the boy sang in a high, resonant voice, as the children in the community center clapped in unison. Ramzi's eyes widened and he broke into a smile. He grabbed a tabla and began tapping out a rhythm. *My heart is broken,* the boy sang.

Ramzi and the French musicians had come to a U.N. school in the Al Fawwar refugee camp, where six thousand people were crowded into a haphazard collection of half-finished cinder-block dwellings a few miles west of Hebron. Narrow broken bands of pavement cut through clusters of two- and three-story buildings. Satellite dishes and black water tanks crowded onto rooftops. An Israeli military base and the adjacent Jewish settlement of Hagai, perched on a nearby hill, looked down at the camp. To the west rose the Israeli separation wall.

As the musicians had prepared to leave Al Fawwar that day, they found their exit blocked by jeeps and tanks. The Israeli army had imposed a curfew and sealed the camp so that no one could leave. Such closures were commonplace across the occupied territories, especially when military authorities suspected an increase in militant activity. In Al Fawwar, closure was a relatively simple procedure. When the army wanted to, it simply lowered the long metal gates at the camp's two entrances, positioned tanks in front of them, and stationed soldiers in the watchtowers, at the ready with machine guns. This made it easier to conduct night raids in search of members of banned militant groups, or suspected suicide bombers. Because of one such closure, the musicians, stuck in Al Fawwar another day, had decided to host more workshops. This is how Ramzi met Oday Khatib.

My heart is broken, Oday sang again, smiling and hamming it up. *Each step makes me more patient.*

Oday's song, "Radi," or "I Am Satisfied," was about what it felt like to be confined to a prison cell. Three of his own brothers were in prison: one suspected of throwing stones, another for resisting arrest, and a third for plotting a suicide bombing at an army camp in Tel Aviv.

Destiny is written on our forehead, the boy sang, his voice soaring over the hand claps and the drums. Oday was short and slight. He wore a T-shirt and jeans. His hair was cut short, except in the front, were it rose in a stylish flip. He smiled cautiously. To the musicians Oday looked barely eight years old, the age Ramzi was when he joined the first uprising in Al Amari; but he was actually twelve.

Ramzi had been searching for something, perhaps a single person or image that could stand for the struggle of children making music under occupation. In the middle of the second uprising, he wanted to capture the imagination of people within and outside of Palestine, much as his own image had during the first.

As Oday finished his song and the room burst into applause, Ramzi was already making a plan. For now, he would keep that plan to himself.

*   *   *

To build a music school, Ramzi knew, required more than the good will of traveling musicians from another land. He would need money, a physical space, and the support of local Palestinians.

Near the end of the summer, as he was preparing to return to the Conservatoire in France, Ramzi went to see Ziad Khalaf at the A.M. Qattan Foundation in Ramallah. They had met before. In their initial meeting, Ziad had been struck by Ramzi's passion, charisma, and the clarity with which he spoke about Al Kamandjati, the name he had chosen for his music school in Palestine. Ziad's foundation had made a small grant to cover the French musicians' travel that summer and was now prepared to become a long-term Palestinian partner. A.M. Qattan was a comparatively small foundation, but it could help leverage substantial funds from European donors. In the years since Oslo, billions of dollars in aid had poured in from European and North American governments and private foundations, both for salaries in the Palestinian Authority and for small Palestinian NGOs focused on politics, media, human rights, and the arts. This created what some saw as overdependence on foreign aid, which ran the risk of undercutting efforts to establish Palestinian sovereignty. Yet Ziad believed Ramzi was blazing his own path and was not at risk of being co-opted by any foreigner's agenda. He also was convinced that Al Kamandjati could be one of the civil society institutions necessary to help create an independent state.

Ziad, much like Soraida before him, had also taken a personal interest in Ramzi. He had seen the famous poster and knew the story of Ramzi and his grandfather sweeping the streets. Ziad was part of a large, wealthy Palestinian family. He wanted to go beyond the role of foundation funder.

Ziad told Ramzi that his extended family owned several abandoned buildings in a neglected neighborhood of Old Ramallah; perhaps, if he could convince his relatives to make a long-term lease to Al Kamandjati, free of charge, the buildings could be shored up and turned into a music school. He knew of a Palestinian historical preservation group, Riwaq, that renovated old buildings with funds from Sida, the Swedish development agency. This seemed like a perfect project for them, and for Al Kamandjati.

Now, on the eve of Ramzi's return to the Conservatoire, things began moving quickly. A series of meetings followed. Riwaq, the cultural and architectural preservation firm, supported the idea. If Ziad could help secure the property from his family, Riwaq could probably get the funds through Sweden. But in order to show his commitment to the project, Ramzi was asked to raise ten thousand dollars toward the renovation—a small percentage of the total cost, but a large sum for a music student.

Ramzi wasn't sure how he would come up with a sum like that, but he didn't hesitate. "Yes," he said. "I will do it."

Fourteen

EDWARD

September 2003
New York City

MARIAM SAID SAT alone on a blue couch in the family room on Riverside Drive, gazing impassively through arched windows to the Hudson River and New Jersey beyond. It was quiet. To the north the George Washington Bridge connected Jersey to upper Manhattan. The windows of the large apartment wrapped around the curve of the high-rise building, and from their bedroom, Mariam could look down on College Walk, the path between the two libraries at Columbia University, where Edward had taught for forty years.

Mariam's hands were folded in her lap. Edward slept in the next room. Compared to her famous husband, Mariam was soft-spoken, with probing, intelligent eyes; she dressed impeccably, and her well-coiffed hair was tinged with red. She shifted her gaze to Edward's empty reading chair, his collection of pipes in a pipe stand, the Cuban cigars he'd picked up at the Beirut airport, a large round glass ashtray, his tortoiseshell glasses, and a magnifying glass. Across from his chair, books lined the shelves: Baldwin, Poe, Twain, Eudora Welty. On the wall facing the picture window hung framed antique maps of Palestine.

Edward's health had been deteriorating since the late spring. The node lodged between his heart and liver hadn't gotten any smaller. The treatment wasn't working. Eating was painful, and walking and breathing more difficult.

September 22 was a Monday, and in the morning, when Mariam was leaving for her job at the bank, Edward said, "Don't go. Stay."

"You look so much better today," Mariam assured him. There would be more time, she believed; there was something very important happening at work that day, a meeting she can now barely recall. Mariam called Edward twice from the taxi, and several more times from work. Najla and Wadie would be checking on him during the day, and a dear friend visiting from Palestine, Rima Tarazi (cofounder of the National Conservatory of Music) was expected to visit at five. In the afternoon, Najla called Mariam. "Daddy's very tired," she reported. "And he's saying strange things."

After work, Mariam picked up a few things for dinner, then rushed home. Wadie was with him. "Edward really looked awful," Mariam remembered. "He would try to say something, he couldn't articulate it. He was able to say a few words, but he could barely walk." They put him in the family car and drove him to the hospital. Doctors rushed to treat him, hoping he would soon revive. Things deteriorated quickly, however, and soon Edward was taken into intensive care.

The next day Daniel flew in from Chicago, where he was music director of the Chicago Symphony Orchestra. He went straight to the hospital. The two had spoken, by Daniel's estimation, every day since they had met by chance in the London hotel lobby ten years earlier. Their friendship, and one byproduct of it—the West-Eastern Divan Orchestra—had survived a decimated peace process, a second uprising, a military siege and reoccupation, and an endless cycle of spilled blood and recrimination between their peoples. Musically, the orchestra was collectively inexperienced—many of its players were still in their early twenties—but audiences responded emotionally to the sight of Arabs and Israelis sharing the stage. For Edward, few things were more important than the Divan—especially as he'd grown weaker over the last year.

"At least, therefore, another world emerges," he had said at the conclusion of a speech in Berkeley—one of his last public appearances.

In our work and planning and discussions, our main principle is that separation between peoples, war between peoples is not a solution for any of the problems that divide them. And certainly ignorance of the other provides no help whatever. Cooperation and coexistence of the kind that music, lived as we have lived, performed, shared and loved it together, might be. I for one am full of optimism, despite the darkening sky and the seemingly hopeless situation for the time being that encloses us all.

Edward's collaboration with Daniel, he told Mariam—most of all the West-Eastern Divan Orchestra and workshop—was "the most important thing I've done."

Mariam told Daniel that Edward was too sick for visitors. She believed he would not want anyone, not even Daniel, to see him in his present condition. The hospital had already given her Edward's clothes, his watch, and his ring, and she knew what that meant. The man widely considered one of the great original thinkers of the twentieth century, who over a spectacular career had written and spoken millions of words, could now offer none. Daniel returned to Chicago.

Edward Said died at 6:25 A.M. on Thursday, September 25, 2003, surrounded by Mariam, Wadie, and Najla. He was sixty-seven years old.

Accolades poured in from around the world. "With his death, the Palestinian nation has lost its most articulate voice in the Northern hemisphere, a world where, by and large, the continuous suffering of the Palestinians is ignored," wrote the British-Pakistani scholar Tariq Ali in the *New Left Review.* "His voice is irreplaceable, but his legacy will endure."

Less glowing comment came from the *New York Times,* which spent much of its obituary recounting attacks on Edward's character, including claims, already discredited, that Edward had "falsified his biography" in his memoir, *Out of Place,* and quoting the conservative Jewish magazine, *Commentary,* which had infamously called Edward a "professor of terror" for his support of the Palestinian cause.

Months later, friends from around the world, including Daniel Barenboim, the actress Vanessa Redgrave, and the South African novelist Nadine Gordimer, gathered in tribute at Columbia. "If the great contemporary intellectuals can be counted on one hand, Edward Said is the index finger," said Gordimer. "Above all, Said had an intelligence of feeling."

As part of the tribute to Edward, mourners were shown excerpts from various films about him and the breadth of his interests—in music, literature, Palestine, and the responsibility to speak truth to power. "The role of the intellectual is to ask questions," said Edward, his recorded voice echoing from the speakers in the packed St. Paul's Chapel on the Columbia campus. "To disturb people, to stir up reflection, to provoke, you might say, controversy and thought. The role of the intellectual is *never* to justify power. *Never*. Always to be critical of power. Whether it's the power of the weak or the power of the strong. Power's power. The role of the intellectual is to challenge power by providing alternative models. And, as important, resources of hope. The individual has to provide perspective. It's not our destiny to be refugees. It's not our destiny to be prisoners of war. It's not our destiny to be commandos. It's not our destiny to be an army of occupation. We have a choice."

Daniel came to the piano to play Schubert's Impromptu in A-flat Major. Afterward, he took the microphone. "Edward understood the world through music," he said. "Very often music has been used to escape from the world. But Edward understood that musical terminology was essential to understanding the world. Everything is interrelated. This is what made his conversation so breathtaking. All his interests were one."

"I think of Edward practically every day," Daniel would say seven years later. "I lost a mentor. Everything Edward said and thought had a reason, had a logic and had a humanism behind it. Edward was a symbol of Palestinian dignity, of Palestinian intelligence, Palestinian culture, ambition, of Palestinian nationalism, patriotism, everything. All the Arabs somehow saw Edward as everything they altogether could maybe one day become. They saw that in the one person. Edward had that very unique quality of having moral authority."

*　　　*　　　*

Daniel arrived in Ramallah to play a concert for the children of the National Conservatory of Music, the Ma'had. He planned to perform Beethoven, to conduct orchestral workshops, and to survey the destruction in the West Bank in the wake of Israeli military operations. His host was Mustafa Barghouti, who, with Edward and Dr. Haidar Abdel-Shafi, in the wake of the Second Intifada, had cofounded the Palestinian National Initiative in 2002. The PNI sought to be a center-left "alternative democratic opposition" to both the Palestinian Authority, which was under increasing international scrutiny for financial malfeasance, and the rising power of Hamas and its extremist fundamentalism. Mustafa planned to challenge Yasser Arafat for the Palestinian presidency in the upcoming elections. His initiative, however, had little if any political base in the villages and refugee camps, where in recent years Hamas's influence had grown, especially given the PA's reputation for corruption and embezzlement. The central political fight in Palestine remained between Fatah, the PA's main political faction, and Hamas.

In the evening Mustafa introduced Daniel at the Friends (Quaker) School in Ramallah, evoking the name of Edward Said and the West-Eastern Divan Orchestra. "We are very proud that you have come here to make music," Mustafa said. "You have cut through the occupation and the embargo imposed on us and you have underlined the fact that the message of music is the message of peace. It has the power to connect peoples. Thank you for being here, Daniel."

Daniel sat before a new Steinway grand piano. A few days earlier, he had arranged for the Steinway company to donate it to the Ma'had; then, in discussion with Israeli authorities, he had helped facilitate its transport through the occupied West Bank. The small auditorium went silent as Daniel began to play Beethoven's haunting Sonata no. 14, the *Moonlight Sonata*, so named for its evocation of moonlight on Switzerland's Lake Lucerne. Two centuries after Beethoven composed the piece, which he originally called *Sonata quasi una fantasia* ("Sonata in the Manner of a Fantasy"), the Israeli pianist began the master's lamentation slowly, his pianissimo notes echoing through the small auditorium.

Afterward, Daniel was surrounded by beaming schoolchildren in uniform, asking for his autograph as if he were a rock star.

"It made me proud that day," Mustafa recalled. "I could see that our kids could differentiate really between a good and a bad person. Between an Israeli who is in solidarity with them and an Israeli who is behaving as an enemy and shelling their places. Because they gave him a wonderful, very warm reception."

"I did not imagine there would be such an immediate and enthusiastic response," Daniel said later. Palestinians, he said, "have shown me so much affection, and so much thirst for music."

*   *   *

Daniel walked alone, across the grounds of the Quaker auditorium, after his performance and the workshops, making his way toward his dressing room on the other side of the school grounds.

A young man approached from behind. "Bravo!" said the young man, smiling and introducing himself. "My name is Ramzi. I play viola, and I study in France."

They had reached the dressing room. The maestro seemed preoccupied; absentmindedly, he handed Ramzi his trousers as he changed into his street clothes. Presently assistants arrived, surrounding Daniel and briefing him on his upcoming schedule in Palestine.

Ramzi saw this was not the right time for a lengthy introduction. He left, determined to meet the maestro another time.

Fifteen

JENIN

October 2003
Angers, France

IN THE FALL OF 2003, after a summer of hectic arrangements with the visiting French musicians, Ramzi returned to France and sank into a deep depression. He no longer faced the violent distractions of a homeland under siege, nor the daily challenge of getting fifteen foreign musicians through military checkpoints and into the refugee camps. In the quiet, sleek, leafy landscape along the Loire, the loss of Rami finally hit him fully. At night, in his flat in Angers, he watched TV until the early hours of the morning, paying no attention to what was on. He put on Tchaikovsky's Fourth Symphony, crying in waves through the slow movements. In the daytime, he managed to get to the practice room at the Conservatoire, but found he could barely play. For hours he would sit in a chair, his head on a table, dozing off, dreaming of Rami. He would step out for coffee and a smoke, come back to the room, play listlessly, and fall asleep again.

"We cannot continue like this, Ramzi," François said one day in Salle 312, as his student gazed blankly through the plate glass window to the Parc Bellefontaine below. "If you keep going in this direction, there's nothing for you here. You'll be finished."

Soon afterward, Ramzi flunked an important examination, putting his future at the Conservatoire, and in France, in doubt. He had recently broken up with Yamna, and he now considered returning home, without his degree, to take care of Sido and the family. How that would affect the prospects for Al Kamandjati wasn't clear, but at the time Ramzi didn't care.

Yet he felt a responsibility to Rami, who he believed was still watching him. After weeks of brooding Ramzi decided that he didn't want to disappoint his little brother. He had long believed that a person's life could be determined by the amount of positive energy he generates, even from the raw material of violence and trauma. Negative experience, even the death of his brother, could be converted into dreams and a plan to implement them.

He went to Richard Lowry, the Conservatoire's director, to ask for another chance. Richard arranged for Ramzi to retake the exam at a nearby conservatory. After weeks of rigorous practice with François, he walked into a small chapel that served as the examination room in the town of Cholet. He performed George Enescu's concert piece for viola and piano, technically difficult, filled with double strings and double stops, imbued with a range of colors. At one point his piano accompanist got lost and began playing the wrong portion. Ramzi quickly adapted, met her where she was, and continued playing. He was still quick on his feet.

After the exam, Ramzi waited outside in the courtyard of the chapel, pacing and smoking. A juror emerged from the examination room. "You passed," she told Ramzi. The jurors, she said, had noted his ability to adapt on the fly. "You're in," she said. Ramzi would be staying in France.

*   *   *

Throughout the late fall of 2003, and into the following spring, Ramzi booked a series of Dalouna concerts across France. He still needed to raise the ten thousand dollars for his share of the renovations for the music school in Ramallah. He called the Palestinian ambassador to France, Leila Shahid, who agreed to host a press conference and benefit concert in Angers.

On the evening of the concert Leila stood in the spotlight of a packed music hall in Angers, speaking glowingly about the boy with the stone in his hand who had transformed his life through music. Dalouna had been founded by two of her own people, Leila said, who were doing such important work in Palestine.

"Come on up to the stage, guys, we're so proud of you," Leila exclaimed to a building wave of applause.

Ramzi, all smiles, stepped onstage, kissing Leila on each cheek. Other members of Dalouna came with him.

At the microphone, Ramzi urged concertgoers to search their attics and garages for old instruments. "It would be much more useful and beautiful to put it in the hands of a child in Palestine, than to have it just sitting in your house," he said.

Ramadan was not in the concert hall that evening. His differences with Ramzi, about the direction of the band and about the establishment of a separate music school in Palestine, had grown deeper. By not appearing on stage with Ramzi and the Palestinian ambassador, he was, in effect, announcing his departure from Dalouna. His friendship with Ramzi, already badly strained, was now finished.

*   *   *

On May 9, 2004, Daniel Barenboim approached the microphone in Israel's Knesset, the nation's parliament. He was the recipient of one of the nation's highest honors, the Wolf Prize for the Arts, bestowed by Israel's Ministry of Education. The award recognizes "achievements in the interest of mankind and friendly relations among peoples." The maestro had been a controversial choice. Israel's political right objected to his long friendship with Edward Said and to his recitals and workshops for Palestinians, including the children of the Ma'had in Ramallah. In the wake of Edward's death, Daniel had decided to continue with the West-Eastern Divan Orchestra. Mariam had agreed to join the project by taking an active role with planning, and to be the liaison to the Arab musicians.

Daniel's work with the Divan, however, was less of an issue in Israel than his violation of the country's informal ban of the music of the great composer Richard Wagner, a virulent anti-Semite and Hitler's favorite. Three years earlier, with the visiting Berlin Philharmonic, Daniel had conducted excerpts of Wagner's *Tristan und Isolde*, causing a furor. The speaker of the Knesset denounced Daniel, saying he had "desecrated the memory" of Holocaust victims. The Knesset Education Committee, citing Daniel's "disgusting deed," declared him "persona non grata" in Israel until he apologized. Three years later, the apology was still an issue, and some members of the Knesset tried to withhold the prize until Daniel issued one. He declined, but told Israel's army radio, "if people were really hurt, of course I regret this, because I don't want to harm anyone." The present-ation of the award would go forward, and its recipient was about to gener-ate another controversy.

Daniel stepped to the podium to accept his prize. "It was in 1952, four years after the declaration of Israel's independence, that I, as a ten-year-old boy, came to Israel with my parents from Argentina," he recoun-ted after thanking the Wolf Foundation for the honor. He then quoted from Israel's declaration of independence, which committed itself to "the principles of freedom, justice and peace" and promised "full equal, social and political rights to all its citizens regardless of differences of religious faith, race or sex."

"I am asking today with deep sorrow," Daniel declared, "can we, despite all our achievements, ignore the intolerable gap between what the declara-tion of independence promised and what was fulfilled, the gap between the idea and the realities of Israel? Does the condition of occupation and domin-ation over another people fit the declaration of independence? Is there any sense in the independence of one at the expense of the fundamental rights of the other? Can the Jewish people whose history is a record of continued suffering and relentless persecution, allow themselves to be indifferent to the rights and suffering of a neighboring people? Can the State of Israel allow itself an unrealistic dream of an ideological end to the conflict instead of pursuing a pragmatic, humanitarian one based on social justice?"

Daniel announced he would be giving the Wolf Prize money—one hundred thousand dollars—to music education projects in Israel and Ramallah.

Outrage in the Knesset immediately ensued, beginning with Israel's minister of education. "As chair of the Wolf Foundation, I wish to express my dismay at the fact that Mr. Barenboim has chosen this arena, this podium to attack the State of Israel," said the minister, Limor Livnat of the ruling Likud Party, raising her voice above the shouting in the Knesset. "I should like to point out, please, I should like ... Control yourselves, please! ... May I propose that we behave in a civilized manner!"

*　　*　　*

A few weeks later, in the late spring of 2004, Ramzi landed in Ramallah to prepare for another musical tour of the refugee camps by his French musician friends. He met with Ziad of the Qattan Foundation. Ramzi told Ziad he had raised the necessary ten thousand dollars in earnest money, in part from the benefit concert with the Palestinian ambassador to France. Ziad reported the conversations with his relatives, most of whom had agreed in principle to lease the family compound of abandoned buildings in Old Ramallah, without charge, for Ramzi's music school. Riwaq, the Palestinian historical preservation firm, had received tentative support from the Swedish development agency to fund the project. Everything appeared to be going smoothly.

Ramzi, Marie, Karim, Ziad, and the architect Khaldun Bshara walked down a narrow street in the old city, past once-stately courtyards of jasmine and twisted grapevines. Neighbors watched in silence, a few of them fingering their prayer beads, others puffing out white clouds from gurgling water pipes. A minaret from the local mosque towered above them. Fifty meters south stood the steeple of the Orthodox church; just below that, a fruit stand displayed precarious pyramids of mangos, cactus pears, and pomegranates. In recent years, the neighborhood had become neglected. Starting in the early twentieth century, local Christians began migrating—some to the United States, others to work in Jerusalem under the British Mandate in the years after the fall of the Ottoman Empire— thus emptying the historic core of the city. Peasant farmers from Hebron moved into the vacant homes, initially as caretakers, working in nearby fields. Over the years they earned the right to stay in their homes, protected by tenant laws that went back to Ottoman times.

In the street, neighborhood kids were playing a game they called Arabs and Jews. In this game boys fashioned foot-long pieces of wood shaped like guns, and played the role of Israelis; girls picked up pebbles or small stones, and played the Palestinians. They divided their identities in this way, they would explain, because boys are stronger than girls.

Ramzi and the others walked past the children laughing and chasing each other with the stones and the toy guns, and moved into a broad, sun-bleached courtyard. The place was a shambles, deserted for years, strewn with rubble and trash. It had been used as an informal dump for the neighborhood. Rats, mice, and stray cats appeared from various layers of trash and scurried back behind the giant pile. "It smelled like shit," remembered Khaldun, the architect from Riwaq. Transforming it would take sweat, shovels, and signed papers from more than a dozen members of Ziad's extended family.

In a far corner of the abandoned building, two girls were playing in the cool shade of a darkened room, far from the mounds of refuse. They had swept the rubble clean and laid out the household items of an ordinary, imagined life. The girls looked up warily as Ramzi walked toward them. He introduced himself. They were sisters: Alá, six years old, and Rasha, twelve. They lived with their parents and four other siblings in a modest house barely twenty meters away. Much of the sisters' childhood had been spent indoors, when Old Ramallah was under strict military curfew and it was often too dangerous even to leave for a few minutes to buy food. Their older brother, Shehada, had learned that two years earlier, in 2002, when at age twelve he and a neighborhood friend, Ali, fourteen, had broken a curfew and snuck out of the house to buy bread. An Israeli soldier's bullet landed in Ali's forehead, killing him instantly. Shehada watched Ali fall.

*   *   *

By the summer of 2004, nearly four thousand people had been killed in the Second Intifada, three quarters of them Palestinian, including about six hundred children; of the Israeli civilian casualties, which numbered close to four hundred, most from suicide attacks, one in every five was a child. In recent months the heaviest killing had been in and around Gaza, where, in March, Israel had assassinated Sheikh Ahmed Yassin, the quadriplegic founder of Hamas, with a helicopter missile attack, as he was being wheeled from a mosque after morning prayers. Nine bystanders and his two bodyguards were killed. Yassin, who Israel said had personally authorized numerous suicide attacks, was from the Palestinian village of al-Jura, depopulated during the 1948 war; later, the Israeli city of Ashkelon was built in part on its ruins. A few weeks after Yassin's death, Israel assassinated his deputy, Abdel-Aziz Rantisi, from the destroyed Palestinian village of Yibna. His car was blown apart by an American-made Hellfire missile fired from an Apache helicopter. Hamas retaliated in the summer, killing sixteen in a suicide bombing in the Israeli city of Beersheba.

Israel, meanwhile, stepped up its construction of the separation barrier, which was found to be a violation of international humanitarian law by the

International Court of Justice in The Hague. Israel, supported by both American presidential candidates, George W. Bush and John Kerry, denounced the decision, declaring Israel's right to protect itself. Israelis cited security as the sole reason for the barrier's existence. Yet the plan for it had been discussed since 1992, at a time of relative peace. Israeli planners had identified another motivation for building the wall: to separate from the Palestinian population in order to preserve the "Jewishness" of Israel. Separation, Israeli planners argued, was necessary to address the perceived "demographic threat" to Israel. The route swerved well over the Green Line and inside Palestinian territory to incorporate an estimated 85 percent of West Bank settlers and, in some cases, to exclude Palestinian populations, or "transfer" their communities to the Palestinian side of the barrier. The separation barrier, Israeli planners argued, could one day define Israel's final border and preserve the state's Jewish majority.

*　　*　　*

In Ramallah, in the summer of 2004, the military siege had eased some-what. Israel's army had withdrawn again to the barricades at the edge of town, and in their wake, Alá and Rasha had begun venturing out beyond their front door. The sisters considered this site their own turf, virtually an extension of their house, and were not eager to see more change.

"Are you a businessman?" Alá asked Ramzi, frowning deeply during one of his visits to the future site of the music school.

"No," he replied. "I am a musician."

They gazed up at him.

"What would you think," Ramzi asked the sisters, "if you learned to play music?"

"Here?" Alá asked. She was still frowning.

"Yes, here, in this place."

"Like the musicians who play with Fairouz?" Rasha responded skeptic-ally. "There is no way we will be able to play like them."

"You don't believe me?" Ramzi replied. "Soon you will see the building, and you'll be able to play music."

For Al Kamandjati to succeed, Ramzi needed to win over children like Alá and Rasha, their parents, and their neighbors in Old Ramallah. But a bigger test was to establish a musical presence in the refugee camps, where swirling militant and religious politics made the relatively calm Ramallah feel more like France. Acceptance from the camps was central to Ramzi's mission for Al Kamandjati. No place would provide a bigger challenge than Jenin. Militants of Jenin had fought back against an occupying army only two years earlier, and it remained a tense and dangerous place, especially for outsiders. Nevertheless, the entourage of French musicians was soon to arrive in Palestine. None of them had ever been to Jenin. The recent battle zone would be one of the first and most important stops on their tour.

*   *   *

On a scorching day in July 2004, Ramzi set off with the French musicians for their workshops at the Jenin camp. They rode in four yellow vans. Many wore matching white T-shirts with the Al Kamandjati logo: a Palestinian keffiyeh in the shape of the treble clef. As they entered the camp, they looked out at the graffiti scrawled on the walls of houses, interspersed with posters of young men staring into the camera, brandishing AK-47s: martyrs of the Second Intifada.

A rock bounced off one of the taxis. Hélèna Cotinier, from the French documentary crew, flinched as the sharp sound echoed in the cab. "Do not be afraid," Ramzi assured her. "They are not used to seeing strangers. For them, a stranger is an Israeli. There are no other strangers."

The first workshop took place at an elementary school. The musicians had to explain that they were from a country called France. "We are French," they explained. "Not Israeli."

"We're not used to seeing visitors here," a girl told them. "This is the first time I held an instrument in my hands. Usually the music and the instruments are only on TV."

The musicians from Europe were trying to make sense of the total lack of order and discipline at the schools; the lives of these children seemed completely out of control. "I recognize that I am totally overwhelmed and powerless," Jessie Nguenang, the singer from Angers, told Thierry Trebouet, a clarinetist. "You get the impression that there's no discipline here. You feel that they can do whatever they want, whenever they want."

"They are stressed," Thierry agreed. "It's a total chaos. It's all we can see. The landscape, the houses, all their environment."

The people of Jenin camp had been under extreme stress since the beginning of the Second Intifada. Across Palestine the camp enjoyed a reputation of resistance in the face of the Israeli siege: Alongside the fifty-two Palestinians killed during the invasion of the camp, militants had claimed the lives of thirteen Israeli soldiers. But the lives and living spaces of the camp residents had also been transformed during the uprising. Four hundred buildings had been crushed by giant Caterpillar armored bulldozers, burying dozens of civilians alive.

Just as shocking to some residents, the Israeli army had begun "walking through walls" in pursuit of the enemy. Military commanders, wary of booby-trapped doorways or militants hiding in narrow alleys, ordered troops to enter homes by smashing down walls with giant hammers, or blowing them apart with explosives, and taking the fight directly into camp residences. For Palestinians living in Jenin and other refugee camps, "walking through walls" further undermined the notion that home was a place of safety, and further heightened the level of paranoia from traumatized residents.

The musicians from France got back into the yellow taxi vans to conduct a workshop at a rehabilitation center for injured and disabled children. Ramzi was tense, with good reason: The camp was now filled with battle-hardened militants, many wanted by Israel, who would not risk their own safety if they saw an approaching stranger whose motives were unclear.

One of those militants, Zakaria Zubeidi, had been living underground, in a three-by-five-foot hole, for much of the previous four years. He had lived deprived of light; his oxygen came via a hose that snaked upward from the hole to the Jenin camp above ground. Zakaria's mother had been shot dead during Israel's 2002 siege of Jenin; she had been looking out the window when a bullet struck her down. A month later his brother had been killed. Zakaria became Jenin chief of the Al Aqsa Martyrs Brigade, which during the Second Intifada carried out numerous deadly attacks against Israeli military and civilian targets. In 2003, he mishandled a homemade bomb; it exploded, embedding a black cloud of tiny black specks into his cheeks and forehead.

Zakaria, twenty-seven years old, was being hunted by the Israeli army, which had already assassinated several of his comrades. In recent months he had begun emerging, warily, to breath air normally, to treat his rashes suffered from so much time in the dank hole, and to do research on the Internet: about his enemy's intelligence capabilities, and about the human capacity for handling stress. He walked the alleys of the camp carefully, lean and unsmiling, in a T-shirt and jeans, with a sidearm strapped in a leather holster. "When you're stressed," Zakaria said, "that will affect how you will make decisions, and most of them, they're going to be wrong."

In his forays above ground, Zakaria would try to sense where the danger zones were, so that he could avoid them and make the proper judgment. But on that hot day in July, when the French musicians came to perform their workshops in the heart of Jenin camp, Zakaria sensed that he was on the wrong street at the wrong time, and that he hadn't taken the proper precautions. Why, he asked himself, was he walking on Al Awda (The Return) Street, in full view of four yellow taxi vans snaking up the dirt road toward him? He looked closely, and saw that everyone inside looked foreign.

Zakaria feared they were special forces sent by the enemy. *Oh, I'm dead,* he thought. *I'm going to die.* He reached inside his belt and pulled out his nine-millimeter Smith & Wesson, ready to fight to the end.

The first two taxis approached a bend in the road, where Zakaria watched them turn left, in the direction of the children's rehab center.

From the backseat of the fourth taxi, Karim, Jessie, Hélèna Cotinier, and the other passengers could see a man pointing something at the third taxi—the one just in front of them. "What's the guy doing there?" Jessie asked. "He has a gun!" she said. Then she laughed. "It's a toy gun!"

"It's not a toy gun," Karim shouted.

Through the open windows Karim, Hélèna and Jessie could hear the man shouting at the driver in the van just ahead of them. "What are you doing in the camp?" the man demanded. Karim could hear no response. The driver kept going, turning toward the rehab center.

Now the man turned his weapon on the fourth taxi, where Karim and the others sat. Karim could see him through the back window. The man was sweating, and his arm was shaking. "We are your friends, I am a Palestinian, there is nothing to worry about!" shouted the driver.

Zakaria was panicking. Palestinian collaborators with the Israeli army said that sort of thing all the time.

Karim put his right hand over his heart. "Get down, get down, get down!" he shouted.

Zakaria fired.

The bullet ricocheted off the metal band on the driver's side, between the front and back windows. The driver hit the gas, hurtling around the turn as two more shots rang out behind them.

Fifty meters on their taxi screeched to a stop at their destination in the Jenin refugee camp. "*Sortez, sortez*, get out, get out!" someone shouted. Jessie and Hélèna could not move. "Trembling," Hélèna recalled. "My legs were like chewing gum." She didn't know who had been shooting at them, and if other snipers awaited. "I was thinking of my sister, my mother, my father. And I was like, oh my God, what am I doing here? I never thought something like that could happen. I was like, okay, I'm going to die. And I'm a stupid girl."

As the musicians came racing inside, Ramzi tore out of the community center, panicked. Fragments of prayer raced through his mind. *Please, God, please protect us, protect the musicians. I hope that the bullet hasn't touched anybody. If it hasn't, I swear that I will stop this crazy project.* He ran in the direction of the shots and saw Zakaria, the gun now down at his side. "Stop, stop, we are Palestinians! And these are French people, they are here to help us!"

A moment later, he returned, having just seen the bullet hole on the doorjamb of the van. "We are not in Ramallah here!" he shouted in French. "We are in Jenin! You have to be careful! You have to listen to me! You have to do what I say! You are not in your country! It's really, really dangerous here.

"*Fuck!* That was a great show, wasn't it? *Now* you understand!"

"That was the very first time the musicians understood they were in Palestine," Karim recounted. "They were in a country which is in war. That's not Paris or Angers or even Marrakech. It's Palestine."

Now the group had to decide: Would they stay and do the workshop, or go back to Ramallah? It was a close vote, but they decided to cancel the workshop and leave.

As they rolled back out of the camp, Zakaria reappeared. This time, his arms were full of plastic cups and bottles of orange soda. "He gave us glasses and said 'please, please, come back.'" Hélèna remembered. "And I remember feeling, we have to stay! We are not afraid of him now. We understand. But we just had the juice in the cab and then gave it back."

"We are sorry," Karim explained, "but some of the musicians just arrived today from France and they are very surprised to be shot at. So they want to go, because it's safe in Ramallah."

"I'll never forget what I've seen on his face and how he was sad to have made a mistake and how he was so sorry, so sorry," Hélèna recounted seven years later, sipping an espresso in a Paris sidewalk café. "Really. I felt it's awful because they were waiting for us, but we didn't give any music, we left, just because we are French people, international people and we think that our lives are important. And we leave them with their everyday life."

On the drive back, Ramzi was quiet. He preferred not to talk about it. Ramzi did not like to linger on his failures, and he never wanted to appear vulnerable. On the long drive home, he replayed the events in his mind, trying to determine their meaning.

Was this some kind of warning to stop, Ramzi asked himself, or a test to continue?

Sixteen

ODAY

Late summer 2004
Al Fawwar refugee camp

RAMZI WAS COLLECTING future students. Alá and Rasha, the sisters from Old Ramallah, were at the top of his list; the summer before, Ramzi met an eight-year-old girl, Bushra, who saw him playing his bouzouk in a Ramallah park, took his hand, and asked him to teach her. More recently, looking at the rushes from the French documentary team, Ramzi had seen the footage of Oday, the boy soprano whose voice had so enchanted him. Ramzi had a plan for Oday, and so the entourage returned to the refugee camp where he lived.

Neighborhood girls found Oday and brought him to the community center at Al Fawwar. "Remember me from last year?" Oday said cheerfully as he sidled up to Ramzi.

Ramzi smiled. "Do you remember the song you sang last year?" Yes, Oday said, he recalled singing "I Accept," the song about a broken-hearted prisoner whose destiny was written on his face. This time he performed a refugee folk song of the occupation. "I can't do anything against what Sharon is doing," Oday sang, his voice strong and high. "I have no more oil, and my torch went out."

Ramzi had been thinking about Oday from the first time he heard him sing. What he had been planning in his head abruptly came out of his mouth.

"Do you want me to take you to France?" Ramzi asked Oday suddenly. "Would you like to go?"

Oday wasn't sure where France was. He shrugged. "Sure," he said. "Why not?"

"I'd like to meet your parents," Ramzi said.

As they left the center, Ramzi put his arm around Oday. They walked down the main street of the camp, beside a long concrete wall covered with graffiti. Ramzi could see himself in Oday. He wanted to find a child to take the international stage as a symbol of the youth of Palestine, and of his music school. Oday could be that child.

"How old are you now, thirteen? Fourteen?" Ramzi asked.

Oday hesitated. He was thirteen. "Fourteen," he said.

"That's old! You don't look like it." Oday looked ten years old or younger.

"We will get you a passport," Ramzi promised. "I play in a group, and there we will record a CD."

They walked into a narrow alley bordered by crudely built cinder-block homes and a stucco house with window frames covered by grates and gray steel shutters. Oday turned into the family courtyard, where creeper vines covered metal fencing and climbed toward the roof. Grape leaves and a palm tree provided shade.

"Go and tell your family," Ramzi said. Presently Oday's mother emerged and invited the group in. Only the mother and her three daughters, Falastin, Tahrir, and Sabrine (Palestine, Liberation, and Patience) were home. Oday's father was, by coincidence, in France, where surgeons were trying to restore movement to the arm of his son, Rasmi. He had been shot by a soldier at an Al Fawwar schoolyard three years earlier, at age twelve, during the early months of the second uprising. Since then, he'd had multiple operations, in Jordan, Iraq, Spain, and France, where doctors remained hopeful he could one day use his left arm again.

On the walls of Oday's home hung framed photos of his four brothers now in prison. It was common in Palestinian families, especially in the refugee camps, to see walls full of images of imprisoned young men. The Khatib brothers' incarceration was tied to the shooting of Rasmi and his subsequent arrest by soldiers who suspected him of throwing a Molotov cocktail with his one good arm. When the soldiers arrived, brother Rostom fought with them, and he in turn was arrested. Rami Khatib, at age seventeen, in the wake of the shooting of Rasmi, abandoned demonstrations and joined the military wing of Islamic Jihad. He vowed to avenge his brother's maiming. Just after midnight on April 25, 2002, Rami Khatib slipped a good-bye note to his family underneath the prayer carpet near his computer. Unbeknownst to them, he was planning, later that day, to travel to a secret location, pick up a belt filled with nails, strap it onto his body, and explode himself at a military barracks near Tel Aviv. An informant in the camp learned of the plan, and soldiers came to arrest Rami at dawn.

Of all the brothers, Oday was the only who had never been to jail.

On an opposite wall, facing the images of the brothers, hung a framed photo of Saddam Hussein, admired for long-standing support of Palestine and for his defiance, even in a losing cause, in the face of the recent U.S. military invasion.

Ramzi and Oday's mother introduced themselves the way many Palestinian refugees do upon meeting: by invoking the names of their long-lost villages in old Palestine, recalling the fragments scattered in memory throughout their diaspora. Oday's mother explained that the family was from Al Faluja, a village on the coastal plain about fifteen miles from Gaza, remembered for its wheat, barley, fruit trees, blue lupine flowers, and village mosque with its three domed halls. Near the end of the war in 1949, the village came under siege, and rumors spread, much like in Sido's village of Na'ani, of impending attacks by Israel's army. Villagers fled or were driven out. In the confusion, family members were separated: Some fled to refugee camps in Gaza, others to the West Bank. With the new state of Israel literally standing between them, many siblings and spouses were unable to reach each other. Husbands and wives started new families. Many of Oday's cousins were still in Gaza. He had never met them. As for the village, all that remained was the foundation of the mosque, a few stones from its walls, and a dilapidated well surrounded by prickly shrubs known as Christ's-thorn. Six years after Oday's family left Al Faluja, eighteen Moroccan Jewish families established the town of Kiryat Gat on village lands. About forty-five thousand Israelis now lived there; these include thousands of Jews from the former Soviet Union. An Intel factory produced computer chips.

A momentary silence enveloped the room. Ramzi broke it with his bold idea: "We would like to invite Oday to sing with us in France," he told Oday's mother.

A year earlier, Oday had told his parents about Ramzi, but he had had no idea Ramzi would return with such a proposal. He had only had time to tell his mother briefly before she invited Ramzi to sit for tea.

She would have to check with her husband, Oday's mother told Ramzi. But she welcomed the idea.

"He'll get on a plane?" she asked Ramzi.

"Yes," Ramzi said. They would leave in the fall. "Is it a problem if he misses some school? I can talk to them and promise that he will catch up on the missed lessons. We want him to sing with us."

Oday's mother smiled and shook her head, absorbing Ramzi's proposal.

"You'll bring me some pictures," said Oday's mother.

"Ensh'allah," Oday replied. God willing.

"Are you taking him to Paris?" she asked Ramzi.

"Yes, we have a big concert in Paris."

"Sing happy songs," the mother instructed her child. "Our life is sad enough."

*   *   *

Late that fall, on November 11, 2004, Yasser Arafat died in Paris after a brief and mysterious illness. Two weeks earlier, he had left his bombed-out Ramallah headquarters, the Muqata, when Israeli prime minister Ariel Sharon lifted the siege to allow Arafat safe passage to leave his homeland. The two had been archenemies for decades; during the siege of Beirut, General Sharon had driven Arafat into exile. Now, uncharacteristically, Sharon said Arafat would be welcome to return once his health improved.

In France Arafat sought medical treatment after inexplicably falling ill with what was variously described as the flu, a stomach virus, gallstones, or a blood disorder. Some Palestinians insisted their leader had been poisoned. American and Israeli officials scoffed at this, but years later, upon exhumation of Arafat's body, the radioactive agent polonium was discovered on his clothes. A team of Swiss examiners determined that the chances were six in seven that Yasser Arafat had been murdered by poison. Later studies by French and Russian teams, however, cast doubt on those conclusions.

Israelis greeted Arafat's death with few tears; to the end, most saw him as a terrorist. Former U.S. president Bill Clinton, who had vowed to Arafat, after the failure of Camp David, "you won't have friendships with anyone," sent both condolences and blame: "I regret that in 2000 he

missed the opportunity to bring that nation [Palestine] into being."
Palestinians remembered him as the revolutionary leader who struggled for
his people's liberation for decades, who later presided over a corrupt and
inept Palestinian Authority, but who, in the end, despite immense pressure
from an American president, refused to surrender Jerusalem.

Thousands of Palestinians gathered at the battered Muqata to greet the
helicopter carrying Arafat's body after his military funeral in Egypt. It was
here, in another helicopter eight years earlier, that Arafat had thunderously
arrived amid great hopes for liberation and statehood. "Al Quuuds!" Arafat
had shouted, evoking his promise to create a Palestinian state with East
Jerusalem as its capital. The Palestinian leader had asked to be buried in
Jerusalem, but Israel would not allow it. Now his body was being lowered
into a stone and marble grave in Ramallah, with soil brought from East
Jerusalem's Haram al-Sharif, the third holiest site in Islam.

*   *   *

Oday's journey from the Holy Land, in the fall of 2004, ended at Charles
de Gaulle airport in Paris, where Ramzi and Yacine Laghrour, an Al
Kamandjati volunteer and Dalouna percussionist, were waiting. When the
boy emerged from the plane he looked tiny, nowhere near the thirteen-
year-old he was. Oday's uncle had put him on the flight in Amman, but
Oday had traveled alone. He had never been on a plane, never journeyed
outside his homeland, never even been to Ramallah, thirty miles and many
checkpoints away from the refugee camp where he lived.

At Al Fawwar, Oday's parents were waiting anxiously for Ramzi's call
confirming that their child had arrived safely. His mother was second-
guessing herself, wondering why she had agreed to let him travel. He was
so young, she reminded herself constantly, and so alone. Oday's father,
Jihad, had agreed to let his son go, provided that his performances in
France be strictly limited to nationalist and liberation songs, not the love
songs or happy music his wife seemed to prefer. Ramzi had agreed to this
condition. Now the family waited. It was midnight; Oday's flight should
have landed by now.

By one A.M. in Palestine, Oday's mother was beside herself. "What have
I done?" she asked. "Oh my God, what will people say? We put our child
on the plane by himself! We will lose him!"

Oday was suffering, too. "Yamma, Yamma!" he called out as he rode toward Paris with Ramzi and Yacine. "Mama!"

Near dawn the phone rang in Al Fawwar. Oday's father seized it. Ramzi began to explain that his cell-phone battery had died, but Jihad, a stout, chain-smoking, mercurial man, cut him off, cursing rapidly at high volume. "You did not call us!" he thundered. "*Inta majnoun?* Are you crazy?"

"I want to talk to my mom," Oday told Ramzi. They were at a pay phone at Montparnasse station. Ramzi handed Oday the phone; when he heard his mother's voice, he started crying again. There were buildings everywhere, he told her, tall buildings, so many tunnels and bridges, the streets so wide with endless traffic, buses and trucks and people moving in every direction. In the distance, he reported, he had seen a beautiful golden tower near a big river with many boats and barges.

*   *   *

At first Oday refused to eat. When he relented, he would only drink tea and eat bread, blackberry jam, and labneh, a delicious yogurt with the consistency of cream cheese that Oday ate every day at home. The smelly blue cheese from France he found disgusting. Eventually he tried a croissant; that was okay, too. As days passed he began to feel more comfortable. He was amazed by the differences. Paris, such a huge place, was so much cleaner than Al Fawwar. People here took better care of the environment they lived in. *Perhaps*, he thought to himself, *they didn't have the occupation to worry about.* As he met new people, Oday noticed the consideration they gave to each other. He was impressed by the way people looked at him, and believed he could tell immediately from their eyes whether they liked him or not. But he remained fearful of the strange urban landscape, and he wanted to stay close to Ramzi whenever he could.

The first concert, sponsored by Musiciens pour la Palestine, was at an Angers nightclub and concert hall called Chabada. On a large dance floor in front of rows of auditorium seating, concertgoers squeezed in, looking up toward Ramzi and his band.

Oday looked out from the backstage curtain. Nearly a thousand people waited to hear him sing. His eyes grew wide. Oday had never seen so many people in one small space. But when Ramzi turned and called Oday to the stage, the boy's fear seemed to vanish. He walked onstage, smiling and waving, a black-and-white checked Palestinian keffiyeh draped around his shoulders.

"I didn't feel he was shy when he was singing," Yacine remembered. "You feel it in the voice, the power in the voice. You don't feel a shy child. You feel a real singer."

This was the first time Oday had sung in public with a band backing him, but he seemed to have no problem using his voice as an instrument to cut through the tabla, oud, clarinet, and bouzouk. He sang his favorite song, "Ghareeb" ("The Stranger"), scanning the crowd to see if he was connecting. Ramzi had told Oday to sing from his heart. "I wanted them to understand my life," he remembered. "I looked into their eyes with a special emotion. They really listened."

A quiet settled over the room. "People were standing there with their mouths open," said Ramzi. "And the ones who understood Arabic started to cry. Even a French girl, who understood the sadness, was crying."

For Oday, the surreal circumstance of his odyssey from a refugee camp in Palestine to performance halls in France was grounded by the sorrow of his family's own experience and the meaning of the words he sang. On stage, first in Angers and then in Paris, Lille, and other French cities, images would flash through his mind: Rasmi at age twelve, bleeding in the schoolyard from a soldier's bullet; soldiers surrounding his house, arresting Rami at dawn; all of his brothers, sitting in separate prison cells across Israel and occupied Palestine. The audience, of course, did not know these details; most of them could not even understand Oday's words. But the crowds were easily captivated by the small boy with the huge voice who seemed to represent all the children of Palestine. For Ramzi, Oday's voice tapped the accumulation of his own loss, trauma, hope, and resistance in Al Amari camp.

"Oday!" the cries echoed. "Oday, Oday, Oday!"

Onstage, Ramzi smiled beneficently, strumming his bouzouk. In several years of Dalouna concerts, during the breaks between songs, he had told his story of growing up in Al Amari, where with his stone he had confronted an occupying army. "And then we'd play another song," Yacine recalled. "Then he would talk about how," as he began to consider the music school, "he saw children drawing tanks and weapons, but after he played music, they drew musical instruments. He was always telling this story. For the public it was very nice, but for us it was always the same story: 'I had a dream to bring music to people like me who come from refugee camps.'" Now, however, with Oday standing and singing right beside them, the meaning had deepened: The dream had a new face.

Oday's journey was playing out exactly the way Ramzi had envisioned. The boy was a huge hit.

Seventeen

CELINE

February 2005
Lille, France

Cᴇʟɪɴᴇ ᴅᴀɢʜᴇʀ ᴛᴏᴏᴋ her seat for the Dalouna concert in the auditorium in Lille. It was February 2005. As the hall began to fill up, Celine, twenty-four, slim and fair with reddish-brown hair, peered intently through round-framed glasses at the photocopy in her hands. The flier described the birth of a new music school in the Holy Land, to be called Al Kamandjati. It showed the picture of little Ramzi throwing the stone, and an older Ramzi playing the viola, and it described, in French, the idea behind the school, and how the Al Kamandjati Association of France was collecting instruments to help launch the enterprise.

Celine was part of a French-Palestinian solidarity group that was sponsoring the concert in Lille that night, but she hadn't known many of these details. "I was just very touched, impressed by what I read," she said six years later.

Celine was born in 1981 in Beirut. When she was a year old, Israel invaded Lebanon, and Celine's early childhood was marked by civil war. She and her sisters, Nicole and Christelle, crafted colorful dough figures, playing quietly in the third-floor hallway, near the elevators, careful not to upset their parents. The family slept in the hall and the entryway to their apartment, to keep away from the windows, through which fragments of shells occasionally crashed. Celine liked to collect them. They were of different shapes and colors and she stored them in three clear plastic bags. Her father, an anesthesiologist, managed to go to work at three different hospitals during the war; her mother, a nurse, mostly stayed home. Celine recalls one New Year's Eve when her mother and father stepped out to celebrate—she in a shining silver dress, he in a dark, well-cut suit—into a brief lull in the explosions. It didn't last; the shells began falling again before the new year.

By 1989, when Celine was eight years old, her parents decided it was time to leave Lebanon. The breaking point was a pitched battle involving a tank, which Celine had nicknamed Victoria, parked just below their window. Celine's parents had long known that the situation could deteriorate enough that they'd have to abandon their home. That is why they had given their daughters French names. They would move to Valenciennes, a town in northern France, near Lille. Her father's Russian medical degree might not be recognized by the French, but a friend said he could find him work in the hospital.

Celine was still peering through her glasses at the Al Kamandjati photocopy when the lights dimmed and the members of Dalouna took the stage.

After the concert, Ramzi was standing in the lobby beside a table stacked with Dalouna CDs and the Al Kamandjati literature. He was shaking hands and smiling, eyes alight and eyebrows raised, talking rapidly. Celine approached him. She considered herself a shy person, but the story she had just encountered, and the music, prompted her to come forward. "I just read this," she told Ramzi, holding the photocopy, "and if I could help you, I would be very happy."

Celine explained she had recently finished a degree in business; she thought her organizational and financial skills could be useful. During business school, she had done consulting work for Decathlon, a French sporting goods chain, to help them establish a policy to prevent sourcing goods from companies and subcontractors that employed child labor.

"And I also play the viola."

"Do you speak Arabic?" Ramzi asked. They were speaking in French.

"Ana Libnaniya," Celine replied. "I'm Lebanese." She wrote down her phone number and e-mail address.

"Okay," Ramzi said, nodding and tucking the scrap of paper in his pocket.

*　　*　　*

Four months later, after seven years at the Conservatoire, Ramzi was a few weeks away from finally receiving his diploma. He was planning a third summer tour of French musicians, which, he hoped, would culminate with the opening of the Al Kamandjati music school in Ramallah. Construction was beginning on the site in the old part of town. Soon a huge container of instruments would be shipped from France to Palestine. Ramzi was beginning to think about how to organize the coming summer of workshops and the preparations for the new school. He needed someone with organizational, musical, and language skills, in Arabic, French, and English. He found the scrap of paper he had stuffed in his pocket in February, and called Celine.

"I just finished my studies and now I'm going back to Palestine, and we're putting together some workshops this summer," Ramzi told Celine. "Would you like to come in July?"

Celine didn't hesitate. "I'd love to," she replied. It would be volunteer work, and Celine would have to pay her own way.

Celine had said yes without really thinking about what that meant. As a member of the pro-Palestinian solidarity group, she kept up with news on the ground. A few months earlier, Mahmoud Abbas, also known as Abu Mazen, had become the new president of the Palestinian Authority. The Second Intifada was finally over, with a cease-fire signed in Egypt by Abbas and Ariel Sharon. Abbas agreed to put an end to violence against Israelis; Israel promised to release nine hundred Palestinian prisoners and gradually withdraw from Palestinian towns it had reoccupied. Yet despite the mutual pledge to forge a new path, the bloodshed and land grabs continued. At a beachfront karaoke nightclub in Tel Aviv, a Palestinian suicide attacker sent by Islamic Jihad killed five Israelis and injured fifty. Ministers in Ariel Sharon's government, meanwhile, had been secretly financing a new wave of settlements on private Palestinian land, connecting them to electricity and water, building houses, and paving roads. These settlement "outposts," unlike "legal" settlements, contravened even Israeli law. They were consistent, however, with Sharon's decades-old strategy of creating an irreversible Jewish presence across the West Bank.

Celine had been following these events as best she could from afar, but she didn't know what to expect when she finally went to Palestine. She had to decide how to tell her parents she was returning, voluntarily, to a Middle Eastern war zone.

Celine was Christian—more by ethnicity than devotion—and had grown up on a Christian street in a Christian neighborhood of East Beirut, where anti-Palestinian sentiment was strong. In the 1970s, Palestinian factions pledging armed struggle against Israel had taken over villages in the south, near the Israeli border, where Celine's parents were born. "They took our homes," Celine's grandparents told her, "and made us leave our villages." This had prompted two invasions by Israel and its occupation of southern Lebanon, and exacerbated sectarian divisions, which played out in the country's long and bloody civil war.

As an adult, Celine had struggled to understand the bigger picture. She read numerous books and articles explaining how the Palestinian Nakba in 1948 had created 750,000 refugees, many of whom ended up in the camps in Lebanon and across the region. Palestinian nationalist factions, many born in those same camps, were fighting to return to lands they believed were rightfully theirs. The Israeli invasions in the south, while welcomed by some Lebanese Christians, had also given rise to Hezbollah, the Islamist militant group fighting to expel Israel from Lebanon. It was far too complicated, Celine came to believe, to blame Lebanon's problems only on the Palestinians. Slowly this political understanding led Celine to join the Palestinian solidarity organization in France, which in turn led her that evening to the Dalouna concert. Finally, despite the reaction she knew would come from her parents, Celine's evolving political consciousness prompted her to take a one-month leave from her job in France and travel back to a place much like the one her family had left: a land of tanks, checkpoints, Molotov cocktails, and random explosions.

* * *

In May 2005, diploma in hand, Ramzi left France and returned to Palestine. Yacine, Karim, Marie, and the French musicians stayed behind in Angers to gather the hundreds of donated musical instruments and pack them in a seaworthy container. The group would follow in a few weeks for the summer tour, and, they hoped, the grand opening of the music school at summer's end.

Over the previous year, a few of Ramzi's friends and teachers in France, and even fewer in Palestine, had learned of Ramzi's surprising personal news, which he and Marie Albert had kept mostly to themselves: In 2004, Ramzi and Marie had married in a quiet ceremony in Angers. They had been working together on Al Kamandjati, but few had seen evidence of their relationship when the two were together or apart.

The reasons for their sense of privacy were complex. For one thing, Ramallah was a conservative culture, and in a place where unsubstantiated rumors abounded, Ramzi wanted to protect himself, and Marie. In general, he did not like to invite his colleagues and friends inside his personal life. And so his relationship to Marie remained a mystery to most. In Palestine, they didn't live together as a couple. Ramzi spent many nights at Sido's, and Marie slept at Rami's old flat, which served as a crash pad for visiting musicians and volunteers. Between Ramzi and Marie there were few if any displays of affection, which in any case had always made Ramzi uncomfortable. "I'm not the guy who could hang out on the street, kissing and hugging. In our culture, you do this in the house."

Ramzi and Marie chose not to share more than the barest details with anyone, including any journalist who asked. One thing was certain, though: By all accounts no one could question Marie's deep commitment to Ramzi's dream, and her own, to build a music school for children in Palestine. Marie was universally admired among her colleagues. She did not believe they were "doing something historical for peace"; rather, they were helping young Palestinians "to experience an aspect of childhood which many others take for granted." Ramzi and Marie's partnership, however unconventional, was genuine.

Ramzi's return home in the late spring of 2005 was delayed at the Allenby Bridge, which connects Jordan and the occupied West Bank. At the metal detectors, Ramzi emptied his pockets, and Israeli soldiers discovered a pamphlet protesting the Israeli separation barrier, and a flyer about Al Kamandjati, written in French. Usually Ramzi was careful to discard such things before crossing, but sometimes a mixture of inattention and defiance would leave him subject to further interrogation. The pamphlet in question caused alarm sufficient to send Ramzi into an interrogation room, where a senior Israeli intelligence officer, who already seemed to know a lot about the young musician, began peppering him with questions. The officer wanted to know Ramzi's address in France, his friends' names, and his plans for the summer.

The officer said to Ramzi, in English, "You mention the wall in your concerts," referring to the Dalouna performances in France. Ramzi was not sure how the man knew that.

"Why should I not mention the wall? It's there."

"That's for the protection of Israel."

"If you had put it on the Green Line"—the pre-June 1967 border between Israel and the West Bank—"I would understand that argument." Israel's security service, the Shin Bet, had recently concluded that the wall had played only a minor role in the recent reduction of suicide attacks; the drop, it concluded, was the result of a truce declared by Hamas. Ramzi also knew that the wall, as designed, was taking an additional 10 percent of West Bank Palestinian land, and was dividing Palestinian farmers from their fields and families from each other. In some cases family members who had lived as next-door neighbors now had to travel miles, through a gate in the wall, just to visit each other.

"Whether you like it or not," Ramzi added to the intelligence officer, "nobody will accept the occupation. We can't live like this."

"Do you think I'm happy to do this?" the officer asked. "Do you think I'm having fun doing this? I would rather be listening to opera."

"Who is prohibiting you from going to the opera?" replied the young man about to open a school for classical and Arabic music. "Please do. This way you can leave us alone and allow us to live our lives in peace."

Before he released Ramzi, the officer brought up the murder of Rami. "Be smart," the officer said, apparently invoking the family's wish for retribution. "Be wise. Think before doing something." Ramzi held his interrogator's gaze and said nothing. Finally the officer allowed him to pass. He clicked through metal turnstiles into the harsh midday light on the outskirts of Jericho.

*   *   *

By the summer of 2005, nearly two years after the death of Edward Said, Daniel Barenboim believed it was time for the West-Eastern Divan Orchestra to perform Richard Wagner, just as Daniel himself had done three years earlier in Tel Aviv. Wagner was widely considered one of the greatest artists in history; the poet W. H. Auden had called him "perhaps the greatest genius that ever lived." Yet Wagner's virulent anti-Semitism during his life, and his association with the Third Reich long after his death, had transformed him into one of history's most polarizing artists and had led to the informal ban on Wagner in Israel, which Daniel had already broken. As a musician, Daniel believed that Wagner's greatness could not be ignored by Jewish or Israeli musicians, "because then we only descend to the level of those people who persecuted us for so many years." Now he sought to bring Wagner to his own orchestra, made up of forty Arabs, forty Israelis, and twenty Spaniards.

The Spanish and Arab musicians agreed with Daniel, and were excited by the prospect of performing portions of the opera *Tristan und Isolde*, with one of the great Wagnerian singers, the German mezzo-soprano Waltraud Meier. At first, many Israelis in the orchestra liked the idea as well; they had been among the first to approach Daniel about it. But things changed after Daniel invited his friend Mustafa Barghouti to talk to the orchestra about the situation on the ground in Palestine. The separation wall, Mustafa told the orchestra, was not for Israel's security; Mustafa himself had easily breached the wall to attend a concert hosted by Daniel in Jerusalem, where, on his way to the performance, he had passed Prime Minister Sharon's house. How much real security, Mustafa asked, could the barrier therefore provide? Rather, he said, this was an "apartheid wall," more about confiscating Palestinian land than protecting Israelis.

Israeli members of the orchestra grew agitated at Mustafa's remarks. A large number of them, perhaps ten or twelve, rose in unison and walked out in the middle of his talk. The atmosphere in the orchestra shifted. Within days many Israelis had developed deep misgivings about playing Wagner. At a rehearsal of the full orchestra in southern Spain, Daniel engaged the Israelis at length, in Hebrew, trying to convince them of the primacy of the music itself. The conversation went on a long time, and after a while, one of the Arab members, a gifted violinist, Maria Arnaout, rolled her eyes and whispered something in Arabic to a colleague. Daniel stopped, looked away from the Israelis, and asked Maria loudly what she had said.

"Never mind," the violinist told the maestro in French. "I'll tell you later."

"No, tell us now," Daniel insisted.

Maria paused. "I said, 'It's always about them,'" she said, referring to the Israeli musicians. She didn't mean only in this moment of the rehearsal, when the conductor was speaking in a language most of them could not understand. She was referring to a growing sense among other Arabs in the Divan that, with Edward gone, and despite Mariam Said's active participation, the balance of power in the orchestra had shifted to the Israeli side.

"Maria, you don't know what you're talking about," Daniel said, waving his hand dismissively. A day or two later, at another meeting called to discuss Wagner, the Israeli maestro and the Syrian violinist got into a shouting match, which culminated in Daniel inviting Maria to leave the orchestra. Soon, feeling unwelcome, she did, traveling back to Syria, eventually to become the director of the Damascus Opera House.

*   *   *

The future location of the music school in Old Ramallah was still piled high with refuse. Now that Ramzi had finally secured the paperwork authorizing a long-term lease and renovation of the historic property, the first job was to clear the site. For two weeks a crew of twenty workers shoveled the trash into thousands of wheelbarrow loads and rolled them to the street. There they piled them into a string of wheeled metal bins connected like train cars to a tractor, which hauled the load away to a new dump site.

One of the workers, fifteen-year-old Shehada Shalalda, lived next door. His younger sisters, Alá and Rasha, had been playing house a year and a half earlier when Ramzi and his entourage had come to examine the place. Ramzi was counting on the sisters to be among his first students, and now their older brother had work there. Occasionally Shehada would see Ramzi come, often with foreigners, to inspect the work. Finally one day they spoke.

"Do you want to learn to play music?" Ramzi asked him. Shehada said he didn't know any instrument. The school would be called Al Kamandjati, Ramzi told him. The Violinist. Shehada said he didn't even know what a violin looked like. But he told Ramzi he liked the idea of the school. Most of all, he liked the work.

Shehada stirred cement in a hand mixer and hauled rocks to rebuild old broken stairways. He learned to cut and chisel stone for the detail work alongside the carved entrances to what would become practice rooms. As the debris vanished, the courtyard began to take shape, bookended by rectangular stone slabs that would serve as benches. Atop the stairway, on the rooftop performance space, the architect Khaldun's vision of flying copper sheets came to life: a giant, rust-colored arm, curved and sheltering, covered with brass rivets that Shehada bolted on with an electric drill.

As Shehada worked throughout the summer of 2005, and as his sisters came over to watch the transformation of the space, recent memories intruded. It had been three years since Shehada broke the curfew during the Second Intifada to get bread; nearly every day he passed the old watermelon warehouse where his friend Ali was felled that April day in 2002 by an Israeli sniper's bullet. Shehada could not shake the memory of looking down to see the fourteen-year-old's mouth filling with blood. A hole from a second bullet remained lodged in the melon seller's doorjamb, now painted over.

During the early years of the Second Intifada, just steps away, the family of eight had been regularly confined in their home: one room plus a kitchen and a bathroom. Israeli soldiers would announce daily curfews by bullhorn, yelling repeatedly in Arabic, "Residents of Ramallah, stay indoors! Curfew!" A tank stood one hundred fifty meters away, its turret pointed toward the house. The army had taken over the mosque, just a few meters behind the family home, where snipers perched in the minaret. Just to the south, a jeep patrolled back and forth.

"Every day they would come to our house and search it and just take my dad," recalled Rasha, a year younger than Shehada. The soldiers were looking for weapons; they jabbed their gun barrels into pillows, and searched the cupboards, pouring out oil, olives, flour, and sugar into a pile on the floor, just as they had done to Ramzi's family during the First Intifada. "My kids want to eat!" screamed Rasha's mother, much like Sido had yelled in Al Amari camp fifteen years earlier. "We don't have anything you're looking for! You're ruining everything."

Frequently the soldiers took the father, Nabeel, away—sometimes in the early morning in his bedclothes; they wouldn't let him dress before leaving. "They used to blindfold him and handcuff him," Rasha remembered.

"I want my daddy back," cried Alá, then four years old, grabbing at her father's shirt as the soldiers were taking him. "He's not coming back!" she yelled. Sometimes Alá would try to follow him out the door, and the soldiers would order her back inside. The children peeked through the metal shutters as their father and the other men in the neighborhood stood handcuffed and blindfolded, sometimes stripped to their underwear.

Three years later, as Rasha watched her brother lay down stones, she thought, *It's strange, seeing this, compared to what we saw every day: the weeping and occupation and killing; our constant state of despair.* Now the relative calm was joined by a complete transformation of the physical space. Rasha felt happy. The music, she hoped, would ease her psyche. *I embrace this idea fully,* she thought. *I want this thing.*

*   *   *

Ramzi was in constant movement: on the phone, sometimes with one in each ear, organizing the concert tour across Palestine or asking about a shipment of instruments; rushing from Sido's place at Al Amari to Rami's old flat, which he was preparing for the musicians, to the site for Al Kamandjati. Soon, he would return to the practice rooms of the Ma'had, where he would begin teaching, as promised back in 1998 when he and Ramadan had set off with scholarships for Angers.

Once back at the Ma'had, he encountered fresh tensions—with Ramadan, who he barely spoke to, and with the Ma'had's leadership, who, he thought, had never believed he could build a music school on his own. Furthermore, Ramzi felt, the Ma'had's attitude was that art is for the elites. To Ramzi, it was a class issue, and he resented it.

"His attitude was, 'You deal with the rich, and we deal with the poor,' and we didn't like that," recalled Nadia Abboushi, the piano teacher at the Ma'had who had been with Ramzi at Apple Hill in 1997. Many of the Ma'had's students came from wealthy Christian families, but not everyone who attended was rich; many students received scholarships. Nadia felt Ramzi was being unfair to the very institution that had helped launch him seven years earlier. "We didn't like him putting us in a corner."

In July, Celine arrived with Karim, Jessie, and the other French musicians, just in time for Al Kamandjati's third summer workshop. Ramzi put Celine in charge of Oday, who was now a regular part of the entourage. Oday was fourteen, but to Celine he still barely looked ten. She would take him by the hand and show him around the city of Ramallah, which, despite his brief taste of France, still seemed like a vast, strange place compared to the narrow confines of Al Fawwar.

As the musicians went from town to village to refugee camp, Celine and Oday were constantly together. She made sure he ate well and got to bed at a reasonable time; when the visiting French documentary crew interviewed him, she translated his Arabic to French. Oday, the other musicians noticed, seemed to treat Celine like a second mom. He never wanted to leave her side.

As they traveled across Palestine, Oday shared his family's story with Celine. Three of his four brothers were in jail then, and Rami, who had plotted the aborted suicide bombing, was in and out of solitary confinement. Once Rami, sitting in his cell, heard Oday singing on a Hebron radio station. In his boy's soprano voice, Oday sang the story of the prisoner whose destiny was written on his forehead. Another time, Oday reached Rami on a cell phone in prison, and sang to him. Oday thought a lot about what would have happened if Rami had managed to carry out his operation at the Israeli military barracks in April 2002.

"Sometimes I think, if he had actually blown himself up, he would have been dead and our life would not have been the same," Oday said. Given the long history of official retribution, it's likely the Israeli military would have demolished the family's home in Al Fawwar as a form of collective punishment, even though they had not been aware of Rami's plans. "And my mom, I can imagine how she would feel all the time. Our life would have been much harder. I even think maybe I would not have met Ramzi and been in music if something like this happened."

"I knew he's very angry," Oday said of his older brother years later, "but I truly believe that there are other ways of fighting back."

Sometimes, as Oday sang in his high pitch onstage, and Celine played the viola behind him, she could sense what he was feeling. His voice would catch, or he'd forget a phrase and cover it by ad-libbing; it was then Celine knew that Oday was feeling overwhelmed, thinking about his family, especially his mother, and the pain she was going through as all but one of her sons sat in prison. Oday had told Celine he felt guilty to be experiencing a new life while his brothers were locked up. He was the only Khatib boy who hadn't spent time in prison. He felt pressure to succeed in the eyes of his family, Al Fawwar camp, and even Palestine. But there were times, he told Celine, when he wanted to live without thinking about occupation. He imagined living an ordinary life, even "just a small part of how people live in those other countries," he said; places like France or the United States.

Oday liked to tease Celine about Ramzi. He thought Ramzi and
Celine would make a lovely pair. "Why don't you marry Ramzi?" he asked
her again and again, enjoying it when she blushed. "I'm afraid that you
will leave. Look at Ramzi. He's a great musician. Why don't you marry
him?" Neither Celine nor Oday had any idea that Ramzi was married
to Marie.

*   *   *

A ship bearing musical instruments was steaming toward Palestine. In Old
Ramallah, as the work progressed on the site of the music school, Ramzi
began to imagine the practice rooms filling up with pianos, ouds, and
timpani, and children toting their horns and cellos in cases slung over their
shoulders. Already dozens of instruments had trickled in, one, two, five,
and six at a time, through informal networks that Ramzi likened to the
relentless work of ants: thousands of creatures, each with its own load,
working constantly, inevitably, to deliver the things they carried. Musicians,
instrument makers, activists, scholars, and religious pilgrims from across
Europe—singularly, in pairs, in larger groups—had traveled thousands of
miles each, ferrying violins, violas, cellos, flutes, and trumpets through
Israeli security and into the West Bank, where friends and supporters of
the coming music school stashed them in their homes. Thus came eighteen
violins from England, dozens of instruments from the north and south of
France, one hundred twenty more on a trip of religious travelers from Italy,
and a half dozen violins from a Palestinian in the American diaspora, made
decades earlier by his Jerusalem-born father.

Soon the instruments would be joined by the biggest shipment of
all. The ship with the container of instruments cut south through the
Mediterranean, bound for the Israeli port of Ashdod.

Workers put in extra time to prepare the music school for its planned
inauguration in late August. Still, it wasn't completely ready. In the courtyard, stone benches needed cutting. On the rooftop, the concert bandshell
stood half-built, and the entrance remained unfinished. Workers awaited
the heavy, slanted, rust-colored door, designed as an iconic signature of Al
Kamandjati. But there was no delaying the opening. Celine and the rest of
the French entourage were about to return home. More importantly, the
container of instruments from France was about to arrive.

*   *   *

Ramzi stood atop a semi truck backing slowly down a narrow street in Old Ramallah, toward the entrance of the new music school. His feet were planted wide for balance, and he held a wooden pole to prod the electrical and telephone wires upward, away from the truck's tightly packed trailer.

Ramzi had grown up barely a mile from here. As the semi eased backward, a thought occurred to him: As a child in Al Amari, the only time he ever saw a truck like this was when relief workers delivered bulk flour, sugar, powdered milk, and cooking oil; fifty-kilo bags would fly off the truck as the refugee families waved their white ration cards, shouting out for their shares.

Now a different cargo rocked gently beneath Ramzi. Gathered from all over Europe, packed in a seaworthy container, shipped from the French city of Angers in the Loire Valley, held by military and civilian authorities in the Mediterranean port of Ashdod, and dispatched to the other side of a vast concrete barrier, the shipment—hundreds of musical instruments— was finally reaching its destination.

Ramzi felt as if he were in the sky, flying.

The truck inched backward toward a falafel stand, where a balding man doused chickpea fritters in a sizzling bath of oil. At a café next door, old men in black-and-white checkered keffiyehs leaned on canes, playing backgammon and sipping Turkish coffee from tiny porcelain cups. Just beyond stood the sand-colored mosque and the empty balcony of the minaret.

The truck driver navigated backward and forward and back again, until finally the street grew too narrow. With a squeak of the air brakes, the truck came to a stop. Ramzi crouched, straddled the trailer and an exterior wall, slid down to the pavement, and walked to the back of the truck. He yanked the metal lever and swung open the red double doors.

The instruments, perhaps a half million dollars' worth, were packed in cardboard boxes marked FRAGILE in red-lettered packing tape. They were cushioned by bubble wrap, old tires, foam mattresses, and clear plastic bags filled with shredded paper. Violins, violas, cellos, double basses, trumpets, French horns, clarinets, bassoons, a piccolo, pianos, timpani, marimbas, a xylophone, a harpsichord: instruments for an orchestra.

"Ya, Ramzi! *Mabrouk habibi!* Congratulations!" someone called out as he started tossing the old tires onto the street. "It's not to start the Third Intifada, but to protect the instruments," he joked as the French film crew—back for their third straight summer—documented the moment.

Near the gate of the school, volunteers formed two lines—one carrying instruments to the practice rooms, the other coming back to the truck for more. Then came the harpsichord, bright red with gold trim, and an upright piano, a Gaveau of Paris, walnut brown with a pair of double lamps over the keyboard, carried in by Ramzi, Jessie, and Thierry.

Alá, now seven years old, watched the spectacle from a distance, unsmiling. She had been suspicious. At first the truck had reminded her of the large army vehicles she had seen during the uprising. But when the piano came out, it looked familiar; she had seen something similar in a Tom and Jerry cartoon.

As he returned to the truck from the courtyard, Ramzi noticed Alá watching warily from a corner. "I am afraid of you," she said. She had been told not to talk to strangers, and despite her sister Rasha's enthusiasm and the fact that she herself had met Ramzi earlier, Alá still did not understand his intentions.

"Here," Ramzi said to Alá, reaching toward her with a soft blue case. "How about if you hold this? It's a violin." Alá gazed at the case for a moment, hesitating as if she were thinking about unzipping it. But she walked the instrument inside and set it on the piano.

At dusk, musicians, supporters, old friends, and curious families from the neighborhood packed the unfinished courtyard and began filing up the refurbished stairway to the concert rooftop. There stood one hundred white plastic chairs in neat rows, before the arched copper arm towering over the stage. It looked like a giant wing, about to take the building into the sky above the old city. Someone had unrolled Oriental carpets atop the stones.

Jessie sang Fairouz, accompanied by Thierry on clarinet, Celine on viola, and Yacine on percussion. Finally Oday, looking a bit stiff in his dark blue shirt and new crisp black pants, sang the words of the great Lebanese composer Marcel Khalife, a song about a little child looking for a string to fly his kite, who looks up in the air to see something glittering in the distance.

Ramzi stood at the back, behind the last row, leaning against the rail above the courtyard. In the street just beyond, neighborhood children had discovered the long, thin strips of white paper that had been stuffed into the plastic bags for cushioning on the journey. Now they dumped them onto the pavement. Dozens of kids were scooping up armfuls of the white strips, racing back and forth, launching them skyward, watching the wind catch them before they settled back to earth.

Ramzi looked down from the rooftop of his new music school. Below, children were laughing and screaming, chasing each other in circles, tossing the shredded paper at each other. As dusk drew near, the entire street was covered in white.

In August, in Palestine, it looked like snow.

END OF SECOND MOVEMENT

INTERLUDE II

THE LEADER OF *the five musicians crouches beside the rope at the base of the vast concrete barrier, arms out, poised for the violin in its soft blue case and determined to catch it before it tumbles to the ground. At that same moment at the Qalandia checkpoint about a kilometer to the north, a bus loaded with musical instruments idles in a blistering parking lot framed by sniper towers and the concrete wall. The bus, carrying visiting musicians from Europe and America, has passed through to the Jerusalem side of the checkpoint. Now the visiting musicians wait for the young Palestinian music students, who have been required to pass on foot through the metal turnstiles and submit their special Jerusalem permits to soldiers for inspection. One by one, the young musicians emerge from an eight-foot metal turnstile, clicking through to the Jerusalem side of the barrier and walking across the asphalt toward the bus. There they join their visiting colleagues and teachers, and another light-skinned fellow student, a clarinetist who the military authorities had mistaken for a foreigner. He was allowed to stay on the bus rather than submit himself for inspection at the checkpoint. "I feel bad, just because my skin is lighter," he says, "while my friends have to go through the checkpoint."*

A group of musicians gathers at the front door of the bus. They have removed their instruments from their cases. Violins, viola, cello, French horn, and clarinet form a Mozart jam session: A Little Night Music. *"Opus baking in the sun," quips a British violinist. The Mozart morphs into "Morrison's Jig," led by a fiddler from Northern Ireland. The musicians lean into each other, forming a tight circle in front of a tableau of gun turrets, spindly red-and-white surveillance towers, and the seemingly impenetrable wall. "It's pretty threatening," says the fiddler, "but not altogether unfamiliar. For the first half of my life, this is what Northern Ireland looked like."*

Now everyone has clicked through the checkpoint—all but the five musicians who were refused passage at Qalandia. Ever since they were denied their permits, no one has heard from them. There was word they would try to cross somehow, but no one knows how, or where. It remains unclear whether the orchestra will cancel the evening Beethoven concert in the Old City.

With all but the five missing musicians accounted for, members of the orchestra reboard the bus, which now swings out of the parking lot and rumbles south. Faces peer from the windows. On their minds are their missing friends.

Third Movement:

PRACTICE

Eighteen

BEETHOVEN

August 2005
Ramallah

IN LATE AUGUST 2005, two days after the grand opening at Al Kamandjati, the West-Eastern Divan Orchestra arrived in Palestine for the first time. It had been six years since Daniel Barenboim, Edward Said, and Yo-Yo Ma met in Weimar in the orchestra's first season. For Arab and Israeli musicians, Daniel considered the trip "an event of historic dimensions: a concert of an orchestra consisting of Palestinians, Israelis, Syrians, Lebanese, Egyptians, and Jordanians in the heart of Palestine." Yet, it was also "truly an impossible undertaking," fraught with complex politics and intricate travel and security arrangements.

"The decision to go," Daniel observed, "touched a nerve central to the entire Israeli-Palestinian conflict, raising all the issues of security, national identity, fear, and the preconceptions of the other party that make political progress so difficult."

Political reality required the orchestra to travel in two groups. Arab musicians, armed with Spanish diplomatic passports secured by the Divan's hosts in Andalucía, flew to Amman and traveled by chartered bus across the Allenby Bridge at the River Jordan. From there they rode north through the occupied West Bank until they reached a VIP checkpoint near Ramallah. There they were met by Mustafa Barghouti, the Palestinian opposition leader and old friend of Edward and Daniel. Mustafa had managed to garner nearly 20 percent in the recent presidential elections, though his campaign was marred when

Mustafa was beaten by Israeli soldiers at a checkpoint during a campaign stop.

Many of the Arab musicians, long banned from entering Israel or the lands under its control, found themselves looking through the bus windows at a place they had only imagined. They had heard about Palestine from their parents and grandparents, but had only seen it on television, in repeated images of Israeli rocket attacks, house demolitions, and the death of innocents. Soon they were walking through bustling downtown Ramallah, chatting with street vendors, struck by the mixture of Palestinian friendliness toward strangers and anger at their occupiers. "I understand how they can be upset," said an Egyptian trumpeter. "They're actually living in a cage."

The Israeli and Spanish musicians flew directly to Tel Aviv, then rode in a European diplomatic convoy across the concrete separation barrier, and into Ramallah with a Palestinian police escort. Many of the Israelis were nervous. They vividly recalled the lynching of an Israeli soldier near the beginning of the Second Intifada, and the horrific sight, shown repeatedly on Israeli television, of his bloody body dragged through the streets of Ramallah. An Israeli violinist had announced he would not go on the trip; after a furious maestro made a withering remark about the young musician's manhood, he had changed his mind, saying he was "more afraid of Mr. Barenboim than I was of Hamas."

Because of the worries over security, the timing of the Israelis' arrival was kept secret, and their whereabouts were not divulged until they appeared onstage, ready for rehearsal, at the Ramallah Cultural Palace. Their Arab and Spanish counterparts were already there, waiting, still a bit stunned at the twisted journeys that had brought them to the same stage. "Going to a land that you think of as Palestine, through an Israeli checkpoint, to meet other Israelis to make music together with them for the freedom of Palestine," recalled the Lebanese cellist Nassib Al Ahmadieh: "It's simply too much to take in all at once."

Reunited onstage, the members of the Divan orchestra faced their ebullient Palestinian host. "I was telling Daniel I feel this is like a dream coming true," declared Mustafa as the orchestra clapped heartily. "This means a lot to us. I'm sure that you will all depart with the strong impression that Ramallah is a very welcoming city."

The Israeli musicians were not allowed to venture into Ramallah, nor did most of them want to; they would rehearse, play the concert, and leave. But in the gardens outside the concert hall, Palestinian policeman invited them to play backgammon. Known as *sheshbesh* in Arabic, the game originated in Mesopotamia perhaps five thousand years ago. During one game, an Israeli oboist, Meirav Kadichevski, asked for a picture with one of the guards. The guard spoke almost no English, but after the photograph, he managed to invite Meirav to his home for a meal. "He gave me a card with his mobile number on it and told me that his mother would cook for us!" declared the astonished oboist.

Yet many in Palestine did not feel so welcoming. Strong opposition to the visit had been building. A new global campaign known as BDS, for Boycott, Divestment and Sanctions, was targeting Israeli commercial, educational, and cultural institutions. The BDS call to arms urged "people of conscience all over the world" to implement "nonviolent punitive measures" in the form of "broad boycotts and . . . divestment initiatives against Israel similar to those applied to South Africa in the apartheid era." At stake, the statement declared, was "the Palestinian people's inalienable right to self-determination." The BDS effort was necessary, the declaration stated, given the failure of peacemaking efforts and Israel's refusal to end the occupation.

The framers of BDS sought to put Israel on the defensive in the international struggle for hearts and minds. "The strategic aim of the Palestinian struggle," wrote Mustafa Barghouti, an early supporter of the boycott movement, "must be to make the costs of the Israeli occupation and its apartheid system so great as to be unsustainable."

The Divan Orchestra, based in Spain, was not an Israeli institution, and few Israelis had been as outspoken as Daniel in defending Palestinian rights, especially in front of his fellow Israelis. Mustafa himself would make this point many times in the years to come.

The orchestra as a whole, however, had not taken the bold political stands of its famous conductor. Many of the Israeli musicians were more conservative than Daniel, and did not want the orchestra to express public solidarity with the Palestinians. This left the Divan open to charges by some Palestinians that it preached coexistence without an outward commitment to justice or an end to the occupation. "Israeli musicians who come to play in Ramallah only months after finishing their service with the occupation army," declared Omar Barghouti, a founder of the BDS movement, and a cousin of Mustafa's, "are only interested in whitewashing

Israel's crimes and covering up its violations of international law by presenting a shining image of 'peace-loving' Israelis to the world." This was "normalization," Omar and other critics charged, when the reality—checkpoints, military patrols, night raids, surveillance towers, expanding settlements, and settlers-only "bypass roads"—wasn't normal at all.

Daniel had heard these arguments and dismissed them. "Before a Beethoven symphony all people are equal," he remarked. To the maestro, the Divan's presence in Ramallah represented "a model of equality that might be achieved between Israel and Palestine."

A major goal of the Divan, added Mariam Said, was about "interaction and coexistence with the other in order to combat ignorance. Music is the language. It's a humanistic idea. That's exactly what Edward wanted."

What Edward Said would have wanted was a subject of intense debate among the various parties fighting over his legacy. The Divan Orchestra, cofounded by Edward, had spawned the Barenboim-Said Foundation in Ramallah, which brought teachers and scholarships for musical education in Palestine. The National Conservatory (the Ma'had) now also bore Edward's name: it was officially known as the Edward Said National Conservatory of Music. But tensions over politics and competition for limited funds were growing between the Barenboim-Said Foundation and the Edward Said Conservatory. Omar Barghouti, whose daughter was a lead violinist with the Edward Said Conservatory, wrote to Mariam, telling her that the Barenboim-Said Foundation was "hijacking" the indigenous musical efforts of the Conservatory. He pointedly asked her to remove her late husband's name from the Barenboim-Said Foundation. "It is time to reclaim Edward Said as our inspiration," he wrote.

"I find this request condescending and quite offensive," Mariam shot back. "Edward's name belongs to me and my family and no one else can claim it. His legacy belongs to everyone and no one. Certainly no one has exclusivity."

The leaders of the Edward Said Conservatory had, like Omar, grown uncomfortable with the Divan's political stance, especially its refusal as a full orchestra to publicly condemn the occupation. Conservatory leaders met to consider removing their endorsement of the Divan's Ramallah concert, and some refused to attend. Rima Tarazi, a cofounder of the Conservatory, decided to support the concert, provided the orchestra play under the large black-and-white banner reading FREEDOM FOR PALESTINE: IN MEMORY

OF PROFESSOR EDWARD SAID. That evening, Edward's spirit and his face hung over the auditorium, a silent witness to the battles over his legacy.

A little after seven P.M. on August 20, 2005, the lights dimmed in the packed Ramallah Cultural Palace. People sat three deep in the aisles and squeezed into the back of the auditorium. One hundred musicians—forty Arabs, forty Israelis, and twenty Spaniards—strode onto the stage. A moment later, out came Daniel Barenboim. A thunderous applause rose, and lasted five minutes before the orchestra played its first note.

They began with Mozart's Sinfonia Concertante for oboe, horn, clarinet, and bassoon, as the hall resonated with "a chorus of clicking shutters."

A short time later, the Cultural Palace filled with the iconic four-note opening of Beethoven's Fifth Symphony.

Ramzi watched from his seat near the stage. It had been nine years since Peter Sulski and the Apple Hill players had come to what was now called the Edward Said National Conservatory of Music, and Ramzi had first encountered a musical concept called harmony. Now, to Ramzi, Beethoven's music stood for artistic and musical freedom, and solidarity with suffering. As the music surged in volume, then fell nearly silent; as it went from violent to warm, gentle to urgent; as the Israeli oboist played her plaintive solo, halfway through the first movement, Ramzi felt the drama and contrast of Beethoven's music to be strangely made for his homeland.

He looked up at the banner with Edward Said's face: FREEDOM FOR PALESTINE, it read. Ramzi was impressed that a group of Arabs and Israelis would come to play a concert in solidarity with his people.

When the applause for the Fifth Symphony finally died down, Nabil Shaath, the Palestinian minister of information, took the stage to declare that Daniel Barenboim was a "humanist and a peacemaker." Then the maestro stepped to the microphone.

"This project that Edward Said and I founded in 1999 has been some-times described in a very flattering way for us as an orchestra for peace," a perspiring Daniel declared from the stage near the end of the concert. "Ladies and gentlemen, let me tell you something. This is not going to bring peace—you know that. What it can bring is understanding, the patience, the courage, and the curiosity to listen to the narrative of the other. We come to you here, today, with the message of humanity. Not with a political message, with the message of solidarity for the freedom that Palestine needs and for the freedom that the whole region needs. It is our belief that there is no military solution to this conflict. It is our belief that the destinies of these two people, of the Palestinian and the Israeli people, are inextricably linked and it is our duty, all of us, to find a way to live together. Because either we all kill each other or we learn what it is to share."

After the concert Ramzi made his way backstage. There he found the maestro surrounded by a throng of friends and well-wishers. This included Rima Tarazi, the chair of the Ma'had board, who had been deeply ambivalent about the orchestra's visit. Only a moment earlier, however, she had found herself rising, with the rest of the audience, in a standing ovation at the end of the concert. Beside her stood her sister-in-law, Tania Nasir, in whose home Daniel and Edward had dined seven years earlier, the night before Daniel's solo performance in West Jerusalem.

Ramzi waited, then finally shook the maestro's hand, but it was not a memorable encounter for either man. Another time, Ramzi determined. They had now had two passing encounters, but Ramzi was certain that eventually, they would meet again.

Nineteen

AL KAMANDJATI

September 2005
Ramallah

MERDE! RAMZI SAID to himself in the late summer of 2005, sitting alone in his new music school. *What have I done?*

The French musicians had all gone home, no documentary crews were following Ramzi around, and the "snow" had long ago been picked up from the street and stuffed into dumpsters. Al Kamandjati was filled with violins, trombones, cellos, kettledrums, ouds, tablas, guitars, pianos, even a harpsichord. But the instruments remained essentially untouched, the practice rooms empty. Ramzi, now twenty-six, envisioned an entire musical presence in Palestine: curriculum, annual music festivals, summer music camps, workshops, a program to study abroad, and a center for making and repairing musical instruments. He envisioned Al Kamandjati in Palestinian refugee camps in Lebanon, and in Jenin, a tough, impoverished place where an infusion of musical culture could make a huge difference. But Ramzi had developed no formal curriculum or teaching pedagogy, and he had hired no faculty. He and Marie spent sixteen-hour days making calls and visits, and writing proposals to bring in funding, but still had no specific plan to recruit students, other than to hope that children would begin to wander into the courtyard.

One afternoon Alá Shalalda followed the sound of a lone stringed instrument drifting from an open doorway to her house. The seven-year-old, in sneakers, jeans, and a T-shirt, her hair pulled back in a ponytail, followed the sound until she reached the entrance of the music school. She felt as though something was tugging at her, encouraging her. She looked through the entrance to see Ramzi, sitting alone on a stone bench, playing unaccompanied. The base of his instrument rested at his heart.

"Why do you hold it like this?" she finally asked him as the echo of the strings faded in the courtyard.

"Because this instrument describes all my emotions," Ramzi replied. "And when I play viola, especially when I'm sad, the viola heals me."

Alá, who lived next door with her parents, her brother Shehada, sister Rasha, and three other sisters, had watched the transformation of the formerly dank, mud-caked rooms that she and Rasha had once explored with candles. She had watched Ramzi carrying young jasmine plants, jacaranda and yucca trees, and a Lebanese cedar to the courtyard, where he planted tiny cacti in old violin cases filled with dirt, for adornment. But Alá remained skeptical; her history warned against enthusiasm. A photograph taken at this precise location in 2001, at the height of the Second Intifada, showed a scowling, three-year-old Alá, pedaling her plastic tricycle outside her front door. It was a rare moment of calm during the siege of Old Ramallah, between the house raids and detentions of her father, and it hadn't lasted. She wasn't sure that this new space would last long, either. Still, she was curious.

"When are you going to start classes?" Alá asked.

"As soon as possible," Ramzi replied. He set down his instrument, smiling at Alá. "How about if I introduce you to Al Kamandjati?"

They walked into rooms Alá remembered. Once filled with garbage, they were swept out clean, the stones shining white. Ramzi explained why he had studied in France for seven years but returned to teach music to Palestinian children. He told Alá about his time in the First Intifada, confronting the occupation army, and how, for him, music had replaced the stone as a form of resistance.

They walked into a large room with a small stairway and domed cross-vault ceilings. In the darkened corner stood the piano, covered by a blanket. Alá removed the blanket and slid her fingers on the white and black keys. Just like in the Tom and Jerry cartoon. She pressed her fingers down; strange chords rang out in the room.

Alá looked up to see her sister Rasha, now thirteen, staring at her from the doorway.

"Go look at the rooms," Ramzi told the sisters. "See what instruments you would like." They visited practice rooms filled with marimbas, timpani, flutes, ouds, and violins. Rasha took turns on different instruments. She loved the five-stringed oud, but she was drawn to the flute. Alá was contemplating the piano, but eventually she chose the violin.

"You have to be sure you want the violin," Ramzi told her. "The violin is really difficult to learn."

"I don't care if it's difficult. At the beginning it will be hard, but then it will become easier." Alá felt herself warming to the idea of the school. *We always think about the occupation*, she told herself. *Why not think about something beautiful?*

* * *

On September 11, 2005, a soldier lowered the Israeli flag on a military base in the Gaza Strip, a near-final act in Israel's long-awaited plan to quit Gaza, which it had first occupied in June 1967. The unilateral disengagement plan, undertaken by Prime Minister Ariel Sharon, included the closure of Israeli military bases and the evacuation of all eight thousand Gaza settlers, many against their will. To many the old hardliner's plan was stunning in its willingness to give up territory, comparable to cold warrior Richard Nixon's visit to China in the 1970s. Pundits understood it as a bold move toward peace in the face of resistance from the powerful settler movement inside Israel. But it was far more complicated than that. Gazans prepared to celebrate the end of the settlements in their territory. Yet Sharon's go-it-alone nature raised serious concerns, which deepened as his broader strategy was revealed. Condoleezza Rice, the American secretary of state, then in the region to promote the administration's Road Map for Peace initiative, declared that the disengagement should not leave Gaza as a "sealed or isolated area, with the Palestinian people closed in after that withdrawal."

Weeks later, however, critics argued that Israel, in controlling access to Gaza and patrolling its skies and shores, effectively continued its occupation of the territory as an "open-air prison."

"Gaza's airport and crossing point to Egypt remain closed," complained Mahmoud Abbas, the new Palestinian president. "Its waters are off-limits to our fishermen; its borders are completely sealed and movement into or out of Gaza is virtually impossible; and no safe passage between Gaza and the West Bank exists."

Sharon's strategy, like that of Israeli leaders before and after him, was driven by his desire to keep the bulk of Israel's settlers in place. Already, he had secured a crucial letter from President Bush, acknowledging the "new realities on the ground . . . including already existing major Israeli population centers"—the settlements. A "final status agreement," Bush wrote, must "reflect these realities." That was precisely what Sharon had sought. Yet in the wake of Israeli military action in Jenin and other Palestinian cities during the Second Intifada, Israel was under increasing pressure internationally, where the "Geneva Initiative" for a two-state solution had picked up momentum, and at home, where soldiers of conscience had begun to refuse to serve in the Occupied Territories. Sharon's team felt he needed to act boldly. By quitting Gaza unilaterally and forcing a relatively small number of settlers to move, Sharon sought to seize the international agenda and put pressure on the Palestinians to show their "seriousness" in quelling "the perpetuation of terrorist acts." The withdrawal from a place most Israelis did not care about helped Sharon convince the Bush administration that in the Palestinians, Israel had "no partner for peace."

Sharon's broader aim in disengaging from Gaza, according to Dov Weisglass, a top aide who helped design the plan, was, ironically, to keep the Israeli settlements in the West Bank in place. By winning praise for acting forcefully and independently in Gaza, Israel sought to delay or eliminate pressure to remove significant numbers of settlers from the West Bank, or what Israel called Judea and Samaria. The disengagement, Weisglass had declared, was therefore "formaldehyde" for the peace process.

"The significance of the disengagement plan is the freezing of the peace process," said Weisglass. "And when you freeze that process, you prevent the establishment of a Palestinian state, and you prevent a discussion on the refugees, the borders and Jerusalem. Effectively, this whole package called the Palestinian state, with all that it entails, has been removed indefinitely from our agenda."

*　　　*　　　*

By October 2005 more children in and around Old Ramallah, including three more Shalalda sisters, joined Rasha and Alá. Later that month, their big brother Shehada returned from a month-long visit to cousins near

Hebron to find all five of his sisters playing music: Rasha on flute, Hanine on clarinet, Ghadir on double bass, Ghayda on cello, and Alá on violin. He was surprised and not entirely comfortable. He especially did not like that Rasha was talking to boys; when he saw Muntasser Jebrini, a twelve-year-old who was learning the clarinet, laughing and chatting with her, Shehada confronted the boy. He didn't want anyone touching his sister.

Ramzi knew that winning over his neighbors in Old Ramallah, including the shabab like Shehada, was crucial to the success of his music school. The intimate courtyards of this conservative neighborhood sheltered the descendants of Muslim fellahin, peasant farmers from Mount Hebron to the south, who had come north in generations past to pick figs. For them, Ramzi was still an unknown quantity. Many of his friends were European. His institutional backing came from a Palestinian charitable foundation, a Palestinian historical preservation firm, and a Swedish development agency. To his neighbors, Ramzi represented uncertain change for Old Ramallah. Ziad Khalaf, his Palestinian benefactor from the A.M. Qattan Foundation, had urged him to "get your neighbors on board as soon as possible, to develop that sense of ownership. They and their children have to be your main partners and beneficiaries."

Shehada, Ramzi noticed, was good with his hands, and so he found him many small jobs. Soon Shehada was fixing doors and stuck windows and laying flagstone from the unfinished courtyard to the street. In the coming months, one young man came looking for a job as a janitor or a guard; another, a local barber, came hoping to learn the oud, and to do whatever odd jobs might be available. Ramzi found work for them. This was becoming his pattern: When faced with a challenge, he found a way to turn it into someone's opportunity.

*   *   *

In January 2006, Celine returned. She had landed in France the previous August, a day after the Al Kamandjati opening. Barely a week later she e-mailed Ramzi. "I really loved my experience," she wrote. "Would you still need someone to help you?"

"As soon as possible," came Ramzi's response. He offered Celine an open-ended contract. She took a one-year leave from her job in France. As expected, her parents did not understand. "We left Lebanon so you could live in good conditions," her mother reminded her. "We left the war, and now you go back?"

But for Celine the decision had been swift and uncomplicated. She was returning to a place where she would feel useful. "Here, not anywhere else," she recalled years later. "Strange, you know?"

Accompanying Celine from France was Elsa Ferrari, who had just graduated from a French university with a degree in music therapy. They moved into Rami's old flat, essentially bare but for a few mattresses. Marie was living there, too. Ramzi was staying mostly at Sido's. On her first day, Ramzi took Elsa to the U.N. school at Al Amari, where he had arranged for an Al Kamandjati visit. A class of forty-six teenage girls awaited her. She would teach this class every week, Ramzi informed her. Elsa felt thrown unaware into chaos. Her spotty Arabic, and the size of the class, meant she was more of a babysitter than an instructor of music therapy.

Celine and Marie worked the phones and computers in a stone, cave-like room in the newly opened school, where Oday occasionally came to serenade them, much to their delight. Ramzi was coming and going from Sido's, and Celine and other co-workers found him brooding, inspiring, mercurial, and possessed by Al Kamandjati and its fragile circumstances. He was given to occasional outbursts, sometimes directed at Celine and Marie, and which sometimes reduced them to tears. Celine had no idea why Ramzi was behaving this way. She had left a good job with an environmental firm in France, consulting with companies to help them comply with new laws in the European Union, and she found Ramzi's behavior shocking. "He was very hard to work with. He was very stressed and tense, always anxious, very demanding. We were always feeling all this pressure because of his way of being. It was difficult to tell him anything." Later she would understand that Ramzi was still dealing with, or not dealing with, the trauma of his brother's murder. This helped explain why Ramzi was in constant motion, as if he couldn't stand the thought of stopping, even for a moment. "He was always making himself busy, in order not to think about things," Celine recalled. "In order not to have any blank space. He was very much protecting himself."

Celine kept working, writing numerous grant requests for office equipment and supplies, teachers' salaries, summer music schools, and to facilitate the travel of visiting performers. Marie, however, decided to return to

France. Over many months in Palestine, and before that in France, she had helped build the new music school's capacity, but in recent weeks her colleagues had noticed she had grown tense and distressed. The multiple pressures to raise money from international donors, pay teachers with limited funds, arrange international music festivals, deal with countless unseen logistical challenges, and, most of all, help manage Ramzi's own stress, had become, at times, overwhelming. She decided to return to Angers. It was heartbreaking, she recalled, but now that Al Kamandjati was becoming stable, and its administration was in Celine's good hands, it was time to leave. "I tried to do my best to sustain Ramzi and the musicians," she said years later. "Al Kamandjati recognizes the right of every kid to have fun, to grow up as slowly as possible. The very act of reaching for a violin and starting to play is itself an act of dignity, an attempt to resist, to stand up to the challenges of being free." In France, Marie would pursue a career in nursing; before long, she and Ramzi would be divorced.

Celine stayed on, making contacts at the refugee camps, organizing Elsa's lessons, and arranging for the teachers' travel to music instruction in Jerusalem. After the marathon days, she returned to Rami's flat and fell asleep.

*　　*　　*

By the spring of 2006, about forty children were taking regular music lessons at Al Kamandjati. Many had simply wandered into the inviting courtyard and peered into the practice rooms filled with instruments. Ramzi took on most of the early students, teaching them violin, viola, musical theory, and bouzouk. But he was already learning that there was little culture of musical education, or even a sense of lesson times. "They didn't have any notion about the time," he said. "Very bad. Their day is light; the night is dark. That's it. The morning, their mothers wake them up, they go to the school. When it's dark, they go to sleep. Two, three, four o'clock doesn't mean anything."

"A child would come for example four times a day," Celine remembered. "They say what time is my lesson? You say, four. He came four times but at four he is not here. Like a really crazy way of thinking. No notion of time."

Now Ramzi had a better idea of how François must have felt in the early years at the Conservatoire, waiting in Salle 312 for his tardy student to begin his viola lesson.

By his own account, Ramzi was a strict teacher; he showed his young students little patience. They had much more opportunity than he ever had at that age, and he didn't want them to waste it. "Why have you come to your lesson without practicing?" Ramzi snapped one day at little Alá. "I don't understand why you're wasting this opportunity."

Rasha and Alá came nearly every day. Rasha had started on flute with her teacher, Miss Abeer, who showed her how to stand up straight, to hold the flute at a ninety-degree angle, and to breathe from her diaphragm, not from her lungs, in order to hold a note for as long as possible. She learned to play in rhythm with a metronome and to stand in front of a mirror to monitor her posture.

Playing, for Rasha, became a necessity, and with it came the ability to face difficulties that had only recently been overwhelming. When she became angry or anxious, she would play; her tensions would empty into her instrument and dissolve. It was as if by holding her flute, she no longer had anything to fear. All her troubles suddenly seemed manageable. When she played, her entire focus was on her flute, and on the world she and her instrument made. "I felt like I was in a forest, all by myself in a little cottage, with no people, no noise, nothing," she recounted. "Mountains, sea, something pure blue, not like the Dead Sea. It was an escape to another world. A better world. I owned that world."

For Rasha even the military occupation seemed diminished. "The conditions that we live in under the occupation affect our personalities. For instance, every time we turn on the TV, we see disturbing images and we hear news from Gaza, West Bank, Ramallah, and Hebron. This changed. We started listening to Fairouz, Umm Kulthum. Everything changed. Everything."

Shehada, Rasha's older brother, remained skeptical of his sisters' musical education. He had tried an instrument himself, the oud, but soon quit. Ramzi wanted to find something useful for Shehada. So far he had easily handled all the odd jobs Ramzi had given him. This gave Ramzi a bigger idea. When a French violin maker came for a visit, Ramzi invited Shehada to the workshop.

*   *   *

In April, Daniel Barenboim returned to Ramallah to conduct the Palestine Youth Orchestra, which was part of the Edward Said Conservatory. After the controversy over the Divan concert the previous September, relations between the Barenboim-Said Foundation and the Said Conservatory had deteriorated. Despite the infighting, Daniel and the Conservatory agreed that he would travel to Ramallah in the spring of 2006 to direct the Palestine Youth Orchestra, which, as it turned out, included Ramzi.

Ramzi took the stage for rehearsals at the Friends Boys School in Ramallah under the baton of Daniel Barenboim. It had been nearly eight years since Daniel and Edward had invited Ramzi, via fax to the Conservatoire in Angers, to participate in the first summer of the Divan, in Weimar. Since then, the Divan had performed in Europe, Asia, and Latin America.

Ramzi sat holding his viola with the Palestine Youth Orchestra, as Daniel went through Haydn's Sinfonia Concertante for violin, cello, oboe, and bassoon. During rehearsal, Ramzi asked Daniel a question in French. The maestro smiled at Ramzi. Later, explaining a rhythm to the youth orchestra, he said, "It's *ta*-ta, *ta*-ta! Like, *Ram*-zi, *Ram*-zi!"

After two passing encounters, Ramzi was making a connection with Daniel Barenboim.

On a break, Daniel approached him. "Where are you from?" Daniel asked, in French.

"I grew up in Al Amari refugee camp," Ramzi replied. "Very close to here." Daniel sized him up. Ramzi imagined the maestro's thoughts: *Why is he not in the Divan?* After all, Ramzi was on a level equal to some of the violists already in the orchestra, and unlike most of them, he was Palestinian. Most of the Arabs in the Divan were either Lebanese, Egyptian, Jordanian, or Syrian. Daniel wanted more Palestinians in the orchestra, especially those who had grown up under occupation.

"You are talented," Daniel told Ramzi. "You are very good." Ramzi anticipated Daniel's next question, but wasn't ready to answer it.

"I would like to invite you for tea at my grandfather's house," Ramzi said abruptly.

Daniel hesitated. He had never been to a Palestinian refugee camp, and he believed they could be dangerous, especially for an Israeli—even one not in uniform. Ramzi noticed that Mustafa Barghouti, Daniel's old friend, had been listening to the conversation. He too appeared worried. A brief discussion ensued, then a phone call; Mustafa agreed that Daniel should accept the invitation, and that two of his friends could accompany them.

Ramzi repeated the invitation. In his mind, any conversation with Daniel Barenboim could not go forward unless the maestro visited his grandfather's house in the refugee camp where he grew up. He kept those thoughts to himself.

"Okay," Daniel said. "Let's go." Then, Ramzi recalls, Daniel turned to the other men and asked, "Are you armed, guys? Yes? Show them to me." Daniel was joking, Ramzi thinks. Or at least, half-joking.

In the alley near Sido's house, children were kicking a soccer ball. The camp walls displayed pasted flyers commemorating fallen martyrs; graffiti welcomed home prisoners held for years in nearby Israeli prisons. The ball rolled toward Daniel; he swung his leg and launched it back to the children. "Don't forget," he told Ramzi with a smile, "I'm from Argentina."

They found Ramzi's grandfather sitting on the stone bench outside the cinder-block home. "*Salaam alaikum*, Sidi," Ramzi said. "I want to introduce a friend of mine." Ramzi invited the maestro up to the roof. They stood amid the feral cats and bent antennae. Before the intifada, Ramzi explained, the family had kept goats and sheep in a small rooftop room.

Ramzi pointed in the distance toward the camp entrance and the four-story building that once served as a military surveillance post. He told Daniel how, nineteen years earlier, he had raced across the rooftops with the soldiers in pursuit.

Daniel gazed out across the rooftops covered with flapping clothes and rows of black water tanks. "Sixty years, this camp has been like this?" Daniel asked.

"These people who came here," Ramzi replied, "were kicked out of their houses."

The maestro was quiet. He stared across the vast space. Despite nearly six decades of existence, it felt impermanent.

They sat for tea with Grandfather Mohammad and Grandmother Jamila, and there, under the poster of Ramzi throwing a stone at an unseen Israeli soldier, Daniel Barenboim learned about Na'ani.

"It was moving to see somebody who had lived through that," Daniel later remembered.

"After that visit, Daniel felt very much that he needed to support Ramzi," recalled Edward's widow, Mariam. "He saw the reality, and decided, This is where we want to extend a hand."

A day or two later Celine walked into the Al Kamandjati office to tell Ramzi there were two older visitors in the courtyard, asking for him. The woman looked like an Arab but about the man, she couldn't tell.

Ramzi walked through the courtyard to the slanted copper door at the entrance. Daniel and Mariam were smiling and looking around admiringly. Ramzi led them back through the courtyard, past the rehearsal rooms and up the steps onto the rooftop concert space that looked out onto Old Ramallah.

They took in the space.

"Why don't you come to the Divan?" Daniel asked.

"I will try," Ramzi replied. "I'm busy in the summer." He was planning a summer camp and a music festival.

"Why haven't you ever auditioned for us?" Daniel asked. Ramzi thought of François, eight years ago, saying, "*You*? Invited by *Barenboim*?"

"Do you have your viola here?" Daniel asked.

"Yes," Ramzi replied.

"Can you play something for me?"

Ramzi retrieved his viola and played, unaccompanied, the concert for piano and viola by George Enescu, the same piece he had played for his examination in the French chapel three years earlier. He felt calm and confident as he played. Joining the Divan had never been a dream of his, Ramzi remembered later, so he had no reason to feel nervous.

"It's fine," Daniel said before Ramzi could finish. "I invite you to come to the Divan."

"I will do my best," Ramzi promised.

Ramzi walked back down the steps and led Daniel and Mariam through a passage to the percussion room, where Samuel Tagardeau, a newly arrived teacher from Angers, was conducting a class. The kids were pounding on tablas, timpani, and snare drums; energy crackled from the room.

"I felt he was giving these kids something that made them happy," Mariam remembered. "It was a joyous moment. I was so happy that there was somebody doing something—just playing music in such a lovely atmosphere. There was a feeling that they cared about what they were doing. It was so genuine."

As the drums echoed off the stone walls in the low-ceilinged room, Mariam looked at Daniel and Ramzi, her eyes wet with tears.

"I wish," she said, "that Edward were alive to see this."

Twenty

ANDALUCÍA

May 2006
Ramallah

A MONTH AFTER Daniel Barenboim left Palestine, Ramzi received an e-mail from the maestro's assistant in Spain, formally inviting him to join the West-Eastern Divan Orchestra for its summer rehearsals and concert series. The season would begin in July in Seville, in the Spanish province of Andalucía. Ramzi sent word that he would be joining the orchestra in time for the rehearsals.

As Ramzi made his plans, larger events conspired against the unity Barenboim preached.

*   *   *

In late June 2006, Hamas militants in Gaza killed two Israeli soldiers patrolling along the Gaza border and captured a third, Gilad Shalit, taking him hostage.

Five months earlier, Hamas had won free and fair parliamentary elections, voted in by Palestinians angry with the corruption in Mahmoud Abbas's Fatah government and its failure to deliver a Palestinian state, or even an easing of Israel's restrictions on travel and commerce. Despite Israel's "disengagement," its military retained control of Gaza by land, sea, and air. Gazans were unable to leave or to cross the "no-go zone" within three hundred meters of the border. They lived increasingly cut off from the rest of Palestine.

After the elections Hamas had reached out to Mahmoud Abbas's Fatah faction to form a broad-based government in Gaza, but the Bush administration strongly pressured Fatah not to join. Israel and "the Quartet"—the United States, the European Union, Russia, and the United Nations—had refused to recognize the outcome of the elections, calling Hamas a terrorist organization. The Quartet suspended economic aid and Israel severely curtailed goods going in and out of Gaza. "It's like meeting with a dietician," remarked Prime Minister Sharon's aide, Dov Weisglass. "We have to make them [Gazans] much thinner, but not enough to die." The punitive measures were to remain in place until Hamas stopped its cross-border rocket attacks, which had begun in 2002 during the Second Intifada and had increased sharply after Israel's disengagement from Gaza, exceeding twelve hundred by 2006, and killing two people in Israel. (Most of the crudely built rockets landed harmlessly, far from their targets.) Under the Quartet's terms, Hamas was also required to recognize Israel and accept all previous agreements based on the Oslo accords.

In the wake of the elections, Hamas was no longer the militant opposition to a ruling Fatah party. Hamas leader Ismail Haniyeh, suddenly responsible for governing, and facing a mounting economic, humanitarian, and political catastrophe, sought to defuse the situation. In June, Haniyeh sent President Bush an appeal for a direct dialogue with the United States. Hamas, in the words of one analyst, was clearly trying to "come in from the cold." In the letter Haniyeh agreed to accept a Palestinian state within the 1967 borders of the West Bank and Gaza—a de facto recognition of Israel—and promised "a truce for many years . . . The continuation of this situation," Haniyeh wrote to Bush, "will encourage violence and chaos in the whole region."

A few lonely voices in the United States and Israeli intelligentsia had urged their leaders to seize the moment with Hamas and coax it toward moderation. Israel itself was formed in part by groups that had committed terrorist acts, the Irgun and the Stern Gang (or Lehi), which in the years before Israel's birth had been responsible for a horrific massacre in the Palestinian village of Deir Yassin and the bombing of the King David Hotel in Jerusalem, which had killed ninety-one people. Leaders of the two organizations, Menachem Begin and Yitzhak Shamir, later became prime ministers of Israel. Similarly, Yasser Arafat, whose Palestine Liberation Organization was considered a terrorist group by Israel and the West, recognized Israel's right to exist in a pivotal 1988 speech, paving the way for the Oslo peace process.

"I believe there is a chance that Hamas, the devils of yesterday, could be reasonable people today," declared Efraim Halevy, former director of the Mossad, Israel's national intelligence agency. "Rather than being a problem, we should strive to make them part of the solution."

Bush did not respond to Haniyeh's letter. Instead, his administration began to explore ways to provide military training and facilitate arms shipments to Abbas's Fatah faction in Gaza. They wanted to bolster Fatah's capabilities against Hamas, allowing it to take control in Gaza.

Israel, meanwhile, stepped up its missile strikes, including one that claimed seven people, three of them children, picnicking on a Gaza beach. The Israeli military increased its targeted assassinations of Palestinian militants, which, according to a senior U.N. official, now numbered forty per month. Hamas launched more waves of rockets across the border. The sanctions remained in place.

In response to the capture of Corporal Shalit, Israel launched Operation Summer Rains. The military dropped leaflets over Gaza, warning residents to stay inside and "follow the orders of the IDF." Israel bombed Gaza's interior ministry, the prime minister's office, the American International School, more than one hundred other buildings, and a power station that was the sole source of electricity for hundreds of thousands of Gazans. In the siege, which Israel pledged to continue until Shalit was released and Hamas ceased its rocket attacks, food supplies grew scarce. Many Palestinians were limited to one meal a day, eaten by candlelight. More than two hundred Palestinians were killed in the first two months of the conflict, at least forty-four of them children. Eleven Israelis were killed. Hamas would not release Shalit, the captured soldier, for another five years, and then in exchange for 1,027 Palestinian prisoners.

In July, Hezbollah fighters penetrated Israel's border with southern Lebanon, ambushed a pair of Israeli military Humvees, killed three soldiers, and captured two others. Israel retaliated with a massive air assault on roads, bridges, village infrastructure, and the country's international airport, killing forty-four Lebanese in the first twenty-four hours. Hundreds of thousands of civilians streamed north along the roads of southern Lebanon to escape the bombing. Their numbers would eventually exceed one million. Israel pledged to crush Hezbollah. Dan Halutz, the army chief of staff, vowed the army would "turn the clock in Lebanon back by twenty years." Hezbollah launched barrages of rockets toward Israeli villages in the northern Galilee. "What we're seeing here," said U.S. secretary of state Condoleezza Rice in a Washington press conference, "is the birth pangs of a new Middle East."

*   *   *

A week later, with the attacks in Gaza and Lebanon unrelenting, Ramzi landed in Spain for his first rehearsals with the West-Eastern Divan Orchestra. Many of the Lebanese musicians had been unable or unwilling to leave home. Some simply could not bring themselves to play alongside Israelis, whose nation's missiles and cluster bombs were falling on their country. Ramzi had his own reservations, but he had made a promise to Daniel, and with deeply conflicting feelings he decided to go. Part of what swayed him was his memory of the Divan Orchestra playing in Ramallah under the banner of Edward Said and the words, "Freedom for Palestine."

The newest member of the Divan Orchestra walked into Seville's Plaza de Toros, the oldest bullfighting ring in the world. There the Divan Orchestra began rehearsals for Beethoven's Ninth Symphony in the heart of Edward Said's beloved Andalucía. For Ramzi, the Ninth, with its humanity, grandeur, and transcendent emotion, was proof that "music can't be neutral. If music is neutral, and art is neutral," he later asked, "why did Beethoven write the Ninth?"

With war raging on two fronts, tensions were high in the orchestra. Already conflict had erupted in the cello section. Its source was a gold pendant on a chain, worn around the neck of a fourteen-year-old Palestinian girl. The pendant represented the map of Israel together with the West Bank and Gaza—but it bore the word, simply, PALESTINE. For Palestinians, especially refugees whose parents, grandparents, or great-grandparents were expelled from their homeland during the Nakba, maps and pendants representing old Palestine were as ubiquitous as falafel stands. It was an expression of history and identity and, for some, a belief that one day there could be a single state for all who lived between the River Jordan and the Mediterranean Sea. Like Ramzi, they still dreamed of that state, and called it Palestine. In its depiction of a single land between the river and the sea, it was no different than many of Israel's own maps, which show the West Bank and Gaza as part of greater Israel.

The Israelis in the cello section were offended by the pendant and demanded that the Palestinian girl remove it. She did as she was told. It was hard to imagine this dynamic playing out had Edward Said still been alive.

Mariam Said had observed the tensions in the orchestra. She approached Daniel. In the wake of the Israeli invasion, she said, the two should make a statement. Daniel said he preferred to discuss a statement that could be endorsed by the entire orchestra. Daniel and Mariam, in consultation with friends, crafted a declaration. After the rehearsal in the bullring, Daniel read it aloud to the orchestra:

> This year, our project stands in sharp contrast to the cruelty and savagery that denies so many innocent civilians the possibility to continue living, fulfilling their ideals and dreams. Israel's destruction of life-giving infrastructure in Lebanon and Gaza, uprooting a million people and inflicting heavy casualties on civilians, and Hezbollah's indiscriminate shelling of civilians in northern Israel are in total opposition to what we believe in . . .

Ramzi listened to Daniel's voice resound in the vast circular space of the Plaza de Toros. When full the arena held more than fourteen thousand people. Now there were just one hundred musicians and a handful of others, in chairs at the center of the dirt circle, engulfed by empty brick bleachers, intricate tile mosaics, and dozens of wooden arches painted yellow and white.

> The refusal to have an immediate ceasefire and the refusal to enter into negotiations for resolving once and for all the conflict in all its aspects goes against the very essence of our project as well . . .

Ramzi found the statement rather tame. He didn't like how it seemed to equate Israel's aerial assault, which would lead to more than eleven hundred deaths in Lebanon and leave more than one million undetonated cluster bomblets across the country, with Hezbollah's Katyusha rocket attacks in Israel, which killed forty-three Israelis. But the statement did condemn the war, and Ramzi could live with it. What he wasn't prepared for was the hostile reaction of many of the Israeli musicians.

"I don't agree with this statement," said one, "but my only alternative is to leave? I don't want to miss out on the whole concert because of this!"

Said another: "But I'm not against the war. I support my government!"

Elena Cheah, a visiting cellist who had arrived from Germany, wondered "how it was possible to support a war against one's own colleagues" while taking part "in a workshop whose sole statement regarding the Israeli-Palestinian conflict is that there is no military solution."

About the time Ramzi arrived in Spain, Israel obliterated most of the tiny village of Qana, in southern Lebanon, killing twenty-eight people, all civilians. Many of the victims had been sleeping. They had taken refuge in the basement of a three-story apartment building when Israeli bombs struck and the building collapsed. As their bodies were dragged out into the light, some of the dead were children in their pajamas. International condemnation was swift, but in the orchestra, aside from the Lebanese violinist who "couldn't stop crying," Ramzi found a strange silence. Finally the statement was approved, but it left everyone unsatisfied, and left Ramzi confused. He recalled the FREEDOM FOR PALESTINE banner that had hung in the Ramallah concert hall during the Divan's performance a year earlier. He had been proud to join an orchestra that, he thought, stood beside his people. Now, amid the angry silence, he began to think that the spirit of this orchestra was not what he had believed.

Ramzi went to Daniel. Despite the orchestra's public statement, he said, "there's too much quiet about what's happening. We are pretending that there's nothing happening. I don't understand."

Daniel counseled patience, encouraging Ramzi to talk to the Israelis. After the orchestra completed its rehearsals and began a tour of Spain, Ramzi engaged in the process of political dialogue. As the buses rolled north out of Andalucía, he sat with his Israeli counterparts, recounting in his broken English the journey of his grandmother during the Nakba of 1948, the resistance during the First Intifada, the destruction during the second, and how the separation wall was stealing more Palestinian land. On the long rides, he unfurled maps he had brought with him, at one point getting into a fierce argument with an Israeli trumpeter that lasted nearly three hours. Ramzi's passion far exceeded that of the orchestra's other Arabs. The Syrians and Egyptians in particular lived in police states and had learned not to speak out. Ramzi's intensity surprised them. "It seemed like the whole Nakba thing happened two hours ago," recalled a trombonist raised in Syria.

But with the war continuing in Lebanon, so many Israeli musicians supporting it, and so many Arab musicians missing from the orchestra, Ramzi could not tolerate the atmosphere. "I can't support this," Ramzi told Daniel. "I'm playing with people who don't want my freedom." In northern Spain, he left the orchestra, traveling into France to be with friends in Angers. There he reconsidered his decision to join the Divan. Finally Mariam and Daniel reached him by phone. The maestro convinced Ramzi to return, promising a more spirited and engaged conversation. "Let's try to do something," Daniel said. "Let's work on it. Let's try to cultivate something."

When he returned, Daniel asked Ramzi to talk to the orchestra about the occupation and to tell his own story. Ramzi showed them *It's Not a Gun*, the French documentary depicting the three summers French musicians traveled to occupied Palestine and culminating in the opening of Al Kamandjati in 2005. At one point, the camera lingers on a French cellist, Catherine de Vençay, sitting on a chair amid the rubble in front of the vast concrete separation barrier. Behind her, a young Palestinian man, perched on the shoulders of another, writes *THE WALL WILL FALL* in spray paint, as Catherine plays the prelude to the Bach Cello Suite no. 1.

Members of the West-Eastern Divan Orchestra, rapt and visibly moved, watched in complete silence.

After the film, Ramzi recounted a childhood of daily flight from soldiers and the death of friends and family: a schoolmate, neighbors at Al Amari camp, his father, his brother.

"When he told us his story we were all in tears," remembered Sharon Cohen, an Israeli, the principal second violinist for the Divan.

For Yuval Shapiro, a trumpeter who grew up in Tel Aviv and who had spent hours on the bus arguing with Ramzi, it was a shock to have a former stone-thrower as a colleague and equal onstage. "When I was a kid in elementary school, you would hear about these stone-throwing kids," said Yuval. "What, are they stupid? And then *this guy* was throwing stones? You basically wanted to kick his ass for what he was telling us."

Yet Ramzi's story confronted Yuval, and other Israeli musicians, with a narrative they hadn't heard.

The rockets in Lebanon fell silent on August 14, 2006, following a cease-fire brokered by the United Nations. Israel had failed in its central mission to destroy Hezbollah; the very survival of the "Party of God" appeared to make it stronger.

Six days later, at the Palacio de Carlos V in Granada, within the medieval fortress known as the Alhambra, Ramzi joined the West-Eastern Divan Orchestra to play an evening concert.

The musicians performed Beethoven's *Leonore* Overture no. 3, op 72a; Fantasia on Themes of Rossini, by Giovanni Bottesini, arranged for cello, double bass, and orchestra; and the Brahms First Symphony. It was at the Alhambra, in 1492, that King Ferdinand and Queen Isabella issued their decree expelling the Jews from Spain. "By the grace of God . . . we . . . order the said Jews and Jewesses of our kingdom to depart and never to return," they declared. As for the Muslims of Spain, the royal couple soon forced them to choose between baptism and exile; in 1609, another Spanish king, Philip III, declared their descendants to be heretics. They were forced out, too, and resettled in North Africa.

Three hundred ninety-seven years after that, Muslims, Christians, and Jews—Israelis, Palestinians, Spaniards, Egyptians, and one Lebanese violinist—played music together in a palace named after the Holy Roman Emperor.

The emotional power of the moment was evident to everyone that night, and some in the audience were moved to tears. As Beethoven's overture raced toward its heroic conclusion, Ramzi sat on the big stage, in the middle of the viola section, playing furiously. The strings rose in tight, dramatic circles, the French horns called, warm and rich, from the back row, and Ramzi was swept away from the Lebanon and Gaza wars, and from the bitterness and disappointment of his first summer in the Divan. The orchestra's sound washed over Ramzi, as Beethoven's passionate *Leonore* carried him to another place.

Twenty-one

PALACES

June 2007
Village of Beit Wazan, near Nablus, West Bank

RAMZI LOOKED OVER his shoulder at the dozens of children following him into the palace. They were stepping off a pair of buses and reaching into the luggage holds, instrument cases slung over their shoulders and music stands in their hands. Behind the buses, Ramzi could see whitewashed buildings sweeping down a broad valley into the Nablus city center, where a large blue-domed mosque gleamed in the sunlight. The city below was quiet, under daylight curfew as Israel launched an operation in search of what it said were bomb-making factories. Nablus remained virtually sealed off by Israeli military order. The young musicians had waited for hours at the checkpoint outside of Nablus. Their ride up the hill into the village was an eerie journey along empty roads.

Ramzi and his entourage walked under a stone arch and into a broad, sunny courtyard of copper, glass, and gleaming white stones. The Qasem Palace was built in 1820 for the family of Sheikh Qasem Al-Ahmad, a governor who collected taxes for the Ottoman Empire. The sheikh and his family could never have envisioned eighty Palestinian children and twenty teachers and organizers from Palestine, Europe, and the United States all squeezing into his courtyard nearly two centuries later.

Al Kamandjati had been operating for nearly two years, and Ramzi was eager to test his vision of expanding it from a school to a full musical presence in Palestine. Already the summer music tours, begun with the French musicians years earlier, had been formalized in an annual Fête de la

Musique. Al Kamandjati now held a winter baroque music festival, which one year hosted the German opera star, mezzo-soprano Waltraud Meier, to sing in the cavernous unheated churches of the West Bank. Ramzi had met Waltraud, a friend of Daniel's, while on tour with the Divan. Master European luthiers were also drawn to Al Kamandjati; Ramzi planned to send Shehada to Italy to learn how to make violins. And he was talking to his former teachers at the Angers Conservatoire about scholarships for his top students, including Shehada's sister Rasha.

Now it was time to try an overnight summer music camp, unlike the roving music festivals the French musicians and others had put on in recent summers. For help Ramzi had reconnected with his former viola teacher, Peter Sulski, who had quit the London Symphony Orchestra and now made regular trips to Palestine as a teacher. Neither man, however, had done anything like this. In addition, Ramzi was pulled in many directions, as usual; he was still recording and touring with Dalouna in France, and soon he had to leave for Salzburg, in another tour with the Divan. Given his experience with the Israeli musicians the summer before, in Andalucía, Ramzi had mixed feelings about the trip. Still, he hadn't given up the hope in encounter with the Israelis. More important, the Divan was an opportunity for Ramzi to reconnect with Daniel, elevate his level of musicianship, and make contacts for Al Kamandjati.

Given Ramzi's constant movement, planning for the summer camp was minimal, and supplies and resources scarce. Teachers drew up sheet music on blank paper with a straight edge and a pen. Someone forgot the spare reeds for the woodwinds, so they fixed old, cracked ones with a knife.

At night the campers filled the stone and tile rooms with bedrolls, four to twelve to a room. Unscreened windows, through which legions of mosquitos would pass each night, prompted shouts of *"Merde!"* as the visiting French instructors slapped themselves in the dark. In the mornings one hundred students and teachers waited in line for the five bathrooms, then returned to stash their bedrolls in a corner. Thus the rooms became practice spaces for individual or group instruction, or orchestral sectionals for violin, trombone, and flute.

Most of the students still played at the most basic level, and the visiting teachers often didn't know where to start. Fany Maselli, an Italian bassoonist living in Paris, showed them how to tap out rhythms on their bodies. When they finally picked up their instruments, the students were so raw,

Fany often had to point to each note: "You have to play this, this, *this*!" Eventually they began working on a deceptively simple piece to teach: the third movement of Mahler's First Symphony, first performed in 1889. The first part of the movement was based on the French folk song "Frère Jacques," converted by minor chords to an ominous dirge. Its trancelike pace depicted the funeral of a hunter followed by a procession of animals. But it remained an accessible children's song, easy to grasp while allowing the kids a measure of emotional expression. Because of the repetitive phrases—it was a round, like "Row, Row, Row Your Boat"—it was relatively easy to teach; young violinists like Alá, now nine, or flutists like Rasha, fifteen, could enter the music when they wanted, and their mistakes would be less noticeable.

Thus, on a sunny June afternoon in Palestine, the sounds of a French folk song, converted to a funeral dirge in Budapest by a Jewish composer from Bohemia, came to life in the two-hundred-year-old courtyard of an Ottoman sheikh, performed by Palestinian children, themselves surrounded by Israeli tanks and settlements just beyond the palace walls.

In the evenings Shehada and the other shabab brought in platters of rice, chicken, soft round bread, salads of tomatoes, cucumbers and mint, and slices of watermelon. The campers dined in the courtyard, in stairwells, or atop the low walls of the rooftop veranda, which afforded a spectacular view of the hills of northern Palestine. In the early evening they gazed toward the Mediterranean fifteen miles away, the sun descending on the long ships shimmering on the water. The sea, like much of the Palestinian landscape before them, was off-limits to nearly all of the students.

The view from Sheikh Qasem's rooftop offered dramatic evidence of the fragmentation of Palestine. A string of Jewish settlements ran along the hilltops from north to south. They were connected by a settlers-only road, a half mile away, which Palestinians were prohibited from crossing. Local residents who wanted to visit family in Zawata, a village barely half a mile away, were required to drive nine miles.

Thus did settlements and exclusive roads splinter Nablus and surrounding villages into small islands of quasi-sovereign Palestinian territory, surrounded by a sea of Israeli military control. The city of 130,000 was ringed by fourteen Israeli settlements and twenty-six informal Jewish "outposts." Fourteen years after the Oslo accords, Palestinians exercised nominal sovereignty over 18 percent of the West Bank. The West Bank, in turn, made up barely one fifth of historic Palestine. Thus Palestinians, whose national liberation movement had, for decades, sought to reclaim all the land between the Mediterranean and the River Jordan, now had semiautonomous control over 4 percent of it.

The Gaza Strip was cut off entirely. In recent weeks Gaza had been roiled with street battles between Fatah and Hamas militias. The two factions had sought to form a unity government, despite American objections and threats to Mahmoud Abbas, but talks collapsed, in part over disagreements over peace talks with Israel. In June the Battle of Gaza claimed more than one hundred lives. Senior American officials were encouraged by the de facto civil war. An American envoy told his U.N. counterpart, "I like this violence," explaining that this indicated Fatah was willing to fight and perhaps would take power in Gaza. Yet despite American involvement in arranging arms shipments and covert aid to Fatah, Hamas prevailed, routing Fatah forces and assuming full control of Gaza. Curiously, this outcome was welcomed by some Israeli officials. Israel's director of military intelligence told the American ambassador in Tel Aviv that a Hamas victory would allow Israel "to treat Gaza" as a separate, "hostile country," and that he would be "pleased" if Abbas "set up a separate regime in the West Bank." The prospect of a Palestinian state that included the West Bank and Gaza seemed more remote than ever.

After dinner at the palace, the students sat on the rooftop to play the music of their homeland. During the day, most studied European classical music, but at night, especially, the music of Palestine and the broader Arab world took hold.

Rasha brought her flute and Alá, her little violin. Alá wore pink sandals and a T-shirt adorned with pink butterflies; a pink rose decal was pasted on her forehead. Scattered dots and strips of light glowed and flickered in the distance: white, from the Palestinian villages; green, from the mosques; high-intensity yellow, from the settlements and military bases; blinking reds, from the army surveillance towers.

Their backs to this tableau, the Palestinian musicians turned inward, facing each other, and began to play. The sounds of ouds and strings, flute, clarinet, bouzouk, and tablas filled the night air. As the delighted Europeans clapped in rhythm, Oday stood up, humming a long *mawal*, the undulating prelude to the prison song "Oheina Ilil Ghubsi Omi" ("I Yearn for My Mother's Bread"), a favorite song among Palestinian prisoners. For more than a year, Ramzi had instructed Oday to rest his voice while it changed. Now, at age sixteen, he sang like a man. Oday's voice rode above the Arabic strings, the clarinet and tabla, carrying over the valley of Beit Wazan and rising toward a black sky studded with pinholes of light.

After the concert Rasha sat with three of her fellow students—Mahmoud, a violinist, Amir, a guitarist, and Muntasser, the clarinetist—and a few of the French teachers. Their legs were crossed atop the cool pavement stones; they craned their necks toward the night sky.

All four students, the stars of Al Kamandjati, dreamed of going to France, like Ramzi had, to study music, then returning to Palestine as Al Kamandjati teachers. Rasha knew she faced the biggest challenge. Two of her uncles, including one in prison, disapproved of her mixing with boys, and would surely oppose her studying in France. Shehada, as the older brother, also withheld his approval, as did her father, Nabeel. But Rasha had told Ramzi she wanted to go to France. He knew it would be difficult, but he had a plan in mind.

Rasha herself seemed surprised at her own attitude. It was only two years earlier that she had told Ramzi she would never sit next to boys at Al Kamandjati. But Rasha, and everyone around her, had witnessed her transformation from an angry, submissive child to a confident, expressive, self-respecting musician.

Rasha could not precisely describe the feeling this music gave her—Ramzi himself would laugh and say, "If I could tell you what I feel when I play, I wouldn't need to play"—but she did know that Bach's Sonata no. 2, arranged for flute, affected her most deeply. Others have described Bach's sonatas and partitas as his most brilliant and emotional: "like a prayer book," "a lifetime's journey," "a whole world of the deepest thoughts and most powerful feelings," "the incredible depth and mystery in his music that brings us close to the very nucleus of existence," "perhaps the greatest example in any art form of a master's ability to move with freedom and assurance, even in chains." Rasha, playing the Sonata no. 2, adapted for her flute, nearly three centuries after it was written, simply thought: *It makes me happy.*

The musicians' reverie was broken by the sound of gunfire and the thump of rotor blades from Israeli helicopters in the valley near Nablus.

Their flashing lights were plainly visible from the rooftop. Israel's operation had intensified in recent days. Nablus and the adjacent Balata refugee camp remained focal points of militant resistance to the occupation. Nightly incursions by the army had led to arrests of dozens of youths; Israel reported finding stashes of rifles and explosives, and reserved the right "to take any necessary action to prevent terrorism against Israelis." Officials in the Palestinian Authority, attempting to rein in the militants, found themselves caught in the middle. On the one hand, they struggled to comply with American and Israeli demands for order, and their commitment to the Oslo process. On the other, they faced a restive Nablus population, which saw no end to the occupation, Israel's collective punishment, or the expanding settlement project all around them.

On the fourth day of the summer camp, the French consulate in East Jerusalem sent diplomatic cars to the palace to retrieve the French musicians. They left the summer camp early, embarrassed and upset with their embassy and unable to explain to their students why they had to go, and leave them behind.

*   *   *

In mid-July Ramzi landed in Salzburg to perform with the West-Eastern Divan Orchestra, under the direction of Daniel Barenboim, in one of the world's most celebrated music festivals. Scarcely two weeks earlier he had been looking out at the lights of Palestine from the rooftop of Sheikh Qasem's palace as gunfire erupted in the distance. Now, in the city of Mozart's birth, he strolled freely along the Salzach River through the old city, past ancient spires, domes, and palaces.

The Divan was now eight years old, and many of the players had been together since its inaugural summer in 1999. Many were still only in their early twenties. Yet it was no longer a youth orchestra, and audiences and reviewers were beginning to take its work seriously. The orchestra's Salzburg program for the summer of 2007 included Beethoven's *Leonore* Overture no. 3, pp. 72; Schoenberg's Variations for Orchestra, pp. 31; and Tchaikovsky's Symphony no. 6 in B Minor, op. 74, the *Pathétique*.

For Ramzi the Divan presented an annual opportunity to return to serious personal musicianship, away from the worries of running a music school, where all of the logistics and planning kept him away from his instruments far too much. Compared to his fellow musicians, however, he was out of practice. Many of them were full-time orchestral or chamber musicians in Amman, Tel Aviv, Jerusalem, Cairo, Damascus, Beirut, Berlin, Frankfurt, Lisbon, and San Antonio, Texas. They were constantly sharpening their skills; Ramzi, less so. As each year went by, this was increasingly evident. Ramzi's days were taken up largely with administrative and organizing duties. Musically, he was playing more bouzouk in Arabic ensembles than viola in orchestral settings. Yet Ramzi's seven years of classical training in Angers meant he could still hold his own in the Divan, and his ambivalence about coming to Salzburg had little to do with his musicianship.

Ramzi's admiration for Edward and Daniel had brought him into the orchestra. "I couldn't say no to Daniel when he came to Palestine," he remembered. He appreciated Daniel's humanity and generous spirit, and his political courage in support of the Palestinians. Ramzi would never forget Daniel visiting his home at Al Amari camp. But this human connection was not enough to eliminate Ramzi's misgivings about playing in the Divan. Even the chance to play for one of the world's great conductors, and to receive special training on the viola in Germany, as Daniel had offered, was not enough. For Ramzi there was a surreal gap between the unrelenting military occupation, which he had just come from, and the splendid orchestra in Salzburg, which evoked the symbol of peace but refused, in his view, to publicly stand with the Palestinians.

"All of them want to make peace, but they stop at that word," Ramzi said. "They don't want to go into detail, and say the occupation should stop." For this reason, some Palestinians already classified the Divan Orchestra as a normalization project. For these critics, the Divan's refusal to criticize the occupation meant it tacitly accepted the situation as "normal." Ramzi, whose own music school was still getting a foothold in Palestine, could not afford such associations. The best way to counter the normalization charges, he believed, would be for the Divan Orchestra to draft a document denouncing Israel's military occupation of his homeland. That, Ramzi believed, more than music, was his work in Salzburg.

"I went to the Divan," Ramzi declared, "to make them take a stand."

Daniel was eager to give Ramzi a platform, in front of both the international press and the orchestra itself. Daniel and Ramzi often sat side by side at press conferences across Europe. Ramzi was ambivalent about the appearances. He was constantly alert to being used as a token Palestinian and didn't want anyone to think that by participating in the orchestra, he somehow endorsed the status quo in Palestine. Yet Ramzi's story, and the savvy with which he told it, captivated the European press, and he often used the occasions to advocate for the Palestinian cause. For Daniel, Ramzi's presence gave his efforts more credibility: Here, after all, was one of the few Divan musicians who actually lived under occupation in Palestine. Edward Said had been gone since 2003, and while Ramzi would never replace Edward, his presence alongside Daniel gave the Divan an eloquent and outspoken Palestinian presence it had lacked for years.

Yuval Shapiro, the Israeli trumpeter who initially wanted to "kick this guy's ass" for throwing stones, now found himself drawn to Ramzi's story. "He kind of opened my mind," he said. Yuval began to reflect about "what this occupation means. He's living in distress. His life is seriously affected by this system." As Ramzi and others brought new perspectives to the orchestra—as the musicians heard tales of checkpoints and settlements and saw maps of an increasingly occupied Palestine—Yuval began to soften. He considered the downside of the concrete barrier his country was building to separate the two peoples. "My reaction was, I think the wall [the barrier is part wall and part series of fences] is there and it's doing its job. I was like, keep them over there. I had no idea what that fence was all about." Soon he was asking himself why he kept calling it a fence. "You know, a six-[actually eight-]meter concrete barrier is not a fence."

Ramzi kept pressing in the hopes he could convince the entire Divan to make the statement against the occupation. At times he felt he was making progress. Other times, he wondered why he had ever agreed to join the orchestra. When he suggested that the group light candles for the children under siege in Palestine, Israeli musicians countered, *What about the Israeli children?*

Daniel believed it a mistake to force everyone to adopt an official position if some in the group felt uncomfortable about it. The simple existence of the orchestra, he was convinced, showed what equality could mean. From that would come a fierce and uncompromising commitment to the music. In this way the Divan could carve a path around the politics, or through it. "I think that these kinds of conflicts, in a way, cannot be solved by political means," Daniel said. "A politician can only work and do good if he masters the art of compromise . . . whereas the artist's expression is only determined by his total refusal to compromise in anything." This, Daniel said, was "the element of courage. Courage in the act of music-making."

In Salzburg, audiences received the Divan's performances in that spirit.

"The woodwinds shone, the brass imposed, the kettledrums thrilled," wrote a reviewer of the Divan's rendering of Beethoven's *Leonore* in Salzburg. "And then, of course, there was the trumpet call. There was never to be any question that this meant something more than words, more than politics, more than any mortal, could ever express. The stunned silence of the hall, as its echoes resounded, spoke more truly than any politician could ever imagine. The quality of freedom is not strained, as Beethoven knew only too well. So did his performers."

For Ramzi, in Salzburg as in Spain, the political discord dissolved in the music, at least for the time it was played. In the first notes of the program's finale, Tchaikovsky's 1893 *Pathétique*, Ramzi leaned forward into his downbow, joining double basses and cellos in a foreboding line rising from the opening phrase of a solemn bassoon. In its Russian context, *pathétique* was understood as "impassioned suffering," and as he produced the dark colors, Ramzi's mind drifted to his family in Palestine. A French horn signaled a shift, and the piece rose in ascending scales and a cascading of flutes, violins, clarinets, and cellos. Tchaikovsky's drama always surprised Ramzi, especially in the *Pathétique* and its immense range of emotions— despair, glory, elation, sadness—even within a single movement. As with other music he loved most, it delivered Ramzi from his immediate surroundings, transporting him even as he helped create the symphony itself.

Then the musicians left the stage.

After the performance, the orchestra and distinguished guests of the Salzburg Festival were dining in a palatial banquet hall, at large round tables covered by white linen, when Ramzi spotted an open chair next to Kyril Zlotnikov, a gifted cellist who was originally from Minsk, Belarus. Around the time of the collapse of the Soviet Union, Kyril and his family became part of the wave of Jewish migration to Israel. They settled in Gilo, on land captured by Israel during the 1967 war. Israel considered Gilo to be a neighborhood or suburb, part of "Greater Jerusalem," just north of Bethlehem. Gilo, however, was built in part on lands seized from the nearby Palestinian villages of Beit Jala, Beit Safa, and Sharafat. Under international law, Gilo was considered an illegal settlement. Kyril, who was already a prodigy when he left the former Soviet Union, arrived in Gilo in 1991, when he and Ramzi were both twelve years old. The two boys grew up ten miles apart.

A few weeks earlier, Ramzi had heard that Kyril was from Gilo. He had been waiting for a chance to confront him. He pulled up a chair at the large banquet table. "I don't understand how come somebody like you can live in a settlement," Ramzi said. Kyril was taken aback. He did not expect to be questioned like this, in the middle of dinner and after such a performance. "I just thought it was an inappropriate moment for him to start accusing me," Kyril remembered. He told Ramzi, "Let's talk about it later. Everybody is so happy. The concert is finished. Let's have a good dinner."

The entire table had fallen silent; musicians and Austrian dignitaries were staring in surprise at the two young men. Ramzi pressed on: "You are actually creating a problem for coexistence. How can you believe in the settlements and participate in such a project as the Divan?"

Kyril explained that his parents had arrived poor from Russia twenty years earlier—six people with a total of nine hundred dollars—and were given a cheap house in Gilo.

"You know why it's cheap?" Ramzi said. "Because it's on stolen land."

Kyril, like many Israelis, believed that Gilo, despite its being built on Palestinian land, was "an integral part of Jerusalem."

"We got used to it," Ramzi recalled Kyril saying. "It's comfortable for us now."

"I don't understand," Ramzi replied sarcastically. "You waited three thousand years to come back to the promised land, but you can't change after twenty years?"

Ramzi was appalled that a settler would be allowed into the Divan Orchestra. He went to Daniel. "In this orchestra there should be no settler," he said. Daniel pointed out that Kyril no longer lived in Gilo. Should everyone be punished for where they once lived?

For Ramzi it didn't matter that Kyril now lived in Portugal. "I don't give a fuck," he said later. "I can also say that I lived in France. This doesn't deny the truth: Your family is there and you grew up there. He still has a chance to take them out of that house, to at least give that house back."

It wasn't likely that Daniel would dismiss Kyril from the West-Eastern Divan Orchestra. The maestro had already lent Kyril the cello played by his late wife, the legendary Jacqueline du Pré, who died prematurely in 1987, fourteen years after being diagnosed with the multiple sclerosis that cut short her brilliant career.

Despite his qualms about Kyril, and his ambivalence about participating in the Divan, Ramzi decided to stay in the orchestra for now. He hadn't given up his efforts to convert his colleagues. His decision to stay created musical opportunities for Al Kamandjati. In Ramallah, the Barenboim-Said Foundation helped provide teachers for Ramzi's school. Daniel and Mariam, through the government of Andalucía, helped secure funds for more instruments for Al Kamandjati. And in the fall of 2007, Daniel himself promised to perform with Ramzi in Ramallah.

Ramzi's decision to stay was also good for Daniel. Many concertgoers seemed to think the Divan Orchestra was only made up of Israelis and Palestinians, even though the vast majority of the Arabs in the orchestra were from other lands. Ramzi's Palestinian identity gave Daniel an authenticity he sought for his orchestra. He didn't want to lose Ramzi.

*   *   *

In September Daniel returned to Al Kamandjati with his son, Misha, first violinist with the Divan. Ramzi arranged a rooftop concert. The event went unpublicized, but word spread quickly, and the roof was packed as the members of the chamber music quintet took their seats at dusk on the mild September evening in Old Ramallah. Daniel sat at the piano, his hands poised at the keyboard. Now the muezzin's voice sliced into the silence before the music, singing the evening prayer from the loudspeakers of the mosque next door.

After a few moments the call to prayer faded, and Daniel looked at Ramzi, ready with his viola. Misha breathed in sharply, the members of the string quartet drew down their bows, Daniel followed with a lilting upward trill, and the strings carried into Schubert's Trout Quintet.

The Trout was one of Ramzi's favorite pieces, and he felt lucky to be playing it—to be collaborating, listening, and creating the harmony of chamber music—with one of the world's most respected musicians. Strangely, though, the elation he had expected to feel was missing, replaced by an ambivalence and by a creeping feeling that he wasn't trying his best. Many in the audience may have simply noted that Ramzi was not in the same league as Daniel, or his son, but Ramzi sensed something else: He was holding back. Again he felt like a token Palestinian—if not for his ethnicity Daniel would have never chosen to play with him—and he worried about conveying a false impression of actual harmony between his people and Daniel's. Never could he let anyone forget the occupation.

It was confusing. He believed Daniel's efforts to reach out to him were sincere; yet Ramzi felt tremendous pressure, given his past, his identity, and the situation on the ground, not to return the embrace of a mentor who offered tremendous opportunity others could not begin to touch. *Opportunity at what price?* he thought as the five musicians played into the deepening dusk. *What's the price?*

Tania Nasir sat in a wooden folding chair on the Al Kamandjati rooftop, listening to Daniel and Ramzi perform. It was Tania who had invited Daniel and Edward to her home in Birzeit for dinner in 1998, and who had attended Daniel's piano recital the next evening in West Jerusalem. After the concert that evening at Al Kamandjati, Tania and Daniel greeted each other warmly, exchanging pleasantries and asking about each other's family. Then Daniel asked, "Why are people being negative about the Divan?"

It had been two years since Daniel had brought the orchestra to Ramallah, and since then, the BDS (Boycott, Divestment and Sanctions) movement had begun to rattle Israeli leaders. An international marketing survey found that "Israel's brand is by a considerable margin the most negative we have ever measured." Worried, Israel's Foreign Ministry launched a "Brand Israel" campaign to change the country's perceptions in the United States. "We need a strategy that includes more positive imaging," declared one of Brand Israel's American advocates. Another compared Israel to "a product undergoing an overhaul to make it more competitive in the marketplace."

Palestinians were skeptical of efforts to buff Israel's image, and some saw the Divan Orchestra through this lens. Yet Daniel did not understand. The Divan was not an Israeli institution, and Daniel himself had perhaps taken more courageous stands than any Israeli public figure. He was stung by the increasing negativity to the orchestra.

"Things are different now, Daniel," Tania told him. "They are so totally different from when your dream with Edward began. You need to understand this. It's just that it doesn't fit anymore. Please, Daniel, just see this. We genuinely respect and appreciate what you're trying to do." The problem, Tania believed, was not with Daniel; it was that the Divan itself was not perceived as an orchestra that had taken a strong stand with the Palestinians, and against the occupation. "Don't think it's personal, Daniel," Tania told him.

But it was difficult for Daniel not to take it personally. As an individual, he had repeatedly put himself on the line in his own country for advocating for the Palestinian cause: declaring solidarity with the plight of occupied Palestine, deploring the occupation in Israel's Knesset, performing repeatedly in the West Bank and Gaza, and, with Mariam Said, generating funds for scholarships for Arab musicians and, through the Spanish regional government, helping to secure funds for Al Kamandjati.

For Palestinians, these acts of solidarity were one thing; the role of the Divan was another. To Tania, Daniel did not seem to grasp how much the political landscape had shifted since the early days of Oslo. Palestinians were less sympathetic to lofty ideals like dialogue toward reconciliation, or witnessing each other's painful history; rather, they simply demanded an end to a brutal four-decade occupation. Because of that, the political situation had changed: Once-popular joint Israeli-Palestinian efforts had fallen out of favor, and the boycott had emerged as a powerful nonviolent tool of resistance. Increasingly Palestinians said they could only support the Divan if it were a "refusenik" orchestra—made up of individuals who denounced the occupation and who, like their conductor, each stood in open solidarity with their Palestinian brethren. That, however, was extremely unlikely to ever happen. Tania and Daniel both knew that.

As they parted that warm night in the courtyard of Al Kamandjati, Tania saw the hurt in Daniel's eyes. She felt overcome by a sense of sadness and loss, and wondered when she'd see Daniel again.

As his old friend Edward might have urged him, Daniel pressed on. A few months later, after a piano recital in Ramallah, Daniel Barenboim accepted Mustafa Barghouti's invitation to become a Palestinian citizen. It was mostly symbolic, of course—there was still no state called Palestine—but to Daniel, it was real. "It is a great honor to be offered a passport," he said, standing next to Mustafa and other Palestinian dignitaries. Daniel was the first person to ever hold Israeli and Palestinian passports. "The destinies are inextricably linked," he said. "We are blessed—or cursed—to live with each other. And I prefer the first.

"I'm a living example that it's possible to be both."

Twenty-two

LUTHIER

Spring 2008
Near Hebron

O NE EVENING, RIDING home from a concert in Bethlehem, Alá,
Rasha, and a few of their fellow musicians suddenly came upon a
military barrier erected hastily in the road. HALT! commanded a sign, in
Arabic and Hebrew. Just beyond, an olive-clad soldier was checking
documents.

"Flying checkpoint," Rasha said. These were temporary barriers the
military erected on the fly for the stated purpose of catching suspected
militants, and those without proper documents, who might try to evade
the fixed checkpoints. Also known as random or "surprise" checkpoints,
they were so ubiquitous that Alá and Rasha were never surprised to
encounter them. "It's normal," Alá said.

More than any single reality in Palestine, checkpoints defined life under
occupation. By 2008, the number of flying checkpoints had reached 90
per week, part of the 630 "closure obstacles" Israel had erected across the
West Bank, a territory the size of Connecticut. Three-fourths of the main
roads leading into the West Bank's biggest cities and towns were now
blocked or controlled by checkpoints. Military authorities said the strict
measures were necessary to protect Israeli lives. Palestinians and humanitarian organizations saw them as a means for Israel to control the occupied
population and protect the movements of settlers who had illegally seized
Palestinian lands. "What was once justified by the Israeli authorities as
a short-term military response to violent confrontations and attacks on

Israeli civilians," declared a semiannual U.N. report on the occupation, "appears to be developing into a permanent system; a system, which is fragmenting the West Bank territory and affecting the freedom of movement of the entire Palestinian population."

Encounters at checkpoints could be deadly, but mostly, for Alá and Rasha, they were humiliating—dehumanizing reminders of who had control. Recently a soldier had ordered Rasha to play her flute at the infamous Huwara checkpoint near Nablus. At Huwara, at the height of the Second Intifada, two pregnant women had been shot on consecutive days; another had given birth to a stillborn baby after waiting for five hours to get to the hospital; a ten-year-old girl had died of a ruptured appendix when soldiers denied her passage; and a man with metastasizing liver cancer, a forty-five year old who worked in a Nablus hummus shop, was denied his wish to die at home. He died at Huwara.

At the "flying checkpoint," the van carrying Alá and Rasha slowed and came to a stop. The sisters gazed at the sign. Behind the soldier a military Humvee blocked the road. The soldier beckoned the van forward. He opened the sliding door.

"What's that?" the soldier asked Alá, pointing to her soft blue instrument case.

"This is a violin," replied Alá, now ten years old.

The soldier told her to step out of the van.

"Do you know how to play?" he asked.

"Yes."

"Play," instructed the soldier.

"Don't play for him!" Rasha yelled in Arabic.

"Play," repeated the soldier.

Alá frowned, looking into the van uncertainly.

Muntasser, the clarinet player, said softly, "It's okay. Play, *habibti.*" Play, my dear.

Ramzi's main purpose for founding Al Kamandjati, he had said many times, was to protect the children from the soldiers. The statement often sounded like a slogan or a sound bite. But Alá, Rasha, and other children of Al Kamandjati had begun to wear their music as a kind of armor, and now, at the flying checkpoint, Alá calmly removed her violin, placed it under her chin, stood erect, and began to play. She had chosen "El Helwadi," or "The Beautiful Girl," a song by Sayed Darwish, made famous by Fairouz.

Ramzi Aburedwan, Al Amari refugee camp, 1988 (Keith Dannemiller)

Ramzi and other youths at Al Amari refugee camp, 1988, in the early months of the first Palestinian intifada (Courtesy Younis Aburish/Al Amari Youth Club)

Ramzi at a musical workshop, Al Amari refugee camp, 2005 (Margarida Mota)

Ramzi Aburedwan, 1987 and 1997, in a poster promoting the National Conservatory of Music in Palestine

Ramzi, Al Amari, 2005 (Margarida Mota)

Musical workshop, 2004
(Arnaud Brunet/NEUS)

Israeli soldiers at the Bethlehem-Jerusalem checkpoint restrict access for Palestinians trying to pass through to pray at Al-Aqsa mosque during the holy month of Ramadan. (Nayef Hashlamoun/ALWATAN CENTER)

Jessie Nguenang and touring French musicians, Al Amari refugee camp, 2004 (Arnaud Brunet/NEUS)

Ramzi and his grandparents, Al Amari refugee camp (Georges Bartoli)

Ramzi and Karim Rissouli with
Yasser Arafat

Al Kamandjati courtyard, 2005

Opening night, Al Kamandjati,
August 2005 (Margarida Mota)

Children with "snow" confetti, Al Kamandjati opening night, August 2005 (Margarida Mota)

Palestinian pedestrian corridor at the barrier between Bethlehem and Jerusalem. Palestinians call the corridor "the chicken-plucking machine." (Sandy Tolan)

Ramzi and Oday Khatib, 2005

Al Kamandjati summer camp, Sheikh Qassem Palace, West Bank, 2007 (Courtesy Al Kamandjati)

Celine Dagher, Al Amari (Margarida Mota)

Al Kamandjati summer music festival, Sebastia, West Bank (Ahmad Odeh)

Palestinian day laborers wait to enter Israel, Taybeh checkpoint, summer 2012 (David Heap/EAPPI/World Council of Churches)

Fadi Basha (Courtesy Al Kamandjati)

Julia Katarina, Al Kamandjati vocal teacher, 2009, guiding a student recital (Suby Raman)

Ramzi and Oday Khateeb, Angers, France

Alá Shalalda, Toulouse, France, 2012 (Nabeel Shalalda)

Benjamin Payen with young violinist, Al Amari refugee camp, 2009 (Courtesy Al Kamandjati)

Charred ouds, Al Kamandjati's Jenin center, 2009 (Courtesy Al Kamandjati)

Alice Howick with violin student at a West Bank Palestinian
refugee camp (Courtesy Al Kamandjati)

Jason Crompton (back to camera) prepares to conduct the Al Kamandjati
Youth Orchestra, Battir, West Bank, 2011 (Vincenzo Cascone)

The widow and son of Mohammad Mahmoud Tarifi, killed by an Israeli
soldier during clashes in Ramallah, summer 2014. Tarifi was the best friend
of Al Kamandjati clarinetist Muntasser Jebrini. (Fadi Arouri)

Shehada Shalalda in his instrument workshop at Al Kamandjati, Ramallah, 2013
(Sandy Tolan)

Celine Dagher (Didier Bizet)

Al Kamandjati instruction, Al Amari refugee camp (Margarida Mota)

Funeral in Gaza, 2014 (Photo by Mahmud Hams/Courtesy AFP)

Alá Shalalda, Al Kamandjati rooftop, summer 2014 (Didier Bizet)

Al Kamandjati courtyard

Ramzi Aburedwan, Celine Dagher, and their children, Hussein (5) and Adam (2),
January 2015 (Fadia Dagher)

A haunting melody floated from Alá's little violin—an "Oriental" sound, as it was called in Israel and the West. Certain and strong, Alá's notes cut through the low rumble of idling cars and floated above the flying checkpoint, into the night air.

"We saw in his eyes, he was shocked," Alá remembered. "It was something he didn't understand."

In the melody, the sisters could recall the words, about a penniless child whose mood is serene, for she has put her life in God's hands. With patience, change will come; all will be better.

Rasha, staring intently from inside the van, felt a surge of pride in her little sister, playing unfazed. "They claim that we are people with no identity, but Alá proved them wrong," she said. Music, Rasha believed, was not only a source of pride; it was a means of assertion, protection, and even, at times, vengeance.

Then the moment turned.

Another soldier walked over to listen. He was smiling and seemed to be enjoying the impromptu concert. "I play, too," he said when Alá finished. "May I try?" Another soldier asked Amir, the guitar student, if he could borrow his instrument.

The soldiers began to play, smiling at Alá and her fellow musicians, who gaped at them in astonishment.

Suddenly, to Rasha, the soldiers seemed like normal people. "I do not know how they can do something like this but at the same time treat people so badly," she said, genuinely confused. "I don't know if they have two personalities, or exactly how it works."

Soon the van was on its way back to Ramallah, leaving its passengers to wonder who those soldiers were, and what it might be like to meet them under different circumstances.

Alá and Rasha had never known a moment without occupation and checkpoints, and when the sisters dreamed, as they often did, of liberation, or spoke wistfully of living in a free Palestine, it was always in the abstract. For fifteen years, though, since the signing of the Oslo agreement, Palestinian, Israeli, and American negotiators had been discussing an actual Palestinian state, which, in theory, would be "viable and contiguous," meaning that it would be whole enough, and sovereign enough, to function as a free and independent Palestine, alongside Israel.

In 2008, nearly eight years after the failure of the 2000 negotiations at Camp David, and the subsequent Road Map discussions, Bush administration officials met with Israeli and Palestinian negotiators in an attempt to finally resolve the matter. By now about half a million settlers lived in the West Bank and East Jerusalem; for the West Bank, this was nearly three times as many as when the Oslo deal was signed. Oslo, it was clear, had done nothing to prevent settlement expansion. If anything, it had facilitated it. To address this issue, some Israeli engineers had drawn up plans for tunnels and bridges to whisk Palestinians under and around the settlements. Palestinian negotiators insisted this was not the kind of "viable and contiguous" state they had in mind. This would make permanent the fragmented Palestinian reality, which was increasingly compared to South African Bantustans during the apartheid era. The two sides agreed to land swaps that would allow some of the settlements to stay and be incorporated into Israel, on its side of the separation barrier. Israel promised a narrow passage to connect the West Bank to Gaza. However, Israel refused to withdraw from two of its largest settlements, Ariel and Ma'ale Adumim, which together held more than fifty thousand settlers deep inside a would-be Palestine. The separation barrier cut halfway into the West Bank to embrace Ariel, and under the Israeli proposal, that would not change. The United States, as the self-described "honest broker," aligned itself with the Israeli proposal.

"I don't think that any Israeli leader is going to cede Ma'ale Adumim," U.S. secretary of state Condoleezza Rice told a senior Palestinian negotiator, Ahmed Qurei.

"Or any Palestinian leader," Qurei replied. For many Palestinians, including Ramzi and thousands of refugee families, even the deal that Qurei held out for was unacceptable, because it didn't include their right to return to their old homelands. Palestinian negotiators appeared willing to forego that right, but to convince a bare majority of their people to accept the current deal, they knew they would need at least to deliver a whole, connected West Bank and Gaza. The Palestinian leadership, Qurei told the Americans, had already agreed to a state on 22 percent of its historic homeland, and his people could not compromise any further.

"Then you won't have a state!" Rice declared, echoing Bill Clinton's words to Yasser Arafat eight years earlier: "You won't have a Palestinian state and you won't have friendships with anyone." Despite Rice's warning,

Palestinian negotiators in 2008 refused to accept such a large settler presence in the middle of their would-be state, and the negotiations, once again, collapsed.

*   *   *

In the summer of 2008 Ramzi secured funds from Italian donors so that Alá, Rasha, and twenty other Al Kamandjati students could travel to northern Italy to play concerts and take part in workshops with local musicians. For many of them, this would be their first trip outside an occupied land. At first it wasn't clear whether the sisters would be allowed to travel on their own to another country, but Ramzi convinced their father, Nabeel, to go along as a chaperone. Shehada, now sixteen, would travel with the group, staying on in Florence with a master luthier to build his first violin, by hand. Ramzi had recognized Shehada's talent and dedication in brief instrument-making workshops at Al Kamandjati; now it was time for the next step.

With the students away in Italy, quiet settled into the Al Kamandjati courtyard. Ramzi and Celine had time to catch up on fund-raising, make final plans for the coming summer music festival—and move in together. Visiting musicians and students alike had noticed that lately, they seemed to be spending a lot of time together, even outside of work. Years earlier Oday had made Celine blush by telling her that she should marry Ramzi. Yet this sort of thing was considered a private matter, especially in conservative Old Ramallah. Ramzi and Celine, a Muslim and a Christian, had kept their relationship to themselves. Now it was no longer a secret; the couple had a home together, in a flat a short walk from the music school.

Ramzi kept up with the Italy trip through e-mails from Nabeel. The children were performing in village squares and making friends along the way. A Palestinian gelato shop owner had treated the family, refusing their money. At the Piazza della Signoria in Florence, the kids gaped at marble statues from the Renaissance period, naked in struggle. In another square, Alá froze, nervous and trying not to laugh, while pigeons landed on her head and arms and her father snapped photos.

For Alá, the freedom of movement in Italy was jarring. One day, riding toward the Mediterranean coast, she asked her father, "Baba, why aren't we being stopped?" They were in a rental car, heading toward Naples. Alá was confused: Nowhere could she see checkpoints, jeeps, or Humvees. *"Habibti,"* Nabeel replied softly. "Darling, this is Italy. This is not Palestine."

In Florence, Shehada was making slow but certain progress in his efforts to build his first violin, modeled on a Stradivarius. His mentor was the master Italian luthier Paolo Sorgentone, who sat beside him at a wooden workbench, showing him how to use a handsaw to slice into a wedge of maple, glue the wood, clamp it, and plane it smooth. From Paolo, Shehada learned how to carve a groove around the circumference and insert three super-thin decorative bands of wood, known as purfling: black ebony, white spruce, black ebony. For the ribs, Shehada soaked thin long strips of maple, and shaped them on a bending iron according to the instrument's dimensions. For the front, he used spruce, tracing the F holes, or sound holes, from a template stamped from X-ray film. He finished them with a delicate knife the size of a fountain pen. After all this meticulous attention Shehada became anxious to finish, but Paolo counseled patience. The violin would be a gift, and it needed proper attention.

After three weeks the entourage returned home, and the courtyard again filled up with conversation, laughter, and the sound of lessons drifting out from the practice rooms. Shehada stayed on with Paolo, working on his violin.

Rasha, back in occupied territory, sat in front of her father's computer, listlessly clicking through hundreds of photos of Italy: crazy clowns walking the streets; Alá in a yellow paper crown with a purple Dumbo on its front; statues of Neptune, Hercules, and the replica of Michaelangelo's David; her father posing in front of the leaning tower of Pisa, smiling and placing his hands just so, appearing to hold it up.

Rasha recalled a moment in Naples with her friend Bushra, a fellow flutist. They had been watching pasty-skinned sunbathers apply lotion to their arms and legs, behavior they found funny and strange. Somehow it made them feel melancholy. "We don't want to go back," Rasha had said, half-joking. "Just let us die over here."

A few weeks later, after a three-hour wait at the Allenby Bridge, during which time Israeli border guards inspected his sharp tools, fingerboards, and wooden sound posts, Shehada returned home. He set his bags down in the family courtyard, embraced his parents and his siblings, and, with a huge smile, handed a black instrument case to Alá. "Here, *ukhti,*" he said. "Here, my sister."

A smile grew slowly on Alá's face as she opened the case and realized what was inside. She looked at Shehada quizzically, then at the violin. Alá turned the instrument slowly in her hands, revealing the hand-carved bridge and above it the scroll, the carefully tapered fingerboard, and the taut metal strings, which, in Stradivarius's time, were made from sheep gut. In the final stages, Shehada explained, he sanded the instrument with dogfish skin, just as Stradivarius had done. For varnish, he whipped egg whites, then dipped a brush made of badger's hair into the liquid below the froth. Gently, he applied the final sheen to his instrument. Beneath a lattice of grape leaves, the violin shone reddish brown in the filtered afternoon light.

Alá peered inside the F holes. There, Shehada had emblazoned his signature:

Shehada Shalalda, de Ramallah Palestina
Firenze, Italia anno 2008

Near the F holes Alá could see a tiny wooden flag of Palestine: maple and ebony, painted black, white, red, and green.

Alá looked up at her brother. Shehada was beaming.

"For me?" she asked.

"Yes, *ukhti*," Shehada replied, touching her shoulder. "This is for you."

Twenty-three

FIRE

Late fall 2008
Ramallah

IN THE QUIET mornings Ramzi and Celine ambled down the four flights of stairs from Ramzi's flat and along the narrow streets of Old Ramallah. They walked toward the shadow of the minaret, past Ibrahim the tabla player's house, Eyad the barber's, Elias's shuttered falafel stand, Ali Baba's coffee shop, the Orthodox church, the competing produce markets with their careful pyramids of fruit, the grapevines in Alá and Rasha's courtyard, and up the stone path to the slanted copper door that marked the entrance to the music school. There a bleary-eyed Ramzi turned the key. Celine walked toward the back office and flipped on the lights while Ramzi inspected the plants. For Ramzi the quiet moments before the students arrived offered time to think. He wandered the courtyard with his watering can, dousing the jasmine and creeper vines.

Soon Ramzi would be a father. Recently he and Celine had shared happy news with their students and colleagues: Celine was pregnant. The baby was due in June.

As Al Kamandjati approached its fourth anniversary, it had begun to feel more like a functioning full-time music school with a professional couple at the helm. This contributed to a sense of stability that had been lacking in the earlier years.

Ramzi was the rainmaker, traveling frequently to perform in Europe, Beirut, and Dubai. He used the international stage to tell the story of Al

Kamandjati and inspire contributions or collaborations. His encounter with a Norwegian rock star led to a donation for a large white van to ferry the children across Palestine. The chance meeting with a fellow Palestinian musician, Iyad Staiti, had led to the creation of an Al Kamandjati branch in Jenin. A British heiress would leave forty-five thousand euros to Al Kamandjati in her will. The queen of the Netherlands would soon invite Ramzi to perform in her palace in Amsterdam. And Ramzi's trips to Beirut had created an opening for an Al Kamandjati presence in the Palestinian refugee camps there.

In Palestine, Al Kamandjati's energy no longer came primarily from international musicians using their vacation time and personal funds to visit Palestine for a few weeks. Those friends still came, for the summer music camps, the annual Music Days and baroque festivals, and for special workshops, but the heart of the day-to-day work was now being done by Celine and her fellow administrators, by Palestinians hired to teach Arabic music, and by the young musicians who had come to Palestine from abroad.

The teachers came from Europe, Palestine, and America, drawn by the story of Ramzi and Al Kamandjati, by the young traveler's spirit of adventure, and by the desire to use their musical talents for work that could make a difference in the world.

Benjamin Payen, a French violinist who played in a Spanish orchestra, had originally gone to Jerusalem to study with a master Israeli violinist. He had lived on the Israeli side of the wall. "Don't go there," Ben was told repeatedly about the Arab side. "You could get killed." Eventually he crossed over and met ordinary people. He traveled through the occupied territories, immersing himself in Palestinian culture and history before returning to Europe and rejoining his orchestra. But Ben, twenty-nine, with long frizzy hair he often wore in a ponytail, missed Palestine. He took his leave from the orchestra and returned. Before long he was teaching at Al Kamandjati and playing music to accompany his collection of old Harold Lloyd and Three Musketeers films, which he would screen on summer evenings in the refugee camps. He was trying to find something to make the children laugh.

Alice Howick, a British violinist with a freshly minted music degree from Cambridge, was looking for challenging work. Alice had first heard about Al Kamandjati from a friend who had founded the Choir of London, which performed occasional concerts in Jerusalem and the Occupied Territories with a combination of European and Palestinian vocalists.

Later, she arrived as a visiting violinist to play in Al Kamandjati's winter baroque festival, where she learned of openings at the music school. After returning home, she wrote to Celine, who hired her immediately.

Maddalena Pastorelli had been studying the flute in Siena, Italy and Lugano, Switzerland, working toward her master's degree, but found the programs too focused on creating standout soloists. She was put off by what she considered cut-throat competition. One night, Maddalena heard Ramzi and his French-Arabic band, Dalouna, at a concert in Siena. Soon after, she sent her CV to Al Kamandjati. She, too, was quickly hired.

Iyad Staiti, an oud player born in Jordan, had grown up dreaming of Palestine, the land of his parents and grandparents. After the opening created by the Oslo peace process, he had moved to Jenin—crying and kissing the ground when he crossed the River Jordan, as so many Palestinians did—and began to give oud lessons. Iyad had a calm, avuncular air; he wore a goatee and dressed in pressed slacks, and button-down shirts that betrayed a slight paunch. In 2003, he had met Ramzi in France in a rambling mansion used by the French Resistance as a safe house during the Nazi occupation. It had become a gathering place for various French and international solidarity organizations. It was here that Ramzi and Iyad had first discussed a new branch of Al Kamandjati, in Jenin, near the refugee camp. Now Iyad, thirty-two, was its coordinator.

Julia Katarina learned about Al Kamandjati the day she went to hear an acquaintance, Peter Sulski, play Brahms and Mozart in an English country mansion. Julia, thirty-one, was making a go as an opera singer. Pale-skinned, with an intense blue-eyed gaze and red hair that flowed halfway down her back, she had grown up in Forest Row, Sussex. There in late summer, purple heather lined country paths, wisteria crawled up brick walls, and weeping willows bent over English country gardens of echinacea and white roses. As a youth Julia worked as a bouncer at clubs, organized paintball games, played guitar in an all-girl punk rock band, picked up flamenco guitar, got inspired by Stravinsky and Tchaikovsky, began to play the cello, and eventually became interested in opera, which, her family and friends believed, was her truest calling. After the chamber music concert, Peter, Ramzi's former viola teacher, showed the French documentary, *It's Not a Gun*, about the building of Al Kamandjati. Julia was so impressed that within weeks she had put her opera career on hold and moved to Palestine to be the school's vocal teacher.

Jason Crompton's introduction to Palestine came on a visit to his sister, who was teaching English in the West Bank in a program sponsored by the American Consulate in Jerusalem. Jason, twenty-nine, was a pianist with degrees in music from the University of Michigan and New York University. He wore sandals and loose-fitting cotton pants, and sported a beard and a thick head of unruly brown hair. He had an open, friendly face and smiled frequently. Jason's sister had come to pick him up in Amman, and soon they crossed back to Jerusalem by land. They sat in the tourist bus at the border crossing. Jason saw Israeli soldiers everywhere; he had never been around so many people with guns. Soldiers with mirrors on long poles searched for bombs under the bus. Eventually, this would come to feel normal, but at the moment, Jason thought, *This is crazy*. Soon Jason would learn about Ramzi and an opening at Al Kamandjati for a piano teacher. What started as a brief visit with his sister evolved to a full-time job teaching music in the occupied territories.

For the Europeans and Americans, many barely out of college, low salaries and modest living conditions were acceptable trade-offs for a deeper sense of purpose at Al Kamandjati, and in Palestine, where they believed their work would be needed and appreciated. They settled in and around Old Ramallah, pairing up as roommates in the spacious, high-ceilinged flats with reddish stone walls and cream-tiled floors. During the days they taught music and learned Arabic. In the evenings they sipped arak and smoked hookah pipes (known locally as *argileh*), looking out from wrought-iron balconies over bustling streets jammed with high-end and discount clothing stores, electronics shops, ice cream parlors, bakeries, pharmacies, snack vendors, and posh cafés with free wireless connections. With East Jerusalem sealed off from most Palestinians, the once-sleepy Christian village had become the de facto capital of Palestine. Its sidewalks were jammed with people from all over the would-be nation. The energy in Ramallah was intense and vibrant.

*   *   *

In 2008, the prospects for Palestinian unity—both physical and political—remained bleak. Hamas and Fatah factions had continued their fighting, and U.S.-brokered peace negotiations had focused only on the fragmented West Bank as Israel treated Gaza, and Hamas, as a separate, hostile country. Israel countered Hamas rocket attacks with repeated air strikes and assassinations of Hamas leaders and lower-level operatives.

Israel and Hamas forged a cease-fire in 2008. A lonely voice in Israel's security establishment urged engagement with Hamas. Retired Brigadier General Shmuel Zakai, former commander of the IDF's Gaza division, implored his country "to take advantage of the calm to improve, rather than markedly worsen, the economic plight of the Palestinians in the [Gaza] Strip . . . You cannot just land blows, leave the Palestinians in Gaza in the economic distress they are in and expect Hamas just to sit around and do nothing." Israel would not heed that advice.

On November 4, 2008, election day in the United States, Israel broke a cease-fire with Hamas by bombing tunnels on the Egyptian border. Smugglers operated the tunnels, seeking to profit and to help ease the effects of Israel's blockade, but Israel saw these as conduits for arms trade and for attempted abduction of its soldiers. In response to the bombing, and to a raid the same day that killed six Hamas operatives, Hamas fired Qassam rockets into Israel. The two sides continued tit-for-tat strikes for weeks. In late December, Israel launched a massive military retaliation, which it called Operation Cast Lead. It lasted twenty-two days and caused more than thirteen hundred Palestinian deaths. Thirteen Israelis died, including three civilians and four soldiers by friendly fire. The Palestinian dead included twenty-seven unarmed police cadets marching in their graduation ceremony, killed by a laser-guided missile; fourteen children taking refuge near a U.N. school; and three daughters and a niece of Izzaldeen Abu al-Aish, a Harvard- and Israel-trained doctor and peace activist, whose home in a Gaza refugee camp was blasted by Israeli tank shells. The Israeli assault also destroyed or damaged twenty-two thousand buildings, including the Palestinian Red Crescent Society building, which housed the new Gaza Music School. The school, not related to Al Kamandjati, was demolished. On day seventeen of Operation Cast Lead, Tzipi Livni, Israel's foreign minister and a candidate for prime minister, declared that it had "restored Israel's deterrence . . . Hamas now understands that when you fire on its citizens it responds by going wild—and this is a good thing."

During a winter tour in Germany with the Divan in early 2009, Ramzi went to Daniel, urging solidarity with the people of Gaza. The maestro told him to speak directly to the orchestra. Most Israelis, Ramzi found, opposed such a statement. "We don't see the importance of a statement like this," several Israeli musicians told him. Ramzi was amazed that they would not at least condemn the destruction of a music school. "That's the big difference between us," Ramzi replied. "For you it's not important because your F-16s are bombing us. For us it's very important, because we are on the receiving end of those bombs."

Undaunted, Ramzi organized a vigil for the children of Gaza in front of the State Opera House in Berlin. One evening before a performance, Ramzi, Mariam, Daniel, many Arab members, and at least one Israeli member of the orchestra marched silently outside the opera house, carrying candles in a silent vigil.

That evening, a statement from the entire orchestra, crafted by Daniel, Mariam, Ramzi, and other musicians, appeared in the musical program for the Divan performances at the State Opera House:

> We, the members of the West-Eastern Divan Orchestra, believe that there is no military solution to the Israeli-Palestinian conflict. The last decades have shown the futility of this way of thinking and we represent an alternate model based on equality, cooperation and justice for all ... We aspire to total freedom and equality between Israelis and Palestinians and it is on this basis that we come together today to play music.
>
> The actions of the Israeli government in Gaza during the past two weeks are not the way to resolve existing differences. The actions of Hamas do not contribute to building mutual trust. We deplore all actions that lead to civilian deaths. We call for an immediate renunciation of all violence, which must lead to honest and just negotiations between all the parties concerned without exceptions.
>
> A sovereign Palestinian state can truly exist only with an end to the occupation. Palestinians must be granted the same freedom and independence that Israel has had since 1948 ... The Israeli-Palestinian conflict is a conflict between two peoples who are profoundly convinced of their right to live on the same piece of land and they have to accept each other's right to do so ...
>
> It is in this spirit that we hope you will enjoy our concert today.
>
> The musicians of the West-Eastern Divan Orchestra

Later, the Barenboim-Said Foundation, established as an incubator for musical talent, donated twenty-five thousand euros to help rebuild Gaza's music school.

Israel's attacks ended just before Barack Obama was inaugurated as the forty-fourth president of the United States. Israel continued to enforce a blockade of Gaza, however, by air, land, and sea, prohibiting the movement of most goods and people in or out of the besieged strip. Israel defended its policy, citing the need to prevent the entry of weapons, including rockets, into Gaza. The blockade drew sharp international criticism. "The whole of Gaza's civilian population is being punished for acts for which they bear no responsibility," declared the normally staid International Committee of the Red Cross. "The closure therefore constitutes a collective punishment imposed in clear violation of Israel's obligations under international humanitarian law." Pressure mounted for Israel to end its siege of Gaza.

*   *   *

By March 2009, in the early weeks after the Gaza War, most of the new teachers had settled into their work. Al Kamandjati's Ramallah center provided the base for daily music lessons, but most days teachers also piled into the new white van to reach the children in the villages and refugee camps. Jenin was the most frequent destination, about two hours away depending on the number of military checkpoints and the mood of the soldiers.

Abu Ayman, Al Kamandjati's gruff, balding, chain-smoking driver, barreled down the Ramallah-Jenin highway, taking corners and straight shots alike as if he were in an international Grand Prix. He sped past the red-roofed Israeli settlements, military jeeps, Humvees, and armored personnel carriers ferrying soldiers from one West Bank base to another, long rows of flagpoles bearing the national colors of Israel, and signs in three languages warning Palestinians against entering the "special security zones" and "closed military areas." Abu Ayman streaked past these reminders of his own occupation, and of the incarceration of his oldest son, twenty years old, who had been taken away at three A.M., a few months earlier. He held his hands in a death grip on the wheel, eyes fixed in front of him, weaving past cars and trucks with inches to spare on the two-lane highway.

Jason, Maddalena, Alice, Ben, and Julia clutched the arms of their seats, looking up from their course notes or sheet music at each near miss. "Abu Ayman!" Julia pleaded with their driver. "Please slow down!" Which he eventually did, as Huwara or one of the other Israeli checkpoints and road-blocks came into view, and Abu Ayman was forced to submit himself and his passengers for inspection. He never spoke to the soldiers in Hebrew, however; Ramzi forbid it. "They are on our land," he said. "They should speak our language."

The mood changed completely once the van pulled up at Al Kamandjati's Jenin center. "Juuuulia!" shouted Fadi Basha, a skinny nine-year-old, racing across the room toward his teacher.

"Marhaba ya Fadi!" Julia smiled back at the boy, taking his hand. *"Keefak inta?* How are you?"

Fadi was Julia's star student. He had started out on a baby violin, but his voice was so pure and strong and, as it turned out, he sang eighteenth-century arias so beautifully, in nearly unaccented Italian, that voice lessons with Julia became the priority.

Anyone who heard Fadi sing for the first time was astonished by the power and tone of the boy's clear soprano. His pitch, and his resonance, seemed to reach inside listeners. In the practice room with Julia, Fadi's voice would soar above the piano, cutting through the ambient din of Jenin: clear and resonant. In recitals, he had a natural dramatic presence, his eyes widening at emotional turns in the piece, as if he understood the original Italian. He memorized his first song, "Sebben, Crudele," written by the Italian baroque composer Antonio Caldara for his 1710 opera, *La costanza in amor vince l'inganno* ("Faithfulness in Love Conquers Treachery"), in a single lesson. The next evening he performed it at a recital for other students, accompanied by Jason on the piano. Julia was stunned. Teachers found themselves on the verge of tears. "A star! A new star at the Kamandjati!" Fadi declared that evening, giddy with his own gifts.

The mixing of Arabic and Western musical and social cultures was inspiring for teachers and students alike. But as more English, German, French, and American volunteers began helping set up film programs, theater workshops, music camps, and solidarity groups in support of the Palestinian olive harvest, which faced regular attacks from settlers, signs of strain became visible. Reports circulated of Western women dating local men, sometimes indiscreetly, with open displays of affection. Others dressed immodestly by local standards, which in some cases meant showing bare arms, or skin below the neck. Al Kamandjati's teachers did not seem to have this reputation, but they were affected by those who did.

"We had been told to watch how we dress all the time, but particularly in Jenin, in refugee camps," remembered Alice, the violin teacher from Cambridge. "Something covering my elbows, that was the general rule. Cover your legs and elbows." Once Alice wore something that Iyad Staiti, Jenin's Al Kamandjati coordinator, considered too low-cut, and he told her she shouldn't leave the center. Iyad had reason to worry. Nearby was Jenin camp, where militants killed thirteen Israeli soldiers at the height of the Second Intifada, and where the French musicians and filmmakers documenting the story of Al Kamandjati had been shot at only four years earlier. Jenin was a tense and conservative place, especially in the wake of Israel's missile strikes in Gaza.

On the morning of March 16, 2009, Alice was sitting alone in her Ramallah flat, drinking her coffee. Petite, green-eyed, smart, and headstrong, her colleagues considered her passionate, impatient, and one of the best violin teachers in Palestine.

Alice's mobile phone rang just after seven thirty. It was Ben, Alice's fellow violin teacher. "Did you hear what happened?" Ben asked urgently. "There's been a fire in the school in Jenin."

Alice hung up and ran up the hill to get a taxi to Al Kamandjati in the old city. From there she and a group of teachers left for Jenin. Abu Ayman would get them there quickly.

Children gazed in shock at pianos whose white keys had turned black; singed and curled-up bass and cello strings; charred ouds, whose thin bands of wood from the concave back had sprung out in the heat. Music stands were covered with ash; the smell of burnt wood hung in the air. The walls were black. Outside the doorway, the police had found matches and an empty gasoline can. The arson had taken place in the middle of the night.

Some of the children were in tears. Iyad, the Jenin coordinator, had been crying, too. "I would have liked to die before seeing this," he said. "All my life, this place has been my dream."

In a corner boys were scrawling slogans with their fingers on the sooty walls. *Al Kamandjati, we will stay!* read one.

Soon Ramzi arrived. He surveyed the damage and gathered everyone, looking carefully at the faces of the children. He noticed something beyond sadness: a guilt, almost, an embarrassment that something like this could happen in their community. "This is like the forest," Ramzi said slowly. "When you burn the forest, it becomes more fertile. There are many seeds. And that's going to be the case for us."

A new Al Kamandjati would rise in Jenin, Ramzi promised. In fact, another building was already in the planning stage. In the meantime, Ramzi and Celine would send out a press release; they would call out every volunteer possible to begin a massive cleanup. Teachers and staff would bring instruments from Ramallah, and the Jenin school would not close, not even for a day.

Alice led the children outside to a garden courtyard. Iyad was nervous, but had reluctantly agreed. Carlo, an Italian trombone teacher, brought out his computer, and began syncopated beats. "We didn't really know what to do," Alice remembered. Many of the instruments had been destroyed, and much of the sheet music was incinerated. But the children with violins and other small instruments had kept them at home, and stood with them now.

Alice picked up her violin. Using her bow as a baton and smiling broadly, she began to play.

"We made a concert outside to show the people that, we are here, we are playing," said Rasha Doulani, a piano student. "And we didn't do anything wrong. And we are just kids and we are just playing. So what's wrong with that? And we just played for them and showed them that we are really sad about what happened and that they did the wrong thing and we will continue. We won't stop."

Alice would remember this day as "one of the most positive days of our teaching. You can really feel this sense of being together. Everyone felt like a little soldier defending the castle. That was—that was Al Kamandjati."

That evening, and for many evenings to come, Iyad tuned the center's radio to the Qur'an radio station, where announcers recited holy verse, and turned it up loud, before he locked the building.

Twenty-four

BIRTH

March 2009
Ramallah

A FEW DAYS after the fire in Jenin, Ramzi turned the key at Al Kamandjati's Ramallah center and swung open the wide copper door.

Off to the left, on the courtyard stones, Ramzi saw an unmarked white envelope. He bent down to pick it up. Inside was a scrap of paper. Ramzi looked over his shoulder to the gap below the door. Someone must have slid the envelope underneath, overnight.

He turned over the sheet of paper to read the handwritten scrawl, in Arabic: *I hope you learned from Jenin.*

Ramzi stuffed the note in his pocket.

Despite the threat, Ramzi did not believe that the arsonists in Jenin were motivated by a fundamentalist interpretation of Islam. Rather he thought the fire was the result of petty jealousies, a kind of village envy that wishes ill to those who succeed. He could have no way of confirming this theory, however, for no one ever stepped forward to claim responsibility for the fire, or for the threatening note.

It was undeniable, however, that Palestine had grown more conservative in recent years, a fact owing in part to the occupation itself. As their lives became more controlled and movements more restricted, people sought political and religious solace in the mosque. Often, outward-looking, Western-sounding attitudes were considered suspect.

Ramzi had been talking to Nabeel, Rasha's father, about the possibility that Rasha, now seventeen years old, could study in France. A scholarship for Rasha in Angers looked likely. Nabeel was open to the idea, if Rasha could live with someone who would watch over her. At first they suggested Shehada. But Shehada, fresh from his workshop in Italy, was scheduled to study in England, at the Newark School of Violin Making. Ramzi had arranged this. Shehada would be leaving in the fall. Rasha, however, would have to study in France, where Ramzi had connections. Ramzi and Celine then came up with another idea: They knew a Muslim family in Angers with close ties to Palestine. Perhaps Rasha could stay with them.

Shehada still did not like the plan. "I'm afraid someone would touch her, would do bad things to her," Shehada said one afternoon in the family's outdoor veranda, smoking a water pipe beneath the shade of grape leaves. "A girl is not like a man, you know? A man is strong. A girl's, like, soft. If you tell her something nice, you can do anything with her after. I don't know, that's what I'm feeling. I've been to Europe and I know that. In Europe, everybody's free. And Arabic culture, we don't let the girls be free. You don't want anyone to touch your sister."

Now word came that Rasha's uncle, still in an Israeli prison, strongly opposed his niece moving to Europe. Nabeel took Rasha aside. "Before anything," Rasha recalled him saying, "I have to consider your uncles' opinions, especially your uncle in prison." Palestinian prisoners were often considered patriots, revered in the society, and their opinions, including about social issues, were given special weight in the family.

Rasha understood this; nevertheless, she was furious. "I am not living my life for him," she told her father. "This is my personal life!"

Rasha wanted to enlist Ramzi's support, but this was a delicate family matter. At a certain point, Ramzi could not intervene.

Soon Rasha's parents came up with another plan. A young man, from the family village near Hebron, had asked for her hand in marriage. He was from a good family, decent and hardworking. He would take good care of her and pay for her university studies. Rasha considered him kind and supportive. She began to grow unsure about France. After much deliberation she agreed to marry the young man, and let go of her idea of studying abroad. However, she insisted to her future husband, she would not give up the flute. Music, she vowed, would remain central to her life.

*   *   *

On June 4, 2009, Barack Obama stepped to the podium in the gilded hall at Cairo's Al-Azhar University and looked out upon the sea of expectant faces. *"Salaam alaikum"* ("Peace be upon you"), he declared in the traditional Arab greeting, to cheering and prolonged applause. Obama sought "a new beginning between the United States and Muslims around the world; one based upon mutual interest and mutual respect" and "common principles . . . of justice and progress; tolerance and the dignity of all human beings."

As for the Holy Land, Obama affirmed America's "unshakeable" friendship with Israel, but declared it "undeniable that the Palestinian people— Muslims and Christians—have suffered in pursuit of a homeland. For more than sixty years they have endured the pain of dislocation. Many wait in refugee camps in the West Bank, Gaza, and neighboring lands for a life of peace and security that they have never been able to lead. They endure the daily humiliations—large and small—that come with occupation." Rarely had an American president spoken so frankly about Palestinian suffering. "The situation for the Palestinian people is intolerable," the president continued. "America will not turn our backs on the legitimate Palestinian aspiration for dignity, opportunity, and a state of their own." The president deplored Israel's continued settlement project, but admonished Palestinians to fight for their independence along a peaceful path. "Violence is a dead end," he said.

In fact, direct nonviolent protests against the occupation and the separation barrier had been taking place in the Palestinian villages of Bi'ilin, Ni'ilin, and Nabi Saleh, and had prompted praise and visits from Desmond Tutu and Jimmy Carter. However, Carter wrote: "While the protests have become a focus for non-violent Palestinian activism, the Israeli Defence Forces (IDF) often respond with force, using tear gas, rubber bullets, stun grenades, water cannons, and sometimes live rounds . . . the IDF have injured over 1,800 anti-wall demonstrators and killed nineteen."

More recently Salam Fayyad, Abbas's prime minister, had been advancing a policy of good governance combined with security and economic opportunity. He was trying to prepare a Palestinian state in advance, applying funds from the United States, the European Union, and the Gulf States for road-paving projects, industrial parks, and planning for a new privately financed city between Nablus and Ramallah. Fayyad worked closely with an American general, Keith Dayton, the United States Security Coordinator for Israel and the Palestinian Authority, who convinced Israel to ease a small portion of the more than six hundred barriers to Palestinian travel within the West Bank; soon, the infamous Huwara checkpoint was empty of soldiers, at least for the time being. One reason for this was Dayton and Fayyad's promise to "professionalize" the Palestinian Authority's security forces, establish rule of law, and neutralize armed opposition following the near-anarchy during the Second Intifada. Ten thousand Palestinians received training, mostly as special forces. Yet the rosy image of the "new men," as Dayton described his trainees to American audiences, was often met with fear and anger on the ground. The new security forces were often seen as tools of the Palestinian Authority to crush its political opposition. Many Palestinians were wary of the PA's "security coordination" with Israel, which focused largely on weakening Hamas in the West Bank. The operations spawned credible reports of torture by PA security forces, and Palestinians increasingly saw the Palestinian Authority as security guards for Israel. In some cases, the targets of stone-throwing shabab were now Palestinian policemen.

Palestinians, meanwhile, remained wary of American promises about statehood, and of the new president's willingness to confront Israel over the settlements. It had been seventeen years, since before the Oslo agreement, that the United States had applied financial leverage on Israel to halt settlement construction. Obama did not appear ready to take such a step. Still, many Palestinians could not help but be encouraged by Obama's words in Cairo, and felt cautiously optimistic.

*   *   *

On June 10, 2009, just after midnight, Celine woke up and shook Ramzi. "I think it's time," she said. They walked down from their fifth-floor apartment and got into their car. Ramzi drove through the empty Manara, the roundabout at the center of town, and to Arab Care Hospital. There Celine gave birth to Hussein Ramzi Mohammad Hassan Hussein Aburedwan. Celine's Lebanese-French mother was with them; she had traveled from France to Palestine, journeying back to the region from which she had rescued her three daughters twenty years earlier. "After that," Celine later said, "it was much easier for her, and for my parents, to imagine me here."

*　　*　　*

Ramzi's grandfather was a few weeks short of his eighty-seventh birthday. He was full of advice for his great grandson. "Eat liver," he would tell Celine. "It's good for the milk." Celine saw a happiness in Sido's eyes when he looked at Ramzi; Sido, Celine sensed, knew that a child would make Ramzi a little less lonely. To his great-grandson, he would say, "I cannot wait for the day when I see you walking."

But Ramzi's grandparents did not praise the boy much; they believed such attention would invite the evil eye for Hussein. When Nawal, the boy's great-aunt, said, "How beautiful he is," Sido would not acknowledge the fact. "He's fine," was as far as he would go; Jamila wouldn't even go that far. "Actually," she said, deflecting the evil eye, "he's ugly." Celine looked at Ramzi, alarmed. "That's just their way of protecting," Ramzi said.

Sido was still sweeping the streets. For years municipal officials had tried to get him to retire, but the old man refused; his work in garbage was a calling, and he could not give it up. He would be too bored, he told Ramzi. Finally, his bosses resorted to taking away his brooms, shovels, and cans, trying to force him into retirement. Undaunted, Ramzi's grandfather went out and bought new ones, cleaning the streets of the town as a volunteer. "I don't want money," he said, "I just want to go on working."

On October 29, 2009, Sido had just finished work and was crossing the Jerusalem road—the same road Ramzi had secretly followed him across twenty-four years earlier. He was in the middle of the road when a truck came speeding around a corner. The rear end swung hard, smashing Mohammad Aburedwan into the pavement. An ambulance came. Grandfather died that day, in a Ramallah hospital.

Ramzi rushed to his side. There was no blood, no visible bruising. Ramzi put his arms around his grandfather. The old man felt warm; it seemed he was still alive. Ramzi kissed him.

For days Ramzi sat alone on the couch, smoking, staring, and thinking, for hours at a time. "I think he felt his support in life disappeared," Celine said. "I felt I could do nothing." And then he would look up and see Hussein. "That really helped him," Celine said. "Something to put his hope into."

*   *   *

Six weeks later, Ramzi flew to Amsterdam to play for Queen Beatrix of the Netherlands. Celine stayed home with Hussein.

On December 16, just after two in the morning, Celine awoke in the flat in Ramallah to a strange sound coming from the front door. She emerged from her bedroom to find the door—a heavy steel multilock security door—jammed partway open and kept that way by a small security bar.

Celine thought burglars were trying to break in. She yelled at them in Arabic to go away. Then she looked through the six-inch opening and spotted ten Israeli soldiers in the hallway. They told her to stand back. They were attaching a special machine to the door. Celine retreated to the bedroom and called a co-worker. "There are soldiers entering my flat," she whispered urgently.

"Don't worry. There is no problem," her colleague replied. "It's normal."

The soldiers stepped through the door, pointing their automatic rifles at Celine. A local Palestinian informant stood near them silently, a black mask pulled over his face to ensure his anonymity.

The commander began to interrogate her. "My name, with whom I live, asking me about the neighbors," she later recalled. Celine flashed her French passport and pleaded with the soldiers to keep their voices down, so as not to wake up Hussein, sleeping in the next room. "I was praying that he would just stay asleep." She told the commander, "I just go from my house to my work, from work to my house." She didn't really know her neighbors, she said.

The soldiers had blown off the door to the wrong flat. They would remove at least three more doors in the building that night, Celine said, before finding their suspect: her seventeen-year-old next-door neighbor. "They stood questioning him for maybe twenty minutes, and then they took him."

Celine stared through the blinds at the street below, where some fifteen jeeps and other military vehicles were parked. Finally, they left with their lights out, and so quietly that she could not even hear their engines. When the flat was silent again, she couldn't sleep. "I was very afraid." Ramzi was coming home soon, so she decided not to call him. A neighbor came upstairs to sit with her until the morning.

Ramzi arrived the next day and put his key in the lock. The door wouldn't open. He looked around the hallway, wondering if he was on the right floor. He tried the key again, then noticed the door was a different color.

Celine came out and told him about the raid.

Ramzi imagined what might have happened if Hussein had been a bit older and had wandered out to the front room to see ten soldiers pointing guns at his mother. Ramzi recalled seeing this kind of thing as a child under occupation in Al Amari refugee camp. But he hadn't thought his family would ever encounter it in Ramallah, in the middle of supposedly autonomous Palestinian territory. "Now you know," Ramzi told Celine with a wry smile, "how we feel."

Twenty-five

SEBASTIA

June 2010
Occupied West Bank

R<small>AMZI SLOWED AS</small> his SUV approached a military kiosk at a break in a dull gray wall. On the other side stood the ancient Palestinian village of Sebastia. Ramzi, Celine, and baby Hussein, now a year old, formed the advance team for Al Kamandjati's Fête de la Musique, or Music Days Festival, in which, for two weeks, one hundred musicians from around the world would perform in orphanages, cultural centers, schools, and concert halls in Ramallah, Jerusalem, Bethlehem, Hebron, in refugee camps, and in isolated villages like Sebastia. The village lay in an archipelago of dozens of Palestinian islands in a sea of Israeli military control. In the Israeli-controlled areas, which represented 60 percent of the West Bank, lay the settlements, surrounding "buffer zones" and military bases, and the exclusive roads—many built during Oslo—that whisked Jewish settlers into Jerusalem and Tel Aviv for work, prayer, shopping, and the beach. To Palestinians, West Bank travelers, and even to some former Israeli soldiers who provided candid accounts, it was clear that acquiring land, more than fighting terrorism, lay behind Israel's policy. "In the West Bank, checkpoints, roads closed to Palestinian traffic, and prohibitions against Palestinian movement from one place to another are measures that effectively push Palestinians off their land and allow the expansion of Israeli sovereignty," declared a group of former soldiers whose published eyewitness accounts challenged the traditional Israeli narrative. The occupation, rather, "is a means of control, dispossession, and annexation."

Sebastia, founded in 876 B.C.E. and conquered by Alexander the Great five centuries later, was, along with neighboring villages, now encircled by checkpoints and concrete barriers topped with looping barbwire. The Music Days Festival was, in part, an effort by Ramzi and his colleagues to penetrate this isolation and create musical bridges between the fractured parts of Palestine. Tonight's performances would take place in the amphitheater built by King Herod around the time of Christ's birth.

Ramzi was in a hurry, but a soldier turned him away from the village entrance, saying, "those are the orders." He directed Ramzi to another entrance, forty-five minutes distant. Ramzi narrowed his eyes, turned around, and circled west and then north, beneath the red-roofed settlement of Shavei Shomron. Just beyond, the family passed below a collection of hilltop trailers recently planted by a new wave of settlers. This outpost was illegal according to Israel's civilian authorities, in contrast to the Jewish West Bank settlements that they deemed legal. This distinction was unique among the world's nations, the rest of which considered the vast majority of the settlements to be violations of international law.

Palestinians who had once embraced the idea that the First Intifada and Oslo would lead to a "viable, contiguous" independent state now recognized that the reality looked nothing like that. Emerging instead was a single state, controlled by Israel, divided between walled-off cantons and privileged hilltop enclaves; between modern cities with high tech and lightrail, and refugee camps strewn with garbage and pasted-up posters of martyrs; between beachfront boardwalks with gleaming discos, and villages bifurcated by an eight-meter wall, where farmers could no longer reach their dying olive trees. In this single regime, some enjoyed full rights as citizens; others had none.

At Anab checkpoint, a few miles from Sebastia, Ramzi slowed and pulled out his green West Bank identification card, submitting himself, his wife, and his baby for inspection. The soldier directed them forward and into Sebastia, where they would meet the Al Kamandjati bus.

Ramzi turned right and pointed the truck up a narrow road, through stony terraces of olive groves and prickly pear cactus. A colonnade of thick Roman pillars marked the entrance to the ancient town; other columns lay fallen, broken into pieces. Nearby stood the ruins of a Crusader church built in 1165. Buried just beyond was the headless body of John the

Baptist. Faded frescoes at a palace ruins depicted his beheading. The head was entombed at a mosque in Damascus.

The center of Sebastia was a wide spot in the road with a couple of restaurants, mostly quiet; a lone customer waited for his kebab. An abandoned tractor baked silently in the searing afternoon sun, as a young man tried to interest scattered visitors in the nine-foot African python he'd bought at a pet store in Israel. The major sign of life at that moment was in a local open-air coffee shop, where village men were sitting in plastic chairs, smoking and shouting as Germany battled Serbia in the World Cup.

The Al Kamandjati bus pulled up at the edge of the clearing. Alá, Muntasser, Julia, Peter, Ben, and dozens of other students and teachers piled out, slung their instrument cases over their shoulders, and walked down a dirt path in the punishing heat. Their destination, as it had been for millennia of musicians, actors, dancers, and orators who came before them, was Sebastia's Roman amphitheater. Nearly twenty-nine centuries after the founding of Sebastia, the curved, stepped, stone ruin would provide witness to another performance.

That late afternoon was probably the first time that the amphitheater had played host to French hip-hop, at least of the "beatboxing" variety— two street musicians from Angers whose vocal tics, shouts, body percussion, microphone mouth play, and repetitive loops through their iPhones were causing a delighted uproar among the children and looks of deep confusion among the older villagers. As the sun touched the horizon, the Frenchmen gave way to Al Kamandjati's Ramallah Orchestra under the direction of Martin Pütz, a German who had come to Ramallah to teach at the Barenboim-Said Foundation and who now conducted the forty musicians through Edvard Grieg's Peer Gynt Suite no. 1, which premiered in Oslo in 1876, and which was composed for Henrik Ibsen's 1867 play.

At dusk, Oday stepped to the microphone, backed by the orchestra, to evoke the poetry and music of the Palestinian resistance. *We are not going to forget our existence*, he sang in the fading light, *and the good days we had, before the occupation.*

Ramzi stood on the top row of the Roman amphitheater, gazing intently at the young man he had first met seven years earlier at Al Fawwar. Hussein was in his arms, asleep on his shoulder. Slowly, Ramzi rocked his son back and forth, patting his back to the rhythm of the music.

*

Ramzi drove through the darkness toward Ramallah. Celine and Hussein slept fitfully in the backseat. The SUV curved along West Bank Highway 60, passing again beneath the settlement of Shavei Shomron, glowing yellow after nightfall. In recent years, settlers had come down from the nearby hilltops, burning Palestinian olive groves and torching mosques. These "price tag attacks," undertaken by extremist Israelis, served as warnings to anyone who would try to challenge the presence of the settlers and the expansion of their settlements.

Presently Ramzi came upon another checkpoint divided into two lanes. Settlers and VIPS bearing yellow license plates were allowed to use the express lane on the left. All others—that is, Palestinians, with the white plates and green lettering—were required to wait on the right side, in the long line of cars idling at the Zatara checkpoint.

Ramzi took one look at the long line of drivers and swung the white-plated SUV around to the left. He pulled up to the guard post reserved for settlers and other Israelis, or the few privileged Palestinians who had special connections. "Why do you come here?" the soldier asked indignantly. "You wait in the other line."

"I would like to know," Ramzi replied in English, "if there is a difference between Israeli babies and Palestinian babies."

"What?"

"I said," Ramzi repeated, his tone sharpening, "is there a difference Israeli babies and Palestinian babies? Between your babies and my babies. I would really like to know the answer to this question."

The soldier peered in at Celine, awake now in the back beside their blue-eyed boy. Hussein snoozed in his car seat. He sported blond locks and a French soccer jersey with his name on the back—a gift from Celine's sister. The young man hesitated, glanced back at Ramzi, then waved him through.

"You have to insist on the positive energy," Ramzi said a few minutes later, his eyes fixed on the white necklaces of lights belonging to the Palestinian villages to the south. He stroked his bearded chin. "The more you believe in what you are doing, the more you keep going on. It's like a snowball." Light pooled in an orb in front of the SUV as he cut through the darkened land. Ramzi shook loose a Gauloises from a half-empty pack, touched the end of it with the orange coil of his car lighter, and cracked open the driver's window. "I see it in the young, who are living in just a whole world of music." To the east, the lights of Beit Wazan came into view; there, three years earlier, at the palace of the Ottoman sheikh, Al Kamandjati had held its first summer music camp. "Their world is music now," Ramzi said of Alá, her sister Rasha, Muntasser, Oday, and their friends at Al Kamandjati. "Their life is now committed to the music."

Teachers and visiting musicians often asked whether Ramzi was more of a musician or an activist, but to Ramzi the question was irrelevant. To him music was intrinsic to the protection of his students, the penetration across splintered landscapes, and the resistance to military domination. Music devoid of politics, Ramzi believed, was impossible under occupation. Now, too, politics was impossible for Ramzi without music.

For the past four years Ramzi had hoped that by conveying the Palestinian reality on the ground, he would convince the Divan Orchestra to publicly condemn the occupation. Its refusal to do so had not only left Ramzi feeling isolated; it had helped prompt him to make his own public stand, putting Al Kamandjati's music directly in the service of political resistance. Ramzi, and many of his students and teachers, saw themselves as part of a larger movement of nonviolent action to protest the occupation, and in support of Palestinian independence.

"Al Kamandjati Association," declared the program for the 2010 Music Days Festival, was organized "under the motto of the boycott of Israeli products as well [as] academic and cultural institutions to end their complicity in denying Palestinian rights." Thus Ramzi aligned himself with the international boycott designed to shame Israel and expose the reality of the occupation. This nonviolent strategy had become more popular with Palestinians, frustrated by their lack of freedom or even prospects for it. Yet the stance increased tensions with Daniel Barenboim. As director of Al Kamandjati, Ramzi had worked closely with the Barenboim-Said Foundation, which had provided the services of several of its teachers, and which was listed as a cooperating organization on the Music Days program. The boycott endorsement was not welcomed by Daniel. "Barenboim called Ramzi to tell him, you cannot have our collaboration if you put that the purpose of these Music Days is to boycott Israeli cultural institutions," recalled Peter Thiemann, a teacher at the Barenboim-Said Foundation who also taught at Al Kamandjati. "There were huge discussions about this." As a result, Ramzi softened some of the wording, but strong language remained in the final program:

> The Israeli Authorities prevent Palestinian culture from spreading in the West Bank, Gaza and among the Palestinians of 48 [i.e., in Israel], and prevent those areas from communicating with each other . . . Because we believe in pacific resistance and in our right to be here, we ask all people who believe in human rights and in freedom, to boycott Israeli products as well as cultural and academic institutions, until Israel understands that it cannot kill a people's will by force, respects the international laws, and ends the occupation.

This was the kind of statement Ramzi had been urging the Divan to make since he had joined the orchestra four years earlier. Recent events had made him feel even more strongly about it. A month earlier, in May 2010, Israeli naval commandos had killed nine foreign nationals aboard a flotilla of six ships steaming toward Gaza. The Gaza Freedom Flotilla carried humanitarian aid; it sought to breach Israel's naval blockade of Gaza and to draw attention to the humanitarian crisis there. Israel claimed that the nine dead, mostly Turkish citizens, were from a "hardcore group" of activists and were armed with iron bars and knives. Eyewitnesses countered with stories of "execution-style" killings by Israeli soldiers. The deaths, together with the Gaza war a few months earlier, drew widespread international condemnation. Turkey broke off diplomatic relations with Israel. Prime Minister Recep Tayyip Erdogan became a hero in Palestine; the Turkish flag could be seen flying from Palestinian homes, where the deaths drew renewed fury against Israel. Prime Minister Netanyahu defended the raid, and the ongoing embargo, invoking fears of weapons entering Gaza and rising influence from Iran. "Israel cannot permit Iran to establish a Mediterranean port a few dozen kilometers from Tel Aviv and from Jerusalem," he declared. The Israeli foreign ministry, meanwhile, facing international isolation, stepped up its "Brand Israel" campaign. A ministry spokesman announced plans to "show Israel's prettier face" overseas through performances, readings, and art exhibitions.

The boycott garnered new support. International artists, including Elvis Costello, Carlos Santana, Dustin Hoffman, and Meg Ryan, canceled appearances in Israel. A small number of European and American trade unions, church groups, and pension funds began to divest from Israeli companies, or those perceived to be profiting from the occupation, including Caterpillar, makers of the D9 bulldozer used to demolish Palestinian homes, and Ahava, a cosmetics company with a factory in an Israeli settlement. These actions were embraced by the BDS movement. Even the Palestinian prime minister, Salam Fayyad, perceived as a moderate by American officials, and not a full supporter of BDS, threw settlement-made products into a large bonfire in a West Bank village, part of the Palestinian Authority's campaign against the settlements.

In this atmosphere, Ramzi believed more than ever that the Divan Orchestra needed to make a strong political statement about the occupation.

"Nobody is exploring the problem," he said. "Everyone avoids speaking about it." Most of the Divan's Arab musicians had not experienced life under occupation. The Israelis in the Divan, on the other hand, not only knew about the occupation; as soldiers under Israeli's compulsory military service, many of them had been part of the occupying army. Perhaps this was why "they are always uncomfortable when I try to talk to them about it." This in turn made Ramzi uncomfortable. In the Divan, Ramzi often said, he might play as an equal beside an Israeli on a European stage, but back home, under occupation in Palestine, this same person could be the soldier at a checkpoint, "not letting me enter to go teach music."

Daniel remained opposed to a statement, despite his strong personal stance; he and Ramzi both knew that this would make many of the Israelis in the orchestra uneasy. Now, Ramzi's frustration was reaching a breaking point. "We have very good relations," Ramzi said of Daniel. "We are very close. But having good relations for me doesn't mean that I have to shut up."

*   *   *

In the late summer of 2010, Ramzi landed in Andalucía, home base for the West-Eastern Divan Orchestra. He had sent a draft statement against the occupation to be circulated before his arrival; it was not well received.

"When I arrived, I felt a very quiet anger toward me," Ramzi recalled. "I felt that the Israelis were very cold." The silence broke in Córdoba, after a rehearsal, when Ramzi stood before his colleagues to make his case. The group was gathered on wooden benches, under date palms curving in the wind.

"I have been waiting for the day when this musical institution can say three words about the bombing of the Gaza Music School," Ramzi declared, recalling the attack of eighteen months earlier. "Three words: 'We are sorry.' But we can't even agree on this."

Ramzi wasn't making many converts. Even Mariam Said had argued against a statement condemning the occupation. "If you want to convince them about ending the occupation, okay, convince them. We don't have to put a statement on the Web site," she told Ramzi before the evening in Córdoba.

"I will not come next year if you don't put it on the Web site," Ramzi responded, "that all the members believe in ending the occupation."

"But the project is not political, Ramzi. It's educational. Either we are about music or we are political. Why do we need to scrutinize every member of the orchestra?"

"I think it would be much better for the Palestinians to engage the Israelis," Daniel argued. "To influence them from the inside. It's an alternative way of thinking. It's not about normalization. In the Divan we don't have a consensus. We have a consensus on the music. We want them to feel that whether united or not, our destinies are inextricably linked."

Yet it was hard to argue that the Divan was completely apolitical. Ramzi had long believed that its projected image of harmony and coexistence was in itself political, because it belied the truth on the ground. "There is no coexistence," he said. "That's a lie. They are putting people in a cage." Beneath the swaying palms of the Córdoba hotel, Ramzi put a fine point on his argument: "In your silence," he said, "you are complicit."

"I think his point is to change the world through a musical statement," recalled Sharon Cohen, principal second violinist with the Divan and a former Israeli soldier who would soon accept a job to play in the Israeli Philharmonic. But "that's not the purpose of this orchestra. I think the people who are running this orchestra"—in other words, Daniel and, to a much lesser extent, Mariam—"have a different agenda."

In the end, Ramzi made it easier for his colleagues to reject his statement. The statement not only denounced Israel's military occupation; it demanded that the full orchestra acknowledge the Palestinian dispossession in the 1948

Nakba and, most crucially, endorse the right of Palestinians to return to their land if they wished to. The last demand was a red line for almost every Israeli. To them, the Palestinian right of return essentially meant the end of Israel. Ramzi did not necessarily see it this way. Most refugees, many Palestian analysts argued, would choose to not return to their old lands, but rather accept compensation for the loss of their land and homes, provided their *right* to return was acknowledged by Israel. The numbers of people who actually returned could be worked out in a final settlement. But such a nuanced position, even if Ramzi had chosen to argue it, would have been lost on nearly the entire orchestra. In the end even many of the Arab musicians could not endorse any statement that included the Palestinian right of return. Ramzi decided there was no point in putting the statement up for a vote.

Ramzi packed his bags. He met privately with Daniel and Mariam, pledging not to return unless the orchestra changed its stance. He departed in the middle of the orchestra's rehearsals, skipping its tour of South America and the Caribbean, where they would play the Beethoven symphonies in Santo Domingo, Caracas, Quito, Bogotá, and Daniel Barenboim's native Buenos Aires.

*   *   *

Ramzi returned to Palestine and immersed himself in the daily duties of running a music school. He no longer had the distraction of the Divan; he was free to plunge deeper into the work on the ground.

Ramzi took note of Alice's work. She was a strong-willed violin teacher who, like her colleagues, had intensified her efforts in the refugee camps since the fire in Jenin. With Ben and Maddalena, she had initiated an "Orchestra of the Camps," searching the refugee camps for students who could take the stage in Al Kamandjati festivals. The work was often frustrating, Alice found, because the camps were so filled with chaos and grief. "Every child has a story," remembered Alice. "Especially the ones in the camps who have been visited in the night by soldiers banging on their doors. Or the two kids in Qalandia who had to stop coming to lessons because the wall was built alongside their house, and now they are on the wrong side of the wall."

Still, Alice felt she and her fellow teachers were making a difference. "If we can bring a degree of normality into these kids' lives, it would make an immeasurable difference. If you can get that kind of engagement and get them to really focus on something, I think it can change their whole concept of the world around them."

Ramzi and Celine began to think that Alice, who now spoke decent Arabic, would be a good candidate to launch the Lebanon program near the end of the year. They asked her to take the job, and she accepted.

*   *   *

Ramzi continued to work with teachers from the Barenboim-Said Foundation and its music school in Ramallah. Teachers there donated their time to Al Kamandjati, but in the wake of his departure from the Divan, relations began to fray. Tensions also rose between Ramzi and the Edward Said National Conservatory of Music. Teachers there had been hearing stories that Ramzi was bad-mouthing the Conservatory, saying it was for the elites of Palestine while Al Kamandjati focused more on the disadvantaged. Ramzi, for his part, was hearing equally disturbing stories about things Conservatory leaders were allegedly saying about him: that, for example, Al Kamandjati was funded by unknown foreign groups. The truth of these stories mattered less than their effects, common in Palestinian society: to divide people and groups who each claimed a more legitimate mantle in their common struggle. Daniel Barenboim had noted this phenomenon in the musical scene: "The problem is that Ramallah is a small town with lots of bickering people. It's ridiculous to have three different musical institutions in a small town like Ramallah. Our center, and Al Kamandjati, and the Conservatory. And they are unable to separate the political thing from the musical thing."

Yet the bickering ceased, at least for a time, during a remarkable show of musical unity at the end of 2010.

"When I become a teacher," Ramzi had told a journalist in 1998, when he was eighteen, "and we have our own symphony orchestra, I hope we will tour the world in the name of Palestine. I want to show the world that we are here, on the map."

Now, in December, Ramzi was about to take part in the inaugural concert of the Palestine National Orchestra. The PNO was the brainchild of Said Conservatory director Suhail Khoury. It was sponsored by the Conservatory (still known locally as the Ma'had) and funded by a grant from the European Union. Suhail had decided that the makeup of the national orchestra should be more than half classically trained Palestinian musicians; he set a goal of 60 percent. To reach that they tapped into the vast Palestinian diaspora, bringing a bass player from Chile, a studio violinist and a cellist from Los Angeles, a French horn player living in Syria, a timpani player whose family was originally from Haifa, a refugee from Syria living in Italy, a soprano who had grown up in Japan and now lived in Paris, and local classically trained musicians like Ramzi and Ramadan. From four continents they arrived for rehearsals in Ramallah.

In late December 2010, however, on the eve of the Jerusalem concert, the orchestra was on the verge of failure before it played its first note. Many of the musicians did not have the proper papers to enter the Holy City. Israel had withheld them. As a result, when the musicians boarded the bus in Ramallah, they risked arrest, deportation, and the collapse of the orchestra. Palestinians with proper visas sat toward the front. It was dark and raining hard when they reached the Jerusalem checkpoint. As luck or destiny would have it, the soldier at the checkpoint, who was wet and grumpy, didn't bother checking all their documents. Hence the orchestra arrived intact at the Alhambra Palace in East Jerusalem.

Hours later, the lights came down and a hush came over the audience.

Suhail Khoury stepped onstage. "Today an orchestra, tomorrow, a state," he declared to sustained cheers from the mostly Palestinian audience, some of whom had traveled from the West Bank with special Israeli-issued Christmas travel permits.

The orchestra, made of the pieces of Palestine scattered around the world, played the Palestinian National Anthem. Ramzi stood on stage, playing from memory. *Amazing,* he thought: *With the touch of a button on a computer, you can gather all of these people. When we meet, when we are gathered, we can be very powerful. We are here. We can do anything.* He looked across the stage to see his old friend Ramadan on the bass. Closer stood Peter Sulski, tonight on violin, part of the 40 percent of non-Palestinian musicians that made up the orchestra. Several Palestinian members of the Divan Orchestra also shared the stage. For this night, at least, the rivalries and divisions among the different musical factions were put to rest.

Mariam Tamari, the soprano living in Paris, stepped onstage to sing the *Exsultate, Jubilate,* composed by Mozart when he was sixteen, and first performed in 1773 in Milan, by Venanzio Rauzzini, an Italian *castrato.*

Mariam had selected the piece because she believed it represented Mozart's vision of peace. For some of the Palestinian musicians, living with a failed Oslo "peace" process that had resulted in an ever-tightening occupation, peace was a dirty word. Yet Mariam saw herself and her fellow musicians as vessels for the composers and their intentions, connecting the emotions and ideas of centuries past to the audiences of the moment. "To bring together the souls that lived centuries ago, and the souls that live today, and to communicate the love and the peace and the experience of oneness in humanity," she said. "That's my motivation in singing."

The friendly day shines forth, Mariam sang in Latin.

Both clouds and storms have fled now
For the righteous there has arisen an unexpected calm . . .
You who feared till now
And joyful for this lucky dawn
Give garlands and lilies . . .
You o crown of virgins,
grant us peace,
console our feelings,
from which our hearts sigh.

As Mariam Tamari bowed before a thunderous ovation, Ramzi stood behind her, beaming and tapping his bow gently against his fingerboard, joining in the applause.

"We all knew how meaningful this was for our country, our culture," Mariam recalled afterward. "It was unlike any other musical experience I ever experienced or probably will experience in my life. Very, very joyous. A real celebration."

END OF THIRD MOVEMENT

INTERLUDE III

*T*HE VIOLIN, IN *its blue case, falls through the air, toward the waiting arms of the violist at the base of the wall.*

He catches it, setting it down gently. Now the two bags of timpani sticks come flying down. Then, one by one, the other four musicians pivot at the top of the wall, grab the rope, and slide down, landing abruptly on the Jerusalem side.

They brush themselves off, laugh, slap each other's backs.

"Yallah," says the violist. "Let's go. We shouldn't be standing here." They need to move quickly away from the wall, where their presence will arouse suspicion. Without valid papers they will face certain arrest.

The five men turn and wave to the smuggler, trotting across the road and blending into the local population.

Fourth Movement:

RESISTANCE

Twenty-six

FRACTURES

May 2011
Jordan Valley, Occupied West Bank

RAMZI RODE IN the backseat of an orange taxi, on the road to Jericho, holding a pair of cell phones to his ears. Into one he was making visa and passport arrangements for the border crossing into Jordan and the subsequent trip, that afternoon, to Beirut, to check on Al Kamandjati's program there. The expansion into Lebanon was part of Ramzi's ambitious vision to reach beyond the borders of Palestine and into the refugee diaspora. Its beginnings had been difficult: one year in, Alice Howick, the British violinist who had moved from Palestine to run the program, was on the verge of quitting. Ramzi hoped a face-to-face meeting might convince Alice to stay.

As the taxi barreled down the long hill and into the Jordan Valley, Ramzi abruptly ended one call and began yelling into the other phone. On the other end of that line was Nabeel Abboud, director of the Barenboim-Said Foundation in Ramallah and a violinist in the Divan Orchestra. Nabeel and Ramzi had been friends for years. Nabeel had grown up in Nazareth, an Arab town in northern Israel. The two shared a common history and love of music, and had sat near each other in the Divan. Nabeel was using his new position to try to groom and recruit new musicians for Daniel and the orchestra. But Ramzi no longer supported this idea. Increasingly the Divan was seen in Palestine as an instrument of "normalization," and Ramzi himself had quit the orchestra the summer before. Now, one of the most talented violinists in Palestine was at the center of a struggle between Nabeel and Ramzi.

Nabeel had been teaching at Al Kamandjati—part of the arrangement between the two institutions. His prize student, and a pride of Al Kamandjati, was Mahmoud Karazon, the gifted eighteen-year-old violinist. Nabeel had spent many hours working with Mahmoud at Al Kamandjati, volunteering his and the Barenboim-Said Foundation's time. "He gave lessons free for one year," Ramzi acknowledged.

But Ramzi had told Nabeel he did not want Mahmoud to join the Divan or to be given any scholarship by Daniel without Ramzi's explicit consent. Now, in the taxi, he had received a call from Mahmoud's family: Nabeel had approached the family with a financial offer to go to the Foundation for lessons, and eventually to join the Divan Orchestra. Ramzi believed Nabeel was trying to steal his student, and he felt betrayed.

"You can't do this!" Ramzi shouted into the phone. "We have already agreed on this!"

"But it's a good opportunity," Nabeel replied. For Nabeel, bringing Mahmoud into the Divan would also be a boon for his boss and maestro, Daniel Barenboim. Few members of the orchestra were from the occupied West Bank, and none from Gaza. For Mahmoud, Nabeel told Ramzi, the benefits of a musical education overseen by Daniel would be significant.

Others were surprised that Ramzi would not recognize this. "Working with Daniel was an opportunity not to be missed," declared Mariam Said. "Had Edward been alive he would have encouraged Mahmoud. Ramzi has to control each and every one of his students. He is afraid to let go."

What Mariam and Daniel apparently did not realize, however, was that the Divan had become a serious political problem for Ramzi. Its message of harmony between traditional enemies obscured the truth on the ground, he believed, and led to the charges of normalization. As a result Ramzi refused to consider sending Al Kamandjati students there. The stakes were too high. Just a few weeks earlier, one of Ramzi's peers—Juliano Mer-Khamis, leader of the Freedom Theatre in the Jenin refugee camp, whose provocative productions seemed to anger all sides in the conflict— had been assassinated, shot point-blank in the head by a masked gunman in front of the theater. Ramzi himself had been receiving threats lately, mainly menacing e-mails, referring to Celine, Ramzi's Christian wife. The threats also castigated Al Kamandjati for teaching boys and girls together, calling this an insult to Islam. The e-mails labeled Ramzi an infidel. Ramzi believed these threats, like the fire in Jenin, were rooted in petty jealousies rather than genuine religious convictions. Nevertheless, they added to his tensions, and to his sense that a feel-good program of musical peacemaking, as represented by the Divan Orchestra, made less sense when peace and harmony had dissolved all around him.

If the Divan, as a full orchestra, had been willing to denounce the occupation, Ramzi would have encouraged Mahmoud to play and to study with Daniel. Instead, Ramzi had made arrangements for Mahmoud to attend a conservatory in France. But Nabeel, Ramzi believed, had gone behind his back.

"This is bullshit," Ramzi said sharply. "You're playing a game, but you're putting our relationship"—personal and institutional—"in danger."

Then Ramzi threatened his old friend.

"If you push this to happen, I'll tell everybody in all Palestine." He would speak out against Nabeel and the Barenboim-Said Foundation, and formally endorse a boycott of the West-Eastern Divan Orchestra. Recently, more international artists and trade unions had joined or endorsed the BDS movement. In the face of the stream of international criticism, an Israeli think tank warned that the "delegitimization challenge" could "develop into a comprehensive existential threat within a few years." Following this, the Israeli Knesset had passed a law effectively criminalizing boycotts against Israel, drawing sharp rebuke from many Israeli critics and further emboldening Palestinian supporters of BDS. The Divan Orchestra and the Barenboim-Said Foundation, Ramzi and Nabeel knew, could ill afford to be targeted for a boycott.

Ramzi's taxi raced deeper into the scorching Jordan Valley, and the line went dead.

At Jericho, Ramzi got out of the taxi and entered a bus, which dropped him at a large passenger terminal built at the beginning of the Oslo process to facilitate travel for Palestinians between Jordan and the West Bank. He stood in line for a ticket on a second bus that would take him from the Palestinian autonomous area to the Israeli-controlled border at the River Jordan in the Palestinian West Bank. Israel had seized this crossing in 1967 and was determined not to give it up. Nearly all of the Jordan Valley was now an Israeli military zone, and Palestinians lived there under severe travel restrictions. Water use was sharply reduced and new construction prohibited. Violators were subjected to house demolitions by the Israeli army. Since 1967, Israel had destroyed twenty-six thousand Palestinian homes in the occupied territories. By 2011, the indigenous Palestinian population of the Jordan Valley had shrunk from three hundred twenty thousand in 1967 to just under sixty thousand.

Ramzi boarded the second bus and arrived at the border, where he emptied his pockets, submitted his Palestinian ID, and put his luggage on a conveyer belt. After waiting about an hour for the proper Israeli permissions and stamps, he boarded a third bus, which took him over the Jordan to the east bank of the river and the Hashemite Kingdom of Jordan. There, he showed his ID again, emptied his pockets again, and put his bags on another conveyor, before emerging into the light and flagging a taxi to the Amman airport and the flight to Lebanon. On the way, he emptied his pockets a third time. He needed to make sure he had no Israeli money. The presence of a single shekel, the currency of Lebanon's enemy, would be sufficient evidence to bar Ramzi from entry at the Beirut airport. He stuffed his Palestinian ID, with the Israeli stamps, deep in the bowels of his backpack, and pulled out his French passport, free of any evidence of Israel.

In the old days, before 1967, when the Jerusalem airport at Qalandia offered commercial flights to Lebanon, travelers could arrive in Beirut in less than forty-five minutes. Now the journey often took all day.

On the flight from Amman, Ramzi recalled his first trip to Lebanon, a few years earlier, after he had received his French citizenship and passport. Lebanon had always been forbidden for Ramzi, just as it had for almost all of his people, except those already living there—people whose families had fled or been driven out of their homes during the creation of Israel in 1948. Lebanon and Israel had been technically or literally in a state of war ever since; hence for Palestinians living under Israeli occupation, and subject to the scrutiny of border guards from both countries, it was essentially impossible to travel between Palestine and Lebanon. Unless, like Ramzi, they were fortunate enough to hold a passport from another country.

At the Lebanese port of entry border security was uneventful. Ramzi hopped into an airport taxi and rode toward Beirut's Corniche, the beloved seaside walkway, and the once-fashionable West Beirut district of Hamra, in the city Arabs and foreigners liked to call "the Paris of the Middle East."

*   *   *

"How are things after Jenin?" Alice Howick asked Ramzi. She had heard about the murder of Juliano and was worried. It's okay, Ramzi assured her. He didn't tell her about the threats he had been receiving.

Alice and Ramzi were sitting in a smoky Beirut café. Alice had just bought a rose from a local Palestinian refugee boy, and it lay there between them on the table. Ramzi looked around at the stylish Beirut denizens—a mix of locals and expats, flitting from table to table. Ramzi dismissed them as party people and fake intellectuals.

Alice picked up the rose, held it to her nose, twirled it in her fingers, and set it back down. The program in Lebanon had been formally launched with her arrival the previous year. When she took the job she agreed to work at Shatila and two other Palestinian refugee camps in Lebanon for three years. But now, scarcely a year later, she had all but decided to go back to England. Ramzi had hoped to convince Alice to stay, but he sensed she had already made up her mind. He let the subject drop, content to spend the weekend observing the Al Kamandjati refugee camp programs with Alice.

The next morning, a Saturday, Ramzi and Alice walked into Shatila camp, moving past jumbles of concrete and rebar with impossible knots of electrical wire crisscrossing overhead. In 1982 this camp, along with the neighboring Sabra camp, had been the site of one of the most horrific massacres in Palestinian history, when hundreds of unarmed residents, many of them women and children, had been slaughtered by a Lebanese Christian militia. Now the two music teachers walked down a narrow alley lined with colorful stenciled images of fish and seahorses, and into a small community center, where their hosts had set aside space for an Al Kamandjati music program.

Ramzi remembered the first time he had visited Shatila, three years earlier, when he first explored the idea for expanding Al Kamandjati to Lebanon. A few minutes after his arrival at the community center, he had excused himself and stepped outside. He had looked up at the mass of wires, so thick they blocked light. Across the alley, mounds of garbage towered seven feet high. A scooter zipped past Ramzi, nearly hitting him. Children screamed and bounced a ball past his feet.

What the hell happened to us? Ramzi had thought on that first visit. He started imagining the lives of all of these people, stuck here with their own stories, just like Sido and Jamila for all those years in Al Amari. Except, at least, his family was still in Palestine. These refugees were truly in exile. Tears welled up and Ramzi had started to cry, then stopped himself, with one word: Music. He walked back to the community center to make plans to begin the program in Shatila.

Now, three years later, the program was approaching its first anniversary, but Ramzi was about to lose his first director. Alice's departure was partly the result of Al Kamandjati's early and aggressive expansion, managed remotely from Ramallah. Alice felt cut off and unsupported. Celine recalled trying to stay in touch as much as possible, but amid "juggling thirty other things" there was a limit to what she and Ramzi could do. Perhaps more important, Alice's short tenure was rooted in the struggles of a young, smart, strong, sometimes impatient Western woman working alone in one of the most impoverished and anguished of all the Palestinian refugee camps, where a sense of unaddressed grievance ran deep. As much as Alice respected the resilience of the people's struggle and the warmth extended to her by her students and their families, some of the values in the camps made her feel uneasy.

A couple of weeks earlier, Alice had shown up to give violin lessons at the community center in Shatila, and walked in on a kindergarten class. The children were getting a history lesson on Palestine. "And they had little books about geography of Palestine, coloring in the flag—and of course to have a natural passion and curiosity about their country is surely something positive. The kids were learning to read. They had lots of words relating to Palestine on the board, amongst them keffiyeh, the scarf, a lot of different cities in Palestine." These were followed by other words: "the words for soldier, gun, exile, Nakba, catastrophe, war. The word for fleeing.

"You see kindergarten kids being taught when they first start learning the letters, you see that the letter for this week is ya, so they will have all the words beginning in ya. Some of these are normal words, like the name Yahya (John) but there will also be Yehud (Jew), or Yaffa (a town in old Palestine). From the beginning they are being taught that they need to feel sad, they need to feel angry. This kind of upbringing makes the victim identity an absolutely central part of their being."

Another time Alice showed up at the community center in Shatila camp to find three children waiting instead of thirty. "What's going on?" she asked the center director. "Where are they?"

"We have a very hard life in Shatila," the director replied. "You know there was the Nakba and then the massacre and these kids have a very hard, difficult life."

"This is why the kids are not here on this Sunday?"

The story of the Palestinian refugee camp is the story of the past—treasured memories of a village long gone, mixed with the trauma of expulsion—and of the future: dreams of a moment when, somehow, the U.N. resolution promising the right of return will finally be implemented, and the refugees will be allowed to go home. Those old homes, in many cases, no longer exist, but the memory of them does, even among children three generations removed.

Alice had been working in Shatila camp with an eleven-year-old boy, Abdallah Qasweh, who was drawn to Beethoven. Once, during a lesson, Alice mentioned to Abdallah that she'd been to Acca, the town in old Palestine, now Israel, where his family had come from. The boy calmly put his violin in its case, pulled up a couple of chairs, and, Alice recalled, "sat me down and said, 'tell me everything about this place. I want to know it, I want to imagine it.' So I tried to describe for him a little about this beautiful city. And he stopped me and said, *'Fi hamam?'* And *hammam* is the word for a bathroom so I thought he was talking about a Turkish bath. And I told him, 'Yes there are, I've never been but I'm sure it's great.' I thought it was a weird question. And he said, 'No, not hammam, *hamam.*' Which means doves. He wants to know if there's doves in the city. I told him, 'It's two hours that way. Everything you have here . . .' I mean, they feel so far away from this country somehow."

Alice found this longing for home beautiful, unbearably sad, and frustrating. Soon, she would be on a plane for London, anguished by her decision to leave, yet relieved to be going home. Her students, and their parents, expressed disbelief at her departure.

Twenty-seven

UNITY

June 2011
Old Ramallah

R AMZI LOOKED DOWN from the rooftop of Al Kamandjati, resting
his arms on the black metal railing and smoking a Gauloises. He
stood beside a thick, blooming bougainvillea, its flowers the color of dark
rose, which he'd planted at the launch of Al Kamandjati six years earlier.
Below him the courtyard was filling up with Palestinian children and
musicians from Europe, Palestine, and the United States. The visitors
rolled in suitcases packed with sheet music, strings, metronomes, tuners,
valve oil, and gifts from faraway places. *"Ahlein!"* someone cried out in
Arabic. "Welcome back!" Alá, now thirteen years old, threw her arms
around Javier Caballero, a cellist from Boston. Majd Qadi, a trombone
student, walked into a bear hug from his American teacher, Doug Weeks,
a barrel-chested trombonist with a gray ponytail. Violinists from London
embraced pianists from New York. New Englanders kissed the shabab
from Old Ramallah on their cheeks, in the Arab style.

"Oh yeah," said Peter, Ramzi's former teacher, surveying the scene. "It's
starting now."

It was the eve of another music festival and summer camp, which again
brought musicians from across Europe and the United States to join the
students and local teachers. Finally, after six years, Al Kamandjati felt in
many ways like a regular music school, with all its inherent tensions,
personalities, and intense musical exchanges, especially in the summer
months. The scene in the courtyard was part of a global summer ritual, as

musicians leave their orchestras, teaching posts, and day jobs to meet at festivals, swap stories, and debate musical theory.

Where are you from? a voice called out. *Really? I heard you just got a new conductor in London. What's he really like?*

Hussein, now two years old, raced through the courtyard with a shiny plastic airplane, *vrooming* along. It was a gift from Oday; today was Hussein's birthday. In a corner of the courtyard Celine was cutting a cake. Ramzi handed out pieces on paper plates. A loud whistle brought silence, and everyone sang "Happy Birthday," first in English and then Arabic: *"Sana helwa ya jamil! Sana helwa ya jamil . . ."* Hussein set down his airplane and licked the chocolate frosting, then picked up a stuffed bear with red eyes. He smacked it on the ground and laughed as the eyes lit up.

The flute teacher, Maddalena Pastorelli, in red balloon pants, heavy black eyeliner, and jangling bracelets, was cutting sheet music with scissors, transposing an aria from a Bach oratorio for flute, cello, and harpsichord to be sung by Julia, the British voice teacher. Alá stood with her arms folded, frowning as a fellow student, a clarinet player, played "Mary Had a Little Lamb" on her violin. The pianist from New York was trying to explain rugby: "It's like a cross between your football and our football," he said.

Fragrant jasmine flowers helicoptered down to the courtyard, landing at the feet of the musicians. "What's the difference between a viola and an onion?" Javier, the cellist, joked with a colleague. "Because nobody cries when a viola is cut in half. And: there's a difference between a viola and a washing machine. At least, when the washing machine vibrates, what comes out is clean." Viola players had long been the butt of orchestral and chamber music jokes. Violists themselves debated whether this was because some in their ranks were failed violin players, or because, unlike the more temperamental violin players, they could take a joke. Javier said it was because centuries earlier, the best chamber music players made first violin; then came the second violinists; violists came after that.

On a stone bench, Eric Culver, pianist and conductor, and Ben Grow, a trumpeter, were swapping stories of the itinerant musician's life, and the thrill and poverty of playing for a living in New York. They had met scarcely five minutes earlier, but were already into a vigorous debate about conveying the beauty of a composition in performance. "The musician doesn't feel it," Eric insisted, "because they're totally focused on the technical. The minute you start to participate, you risk blowing it. He *embodies* the work. If he gets lost in it, it will fall apart. If you're emotional about it, you can't control it, because you're participating in it."

"The whole reason you practice physicality," Ben countered, "is so that you can turn that off and use every other part of your being to express something."

Helen Sherrah-Davies, a violinist from England, joined in, explaining how Carl Jung's "four functions"—intellect, emotion, intuition, and sensation—apply to performance. "It *is* magic!" she said. "Get yourself out of the way."

The conversation moved to the emotions composers arouse through their music. Wagner's "Tristan chord," was so "untethered," so disorienting, when first performed that some audience members fainted or fell ill. Debussy and Stravinsky similarly stirred up their listeners. The conversation was about eliminating barriers between the composer's emotional intent and the audience's ability to receive it—whether that meant ripping out the boxes in opera houses so patrons couldn't dine while listening, or the shared moment in a live performance when the conductor holds the silence for a seeming eternity at the end of a Mahler symphony, so that everyone's feelings can linger.

"You may not have noticed at the time, but the orchestra was also frozen," Ben said. "The bows were in the air, the trumpets were being held on their mouths, nobody did anything at all."

"Just breathing," Eric adds.

"There's nothing like it."

But Eric and Ben disagreed about whether the musician should share that emotion in the moment of performance.

"Ideally you're there emotionally too, in order to play expressively," Ben said.

"Ben is younger than I am," Eric laughed.

Eric was sixty. He had come to the occupied territories for the second time, returning at the urging of Peter, his colleague at the College of the Holy Cross. Eric liked to say that he was "born in a violin case." Both his parents were concert violinists and natives of Rochester, New York, where they enjoyed the largesse of George Eastman, the founder of Eastman-Kodak. In 1925 Eastman donated a thousand musical instruments to Rochester's public schools, and thus initiated a culture of musical education that eventually reached Eric's father, who had come from a line of blacksmiths in upstate New York. "At age seven my dad ended up with a fiddle in his hand, because it was available," Eric said. "They put music in everybody's hands, and my father became a professional orchestra player for the rest of his life. He was like Ramzi, actually." Rochester's Eastman School of Music is one of most respected conservatories in the United States.

The Eastman story brought to Eric's mind El Sistema, Venezuela's elaborate system of making music accessible to children of all backgrounds. El Sistema produced Gustavo Dudamel, the celebrated conductor of the Los Angeles Philharmonic. And yet, Eric said, like Al Kamandjati, El Sistema is "not about 'making musicians.' It's about improving people's lives through music."

In a small corner of the courtyard at Al Kamandjati, the ideals of Palestinian freedom and musical fellowship had yielded to more practical considerations of running a music school. Peter, just arrived from Massachusetts, was facing a disorganized mess. He was annoyed. Ramzi had been away for two weeks, playing concerts in Europe. While Ramzi was gone, the planning for the festival had been neglected. "We've got plenty of other things to do," Peter complained. "We need to be teaching, we need to be working." Lately Peter felt that Ramzi was spreading himself too thin, and that the entire musical curriculum was suffering. It had fallen upon Peter, who in recent years had become a paid strategist and consultant to Ramzi, to pick up the slack.

Peter had arrived at the outset of an ambitious series of chamber music concerts to find that nothing had been arranged. There was no musical program and yet the first performance was scheduled for the following evening. Peter was scribbling down an impromptu program into a small notebook. "Monday in Jerusalem—whatever Bach arias I feel are ready. Julia and Tarek, two or three arias. Then Javi and I will play some Bartók duos. Mozart duos, Jason and Maddalena. Tuesday, Verdi and Bizet. Helen and Javi with the Dvořák. Then on Thursday we have more baroque, because we can take the harpsichord to the French-German cultural center.

"I'm basically doing what they should have done a month ago—for some reason," Peter fumed. "The whole staff is freaking out because Ramzi went away for two weeks. They're trying to be a professional music school."

He took a breath and softened.

"It's fine. You know, even though this is a crazy way of doing it, it's going to be a wonderful program."

Peter's frustrations were part of the periodic tensions between the professional musicians who flew in for a couple of weeks and the generally less-
experienced local teachers who did the everyday work at Al Kamandjati.
That night, over dinner at a long table at Ziryab, a local Arabic restaurant,
Peter vented his frustrations.

"I need you to be an adult," he told Julia, the voice teacher who had
come from England two years earlier. It had been up to her, Peter believed,
to organize the chamber music concerts. She understood things
differently.

"We're dealing with a lot of burnout," Julia replied. "Try teaching in the
camps. It's a whole different ballgame." Lately Julia had been frustrated
that more of Al Kamandjati's resources seemed to be going to high-visibil-
ity public performances than what she considered the more important
work in the camps. "The camps are getting scraps," she said, and this was
taxing the teachers. Emotionally, Julia was overwhelmed by her weekly
teaching at Jalazon camp near Ramallah, where she gathered a group of
children for their weekly choir practice.

The camp stood nearly in the shadow of a West Bank Jewish
settlement, next to an old Arab village called Jifna, which Julia considered
one of the prettiest in Palestine. Jalazon was a poor place, even by the
standards of refugee camps, and prone to the violent reprisals of a land
under occupation. Recently, a resident of the camp had been assassinated
on suspicion of being a snitch, or "collaborator," for the occupying
army.

Julia saw children as "beings from the spiritual world," and in Jalazon
and the other camps she wanted to help give them "a creative focus that all
kids deserve to have: something positive, something idyllic, something
beautiful, something heavenly." But at Jalazon lately she had seen how the
innocence "just gets shattered so early here." *How are they supposed to grow
up properly, in a healthy way?* she asked herself. *If they just have bare concrete
and narrow streets to play in and filth and the only toys they have are rocks to
throw at each other, what kind of start is that?* Lately these questions were
haunting Julia. It was affecting her work.

Julia looked down at her plate. Peter was silent. A few years earlier, Peter,
playing a concert in England, had introduced Al Kamandjati to Julia.

The two colleagues let the subject drop.

*

Julia's concerns about allocation of resources were shared by other teachers. Al Kamandjati was great at publicity, but sometimes teachers found there was no money for spare reeds, for emergency repair of a trombone—one went through summer camp with the spit valve held together by chewing gum—or for basic supplies in the lessons at the camps.

More fundamental was the feeling, especially among many of the full-time teachers, that their work went unappreciated by Ramzi. This was part of the psychology of a nonprofit organization, when young, committed artists, willing to work long hours and forego significant income in order to be part of a cause, expect appreciation in return. "We kind of feel that we don't receive the appreciation we would like to get," said one teacher in a typical comment. "We hardly hear thank you very much." This sentiment was widespread at Al Kamandjati.

Concerns like this had been expressed, even by admirers of Ramzi, for years.

"If you don't take care of your team," said Saed Karzoun, who left Al Kamandjati in 2009, "you are going to lose them. Already he lost a lot of connections. Don't lose more."

Few if any of the teachers, however, were aware of the amount of loss, in the form of abandonment, violence, and murder, that Ramzi himself had had to deal with his entire life, from age five, nor how the cumulative trauma affected his personality. He kept his private anguish to himself; moreover, he had always been determined to convert the negative into positive, but there was a limit to how much anyone, especially those still living inside their trauma, could do that. And now, with the loss of his classical performances in the Divan, an important outlet for joy, creativity, and spirit had also gone missing.

"I am demanding," Ramzi said when asked about these complaints. "But it's not true that I don't appreciate. I always appreciate." But excessive appreciation, Ramzi believed, was not useful: "If you give too much appreciation, then it doesn't have meaning."

Experienced musicians were not surprised by the tensions. "Every nonprofit I've been associated with has had this sort of planetary relationship of personal dynamics," said Eric, the visiting conductor. "You have this vision person who's the sun, who has lots of energy and personal connections." Ramzi, Eric said, assisted by Peter and his resources, was "the thing that holds the planetary system together." It was typical. "New

York City Opera, Metropolitan Opera, all these great huge things, they all have these central people. You can have huge numbers of talented people all around but without that person in the middle nothing happens."

Ramzi was not soft and fuzzy and never would be. He could be mercurial, remote, impatient, controlling, and overly demanding. "Part of him doesn't want to be involved and will happily leave the country for two months," said one teacher. "And yet part of him needs to control what is happening. He comes back and feels so out of control, it's like, 'Why are the chairs here and not there? Why is that boy having his lesson at two thirty?'"

Many teachers felt stressed and put-upon to meet Ramzi's expectations. Some left before their contracts were finished, and a few students went elsewhere to learn music. But most stayed, because they had never encountered anything like Al Kamandjati: the graceful, inviting physical space, crawling with flowering vines and scattered with cacti filling tattered violin cases; the echoes of violin, trumpet, and timpani, mixed with laughter floating beneath stone arches; the safe space for boys and girls to connect with musical mentors; and perhaps most important, the sense that they were part of a larger national vision of freedom through music. No one disputed that Ramzi's fusion of musical and political self-assertion was unsurpassed. In the coming weeks, that would only deepen.

Twenty-eight

RISE, CHILD

Summer 2011
The Road to Bethlehem

THE CHARTER BUS rolled slowly out of Ramallah on its way to
Bethlehem. Music stands, basses, timpani, and other heavy instruments nestled in the hold. Children and their teachers played card games
on their violin cases as the bus rolled south from Old Ramallah toward
Qalandia and the separation barrier. A harp leaned against a seat, covered
by a piece of red felt. Two girls made faces at each other, competing to see
who could best curl her tongue. In the back, a group of teenaged boys
broke out tablas and began singing and clapping in rhythm.

Alá Shalalda stared out as the vast, snaking gray wall came into view.
From point to point, it was fifteen miles from Ramallah to Bethlehem, but
she knew this trip would take about two hours. At Qalandia, the bus
swung east, around the checkpoint, and then south, along the wall and
through Abu Dis, once considered part of East Jerusalem but now cut off
by the barrier, then deep into Wadi Nar, or the Valley of Fire. In past years,
Alá would share the ride with Rasha, but now her sister was married, with
a newborn baby, and living in the family village, Sa'ir, outside of Hebron.

On a recent visit to Ramallah, Rasha had told Alá of a conversation
she'd had at Al Kamandjati with her old friend Muntasser. They had
recalled the common dream of four teenaged friends, spoken at summer
camp four years earlier on the palace rooftop of the Ottoman sheikh:
Muntasser, the clarinet player, Amir, on guitar, Mahmoud, on violin, and
Rasha, flutist, had dreamed of studying together in France. The three boys

were abroad now, in Angers and Toulouse. At night, at home in Sa'ir, Rasha played the flute to her baby son.

"Every night before I sleep, I play for him," Rasha had told Muntasser. "I still play really well. Now I am going to put all of this into my son. Sometimes he likes to hold the instrument. By God's will, my dreams will happen through my son.

"You have this chance, Muntasser," Rasha said. "You have a chance to be a good musician. Keep it with you; hold it close."

The road before Alá plunged toward the valley and then snaked up through the gray-green hills beyond. A Bedouin sheep camp flashed past: black tarps stretched over wooden two-by-fours and held down by old tires. To the right, the separation wall marched down the valley, its gray upright planks splattered with graffiti. In one stenciled image, by the British guerrilla artist Banksy, a pigtailed girl clutched a handful of balloons, floating upward toward freedom. Behind the wall, East Jerusalem was surrounded almost entirely by Jewish settlements, but for one vacant patch of land, near the Palestinian village of Al Ezaria, and known to Israel and much of the world as E-1. This was the last sliver of land that connected Palestine to Jerusalem. Soon, in response to the modest Palestinian U.N. bid for nonmember limited statehood, Israel would announce plans to put a Jewish settlement on this land, too.

Suddenly hundreds of blackened stumps came into view; for decades, perhaps centuries, olive groves had stood there. Israeli military bulldozers had plowed them under. Officials cited security reasons; terrorists, they said, could hide in the groves. An estimated eight hundred thousand olive trees, whose harvests formed the heart of the Palestinian rural economy and culture, had been uprooted since the beginning of the occupation in 1967. Tens of thousands of olive trees were cleared for the path of the separation barrier. Some were transported and replanted in Tel Aviv or the settlements. Palestinian villagers came to fear the sight of Israel's Caterpillar D9 bulldozers rumbling toward their groves.

The bus ascended slowly out of the scorching heat, cactus giving way to pine, and topped the crest of a hill just east of Bethlehem. To the north lay East Jerusalem. Sunlight sparkled off a golden dome in the distance. "Al Aqsa!" someone shouted. There, beside the golden Dome of the Rock, stood Al Aqsa Mosque, part of the Noble Sanctuary or Haram al-Sharif, the third holiest site in Islam and their symbol of Jerusalem. For Palestinian children, Jerusalem was becoming an imaginary city, forever out of reach. Many had family there but could rarely go themselves. Israel had made concerted efforts to restrict access to Jerusalem, and to suppress Palestinian identity there. In 2009, Israeli military police showed up in East Jerusalem to close down a literary festival dedicated to Jerusalem as the "Center of Arab Culture."

As the bus curved south toward Bethlehem, Jerusalem disappeared from view.

A few hours later, Fadi Basha, the twelve-year-old native of Jenin and singer of Italian arias, was holding court in the lobby of Talitha Kumi, a German Christian retreat center. A thin forest of spindly pines surrounded the low-slung two-story stone building on a hill above Bethlehem. A wooden cross hung on the wall above them, and in nearly every other room. The center was named for a miracle performed by Jesus. *"Talitha kumi,"* Jesus proclaimed to a stricken child. "Rise, little girl." And she did.

Fadi held the full attention of a group of visiting French musicians lounging in cushioned wicker chairs in the tiled lobby. "I like Pavarotti," he announced, repeating the name of the only opera singer he cared to listen to.

"What about Carreras?" asked Étienne Cardoze, a cellist who had been coming to Al Kamandjati every summer since 2005 with fellow members of the Ensemble Orchestral de Paris. "What about Plácido Domingo?"

"Flamingo?" Fadi replied to laughter. *"No.* Pavarotti," he declared, an index finger pointed to the ceiling. "His voice is *fantastico.* Did you know he wanted to be a famous football man, World Cup? But he was so fat, so he cannot! I read it in the computer!"

"For the opera I made with him," Étienne said, "they built him a special chair."

"He bring it with him all the time, ah?" Fadi laughed.

Fadi was still a skinny kid, small for his age. When he was younger, growing up in Japan while his father, Walid, worked on his Ph.D., Fadi had learned how to make origami; once back in Palestine, he had helped his dad fold a thousand cranes, for a project to honor Japan's victims of the Fukushima Daiichi nuclear disaster. "If you can do one thousand cranes," Fadi's father had told him, "all your dreams will come true."

Fadi had just lost his teacher, Julia Katarina, the soprano from England. She had left Al Kamandjati under disputed circumstances after growing mutual tensions. Julia didn't get into the details with Fadi. She just told him she needed to go back to England. Eric Culver, the conductor from Massachusetts, took over Fadi's lessons until the replacement vocal teacher arrived.

The next day, the children took their lessons in sun-filled classrooms in the sprawling stone arms of Talitha Kumi. Alá, in a ponytail and Hello Kitty T-shirt, her toenails painted white, frowned at her sheet music, propped on four stacked chairs in an open violin case. Her teacher, Mirana, a Romanian-French violinist, stood beside her, playing forcefully in a slow, flowing arc. Alá tried to imitate her. A cat dozed in a bookcase in the corner.

Down the hallway, in a near-empty chapel, Eric sat at the grand piano on the altar. Fadi stood beside him. Behind them two large candles flanked a wooden crucifix; above that, on the wall, a stunning tile mosaic depicted the Virgin Mary cradling baby Jesus.

"Did you warm up yet?" Eric asked. Yes, Fadi said, he had.

Eric brought Fadi through "Ave Maria," stopping him frequently. "You don't want to push that top note, just touch it." Eric sang the scale. "Just a little bit of touch on that note."

As they moved into the Italian arias—the ones the young singer had begun with Julia—Eric said, "You're a singing actor, Fadi. What is the story of this? When you say, 'I don't think my girlfriend loves me,' your face should change a little bit. Or when you say, 'If you open my heart, you would see written your name,' you should get a different look on your face. This is acting."

Before concluding the lesson, Eric said Fadi had to take control of the musicians behind him: "You have to make sure to know when it's too loud. Then turn around and say to them that it's too loud. Because when you come down in your voice, it's hard to hear it. You have to make sure you can always be heard. If it makes you sound bad, then you have to know that you have to protect yourself and say this doesn't make me sound good."

At that evening's recital, Fadi waited as the mix of professional and student chamber music groups, Arabic ensembles, solo pianists, cellists, oboists, and Palestinian rappers took their turns. When his time came, he strode to the stage with tabla and oud players from the Oriental Ensemble of Jenin. He launched into a traditional Palestinian folk song, looking around him at his accompanists, pushing his palms toward the ground. Their music softened, and Fadi's voice soared over it. As the song ended, Fadi smiled, bowed, and basked in the loud applause. "This is the best student I've ever had," Eric said to himself.

The guest of honor at Talitha Kumi that evening was the United States Consul General and Chief of Mission in Jerusalem, Daniel Rubinstein. He had arrived an hour earlier, as quietly and unobtrusively as an American diplomat could to a summer music camp in occupied territory: In a bullet-proof sedan, trailed by a pair of security officers in dark suits with earpieces, speaking into their sleeves, and accompanied by a small team of American minders.

The Americans were funding the summer camp, and the accommodations at Talitha Kumi, thanks in large part to Peter's efforts and contacts. The consulate eagerly supported the school, but, as with the Divan Orchestra, Ramzi felt in an increasingly difficult position.

In recent months the Americans had removed pressure from Israel to freeze its settlements, while threatening to veto the Palestinian attempt to establish an independent state through the United Nations. If the United States followed through on that promise, Ramzi knew he might have to decline future American support for his school, which this summer was substantial: Nearly every American musician was here because of American money. But at some point it would be untenable to accept funds from a government that had directly blocked his own people's deepest aspirations.

The consul general sat in the front row, listening to a Mozart sonata performed by Eric, a Palestinian resistance song, "The Stranger," sung by Oday, chamber music performed by a French quartet, a rap song by a blind boy from Jenin, and the Italian aria, belted out by little Fadi.

At a pause in the music, Ramzi dispatched Yanal Staiti, an eighteen-year-old percussion student, to formally welcome the American consul to the concert.

Yanal stood before Daniel Rubinstein, bowing deeply. "On behalf of the students of the Kamandjati Foundation, we would like to welcome Mr. Daniel, and thank the consul for his support of the Kamandjati Foundation, especially the annual summer camp," Yanal said in his native Arabic, which the consul understood perfectly. "We are very pleased that you are with us tonight. The students of Kamandjati will perform a few pieces that they worked on during the summer camp. God willing you will enjoy it. Welcome to all of you." Yanal paused to let the polite applause die down. He looked directly into the consul's eyes.

"But we would like to take this opportunity also to convey our message. We would like to have a state and it's about time to have our freedom. This is not only the will and the wish of the government; it's the wish of every child and every student and every adult present and the whole Palestinian nation."

As the children began whooping and clapping, Yanal continued: "While we are here in your gracious presence we would wish of you to deliver a message to the American government: that it has been long enough that America has used their right of veto against Palestinian freedom, against our freedom. Please, do not use the veto against us anymore."

The message was delivered in a clear, soft voice, with the utmost grace, and its content and tone came off as utterly reasonable.

"The message has been received," the consul replied in perfect Arabic, and with equal restraint. But for the consul and his staff, there to enjoy the fruits of American generosity, it was a diplomatic faux pas. They had come with the understanding there would be no politics inserted into the evening's music.

For Ramzi, that was impossible. He could not pass up the chance to use music in the pursuit of his people's national dreams.

The consul general listened politely to another piece or two. Then, with thanks, his entourage rose and returned to Jerusalem.

*   *   *

A few weeks earlier, on May 15, 2011, Palestinians had observed "Nakba Day," which commemorated the sixty-third anniversary of their dispossession. At the border between Syria and the Israeli-occupied Golan Heights, hundreds of Palestinian refugees living in Syria crashed the fences, forcing their way over the border near the village Majdal Shams in the northern Golan. An Israeli patrol responded with live fire. Four refugees were killed before the border was resealed.

In Israel, the breaches produced deep anxiety. The Nakba was largely a taboo subject in Israel. Recently, the Knesset had approved the "Nakba Law," which sanctioned fines against communities within Israel that observe Nakba Day. Israel's education ministry had already banished the word *Nakba* from textbooks, including those that serve Palestinian children in Israel. But the border breaches generated many headlines about the possibility of a third intifada. Defense Minister Ehud Barak warned of future incursions.

"This is huge," Ramzi said, the day after the refugees crashed the Golan border. "To surround yourself with walls—that is a short-term solution. Not long term. In the long term, we will integrate, and everyone will have their rights."

*   *   *

One evening, near the end of the recitals at the Bethlehem summer camp, Ramzi had a proposal for the group: What did they think about traveling to a beautiful old village called Battir, on the border with Israel? There, amid the ancient agricultural terraces dating to Roman times, they would perform Mozart and Bizet. They would do so, Ramzi proposed, across the West Bank border, in Israel, thus asserting the refugees' right to return to their homeland of old Palestine. There was cheering, and there were some worried looks. "Check with your parents," Ramzi said.

Some players—children and adults—were nervous. Crossing the border could risk arrest, jail time, and possibly deportation of the visiting players. But ever since he was eight years old and holding a stone, Ramzi had looked for chances to provoke Israel. At his core was the desire to live in his homeland and to return to the place where his grandfather was born, which he had spent his whole life hearing about, but never experienced, except through stories. "I lived it fully, with my grandfather," Ramzi said. "And I think all the grandfathers and grandmothers, each one transmits their village, and gives fantastic detail to their grandchildren." Even when the grandparents die, many families continue to pass on the oral history. Each year, the apricots grow larger, the oranges sweeter, and the villages, which no longer exist, are still mapped out on blank sheets of paper, emblazoned into the minds of Palestinian children.

"We are the refugees," Ramzi said. "And they want to solve our problems without really thinking. Many people think you can solve a problem without involving the ones who are most directly concerned." Ramzi wanted to give the children, many of whom came from villages and towns in what was now Israel, the opportunitty "to see this beautiful landscape, which was their landscape, which belonged to them." But he insisted this dream of return was not a fantasy. "There is no fantasy. It's a right. But you know you can't get anything you want in one second. You need really to wait. And you never work for it to see it yourself. Maybe for my son. Or for the son of my son."

Ramzi considered his life's work a form of resistance to occupation, and the proposed action in Battir bore similarities to the border crashing in the Golan of a few weeks earlier.

Not everyone, however, was comfortable recruiting musicians, especially children, to participate. A few dropped out. One, a visiting instructor from Britain, felt the politics were too brazen, and that the effort clouded their mission of musical education. Fadi also declined to go. His father, Walid, did not want his son to participate in such a risky confrontation. Fadi would stay at the summer camp.

*   *   *

That night—the eve of departure to Battir—Ramzi dreamed of music drifting into a westbound train, which would pass through the village and roll past the ruins of Na'ani, his ancestral home, carrying song into old Palestine on its way toward the Mediterranean Sea. The passenger train followed much the same line as previous trains in old Palestine: from Jerusalem, along the coastal plain, toward Jaffa and Tel Aviv. Now, the train was Israeli. "I would love to send my music and my love through this train to Na'ani," Ramzi said, the rims of his eyes turning red. "Through space. Through the train. Through imagination. At the time the train would pass I don't know which music will be playing. It's just a message from me to my village and to everybody. Many people think this is too much dreaming. Or too much philosophy. But it's not dreaming at all. I have spoken with many farmers. And they say, when you come in the morning to your land, and you speak with the trees and you say good morning, I hope you are fine and you address your love to your land, all of them say that the trees become stronger and bigger. And that's why I always give importance to my land. You have the right to dream. Everything is possible."

The caravan of buses, vans, and taxis left in the warm afternoon, bearing eighty young musicians and their teachers. They rode down from the terraces of Talitha Kumi toward the old Palestinian village of Battir. They crossed a maze of jurisdictions, moving through tiny Palestinian village islands in the larger Israeli-controlled sea.

The lead bus moved slowly down across the broken pavement, toward a long tunnel connecting one Palestinian village to another. On the restricted road above, cars with yellow plates zipped past, carrying Jews from one settlement to another. Thus was the land being carved up not only horizontally, but vertically, with Palestinians occupying the understory of the West Bank landscape.

The bus stopped in the village, at the edge of the border with Israel. Here was one of the few places where no separation barrier carved into the landscape at the edge of the West Bank. The village seemed to spill across both sides of the Israeli border; houses on one side, farms on the other. Whitewashed stone buildings crawled up the juniper-studded hillsides. The stone glowed a soft yellow in the afternoon light. Terraced olive groves, some of the oldest in the Middle East, stepped gently up the hillsides. It was as quiet and peaceful as a Palestinian village could be, all the moreso for the absence of the gray concrete wall. That barrier was nowhere in sight; its absence evoked another time and invited a softening of the hard realities of the present. The Palestinian Authority, joined by Israeli environmentalists, planned to petition UNESCO to declare Battir a World Heritage site, which, they hoped, would end plans to drive the barrier through the village.

For generations of Palestinian refugees who still dreamed of going home, Palestine seemed to be united again by the apparent absence of a border at Battir. Reclaiming the homeland, to Ramzi and many of the young musicians, seemed as simple as walking across the railroad tracks and playing music for the hills and the westbound train. Yet the border between the West Bank and Israel was real, and crossing it carried immense risks for Ramzi, his teachers, their students, and, it could be argued, for the future of Al Kamandjati.

A small group of teachers stood in a dirt clearing under the sun, heatedly debating the wisdom of crossing into Israel. Surveillance cameras kept watch at the power station along the railroad tracks and would surely detect an entire orchestra crossing the border. Ramzi still wanted to go; he returned from scouting a location on the other side. Peter warned him that students could face arrest, and teachers could face deportation, by Israel. "And let's say they blacklist four of us internationals, and two of them happen to actually be full-time teachers. Where does that leave your organization in September? I mean it's an obvious choice, you just don't mess with it."

Ramzi relented. They would stay on the West Bank side of the railroad tracks, not risking their own arrest or that of the children.

The members of the Al Kamandjati's youth orchestra—a Palestinian trombonist, a French cellist, a Greek oud player, an American violinist, and dozens of other Palestinian and Western musicians—trudged up a gravel road, into the hills above Battir. Carrying their instruments and music stands, they walked away from the village along a shiny steel fence and into the shade of a hillside in the late afternoon.

The orchestra assembled near the bend of the deserted mountain road. They tuned, and fell silent as Jason raised his hands.

The sound of Mozart's Sixth Symphony rose into the hills above Battir. Behind them, to the east, the village was awash in the late afternoon light. The setting was idyllic, and the only one who seemed disappointed was Wassim Daraghmeh, at nine years old the youngest member of the orchestra. He was upset because nobody came to listen.

"I want people to hear music, and to be able to know what music is," said the young violinist.

During the performance, a train passed quietly beneath them, heading west.

"This railway passes through many villages that we are from," Ramzi said just after the concert. "Many of us think that we don't have enough power, but I think the music is a very big power. And I am sure that our villages will receive this sound that we've played. I myself believe in the music," he said, "and I believe that we will one day go back to our homes."

Twenty-nine

ODE TO JOY

August 2011
Cologne, Germany

A MONTH AFTER THE Bethlehem summer camp, in Cologne, two thousand miles to the north, a German chorus of 104 filed into the three balcony rows behind the West-Eastern Divan Orchestra. On the stage below, Daniel Barenboim welcomed his old friend, Waltraud Meier, just arrived from Berlin to rehearse the fourth and final movement of Beethoven's Symphony no. 9, the "Ode to Joy," for the evening's performance. It was the last day of a week of Beethoven's nine symphony performances in a concert hall on the Rhine River.

The musicians, dressed in jeans, T-shirts, and tennis shoes, looked up at the maestro as he suspended his baton above his head.

Low strings emerged from the void of silence, growing slowly louder, moving toward the choral surge. "It has all been likened to the creation of the world," wrote the music historian Christopher H. Gibbs of the Ninth Symphony. "Certainly no symphony before had sounded anything like it." The Ninth, composed by a man who grew up during the French and American revolutions, was a kind of freedom symphony, and nearly two centuries later it was considered by some to be one of the greatest works of art ever created.

"This music speaks a universality of thought, of human brotherhood, freedom, and love," conductor Leonard Bernstein had declared. This was why the Ninth had been embraced by the Olympic Games, by protesters at Tiananmen Square, by the European Union for its anthem, and by

Bernstein himself, when he conducted the symphony in Berlin in 1989, at the fall of the Berlin Wall.

In Germany, the Ninth Symphony performed by the Divan took on extra meaning. That evening in Cologne, 40 Arabs, 40 Jews, 20 Spaniards, and 104 Germans strode onstage and into the first rows of the stage balcony. Their Jewish conductor raised his baton, creating utter silence at the beginning of a sustained call for universal freedom. Forty-five minutes later, poet Friedrich Schiller's words rang out in Beethoven's thunderous melody. "Joy, beautiful spark of the gods . . . All men become brothers, under thy gentle wing," sang Waltraud and the choir above her: the finale of the Ninth, completed in 1824 by a native son, conducted by a Jew, and performed by Arabs and Israelis in a concert hall along the Rhine. Now in its twelfth year, the Divan Orchestra commanded greater critical acclaim than during its early days as a youth orchestra, even if its fame was largely related to its novelty and its famous conductor. "It felt as if the enthusiasm is as much for the noble cultural project and the great man at its helm as for the performances themselves, which are sometimes, it needs to be said, rather patchy and underachieved," a British reviewer declared. Yet in the Cologne orchestra hall that evening, no words or analysis could measure the feeling in the air, or the duration and emotion of the standing ovation.

*   *   *

Missing at the Divan this year was Ramzi. Mariam Said told the orchestra that Ramzi had said he was too busy with Hussein and the music school, but they knew his reasons were more complex. Ramzi himself had told Daniel and Mariam he would not be coming back unless the Divan stood up publicly against the occupation of the Palestinians.

"He's constantly in friction within himself," said Daniel, sitting in a sun-dappled outdoor café in an old church square just above the Rhine. "On the one hand, what he wants to do for his people and on the other hand what he wants to do for himself, for his own development." Daniel paused, taking a puff of his cigar, already nearly down to a stub. He had a broad, open face, and he gestured by opening his palms toward each other. He wore a dark suit with a pink, polka-dotted tie; he was about to attend a ceremony at which the town fathers would give him the key to the city.

"I have a lot of affection for Ramzi," the maestro said. "Ramzi came with us on tour. I took him on every press conference. In London. In Salzburg. In Berlin. He could say whatever he wanted. And he did. I never said, 'No you can't say that.' I never did. So he had a fantastic platform. It was an internal problem for him."

Daniel and Mariam believed Ramzi had gotten caught up in the forces of the boycott, and been swept away. "I'm sorry for him. And I'm sorry that he doesn't see the Divan for what it is. This is not about normalization. The minute they [boycott supporters] hear the word Israel or Israeli they say no. But the world is not made up only by systems of government, but by people.

"In the orchestra, there is equality. In the orchestra, there are no checkpoints. There is no occupied territory. There is no occupier and occupied. And I think that this is in that respect an alternative way of thinking. That was Edward's idea. And they agree about the music one hundred percent. This is the most homogeneous orchestra I've ever conducted. Musically. They don't agree about everything else, but they listen to each other."

* * *

Ramzi would smile when he heard that Mariam said his fellow musicians in the Divan were asking about him, and that she'd reported, "They love Ramzi. Really they love Ramzi." As his Divan colleagues were rehearsing in Cologne, Ramzi seemed to long for the fellowship of the orchestra, and of Daniel.

"We always had nice relations," Ramzi said about Daniel, in the quiet courtyard of Al Kamandjati, long after the summer camp had ended and the visiting musicians had rejoined their orchestras in Europe. "I never have been shy to tell him anything, and he always was surprised by my frankness. I never hide anything. Yeah, I wish that we could have a personal friendship but I know it's not easy. I think because he's just—he's a very busy man. And he wants me for a certain reason. And that's sad."

Did he miss Daniel? "Yes," Ramzi said. "Very much. As a musician and as a human being."

Yet Ramzi did not appear to regret his decision to leave the Divan. His choice mirrored the deterioration of relations between Israel and the Palestinians, since Oslo and especially in more recent years. As hopes for a genuine Arab-Israeli reconciliation faded, many of the other Arab musicians in the orchestra also found it difficult to participate in the Divan. Some would not agree to interviews; others requested that they only be identified by their first names, for fear of recriminations back home. Auditions were held in undisclosed locations in the Arab countries, and some musicians were interrogated by national intelligence agencies about their participation. Because the orchestra, as a group, had not taken a stand against the occupation of the Palestinians, it was increasingly seen in the Arab world as a collaborator with Israel. One Divan violinist described a breakup with his fiancée, who had demanded that he quit the orchestra in support of the boycott. Even Edward Said, intent on forging his alternative vision for peace, may not have expected the fierce and widening divisions that confronted some orchestra members, even within their own families. Or, perhaps he would have.

For the orchestra, in the end, the Divan was about the music; for audiences, extra resonance came from what it seemed to represent. In the applause in Cologne, or in the summer of 2012 at the Royal Albert Hall in London, or in early 2013 at Carnegie Hall in New York City, the very national, ethnic, and religious composition of the orchestra moved people in ways that could not only be explained by the music. "In the finale of the Ninth," wrote a restrained reviewer in the *New Yorker*, "Beethoven's plea for universal brotherhood registered even more strongly than usual." And when Daniel himself, after the finale of the Ninth, stood on stage at the Royal Albert Hall, explaining that the orchestra's hopes to play in East Jerusalem, in support of Palestinian civil society, had been quashed by a Palestinian-led boycott, Daniel nevertheless held the rapt audience in his hands.

"There were factions, Palestinian factions who protested about this concert, and [so] we are not going," a perspiring Daniel said.

"Awwww," the crowd responded in unison.

"Never mind the concert, much worse is the reason. The reasoning behind it is that we represent for them an instrument of 'normalization.' In other words, of accepting the present status quo with the occupation, the settlements, and all that that means. And I want to tell you one thing. We are not a political project, we don't have a political program, but we have a certain amount of social conscience and solidarity with civic societies who suffer."

"Bravo, sir!" cried a man in the crowd.

"And what makes this orchestra, besides the individual talent and the musicianship and the hard work and dedication of each one of these members, is that they play together with this homogeneity because here in our West-Eastern Divan Orchestra, they are all equals."

A long cheer rose up from the audience.

Thirty

A MUSICAL INTIFADA

Summer 2013
Near Hebron, West Bank

Rasha shalalda, the young Palestinian flutist, smiled at her visitors from an open doorway, quickly beckoning them forward and up the stairs of her house in the family's ancestral village of Sa'ir. Upstairs she directed the visitors to an overstuffed gold couch tossed with embroidered Palestinian pillows, beneath framed quotations from the Qur'an and a framed inscription in Arabic: "The heart of a mom is a flower that never dies." She brought juice and cookies, then pulled out a photo album. Rasha flipped through pictures of her parents, of Shehada, Alá, and their sisters in younger days, and of her grand wedding in Sa'ir three years earlier. In one picture Rasha and her groom stood under a flowered arch covered with shining leaves. LOVE STORY, read the caption, in English. As she turned the pages, Rasha's son, Amir, two years old, picked up a blue toy car, dropped it, and began to stomp on it, sending bits of plastic flying across the tile floor.

Rasha paused at photos from Italy. "I want to go back there," she said wistfully. "The two important things in Italy were respect and freedom. Then coming back here, and looking at how things are, I wish I hadn't gone."

Rasha agreed to play. She retrieved her flute, pulled out sheet music from a green file folder, and taped it to a wall, at eye level: Bach's Sonata no. 2, arranged for flute. She had learned it from her favorite Al Kamandjati flute teacher, Irena from Italy, who had been able to determine Rasha's moods depending on how she played. "I'm out of practice," Rasha said. Still, her notes danced; then they were long and steady.

Presently Rasha's husband came home from his job in a nearby Israeli settlement, Ma'ale Adumim, where he worked in construction. He was one of more than twenty-six thousand Palestinians who worked in the settlements, about one third of them illegally and most for less than the Israeli minimum wage of $6.55 per hour. In their work, especially in building new settlement housing, they were helping to fuel their own dispossession. But their families had to eat. Every day, riding a van to and from the settlement, Rasha's husband was confronted by the contrasts. "Israeli kids, they have security, parks in front of their houses. Palestinian children, they have none of that. You can't find a house here where you don't have one or two martyrs, one or two prisoners." He found his work humiliating. Once, he said, a young daughter of a settler wandered into a construction site, and a co-worker gently warned her, in Arabic, to stay away. The father, armed, stormed over, screaming at the man for speaking to his child. This man was only trying to protect your girl, Rasha's husband had explained in broken Hebrew. He would like to quit his job, but his family needs the one hundred eighty dollars per week he brings home for Rasha and Amir. So he preferred not to have his picture taken, or to have his name printed in this book.

Before the visitors left they were treated to a feast prepared by Rasha's hand: chicken stuffed with rice and ground beef and sprinkled with pine nuts and Arabic spices; stuffed grape leaves and eggplants; hummus; fresh warm flatbread; and orange soda.

Rasha worried that her people no longer cared about the Palestinian struggle. "For sixty-five years we were under occupation, then people come and tell us to dream. We can dream if someone helps us. I want freedom. I want to go to the sea. When the occupation is over, then I'll allow myself to dream."

*　　*　　*

On March 19, 2013, Oday Khatib, the singer who Ramzi had found in the Al Fawwar refugee camp, was arrested by Israeli soldiers, taken to Ofer Prison near Ramallah, and charged with throwing stones. Soldiers claimed that Oday was part of a group of youths hurling rocks in the camp that day. Oday and his family maintained that he was waiting for a friend on a hill in Al Fawwar, and not connected to the stone-throwing shabab. They said that Oday's cell phone records would confirm a recent call to his friend.

For many Palestinians, throwing stones at occupying Israeli soldiers is still considered legitimate resistance to a military occupation that is nearly half a century old. Oday's brothers had clashed repeatedly with Israeli soldiers since at least 2002, after brother Rasmi was shot in the shoulder in an Al Fawwar schoolyard and lost the use of his left arm. Yet Oday had found his resistance to the occupation in his voice. At age twenty-two, Oday, alone among his brothers, had never before been arrested. "Oday is not like any of my other sons," his father, Jihad, told the military court when the charges were brought against his son. "He is not interested in throwing stones or getting involved in this. Since he was nine years old he was interested only in music." Oday also maintained he would not put his budding singing career at risk by throwing stones. "I have my life and my work to worry about," he told the court. He was one of the stars of Al Kamandjati, and had recorded and toured with various Arabic music ensembles in France, Belgium, Lebanon, Norway, Italy, Palestine, Dubai, Algeria, and Austria. In an interview, Jihad said, "For our family, Oday is the free bird. We're the prisoners, and now he's captured."

Oday was charged under Section 212 of Israeli Military Order 1651, which states that anyone convicted of throwing stones "[a]t a person or property, with the intent to harm the person or property shall be sentenced to ten years imprisonment." Children as young as fourteen could be charged under the law, according to UNICEF. The conviction rate in such military trials was 99.74 percent, or 399 of 400.

Faced with the prospect of a long prison term, Oday agreed to plead guilty in exchange for a three-month term. And so he joined the 4,700 Palestinians being held by Israel. Since 1967, an estimated 650,000 Palestinians, or 40 percent of the adult male population, had spent time in an Israeli prison.

On Oday's first day of incarceration, a fellow inmate, learning Oday was from Al Fawwar, asked if he knew a young man, also a singer from that camp. The inmate had seen this singer on TV, in a documentary called *It's Not a Gun*.

"That's me," Oday said, smiling.

Oday's fellow inmates insisted he sing rather than perform daily chores in the cellblock. "I tried my best to change the atmosphere of the prison and make a pleasant mood for everyone," he said. "I started singing for them and telling them that we should pretend we were in a summer camp, not a prison, just to lighten things up." Yet the songs were rarely happy ones.

Once an old man came and asked Oday to sing a song about mothers. While in prison, the man's mother had died. "I yearn for my mother's bread," Oday sang, from the poem by the great Palestinian poet Mahmoud Darwish. "I yearn for my mother's coffee. I yearn for my mother's touch, and the childhood memories that grow inside me, day after day." And he sang "Haddy ya Bahar" ("Calm Down, Sea"), about a sailor who implores the sea to be still; that he and his shipmates will be coming back one day, however long the journey.

After three months Oday was released. His feelings were mixed. "When all my family and friends met me at the checkpoint," Oday said, "I told them that they did not have to do all of this. I mean I barely spent any time in prison." He could not stop thinking about his fellow prisoners. "I feel like I am abandoning the guys," he said. "I feel guilty. I'm ashamed for spending only three months in prison."

Nevertheless, Oday began to make plans, starting with a birthday party for Hussein, Ramzi and Celine's son, now four years old. He had performances scheduled in France and Dubai, and was considering entering the "Arab Idol" singing competition, which had been won by a Gazan in 2013, sparking rare jubilant celebrations across Palestine. "And to get engaged," Oday added. "There are some plans for that."

*   *   *

By January 2014 Israel's separation barrier was nearly finished. Officials announced that its last portion would go through Battir, the Palestinian village where Al Kamandjati students had performed Mozart a few summers earlier. The barrier would destroy the livelihood of most Battir villagers, whose delicate agricultural terraces, famous for their aubergines, or eggplants, have been watered by stone canals since Roman times.

The plan to build the barrier through Battir was due in part to the American-backed peace negotiations led by U.S. secretary of state John

Kerry. The Palestinian Authority planned to submit Battir for recognition as a UNESCO World Heritage site, thus slowing or even stopping the separation barrier. The bid had the backing of Israeli environmental groups and even a nearby Israeli settlement. Under American pressure, however, Palestinian President Mahmoud Abbas agreed not to submit the proposal. The World Heritage application, the Palestinian delegation was told, would harm talks with Israel. It was deemed necessary to destroy the village in order to save the peace process.

The peace negotiations collapsed anyway, even though Abbas, under pressure from the United States, had also dropped his demand for a freeze on Israeli settlements. President Obama's attempts to secure such a freeze had long since failed. Instead, mere hours after Vice President Joe Biden, on a visit to Israel, pledged America's "absolute, total, unvarnished commitment to Israel's security," Prime Minister Netanyahu announced the construction of sixteen hundred new apartments in East Jerusalem. Now, in the negotiations with Abbas, Netanyahu had another demand, again backed by the United States: to recognize Israel as a Jewish state. This demand was connected to a broader issue in Israel. Israelis saw Palestinians as a "demographic threat" to the state's Jewish identity and debated ways to increase the nation's percentage of Jews. The foreign minister, Avigdor Lieberman, pressed for loyalty oaths for non-Jewish citizens and advocated moving the separation barrier to exclude Israeli Arab communities and incorporate more settlers. Yet for Abbas to accept Israel's Jewish-state demand would amount to a denial of Palestinian history and a declaration of surrender. One of every five Israeli citizens was a Palestinian, and the roots of all four million Palestinian refugees worldwide lay in the flight and expulsion during the creation of Israel in 1948. Formal Palestinian recognition of Israel, Abbas said, had been built into previous agreements dating to Oslo's Declaration of Principles in 1993. This new demand, Palestinians believed, was an attempt to rewrite those agreements. Abbas refused it, and the peace talks collapsed.

As a direct result, prospects for Battir improved. The Palestinian Authority, with little to lose, submitted its proposal to UNESCO, which approved the bid in April 2014. Battir, along with the Church of the Nativity in Bethlehem, was now a Palestinian World Heritage site.

With newfound freedom from the demands of the United States and Israel, Abbas now inked a reconciliation pact with Hamas. The Islamic organization, severely weakened by its fractured alliances with former supporters Egypt, Syria, and Iran, appeared desperate to reach out. In the reconciliation pact it agreed to hand over power, including that of the prime minister and all major cabinet postions, to Abbas's West Bank factions. Most significant, it pledged to recognize Israel, adhere to nonviolence, and abide by past agreements under the Oslo process. These were precisely the measures the United States and Israel had been demanding of Hamas. In its specifics, the unity deal was far more conciliatory than what Hamas had offered in its secret letter to George Bush in 2006.

"The era of discord is over," declared Hamas leader Ismail Haniyeh, standing with Fatah officials. For Palestinians, the unity pact was an effort to fight political and physical fragmentation and build toward a connected Palestine. For Israel and the West, it appeared to be a rare opportunity to seize the chance for a long-term peace.

Instead, Benjamin Netanyahu denounced the agreement, suspended the already moribund peace talks, and accused Abbas of collaborating with "a terrorist organization bent on the destruction of Israel." Crushing Hamas remained a national priority.

A few weeks later, in June 2014, three Israeli teenagers, Gil-Ad Shaer, Naftali Fraenkel, and Eyal Yifrah, were kidnapped while hitchhiking from Jewish seminaries in a West Bank settlement to Jerusalem. Israel quickly blamed Hamas. Hamas, often quick to claim responsibility for attacks, denied its involvement. Undeterred, Israel launched Operation Brother's Keeper. More than two thousand soldiers conducted dozens of raids across the West Bank, searching twenty-two hundred homes and arresting some four hundred Palestinians, more than a third of those without charge or due process.

Most of those were Hamas members and only a small portion were interrogated about the kidnapping. Evidence suggested that the Israeli authorities knew within a day that the teens had been murdered, and that Netanyahu's government was using the pretext of their abductions to cripple Hamas.

After eighteen days the tragedy was confirmed: The teens' bodies were found, buried in a field near Hebron. A wave of grief and rage swept across Israel. Tens of thousands of Israelis attended the funeral, where Netanyahu declared, "May God avenge their blood." An Israeli Facebook page, "The People of Israel Demand Revenge," quickly garnered thirty-five thousand "likes." A member of the Knesset from a party in the nation's ruling coalition posted an article by Netanyahu's late former chief of staff, calling for the killing of "the mothers of [Palestinian] martyrs" and the demolition of their homes: "Otherwise, more little snakes will be raised there."

Israel's ambassador to the United States, Ron Dermer, declared, "You're talking about savage actions . . . In the case of Israel, we take legitimate actions of self-defense, and sometimes, unintentionally, Palestinian civilians are harmed." That day Palestinian teenager Mohammed Abu Khdeir was abducted and murdered, his body set ablaze. This was another "price tag" attack, and it sparked furious protests in Arab East Jerusalem amid talk of a third intifada.

In the wake of the four deaths, an American organization, Jewish Voice for Peace, unearthed a little known statistic: Since 2000, 1,384 Palestinian children had been killed by Israel's military—an average of one every three or four days for fourteen years. "All lives are precious," the group declared. Within weeks, hundreds more Palestinian children would be killed.

In response to Israel's raids and arrests, Hamas launched rockets over the Gaza border. Israel responded with massive airstrikes on Gaza, followed by a ground invasion. The dead included nine men watching the World Cup in a Gaza beachside café, twenty-one people taking refuge in a U.N. school, four boys—cousins aged nine, ten, and eleven—playing hide-and-seek in the fishing shacks along the Mediterranean, and seventy people in the Shejaiya neighborhood, much of which was leveled by Israeli shells in less than an hour.

Finally the two sides agreed on an apparently long-term truce. By then Israeli airstrikes had destroyed more than eighteen thousand homes and buildings, left one hundred thousand Gazans homeless, and killed more than twenty-one hundred people. Nearly three-quarters of these were civilians, by U.N. estimates, including nearly five hundred children. On the Israeli side, sixty-four soldiers and five civilians died.

As Israel, backed by the United States, again asserted its right to defend iself and to target militants in crowded urban neighborhoods, the United Nations' human rights groups called for war crimes investigations.

Near the war's end Israel declared it had successfully sealed tunnels Hamas had dug into Israel. But its attempts to crush Hamas or destroy its military capacity had failed, just as they had with Hezbollah in Lebanon eight years earlier. Nor had Israel presented compelling evidence that Hamas leaders ordered the killing of the three Israeli teens, or had known in advance of their kidnappings. A Hamas official in Turkey declared its leaders were responsible, but other experts were skeptical; more important, Israeli intelligence officials saw the operation as local, not ordered from above. In other words, evidence of Hamas leaders' involvement in the deaths of the three teens—which Israel had cited as a central justification for its bombing of Gaza—appeared tenuous. One publication chided Israel for the "WMD of the Gaza onslaught."

Ironically, the Palestinian unity agreement—Israel's response to which had prompted the latest cycle of destruction and loss of life—remained intact. Despite obstacles, officials from both Fatah and Hamas pledged their determination to form a joint governing coalition, and fight the separation between Gaza and the West Bank.

Experts, meanwhile, predicted it would take years for Gazans to rebuild and recover, if they ever could.

In the sheer amount of destruction in Gaza, Israel did, however, appear to succeed in one long-term strategic objective, which could be traced back a generation to Ariel Sharon: physically dividing Palestinians from one another, thus undermining any chance for Palestinian self-determination in a "viable and contiguous state." President Obama's Middle East team had already cited Israeli intransigence in the collapse of the Kerry peace talks; a few months later, in the midst of the Gaza war, a senior U.S. official, speaking in Tel Aviv, vented U.S. frustrations. "How will Israel remain democratic and Jewish if it attempts to govern the millions of Palestinian Arabs who live in the West Bank?" asked Philip Gordon, White House coordinator for the Middle East, in an unusually strong diplomatic rebuke of a close ally. "How will it have peace if it is unwilling to delineate a border, end the occupation, and allow for Palestinian sovereignty, security, and dignity? It cannot maintain military control of another people indefinitely."

Three days later at a press conference, Netanyahu made it clear that he had no intention of heeding the White House's words or of allowing a sovereign Palestinian state. "There cannot be a situation, under any agreement, in which we relinquish security control of the territory west of the River Jordan," he said on July 11, referring to the entire West Bank and Gaza. Israel's prime minister had finally stated what had been clear to so many for so long: Israel has no interest in a two-state solution. This was further confirmed in late summer, when Israeli officials announced the annexing of one thousand acres in the West Bank, and in the fall, when they revealed plans for fifteen hundred new Jewish housing units in East Jerusalem. President Obama's spokesman warned such moves would invite international condemnation of Israel and "call into question" its commitment to peace. On the ground, Palestinian youths angered by the new land grabs and by the Israeli soldiers who blocked their access to pray at Al Aqsa Mosque, poured into the streets of East Jerusalem. As clashes erupted yet again in the would-be capital of Palestine, an anonymous U.S. official called Netanyahu a "chickenshit." United States–Israeli relations plunged toward an all-time low.

Europeans responded differently. Parliaments in Ireland and the United Kingdom issued nonbinding votes to recognize an independent Palestinian state. Sweden's prime minister declared his nation's formal recognition of Palestine, becoming the 135th country to do so. Other European nations appeared ready to join the list. The United States did not.

*   *   *

That same summer of 2014, as Israel's search-and-arrest operation continued across the West Bank, Ramzi decided to go forward with Al Kamandjati's annual summer music festival and camp. Teachers were already arriving from Europe and America; Alá, Mahmoud, Muntasser, and their fellow students were rehearsing Beethoven's Fifth Symphony and were excited at the prospect of performing it in Jerusalem, Haifa, and across the West Bank. Ramzi recalled the time in 2003 when he had led French musicians across Palestine in the middle of the Second Intifada. He knew the situation would never be normal, and that canceling the summer music celebrations would not make anything better. Out of respect for the hunger strike by Palestinians in Israel's prisons, however, Ramzi invited former prisoners to speak before the evening performances. They described Israel's "administrative detention" policy, which allows Palestinians to be jailed for months at a time without charge or due process, and which was at the heart of the hunger strike.

The musicians' movements were even more restricted and their proximity to live fire even closer than usual. The buses carrying Al Kamandjati musicians were ordered to turn around at a checkpoint on their way to the Jerusalem performance of Beethoven's Fifth, and the orchestra canceled a trip to Haifa; they played in Ramallah. Yet even Ramallah was not safe. After midnight, Al Kamandjati students and teachers could hear the sound of shouting and gunfire near the Manara. Israeli and Palestinian forces— "security coordination" teams sanctioned as part of the Oslo process— entered downtown Ramallah, which many people had thought was an autonomous Palestinian zone, as part of Israel's operation against Hamas. Shabab gathered in large numbers, yelling and pelting both Israeli personnel carriers and Palestinian security vehicles with rocks, enraged that their own policemen were aiding Israel's army. Periodically gunfire erupted, and the young men scattered.

On the morning of June 23, Muntasser Jebrini, Al Kamandjati's clarinet player, on summer break from his French conservatory, woke to learn that his best friend, Mohammad Mahmoud Tarifi, had been killed on the roof of a Ramallah building the night before. He had died, according to reports, after being shot by an Israeli M-16. As he lay bleeding, an ambulance was barred from entering the area. Tarifi bled to death. He left a wife and a son, four years old. "Sorrow remains in the heart," Muntasser wrote in a Facebook message, "and needs time to enter and end the pain."

Celine had grown frightened, especially for Hussein, now five, and his little brother, Adam, born in December 2012. After midnight, Celine and Ramzi could hear the shouting and automatic weapons fire just down the street. It reminded Celine of her childhood in Beirut. Like her own mother twenty-five years earlier, she wanted to take the children to France, until it was safe again. For Celine, it was not only the nearness of the clashes; it was the realization that, even in semiautonomous Ramallah, "the soldiers could enter the home during the night and ransack it in front of my children, with their guns."

"I understand," Ramzi said. "Let's wait for a week, and if this continues, I will take you to Jordan and put you all on a plane to Paris." After a few more days, the clashes ended, but Celine wondered when they would begin again.

"I am really thinking of leaving in the coming years, in spite of my love for Palestine and for Al Kamandjati," she said. "I do not want my children to be exposed to that. And I was thinking, actually, I would be doing the same as my mother did."

*

In late June the students took refuge at the summer camp, held ten minutes outside of Ramallah in a place called Star Mountain. Ramzi came for recitals in the evening, but mostly he was in the office, strategizing over ways to build an endowment to keep Al Kamandjati afloat. The music school had broken relations with the Divan and the Barenboim-Said Foundation, and in the wake of the U.S. refusal to support the Palestinian bid for statehood, Ramzi was no longer soliciting U.S. government funds, either, though he remained open to donations from American foundations and individuals. He needed to find other sources of support, especially within the changing political context of Palestine.

Like many Palestinian organizations, Al Kamandjati had formally endorsed the Palestinian BDS strategy as the best way to bring the reality of Israel's long occupation, and the plight of the Palestinians, to the world. Recently the BDS campaign had claimed several major victories. In May 2013 the renowned physicist Stephen Hawking canceled a visit to a conference in Israel; the actress Scarlett Johansson was forced to resign as an Oxfam global ambassador in early 2014 when she refused to cut ties with the beverage maker SodaStream, which had a factory in the occupied territories. The boycott appeared to threaten the company's financial health. Its share price dropped by nearly a third in the first half of 2014. Soon the company would announce the closure of its West Bank plant. In June, the Presbyterian Church USA, in a controversial decision, narrowly voted to divest from Caterpillar, makers of the D9 bulldozer, and two other companies linked to profiteering from the occupation.

Supporters of BDS were encouraged to cut ties with any organization that promoted "normalization," which BDS saw as, in many cases, well-intended efforts that brought Israelis and Palestinians together but ultimately created the illusion that all was well on the ground. These were now seen as part of a failed Oslo era of "dialogue" that led not to freedom but rather to more occupation, settlers, and restrictions on Palestinian movement. Instead, boycott supporters believed, Palestinian freedom required direct nonviolent protest and the language of economic pressure and international condemnation. It required groups to directly denounce the occupation. Ramzi had had the same discussion with Daniel for years before finally leaving the Divan Orchestra.

For Ramzi this sharpened strategy meant ending Al Kamandjati's relationship with Apple Hill and its Playing for Peace program in New

Hampshire. Ramzi himself had taken part in the program seventeen years earlier, with his triumphant performance of Mozart's Piano Quartet in G Minor. Reluctantly, he wrote to his former viola teacher, Lenny Matczynski, now the director of Apple Hill, that he could no longer send Al Kamandjati music students to New Hampshire as long as Israelis and Palestinians played under the banner of "peace." "Although we understand Apple Hill's positive intention of the program," Ramzi wrote, "we believe that it would do more harm than good."

"I was truly sad to read your letter not just because of individual losses but because of the hopelessness Palestinians must feel," Lenny wrote back. "We recognize and empathize with your situation, and we understand and respect your need to take a stand in whatever way you feel necessary . . . I wish you all the best and trust that Al Kamandjati is thriving. What you have accomplished is truly amazing." In an interview later, Lenny lamented, "It is just such a shame that the benefits of programs like Apple Hill will not be available to them."

For Ramzi it was a painful decision: It was at Apple Hill that he had first begun to dream of building a music school in Palestine. But he felt he could no longer justify sending his students to convey a message of "playing for peace" when Palestine was under siege.

For Palestinians not interested in taking up arms, which was the vast majority of the population, few choices remained beyond BDS and direct nonviolent protest. With the "two-state solution" nearly extinguished—in large part because of the United States' inability or unwillingness to stop Israel's settlement expansion—the conversation began to change. Palestinians themselves, in the Holy Land and the diaspora, debated whether a single or binational state could ever be implemented. Others advanced more experimental ideas like "parallel states," where Palestinians and Israelis would live interspersed within the same piece of land. Still others dreamed of a broad confederation of states in a wider Middle East at peace. Increasingly, though, the word *apartheid* was spoken not only among Palestinians and their supporters, but by pundits and even Israeli and American leaders. The facts on the ground told the story of a single state controlled by Israel. Now the struggle focused on civil rights and international recognition. In the meantime, Palestinians argued for *sumud*, or steadfastness on the land. "Existence," said the popular Palestinian slogan, "is resistance."

For Ramzi, the tactics of resistance had changed since the day in 1988 when a photographer snapped his picture hurling a stone at an unseen soldier. But the spirit behind it was essentially the same.

We are here.

*   *   *

"This is a musical intifada," Ramzi declared on a warm June morning, standing at the front of a bus heading south. He was preparing the students to once again confront the decades-long occupation by reclaiming space through music. The operation had begun a half hour earlier, at eleven A.M. in Ramallah, when some two dozen young musicians, all members of the Al Kamandjati youth orchestra, many dressed in black shirts and pants, began piling into the bus, carrying their violins, cellos, trombones, and clarinets. Into the belly of the bus went snare drums, cymbals, timpani, backpacks, and sheet music. They were about to confront the occupation in perhaps its bleakest place: the wall and military checkpoint at Qalandia. The musical intifada was to be the culmination of the summer music festival.

Jason Crompton and a couple of his colleagues had come to Ramzi with the idea. They had heard the story of the French cellist performing the Bach suites, alone, in front of the separation wall. But they all knew that Qalandia was under full Israeli military control. Setting up a Palestinian orchestra in a military zone—just steps from the steel corridors, revolving metal gates, and X-ray machines—was an uncertain prospect. They worried about the reaction of the soldiers.

Ramzi stood at the front of the bus and faced the musicians. He designated a half dozen of the older students and staffers for early logistics: As soon as the bus arrived at Qalandia, these six would quickly assemble the music stands and mount the large percussion. For the rest, "You stay on the bus. Please don't go out. We don't want to attract any attention. Once the stands and the big instruments are ready, everybody come with his music, his instrument, and we'll start immediately. If you can tune on the bus, that would be amazing."

What if the soldiers come and order the children to stop playing? "We don't listen," Ramzi said. "Exactly as if they are not there. If they say something on the loudspeaker, we don't listen. We produce sound. That's it. Just play."

The bus rolled past Lovely Toys, a children's store brightly festooned with stuffed tigers, scooters, beach balls, and racing cars; then the wall and checkpoint towers came into view. The bus swung left through a round-about, and right, into the parking lot. Ramzi ran off to find Jason, who had come in a car with two dozen music stands.

The early logistics team assembled the percussion and music stands, according to plan. There they stood, black metal sentries in the hot sunlight outside the "passenger terminal," apparently out of the range of military surveillance cameras. Nearby, through the open windows of the bus, came the sounds of children tuning their instruments.

And then it started. In two lines, from the front and rear bus doors, the young musicians filed out, their instruments out of their cases and ready. Ramzi directed them to the side of the building, where they were to grab a music stand and enter the terminal.

They strode determinedly past the red metal benches and toward the far corner of the terminal, in front of a long row of blue horizontal bars. On the other side, in a small building behind bulletproof glass, soldiers seemed unaware of the unfolding musical drama.

Now Jason stood, arms raised, before the musicians—about twenty-five children, and perhaps half as many teachers. The orchestra was poised, bows and brass in position.

The sound of Mozart's Symphony no. 6 in F Major filled the terminal. Immediately Palestinians stopped, stared, and smiled in amazement. They came closer, pulling out cell phones and snapping photos. Soon perhaps a hundred people were gathered around the Al Kamandjati youth orchestra, transfixed. "People were listening fully," Ramzi would say later. He was playing viola. "The crossing stopped." Helen Sherrah-Davies, a visiting violinist from the United Kingdom, remembers having to fight back tears as she played. "I wonder how many times joy has entered that space," she said.

At first the soldiers seemed to pay no attention. But as the Mozart symphony built—Allegro, Andante, Minuet, and the Allegro last movement—they started to take notice. By the time the orchestra launched into Georges Bizet's "Danse Bohème" from *Carmen*, a soldier appeared, looking out through the blue bars.

In the violin section, sixteen-year-old Georgina Mukarker from Bethlehem felt herself relax. At first she had been tense and distracted, and the place felt depressing. *Why am I here?* she often wondered. *Why am I a Palestinian? Why am I Christian? What does God want from me? I was born in Jerusalem but never got the ID. I am still looking for a dream.* As she played at Qalandia, she began to feel brave and happy: "I am in front of the soldiers. They see me and can do nothing about it. They can't shoot me. I'm strong, I have music. That's my weapon." This gave way to other thoughts, passing through her mind as she played, hyperaware of the men and women on the other side of the steel bars, holding machine guns: *Do they really want us to not exist? I don't think they really hate us. They are working as soldiers but they're humans. They actually have hearts, and they feel. What are they feeling when they hear us play? What's in their hearts, really?* Later, a few of the players would insist they had seen two soldiers dancing.

The orchestra played on, reprising Bizet's Farandole from *L'Arlésienne* Suite no. 2, to enthusiastic applause. For a long moment, the cheering resounded. A feeling of euphoria hung over the reclaimed space. The players looked at each other in amazement.

Sweat beaded up on Jason's forehead, the result of his energetic conducting. Now he was facing the cameras; someone had advised them to come quickly to the checkpoint. "Do you think the music can make a solution for peace between the nations?" a local Palestinian reporter wanted to know.

"I wish it were that simple, really," Jason said with a laugh. "I don't know if it can bring a solution but I think it can bring a lot of good things to people. It brings really great things to these kids here. And to be a part of that, I can't ask for anything more, really. It's amazing. To play here today—I feel so good."

At the bus there was jubilation. In the parking lot, Jason went window to window, jumping up to yell gleefully to the kids, who responded each time with whoops and screams.

They headed back to Ramallah, to the sound of much singing, tabla, and oud.

"This was the best concert of my life," said Alá. Three years earlier, at the checkpoint near Nablus, she had been forced to open her violin case and play a song before the soldier would let her pass.

Now, Alá looked out of the bus window at the landscape of Palestine, a peaceful and uncomplicated smile on her face.

Ramzi sat in the front of the bus, absently stroking his beard, staring through the broad windshield at the road back to Ramallah. It had been only a few years since a wary Alá had walked through the slanted copper door at Al Kamandjati and asked for her first lesson. After her, hundreds had come, from the towns, villages, and refugee camps, learning their Bach, Mahler, and Fairouz; their clarinets, ouds, darbukas; their drumming circles and string quartets; their Mozart and Beethoven symphonies. They had played at music festivals in Jerusalem, in ancient stone ruins in pre-Christian villages, in rehab centers for injured children in the camps, and at impromptu concerts in front of one of the world's mightiest armies.

Ramzi wasn't the gentlest teacher, or the easiest leader to work with. But on the bus home, he allowed himself a smile. This is what he had wanted for half his life, and what he had built, with the sweat, pain, and joy of hundreds of others who had played, taught, and planned beside him. They had made something so that children could experience the beauty that Ramzi and his generation, the children of the stones, had missed in their own childhoods. Now another generation of children had let the music enter them. It was reconfiguring them, forming a new core; rewiring a new generation. The music they absorbed was their protection, Ramzi kept telling anyone who would listen. Now, he was certain, they would use that music as shield and sword, toward the freedom of their people.

Postlude: Over the Wall, to Play Beethoven

Near Qalandia military checkpoint

*T*HE BUS FULL *of musicians rolls south along the wall, approaching the Palestinian town of Beit Hanina, just north of Jerusalem. A cell phone rings, and a short time later, the driver slows, stops, and opens the door.*

The five musicians bound up the steps, giddy and smiling as the bus fills with cheers.

"How did you—" someone starts to ask.

"What the—" says another.

From his cell phone, one of the timpanists plays a video showing a ladder and a wall, and two musicians climbing toward the sky: proof of their deed. They settle into their seats, still breathing hard, smiling, accepting congratulations.

Twenty minutes later, the orchestra enters the tranquil grounds of St. Anne's, a French church built during Crusader times. Tourists wander quietly through the gardens, or rest on shaded benches. An old French priest welcomes the orchestra with a soft smile and a thick English accent. A French flag flaps from the steeple. Qalandia and the wall are part of another world.

The musicians disappear into the cavernous church to rehearse Beethoven's Symphony no. 4 in B-flat Major and a Mendelssohn concerto. The sound of a violin floats out from the open church doors, joined now by the entire orchestra: trombone, oboe, flute, and the pounding of the timpani.

A little after eight o'clock, thirty-six musicians sit silently as the visiting French conductor raises his arms. Strings whisper the haunting first notes of Beethoven's Fourth, in a minor key, as two hundred visitors watch from the packed rows of chairs in the old church. The violist, in the middle of the small orchestra, thinks of Beethoven. What would he think about an orchestra like this, playing his symphony in such a context? He looks out to the audience, sitting peacefully in the neat rows of plastic chairs. They would never know what it had taken to get to Jerusalem to perform. But they do know, it seems, that they are in the presence of something extraordinary. Moments after the conductor makes his final thrusts and the orchestra reaches Beethoven's six-note triumphal ending, the audience rises in sustained applause. The joyful ovation fills the church, echoing off the stone walls and out into the cobbled streets of the Holy City of Jerusalem.

ACKNOWLEDGMENTS

Children of the Stone could not have been written without the generous cooperation, insight, and support of a large group of musicians, teachers, students, parents, researchers, historians, journalists, and friends in the West Bank, Jerusalem, France, the United Kingdom, Germany, and the United States. Research and reporting originated in 1998, for my story on Ramzi Hussein Aburedwan, which aired that March on National Public Radio. Over five additional trips to Palestine, beginning in late 2009 with a chance encounter with Ramzi in a Ramallah restaurant, and in numerous journeys to France, Britain, Germany, and New York City, I gathered the material for this book. The number of people who helped facilitate the telling of this story, including the more than 230 people I interviewed, are too numerous to mention. I remain, however, grateful to each of them.

Along with Ramzi, his wife Celine Dagher, and the inspiring team of teachers and students at Al Kamandjati, I am especially indebted to: Lamis Andoni, who introduced me to Ramzi and facilitated our meetings in 1998; Anan AbuShanab and Eman Musleh, my indefatigable West Bank researchers and Bard College/Al Quds University graduates who spent many hours facilitating, translating, and transcribing interviews with children of the music school and veterans of the Palestinian struggle; Mariam Said, widow of the late Palestinian intellectual Edward Said and a coordinator and liaison for the West-Eastern Divan Orchestra, founded by Edward and Daniel Barenboim, who spent dozens of hours discussing the Divan and her late husband's legacy; Peter Sulski, violist and teacher, who was unfailingly willing to discuss music, teaching, and strategizing for Al Kamandjati; Rima Tarazi, cofounder of the Edward Said National

Conservatory of Music in Palestine, who generously gave hours of her time; Tania Nasir, who, with Hanna Nasir, opened up her elegant Birzeit home and shared many memories; Eric Culver, Donato Cabrera, and Jordan Nelson, who served as musical mentors; and the families of Alá, Rasha, and Shehada Shalalda and of Oday Khatib, who invited me into their homes, in Old Ramallah and Al Fawwar camps respectively, many times, including for iftar meals during the holy month of Ramadan. Thank you also to Tarek, Maryna, Rasha and Radi Doulani of Jenin, and to Walid and Fadi Basha, also of Jenin.

Numerous people generously read and commented on all or parts of various drafts for this book, including: Anan AbuShanab, Ibtisam Barakat (special thanks), Hatem Bazian, Joel Beinen, Donato Cabrera, Hillel Cohen, K. C. Cole, Eric Culver, Celine Dagher, Jessica Boucher Dias, Julian Foley, Erica Funkhouser, Patricia Golan, Alex Killian, Leonard Matczynski, Jordan Nelson, Shannon Nickerson, Geneva Overholser, Michael Parks, Nicola Perugini, Andrea Portes, Danny Rubinstein, Stephanie Saldaña, Eric Stumacher, Peter Sulski, Salim Tamari, Kathleen Tolan, Chris Whitman, and George Bisharat, who hauled his laptop on a fishing trip to Bolivia so that he could send me timely feedback.

Others facilitated and translated interviews in the Holy Land, Lebanon, and France, including Nidal Rafa, Thana Alqam, Lubna Takruri, Rajy Khaznadar, Sarah Tuttle-Singer, Maha Alami, Jane Blumer, and Paraska Tolan, who also conducted core research and compiled an advanced draft of the source notes for *Children of the Stone*.

Transcripts for the dozens of hours of recorded interviews came to more than three thousand pages; most were compiled by a small brigade assembled by Jessica Boucher Dias, and included Jessica and: M. C. Abbott, Jeffrey Baker, Tamer Bataymeh, Leona Deckelbaum, Doug Ferguson, Molly Flynn, Ben Gottlieb, Alex Killian, Courtney McBride, Carina Molnár, Wafa Nazzal, Emily Scheff, Magda Socha, Chelsea Souter, Doug Sparling, Eve Sturges, SeMe Sung, and Alice Taylor.

I am grateful to the producers and directors of three documentaries, who provided access to raw footage and/or field notes. They are Hélèna Cotinier and Pierre-Nicolas Durand of *It's Not a Gun*, and Dimitri Chimenti of *Just Play*, both about Al Kamandjati; and Paul Smaczny, of *Knowledge Is the Beginning*, about Daniel Barenboim, Edward Said, and the West-Eastern Divan Orchestra.

From the Barenboim-Said Foundation and Divan Orchestra, Carsten Siebert, Tabaré Perlas, and Judith Neuhoff facilitated interviews, especially with Maestro Daniel Barenboim, to whom I am grateful. Mr. Barenboim also approved my backstage and rehearsal access. More than a dozen members of the Divan also agreed to interviews.

At Angers, France, François Hetsch, Ramzi's former viola teacher, and Richard Lowry, until recently the director of the Conservatoire à Rayonnement Régional d'Angers, where Ramzi studied, made themselves available on multiple occasions, and put me in touch with many others. François interrupted a family vacation in the French Alps to meet with me there and review portions of the manuscript for accuracy. Yacine Laghrour of Angers was a huge help in facilitating many interviews there. My brother John and sister-in-law Michelle Szkilnik, who live in nearby Nantes, provided me meals and a bed on many nights, including in their Paris flat; thank you so much. And thank you to Alice Howick and Benjamin Payen for hosting me in the South of France.

In Weimar, Divan trombonist Rajy Khaznadar helped me navigate the town and proved a sensitive guide to the devastating experience of the nearby Buchenwald death camp. In Berlin, my old friends Raj Kamal Jha and Suj Bose were warm and welcoming hosts.

At the University of Southern California's Annenberg School for Communication and Journalism, where I am fortunate to teach, I had strong support from Dean Ernest Wilson and directors Geneva Overholser and Michael Parks, both of whom supported my taking time away from teaching to complete the book.

To my USC colleague Tim Page, thank you for the collection of Beethoven symphonies, which helped launch me on this project. I am grateful to Tim and Will Page for the wonderful rambling house in Chester, Nova Scotia, where I wrote the first portion of the book. Thanks to Christie and David Chaplin-Saunders for their kindness in Chester.

And thank you to my friends Nubar Alexanian, Rebecca Koch, Maria Blanco, Erna Smith, Erica (Ricky) Funkhouser, Mariam Shahin, George Azar, Nidal Rafa, and my production company partners, Bear Guerra, Ruxandra Guidi, Jonathan Miller, Cecilia Vaisman, and Alan Weisman. To Anthony Weller and Kylee Smith: You inspire. And, thank you to my piano teachers, Dina Shilleh in Palestine and Grace Lee in Los Angeles.

I am especially grateful to the teachers of Al Kamandjati in Ramallah, Jenin, and Lebanon, who shared their histories, experiences, and insights. These included: Jason Crompton, Alice Howick, Dimitri Mikelis, Benjamin Payen, Maddalena Pastorelli, Iyad Staiti, and Julia Katarina. Julia in particular spent countless hours telling her story and sharing her delight at the "discovery" of the young singing sensation, Fadi Basha. At the Edward Said National Conservatory, director Suhail Khoury and cofounder Nadia Abboushi shared important history and perspective. Al Kamandjati's administrative team, including Khalil Ghneim and Iyad Jaradat, made things much easier for me. Celine Dagher, with her great spirit, warmth, and competence, provided reams of documents and photographs for me to peruse.

The biggest help of all, of course, was Ramzi himself, who has spent hundreds of hours with me since I met him again in late 2009. Shortly thereafter, I determined there was a book in the story of Ramzi and Al Kamandjati. Ramzi understood that I could only write it as a full journalistic account, not as a promotional tale or hagiography. He made a decision to trust me with his life's story and to spend the time necessary to answer my endless questions—including those about tiny details of life at age five in the Palestinian refugee camp of Al Amari. I am deeply grateful to Ramzi for all the time, vision, and insights he shared.

Deepest thanks to my friend and agent, David Black, who is always there for me. Kathy Belden, the best editor a writer could ever wish for, provided in-depth feedback on multiple drafts, even when the manuscript was barely more than notes. Her clear view, patience, intelligence, compassion, and insight are a writer's gift.

Finally, family: To Tom, Kathleen, Mary, John, Yam, and my dear mother, Sally Tolan in Wisconsin: Thank you for your love and support. And most of all, to five-year-old Wyatt and his mother, my life partner, Andrea Portes: You have brought me so much happiness. It is a gift to live with another writer, particularly a kind and patient one with a generous spirit and great instincts, who often knew what I needed to do to finish this book, even before I did. I am eternally grateful, my dear Andrea.

Source Notes

Children of the Stone is entirely a work of nonfiction. The narrative was created from all available sources, including books, newspaper and magazine articles, films, human rights reports, policy papers, political speeches, diplomatic cables, official state and United Nations proceedings and investigations, historical archives, blogs, government and NGO Web sites, unpublished manuscripts, my personal observations based on on-the-ground reporting, and, most important, my interviews with 230 people in Palestine, Israel, Lebanon, Jordan, France, Germany, Britain, and the United States. It is in these documents and interviews entirely that *Children of the Stone* is grounded.

These notes reflect many hundreds of hours of research and fact-checking done over the course of my twenty years as a journalist working in the West Bank, the Gaza Strip, and Israel. Most of the documentation was done since December 2009, when I remet Ramzi Aburedwan nearly twelve years after having produced a profile of him, "From Stones to Songs," for National Public Radio's *Weekend Edition*, in 1998. That program was the seed for this book.

Much of the research, in particular the fact-checking, was done in conjunction with Paraska Tolan, my niece, currently a Ph.D. candidate in African Studies at the University of Pennsylvania. Paraska's natural rigor, her gifts as a scholar, and her experience working and traveling in Israel/Palestine all proved immensely helpful, especially during the fact-checking stage. Working with my notes, and excavating countless other facts and sources, Paraska prepared an advanced draft of these Source Notes. I have overseen the process, and if there are any errors, they are my responsibility.

In most cases, the notes serve as corroboration and verification of specific facts and historical occurrences mentioned in the text. In cases where there are no corresponding source notes, that is because the source of the narrative is the person or people who are recalling a specific incident or memory, and/or my own personal observation on the ground.

The notes also reflect my intention to not only document each pertinent fact but, in many cases, to provide further background for interested readers—for example, the backstory of various peace negotiations; the early intent of Israel's occupation of the

West Bank and Gaza; the background behind the decades of enmity in Hebron; the reasons, beyond security, for the construction of Israel's separation barrier; or the value of music therapy in resolving trauma in conflict zones.

The title of the book is grounded in Ramzi's history as one of the *atfal al hijara*, or "children of the stones," as the Palestinian youth of his generation came to be known. That is also echoed in the title of Nizar Qabbani's famous poem, "Children Bearing Rocks." The use of the singular in this book's title, to evoke the stone of *Terra Sancta*, is intentional.

Introduction

I was standing with two fellow journalists: My colleagues that evening were Lubna Takruri, then working as a freelance journalist in Ramallah and also with me as a translator and guide in the West Bank that December, and Ben Hubbard, then with the AP and now a Beirut-based correspondent with the *New York Times*. Both had been journalism graduate students at UC Berkeley when I taught there. I recall that Lubna was looking for another restaurant a little further down, but that we had decided at the last moment to go to Pronto. Because we did, I met Ramzi again.

I sought out Ramzi in the refugee camp: My meeting with Ramzi was facilitated by Lamis Andoni, a Palestinian journalist whose own curiosity and compassion toward an eighteen-year-old aspiring musician, and his family in the refugee camp, helped me create an early bond with Ramzi, making it only natural to reconnect with him in the Ramallah restaurant eleven years later.

I want to see many conservatories: This, and other quotes of Ramzi from the introduction, come from my interviews with him in Al Amari refugee camp and in Ramallah in the early months of 1998. The interviews were for the NPR broadcast "From Stones to Songs," which aired on *Weekend Edition* on May 23, 1998. Summary at http://www.npr.org/templates/story/story.php?storyId=1000955

"The role of the intellectual": These remarks are excerpted from the 2004 film *Selves and Others: A Portrait of Edward Said*, directed by Emmanuel Hamon. Video can be viewed at http://www.columbia.edu/cu/news/media/04/280_edward Said_memorial

Prelude

The story told in the prelude (and the interludes and postlude) is as rigorously reported as any other facts or scenes in the book. For obvious reasons—the young men in question are scaling Israel's separation barrier—their real names, and the name of the smuggler, have been changed. All other facts in these sections are either based on my personal observation or verified with multiple interviews and additional reporting. These events are also chronicled in my piece "Over the Wall to Play Beethoven in Jerusalem," on Al Jazeera America's Web site, August 2013, http://america.aljazeera. com/articles/2013/8/14/over-the-wall-toplaybeethoveninjerusalem.html

First Movement: Stone

Chapter 1: Pushcart

A light rain fell: The account of the pushcart was related to me in interviews with Ramzi during the summer of 2011, and subsequently in follow-up interviews, and with his mother. In an interview on September 20, 2014, conducted by Anan AbuShanab from questions submitted by me, Umm Ramzi (mother of Ramzi) said: "Hussein [Ramzi's father] used to beat me all the time. He used to drink and was always drunk, and he hit me . . . Almost every day I had to go to Ramallah Hospital, either he cut my face or hurt me in my body. Even when I was pregnant with Ramzi, he would beat me."

Both Ramzi and his mother recall a time when Ramzi awoke to see his father beating his mother, and that the boy tried, at age four, to intervene. "Ramzi, may God bless him . . . woke up that day with his father beating me. Ramzi ran after his father, he held rocks and a stick and he wanted to hit him, but his father was [running] away. But he did that because he saw him hitting me. This is something Ramzi cannot forget. Then I went back to my parent's house—they came to get me. This was my life, always upset and back to my parents' house."

Set fire to their home: The 1985 divorce decree of Ramzi's parents, translated from the Arabic by Nidal Rafa and Anan Abushanab, cites the fire and domestic violence as reasons Ramzi's mother asked for a divorce. Ramzi verified this in subsequent interviews. About the fire Umm Ramzi said in an interview on September 20, 2014: "This happened when I was upset with him and left to my parents' house. Because I went to them, Hussein was upset and he came to burn the [parents'] house."

"No," Ramzi had heard his mother say: The truth was far more complicated. In her September 20, 2014 interview, Umm Ramzi makes it clear she felt trapped by her desire to keep her children and the wishes of her own father, who wanted to protect his daughter and keep her away from Ramzi's father, Hussein. "We gave him first, second, and third chances but it was all for nothing," she recalled. "My father answered that he doesn't want anything to do with him, all he wants for him to take 'this evil' away from my daughter. At that moment I was scattered in between, on one side with my parents and on the other there was my children. My family didn't want my kids, but I wanted to keep them. My parents didn't want them, but I want them. They are my kids." Umm Ramzi confirmed that her father-in-law "said that he will open a house for me, and he will pay for anything. My family said, How do you want her to live with you? She is divorced. How is she going to live with her in-laws? How can that happen? My father-in-law said you'll keep the kids and I will pay anything for them, but I was scared of Hussein Aburedwan, how can I live in the house? My father told him no."

Chapter 2: Grandfather

Ramzi pretended to sleep: The story of Ramzi following his grandfather to work was recounted in multiple and extensive interviews with Ramzi over the period of four summers, 2010–13. Some of the details were corroborated by additional interviews with Ramzi's aunts, Widad and Nawal.

Temporary shelter in the aftermath of mass expulsions: According to the United Nations Relief and Works Agency (UNRWA)'s Amari camp profile, the camp was established in 1949 by the Red Cross. The inhabitants came from the cites of Lydda, Jaffa, and Ramle, and from the villages of Beit Dajan, Deir Tarif, Abu Shoush, Sadoun Janzeh, Beit Naballa, and Na'ani, the village of Ramzi's grandparents. "Amari Refugee Camp Profile, Camp Development Research Project," UNRWA, October 2008, p. 1. Published by the United Nations Office for the Coordination of Humanitarian Affairs, http://www.ochaopt.org/documents/opt_campprof_unrwa_amari_oct_2008.pdf

Voted to divide the land: The United Nations 33-13 vote represented a triumph for the Zionist movement, which for decades had been fighting for a Jewish homeland. "The UN partition plan divided the country in such a way that each state would have a majority of its own population, although some Jewish settlements would fall within the proposed Palestinian state and many Palestinians would become part of the proposed Jewish state. The territory designated to the Jewish state would be slightly larger than the Palestinian state . . . on the assumption that increasing numbers of Jews would immigrate there. According to the UN partition plan, the area of Jerusalem and Bethlehem was to become an international zone." See "The United Nations Partition Plan," *Middle East Report* (Middle East Research and Information Project), January 2001, http://www.merip.org/palestine-israel_primer/un-partition-plan-pal-isr.html. The "partition resolution," or United Nations General Assembly Resolution 181, is available in its entirety in Michael J. Cohen's *The Rise of Israel*, Vol. 37 (New York: Garland Publishing, Inc., 1987).

The indigenous Arabs rejected the partition plan: In *Before Their Diaspora*, the Palestinian scholar Walid Khalidi writes: "The Palestinians failed to see why they should be made to pay for the Holocaust . . . why it was not fair for the Jews to be a minority in a unitary Palestinian state, while it was fair for almost half of the Palestinian population—the indigenous majority on its ancestral soil—to be converted overnight into a minority under alien rule in the envisaged Jewish state according to partition." See *Before Their Diaspora: A Photographic History of the Palestinians* (Washington, D.C.: Institute for Palestine Studies, 2010), pp. 305–6.

Arabs of Palestine were weak and unprepared: This reality runs counter to the myth of a monolithic and united Arab presence prepared to wipe Israel off the map. Because of the devastating effects of the British crackdown on Palestinian resistance during the Arab Rebellion, and sharp internal and often murderous disagreements over how to contend with the Zionist movement, the divisions among Palestinians were sharp. Both factors, along with how ill-equipped the Palestinians were for battle and, as important, word of a horrific massacre in the Palestinian village of Deir Yassin, contributed to their exile. See Benny Morris, *Righteous Victims*, pp. 191–214; Hillel Cohen, *Army of Shadows: Palestinian Collaboration with Zionism, 1917–1948*, pp. 121–68 and 230–68; my book *The Lemon Tree*, pp. 43–69; and Avi Shlaim, *Collusion Across the Jordan: King Abdullah, the Zionist Movement, and the Partition of Palestine*.

Their numbers were limited: The claim that Arab troops outnumbered Israeli forces on the ground during the 1948 war is inaccurate, as shown in multiple Israeli accounts.

In *Clash of Destinies*, Jon Kimche and David Kimche estimate that the total strength of the invading Arab armies was twenty-four thousand, compared to thirty-five thousand for Israel. In *1948 and After: Israel and the Palestinians*, Benny Morris writes that during the 1948 war, "Jewish coordination, command and control . . . were clearly superior to those of the uncoordinated armies of Egypt, Syria, Iraq, and Lebanon." He adds: "The atlas map showing a minuscule Israel and a surrounding giant Arab sea did not, and, indeed, for the time being, still does not, accurately reflect the true balance of military power in the region . . ." For additional background, see Avi Shlaim's *Collusion Across the Jordan* and pp. 43–69 of my book *The Lemon Tree*.

Hundreds of thousands of Palestinian Arabs had fled or been driven out of their homes: According to a United Nations General Assembly report, "the estimate of the statistical expert, which the Committee believes to be as accurate as circumstances permit, indicates that the refugees from Israel-controlled territory amount to approximately 711,000." See "General Progress Report and Supplementary Report of the United Nations Conciliation Commission for Palestine, Covering the Period from 11 December 1949 to 23 October 1950." Official Records: Fifth Session Supplements No. 18 (A/1367/Rev.1), New York, 1951. In the *Final Report of the United Nations Economic Survey Mission for the Middle East*, the United Nations Conciliation Commission used a figure of 726,000. Subsequent estimates, from both Palestinian and Israeli sources, put the number at 800,000. Many other estimates, including other citations from the United Nations, put the total number of Palestinian refugees from the creation of Israel at 750,000.

Two thousand refugees, mostly poor villagers, took shelter in Al Amari: Israeli historian Benny Morris writes: "The arrival in Ramallah—population 10,000—of as many as '70,000' refugees severely undermined civilian morale. The acting mayor, Hana Khalaf, appealed to the king to order them to leave town: they are 'dispersed in the town streets, most of them poor, they suffer from great want of basic goods and water and pose a serious threat to health.' Abdullah advised 'patience.'" See Benny Morris, *The Birth of the Palestinian Refugee Problem Revisited* (Cambridge: Cambridge University Press, 2004), p. 435. See also my book *The Lemon Tree*, p. 315.

Cinder block, plaster, and corrugated tin: According to a profile of Al Amari refugee camp by the United Nations Office for the Coordination of Humanitarian Affairs in the occupied Palestinian territory (OCHAoPt), the shelters were made variously of stone, concrete, cement bricks, asbestos, wood, zinc, cloth, mud, straw, and other materials. See "Amari Refugee Camp Profile, Camp Development Research Project," UNRWA, October 2008, p. 3, http://www.ochaopt.org/documents/opt_campprof_unrwa_amari_oct_2008.pdf

The United Nations now ran the camp: In 1950 the United Nations Relief and Works Agency (UNRWA), created solely to deal with the Palestinian refugee crisis, had taken over from the Red Cross. In Al Amari UNRWA workers built multiple housing blocs for 80 families each—710 units total, with communal bathrooms for every seven or eight families, and showers for about one in every twenty (Al Amari figures drawn from interviews with UNRWA officials in Al Amari camp). "The norm for the provision of public latrine seats was 3 per 100 camp population . . . Living conditions in the tents and other primitive accommodation made it necessary to construct bath houses to enable the camp inhabitants to have a hot bath at least once a week to maintain their personal hygiene . . . Hot and cold water was available daily; soap was also provided." See N. Shabak, "Environmental Sanitation Services and Development in Palestinian Refugee Camps: The UNRWA Experience," *Proceedings of the Regional Workshop on Environmental Health Management in Refugee Areas* (http:// helid.digicollection.org/en/d/Jh0222e/2.13.html). By 1968, fifty-nine Palestinian refugee camps had sprung up across a vast space of exile—the West Bank, Gaza, Jordan, Lebanon, Syria, and Egypt. Under its U.N. mandate, UNRWA built schools, health centers, hospitals, bulk food distribution centers, and housing for successive generations of families.

The camp had doubled in size: According to the United Nations Office for the Coordination of Humanitarian Affairs on the occupied Palestinian territories, Al Amari's population, originally two thousand, doubled to four thousand residents by 1955 and increased to more than six thousand by 1985. However, the camp itself could not add space; its 25 acres (101 dunums) of land were wedged between Ramallah and the adjacent village of Al Bireh. See "Amari Refugee Camp Profile, Camp Development Research Project," UNRWA, October 2008, p. 2, http://www.ochaopt. org/documents/opt_campprof_unrwa_amari_oct_2008.pdf

Na'ani, like more than four hundred other Palestinian villages, had been eliminated by Israel: For sources on the destruction of the Arab villages, see pp. 165–67 in Meron Benvenisti's *Sacred Landscape: The Buried History of the Holy Land Since 1948*. Also Aharon Shai of the Hebrew University of Jerusalem, using records from the Archaeological Survey of Israel (now part of Israel's Antiquities Authority) documented an extensive program conducted in conjunction with the Israel Land Authority to demolish abandoned Arab villages in "efforts to clear the country of deserted villages . . . Most of the abandoned Arab villages inhabited until 1948 and abandoned in the course of the War of Independence . . . disappear[ed] . . . as a result of a clear and well-designed plan originating with the ILA." See also my book *The Lemon Tree*, pp. 323–24. Israeli historian Benny Morris quotes Yosef Weitz, director of the Lands Department of the Jewish National Fund, ordering two settlement officials "to determine in which villages we will be able to settle our people, and which should be destroyed." See *1948 and After: Israel and the Palestinians*, p. 122. See also the *Haaretz* article of April 4, 1967, which quotes Moshe Dayan (then about to be appointed Israel's minister of defense) saying "There is not a single Jewish village in the country that has not been built on the site of an Arab village." See also Ian Black, "Remembering the Nakba: Israeli Group Puts 1948 Palestine Back on the Map," *Guardian*, May 2, 2014, http:// www.theguardian.com/world/2014/may/02/nakba-israel-palestine-zochrot-history

Old families of Al Bireh and Ramallah, many of them Christian: Ramallah's roots as a Christian hill town are documented through my numerous interviews with scholars and Ramallah residents over the last fifteen years.

Mr. Foreigner Shlomo: I first heard the story of Khawaja Shlomo in 1998 in the Al Amari refugee camp near Ramallah from a Palestinian native of Na'ani: Ramzi's grandmother Jamila. In 2004, Dr. Shimon Gat, whose Ph.D. is on ancient Ramla and who is a lifelong resident of Kibbutz Na'an (near the ruins of Na'ani), corroborated the story. The real name of the man on horseback, Gat told me, was Moshe Ben Avraham of Kibbutz Na'an. Two of Ben Avraham's children also confirmed the story of their father's journey into Na'ani in 1948. Gat told me that Ben Avraham worked for the intelligence arm of the Haganah, and speculated that the ride into Na'ani in May 1948 was likely part of a military psychological operation to induce villagers to flee. This was a common tactic of the Zionist movement in Palestine in 1947–48. Israeli commander Yigal Allon, in the 1948 *Journal of the Palmach* (the "strike force" of the Haganah, which later became the Israel Defense Forces), describes psychological operations whereby local kibbutz leaders would "whisper in the ears of some Arabs, that a great Jewish reinforcement has arrived," and that "they should suggest to these Arabs, as their friends, to escape while there is still time. The tactic reached its goal completely." (*Ha Sepher Ha Palmach* (Hebrew), Vol. 2, p. 286, as cited in David Hirst, *The Gun and the Olive Branch*, p. 267.)

Taking with them little besides Jamila's gold: The story of Sido and Jamila's flight from Na'ani, Jamila's subsequent trek through the hills toward Ramallah, and other details, including Sido's incarceration and his burying of valuables before fleeing Na'ani, come from interviews with Ramzi in 1998 and 2010–14, and with Jamila at Al Amari refugee camp in 1998. Additional details are corroborated by local Na'an and Israeli national archives, as well as by the aforementioned interview with Shimon Gat of Kibbutz Na'an. Additional sources include: *Palmach 67* (1948); Spiro Munayyer, "The Fall of Lydda," *Journal of Palestine Studies* (Summer 1998), pp. 80–98; Alon Kadish, *The Conquest of Lydda*; Tom Segev, *1949*; Benny Morris, *1948 and After*, pp. 1–2; John Bagot Glubb, *A Soldier with the Arabs*, pp. 151–70; Yoav Gelber, *Palestine 1948*, p. 159; and the July 11 and 12, 1948 editions of the *New York Times, Chicago Tribune*, and *New York Herald Tribune*.

An internment camp: According to historian Benny Morris, during the Israeli military intervention in Ramle, the Operation Dani headquarters instructed one of its brigadiers to allow the women, elderly people, and children to flee but to detain the men of military age. See *The Birth of the Palestinian Refugee Problem Revisited*, p. 425. Numerous sources confirm the taking of local men and youths from Ramle and Lydda by Israel's army during and in the immediate aftermath of July 1948. Benny Morris, in "Operation Dani and the Exodus of Palestinians from Lydda and Ramle," *Middle East Journal* 40, no. 1 (Winter 1986), pp. 82–109; tinyurl.com/mo9g1zo, describes how "Israeli troops in both towns began to round up able-bodied males who were placed in temporary detention centers in mosques and churches, prior to being questioned and sent off to POW camps . . ." Yoav Gelber, *Palestine 1948*, p. 161, states: "Yigal Allon [commander of the Palmach, or Israeli army] had ordered that all males of military age be detailed as prisoners-of-war and the rest be deported across the lines." It is not clear exactly where Sido Mohammad was incarcerated. Ramzi recalled that his grandfather "told me that he was arrested and moved in an army bus to a jail in an airport. Mostly up in the north. A prison near an airport. Military airport. Possibly around Haifa, or maybe Ben Gurion." This would likely have been Lydda Airfield (now Ben Gurion airport) or RAF Ramat David, a military airfield in the north.

One-hundred-degree heat of mid-July: John Bagot Glubb, British commander of the Arab Legion, mentioned the one-hundred-degree heat on p. 162 of *A Soldier with the Arabs*. See also Reja-e Busailah in his *Arab Studies Quarterly* report, p. 142. Israeli historian Benny Morris writes "the exodus, under a hot July sun, was an extended episode of suffering." See *The Birth of the Palestinian Refugee Problem Revisited*, p. 432.

"Go to Abdullah! Go to Ramallah!": Soldiers yelling "Go to Abdullah" is a common theme in countless interviews I have done with 1948 Arab residents of Ramle and Lydda, many of whom now live in the Al Amari camp. Reja-e Busailah also mentions this heckling on p. 140 of his *Arab Studies Quarterly* article, "The Fall of Lydda, 1948: Impressions and Reminiscences," published in 1981.

Fifty thousand of them from Ramle, Lydda, and their surrounding villages: Both Glubb, in *A Soldier with the Arabs*, p. 162, and David Ben-Gurion, in his diary of July 15, 1948 (quoted in Tom Segev's, *1949*, p. 27), mention a figure of thirty thousand. Researchers later have increased that estimate to at least fifty thousand. Benny Morris, in "Operation Dani," *Middle East Journal*, p. 83, and author Alon Kadish (interview with me, June 2004) estimate that there were between fifty thousand and sixty thousand Palestinians in the two towns of Lydda and Ramle in July 1948, including refugees who had arrived from Jaffa and nearby villages such as Sido and Jamila's home village of Na'ani.

Thirsty and unsure of the way: The story of the march through cactus and Christ's-thorn from Ramle and Lydda toward Ramallah was recounted in more than a dozen interviews, including one with Ramzi's grandmother Jamila, which I have conducted with refugees from those areas since 1998. The events are corroborated by numerous other historical accounts, including from Benny Morris, who wrote: "One Israeli soldier (probably 3rd Battalion), from Kibbutz Ein Harod, a few weeks after the event recorded his vivid impression of the refugees' thirst and hunger, of how 'children got lost' and of how a child fell into a well and drowned, ignored, as his fellow refugees fought each other to draw water. Another soldier described . . . the slow-shuffling columns . . . [jettisoning] utensils and furniture and in the end, bodies of men, women and children, scattered along the way.' Quite a few refugees died on the road east— from exhaustion, dehydration and disease—before reaching temporary rest near in Ramallah." See *The Birth of the Palestinian Refugee Problem Revisited*, p. 433.

United Nations Resolution 194: For the complete text of the United Nations Resolution 194 see the Palestine Progress Report of the United Nations Mediator, U.N. General Assembly, December 11, 1948, Measure 194, Article 11.

Israel rejected the resolution: In *Sacred Landscape*, p. 150, Meron Benvenesti writes: "The official decision to block the return of the displaced Palestinians was made on 16 June 1948 without a vote; nor did it have officially approved wording. The Israeli cabinet made do with the statements of the prime minister and foreign minister. Prime Minister David Ben-Gurion had proclaimed: 'I do not want those who flee to return. Their return must be prevented now. Because after the war, everything will depend on the outcome of the war—I will be in favour of their not returning even after the war.' Foreign Minister Moshe Sharett (Shertok) stated simply: 'This is our policy: they are not coming back.'" See also: The Seventeenth International Red Cross Conference, Stockholm, August 1948, http://www.loc.gov/rr/frd/Military_Law/pdf/RC_XVIIth-RC-Conference.pdf

Delineating the new boundaries in green ink: Yoav Gelber describes the armistice agreements in *Palestine 1948: War, Escape and Emergence of the Palestinian Refugee Problem*, p. 298. Yezid Sayigh's *Armed Struggle and the Search for State: The Palestinian National Movement, 1949–1993* also mentions the armistice agreements on pp. 4 and 58.

"Green Line": For more on this division of land and on the "Green Line," see the United Nations Permanent Observer report, http://www.unispal.un.org/unispal.nsf/2f86ce1831 26001f85256cef0073ccce/f03d55e48f77ab69852643b0068d34?OpenDocument

Nasser was beloved across the Arab world: To read more on Nasser as a hero of the Arab masses, see Mohamed Heikal, *Secret Channels: The Inside Story of Arab-Israeli Peace Negotiations*, pp. 100–38, and Bassam Abu-Sharif, *Best of Enemies* (Boston: Little, Brown & Co., 1995), pp. 28–30. See also "How Suez Made Nasser an Arab Icon," BBC News, July 25, 2006, which states: "Nasser was seen as a new breed of ruler ready to stand up to the old colonial order." http://news.bbc.co.uk/2/hi/middle_east/5204490.stm.

The Arabs' humiliating defeat in the Six Day War in 1967: For further information on the 1967 war and its aftermath, also known as the Six Day War, see Tom Segev, *1967*; Chaim Herzog, *The Arab-Israeli Wars*; Avi Shlaim, *The Iron Wall: Israel and the Arab World*; Mohamed Heikal, *Secret Channels*; Samir Mutawi, *Jordan in the 1967 War*; and Yezid Sayigh, *Armed Struggle and the Search for State*.

Israel annexed East Jerusalem: Israel annexed East Jerusalem on June 28, 1967, by a vote of the country's Knesset. The de facto annexation, which the Knesset preferred to call "unification," was a violation of the fourth convention of the 1949 Geneva Conventions, which prohibited annexing land won by military conquest. See Karen Armstrong, *Jerusalem: One City, Three Faiths* pp. 400–3.

"Eternal capital": Among the many Israelis who declared Jerusalem to be Israel's "eternal capital of Israel" was Prime Minister Levi Eshkol, in June 1967. See Karen Armstrong, *Jerusalem: One City, Three Faiths*, p. 402.

Return to "armed struggle": For more on the years of Palestinian attacks and hijackings in the post–1967 era, and of Arafat's travels in the West Bank during that era, see David Hirst, *The Gun and the Olive Branch*, pp. 437–57; Said Aburish, *Arafat: From Defender to Dictator*, pp. 68–133; Bassam Abu-Sharif and Uzi Mahnaimi, *Best of Enemies*, pp. 56–150; Yezid Sayigh, *Armed Struggle and the Search for State*, pp. 143–281; and my book *The Lemon Tree*, pp. 150–51 and 170–75. Abu-Sharif, in an interview with me in 2003, described the hijacking and other "spectaculars" of the era, and the Israeli response of assassinations and letter bombs, one of which exploded in Abu-Sharif's face, disfiguring him. Another prominent member of a Palestinian faction told me of his faction's opposition to the "spectaculars" and how they were giving the Palestinians reputations as terrorists.

Sido Mohammad was recruited: This comes from interviews with Ramzi, 2012–14. For historical context, see the sources in the **Return to "armed struggle"** note, above.

Renamed it Psagot: According to Peace Now, the Israeli peace group which promotes at two-state solution and opposes settlement construction, Psagot was created in 1981 and is situated 9.6 kilometers (about 6 miles) from the Green Line, in the Ramallah district. See "Psagot" on the Peace Now Web site, http://peacenow.org.il/eng/content/psagot.

"We'll insert a strip of Jewish settlement in between the Palestinians": The journalist who recalled these remarks was Winston Spencer Churchill, a former British MP, grandson of the late prime minister, coauthor with his father, Randolph Spencer Churchill, of the 1967 book *The Six Day War*, and a strong supporter and admirer of Israel. He cited his 1973 conversation with Sharon in remarks at the National Press Club in Washington, D.C., in October 2002. The remarks are taken from the transcript of Churchill's talk, provided to me by the National Press Club, and are cited in "Sharon's New Map," Foundation for Middle East Peace, http://fmep.org/reports/archive/vol.-12/no.-3/sharons-new-map. There was, of course, no formal "Pastrami Sandwich" policy, but Sharon's candid remarks revealed his thinking in the years after the Six Day War. More important, this thinking would be transformed into facts on the ground in the years to come. Those facts went well beyond the more formal policy known as the "Allon Plan," named for former IDF general and Israeli government minister Yigal Allon. The Allon Plan, proposed in a 1976 *Foreign Affairs* article, stated, according to Israel's Knesset Web site, "that Israel will have sovereignty within the occupied territories over territories that are necessary for its defense." http://www.knesset.gov.il/lexicon/eng/alon_eng.htm A map is available at http://azure.org.il/download/files/az21_diker_map.pdf. Notably, Israel's settlements on the ground have gone well beyond the Allon Plan's vision.

Red-roofed buildings towered over Ramallah: Settlements began to spring up in the West Bank and East Jerusalem after the 1967 war, slowly at first. According to a U.N. report, "Early settlement development was concentrated in and around East Jerusalem, along the Jordan Valley and on the eastern and western slopes of the northern West Bank mountains. Settlements were also established in and around Hebron and later in the southern Hebron hills and near the 1949 Armistice Line, commonly known as the 'Green Line.' The establishment of new settlements was particularly prolific in the decade between 1977 and 1987." In 1987, there were 128 existing settlements with 169,200 Israeli settlers in the West Bank and East Jerusalem. See "Israeli Settlements and Other Infrastructure in the West Bank," *The Humanitarian Impact of Israeli Infrastructures, the West Bank, Chapter 1,* The United Nations Office for the Coordination of Humanitarian Affairs, occupied Palestinian Territory, April 2007, pp. 16–20, http://www.ochaopt.org/documents/TheHumanitarianImpactOfIsraeliInfrastructureTheWestBank_ch1.pdf

Their occupation would be benign and "inconspicuous": "We must ensure that the areas of friction between the two peoples are minimal," defense minister Moshe Dayan declared in a November 1967 meeting with Shlomo Gazit, the brigadier general he'd put in charge of overseeing the occupied territories. "We have to make it a goal of our military administration that a local Arab can live a normal life . . ." (Shlomo Gazit, *Trapped Fools: Thirty Years of Israeli Policy in the Territories,* Chapter 5, Kindle location 1204). In the first years after the Six Day War, this "liberal attitude towards the occupied population" (Gazit, Chapter 6, Kindle location 1659) led to significant social improvements. Occupation authorities improved access to health care, built sewage systems, installed new telephone service, and opened the borders for day workers, providing Israel with cheap labor and significantly raising the standard of living in the West Bank. (See Neve Gordon, "From Colonization to Separation: Exploring the Structure of Israel's Occupation," in Ophir, Givoni, and Hanafi's *The Power of Inclusive Exclusion,* pp. 246–7). Yet Israeli leaders actively suppressed any Palestinian industry or agriculture that might have competed with their own economy. "The civilian planners had one goal—to reduce as much as possible the economic burden of maintaining the Territories and to prevent the economy of the Territories from competing with, or harming, Israeli economic interests." (Gazit, Chapter 2, Kindle location 670). Palestinian independence, or even self-reliance, was not under consideration, as Defense Minister Yitzhak Rabin declared: "There will be no development in the occupied territories initiated by the Israeli Government, and no permits will be given for expanding agricultural or industry which may compete with the State of Israel." As quoted in Yezid Sayigh, *Armed Struggle and the Search for State,* p. 608, from a February 15, 1985 article in the *Jerusalem Post.* For more on the growing violence of the occupation see Gazit, Chapter 7.

Six Palestinians were wounded: Jesus Rangel, "Man Sought in Israel for Attacks on Arabs Is Seized," *New York Times,* January 16, 1986, http://www.nytimes.com/1986/01/16/nyregion/man-sought-in-israel-for-attacks-on-arabs-is-seized.html

At night he drank: According to Hatem Bazian, cofounder of Zaytuna College (the first Muslim liberal arts college in the United States, in personal communication with me): "[D]rinking . . . is prohibited in the Qur'an; nevertheless throughout history we find Muslims violating the restrictions. In the modern period, and as the debate and tension between secular and religious outlook developed, it was a mark of sophistication, modernity, and secularity to drink and insist upon it as a way to express departure or distance from Islam. This trend was also promoted by the emerging secular independent nation-state so as to cement their hold on power by constructing a modern (one can say a misunderstanding of Western) image failing to have any epistemic roots in Islamic tradition. Another aspect to Muslim culture in Palestine, Syria, and Lebanon is that problems and challenges have often resulted in seeking refuge in drinking in a similar way we find in America during hard economic times, so it would not be surprising for it to occur despite the restrictions in the Qur'an."

U.N. elementary school in Al Amari: The United Nations Relief and Works Agency operates ninety-nine educational facilities across the West Bank, which reach more than fifty thousand students. See "Education in the West Bank," United Nations Relief and Works Agency for Palestine Refugees in the Near East Web site, http://www.unrwa.org/activity/education-west-bank. Al Amari refugee camp has two primary schools, one for boys and one for girls. Amari Refugee Camp Profile, Camp Development Research Project, UNRWA, October 2008, page 5, http://www.ochaopt.org/documents/opt_campprof_unrwa_amari_oct_2008.pdf

Sido Mohammad was born in 1922: The actual year of Sido's birth is unclear. Ramzi recalls Sido telling him that he, Sido, had been "very young" when his father was killed in 1936 (see note on Hasan Abu Askar below). Ramzi believes that Sido's actual birth year may have been 1929, but that he may have lied about his age in an attempt to find work in the Al Bireh municipality near Ramallah in 1949. However, Sido's official documents stated his birth year as 1922, and I am using that birth year throughout the book.

In the 1917 Balfour Declaration: The text of the declaration, notably, did not mention the Arab Palestinian population, except by reference as "non-Jewish communities in Palestine." The full text: "His Majesty's Government view with favour the establishment in Palestine of a national home for the Jewish people, and will use their best endeavours to facilitate the achievement of the object, it being clearly understood that nothing shall be done which may prejudice the civil and religious rights of existing non-Jewish communities in Palestine, or the rights and political status enjoyed by Jews in any other country." See more at http://unispal.un.org/UNISPAL.NSF/0/E210CA73E38D9E1D052565FA00705C61

Boats filled with European Jews kept coming: To consult specific figures of Jewish immigration pre-1948, see *A Survey of Palestine: Prepared in December 1945 and January 1946 for the Information of the Anglo-American Committee of Inquiry.* Vol. I (Jerusalem: The Government Printer, 1946), pp. 149, 185.

Arab Rebellion: Ted Swedenburg, *Memories of Revolt: The 1936–1939 Rebellion and the Palestinian National Past* is an excellent source for the Arab Rebellion. See also Palestine and Transjordan Administrative Reports, Vol. 6., pp. 19–39, for the sequence of events of the Arab Rebellion; David Hirst, *The Gun and the Olive Branch*, pp. 198–230; and my book *The Lemon Tree*, pp. 12–21.

Sido's father, Hasan Abu Askar, took up arms: It appears that Sido's father was killed by British troops in 1936 during the Arab Rebellion. Ramzi recalls being told by Sido that Hasan had been killed in a British aerial bombing. This fits with this historical record: Royal Air Force bombers were deployed during the rebellion from 1936 to 1939 and bombed rebel positions. See the RAF web page at http://www.raf.mod.uk/ organisation/14squadron.cfm. The Israeli author and journalist Danny Rubinstein, in personal correspondence with me, reports finding Hasan Abu Askar's name from "Naane village in the list of the Palestinian fighters of 1936." This list can be found in M. Kabha and N. Sirhan, *Lexicon of Commanders, Rebellions and Volunteers of the Palestinian 1936–1939 Revolt.* Dar al-Huda: Kafr Qari' (Arabic, translation of the title from openlibrary.org).

Ramzi's father suffered severe head trauma: Ramzi provided me with the medical report dated July 24, 1987, from a "Dr. Kidess" in the Jerusalem hospital, which listed "severe head trauma" and "decerebration" as a consequence of the accident, thus, according to doctors, indicating brain damage. This in turn is consistent with Ramzi's description of the profound change in his father's behavior after the accident.

Chapter 3: Uprising

An Israeli truck had veered into a long line of vehicles: This traffic accident is commonly seen as the spark that started the First Intifada. A few days later, on December 15, a *New York Times* article mentions the December 8 accident as the catalyst for a violent round of clashes between Palestinians and the Israeli army; "the current round of clashes, part of an increasing cycle of violence in the last year, began after a traffic accident last Tuesday in which an Israeli Army truck collided with two vans bringing day laborers back home to Gaza, killing four Palestinians." See John Kifner, "Arab Is Killed in Gaza and Another Dies of Wounds," the *New York Times*, December 15, 1987. A more recent article in the *Jerusalem Post* describes the accident as "what may have been the most consequential traffic accident in both Israeli and Palestinian history." (Michael Omer-Man, "The Accident that Sparked an Intifada," *Jerusalem Post*, December 4, 2011.)

Tinder for a fire that had been smoldering for years: Other incidents that may have helped spark the First Intifada include a November 1987 Palestinian hang-glider attack on an Israeli military base, which killed six soldiers (Morris, *Righteous Victims*, p. 561), and an uprising at Balata refugee camp near Nablus (Morris, *Righteous Victims*, p. 573; and Schiff and Ya'ari, *Intifada*, pp. 59–62).

Protests broke out in Gaza that evening and spread quickly across the West Bank: "Demonstrators hurled rocks, gasoline bombs, and other objects at Israeli troops, [drove] them back with live ammunition . . . The few IDF troops regularly stationed in the Gaza Strip could not cope with either the scale or intensity of the disturbances . . . On Thursday, December 10, the mass unrest spread to the West Bank." See the American Jewish Yearbook's AJC Archives, Vol. 89, p. 378, http://www.ajcarchives.org/ AJC_DATA/Files/1989_12_Israel.pdf

Ruth Margolies Beitler, professor of international relations at the U.S. Military Academy at West Point, writes, "The growth of grassroots movements, coupled with the frustration of living under an occupation, altered the Palestinians' choice of tactics." See *The Path to Mass Rebellion: An Analysis of Two Intifadas* (New York: Lexington Books, 2004), p. 100.

Israel controlled West Bank and Gaza borders, streams: In her paper entitled "Water as a Human Right: The Understanding of Water in Palestine," Dr. Karen Assaf writes: "In 1964, Israel took advantage of its control over much of the headwater area without recognition of other riparian users' needs or rights in the Jordan River Basin when it implemented the first 'out of basin' transfer (National Water Carrier System) of the Jordan River waters to the Negev and southern coastal areas of Israel. After 1967, with the annexation of the Golan Heights and the occupation of the West Bank, Israel increased its control over both the headwaters and the lower Jordan River . . . Further exploitation of the resources of both the upper and lower reaches of the Jordan River continued over this period with total disregard for other riparians until the Peace Treaty with Jordan in 1994. Meanwhile, colonisation of the West Bank and Gaza was carried out by the construction of settlements. These settlements, in addition to utilizing a disproportionate part of the available aquifer, discharged untreated domestic, agricultural and industrial waste into nearby valleys, resulting in significant harm to the environment." See Global Issues Paper No. 11, Heinrich Böll Foundation, 2004, p. 138, http://www.boell.de/sites/default/files/assets/boell.de/images/download_de/interna tionalepolitik/GIP11_Palestine_Karen_Assaf.pdf. See also Martin Asser, "Obstacles to Arab-Israeli Peace: Water," BBC News, September 2, 2010, http://www.bbc.com/news/world-middle-east-11101797, and "Israel Controls 80% of Palestinian Water," IMEMC, Janury 8, 2007, http://www.imemc.org/article/46460

Israel . . . levied occupation taxes: According to a 1990 report on the system of taxation in the West Bank and in Gaza, "In 1976, when a value added tax (VAT) was introduced in Israel, the same law was extended to the territories by means of an order known as 'Excise Added Tax' . . . In 1981 the authorities attempted to enforce the law more vigorously, requiring businesses in the territories to keep books and submit tax statements." See "The System of Taxation in the West Bank and Gaza Strip as an Instrument for the Enforcement of Authority During the Uprising," B'Tselem, February 1990, http://www.btselem.org/download/199002_taxation_system_eng.doc

During the First Intifada, in order "to defy the Israeli authorities, many Palestinians refused to pay their taxes, forcing the civil administration to clamp down on tax collection. As a response to Palestinian defiance, the civil administration ruled that businessmen could not obtain import or export licenses until they paid their taxes." See Ruth Margolies Beitler, *The Path to Mass Rebellion*, p. 110.

Israel . . . censored Arabic-language media: "In late 1988, Israeli authorities, suspecting Palestinian journalists of involvement in the *intifadah*, censored and shut down many Palestinian newspapers and magazines in the West Bank and the Gaza Strip and arrested Arab journalists, including several members of the board of the Arab Journalists' Association." See "Israel: Communications Media," http://www.country-data.com/cgi-bin/query/r-6816.html. Anna Saraste, in her study, "Media Regulation and Censorship in Occupied Palestine," writes: "When Israel occupied the West Bank and Gaza in 1967, it immediately established laws restricting the freedom of the press . . . a license from the Israeli government was needed to publish a newspaper in the West Bank and Gaza strip . . . newspapers were closed down if they were deemed harmful to Israeli state security as defined by the Israeli authorities." (University of Tampere, ICAHD Finland, p. 5, http://icahd.fi/wp-content/uploads/2010/05/media_regulation_and_censorship_in_palestine.pdf) Veteran Israeli journalist Danny Rubinstein writes: "The Palestinian press has a long history stretching back to the start of the century . . . This press was, and to some extent still is, centered in East Jerusalem, which is annexed to the State of Israel . . . The editors and writers could exploit the freedom of the press practiced according to Israeli law . . . The Israeli administration's military-political censorship found it difficult to supervise the Palestinian press, and the most effective way of punishing these papers for censorship offenses was to prevent their distribution in the areas of Israeli military government in the West Bank and Gaza." See Danny Rubinstein, "Palestinians and Israelis: An Uneven Curiosity," Palestine-Israel Journal 5, nos. 3 and 4 (1988), http://www.pij.org/details.php?id=373

Israel . . . issued or denied precious travel permits: According to a 1989 report by B'Tselem, "Every resident of the West Bank and Gaza over the age of 16 is obliged by order to carry his identity card with him. A resident without his identity card commits a criminal offence and can be arrested." See "Information Sheet: Update May 1, 1989," p. 8, B'Tselem, http://www.btselem.org/sites/default/files2/update_may_1.1989.pdf

During the First Intifada, in order "to quickly identify Palestinians who entered Israel, the civil administration issued new license plates for vehicles from the territories. In tandem with the new licenses, Israel distributed plastic identification cards that were mandatory for any person entering Israel proper and directed that only Palestinians who had paid their taxes were eligible to receive the card." See Ruth Margolies Beitler, *The Path to Mass Rebellion*, p. 110.

Birth certificates, and death certificates: From an interview with Ghassan Abdullah, summer 2010, Ramallah: "Imagine that when my grandmother died, and in order to bury my grandmother, I had to get a death certificate from the Israeli forces. To get a driving license, I have to have this clearance. To get a birth certificate for my child, I need their clearance."

Closed schools and universities at will: The late Gabi Baramki, former president of Birzeit University, in an interview in the summer of 2011, recalled that the university had been ordered closed for fifty-one consecutive months during the First Intifada. Of the school closures, by military order and for long periods of time, wrote Baramki: "Closures varied in length and nature . . . from 1979, the closures usually lasted for a minimum of two months. With time, three- to four-month closures became the norm." See Gabi Baramki, "Palestinian University Education Under Occupation," *Palestine-Israel Journal of Politics, Economics and Culture* 3, no. 1 (1996), http://www.pij.org/details.php?id=569

"Occupation . . . interferes in every aspect of life and of death": Mourid Barghouti, *I Saw Ramallah*, p. 48.

Their eyes and ears in the camp: For a detailed and chilling report on the system of Palestinian collaborators with Israel, see B'Tselem, "Collaborators in the Occupied Territories," researched and written by Yizhar Be'er and Dr. Saleh Abdel Jawad. B'Tselem, January 1994, http://www.btselem.org/publications/summaries/199401_collaboration_suspects

Abdel Jawad, the former dean of the law school at Birzeit University in the West Bank, described Israel's recruitment tactics to me in detail in an interview in the summer of 2011, and in subsequent discussions in 2013 and 2014.

"We must set the ground burning under the feet of the occupiers": From Schiff and Ya'ari, *Intifada*, p. 193.

Organized secret classes in a musty shack: Many of the details from this section (including the musty shacks) come from Lindsey Cook, an American schoolteacher teaching at the Friends Girls School in Ramallah during the First Intifada. During the school closures Lindsey started a twice-a-week English class at Al Amari. "Our enthusiastic students, all teenager girls, create a makeshift classroom out of a musty shack in a jagged open courtyard . . . A cluster of old mattresses piled high form a sofa, and a green door serves as a blackboard. The students bring chairs, damp chalk and a rag. We close the rusted metal shutters . . . (boys will warn if soldiers come near). If caught teaching during the ban on education, we could be imprisoned or deported." Taken from "A Journey Through Palestine and Israel, 1987–1997," an unpublished manuscript by Lindsey Fielder Cook.

The children stuffed their forbidden notebooks under the mattresses: "'UP THE ALLEYWAY! THEY'RE SEARCHING HOUSES!' scream the boys outside and, like clockwork, the girls shove notebooks and pencils deep between damp mattresses. The blackboard is wiped clean and reborn as a broken door resting against a wall." From "A Journey Through Palestine and Israel, 1987–1997," unpublished manuscript by Lindsey Fielder Cook, p. 48.

Rabin dismissed the early protests as local and insignificant: "'The majority of the population in the areas is interested in public order, but is exposed to the terrorism of a few,' said a Cabinet communiqué [which] said the army was in control of the situation, 'in contrast with greatly inflated descriptions' . . . Brig. Gen. Shaike Erez, head of the military government in the West Bank, said, 'We have known much worse.'" See "11 More Hurt in West Bank and Gaza," *New York Times*, December 14, 1987. The next day the *Times* reported: "Prime Minister Yitzhak Shamir Dismissed the Clashes as the Work of 'Terrorists and Delinquents.'" See "Arab Is Killed in Gaza and Another Dies of Wounds," John Kifner, *New York Times*, December 15, 1987.

The Israelis had to revise their strategy: Indeed, soon afterward Yitzhak Rabin declared, upon his return from meetings in Washington, D.C., that he intended to "adopt steps that will improve order, even if those are painful and will not gain us sympathy in the world." See "Fractious Israeli Leaders Are Circling the Wagons," John

Kifner, *New York Times*, December 23, 1987. He later told *Haaretz* newspaper: "Even if we are forced to use massive force, under no circumstances will we allow last week's events to repeat themselves." See John Kifner, "Israeli Vows to Stress Riot Training," *New York Times*, December 30, 1987. The article adds: "The commander, Gen. Dan Shomron, the Chief of the General Staff, said in a briefing for Israeli defense correspondents and in an interview with the army radio that his men had been taken by surprise by the scope and intensity of the rioting that swept through the occupied West Bank and Gaza Strip this month."

Soldiers filled fifty-five-gallon drums: Details from Al Amari camp during this period come from multiple interviews with Ramzi and also from numerous other organizers and activists at the camp during the First Intifada.

Each day, jeeps and armored trucks entered Al Amari: See, for example, "Use Less Force, U.S. Tells Israel: Crackdown on Agitators Seen; Strife Goes On," *Los Angeles Times*, December 23, 1987, which reported that Israeli security forces were making "house-to-house searches for suspects in the Al Amari refugee camp near Ramallah." The next day John Kifner of the *New York Times* reported that "troops also surrounded the Amari refugee center near Ramallah." See "Israel Bears Down to Stop Protests in Occupied Areas," *New York Times*, December 24, 1987.

Military authorities imposed periodic curfews: Ruth Margolies Beitler writes: "Extended curfews affected the economic viability of the West Bank and refugee camps. In some areas, round-the-clock curfews made it almost impossible for the local population to support themselves financially. In addition, Rabin threatened to ban food shipments into the area unless shopkeepers agreed to open their stores. The military government hoped that the economic sanctions would persuade the majority of the local population that the price of sustaining the Intifada was too great." See *The Path to Mass Rebellion*, p. 110.

Rice, lentils, potatoes, and olive oil were hidden in neighborhood caches: The information on Palestinian organizing during the First Intifada comes from more than a dozen interviews I conducted during the summers of 2011–13 with organizers and "ordinary" residents in Al Amari and Ramallah. Other sources include "A Journey Through Palestine and Israel, 1987–1997," Lindsey Fielder Cook's unpublished manuscript, in which she writes (p. 36): "Arresting those involved is proving an embarrassing operation for the IDF, especially when university professors were arrested for advising the community on how best to plant 'intifada gardens.' [If] clashes develop in my neighbourhood, there is now a 'secret clinic' in someone's living room that is stocked with first aid needs. A local doctor is on call. A welfare committee distributed food to the needy . . . Lawns and forgotten fields are attacked with plows and seeds. Old and young pool labour skills on weekends and during general strikes to gather with picks, shovels and spades and return at dusk with faces caked in dirt."

Palestinian shopkeepers, en masse, refused to pay taxes to the occupying authorities: Benny Morris, *Righteous Victims*, p. 580; and Ruth Margolies Beitler, *The Path to Mass Rebellion*, p. 110.

Slick and dangerous for the incoming army jeeps: Benny Morris, *Righteous Victims*, p. 580.

Live ammunition to disperse the crowds: In *The Path to Mass Rebellion*, p. 109, Ruth Margolies Beitler writes, "by March . . . the rules of engagement were modified, allowing soldiers to fire at petrol bomb throwers. Previously, soldiers were only permitted to fire at protesters when their lives were in immediate danger. As time progressed the Israeli army continued to amend its rules of engagement to clarify when soldiers were permitted to shoot at rioters . . . By September 1989, the IDF issued new orders defining unarmed, but masked, Palestinians as suspects at whom soldiers may fire with live ammunition. The soldiers were still required to warn the suspect, shoot in the air, and then aim at the suspect's legs. The Israelis posited that if the Palestinians understood the rules of engagement and that soldiers were permitted to shoot, they would be deterred from participating in any type of demonstration." For more information about the changing rules of engagement see the B'Tselem report on the matter, http://www.btselem.org/sites/default/files/the_use_of_firearms.pdf

Confronting an unseen army: "Television screens throughout the world presented the Israeli military occupation in the most ugly light," observed Shlomo Gazit, the Israeli brigadier general, "with Israel's armed, well-protected and clumsy soldiers trying in vain to deal with agile Palestinian kids throwing stones at them and making fools out of them. It was a David and Goliath battle of sorts, this time with the Palestinians in the role of David and receiving the world's sympathy." See *Trapped Fools: Thirty Years of Israeli Policy in the Territories*, Chapter 17.

The soldier aimed his Galil: Former Israeli soldiers who had been stationed in or near Ramallah and Al Amari during the First Intifada and were interviewed for this book recall the use of Galils. At the time, according to Small Arms Defense Journal (http://sadefensejournal.com/wp/?p=1927), the M-16, another relatively lightweight assault rifle, was already replacing the Galils, though that rifle was still used by some branches of the Israeli security forces. See Iris Giller, "Death Foretold: Firing of 'Rubber' Bullets to Disperse Demonstrations in the Occupied Territories," B'Tselem Information Sheet, December 1998, p. 19.

The soldier lowered his rifle: It seems that the Israeli soldier, in deciding not to shoot at Ramzi, was following the rules of engagement as dictated by the IDF handbook, which stated: "It is forbidden to open fire on stone throwers, except as part of the apprehension of suspects procedure and only when the stone-throwing constitutes a real and immediate danger." See Ronny Talmor, "The Use of Firearms by the Security Forces in the Occupied Territories," B'Tselem, July 1990, p. 11, http://www.btselem.org/sites/default/files/the_use_of_firearms.pdf

Syrian poet Nizar Qabbani: Qabbani, as cited in Collins, *Occupied by Memory*, p. 40. See also "Children Bearing Rocks," translated by Sharif Elmusa and Naomi Shihab Nye, p. 147, http://www.btselem.org/sites/default/files/the_use_of_firearms.pdf

Israeli officials saw Palestinian liberation as a basic threat: For a discussion of strategic depth, see Benny Morris, *Righteous Victims*, p. 602, and Schiff and Ya'ari, *Intifada*,

p. 169. To read more about the fears of Palestinians wanting more, see Morris, p. 606, and Schiff and Ya'ari, p. 193. For more on Hamas's emergence, see Morris, p. 579; Yezid Sayigh, *Armed Struggle and the Search for State* p. 631; and my book *The Lemon Tree*, p. 194. Ironically, Israel initially sought to encourage the formation of Hamas in order to weaken the PLO. See Avi Shlaim, *The Iron Wall*, p. 459.

Ramzi woke up to the sound of armed men: Israeli soldiers stationed in Ramallah in 1988 recalled in interviews with me in the summer of 2011 the three basic tasks ordered by superiors: remove all Palestinian flags and obliterate graffiti, find and detain suspected organizers and militants, and chase the children and young men throwing stones. Job one was obliterating any expression of nationalist sentiment, especially the Palestinian flag. Each morning soldiers would find the flags flapping from telephone or electrical poles. They'd pound on a few doors, order the men out, and command them to select a volunteer to climb up and take down the banned national colors. They ordered the women to remove the slogans and directives splashed nightly on the camp walls. Graffiti removal was so common, one former soldier recounted to me, that some families kept a bucket of white paint by the door.

Poured the food in the sink and dumped jars of tea and vegetables on the floor: One soldier of the day recalled: "It would basically depend on the whim of the commander on that night. If he was unhappy with his life, or his girlfriend, or if he just wanted to go back, or if he was just angry at something, he could take it out on the Palestinians. And it wasn't just the commander. Soldiers would take out their personal grief on whoever was around, because they were in a position of power. Because they could." (Interview with former Israeli soldier Tal Frankl, Tel Aviv, August 2011.)

Having found no weapons: "During the First Intifada I never saw any Palestinian carrying a weapon," Ramzi remembers. "There were no weapons during the First Intifada. And the Israelis knew this." "The Palestinians rarely used firearms," acknowledged an Israeli brigadier general of the day, "partly because they hardly had any." See Shlomo Gazit, *Trapped Fools*, Chapter 11.

Punching and kicking them: During my interview with Tal Frankl in Tel Aviv in August 2011, the former Israeli soldier stated: "Pulling people out of houses is . . . probably the worst thing that I did. I definitely felt it was a terrible act, thinking back on it . . . Or tying people up on the street because someone threw a stone at you, and leaving them out there for six hours in the sun, and inevitably someone confesses, just to let everyone else go."

Ten thousand children suffered broken bones: According to a May 1990 report by the Swedish branch of Save the Children, *The Status of Palestinian Children During the Uprising in the Occupied Territories*, in the first two years of the intifada, "23,600 to 29,900 children required medical treatment for their beating injuries," and nearly a third of those "sustained broken bones, including multiple fractures." As cited in John Mearsheimer and Stephen Walt's *The Israel Lobby*, p. 100.

Far less frequently, Molotov cocktails: According to Benny Morris's *Righteous Victims*, p. 580, Molotov cocktails were used heavily "for a time, mainly against [settler] traffic, though occasionally against troops." Schiff and Ya'ari, in *Intifada*, pp. 144–5, describe Rabin's issuance of "unequivocal orders to shoot anyone hurling a Molotov cocktail, regardless of the circumstances" and his insistence that those suspected of throwing the cocktails be given "harsh punitive measures, including the demolition or sealing of their houses." Firebombs were used less frequently—perhaps three or four a day during a surge in such use, according to one estimate (Schiff and Ya'ari, *Intifada*, p. 113).

The soldiers were coming unglued: Indeed the Israeli military was facing a crisis within its own ranks. Stories of the soldiers' fury were raising internal concern. On May 25, 1989, the IDF's judge-advocate general put four soldiers on trial. They were accused of beating an unarmed Gazan to death. The soldiers, wearing the purple berets of the elite Givati Brigade, had burst into the home of Hani Al Shami, in the Jabaliya refugee camp, in search of his sons. When he tried to shield them, the soldiers seized Al Shami, "beat him mercilessly for 15 minutes with rifle butts and a broomstick," blindfolded him, and administered "a vicious 'karate kick' in the chest which hurtled him with brute force against a wall. He died soon afterward." See the American Jewish Year Book's AJC Archives, Vol. 91, p. 365, http://www.ajcarchives/org/ajc_data/files/1991_11_Israel.pdf

Underwent a mental metamorphosis: The military court asserted that the beating death of Hani Al Shami was part of a pattern, especially of the feared Givati Brigade: "We were appalled to hear some of the witnesses express hatred and contempt for the value of the life of the population which is ruled by the [IDF]. We shuddered when witnesses who are soldiers in the army [related how they] watched the humiliating spectacle of the beating of bound and helpless prisoners in an army camp, indifferent to what they saw and shutting their ears to the ghastly outcries of those being beaten . . ." (AJC Archives, Vol. 91, p. 366.)

Frequent Israeli use of live ammunition against demonstrators armed only with stones: Numerous reports and eyewitness accounts, including Ramzi's and his Aunt Widad's, described soldiers' frequent use of live ammunition at stone-throwing demonstrators and bystanders. The *New York Times* reported: "Defense Minister Yitzhak Rabin announced tough new measures today against Palestinians accused of throwing stones in the occupied territories. The measures include allowing a greater number of soldiers to fire on demonstrators, sealing or destroying the homes of stone throwers and confiscating the cars and other property of those who take part in the uprising." See Joel Brinkley, "Israel Orders Harsher Tactics in Palestinian Revolt," *New York Times*, January 18, 1989.

Greater use of plastic bullets: Yitzhak Rabin, the defense minister, authorized a partial shift to plastic bullets, which soldiers were authorized to fire at the legs of "leaders of a riot" or of protesters who erected concrete barriers. See American Jewish Year Book's AJC Archives, Vol. 91, http://www.ajcarchives/org/ajc_data/files/1991_11_Israel.pdf At a press conference on September 21, 1988, Rabin stated that use of plastic bullets was designed to increase injuries among Palestinians, and that he was "not worried" about the sharp increase in such casualties from the clashes. "This is precisely our aim," he said. (U.N. report of July 13, 1989, quoting the *Jerusalem Post*, September 28, 1988.)

This way, he added, the uprising would grow more quiet, and the overall level of violence would eventually decline. See also "Rabin Defends Plastic Bullets," *Chicago Tribune*, September 28, 1988.

The rules of engagement were unclear: This statement is confirmed by Morris, *Righteous Victims*, p. 588, who states: "From the start, regulations governing open-fire procedures were a hot moral and political issue . . . The radically changed circumstances of the Intifada inevitably gave rise to new definitions of what was permissible . . . In general, the IDF tried to restrict the use of firearms to life-threatening situations—but trigger-happy troops, provocation, or complex situations often resulted in the death of Arabs, even though no Israeli life had, in fact, been threatened." According to another account, "the written rules appear to be unchanged. However, policy vis-à-vis the rules has certainly changed, the thrust being toward a relaxation of the existing regulations." See Ronny Talmor, "The Use of Firearms by the Security Forces in the Occupied Territories," B'Tselem, July 1990, p. 22. For more information on the modifications in the policy of opening fire at persons engaged in intifada-related actions, see the B'Tselem report on the matter, http://www.btselem.org/sites/default/files/the_use_of_firearms.pdf

"The development of an insensitivity to human life": Shlomo Gazit, *Trapped Fools*, Chapter 17.

Massacres of Palestinians at the refugee camps of Sabra and Shatila: The executioners at Sabra and Shatila were Phalangist Christian militia who had entered the camps after the murder of Lebanese Christian president Bashir Gemayel, who Israel, which had invaded Lebanon, had hoped to install as a friendly head of state. The Phalangist militia entered the camp at the encouragement of Ariel Sharon and other Israeli officers. The militia sought to root out two thousand militants allegedly still in hiding. Sharon and Israeli troops stood by outside the camp. Israeli forces launched night flares to aid the Phalangist mission. According to reports, the militia killed not only militants, but every living creature in the camps, including babies, even dogs and donkeys. See my account in *The Lemon Tree*, pp. 204–5. Loren Jenkins of the *Washington Post* entered the camps shortly after the forty-eight-hour killing spree:

> *The scene at the Shatilla camp when foreign observers entered Saturday morning was like a nightmare. Women wailed over the deaths of loved ones, bodies began to swell under the hot sun, and the streets were littered with thousands of spent cartridges. Houses had been dynamited and bulldozed into rubble, many with the inhabitants still inside. Groups of bodies lay before bullet-pocked walls where they appeared to have been executed. Others were strewn in alleys and streets, apparently shot as they tried to escape. Each little dirt alley through the deserted buildings, where Palestinians have lived since fleeing Palestine when Israel was created in 1948, told its own horror story. (Washington Post, September 23, 1982.)*

The United Nations General Assembly declared that it was "appalled at the large-scale massacre of Palestinian civilians in the Sabra and Shatila refugee camps situated at Beirut" and resolved "that the massacre was an act of genocide." See United Nations General Assembly, A/RES/37/123, December 16, 1982, http://www.un.org/documents/ga/res/37/a37r123.htm. For more on the Sabra and Shatila Massacre and on the varying death count, see the Institute for Middle East Understanding Fact Sheet, http://imeu.org/article/the-sabra-shatila-massacre

No one, apart from soldiers, could be seen along the main camp road: Widad recalls some of the details differently: demonstrators still in the streets, stones flying, and teargas and live ammunition incoming from the soldiers. "The *shabab* were there," she remembered. The collective memory of aunt and nephew, however, converge over what happened next.

Died of her wounds: Nahil Tukhi's death drew brief mention in the international press, in longer dispatches about the ongoing violence. "A 13-year-old Palestinian girl died today of wounds suffered in an earlier clash with troops," the *New York Times* reported on September 25, 1988, in an article headlined, "7 Cases of Polio Reported in Israel." "Nahil Tokheh, 13, died a week after being shot in the head during a clash in the Amari refugee camp, the army confirmed." See "Israelis Kill 3 Guerrillas; 6 Arabs Hurt in Clashes," *Los Angeles Times*, September 25, 1988. Reports of Nahil's age varied; her mother, who I interviewed, says she was 12. Ten months later her death was mentioned in U.N. human rights proceedings (United Nations General Assembly, "Report of the Special Committee to Investigate Israeli Practices Affecting the Human Rights of the Population of the Occupied Territories July 13, 1989"). The Israeli army conducted a routine review of the shooting. For Nahil's death, "the file was closed with no legal steps taken," according to a report from the respected Israeli human rights group B'Tselem. The report quoted the military spokesman saying that the soldier's rifle fire in the incident had been "according to regulations." See B'Tselem, "Human Rights Violations in the Occupied Territories, 1992/1993, http://www.btselem.org/sites/default/files/human_rights_violations_in_the_occupied_territories_1992_1993.pdf

Brought the death toll to at least 250 Palestinians in the first nine and a half months of the uprising: See "Israelis Kill 3 Guerrillas; 6 Arabs Hurt in Clashes," *Los Angeles Times,* September 25, 1988. Many of the dead were children. According to a May 1990 report by the Swedish branch of Save the Children, *The Status of Palestinian Children During the Uprising in the Occupied Territories,* during the first two years of the First Intifada, 106 children died by Israeli fire, almost all of them "hit by directed—not random or ricochet—gunfire." Most of the children "were not participating in a stone-throwing demonstration when shot." According to a B'Tselem report, from the beginning of the intifada in December 1987 to the end of October 1988, six Israeli civilians were killed in the Occupied Territories, three of whom were minors under seventeen. See "Fatalities in the First Intifada," B'Tselem, http://www.btselem.org/statistics/first_intifada_tables

5,000 Palestinians were injured, 18,000 were arrested, and 2,500 were taken into administrative detention: These statistics come from Carmel Shalev, "The Price of Insurgency," report of the West Bank Data Project, October 1988, cited in the U.N.

Report of the Special Committee to Investigate Israeli Practices Affecting the Human Rights of the Population of the Occupied Territories, July 13, 1989, http://unispal.un.org/UNISPAL.NSF/0/BB7D35D91ADB56920525660500535C45. Wendy Pearlman, in "Conditions in Israel and the Occupied Territories: A Middle East Watch Report" (Human Rights Watch, 1991), cites a figure of 10,000 placed under administrative detention by the end of 1988 alone.

The revolutionary Arafat had softened his political stance: The previous December in Geneva, Yasser Arafat, the PLO chairman-in-exile, had advocated for Palestinian statehood at a special session of the United Nations. (U.S. officials had refused to grant Arafat a visa to travel to New York.) In his speech, Arafat declared the PLO's support for U.N. Resolution 242, which recognized Israel's right "to live in peace within secure and recognized boundaries free from threats or acts of force." The speech represented a monumental compromise by the PLO. Arafat was recognizing Israel's right to exist and, by implication, agreeing to seek an independent state not on all of historic Palestine, which included Israel, but on the 22 percent of it that remained after the 1948 war: the West Bank and Gaza. Arafat was, in essence, embracing the "two-state solution." How this would affect the refugees, who after forty years still had every intention of returning to their homes, was left unclear. In his U.N. speech, Arafat crucially renounced "all forms of terrorism, including individual, group, and state terrorism." For the full speech, see the Jewish Virtual Library, https://www.jewishvirtuallibrary.org/jsource/Terrorism/plotstate2.html. It was this pledge, especially, that prompted the United States to open a dialogue with the PLO. This in turn rattled Israeli leaders, who had no such inclination. Israeli leaders insisted that terms were to be negotiated with local Palestinian leaders, not the PLO. Local leaders rejected the overture, insisting that the PLO was the sole representative of the Palestinian people. The uprising continued.

Literally had the future of Palestine in their hands: Across the West Bank and Gaza, families like Ramzi's struggled to control their children. As commentators and scholars praised the "new spirit" and "truly revolutionary action" of the children of the stones (John Collins, *Occupied by Memory*, pp. 40–1), parents found it increasingly difficult to discipline their boys and young men. Studies showed, on the one hand, a rise in aggression and disobedience (pp. 44–5, 68–72) and on the other, a shift in family dynamics, a "terminal upheaval" (p. 38) in which "children increasingly respond to a locus of authority outside the home, and the parents' authority is reduced." See also Kate Rouhana, *Journal of Palestine Studies*, 18:4, 110–21, as quoted in Collins, p. 69.

Red roofs of the settlement of Psagot: According to Peace Now, Psagot was created in 1981 and is situated 9.6 kilometers (or roughly six miles) from the Green Line, in the Ramallah district. See "Psagot" on the Peace Now Web site, http://peacenow.org.il/eng/content/psagot

Raw sewage trickling down the hillside: It is not uncommon to see raw sewage flowing down from the settlements toward Palestinian lands and villages. See, for example, "Settlers Dump Sewage on Palestinian Land," *Daily Beast*, March 8, 2013, http://www.thedailybeast.com/articles/2013/03/08/settlers-dump-their-sewage-on-palestinian-land.html. For a report on Psagot's raw sewage flowing down the old hill at Jabal Al Tawil, see the article by Amos Harel in *Haaretz*, July 9, 2009, referenced at *The Magnes Zionist*, http://www.jeremiahhaber.com/2009/07/reading-for-three-weeks-how-settlements.html

Even a gazelle: Ramzi's memory of seeing a gazelle is vivid, and is backed by confirmation of the species' existence in the West Bank. "The mountain gazelle and dorcas gazelle are spread around different areas of the West Bank," writes Stefan Szepesi, author of *Walking Palestine: 25 Journeys into the West Bank*. "Encountering gazelles on a walk is not uncommon . . ." Raja Shehadeh, in his lovely, bittersweet memoir *Palestinian Walks*, also reports encounters with gazelles.

Chapter 4: Father

Launched firebombs at Jewish vehicles: "In East Jerusalem today, an Israeli bus was destroyed by a firebomb thrown at it." See "Troops in West Bank Kill Teen-Age Arab; A Gaza Youth Dies," *New York Times*, January 17, 1989, http://www.nytimes.com/1989/01/17/world/troops-in-west-bank-kill-teen-age-arab-a-gaza-youth-dies.html. See also "Inter-Arab Violence Growing in Occupied Areas," *New York Times*, September 11, 1989, http://www.nytimes.com/1989/09/11/world/inter-arab-violence-growing-in-occupied-areas.html. The Israeli army "installed anti-riot devices on some of their military vehicles to deal with stone and fire-bomb throwing demonstrators. See "Israelis vs. Palestinians: Tactics Are Refined," *New York Times*, March 30, 1989, http://www.nytimes.com/1989/03/30/world/israelis-vs-palestinians-tactics-are-refined.html

An Israeli soldier was caught in a lethal ambush in the old city of Nablus: "On February 24, Sgt. Binyamin Meisner, 25, became the fifth Israeli soldier killed there since the start of the uprising, when an IDF patrol walked into a well-executed ambush in Nablus's labyrinthine old city. A ten day curfew was imposed on the city's 100,000 inhabitants as security forces hunted the perpetrators of the ambush. In early March, two suspected perpetrators, aged 19 and 22, were arrested . . . and their homes were demolished." See the American Jewish Year Book's AJC Archives, Vol. 91, p. 355, http://www.ajcarchives/org/ajc_data/files/1991_11_Israel.pdf

Shepherds had stabbed a Jewish man to death: "Three Palestinians said they met a Jewish settler who was hiking in the occupied West Bank, chatted with him, posed for a picture and then stabbed him to death." See "3 Arabs Allegedly Chatted with Settler Before Slaying Him," *Los Angeles Times*, June 21, 1989. Jewish settlers vowed revenge, and "hundreds of settlers raided Arab villages, doing large property damage." See the American Jewish Year Book's AJC Archives, Vol. 91, p. 359, http://www.ajcarchives/org/ajc_data/files/1991_11_Israel.pdf

Home of suspected perpetrators, order everyone out, load it with explosives, and blow it up: This accelerated a policy dating back to the "emergency regulations" of British Mandate rule from 1917 to1948. In 1988, 101 homes were "totally demolished," according to a U.S. State Department human rights report; the next year, the number rose to 138. Israel rejected arguments by the United States that the demolitions were a violation of the Fourth Geneva Convention, which prohibited such collective punishment: "No protected person may be punished for an offence he or she has not personally committed. Collective penalties and likewise all measures of intimidation or of terrorism are prohibited." See Article 33, Fourth Geneva Convention for the Protection of Civilian Persons in Times of War, August 12, 1949, http://www.icrc.org/ihl/WebART/380-600038. According to a B'Tselem report on house demolitions and sealing as a means of punishment during the First Intifada, "the demolition is usually carried out at night, by either the use of explosives or a bulldozer, depending on the conditions of the area and the nature of the building, and after imposing a curfew in the area around the house designated for demolition. The tenants of the house have a very limited amount of time to gather and remove their possessions. In some cases, houses have been demolished or sealed before the families were able to remove their belongings. . . . The family is not allowed to rebuild the house or to break the sealed openings." See, "Demolition and Sealing of Houses as a Punitive Measure in the West Bank and Gaza Strip During the Intifada," Ronny Talmor, B'Tselem, Jerusalem, September 1989, www.btselem.org/download/198909_house_demolitions_eng.rtf

Subjected instead to substantial fines: "Families whose children were accused of throwing stones faced financial penalties such as fines or stiff bails to release the youths from custody." See Wendy Pearlman, *Conditions in Israel and the Occupied Territories: A Middle East Watch Report* (Human Rights Watch, 1991).

The young people, mostly from the refugee camps, who had paid the highest price: Compared to the middle-class and wealthy Palestinian kids, many more of the camp children had been killed or maimed, or, like Ramzi, had seen schoolmates die. It was the camp children who were subjected to the greatest trauma, and who had lost the most time in school. Ramzi himself had missed months' worth of instruction in the U.N. school in Al Amari, and the impromptu classes held in secret made up for only a fraction of those.

It had been closed by Israeli military order: According to Wendy Pearlman, in "Conditions in Israel and the Occupied Territories": "Israel closed Palestinian universities for most years of the Intifada and West Bank schools for a total of 12 months." A report for UNESCO stated: "In 1990, children were not able to begin their school year until January, four months after the usual start . . . in 1991 . . . there were reportedly closures for as long as six months at a time. Moreover, according to Al Zaroo and Hunt, 'a tenth of the schools were used [by Israel] as military camps and detention centres during the closure period'" See Susan Nicolai, *Fragmented Foundations: Education and Chronic Crisis in the Occupied Palestinian Territory*, UNESCO International Institute for Educational Planning (London: Save the Children UK, 2007), p. 37, http://unesdoc.unesco.org/images/0015/001502/150260e.pdf. See also Gabi Baramki, "Palestinian University Education under Occupation," *Palestine-Israel Journal*, 3, no. 1

(1996), http://www.pij.org/details.php?id=569; and his book, *Peaceful Resistance: Building a Palestinian University under Occupation.*

One of hundreds in a long tradition of Palestinian protest music: For background on the history of Palestinian protest music, see David A. McDonald, *My Voice Is My Weapon: Music, Nationalism, and the Poetics of Palestinian Resistance.* See also "Palestine: The Sound of Resistance," from the Web site Cultures of Resistance, http://www. culturesofresistance.org/sound-of-resistance-palestine

It was Land Day: Land Day, March 30, is a holiday Palestinians commemorate for the loss, among other things, of their land to Israel in 1948. In "Remembering Land Day" (*Al Ahram Weekly*, April 7–13, 2005; http://weekly.ahram.org.eg/2005/737/op3.htm), Nayef Hawatmeh writes: "[What] immediately sparked the Land Day uprising was the Ministry of Finance decision of 29 February 1976 to confiscate 21,000 dunams of Palestinian land in Galilee. These vast tracts of land were to be turned over to the construction of eight Jewish industrial villages, in implementation of the so-called Galilee Development Plan of 1975. In hailing this plan, the Ministry of Agriculture openly declared that its primary purpose was to alter the demographic nature of Galilee in order to create a Jewish majority in the area." For additional background, see "Israeli Arab Groups Mark Land Day," BBC, March 30, 2005, http://news.bbc.co.uk/2/hi/middle_east/4394245.stm; and "Israel's Arabs to Mark Land Day," *Jerusalem Post*, March 30, 2006, http://www.jpost.com/Israel/Israels-Arabs-to-mark-Land-Day

Estimated seventy-five hundred children wounded by Israeli gunfire in the first two years of the intifada: The Swedish branch of Save the Children, in a May 1990 report, *The Status of Palestinian Children During the Uprising in the Occupied Territories*, estimated that between 6,500 and 8,500 children were the victims of gunshot wounds during the first two years of the First Intifada. As cited by Mearsheimer and Walt, *The Israel Lobby*, p. 100.

Israeli soldiers had killed 574 Palestinians: See "First Intifada Fatalities," B'Tselem, http://www.btselem.org/statistics/first_intifada_tables

"Excessive force" on the part of the Israel Defense Forces: "At the start of the uprising, Mr. Rabin attracted wide attention when he said that Israeli soldiers would use 'force, might and beatings' to quash the Palestinian revolt." See "Israel Declines to Study Rabin Tie to Beatings," *New York Times*, July 12, 1990, http://www.nytimes.com/1990/07/12/world/israel-declines-to-study-rabin-tie-to-beatings.html. See also Yezid Sayigh, *Armed Struggle and the Search for State*, p. 619, Avi Shlaim, *The Iron Wall*, p. 453; Dilip Hiro, *Sharing the Promised Land*, p. 186; Benny Morris, *Righteous Victims*, pp. 589–92, and my book *The Lemon Tree*, p. 195.

Rabin believed more force would break the intifada: On September 27, 1988, Rabin declared, "Those who participate in violent activities suffer more casualties in terms of wounded . . . Our purpose is to increase the number [of wounded] among those who take part in violent activities, but not to kill them." See "Rabin Defends Plastic Bullets, Wounded Toll," *Los Angeles Times*, September 28, 1988. See also: Yezid Sayigh, *Armed Struggle and the Search for State*, p. 619; Avi Shlaim, *The Iron Wall*, p. 453; Dilip Hiro,

Sharing the Promised Land, p. 186; Benny Morris, pp. 589–92; and my book *The Lemon Tree*, p. 195.

Nearly as many Palestinians died at the hands of other Palestinians: Three different sources put the number of Palestinians killed by other Palestinians at no less than 72 percent of the number killed by Israel. B'Tselem, the respected Israeli human rights group, cites an Associated Press figure of 771 and quotes the IDF estimate of 952. In an interview with me in the summer of 2012, Dr. Saleh Abdel Jawad, coauthor of the B'Tselem report and former dean of the law school at Birzeit University in the West Bank, estimated the total number to be eleven hundred, which included collaborators, suspected collaborators who may have been innocent, and criminals and prostitutes condemned and executed for immoral behavior. This number slightly exceeds the 1,070 Palestinians killed by Israeli soldiers during the First Intifada, according to B'Tselem. The subject of internecine killings during the First Intifada is extremely sensitive for many Palestinians. It attests not only to the level of suspicion and paranoia felt during the uprising, and the brutal means by which the resistance to Israel's occupation dealt with suspected collaborators, but also to the extent to which Israel's collaboration regime had penetrated Palestinian society. Abdel Jawad and B'Tselem point out that since 1967 Israeli security forces "have recruited tens of thousands of Palestinians from the territories to serve as collaborators. This was made possible in part by the great dependence of the Palestinians on services provided by the Israeli administration. In recruiting collaborators, the security forces used methods that contravene international law." Indeed, Article 51 of the Fourth Geneva Convention states: "The Occupying Power may not compel protected persons to serve in its armed or auxiliary forces. No pressure or propaganda which aims at securing voluntary enlistment is permitted." See Saleh Abdel Jawad and Yizhar Be'er, "Collaborators in the Occupied Territories."

These collaborators were recruited by Israel: See B'Tselem, "Collaborators in the Occupied Territories."

Were sometimes taken into detention and raped: Ibid.

Children were also targets: See, for example, "Use of Children in the Occupied Territories," Defence for Children International, July 2004, https://www.essex.ac.uk/armedcon/story_id/000205.pdf; and "Spotlight Shines on Palestinian Collaborators," Al Jazeera, February 17, 2014, http://www.aljazeera.com/indepth/features/2014/02/spotlight-shines-palestinian-collaborators-201421611151157762.html

There were no independent Palestinian police, detention facilities, or courts: In the absence of sovereign instruments of justice and punishment, an essentially vigilante system of justice emerged. The crude punishment often meted out was a direct result of Israel's military occupation, the Palestinians' refusal to recognize it, and the willingness of Palestinian individuals and groups to accept self-administered violent outcomes often based on suspicion alone. Many of the killings were carried out by cells and strike forces associated with various Palestinian factions, including Fatah and the Popular Front for the Liberation of Palestine. Sometimes the individuals and groups operated independently of the PLO in exile; other times, with its at least tacit approval, and that of the Unified National Leadership of the Uprising (sometimes also known as the Unified National Command). One of the group's leaflets urged collaborators to repent, and later missives called for prior warnings and urged against "hasty sentencing." An estimated 107 of the Palestinians killed were women, many for alleged "immoral behavior" such as having multiple sexual relations. For more, see Saleh Abdel Jawad and Yizhar Be'er, "Collaborators in the Occupied Territories."

Five shabab, most apparently in their late teens, knocked on the door of Sido's house: The story of Ramzi's father and the events of February 19, 1990, were conveyed to me in multiple interviews with Ramzi during 2013 and 2014. A number of details were corroborated in interviews in Al Amari camp during the summer of 2013, and with a legal expert and human rights advocate in Ramallah. Details on religious customs, and on the role of the mosque as a community center during the First Intifada, come from Dr. Hatem Bazian, cofounder of Zaytuna College, America's first Muslim liberal arts college, and a senior lecturer in the departments of Near Eastern Studies and Ethnic Studies at the University of California, Berkeley.

Was one of the estimated 60 percent of Palestinians killed by other Palestinians during the intifada: Interview with Dr. Saleh Abdel Jawad, Ramallah, July 6, 2013. The 60 percent figure is an estimation by Abdel Jawad, who is arguably the world's leading expert on the subject and is the former dean of the Birzeit University Law School in the West Bank. Abdel Jawad, in a subsequent interview with me in September 2014, emphasized that the 60 percent figure represented those for whom there was no "solid evidence" to mete out punishment. The chance that Hussein Aburedwan was a collaborator for Israel appears to be extremely small. For one thing, as mentioned, his mental capacity had been severely reduced because of the brain damage he suffered as a result of his drunk-driving accident. Additionally, according to West Bank sources, it would have been very unusual for a killing of a Palestinian collaborator to be ordered from the PLO in exile, as Ramzi's family was told later. Many Palestinian-on-Palestinian killings during the First Intifada, according to Abdel Jawad, included revenge for a past transgression. Ramzi believes the killing was revenge for an assault his father had made after a traffic altercation years earlier. For additional background, see Abdel Jawad and Yizhar Be'er, "Collaborators in the Occupied Territories." See also Abdel Jawad's article on how Israelis have used the idea of collaboration as a way to discredit the popular nature of the intifada: "The Issue of Collaborators in Palestine," Palestine Academic Society for the Study of International Affairs (PASSIA), http://www.passia.org/publications/dialogue_series/collaborators/saleh.html).

In an interview on September 20, 2014, Umm Ramzi (mother of Ramzi) also stated her strong belief that her former husband could not have been a collaborator. "No it is not possible," she said. "He was a drunk, he used to beat me, he burned the house, but this [claim that Hussein was a collaborator] is not true. He was a beggar, he stole my gold, he used to go take from his father, his uncles, but to be a collaborator it is not possible. I know Hussein, it is impossible for him to be a collaborator." In an interview in November 2014, Ramzi added: "I hope that in the future, once we have a Palestinian state, the leaders will re-open the files and investigate the cases of people killed without justification, in order to restore the honor to these families. They have suffered not only from the occupation, but from their leadership in the PLO."

Organs had been removed: The fear of organ removal was not simple paranoia; such cases were frequently reported in the Occupied Territories during the First Intifada, and later evidence, reported in the Israeli and British press and in American academic papers, indicates that the removal of organs—from the bodies of Palestinian victims, Israeli soldiers, and others—was part of a widespread scandal. A 2009 article in the *Guardian* stated, "Israel has admitted pathologists harvested organs from dead Palestinians, and others, without the consent of their families—a practice it said ended in the 1990s—it emerged at the weekend." "Doctor Admits Israeli Pathologists Harvested Organs Without Consent," *Guardian*, December 21, 2009, http://www.theguardian.com/world/2009/dec/21/israeli-pathologists-harvested-organs

The article cites an interview with Dr. Yehuda Hiss, "former head of the Abu Kabir forensic institute near Tel Aviv," who resigned following the revelations. In the interview with Nancy Scheper-Hughes, a professor of anthropology at the University of California, Berkeley, Hiss states that organs were mined from the bodies of Palestinians, as well as Israeli soldiers and others, in what Scheper-Hughes called a "'don't ask, don't tell' policy concerning the source of needed tissues, skin, and solid organs taken from dead bodies without the consent or knowledge of their family members." The longer interview with Scheper Hughes can be found in the *Brown Journal of World Affairs* 19, no. 2 (Spring/Summer 2013). See also "Chief Pathologist Tapped to Replace Disgraced Hiss," *Haaretz*, March 4, 2013, http://www.haaretz.com/news/national/chief-pathologist-tapped-to-replace-disgraced-hiss.premium-1.509223; and the paper by Dr. Hiss's replacement, Chen Kugel, "Defending the Bodies of the Dead: The Case of Abu Kabir," presented at the Organs Watch conference in Berkeley on May 10, 2010.

Chapter 5: Accord

"Seven Stars" plan: For a discussion of Seven Stars and the Geneva Convention, see David Kretzmer, *The Occupation of Justice: The Supreme Court of Israel and the Occupied Territories*, pp. 76–7. For Sharon's strategy for Seven Stars and its intended absorption of former Soviet Jewry, see Clive Jones, *Soviet Jewish Aliyah: Impact and Implications for Israel and the Middle East*, pp 104–05.

A permanent agreement based on U.N. Resolution 242: The result of these talks in the Norwegian capital came to be known as the Oslo accords, including, initially, the Declaration of Principles, the text of which is on pp. 145–50 of *Documents on Palestine*, Vol. 2, published by the Palestinian Academic Society for the Study of International Affairs (PASSIA). See also my book *The Lemon Tree*, p. 342.

This represented a monumental compromise: This was not the first time Arafat recognized Israel; but it was the most important, as it set the stage for the Madrid and Oslo peace talks that followed.

Arafat, disastrously, had supported Saddam Hussein: U.S. President George Bush, in remarks to the Arab press on March 8, 1991, declared: "Arafat bet on the losing horse at the wrong time and in the wrong place." See Mahdi Abdul Hadi, "Post Gulf War Assessment: A Palestinian Perspective," PASSIA, http://www.passia.org/about_us/MahdiPapers/golfwar.html. According to the Middle East Research and Information Project, the PLO only accepted this "deeply flawed agreement with Israel because it was weak and had little diplomatic support in the Arab world. Both Islamist radicals and local leaders in the West Bank and the Gaza Strip challenged Arafat's leadership. Yet only Arafat had the prestige and national legitimacy to conclude a negotiated agreement with Israel." See "The Oslo Accords," *Middle East Report* (Middle East Research and Information Project), January 2001, http://www.merip.org/palestine-israel_primer/oslo-accords-pal-isr-prime.html. See also "Arafat's Costly Gulf War," Al Jazeera, August 2009, http://www.aljazeera.com/programmes/plohistoryofrevolution/2009/2009/08/200981294137853350.html; and "The Gulf War," Jewish Virtual Library, http://www.jewishvirtuallibrary.org/jsource/History/Gulf_War.html. In addition, because of the end of the Cold War, the PLO lost its Soviet sponsorship and a million Russian Jews were allowed to immigrate to Israel. See also Avi Shlaim's summary of the Oslo accords process in "The Rise and Fall of the Oslo Peace Process," in Louise Fawcett, ed., *International Relations of the Middle East*, pp. 241–61.

Expulsion of two hundred thousand Palestinian wage earners from Kuwait: "From March to September 1991, about 200,000 Palestinians were expelled from the emirate in a systematic campaign of terror, violence, and economic pressure while another 200,000 who fled during the Iraqi occupation were denied return. By September 1991, Kuwait's Palestinian community had dwindled to some 20,000." Steven J. Rosen, "Kuwait Expels Thousands of Palestinians," *Middle East Quarterly* (Fall 2012), pp. 75–83, http://www.meforum.org/3391/kuwait-expels-palestinians

Ninety-four Israeli civilians, compared to nearly eleven hundred Palestinians: For more information on Israeli and Palestinian casualties of the First Intifada, see "Fatalities in the First Intifada," B'Tselem, no date given, http://www.btselem.org/statistics/first_intifada_tables. The number, through the official end of the intifada on September 13, 1993 (date of the signing of the Oslo accord), is 1,070.

Growing numbers of Israelis had come to believe that the Palestinian quest for statehood was legitimate: See, for example, Shay Fogelman, "Journey Back to the First Intifada," *Haaretz Weekend Magazine*, December 15, 2012: "Of course, the intifada also had a powerful impact on Israeli society. Besides causing economic harm and eroding personal security, it created a tectonic shift between right and left in the country. In its wake, the occupation lost its legitimacy in the eyes of large segments of the Jewish population. In 1992, after a decade of extensive settlement building under right-wing governments, Yitzhak Rabin was elected prime minister, with the promise that he would bring peace."

Hopeful Israelis who believed the veteran soldier and his Labor Party coalition could bring a lasting peace: From Michael Parks, former Jerusalem correspondent for the

Los Angeles Times, in personal correspondence to me: "Rabin was betting on peace with Syria, [Shimon] Peres [the foreign minister] was betting on peace with the Palestinians, and the Oslo initiative was almost a rogue operation within and outside the Israeli foreign ministry. When Peres and [Dr. Yossi] Beilin [deputy foreign minister] brought a real prospect of an agreement with the PLO, Rabin said yes."

Yasser Arafat and Yitzhak Rabin shook hands on the White House lawn: On September 13, 1993, the *New York Times* headline read: "Rabin and Arafat Seal Their Accord as Clinton Applauds 'Brave Gamble.'"

Israel and the PLO had just agreed on the Declaration of Principles: The text of the Declaration of Principles is widely available, including via a U.S. State Department dispatch, http://dosfan.lib.uic.edu/ERC/briefing/dispatch/1993/html/Dispatchv4Sup4.html

Thousands who had been in exile for a generation, including Arafat, would soon be returning home: See Juliane Hammer, *Palestinians Born in Exile: Diaspora and the Search for a Homeland*, in which she states: "In the decade following the 1993 Oslo Peace Accords, some 100,000 diasporic Palestinians returned to the West Bank and Gaza. Among them were children and young adults who were born in exile and whose sense of Palestinian identity was shaped not by lived experience but rather through the transmission and re-creation of memories, images, and history." A headline in the September 9, 1993, edition of the *New York Times* declared: "Mideast Accord; Israel Confirms That Deportees Are to Return Today," (http://www.nytimes.com/1993/09/09/world/mideast-accord-israel-confirms-that-deportees-are-to-return-today.html).

And a new player had emerged: Ironically, Israel initially sought to encourage the formation of Hamas in order to weaken Arafat and the PLO. See Avi Shlaim, *The Iron Wall*, p. 459.

Mahmoud Darwish, the great Palestinian poet, resigned from the PLO executive committee: Darwish did not oppose peace with Israel or the two state solution. However, he recalled later that "there was no clear link between the interim period and the final status, and no clear commitment to withdraw from the occupied territories. I felt Oslo would pave the way for escalation. I hoped I was wrong. I'm very sad that I was right." See Adam Shatz, "A Poet's Palestine as Metaphor," *New York Times*, December 22, 2001, http://www.nytimes.com/2001/12/22/books/a-poet-s-palestine-as-a-metaphor.html

Polls within the Occupied Territories: Polls taken of Palestinians living in the Occupied Territories around the time of the Rabin–Arafat handshake indicate a strong support for the Oslo "peace process." See, for example, "Public Opinion Poll #1, The Palestinian–Israeli Agreement: 'Gaza-Jericho First' September 10–11, 1993," by the Palestinian Center for Policy and Survey Research, cited at http://www.pcpij.org/details.php?id=770. In general, Palestinians in the West Bank and Gaza were more amenable to a two-state solution as it indicated a possible end to the Israeli military occupation. In the diaspora, however, and in the refugee camps inside and outside

Palestine, more people oppose the two-state solution, which they see as sacrificing their right of return to their homelands in what is now Israel.

Give Oslo, Arafat, and the two-state solution a chance: This conclusion comes from scores of interviews in the West Bank during research for this book, as well as contemporary articles of the time. Even people who quickly grew skeptical of Oslo acknowledged the Palestinian support that the peace process, and Arafat, received in the early days. Mourid Barghouti, in his 2000 memoir, *I Saw Ramallah* (p. 120), states: "The majority who gave their voice to Yasser Arafat are a real majority. But they are a majority who believed in the historic promises they were given and are waiting for them to be fulfilled . . . Palestinian society as a whole is still waiting. It has not closed its eyes yet."

People gathered in joyful celebration: "Throughout the West Bank and the Gaza Strip today Palestinians took to the streets in rapturous and noisy celebrations of the Palestine Liberation Organization accord with Israel and what they said was the cornerstone of their future state," declared the *New York Times*. "All day and into the night they sang, danced and marched, savoring a new reality few had dared to imagine just a few weeks ago. In Gaza they handed flowers to Israeli soldiers. In East Jerusalem they shouted, 'Shalom!,' Hebrew for peace, to Israeli well-wishers and not the Arabic Salaam." See Joel Greenberg, "Mideast Accord: Jericho Israelis Are Transfixed; Palestinians Run From the Rapturous to the Furious; 'We Are Feeling Freedom,'" *New York Times*, September 14, 1993.

Chapter 6: Viola

Departing soldiers: "Ramallah, West Bank, Dec. 27—Under a final cascade of stones, Israeli troops withdrew today from Ramallah, completing a pullout from six West Bank cities and their neighboring villages in preparation for Palestinian elections next month. 'Out!,' shouted youths as a column of Israeli jeeps moved away from a police station downtown, trailed by scores of cheering Palestinians. As stones pitched by the crowd arched toward the receding vehicles, Palestinian officers entered the station, raised a flag and greeted the throng from the roof, waiving their rifles." Joel Greenberg, "Palestinians Take Control of Ramallah, *New York Times*, December 28, 1995. See also Nigel Parry, "Waiting for the Israelis to Go," Ramallah Diary: A Personal Diary of the Israeli-Palestinian Conflict (blog), December 27, 1995, http://nigelparry.com/diary/ramallah/depart.html

In full control of approving or denying each entry: Details of protocol at border crossings are discussed in the Gaza-Jericho Agreement, Annex I, "Protocol Concerning Withdrawal of Israeli Military Forces and Security Arrangements." Article X of the Annex states that passengers in the "Palestinian wing" of the terminals "will be checked by an Israeli officer who will also check their identity indirectly in an invisible manner." The document is widely available, including at the Israel Ministry of Foreign Affairs, http://www.mfa.gov.il/mfa/foreignpolicy/peace/guide/pages/gaza-jericho%20agremeent%20annex%20i.aspx

Thousands repeated his jubilant promise: For a description of the gathering in Ramallah see "Arafat Visits Ramallah" from Nigel Parry's Ramallah Diary (blog), December 30, 1995, http://nigelparry.com/diary/ramallah/afatvst.html. On December 31, 1995, in "Arafat Exults at Takeover of Ramallah," the *New York Times* reported Arafat's remarks: "'Let us, every individual, woman and man, make a pledge together to liberated Palestine—to Palestine, the independent state,' Mr. Arafat shouted to a cheering crowd of thousands from the roof of the former Israeli military headquarters here. 'I declare Ramallah and El Bireh liberated cities forever, forever, forever!' he said."

When Israel annexed East Jerusalem: Karen Armstrong, in *Jerusalem: One City, Three Faiths* (p. 403) points out that in passing the "law and Administration Ordinance of June 28, 1967, Israel's Knesset 'carefully avoided using the word annexation.' Israelis preferred the more positive term 'unification.'"

"Eternal capital of Israel": Prime Minister Levi Eshkol so referred to Jerusalem in June 1967; many after him would repeat these words.

Evicting more than six hundred Palestinians: Karen Armstrong, in *Jerusalem* (pp. 402–3), says 619 residents of the quarter were evicted, an act "which contravened the Geneva Conventions." It was done "in order to create a plaza big enough to accommodate the thousands of Jewish pilgrims who were expected to flock to the Western Wall." See also Rashid Khalidi, *Palestinian Identity,* p. 17, or his more detailed account in *The British Journal of Middle Eastern Studies,* 19 (Fall 1992), pp. 133–43. Khalidi puts the number of evictions at one thousand. See also "Jerusalem 1967," *Journal of Palestine Studies,* http://www.palestine-studies.org/sites/default/files/jps-articles/9704.pdf; and Mick Dumper, "Jerusalem Then and Now," *Middle East Report* #182, Middle East Research and Information Project, http://www.merip.org/mer/mer182/jerusalem-then-now

Prohibited from praying there: See Karen Armstrong, *Jerusalem,* p. 407.

Rushed to the site: Karen Armstrong, in *Jerusalem,* describes (pp. 397–404) that after the 1967 war, "Israeli soldiers and officers had one objective: to get as quickly as possible to the Western Wall." She describes the religious fervor and sense of belonging sparked by the soldiers' presence at the wall, "that reached right down to the core of each soldier's Jewish identity." Yet, she adds, "Israel's claim to the city [East Jerusalem] was dubious . . . It was no longer possible in international law to permanently annex land conquered militarily . . . Palestinians were suffering their own exile, homelessness, and separation. They could not share the Kabbalistic dream . . . The international community was also unwilling to accept Israel's annexation of Jerusalem."

Same stone: For more on the clashing of identities at Haram al-Sharif/Temple Mount, see Rashid Khalidi in *Palestinian Identity,* pp. 15–18, and Karen Armstrong's *Jerusalem,* pp. 397–430.

"The Jerusalem of houses and cobbled streets": Mourid Barghouti, *I Saw Ramallah,* pp. 142–3.

Thirty thousand strong: The thirty thousand figure comes from Annex I of the Israeli-Palestinian Interim Agreement on the West Bank and the Gaza Strip, widely known as

Oslo II, which also states: "The Palestinian side will notify Israel of any candidate for recruitment to the Palestinian Police. Should Israel object to the recruitment of any such candidate, that person shall not be recruited." The Oslo II text is widely available, including on the Web site for the Israeli parliament, or Knesset, http://www.knesset. gov.il/process/docs/heskemb2_eng.htm

The army's withdrawal from Ramallah consisted of retreating one kilometer: Israel had simply "redeployed" to just outside of Ramallah and other Palestinian cities, while retaining full military control of a large majority of the West Bank. The Oslo agreements carved the West Bank into three separate areas: Area A, the so-called Palestinian autonomous region around West Bank cities; Area B, in which Palestinians and Israelis would share control; and Area C, which would remain under full Israeli military control. In the first agreement, Area C covered 72 percent of the West Bank. Under Oslo II, the 1995 agreement that led to the redeployments, Area C shrank slightly, to 60 percent. Palestinians hoped that negotiations toward a final settlement would transfer more land into their hands; as of this writing, in November 2014, Area C remains at 60 percent. See pp. 145–50 of *Documents on Palestine*, Vol. 2, published by the Palestinian Academic Society for the Study of International Affairs (PASSIA).

Tens of thousands of Palestinians long exiled by Israel were finally coming home: For more information on the Palestinians "returnees" after the Oslo Accords, see the *Middle East Report* (Middle East Research and Information Project) article by Ward Sayre and Jennifer Olmstead entitled "Economics of Palestinian Return Migration," http://www.merip.org/mer/mer212/economics-palestinian-return-migration. In footnote 5 of the article, the authors cite several different statistics for the number of Palestinian returnees after Oslo. Michele Chabin's "An Uneasy Homecoming" (*Jerusalem Post*, July 21, 1998), quotes official estimates of legal returnees at 40,000 to 50,000. Abbas Shiblak of the Palestinian Diaspora and Refugee Centre (*Shaml*) reports an estimate of 60,000 in the preface to *Reintegration of the Palestinian Returnees*, Monograph 6 (Bethlehem: Shaml, 1997), cited at http://108.165.20.117/mer/ mer212/economics-palestinian-return-migration. See also Ward Sayre and Jennifer Olmstead, "Economics of Palestinian Return Migration," *Middle East Report* #212 (Fall 1999, Middle East Research and Information Project), in which they state, "Estimates of the number of post-Oslo returnees range from 40,000 to 100,000." http://www.merip.org/mer/mer212/economics-palestinian-return-migration

"There were none who knew me": Mourid Barghouti, *I Saw Ramallah*, p. 66. Barghouti's beautiful memoir contains laments of return from exile that are both universal and particularly Palestinian. He also notes the practice of caretaking of property performed by families during exile, and the problems that occasionally developed: "Everybody here fears for what they have. Many people have registered their possessions in the names of their relatives so that the Occupation cannot confiscate those possessions as belonging to absentees. This is how the Palestinian lands and homes, whose owners work in the Diaspora, were saved. This is how the olive groves were maintained and how the land was looked after and ploughed and turned and combed and watered." And yet: "There are dazzling stories of the faithfulness and commitment of the 'caretakers' to the rights of the absent owners; rights not registered in contracts or through powers of attorney. But there were also stories about residents who actually took possession of properties that they were holding in trust and refused to return them to their original owners." *I Saw Ramallah*, p. 104.

Arrest and subsequent torture by Israeli authorities: In an interview with me in the summer of 2011, Suhail Khoury described his arrest at an Israeli roadblock, where military police found thousands of the "Intifada Tapes"—a homemade, underground hit recording championing the "war of the stone"—in the trunk of his car. They took him to the infamous Muscovia jail. Khoury described undergoing torture for twelve days; this included beatings, shock, and the placement of feces- and/or urine-lined hoods over his head. While it is impossible to corroborate this, the story is consistent with the forms of torture undertaken by Israeli interrogators, as has been widely documented by numerous organizations, including the respected Israeli human rights group B'Tselem. According to B'Tselem's report "Torture and Abuse Under Interrogation" (http://www.btselem.org/torture/background), "The methods of interrogation included several techniques: depriving the interrogee of sleep for a number of days by binding him or her in painful positions; playing loud music; covering their head with a filthy sack; exposing the interrogee to extreme heat and cold; tying them to a low chair, tilting forward; tightly cuffing the interrogee's hands; having the interrogee stand, hands tied and drawn upwards; having the interrogee lie on his back on a high stool with his body arched backwards; forcing the interrogee to crouch on his toes with his hands tied behind him; violent shaking of the detainee, the interrogator grasping and shaking him; using threats and curses, and feeding him poor-quality and insufficient amounts of food." In addition, the *Berkeley Journal of International Law*, summarizing the findings of numerous international, Israeli, and Palestinian human rights organizations, found that Israel's interrogation methods of arrested Palestinians included: ". . . violent shaking; the 'frog crouch,' excessive tightening of handcuffs and prolonged sleep deprivation . . . electric shock, beatings to all areas of the body (often with the use of instruments), sexual assault, application of burning cigarettes, partial suffocation, prolonged exposure to temperature extremes, prolonged abusive body positioning . . . and a multitude of methods of psychological torture including threats of death and rape." ("Moderate Torture on Trial: Critical Reflections on the Israeli Supreme Court Judgment Concerning the Legality of General Security Service Interrogation Methods," *Berkeley Journal of International Law* 19, no. 2 (2001), http://scholarship.law.berkeley.edu/cgi/viewcontent. cgi?article=1202&context=bjil. Indeed, according to a London *Sunday Times* article: "Israeli interrogators routinely ill-treat and often torture Arab prisoners. Prisoners are often hooded or blindfolded or hung by their wrists for long periods. Many are sexually assaulted. Others are given electric shocks. At least one detention centre has (or had) a specially constructed 'cupboard', about two feet square and five feet high, with concrete spikes set in the floor." See "Israel Tortures Arab Prisoners," *Sunday Times* (London), June 19, 1977, retrieved from the U.N. General Assembly Web site http://unispal.un.org/ UNISPAL.NSF/0/FE3D603D74F5729B85256FE0006CC519. Khoury's story of the tapes is also recounted in "Rhythms of Resistance," Al Jazeera, April 4, 2010, http://www.aljazeera.com/programmes/general/2010/03/2010325132736122581.html

Gaza International Airport: See Globalsecurity.org, "Gaza International Airport," http://www.globalsecurity.org/military/world/palestine/gip.htm

Chapter 7: Harmony

The story of the Palestine National Conservatory of Music, of Ramzi's early training there, and of the visit of the American musicians in 1996 is crafted through multiple interviews between 2010 and 2014, including with Ramzi, Ramadan Khatib, Peter Sulski, Richard "Dobbs" Hartshorne, Eric Stumacher, Suhail Khoury, Rima Tarazi, Mohammad Fadel, and Nadia Abboushi.

Israeli Prime Minister Yitzhak Rabin had been assassinated at a peace rally: "Mr. Rabin, 73, was struck down by one or two bullets as he was entering his car," the *New York Times* reported. "Police immediately seized a 27-year-old Israeli law student, Yigal Amir, who had been active in support of Israeli settlers but who told the police tonight that he had acted alone." See "Assassinatoin in Israel: The Overview; Rabin Slain After Peace Rally in Tel Aviv," *New York Times*, November 5, 1995, http://www.nytimes.com/1995/11/05/world/assassination-israel-overview-rabin-slain-after-peace-rally-tel-aviv-israeli.html?pagewanted=all&src=pm. For the international community's reaction see the "Speakers express great shock over assassination of Israeli Prime Minister," United Nations Press Release, November 6, 1995, http://domino.un.org/UNISPAL.nsf/fd807e46661e3 689852570d00069e918/06a2d36c0ea3fbb285256c8d006a2dd7?OpenDocument

Israel was not restricted from building new West Bank settlements: In the Oslo documents, no explicit restrictions were placed on Israel for settlement building. Perhaps the closest admonition is in Article XI of Oslo II, which states: "The two sides view the West Bank and the Gaza Strip as a single territorial unit, the integrity and status of which will be preserved during the interim period." The Palestinians did, however, receive written assurances, in a "Letter of Assurances" by U.S. Secretary of State James Baker, stating American opposition to settlement activities: "The United States has long believed that no party should take unilateral actions that seek to predetermine issues that can only be resolved through negotiations. In this regard the United States has opposed and will continue to oppose settlement activity in the territories occupied in 1967, which remains an obstacle to peace . . . The United States will act as an honest broker in trying to resolve the Arab-Israeli conflict." Cited in *Brokers of Deceit*, by Rashid Khalidi. For a full text of the Baker letter, see Appendix M of William Quandt's *Peace Process: American Diplomacy and the Arab-Israeli Conflict Since 1967* at http://www.brookings.edu/~/media/Press/Books/2005/peaceprocess3/Appendix%20M.pdf

As a result of the Oslo Accords' failure to prohibit settlement expansion, in the early years of Oslo, Israel announced plans for thousands of new housing units in East Jerusalem and continued building and expanding West Bank settlements and the military and Israeli civilian infrastructure that accompanied that, including settlers-only "bypass roads" connecting the settlements to Jerusalem and Tel Aviv. According to a B'Tselem report, "since signing the Declaration of Principles, Israel [had] established thirty settlements in the Occupied Territories." See Na'ama Carmi, "Oslo: Before and After, The Status of Human Rights in the Occupied Territories," B'Tselem, May 1999, p.7, http://www.btselem.org/sites/default/files/oslo_befor_and_after.pdf. See also PASSIA, "Documents on Palestine," pp. 371–88.

No apparent plans, and no explicit requirement under Oslo, to relinquish it: The language of the agreements, including Oslo II or the Israeli-Palestinian "Interim Agreement on the West Bank and the Gaza Strip," states in Article X that "Israel shall continue to carry the responsibility for external security [i.e., anyone crossing into the West Bank or Gaza], as well as the responsibility for overall security of Israelis [including settlers] for the purpose of safeguarding their internal security and public order." Gaza-Jericho Autonomy Agreement of May 4, 1994," Annex 1, Article 10, http://mfa.gov.il/MFA/ForeignPolicy/Peace/Guide/Pages/Gaza-Jericho%20Agremeent%20Annex%20I.aspx. According to a B'Tselem report, "The Oslo Accords stipulate Israeli control of the border crossings from PA-controlled areas: between Gaza and the West Bank and between PA areas and Israel, Jordan and abroad. Israeli military forces are even stationed between the Gaza Strip and Egypt. Thus, Israel maintains sole control over the freedom of movement of Palestinians, using this power to arbitrarily deny their freedom of movement." See Na'ami Carmi, "Oslo: Before and After, The Status of Human Rights in the Occupied Territories," B'Tselem, May 1999, p. 7, http://www.btselem.org/sites/default/files/oslo_befor_and_after.pdf. According to the Declaration of Principles, the control of borders was to be discussed during the permanent status negotiations, to commence "not later than the beginning of the third year of the interim period," and would cover "remaining issues, including: Jerusalem, refugees, settlements, security arrangements, borders . . ."

"Official Palestinian consent to continue occupation": Edward Said, "Middle East Peace Process," from *Peace and Its Discontents*, p. 148.

Edward Said: A short biography of Edward Said and a list of his publications and lectures are available on Columbia University's Center for Palestine Studies page, http://www.columbia.edu/cu/palestine/resources/edwardsaid.html.

"An instrument of Palestinian surrender": Edward Said, *Peace and Its Discontents*, p. 17.

"A kingdom of illusions": Ibid., p. 148.

"Kind of small-town government": Ibid., p. 4.

"Further from realization than today": Ibid., p. 159.

"Are still masters of the place": Mourid Barghouti, *I Saw Ramallah*, p. 38.

Palestinians believed the digging: See, for example, Ramzy Baroud, "Saving Al Aqsa Mosque," Al Jazeera, March 6, 2014, http://www.aljazeera.com/indepth/opinion/2014/03/saving-al-aqsa-mosque-2014355375242745.html

Uncovering archaeological remains and **"severe aggression":** United Nations, "Chronological Review of Events Related to the Question of Palestine: September

1996 (entry for September 24), http://domino.un.org/unispal.nsf/9a798adbf322aff3
8525617b006d88d7/77be000dabe3090c852563e9005698ee

Har Homa: Settlement construction on the hill known to Israelis as Har Homa, and which the Palestinians call Jabal Abu Ghneim, began in 1997. Today the population is twenty-five thousand. See "Har Homa: Netanyahu Wins First Round of the Battle for Jerusalem," Foundation for Middle East Peace, Settlement Report, May–June 1997, http://www.fmep.org/reports/archive/vol.-7/no.-3/har-homa-netanyahu-wins-first-round-of-the-battle-for-jerusalem

"The battle for Jerusalem has begun": Ibid.

Diagnosed with leukemia: Edward Said was diagnosed with incurable leukemia in 1991. In 1994 he started chemotherapy and the writing of a memoir concurrently. See Janny Scott, "A Palestinian Confronts Time; For Columbia Literary Critic, Cancer Is a Spur to Memory," *New York Times*, September 19, 1998, http://www.nytimes.com/1998/09/19/arts/palestinian-confronts-time-for-columbia-literary-critic-cancer-spur-memory.html

Yellow license plates: Cars registered in Israel have yellow license plates and are thus easily recognizable in the Palestinian territories. "When a local military commander in the West Bank or Gaza Strip deems it necessary, he can declare a field, a road, or an entire town, a closed military area, and deny access to that area to anyone he wants to keep out . . . Israeli settlers, driving cars with easily identifiable yellow license plates, have never been delayed at Army roadblocks." See "Israel Acts to Keep Jewish Settlers Out of Palestinian Towns," Peter Ford, *Christian Science Monitor*, December 20, 1993, http://www.csmonitor.com/1993/1220/20032.html/%28page%29/2. For more on license plates in Israel and the West Bank, see Nigel Parry's Ramallah Diary (blog), http://nigelparry.com/diary/ramallah/plates.html

Mini Uzi: For more on the Mini Uzi, see the Israel Weapon Industries Web site, http://www.israel-weapon.com/default.asp?catid=%7B172FA0DF-0A2F-49CD-BE3A-BA92809A441A%7D. Search for "Mini Uzi sound" on YouTube.com to hear the sound of its rapid gunfire.

Nearly 1,100 Palestinians had been killed by Israeli soldiers: According to a B'Tselem report, 1,070 Palestinians were killed in the Occupied Territories (including East Jerusalem) from December 9, 1987, to September 28, 1993, 237 of which were minors under seventeen. See "Fatalities in the First Intifada," B'Tselem, http://www.btselem.org/statistics/first_intifada_tables. According to the Palestine Human Rights Information Center, 1,283 Palestinians were killed between December 9, 1987, and December 31, 1993. See Palestine Human Rights Information of Jerusalem and Washington, "Living Under Israeli Occupation," *Washington Report on Middle East Affairs* (April/May 1994).

More than 130,000 Palestinians were injured: Statistics for the number of people injured vary depending on the definition of injured, but, according to the Palestine Human Rights Information Center, between December 9, 1987, and December 31,

1993, approximately 130,472 Palestinians were injured to the point that they required hospitalization. See Palestine Human Rights Information Center of Jerusalem and Washington, "Living Under Israeli Occupation," *Washington Report on Middle East Affairs* (April/May 1994), cited in Donald Neff, "The Intifada Erupts, Forcing Israel to Recognize Palestinians," *Washington Report on Middle East Affairs*, December 1997, pp. 81–3, http://ww.wrmea.org/1997-december/middle-east-history-the-intifada-erupts-forcing-israel-to-recognize-palestinians.html

Twenty-five hundred houses had been demolished, and 184,000 olive trees uprooted: According to the Palestine Human Rights Information Center, between December 9, 1987, and December 31, 1993, 2,533 houses were demolished or sealed, and 184,257 trees uprooted. See "Living Under Israeli Occupation," *Washington Report on Middle East Affairs*, cited in Donald Neff's 'article, "The Intifada Erupts, Forcing Israel to Recognize Palestinians," pp. 81–3, http://ww.wrmea.org/1997-december/middle-east-history-the-intifada-erupts-forcing-israel-to-recognize-palestinians.html

At least 750 Palestinians, including Ramzi's father, had died by Palestinian hands: Three different sources put the number of Palestinians killed by other Palestinians during the First Intifada at least 72 percent of those killed by Israel. B'Tselem cites an Associated Press figure of 771 and quotes the IDF estimate of 952. In an interview, Dr. Saleh Abdel Jawad, coauthor of the B'Tselem report and former dean of the law school at Birzeit University in the West Bank, estimated the total number to be 1,100, which slightly exceeds the number of Palestinians killed by Israeli soldiers during the First Intifada. As stated above, the 1,100 number included collaborators, suspected collaborators who may have been innocent, and criminals and prostitutes condemned for immoral behavior. See http://www.btselem.org/publications/summaries/199401_collaboration_suspects

Convert his trauma into positive energy: "Active participation in the conflict may enhance self-esteem and shield children from development of psychological symptoms." See Ahmad A. Baker, "The Psychological Impact of the Intifada on Palestinian Children in the Occupied West Bank and Gaza: An Exploratory Study," *American Journal of Orthopsychiatry.* For an excellent review of the phenomenon of heroism and victimization, see John Collins, *Occupied by Memory*, pp. 40–50.

Complete personal transformation: In Julie P. Sutton, ed., *Music, Music Therapy and Trauma: International Perspectives*, Michael Swallow writes about the possible biological effects of music on patients suffering from various ailments. "Music," he writes in his essay, "The Brain: Its Music and Its Emotion: The Neurology of Trauma," can, "by raising the threshold for anxiety, reduce the likelihood of resurgence of traumatic memories."

Marie Smyth, in "Culture and Society: The Role of Creativity in Healing and Recovering One's Power after Victimization," an article about Northern Ireland, explains the impact of creativity on healing and in recovering one's power after victimization. "Creativity is resistance to oppression," she asserts, "it is the refusal of victimhood and helplessness. Creating something new is an act of defiance in the face of destruction."

Mercédès Pavlicevic, in "South Africa: Fragile Rhythms and Uncertain Listenings: Perspectives from Music Therapy with South African Children," writes that music therapy in South Africa can "manag[e] and evok[e] the difficult, frightening, playful and creative feelings and tap . . . into the child's own potential for healing," and can "potentially engage, stimulate and evoke the child's imagination, offering an opportunity to 're-create' and 're-imagine' life." And in "Music and Human Rights," Matthew Dixon writes: "Music created through a process of interaction between people can take on a life of its own, and in turn transform those who create it. The transformation is temporary, but the experience of having been transformed, and the discovery of new possibilities, are more permanent."

"I love him": This quote comes from Ramzi's interview with me in early 1998, for my NPR feature piece on Ramzi, translated by Lamis Andoni.

Muscle memory was the path to that transformation: The language on muscle memory is inspired by an exchange with Stephanie Saldaña, a lifelong musician and author of the lovely memoir *Bread of Angels*, about learning Arabic in Syria. For more, see the previously cited research under "**Complete personal transformation**" above.

Apple Hill Chamber Players: For more on the Apple Hill Center for Chamber Music and the Playing for Peace program, check out their Web site, http://www.applehill. org/playforpeace/pp_description.htm

Chapter 8: Mozart

The narrative and factual details for this chapter come from my trip to Apple Hill in the summer of 2011, and my interviews with more than a dozen teachers, campers, visiting musicians, and administrators who were at Apple Hill in 1998, in particular Ramzi, Peter Sulski, Leonard Matczynski, Eric Stumacher, Richard "Dobbs" Hartshorne, and Nadia Abboushi. As such there is little formal factual documentation beyond the interviews for this chapter. The interviews were conducted from 2009 to 2014, and in 1998, with Ramzi in the West Bank. For additional background, see Zoe Kemmerling, "Apple Hill: More Music in Bucolic New Hampshire," *Boston Musical Intelligencer*, June 29, 2012, and reprinted in the Apple Hill Blog. My piece about Ramzi, which contains portions of his Mozart performance in New Hampshire, was broadcast on NPR's Weekend Edition Saturday on May 23, 1988, http://www.npr. org/templates/story/story.php?storyId=1000955

Chapter 9: Symbol

Something of a celebrity: The poster, in fact, was what drew me to Ramzi in the first place. I was in Ramallah researching a story on the fiftieth anniversary of what Palestinians call the Nakba, or Catastrophe, and Israelis call their War of Independence. That research led to a radio program for NPR's Fresh Air and eventually to my book

The Lemon Tree. But during my time in Ramallah, I kept seeing Ramzi's poster; that story was also too compelling to resist.

"As a result, these areas are almost totally severed from each other": According to a 1998 B'Tselem report, "The closure also prevents Palestinians from entering East Jerusalem. Israel ignores international law and the position of the international community, which hold that the status of East Jerusalem is identical to that of the rest of the West Bank. This superficial severance of East Jerusalem from other areas of the West Bank severely prejudices the lives of Palestinian residents inasmuch as East Jerusalem is the center of medical, economic, religious, and educational activity in the Occupied Territories." See Noga Kadman, "1987–1997: A Decade of Human Rights Violations, Information Sheet," B'Tselem, January 1998, p. 19. The report also notes that "the permanent closure imposed on the Occupied Territories since 1991 prevents movement of Palestinians between the Gaza Strip and the West Bank. In signing the Oslo Accords, Israel undertook to enable safe passage between the Gaza Strip and the West Bank, but Israel has not arranged this passage. As a result, these areas are almost totally severed from each other, although under the Declaration of Principles, signed by the parties in 1993, they comprise one territorial unit. This severance harms population groups, among them families living apart, businesspeople, and students."

An increase of almost half, to more than 163,000: For background, see Central Bureau of Statistics, *Statistical Abstract of Israel,* 1992–2006, and "List of Localities, the Populations, and Symbols, 1995–2005," *Statistical Yearbook of Jerusalem,* Jerusalem Institute for Israel Studies, 1991–2004, cited at "Israeli Settler Population, 1972–2006," Foundation for Middle East Peace, http://www.fmep.org/settlement_info/settlement-info-and-tables/stats-data/israeli-settler-population-1972–2006

"They have already taken my land": From one of my interviews with Ramzi, winter 1998.

"No real and lasting peace": Edward Said, *Peace and Its Discontents,* p. 164. Within the "peace process" alliance of Americans, Israelis, and the Palestinian Authority, Said was considered a pariah: a negative force obstructing real, if incremental, progress. A few years earlier, Yasser Arafat, who rode the wave of optimism of the intifada to his limited power in a would-be emerging Palestine, had attacked Edward publicly. "He, in America does not feel the suffering of his people," Arafat wrote, "does not understand the size of the greatest uprising in the modern age, which is considered to be the completion of the Palestinian revolution." (*Peace and Its Discontents,* p. 165.) In an interview, Said shot back that Arafat did not seem to understand the difference between limited autonomy and national liberation, and that he therefore had "erase[d] with the stroke of a pen many of the inalienable rights of the Palestinian people, including their right to independence." (Ibid., p 167.) Before Oslo, the Palestinian struggle for freedom had been a largely unified one; now, Palestinians were divided over the compromises in the accord.

A Palestinian home had been demolished by Israeli bulldozers: According to a 1998 B'Tselem report, between 1988 and 1998 more than eighteen hundred houses were demolished in the West Bank, not including East Jerusalem: "Over the years, Israel has created a situation in the Occupied Territories whereby thousands of Palestinians have been unable to obtain permits to build houses on their land, compelling them to build without a permit. Rather than change this situation, Israel adopted a policy of mass demolition of Palestinian houses." Settlers in the West Bank, on the other hand, built houses without permits that were allowed to stand: "The authorities have retroactively approved thousands of houses built without permits." See Noga Kadman, "1987–1997: A Decade of Human Rights Violations, Information Sheet," B'Tselem, January 1998, p 17. Punitive house demolitions date back to the British Mandate, specifically Regulation 119 of the Defence Emergency Regulations, which authorized house demolitions. See "Rules of IHL applicable to the conduct of military operations in urban areas," Briefing Paper, Harvard Program on Humanitarian Policy and Conflict Research, May 2004, http://www.hamoked.org.il/items/3554_eng.pdf. This report also includes statistics about housing demolitions during the First Intifada.

"Who is giving these people peace?": *In Search of Palestine: Edward Said's Return Home*, BBC production, 1998, http://www.youtube.com/watch?v=ksTgAL-e9yo

"Palestine and Palestinians remain": Edward Said, "Palestine Has Not Disappeared," *Le Monde Diplomatique*, May 1998, http://mondediplo.com/1998/05/01said

Daniel Barenboim: For more about Daniel Barenboim visit Barenboim's Web site, http://www.danielbarenboim.com/index.php?id=7

His new best friend: According to Daniel Barenboim's Web site: "In the early 1990s, a chance meeting between Barenboim and the late Palestinian-born writer and Columbia University professor Edward Said in a London hotel lobby led to an intensive friendship that has had both political and musical repercussions." See http://www.danielbarenboim.com/index.php?id=7

A musical enterprise based on listening and common ground: According to Barenboim's Web site, Said and Barenboim "decided to continue their dialogue and to collaborate on musical events to further their shared vision of peaceful co-existence in the Middle East." See http://www.danielbarenboim.com/index.php?id=7

Before Palestinians fled or were driven out: In the War of 1948, Arab Legion forces captured East Jerusalem, and Israelis, West Jerusalem. Jews from the Jewish Quarter were expelled by Arab forces (http://cdn.worldheritage.org/articles/1948_Arab-Israeli_War#cite_note-138); Palestinians living in the west fled or were driven out by Israel. Edward Said was not one of them; as he wrote in his memoir *Out of Place*, his family, though from Jerusalem, was from the mid-1940s living in Cairo. But like all other Palestinian West Jerusalemites, he was not allowed to return. For more, see "The De-Arabization of West Jerusalem, 1947–50," *Journal of Palestine Studies* (Winter 1998), pp. 5–22, http://www.jstor.org/discover/10.2307/2538281?uid=2&uid=4&sid=21104340210577

Charged with "security violations" following university protests against Israeli rule: "Deportation Statement of Hanna Nasir," November 1974, in Gabi Baramki, *Peaceful Resistance*, p. 169.

Israel had allowed Hanna to return: See Michael Parks, "Profile: Exiled Palestinian Comes In From the Cold: 'This is where I belong,' Says University President Hanna Nasir, Home after 18 Years," *Los Angeles Times*, May 25, 1993, http://articles.latimes.com/1993-05-25/news/wr-39490_1_hanna-nasir. The *New York Times* also mentioned Hanna Nasir's return in an article on December 10, 1993, http://www.nytimes.com/1993/12/10/world/among-palestinians-worry-and-rage.html

"Driven for seven hours towards an unknown destiny": "Why Israel Closed Palestinians' University," *New York Times*, December 28, 1981, mentions Nasir's deportation: "In 1974, Bir Zeit was closed and its president, Dr. Hanna Nasir, was deported." http://www.nytimes.com/1981/12/28/opinion/why-israel-closed-palestinians-university.html

Travel permits: Stories of Palestinians waiting for travel permits are legion. Mourid Barghouti, the Palestinian poet, recalls: "Here my mother stood for as long as the sun was in the sky to get pieces of paper from the Israeli Military Governor. A new permit each time to visit her sons in Doha, Cairo, Beirut, Paris, or Budapest, or her brother in Kuwait, or to meet everyone in a hotel in Amman . . . Here she put in requests for 'reunion' and requests for permits for us to visit her that were always refused. This is the location for the daily exhaustion and bitterness for thousands of Palestinians throughout the years that Ramallah was occupied . . ." (*I Saw Ramallah*, p. 48.) For more on Israel's use of permits as a way to hinder the mobility of Palestinians, see Chaim Levinson, "Israel Has 101 Different Types of Permits Governing Palestinian Movement," *Haaretz*, December 23, 2011, http://www.haaretz.com/print-edition/news/israel-has-101-different-types-of-permits-governing-palestinian-movement-1.403039

The project still hadn't taken shape: The meeting at Tania and Hanna Nasir's was part of a series of conversations that eventually led to Barenboim's first concert on the West Bank, a piano recital at the Palestinian Birzeit University in February 1999. These and other conversations helped prepare the ground for the workshop for young musicians from the Middle East that would take place in Weimar, Germany, in August 1999. See http://www.danielbarenboim.com/index.php?id=7

Torn page of the Qur'an: Daniel Barenboim and Edward Said, *Parallels and Paradoxes*, p. 7.

Late the next afternoon Tania: The story of Tania's trip to Jerusalem, as well as of the dinner the evening before, was built from multiple interviews, most prominently with Tania herself over several sessions at the Nasir family home in Birzeit, where many of the details of the house were recorded. Additional interviews, with Daniel Barenboim, Mariam Said, and Rima Tarazi, filled out the narrative.

Also central to the telling was Tania's September 2003 article, "No Ordinary Concert," in *Al Ahram Weekly*, the Cairo newspaper, http://weekly.ahram.org.eg/2003/654/feature.htm

Richard was undergoing similar questioning: For all of the twenty years that I have been traveling to Israel and the Occupied Palestinian Territories, visitors to the West Bank have been subjected to extended questioning by Israel's Shin Bet (or General Security Service). Indeed, for West Bank visitors it is rare to hear a story of someone who has not been questioned. As the experiences of Hetsch, Lowry, and many contemporary European and American musicians indicate, the extensive questioning is part of a broad security screening conducted by the Shin Bet. The interrogations tend to be lengthier for Palestinians or people with Muslim-sounding names. More recently Israeli courts upheld the rights of Shin Bet to read through e-mails of visiting tourists, especially those with Arabic surnames. For more, see *Haaretz*: http://www.haaretz.com/israel-airport-security-demands-access-to-tourists-private-email-accounts.premium-1.434509#, or this story from the Associated Press: http://bigstory.ap.org/article/israel-asks-arab-visitors-open-emails-search. See also Amira Hass, "Israel Airport Security Demands Access to Tourists' Private Email Accounts," *Haaretz*, May 6, 2012, http://www.haaretz.com/news/diplomacy-defense/israel-airport-security-demands-access-to-tourists-private-email-accounts.premium-1.434509

The duo played in an unheated auditorium: The story of the concert with Scheherazade and falafel is based on my own observations of Ramzi, Ramadan, and the visiting French-Vietnamese violin and viola teacher, Antoine Pham, in the cold Ramallah church auditorium in the winter of 1998.

SECOND MOVEMENT: INSTRUMENT

Chapter 10: Conservatoire

The narrative of this chapter is shaped by numerous interviews with Ramzi, and with his former teacher, François Hetsch, in several locations in France during the summers of 2010–12. Additionally I spoke with a score of former Conservatoire students, teachers, and colleagues, many of whose names appear in this chapter, and with Ramzi's early hosts in Angers, John and Francine Cassini. Some of the viola instruction techniques come from interviews with Ramzi and François; others from Peter Sulski, or from the British violinist Simon Hewitt Jones, who proved his patience by giving me my first (and only) violin lesson, which at least proved useful for this book. The section on the Divan Orchestra is similarly constructed from multiple sources, including interviews with Daniel Barenboim, Mariam Said, numerous interviews with the members of the West-Eastern Divan Orchestra, conversations between Daniel and Edward captured in their book *Parallels and Paradoxes*, and the documentary *Knowledge Is the Beginning*.

Closest to a human voice: This comes from interviews with the violist Peter Sulski, formerly of the London Symphony Orchestra and now a viola teacher at The College of the Holy Cross who travels frequently to the West Bank to teach. American violist Lawrence Dutton agrees that "the sound of the viola is closest to the sound of the human voice." See *The Strad*, September 2012, p. 14. Also see Rian Evans's article, "Jordi Savvall-Review," *Guardian*, December 9, 2003, which states: "It was in the 17th century when Marin Mersenne, father of acoustics, noted the subtle parallels between the sound of the viola and that of the human voice" (http://www.theguardian.com/music/2013/dec/09/jordi-savall-review). Cynthia Phelps, the principal violist of the New York Philharmonic, explains that the viola is often politely referred to as the "inner voice" because it is discreet and rarely plays the principal melody. See http://www.npr.org/templates/story/story.php?storyId=6836307

"Can I come too?": Recollection of Daniel Barenboim in an interview with me in Cologne, Germany, summer 2011.

"You cannot be a lukewarm musician": Daniel Barenboim, from *Music Quickens Time*.

"The proximity of such sublimity to such horror": This and other quotes in this section come from *Parallels and Paradoxes*, edited conversations between Edward Said and Daniel Barenboim, facilitated by Ara Guzelimian, provost and dean of the Juilliard School.

"Poems based on his enthusiasm for Islam": Ibid, p. 7.

Inspiration for their new project's name—the West-Eastern Divan Orchestra: See Marina Warner, "In the Time of Not Yet: Marina Warner on the Imaginary of Edward Said," *London Review of Books* 32, no. 24, December 16, 2010, pp. 15–18, http://www.lrb.co.uk/v32/n24/marina-warner/in-the-time-of-not-yet

His leukemia resurfaced: Edward Said suffered from leukemia, which would flare up, go into remission, and return, for twelve years. The treatments were physically and emotionally excruciating and painful for his surviving family members, especially his widow Mariam, to recall. Nevertheless Mariam Said demonstrated remarkable grace and patience with me in describing the details of Edward's physical challenges, to the extent that they were necessary for the narrative of this book.

"The quality is not half bad!": Handwritten card from Yo-Yo Ma to Edward Said, found in the Edward Said Archives at the Rare Book and Manuscript Library, Columbia University.

Open the shutters on a sunny day: This phrase and other descriptions of Beethoven's Seventh Symphony comes from Donato Cabrera, resident conductor of the San Francisco Symphony, who served as a musical mentor for me during the process of writing and researching.

"What gives you the right to play Beethoven?": Edward Said, from *Parallels and Paradoxes*, p. 9.

"Ethnic cleansing is ethnic cleansing whether it is done by Serbians, Zionists, or Hamas": Edward Said, "Israel-Palestine: A Third Way," *Le Monde Diplomatique*, September 1998, http://mondediplo.com/1998/09/04said. Neither Said's idea nor the title of the article should be confused with Mitchell Plitnick's blog A Third Way, which may be familiar to some readers. See http://mitchellplitnick.com

"A horror that afflicts all of humanity": Edward Said, in "Setting the Record Straight," *Atlantic Unbound*, Interviews, September 22, 1999, http://www.theatlantic.com/past/docs/unbound/interviews/ba990922.htm

"Jedem das Seine": The translation here, as well as many other details from the grounds of Buchenwald, were taken from my visit to the former death camp in the summer of 2013. My guide to the camp was Palestinian musician Rajy Khaznadar, a trombonist with the Divan Orchestra, who is fluent in German and lives in Weimar.

"Little Camp": According to the Buchenwald and Mittelbau-Dora Memorials Foundation, the "little camp" of transition camps was built following the Germans' defeat in Stalingrad in 1943, when the SS started leasing out the concentration camp inmates to the German armament industry as well as putting them to work on construction projects of their own. "In Buchenwald the SS had twelve windowless Wehrmacht stables set up downhill from the main camp. Each of these wooden barracks was 40 m (131′) long and just under 10 m (33′) wide. There were neither sanitary facilities nor even beds in the interiors; rather, shelf-like boxes were built out of raw wood on either side of a narrow central aisle from one end of the building to the other. Each of these stables had originally been designed for approximately fifty horses. In Buchenwald, 1.000—sometimes nearly 2.000—human beings were crowded into each of these stables." See "The 'Little Camp'—Transit Camp," Buchenwald and Mittelbau-Dora Memorials Foundation Web site, http://www.buchenwald.de/en/942/#sthash.aHH2aqey.dpuf

Bodies hung on meat hooks before being fed to the ovens: According to the Buchenwald and Mittelbau-Dora Memorials Foundation, one of the camp's execution sites was the cellar, where the SS had "some 1,100 men, women, and adolescents hanged on hooks in the walls." See "The Crematorium," retrieved from the Web site of the Buchenwald and Mittelbau-Dora Memorials Foundation, http://www.buchenwald.de/en/539/. For more on the various explanations for the hooks in the "corpse cellar," see http://www.scrapbookpages.com/Buchenwald/Atrocities3.html. For a photo gallery of the objects found in the Buchenwald Camp, see the Buchenwald and Mittelbau-Dora Memorials Foundation Web site at http://www.buchenwald.de/fileadmin/buchenwald/fundstuecksammlung/index_findbuch.html

Holocaust could not be used as a justification: For reference to this quote and other writings, see Robert Fisk's essay on Said in the *Independent* (UK) at http://www.independent.co.uk/arts-entertainment/books/book-review--pirouettes-of-an-exvisionary-robert-fisk-considers-edward-saids-admirable-essays-during-a-decisive-week-in-palestinian-history-1412695.html

"Cries of the people of Gaza": Edward Said, *The Politics of Dispossession*, pp. 171–2.

"That there's less of it.": This quote by Edward Said, and many of the other observations from this chapter, are taken from the documentary *Knowledge Is the Beginning*, about the friendship between Edward Said and Daniel Barenboim and the development of the West-Eastern Divan Orchestra. Director Paul Smaczny generously provided me with additional transcripts of the raw interviews his team recorded, which added important detail for this section.

Chapter 11: Adaptation

Ariel Sharon marched onto the most contested piece of ground: The next day the *New York Times* reported, "Mr. Sharon entered as a police helicopter clattered overheard and a thousand armed policemen were positioned in and around the Temple Mount, including antiterror squads and ranks of riot officers carrying clubs, helmets and plastic shields. Throughout the tour, Mr. Sharon was ringed tightly by agents of the Shin Bet security services." See "Sharon Touches a Nerve, and Jerusalem Explodes," *New York Times*, September 29, 2000, http://www.nytimes.com/2000/09/29/international/29ARAFAT.html. While the *New York Times* article says one thousand police were in place for Sharon's visit, the Israeli government, in statements to the Sharm El-Sheikh Fact-Finding Committee, declared that fifteen hundred Israeli police were present. See http://mfa.gov.il/MFA/MFA-Archive/2000/Pages/Sharm%20el-Sheikh%20Fact-Finding%20Committee%20-%20First%20Sta.aspx. The Sharm El-Sheikh Committee, chaired by former U.S. senator George Mitchell, was established to investigate the causes of the Second Intifada and to make recommendations to cease hostilities. Its final report, better known as the Mitchell Report, also found that "Mr. Sharon made the visit on September 28 accompanied by over 1,000 Israeli police officers." See http://2001-2009.state.gov/p/nea/rls/rpt/3060.htm

Investigative commission had found him indirectly responsible for the massacres of hundreds of Palestinians: The recommendation section of the Kahan Commission's report declared that "that the Minister of Defence bears personal responsibility" and "if necessary, that the Prime Minister consider" removing Sharon from office. See the "Report of the Commission of Inquiry into the Events at the Refugee Camp in Beirut," *Jewish Virtual Library*, February 8, 1983, http://www.jewishvirtuallibrary.org/jsource/History/kahan.html. Between Sharon's resignation as defense minister in 1983 and 2000, he served as Minister of Industry and Trade, Minister of Construction and Housing, Chairman of the Ministerial Committee on Immigration and Absorption, a member of the Knesset's Foreign Affairs and Defense Committee, and Minister of National Infrastructure. In 1998 he was appointed Foreign Minister, and in September 1999 he was elected Likud Party chairman. See "Ariel Sharon Biography," *Jewish Virtual Library*, http://www.jewishvirtuallibrary.org/jsource/biography/sharon.html. See also John Kifner, "Arafat Always Seems to Survive. Peace May Not," *New York Times*, October 8, 2000, http://www.nytimes.

com/2000/10/08/weekinreview/the-world-arafat-always-seems-to-survive-peace-may-not.html

Arabs to be the stewards of Haram al-Sharif: The control over access to the Haram al-Sharif is among the most contested of all the issues that divide Israel and the Palestinians. Under the 1994 peace treaty between Jordan and Israel, the "Jordanian Waqf Authority" was to retain partial control over visitors to the Haram al-Sharif. See Ora Ahimeir and Marshall J. Berger, eds., *Jerusalem: A City and Its Future*, p. 163. The Palestinian Authority, as the book points out, has tried unsuccessfully to assert its influence but has been consistently opposed by Israel, which refused to grant any Palestinian sovereignty in East Jerusalem. See also Daoud Kuttab, "Jordan's Waqf No Match for Israelis in Jerusalem," *Huffington Post*, April 4, 2013, http://www.huffing tonpost.com/daoud-kuttab/jordans-waqf-no-match-for_b_3011544.html

"Let hell break loose and live with the consequences": For a detailed narrative account of the failed 2000 summit at Camp David, based on multiple first-hand accounts, see my book *The Lemon Tree*, pp. 234–9. The exchange between Clinton and Arafat is included in accounts in books by former secretary of state Madeleine Albright, U.S. Middle East envoy Dennis Ross (p. 296), former U.S. ambassador to Israel Martin Indyk (pp. 334–5), and journalists Charles Enderlin (p. 239) and Clayton Swisher (p.299), and in an extensive interview by former Israeli prime minister Ehud Barak given to Israeli historian Benny Morris and published in the *New York Review of Books*, http://www.nybooks.com/articles/archives/2002/jun/13/camp-david-and-after-an-exchange-1-an-interview-wi/. The "Let hell break loose" comment comes from Martin Indyk's *Innocent Abroad* (p. 335) and numerous other sources, including the aforementioned Swisher account, and Robert Malley and Hussein Agha's excellent summary, "Camp David: Tragedy of Errors," in the *New York Review of Books*, August 9, 2001, http://www.nybooks.com/articles/archives/2001/aug/09/camp-david-the-tragedy-of-errors/

The bloodiest fighting between Israel and the Palestinians: According to "Battle at Jerusalem Holy Site Leaves 4 Dead and 200 Hurt," Deborah Sontag's September 30, 2000 account in the *New York Times*, http://www.nytimes.com/2000/09/30/world/battle-at-jerusalem-holy-site-leaves-4-dead-and-200-hurt.html: "Wearing full riot gear, Israeli police officers today stormed the Muslim area, where they rarely set foot, to disperse Palestinian youths who emerged from Friday prayer services to stone first a police post at the Moghrabi Gate and then Jewish worshipers at the Western Wall." For in-depth findings of the events of September 29 and after, consult the impartial Sharm El-Sheikh Fact-Finding Committee, better known as the Mitchell Commission after its chair, former U.S. senator George Mitchell, see http://2001-2009.state.gov/p/nea/rls/rpt/3060.htm. The report indicated the Palestinian demonstrators did not fire weapons on September 29. More details can be found in the report, "Israel and the Occupied Territories: Excessive Use of Lethal Force," Amnesty International, October 19, 2000, http://www.amnesty.org/en/library/asset/MDE15/041/2000/en/0081a385-dd24-11dd-8595-5f956bd70248/mde150412000en.html

Scenes were reminiscent of the days many had hoped and believed were long past: "The first day of the Jewish New Year, normally celebrated as a day of reflection and prayer, was instead marked by sending Israeli troops throughout Jerusalem, Gaza, and the West Bank." See "At Least 12 More Arabs Die in Confrontations with Israelis," *New York Times,* September 30, 2000, http://www.nytimes.com/2000/09/30/world/01CND-MIDEAST.html. Two days later, the *New York Times* reported: "Palestinian mourners proceeded directly from village graveyards to the junctions between Israeli and Palestinian-ruled areas, where they jumped from pickup trucks adorned with wreathed pictures of the dead to collect and hurl stones at Israeli soldiers dressed in riot gear." See "Israeli, Palestinian Troops Battle," *New York Times,* October 2, 2000, http://www.nytimes.com/2000/10/02/continuous/02CND-MIDE.html

A "grand plan" of terror: Israelis believed that Arafat was purposefully orchestrating the violence after the failure of Camp David. "We know, from hard intelligence, that Arafat intended to unleash a violent confrontation, terrorism," claimed Ehud Barak. "The intifada," he continued, "was pre-planned, pre-prepared." See Jeremy Pressman, "Visions in Collision: What Happened at Camp David and Taba?" *International Security* 28, no. 2 (Fall 2003), pp. 13–14, retrieved from http://polisci.uconn.edu/people/faculty/doc/Visions_pressman.pdf. The impartial Mitchell Report found no evidence for such claims; see http://2001-2009.state.gov/p/nea/rls/rpt/3060.htm

Few Palestinians were armed: Nearly three-fourths (73 percent) of the early demonstrations, from September 29 to December 2, 2000, "did not include Palestinian gunfire," according to the IDF's own figures, according to the findings of B'Tselem in its December 6, 2000 report "Illusions of Restraint," http://www.btselem.org/press_releases/20001206

264 Palestinians died in the occupied territories: In nearly three-fourths of the demonstrations, according to the IDF's own figures, no gunfire came from the Palestinian side (cited in the Sharm El-Sheikh Fact-Finding Committee of April 30, 2001, http://2001-2009.state.gov/p/nea/rls/rpt/3060.htm). On December 2, 2000, B'Tselem reported that in the previous 64 days, 264 Palestinians had been killed in the Occupied Territories during the second uprising, most by Israeli soldiers, including "73 minors aged 17 and under." See "Illusions of Restraint," B'Tselem, December 6, 2000, http://www.btselem.org/press_releases/20001206. During the same period, 29 Israelis were killed, including 16 soldiers. For more information and details, see "Report of the Sharm El-Sheikh Fact-Finding Committee," UNISPAL, April 30, 2000, http://unispal.un.org/UNISPAL.NSF/0/6E61D52EAACB860285256D2800734E9A. Thousands of Palestinians were wounded as Israel adopted a "shoot to maim" policy in which soldiers aimed for demonstrators' legs. See Lamis Andoni and Sandy Tolan, et al., "Shoot to Maim," *Village Voice,* February 19, 2001, http://www.villagevoice.com/2001-02-20/news/shoot-to-maim/full/

The weak, compliant government it has spawned: According to an October 8, 2000, *New York Times* article, "Arafat Always Seems to Surive. Peace May Not," John Kifner writes: "'Arafat's authority has eroded over the years,' said a Western expert on the region who has dealt closely with him. 'There is a tremendous frustration among Palestinians, a lot of very angry people out there, an awful lot of rage. He negotiated these agreements with the Israelis, and Palestinians just don't believe in them anymore.'" See http://www.nytimes.com/2000/10/08/weekinreview/the-world-arafat-always-seems-to-survive-peace-may-not.html

"What of the much-vaunted peace process itself?": Edward Said, "Palestinians under Siege," *London Review of Books*, December 14, 2000, http://www.lrb.co.uk/v22/n24/edward-said/palestinians-under-siege

Edward and Wadie had engaged in a stone-throwing competition: In an interview with Ari Shavit of *Haaretz*, Edward said his son and other young men had been having a stone-throwing competition. See *Mid-East Realities*, Washington, August 25, 2000, http://h-net.msu.edu/cgi-bin/logbrowse.pl?trx=vx&list=h-radhist&month=0008&week=e&msg=nY%2B/t%2BkE9pOqjTxZIFSnsw&user=&pw=. Earlier, in a *Columbia Spectator* article of July 19, 2000, Edward had said, "There were many people [at the border] . . . elated by the absence of Israeli troops . . . For a moment, I joined in: the spirit of the place infected everyone with the same impulse, to make a symbolic gesture of joy that the occupation had ended." According to the article Columbia University declined to comment on Said's actions, noting that it did not pass judgment on the outside activities of its faculty members. See Sunnie Kim, "Edward Said Accused of Stoning in Southern Lebanon," http://www.columbiaspectator.com/2000/07/19/edward-said-accused-stoning-south-lebanon. Two months after the event, in an open letter to the Columbia community, provost and dean Jonathan Cole wrote, "To my knowledge, the stone was directed at no one; no law was broken; no indictment was made; no criminal or civil action has been taken against Professor Said." See Karen Arenson, "Columbia Debates a Professor's 'Gesture,'" *New York Times*, October 19, 2000, http://www.nytimes.com/2000/10/19/nyregion/columbia-debates-a-professor-s-gesture.html

"Symbolic gesture of joy": "Palestinian writer defends stoning," Associated Press, July 13, 2000.

More than thirty Israelis were injured: The estimates for the number of wounded vary depending on the reports. The *Jerusalem Post* on June 12, 2005, reported thirty-four wounded (http://www.jpost.com/LandedPages/PrintArticle.aspx?id=6663); the *Jewish Telegraphic Agency* also reported about thirty. The Israeli Ministry of Foreign Affairs, however, reports sixty injured and one death, most likely one of the terrorists involved in the attacks, the Web site claims. See "Suicide and Other Bombing Attacks in Israel Since the Declaration of Principles (Sept 1993)," Israeli Ministry of Foreign Affairs, http://www.mfa.gov.il/mfa/foreignpolicy/terrorism/palestinian/pages/suicide%20and%20other%20bombing%20attacks%20in%20israel%20since.aspx

Four similar attacks in the previous two years: According to the Jewish Virtual Library, on November 2, 2000, two Israelis were killed in a car-bomb explosion in Jerusalem; on November 20, 2000, two Israelis were killed in a roadside bomb explosion; on November 22, 2000, two Israelis were killed in a car-bomb explosion in Hadera; and on December 28, two Israelis, two people, one an IDF captain and the other a policeman, were killed trying to dismantle a bomb. "Major Palestinian Terror Attacks Since Oslo," Timeline, *Jewish Virtual Library*, http://www.jewishvirtuallibrary. org/jsource/Terrorism/TerrorAttacks.html

"Weapon of the weak": See, for example, Mary Kaldor, "Armageddon Myths," in New Statesman, May 26; Graham Fuller, *A World Without Islam*; and Yoram Schweitzer's "The Rise and Fall of Suicide Bombings in the Second Intifada."

Three dozen more such attacks: See "Major Palestinian Terror Attacks Since Oslo," Timeline, *Jewish Virtual Library*, http://www.jewishvirtuallibrary.org/jsource/ Terrorism/TerrorAttacks.html; and "Suicide and Other Bombing Attacks in Israel Since the Declaration of Principles (Sept 1993)," Israeli Ministry of Foreign Affairs, http://www.mfa.gov.il/mfa/foreignpolicy/terrorism/palestinian/pages/suicide%20 and%20other%20bombing%20attacks%20in%20israel%20since.aspx

Suspension of the last-ditch peace talks: "The negotiations at Taba were interrupted by Mr. Barak after two Israelis were killed in the West Bank," wrote Deborah Sontag of the *New York Times* in her essay "Quest for Mideast Peace: How and Why it Failed," July 26, 2001, http://www.nytimes.com/2001/07/26/world/and-yet-so-far-a-special-report-quest-for-mideast-peace-how-and-why-it-failed.html. See also "Progress in Taba Peace Talks Cut Short by West Bank Murders," *Jewish Telegraphic Agency*, January 24, 2001, http://www.jta.org/2001/01/24/archive/progress-in-taba-peace-talks-cut-short-by-west-bank-murders#ixzz2q6YC5AsY

He stepped up incursions into Palestinian territory: "The main task that lay in front of him was dealing with the wave of Palestinian terror that engulfed Israeli cities," wrote Haaretz. "Sharon took a hard line in the military struggle against the Palestinians and authorized the policy of 'targeted killings.'" See Jonathan Lis, "Ariel Sharon, Former Israeli Prime Minister, Dies at 85," *Haaretz*, January 11, 2014, http:// web.archive.org/web/20140111174341/http://www.haaretz.com/news/national/ 1.546747

Tanks and, on occasion, American-made Apache helicopter gunships: Multiple accounts of tanks and helicopters during the Second Intifada include those from Ramzi, and from his brother Rami's reports over the phone. For additional documentation, see, for example Joel Brinkley, "As Tanks Leave City, Ramallah Is Defiant," March 16, 2002. For the use of Apache helicopters, see, for example, Avery Plaw, *Targeting Terrorists: A License to Kill?*, pp. 68–9.

Orders to intimidate the local population: The definition of "demonstration of presence" comes from *Our Harsh Logic*, a collection of eyewitness accounts by Israeli soldiers who served in the occupying army during the Second Intifada, published by Breaking the Silence, "an organization of veteran combatants who have served in the Israeli military since the start of the Second Intifada and have taken it upon themselves to expose the Israeli public to the reality of everyday life in the Occupied Territories."

The book asserts that "a significant portion of the IDF's offensive actions are not intended to prevent a specific act of terrorism, but rather to punish, deter, or tighten control over the Palestinian population. 'Prevention of terror' is the stamp of approval granted to any offensive IDF action in the Territories, obscuring the distinction between the use of force against terrorists and the use of force against civilians." Field commanders considered the patrols "harassing activity" or "disruption of normalcy . . . they are not dependent on intelligence regarding a specific terrorist activity. Missions to 'demonstrate presence' prove that the IDF sees in every member of the Palestinian population—whether involved in opposition efforts or not—a target for intimidation, harassment, and instilling of fear." Individual accounts report numerous occasions of night raids with no apparent specific purpose. Breaking the Silence's children and youth testimonies, p. 28, includes this from a soldier stationed in Hebron in 2006–7:

"So there's a school there. We'd often provoke riots there. We'd be on patrol, walking in the village, bored, so we'd trash shops, find a detonator, beat someone to a pulp, you know how it is. Search, mess it all up. Say we'd want a riot? We'd go up to the windows of a mosque, smash the panes, throw in a stun grenade, make a big boom, then we'd get a riot.

And the locals were praying at the time?

Yes, possibly. Everything goes. It's best, in the middle of prayers. That annoys them the most. You know what it's like. Soldiers are bored. They want action. Some are already waiting for the Palestinians outside, to fire rubber ammo as soon as they come out. Once we came—actually this was not planned—one of our guys went up to the window of the mosque, smashed it, and suddenly a riot broke out. So we came, shot rubber ammo, and they all scurried back inside. So a soldier went up and threw a gas canister inside.

Into the mosque?

Sure. Can you imagine what sort of riot broke out there? I tell you, I never saw one like that. . . . You know, they'd get really upset at us when we threw stun grenades into their holiday prayers."

See more at http://www.breakingthesilence.org.il/wp-content/uploads/2012/08/ Children_and_Youth_Soldiers_Testimonies_2005_2011_Eng.pdf

In the fall of 2000, Ramzi and Ramadan: The accounts of the development of Dalouna, and life at the Conservatoire, are based on interviews with Ramzi, Ramadan, Jessie, François Hetsch, Richard Lowry, and numerous other teachers, students, and fellow musicians, as well as with members of the National Conservatory of Music in Palestine, including Suhail Khouri and Rima Tarazi.

"Cruel and bloodthirsty enemy": See, for example, Ross Dunn, "No Talks, Just Pain, Vows Sharon," *The Age* (Melbourne, Australia), March 6, 2002, http://www.theage. com.au/articles/2002/03/05/1014705049494.html

"Patriarch of terror": Ibid.

Global war on terror in the wake of the attacks made on the United States on
September 11: Sharon adopted the rhetoric of the "war on terror," implemented
following September 11, in order to justify his actions against Palestinians. See, for
example, "Sharon Vows to Continue 'War on Terror,'" *Guardian*, March 22, 2004,
http://www.theguardian.com/world/2004/mar/22/israel3

"We must cause them losses, victims, so that they feel the heavy price": See, for
example, "Streets Red with Blood," *Time*, March 18, 2002, http://www.time.com/
time/magazine/article/0,9171,1002012,00.html, and "Israel and the Occupied
Territories: The Heavy Price of Israeli Incursions," Amnesty International, http://
www.amnesty.org/en/library/asset/MDE15/042/2002/en/cd1f0393-d85e-11dd-
9df8-936c90684588/mde150422002en.html

"If you declare war": See the *Philadephia Inquirer*, "As Israel Girds for War, U.S.
Chafes: Sharon Must Look Hard at His Policies, Powell Said of the
Leader's Call to Cause 'Losses-Victims' for Palestinians; U.S. Chafes at Israeli
Stance," Philly.com, March 7, 2002, http://articles.philly.com/2002-03-07/news/
25340559_1_palestinian-leader-yasir-arafat-saeb-erekat-palestinian-targets

Thirty people died, most in the midst of a Passover seder: On March 27, 2002, thirty
people were killed and one hundred forty injured—twenty seriously—in a suicide-
bombing attack at the Park Hotel in Netanya during a Passover Seder with two
hundred fifty guests. Hamas claimed responsibility. "Passover Suicide Bombing at
Park Hotel in Netanya-27-March-2002," Israel Ministry of Foreign Affairs, March 27,
2002, http://mfa.gov.il/MFA/MFA-Archive/2002/Pages/Passover%20suicide%20
bombing%20at%20Park%20Hotel%20in%20Netanya.aspx

In a statement following the attack Prime Minister Ariel Sharon declared,
"Israel will act to crush the Palestinian terrorist infrastructure, in all its parts and
components, and will carry out comprehensive activity to achieve this goal. Arafat,
who has established a coalition of terror against Israel, is an enemy and at this point
he will be isolated." See "Statement by PM Sharon and DM Ben-Eliezer at press
conference," Israel Ministry of Foreign Affairs, March 29, 2002, http://mfa.gov.il/
MFA/PressRoom/2002/Pages/Statements%20by%20PM%20Sharon%20and%20
DM%20Ben-Eliezer%20at%20pres.aspx

Two days after the Passover bombing, the IDF called up thirty thousand reserve
troops: The thirty-thousand figure comes from numerous sources, including Matt
Rees, "The Battle of Jenin," in *Time*, http://content.time.com/time/magazine/article/
0,9171,1002406,00.html. The Jewish Virtual Library says the battle marked "the
largest such action since the 1982 Lebanon War, and put the army and air force on
high alert," adding, "On March 29, IDF infantry and armor, supported by air force
helicopters, made their way into a number of the major Palestinian cities of the West
Bank, including Bethlehem, Nablus, Ramallah, Tulkarem, Qalqilya, and Tubas, to
initiate Operation 'Defensive Shield' . . . The IDF decided to send infantry soldiers
and tanks to conduct house to house fighting in order to minimize civilian casualties

and collateral damages." See "Operation Defensive Shield," Jewish Virtual Library, http://www.jewishvirtuallibrary.org/jsource/History/defensiveshield.html. According to a 2002 B'Tselem report: "In some cases, curfews remained in place for weeks and months on end, with only short breaks given to allow residents to stock up on basic supplies." The report said the IDF regularly used "live ammunition as a means of enforcing the curfew, which has left more than twenty Palestinians dead, including twelve minors, and dozens more injured . . . Palestinians who have left their homes to stock up on supplies often find themselves under fire because they were unaware that curfew had been reinstated." See "2002 Activity Report," B'Tselem, http://www. btselem.org/download/2002_activity_report_eng.pdf. The report also cited the "IDF's use of civilians as human shields. Soldiers have compelled Palestinian civilians to walk in front of them as protection against gunfire, to enter houses to check if they were booby-trapped, or to remove suspicious objects from the road."

In five weeks, seven thousand Palestinians were arrested, many under Military Order 1500: A 2002 report of the U.N. Secretary General stated: "By 6 May, an alleged 7,000 Palestinians had been arrested under Operation Defensive Shield, many of them held for long periods with little or no outside contact. In many instances, the IDF followed a pattern of using loudspeakers to summon males between the ages of 15 and 45. According to human rights reports, significant numbers of the men arrested were blindfolded and handcuffed, not allowed to use a lavatory, and deprived of food or blankets during their first day in detention." According to B'Tselem more than five thousand Palestinians had been detained by May 12, see http://www.btselem.org/statistics/detainees_and_prisoners

Making it impossible to assess the precise level of loss: According to a 2002 B'Tselem report, "The al-Aqsa Intifada, which began in September 2000, ushered in a severe deterioration in human rights in the Occupied Territories . . . Israel conducted widespread ground and air assaults in Palestinian population centers, restricted almost all movement for Palestinians within the West Bank, prevented access to medical treatment and humanitarian aid, and detained thousands of Palestinian civilians—in many cases arbitrarily . . . The lack of credible information has been further exacerbated by limits on access to areas of military operation imposed by Israel . . . During the operation, all access for journalists and human rights workers was prohibited to areas in which military operations were being conducted, and the Israeli press entirely refrained from covering the Palestinian reality. As a result, virtually no information was available on the widespread human rights violations being committed and the impact of IDF actions on the Palestinian civilian population." "2002 Activity Report," B'Tselem, http://www.btselem.org/download/2002_activity_report_eng.pdf, pp. 1, 5.

500 Palestinians were killed: According to a United Nations report, 497 Palestinians were killed in the course of the IDF reoccupation of Palestinian Area A from March 1 to May 7, 2002, and in the immediate aftermath. For the same period about 1,447 Palestinians were wounded. Over the same period "over 2,800 refugee housing units were damaged and 878 homes were demolished or destroyed . . . leaving more than

17,000 people homeless or in need of shelter rehabilitation." "United Nations, Report of the Secretary-General Prepared Pursuant to General Assembly Resolution ES-10/10 (Report on Jenin), July 2002," http://unispal.un.org/UNISPAL.NSF/0/ FD7BDE7666E04F5C85256C08004E63ED

"Target and paralyze anyone who takes up weapons": See "PM Sharon: Anti-Terror Efforts Will Continue until Completion," *Israel National News*, April 8, 2002, http:// www.israelnationalnews.com/News/News.aspx/21423; and "Déclaration Politique d'Ariel Sharon à la Knesset, *Le Monde Diplomatique*, April 9, 2002, http://www. monde-diplomatique.fr/cahier/proche-orient/declsharon20020408

Destroying any emergence of a free Palestinian society: In "Attacks Turn Palestinian Plans into Bent Metal and Piles of Dust," Serge Schmemann wrote in the *New York Times:* "There is no way to assess the full extent of the damage to the cities and towns . . . while they remain under a tight siege, with patrols and snipers firing in the streets. But it is safe to say that the infrastructure of life itself and of any future Palestinian state—roads, schools, electricity pylons, water pipes, telephone lines—has been devastated." *New York Times*, April 11, 2002, http://www.nytimes. com/2002/04/11/world/mideast-turmoil-rubble-attacks-turn-palestinian-plans-into-bent-metal-piles-dust.html. The World Bank would estimate the rebuilding costs at $361 million, much of it for structures Western donors had already paid for once. See "United Nations, Report of the Secretary-General Prepared Pursuant to General Assembly Resolution ES-10/10 (Report on Jenin), July 2002," http://unispal.un.org/ UNISPAL.NSF/0/FD7BDE7666E04F5C85256C08004E63ED

"Trying to eliminate them as a people with national institutions?": Edward Said, *From Oslo to Iraq and the Road Map*, p 174.

Encountered stiff and unexpected resistance: See Suzanne Goldenberg, "Toll of the Bloody Battle of Jenin," *Guardian*, April 9, 2002, http://www.guardian.co.uk/ world/2002/apr/10/israel

"This group of suicide bombers has refused to surrender": Ibid.

Fifty-two Palestinians were killed in the Battle of Jenin: Suzanne Goldenberg, "Toll of the Bloody Battle of Jenin," *Guardian*, April 9, 2002; See also Matt Rees, "Untangling Jenin's Tale," *Time*, May 13, 2002, http://content.time.com/time/ magazine/article/0,9171,1002406,00.html; "Israel and the Occupied Territories: Shielded from Scrutiny: IDF Violation in Jenin and Nablus," Amnesty International, November 4, 2002, http://www.amnesty.org/en/library/info/MDE15/143/2002; and "Civilian Casualties and Unlawful Killings in Jenin," Human Rights Watch, 14, no. 3E (May 2002), http://www.hrw.org/reports/2002/israel3/israel0502-05. htm#P234_38516

The United Nations called off the investigation: See William Orme and Mary Curtius, "Annan Urges U.N. to Drop Jenin Probe," *Los Angeles Times*, May 1, 2002, http://articles.latimes.com/2002/may/01/world/fg-un1; "Jenin Mission Delayed until Sunday," BBC News, April 27, 2002, http://news.bbc.co.uk/2/hi/middle_east/

1952508.stm; "UN Condemns Israel over Jenin," BBC News, May 8, 2002, http://news.bbc.co.uk/2/hi/middle_east/1974389.stm; and "Ben-Eliezer, Peres to Annan: Israel Unhappy with Jenin Delegation, *Haaretz*, April 22, 2002, http://www.haaretz.com/news/ben-eliezer-peres-to-annan-israel-unhappy-with-jenin-delegation-1.47169

Which had killed several hundred: For background, see Mideast Web's Second Intifada timeline, http://www.mideastweb.org/Middle-East-Encyclopedia/second_intifada.htm. A United Nations investigation put Palestinian deaths at 497; other sources say the death toll was about half that. Jerusalem Media and Communication Centre, timeline for the Second Intifada, updated March 25, 2010, http://www.jmcc.org/fastfactspag.aspx?tname=88

New suicide bombing: See the Jerusalem Media and Communication Centre, timeline for the Second Intifada: "May 7, 2002: Suicide Bombing in Rishon Letzion Kills 16 people. Hamas Claims Responsibility." http://www.jmcc.org/fastfactspag.aspx?tname=88

A vast barrier, which they would call a security fence: For more information see Mideast Web, Second Intifada timeline, http://www.mideastweb.org/Middle-East-Encyclopedia/second_intifada.htm

Center for Rehabilitation: See the school's Web site: http://www.cbm.org/programmes/Star-Mountain-Rehabilitation-Centre-303406.php

"Cave à vins Psagot": From J Wines, "the premiere Kosher wine store": "While the first bottles of Psagot Wine were introduced in 2002, the winery makes use of facilities that date to antiquity. Psagot Wine is aged in a special cave containing winemaking implements that date to at least the time of the Second Temple. The combination of ancient tradition and sophisticated technology adds to the allure and mystique of this boutique winemaker. The local vineyards yield a distinctively mineral-tasting grape, which surprises and delights the palate. All Psagot Wine labels bear the image of the ancient cave now used as the aging room, a reminder of the long tradition and hard work that bring this heavenly bottle to your table." http://jwines.com/wines/psagot-wine.html

Chapter 12: Brother

The first meeting: The development of the Al Kamandjati Association is documented through multiple interviews of early board members and supporters, including Ramzi, Karim Rassouli, Yamna Amraoui, Marie Albert, Marie-Paule Bocher, Catherine Bocher, and Elsa Ferrari. Many of these interviews were facilitated by Yacine Laghrour of Angers, France.

International Solidarity Movement: The ISM remains the most high-profile of the international solidarity organizations. Founded during the Second Intifada, the ISM's work has consisted of orange-vested volunteers, mostly young Westerners, escorting Palestinians in conflict zones to school, standing watch at olive groves subject to attack by nearby Israeli settlers, or standing in the way of bulldozers coming to demolish a

Palestinian home. Its critics include the staunchly pro-Israel Anti Defamation League, which says the ISM "seeks to delegitimize Israel by spreading anti-Israel propaganda" and "engage[s] in confrontational tactics such as obstructing the activities of the Israeli military." See http://archive.adl.org/main_anti_israel/international_solidarity_movement.html#.UwI_XkJdWZ4

On its Web site, http://palsolidarity.org/about/, the ISM describes itself as a "Palestinian-led movement committed to resisting the long-entrenched and systematic oppression and dispossession of the Palestinian population, using non-violent, direct-action methods and principles." Also for background on solidarity organizations, see Julie Norman, *The Second Palestinian Intifada: Civil Resistance.* For more information about the Association France Palestine Solidarité, see their Web site, http://www.france-palestine.org/

Rachel Corrie: Rachel Corrie, an ISM activist, was killed on March 16, 2013, a few months after the Al Kamandjati meeting described here. She was crushed after a Caterpillar D9 armored bulldozer operated by an Israeli soldier ran over her twice during protests against the military's house demolitions in Rafah, in the Gaza Strip. The homes were being demolished in a military operation whose stated purpose was to seal tunnels suspected of being arms conduits on the border between Gaza and Egypt. Corrie was standing in front of the bulldozer, wearing a bright orange vest, and had been speaking into a bullhorn until minutes before her death. An Israeli court ruled that the death was accidental. An eyewitness to Corrie's death, journalist Tom Dale, told the *New York Times*: "It is inconceivable that at some point the driver did not see her, given the distance from which he approached, while she stood, unmoving, in front of it . . . just before she was crushed, Rachel briefly stood on top of the rolling mound of earth which had gathered in front of the bulldozer: her head was above the level of the blade, and just a few meters from the driver." "Witness to Rachel Corrie's Death Responds to Court Ruling Absolving Soldier," the *New York Times*, "The Lede" blog, August 28, 2012, http://thelede.blogs.nytimes.com/2012/08/28/witness-to-rachel-corries-death-responds-to-israeli-court-ruling-absolving-soldier. For a picture of Corrie confronting the bulldozer, see *Electronic Intifada*, March 16, 2003, http://www.electronicintifada.net/content/photostory-israeli-bulldozer-driver-murders-american-peace-activist/4449

New concerts planned for Morocco, Mexico, and South America: See the orchestra's Web site for more information at http://www.west-eastern-divan.org/past-performances/

Whose twenty-four books: For more on Said's publications, see http://www.lib.uci.edu/about/publications/wellek/said/

". . . and whose minds we might change?" For the full text of Edward Said's award speech in Oviedo, Spain, go to http://www.fpa.es/en/prince-of-asturias-awards/awards/2002-daniel-barenboim-y-edward-said.html

Ariel Sharon declared that Israel was prepared to "allow" a Palestinian state on less than half of the West Bank: "Israel will allow the establishment of a Palestinian state with temporary borders," Sharon said. As quoted in the *Guardian*, December 6, 2002.

The article also states that under Sharon's proposal, the borders "would be defined by the 42% of the West Bank that falls under direct Palestinian administration under the Oslo agreement—known as Areas A and B—'except for areas vital for security,' and 70% of the Gaza strip." According to the December 6 *Guardian* article, "Ariel Sharon has laid out his terms for Palestinian independence with a vision of an emasculated and demilitarised state built on less than half the land of the occupied territories, and without Yasser Arafat as its leader." See "Sharon's deal for Palestine: no extra land, no army, no Arafat," http://www.theguardian.com/world/2002/dec/06/israel. See also the Annual Edmond Benjamin de Rothschild Herzliya Conference series on "The Balance of Israel's National Security," http://www.herzliyaconference.org/eng/_uploads/142002conclusions-pdf.pdf, p. 35.

"I've been very deeply distressed": Bishop Desmond Tutu, "Apartheid in the Holy Land," the *Guardian*, April 28, 2002, http://www.theguardian.com/world/2002/apr/29/comment

Road Map for Peace: Numerous accounts document Israel's hundred initial objections to the Road Map. See "Israel Grudgingly Accepts Road Map," UPI, May 25, 2003, http://www.upi.com/Business_News/Security-Industry/2003/05/25/Israel-grudgingly-accepts-road-map/UPI-45841053897279/. Eventually these objections were reduced or consolidated to fourteen main objections. See "Israel's Road Map Reservations," *Haaretz*, May 27, 2003, http://www.haaretz.com/print-edition/news/israel-s-road-map-reservations-1.8935. For the full text of the plan, see http://www.un.org/News/dh/mideast/roadmap/122002.pdf. For further questions, see Sharon Otterman, "Middle East: The Road Map to Peace," Council on Foreign Relations, Febuary 7, 2005, http://www.cfr.org/middle-east-and-north-africa/middle-east-road-map-peace/p7738

Tanks still blocked the entrances to some of the camps: According to a July 2003 United Nations OCHA humanitarian update, "On 27 July, the IDF removed six physical barriers at important road junctions in three West Bank areas: Ramallah, Hebron, and Bethlehem—the first time some of these roadblocks had been removed since March 2001. Despite these measures, movement still remains restricted. Several of the roadblocks were replaced by permanent and/or roaming IDF checkpoints that continue to significantly limit Palestinian access. Even where the IDF has removed some roadblocks—Ramallah, Bethlehem, and Hebron—the nearby cities and villages still remain virtually surrounded by dozens of other roadblocks, checkpoints, and other barriers." Humanitarian Update, OCHA Occupied Palestinian Territories, July 31, 2003, http://unispal.un.org/UNISPAL.NSF/0/5D2F25EB40D05CAB85256D7F0051CA7E#sthash.KHhRonTK.dpuf

Reduced to a single besieged building: See "Inside Arafat's Compound of Rubble," BBC News, September 22, 2002, http://news.bbc.co.uk/2/hi/middle_east/1902566.stm. See journalist Ian Buruma's interview with Arafat, in which Arafat's compound is described as "a grotesque sight: the facade of one large building has been blown away to reveal half-furnished rooms with pictures of Arafat still hanging on the walls, like a ruined doll's house. Nearby is the skeleton of an elevator shaft, standing alone in a pile of concrete and twisted steal." "More Tea, Mister Chairman?" the *Guardian*, August 8, 2003, http://www.theguardian.com/ world/2003/aug/08/israel. According to the Jewish Virtual Library entry on Operation Defensive Shield: "With tanks and soldiers stationed completely around the structure, Arafat was effectively cut off from leading an insurgency and was cordoned off, along with a number of his advisors and security personnel, to a small section of the building." http://www.jewishvirtuallibrary.org/jsource/History/ defensiveshield.html

Badly weakened the Palestinian Authority's security apparatus: In "The Battle for Palestinian Security Services" (Conflict Studies Research Center, Defence Academy of the United Kingdom, October 2006), Gordon Bennett writes: "The Israelis practically destroyed the Palestinian security apparatus in the West Bank campaign in early April 2002, when the Israeli Army took over the Palestinian Preventive Security Service HQ in Batuniya, near Ramallah. They took about 200 prisoners, including Abu-Awwad, the commander of the elite Force 17 in Ramallah and several other security officials." See http://www.isn.ethz.ch/Digital-Library/Publications/Detail/?ots591=0c54e3b3-1e9c-be1e-2c24-a6a8c7060233&lng=en&id=28893. See also Israel Ministry of Foreign Affairs, "Information Concerning Detainees Captured in the Palestinian Preventive Security Service Headquarters in Betunia," April 3, 2002, http://mfa.gov.il/ mfa/pressroom/2002/pages/information%20concerning%20detainees%20 captured%20in%20the%20p.aspx

Brought nearly two hundred Palestinians . . . into custody: Bennett, "The Battle for Palestinian Security." See also Israel Ministry of Foreign Affairs, "Information Concerning Detainees Captured in the Palestinian Preventive Security Service Headquarters in Betunia," cited above.

Lawlessness had spread throughout the Occupied Territories: See Nu'man Kanafani, "As If There Is No Occupation: The Limits of Palestinian Authority Strategy," *Middle East Report* (Middle East Research and Information Project), September 22, 2011, http://www.merip.org/mero/mero092211

Before sunrise the next morning: The story of the death, mourning, and burial of Rami Aburedwan, Ramzi's younger brother, is told through interviews with Ramzi, Ramadan, Karim Rassouli, and Yamna Amraoui. Dr. Hatem Bazian, cofounder of Zaytuna College, America's first Muslim liberal arts college, and a senior lecturer in the Department of Near Eastern and Ethnic Studies at the University of California, Berkeley, provided insight into Palestinian Muslim religious customs and burial.

Chapter 13: Troubadours

Two documentary filmmakers: The filmmakers, Hélèna Cotinier and Pierre-Nicolas Durand, would document the development of Ramzi's dream for a music school over three summers, in France and mostly the West Bank, resulting in the 2006

documentary *It's Not a Gun*. Hélèna was extremely helpful to me in my research, sitting for interviews and providing raw field notes from shooting days, which helped me add crucial detail to the narrative, especially around the travel of the French entourage during the summers of 2003–05.

The Palestinian proprietor offered Turkish coffee: Details from this scene and others throughhout this chapter come from interviews with Ramzi, Karim Rissouli, Yamna Amraoui, Jessie Nguenang, Hélèna Cotinier, Julien Leray, and other members of the French entourage, and from the transcripts and footage of the documentary *It's Not a Gun*.

Final draft of the Road Map: For the full text of the Road Map, see the United Nations Report "A Performance-Based Roadmap to a Permanent Two-State Solution to the Israeli-Palestinian Conflict," at http://www.un.org/News/dh/mideast/roadmap122002.pdf. For background, see Sharon Otterman, "Middle East: The Road Map to Peace," Council on Foreign Relations, February 7, 2005, http://www.cfr.org/middle-east-and-north-africa/middle-east-road-map-peace/p7738#p4

"What do you want, for a pregnant woman to have an abortion just because she is a settler?": See "Sharon Rejects US Pressure on Settlements," the *Guardian*, May 14, 2003, http://www.theguardian.com/world/2003/may/14/usa.israel and "Powell Visit Highlights Problems," BBC News, May 12, 2003, http://news.bbc.co.uk/2/hi/middle_east/3020335.stm

Move to the settlements with generous subsidies: B'Tselem, the Israeli human rights organization, states that "The Israeli governments have implemented a consistent and systematic policy intended to encourage Jewish citizens to migrate to the West Bank. One of the tools used to this end is to grant financial benefits and incentives to citizens—both directly and through the Jewish local authorities. The purpose of this support is to raise the standard of living of these citizens and to encourage migration to the West Bank . . . These benefits are provided by eight government ministries: the Ministry of Construction and Housing (reduction of price of the land and generous loans for the purchase of apartments, part of which is converted to a grant); the Israel Lands Administration (significant price reductions in leasing land); the Ministry of Education (Compulsory Education Law from Age Three, the long school day, extension of the school year, incentives for teachers, and subsidized transportation to school); the ministries of industry and trade, tourism, and agriculture (grants for investors, development of infrastructure for industrial zones, indemnification for loss of income resulting from custom duties imposed by countries of the European Union); the Ministry of Labor and Social Affairs (incentives for social workers); and the Ministry of Finance (reductions in income tax for individuals and companies). In 2003, the Ministry of Finance cancelled the income tax reduction that residents of settlements previously received." http://www.btselem.org/settlements/migration. See also "Israel Expands West Bank Subsidies," the *Washington Post*, August 4, 2013, http://www.washingtonpost.com/world/israel-expands-settlement-subsidies/2013/08/04/b01a4faa-fd1d-11e2-96a8-d3b921c0924a_story.html; and "Israeli Settlers Lured by

Subsidies," Al Jazeera, August 23, 2012, http://www.aljazeera.com/indepth/features/2012/08/201282211420708214.html

Fulfilling a demand Sharon had been pressing for months: One of the fourteen reservations set up by Sharon and the Israeli government in order to even consider the Road Map was a change of Palestinian leadership. Sharon saw in Abbas a weak opponent, and thus favored him to Arafat, who, though he had already made many concessions, was perhaps less likely to let Sharon decide what the Road Map plan would look like. See Akiva Eldar, "Who Could Lead Palestinians Better than Abbas?" *Haaretz*, January 17, 2011, http://www.haaretz.com/print-edition/opinion/who-could-lead-palestinians-better-than-abbas-1.337443

This was because of the *hudna*: For more on the truce of 2003, see "Words of Hamas, Fatah, and Islamic Jihad: 'Just, Lasting, and Comprehensive Peace'," the *New York Times*, June 30, 2003, http://www.nytimes.com/2003/06/30/world/words-of-fatah-hamas-and-islamic-jihad-just-lasting-and-comprehensive-peace.html; and an analysis on *+972 Magazine*, "Hamas: Political Pragmatists or Islamic Dogmatics?," May 1, 2014, http://972mag.com/hamas-political-pragmatism-or-dogmatism/90187/

439 miles long: Calculations are gleaned from the Web site of the Israel Ministry of Defense, including its page "Israel's Security Fence," and are based in part on figures for the initial 225-kilometer stretch of the barrier (http://www.securityfence.mod.gov.il/Pages/ENG/execution.htm#1). Additional figures come from the ministry's "Security Fence Numbers: Valid Summary at End of 2006," translated from the Hebrew. The 439-mile (or 708-kilometer) figure comes from numerous sites, including from B'Tselem: http://www.btselem.org/separation_barrier

A series of ditches, trenches, electronic fencing: For a detailed description of what Israel calls its "security fence" and Palestinians the "apartheid wall," see p. 21 of *Extreme Rambling: Walking Israel's Barrier. For Fun.*, Mark Thomas's first-person nonfiction account of a journey on foot along the route of the barrier in Israel and Palestine.

Annex more than 130,000 acres, or nearly 10 percent of West Bank land: The 130,000 figure is calculated by dividing the total acreage of the West Bank (1,393,000) by the amount of West Bank land incorporated—in essence, annexed—onto the Israeli side of the barrier. Conservative estimates put that number at 9.5 percent. See "The Separation Barrier," B'Tselem, January 2011, http://www.btselem.org/separation_barrier. The article states: "In setting the Barrier's route, Israeli officials almost entirely disregarded the severe infringement of Palestinian human rights. The route was based on irrelevant considerations completely unrelated to the security of Israeli civilians. A major aim in planning the route was de facto annexation of part of the West Bank: when the Barrier is completed, 9.5 percent of the West Bank, containing 60 settlements, will be situated on its western, 'Israeli' side. Israeli politicians already consider the Barrier's route as Israel's future border."

757 checkpoints, roadblocks: "Humanitarian Update: Occupied Palestinian Territories 16–31 Oct 2003," United Nations Office for the Coordination of Humanitarian

Affairs(OCHA),http://css.static.reliefweb.int/report/israel/ocha-humanitarian-update-occupied-palestinian-territories-16-31-oct-2003

Old city in Hebron, the most surreal tableau in the entire Israeli-Palestinian tragedy: For background, see "The Closure of Hebron's Old City," OCHA, July 2005, http://www.ochaopt.org/documents/ochaHU0705_En.pdf; and "Humanitarian Update, Occupied Palestinian Territories 16–31 Oct 2003," OCHA, http://css.static.reliefweb.int/report/israel/ocha-humanitarian-update-occupied-palestinian-territories-16-31-oct-2003; as well as Sarah Lazare and Clare Bayard, "Hebron's Architecture of Occupation," *Electronic Intifada*, November 23, 2009, http://www.electronicintifada.net/content/hebrons-architecture-occupation/8548. For more on the situation in Hebron, see "Hebron, Area H-2: Settlements Cause Mass Departure of Palestinians, August 2003," B'Tselem, http://www.btselem.org/publications/summaries/200308_hebron_area_h2; "The Occupying Force Continues to Contravene International Law, Supreme Court Legalizes Illegal Settlement in Hebron/Palestine," Geneva International Center for Justice, http://www.gicj.org/index.php?option=com_content&task=view&id=361&Itemid=41; "Ghost Town: Israel's Separation Policy and Forced Eviction of Palestinians from the Centre of Hebron, May 2007," B'Tselem, http://www.btselem.org/publications/summaries/200705_hebron; and "Hebron City Profile," Applied Research Institute in Jerusalem, 2009, http://vprofile.arij.org/hebron/pdfs/Hebron%20City%20profile.pdf

For hard-hitting first-hand accounts from former soldiers of the violence committed against Palestinian residents of Hebron, see http://www.breakingthesilence.org.il/testimonies/database?is=1&as1=hebron

Pushing a baby stroller down an empty street: Observation from Max Blumenthal, *Goliath*, p. 270.

Scaled their buildings with a rope: Sarah Lazare and Clare Bayard, "Hebron's Architecture of Occupation."

Settlers in downtown Hebron: Israel had allowed settlers to establish a foothold in 1980, and their continued presence was sanctioned by an agreement the Palestinian Authority had signed with Israel in 1997, with the encouragement of the United States. It was part of the ongoing Oslo peace process. See "Protocol Concerning the Redeployment in Hebron," http://unispal.un.org/UNISPAL.NSF/0/C7D7B824004FF5C585256AE700543EBC

Bags of human feces: Sarah Lazare and Clare Bayard, "Hebron's Architecture of Occupation." For more, see "Hebron Settlements," Temporary International Presence in Hebron, http://www.tiph.org/en/About_Hebron/Hebron_today/Settlements/. In my experience, these images, shocking as they are, become unsurprising after some time spent in Hebron.

The enmity went back decades: The settlers and their supporters had long argued that the killing of Jews in Hebron by Palestinians in 1929, and the presence of Jews there in centuries past, justified their presence. Palestinians point out that many of the current settlers came from the United States and have no connection to earlier Jewish families in Hebron. Many Palestinian residents sheltered and saved hundreds of Jews during the 1929 massacre, which came during riots against Jewish immigration to Palestine and began after rumors "that Jews were killing Arabs" (Israeli historian Tom Segev, *One Palestine, Complete*, p. 319). On p. 325 Segev writes: "Most of Hebron's Jews were saved because Arabs hid them in their homes." Yona Rochlin, a descendant of a Jewish family with a five-hundred-year history in Hebron, whose uncle was murdered in 1929, organized a group of fellow descendants, forty of whom signed an open letter to the Israeli government. The letter called for the removal of the current Israeli settlers "at once, before they succeed in exploding the peace process and destroying the prospects of peace." In an interview with the *Christian Science Monitor*, Rochlin said, "The settlers have taken two days and erased 500 years. While they live in Hebron in the name of the old Jewish community, they don't represent its way of life, which was a way of peace." See Lital Levy, "Peacemaker in Hebron," *Christian Science Monitor*, May 20, 1997, http://www.csmonitor.com/1997/0520/052097.opin. opin.1.html. For a personal reflection on the massacre, and the saving of a family by Hebron Arabs, see Meyer Greenberg, "The Hebron Massacre of 1929: A Recently Revealed Letter of a Survivor," http://hebron1929.info/Hebronletter.html

Baruch Goldstein: The story of Goldstein's massacre of twenty-nine Muslim worshipers is well documented by news accounts of the day. For additional background, see Jeff Klein, "A Visit to the Grave of Mass Murderer Baruch Goldstein," *Mondoweiss*, July 4, 2013, http://mondoweiss.net/2013/07/murderer-baruch-goldstein.html

The village of Azzoun: The map of Qalqilya village close, to Azzoun, prepared by the U.N. Office for the Coordination of Humanitarian Assistance (OCHA) strikingly demonstrates how it and other nearby villages like Azzoun are surrounded by the wall and other barriers; see http://www.ochaopt.org/documents/ocha_opt_the_closure_ map_2011_12_21_qalqiliya.pdf. The financial and agricultural impact of the barrier on Qalqilya is demonstrated in the Jerusalem Fund's "Fact Sheet 3," part of a series on the costofIsrael'soccupation(http://thejerusalemfund.org/ht/a/GetDocumentAction/i/3067). For a comparison with the Berlin Wall, see the Cold War Museum's "Berlin Wall timeline" for August 13, 1961, http://www.coldwar.org/articles/60s/BerlinWallTimeLine.asp

"I would not feel like playing bass": This discussion, the subsequent conversation between the French musicians in Gaza, and the scenes with Oday at Al Fawwar Refugee Camp are taken from Hélèna Cotinier and Pierre-Nicolas Durand's documentary *It's Not a Gun.*

Al Fawwar refugee camp: For Al Fawwar Refugee Camp demographics, see this census conducted by the Palestinian Central Bureau of Statistics: http://www.pcbs.gov.ps/ Portals/_Rainbow/Documents/hebrn.htm. See also the fact sheet at http://vprofile. arij.org/hebron/pdfs/Al%20Fawwar%20Camp.pdf; and "Al Fawar Refugee Camp Profile," Applied Research Institute of Jerusalem, 2009, http://vprofile.arij.org/ hebron/pdfs/Al%20Fawwar%20Camp_pr_en.pdf

Sealed the camp so that no one could leave: For context and a broader view of Israel's closure practices, see, for example, "OCHA Humanitarian Update Occupied Palestinian Territories 1–15 Aug 2003," http://reliefweb.int/report/occupied-palestinian-territory/ocha-humanitarian-update-occupied-palestinian-territories-1-15

Overdependence on foreign aid: For a discussion of aid dependence see "Does the International Aid System Violate Palestinian Rights?," Dalia Association, http://www.dalia.ps/node/123

Chapter 14: Edward

Edward's health had been deteriorating since the late spring: The story of Edward Said's illness and death was relayed to me by Mariam Said over many conversations from 2011 to 2014. Despite the painful memories, Mariam never once betrayed a lack of patience or grace, and I remain grateful to her.

"I for one am full of optimism": For a video of Edward's speech, "Memory, Inequality, and Power: Palestine and the Universality of Human Rights," at the University of California, Berkeley, on February 19, 2003, see this YouTube link: http://www.youtube.com/watch?v=Pb2pYStv8x8

"His voice is irreplaceable, but his legacy will endure": See Tariq Ali, "Remembering Edward Said, 1935–2003," *New Left Review* 24 (November-December 2003), http://newleftreview.org/II/24/tariq-ali-remembering-edward-said

Claims, already discredited, that Edward had "falsified his biography": "Edward W. Said, Polymath Scholar, Dies at 67," *New York Times*, September 26, 2003, http://www.nytimes.com/2003/09/26/obituaries/26SAID.html?pagewanted=1. See also Edward Alexander, "Professor of Terror."

"Professor of terror": See Christopher Hitchens, "A Valediction for Edward Said," *Slate*, September 26, 2003; and Edward Alexander, "Professor of Terror," *Commentary*, August 1989, http://www.commentarymagazine.com/article/professor-of-terror/

"Above all, Said had an intelligence of feeling": "St. Paul's Chapel at Columbia University was filled to the brim on March 3, as family, close friends and colleagues of Edward Said gathered to remember and celebrate his life." Colin Morris, "Friends and Family Celebrate the Life and Work of Columbia Luminary Edward Said," *Columbia News*, March 24, 2004, http://www.columbia.edu/cu/news/04/03/edwardSaid.html

"We have a choice": These remarks are excerpted from the film *Selves and Others: A Portrait of Edward Said*, directed by Emmanuel Hamon. Video of the excerpts, as well as remarks from Nadine Gordimer, Vanessa Redgrave, Daniel Barenboim, and others at Edward's Columbia memorial service, can be viewed at http://www.columbia.edu/cu/news/media/04/280_edwardSaid_memorial/. Edward's remarks are also cited in John R. MacArthur, "Columbia College Class Day Keynote Speech," *Harper's Magazine*, May 15, 2012, http://harpers.org/blog/2012/05/columbia-college-class-day-keynote-speech/

"All his interests were one": Colin Morris, "Friends and Family Celebrate the Life and Work of Columbia Luminary Edward Said."

"I think of Edward practically every day": This quote from Daniel Barenboim comes from my 2011 interview, in Cologne, with Barenboim.

"Edward had that very unique quality of having moral authority": From the documentary film *Knowledge Is the Beginning* by Paul Smaczny.

Palestinian National Initiative: For background, see the PNI Web site: http://www.almubadara.org/new/english.php. A background article on PNI states that the organization "published its original manifesto in November, 2000 espousing a non-violent, non-militarized Intifada. It was established as a formal political group in June, 2002 by prominent Palestinian politicians, activists and academics, including Dr. Mustafa Barghouti, the late Prof. Edward Said, the late Dr. Haidar Abdel-Shafi and Ibrahim Dakkah . . . The PNI has emerged as an alternative to Fatah and Hamas, its platform calls for improved democratic governance within the PA, the establishment of a viable Palestinian state within the pre-1967 internationally recognized borders, the withdrawal of all Israeli occupation forces, and the recognition of the right of all Palestinian refugees to return to their homeland . . . Unlike the majority of Palestinian political factions, the PNI has no armed wing and practices peaceful resistance to the occupation—though it recognizes the right to resistance." "Factsheet: The Palestinian National Initiative and Dr. Mustafa Barghouti," Canadians for Justice and Peace in the Middle East, CJPME, Factsheet Series No. 80, May 2010, http://www.cjpmo.org/DisplayDocument.aspx?DocumentID=819

"It has the power to connect peoples" and "so much thirst for music": These quotes from Daniel are from the transcript of Paul Smaczny's documentary *Knowledge Is the Beginning*, about the formation of the West-Eastern Divan Orchestra. Smaczny generously provided me with numerous transcripts, both of the finished documentary and of raw footage.

Chapter 15: Jenin

Ramzi . . . sank into a deep depression: The story of Ramzi's depression, failed performance exam, and new exam at the conservatory in Cholet were recounted in interviews with Ramzi, François Hetsch, and Richard Lowry.

Leila Shahid: Leila Shahid was the representative of the PLO and then the Fatah in Paris from 1993 to 2005, at which point she was sent to Brussels (the parliamentary capital of the European Union) by the new Palestinian Authority of Mahmoud Abbas. See http://www.lalibertedelesprit.org/spip.php?article49

Wolf Prize for the Arts: Barenboim received the Wolf Prize on May 9, 2004, about eight months after Edward Said's death.

"Achievements in the interest of mankind and friendly relations among peoples": See "About," Wolf Foundation Web site (http://www.wolffund.org.il/index.php?dir=site&

page=content&cs=3000). See also "Daniel Barenboim Winner of Wolf Prize in Music, 2004," Wolf Foundation Web site (http://www.wolffund.org.il/index.php?dir=site&p age=winners&cs=397)

Violation of the country's informal ban of the music of the great composer Richard Wagner: "Wagner has become Mr. Barenboim's calling card," wrote James R. Oestreich in "Musing on the Barenboim X-Factor," *New York Times*, March 2, 2007, http://www.nytimes.com/2007/03/02/arts/music/02bare.html?n=Top% 2fReference%2fTimes%20Topics%2fPeople%2fB%2fBarenboim%2c%20Daniel. See also "Daniel Barenboim to Apologize, Receive Wolf Award," *Haaretz*, December 16, 2003, http://www.haaretz.com/news/daniel-barenboim-to-apologize-receive-wolf-award-1.108908; and "A Semiapologetic Barenboim to Get Israeli Prize After All," *New York Times*, December 17, 2003, http://www.nytimes.com/2003/12/17/ world/a-semiapologetic-barenboim-to-get-israeli-prize-after-all.html?n=Top% 2fReference%2fTimes%20Topics%2fPeople%2fB%2fBarenboim%2c%20Daniel

"Control yourselves, please!": A video of the speech is available at http://rutube.ru/ video/9b8eec2d5b68ad6101657add1aef2287/. See also "Barenboim's Attack on Israel Angers Katsav, Livnat," *Haaretz*, May 9, 2004, http://www.haaretz.com/news/ barenboim-s-attack-on-israel-angers-katsav-livnat-1.121922

Local Christians: See Mitri Raheb, *Palestinian Christians in the West Bank: Facts, Figures and Trends*, http://www.amazon.com/Palestinian-Christians-West-Bank-Figures/dp/1478397470

Nearly four thousand people had been killed in the Second Intifada: See "Intifada toll 2000–2005," BBC, http://news.bbc.co.uk/2/hi/middle_east/3694350.stm

Israel had assassinated Sheikh Ahmed Yassin: According to the Jewish Virtual Library, Sheikh Ahmed Yassin was "killed in an Israeli helicopter missile strike on his car as he was leaving a mosque in the northern Gaza Strip." See "Ahmed Yassin," Jewish Virtual Library, http://www.jewishvirtuallibrary.org/jsource/biography/yassin.html. See also "Hamas Founder Killed in Israeli Airstrike," CNN, http://www.cnn.com/2004/ WORLD/meast/03/21/yassin/; and "Hamas Chief Killed in Airstrike," BBC, http:// news.bbc.co.uk/2/hi/middle_east/3556099.stm, which mention the seven bystanders.

Abdel-Aziz Rantisi: See "Profile: Hamas Leader Rantisi," BBC News, April 17, 2004, http://news.bbc.co.uk/2/hi/middle_east/2977816.stm; and Derek Brown, "Abdel-Aziz al-Rantissi," the *Guardian*, April 19, 2004, http://www.theguardian.com/news/ 2004/apr/19/guardianobituaries.israel

Killing sixteen in a suicide bombing: See "16 Killed in Suicide Bombing on Buses in Israel," CNN, September 1, 2004, http://edition.cnn.com/2004/WORLD/ meast/08/31/mideast/; "Twin Blast Kills 16 in Israel; Hamas Claims Responsibility," *New York Times*, September 1, 2004, http://www.nytimes.com/2004/09/01/international/ middleeast/01mideast.html?pagewanted=2&_r=0); and "Be'er Sheva Bus Bombers Were Part of Hamas Cell in Hebron," *Haaretz*, September 1, 2004, http://www.haaretz.com/ news/be-er-sheva-bus-bombers-were-part-of-hamas-cell-in-hebron-1.133345

A violation of international humanitarian law: For further information, see: International Court of Justice,"Legal Consequences of the Construction of a Wall in Occupied Palestinian Territory," July 9, 2004, http://www.icj-cij.org/docket/index. php?pr=71&code=mwp&p1=3&p2=4&p3=6

"Demographic threat" to Israel: The political and intellectual arguments for Israeli separation from Palestinians on demographic grounds come largely from the demographer Arnon Sofer, professor at Haifa University, who is widely credited (or blamed) with convincing Prime Minister Ariel Sharon to begin construction of the separation barrier. Beyond just security, Sofer's reasons were demographic: Citing "the grave demographic data [that] were put on your desk many months ago," Sofer warned Sharon that, "In the absence of separation, the meaning of such a majority" of Arabs "is the end of the Jewish state of Israel." Hence the Israeli argument for a physical separation barrier, and for its twisting route that pays heed to Israeli demography rather than to the West Bank boundary. See *Haaretz*, June 27, 2002, http://www. haaretz.com/print-edition/features/a-jewish-demographic-state-1.41134. The article also states: "Richard Harris, the head of the planning department at the U.S. State Department, some time ago asked Arnon Sofer what percentage of his separation map is based on security and what percentage on demography. 'One hundred percent demography,' replied Sofer." Another influential figure advocating physical separation was Daniel Scheuftan, a senior policy advisor to Sharon and author of the influential book *Disengagement, Israel, and the Palestinian Entity* (from the Hebrew, Zmora-Bitan Publishers & Haifa University Press, 1999). According to Israeli analysts Gershon Baskin and Sharon Rosenberg, Scheuftan long advocated that Israel "should remove as many Palestinians as possible from the Israeli side." In "New Walls and Fences: Consequences for Israel and Palestine" (Center for European Policy Studies, June 2003), they write, "Scheuftan's book was adopted as the background for the separation policy adopted by Israel's National Security Council where Scheuftan serves as an advisor. This book seems to be the working manual for the IDF and wide Israeli political circles for the implementation and construction of the unilateral construction of walls and fences." See http://www.ceps.eu/files/book/1037.pdf; For an analysis of the demographics of separation, see also Max Blumenthal's *Goliath*, pp. 351–8.

85 percent of West Bank settlers: See the interview with Arnon Sofer in Mark Thomas's *Extreme Rambling*, p. 143: "My plan, the demarcation . . . was a great victory because eighty-five percent of all the settlers in the West Bank are now inside Israel; they are west of the Wall . . . Only by taking them back home and leaving the Palestinians can we live together."

Military siege had eased somewhat: This statement comes from personal observation and the experience of members of the French entourage, and Palestinian musicians affiliated with Ramzi's project. This is despite the rise in the number of rocket and mortar attacks from Hamas and the large number of political assassinations Israel continued to carry out. See Bader Araj and Robert J. Brym, "Opportunity, Culture and Agency: Influences on Fatah and Hamas Strategic Action During the Second

Intifada," *International Sociology* 25, no. 6 (November 2010), pp. 842–68, http://projects.chass.utoronto.ca/soc101y/brym/ArajBrymIntSoc.pdf

On a scorching day: The story of the musicians in Jenin in the summer of 2004 is told through more than a dozen interviews with musicians and other members of the French entourage that day, with Ramzi, and with Jenin resident Zakaria Zubeidi. A few of the quotes ("they are stressed," for example) are from the French documentary *It's Not a Gun*, by Hélèna Cotinier and Pierre-Nicolas Durand.

The people of Jenin camp had been under extreme stress: According to the UNRWA statistics, during the ten-day battle of Jenin, 52 Palestinians and 23 Israeli soldiers were killed, approximately 150 buildings were destroyed, and about 435 families were left homeless. See "Jenin Refugee Camp," UNRWA, November 24, 2009, http://www.unrwa.org/newsroom/features/jenin-refugee-camp. See also Human Rights Watch, "Jenin: IDF Military Operation, Summary," http://www.hrw.org/reports/2002/israel3/israel0502-01.htm#P49_1774. According to a U.N. report, the cost of the destroyed property was estimated at twenty-seven million dollars. "Illegal Israeli Actions in Occupied East Jerusalem and the Rest of the Occupied Palestinian Territory," Report of the Secretary-General Prepared Pursuant to General Assembly Resolution ES-10/10 (Report on Jenin), http://web.archive.org/web/20080911045522/http://www.un.org/peace/jenin/index.html

"Walking through walls": "This manoeuvre," wrote the Israeli architect Eyal Weizman in *Hollow Land*, p. 186, "turned inside to outside and private domains to thoroughfares. Fighting took place within half-demolished living rooms, bedrooms and corridors." Israeli Brigadier General Aviv Kovachi added: "This is why we opted for the method of walking through walls . . . Like a worm that eats its way forward, emerging at points and then disappearing. We were thus moving from the interior of homes to their exterior in unexpected ways and in places we were not anticipated, arriving from behind and hitting the enemy that awaited us behind a corridor . . . I said to my troops, 'Friends! This is not a matter of your choice! There is no other way of moving! If until now you were used to moving along roads and sidewalks, forget it! From now on we all walk through walls!'" "Walls," explains Eyal Weizman, "in the context of the Israeli-Palestinian conflict, have lost something of their traditional conceptual simplicity and material fixity, so as to be rendered—on different scales and occasions—as flexible entities, responsive to changing political and security environments; as permeable elements, through which both resistance and security forces literally travel; and as transparent mediums, through which soldiers can now see and through which they can now shoot." From Eyal Weizman, "Walking Through Walls: Soldiers as Architects in the Israeli Palestinian Conflict, *Public Space* (November 2005), http://www.publicspace.org/en/text-library/eng/b018-walking-through-walls-soldiers-as-architects-in-the-israeli-palestinian-conflict. For more, see also Amnesty International, "The Heavy Price of Israeli Incursions," http://www.amnesty.org/en/library/asset/MDE15/042/2002/en/cd1f0393-d85e-11dd-9df8-936c90684588/mde150422002en.html

Zakaria Zubeidi: "Shot dead" and other details in this article come from Christine Toomey, "Date with Terror," in the *Sunday Times* (London), June 11, 2006, http:// www.christinetoomey.com/pdfs/Zakaria_Zubeidi_Date_with_Terror.pdf. Additional details on his mother's death come from numerous sources, including "The Penitent of Jenin" from *Tablet: A New Take on Jewish Life*, September 21, 2012, http://www. tabletmag.com/jewish-news-and-politics/112489/the-baal-teshuva-of-jenin. My interviews with Zakaria were facicitated and translated by Nidal Rafa and Anan Abushanab.

Pulled out his nine-millimeter Smith & Wesson, ready to fight to the end: The details come from Christine Toomey's "Date with Terror."

Chapter 16: Oday

Neighborhood girls found Oday: The details from this section were gathered from my multiple interviews with Ramzi, Oday, and Oday's parents and brothers during several visits to the family home in Al Fawwar. Additional detail is gathered from the documentary *It's Not a Gun*.

On the walls of Oday's home: Details of the Khatib family home, and of their history, come from my multiple visits to the home and from interviews with Oday, his parents, and his brothers. The story of Oday's brother Rami Khatib and his foiled suicide attack came from my interview with Rami in the summer of 2012. Rami Khatib told me he had served his time for planning the attack and that he had no reservations in telling the story. For background on the families of suicide bombers, see Lamis Andoni, "Searching for Answers: Gaza's Suicide Bombers," *Journal of Palestine Studies*, Vol. 26, no. 4, Summer 1997, pp. 33–45.

Al Faluja: Details about Al Faluja village come from Walid Khalidi, et al., *All That Remains: The Palestinian Villages Occupied and Depopulated by Israel in 1948*, Institute for Palestine Studies (2006), pp. 95–7.

Rumors spread . . . of impending attacks: Details are from Walid Khalidi, et al., *All That Remains*, pp. 95–7. Benny Morris cites Moshe Sharett, the Israeli foreign minister, as saying the IDF was undertaking a covert "'whispering propaganda' campaign among the Arabs, threatening them with attacks and acts of vengeance by the army, which the civilian authorities will be powerless to prevent. This whispering propaganda (*ta'amulat lahash*) is not being done of itself. There is no doubt that here there is a calculated action aimed at increasing the number of those going to the Hebron Hills as if of their own free will, and, if possible, to bring about the evacuation of the whole civilian population . . ." (Sharett to Dori, 6 Mar. 1949, Israel State Archives FM 2425\7.) Cited by Morris in *The Birth of the Palestinian Refugee Problem Revisited* (Cambridge: Cambridge University Press, 2004), p. 523.

As for the village, all that remained: According to Benny Morris, the decision to destroy Al Faluja was made by Yitzhak Rabin on April 27, 1949. (Rabin to 3rd Brigade, 26 April 1949, IDFA 979\51\\17.) Cited by Morris in *The Birth of the Palestinian Refugee Problem Revisited*, p. 524.

Eighteen Moroccan Jewish families established the town of Kiryat Gat: See "Kiryat Gat," Jewish United Fund, http://www.juf.org/p2g/kiryat_gat.aspx. For the Intel factory, see Intel's Web site, "Israel Locations: Kiryat Gat," http://www.intel.com/content/www/us/en/jobs/locations/israel/sites/qiryat-gat.html

Yasser Arafat died: "Mr. Arafat, who was the symbol of the Palestinian revolution and aspiration for an independent state for some 40 years, died at about 3:30 a.m. Paris time of complications from an unknown disease after lingering in a coma for days, as his wife and closest aides struggled over his political and financial legacy," the *New York Times* stated on November 11, 2004 in "Arafat Dies at 75; No Sucessor Set; West Bank Burial," http://www.nytimes.com/2004/11/11/international/middleeast/11mideast.html

Murdered by poison: For more information about the investigations into Arafat's death, see: "Q&A: François Bochud on the Arafat Report," Al Jazeera, November 8, 2013, http://www.aljazeera.com/investigations/killing-arafat/qa-francois-bochud-arafat-report-2013117184743478799.html. See also "Yasser Arafat Wasn't Poisoned by Polonium, Russian Probe Concludes," Associated Press story at the Canadian Broadcasting Corporation Web site, December 26, 2013, http://www.cbc.ca/news/world/yasser-arafat-wasn-t-poisoned-by-polonium-russian-probe-concludes-1.2476563

"I regret that in 2000 he missed the opportunity to bring that nation into being": "Statement: Death of Yasser Arafat," Clinton Foundation, November 11, 2004, https://www.clintonfoundation.org/main/news-and-media/statements/statement-death-of-yasser-arafat.html

Israel would not allow it: "Aides Seeking Arafat Burial in West Bank," *New York Times*, November 9, 2004, http://www.nytimes.com/2004/11/10/international/middleeast/10arafat.html

His body was being lowered: Details from the BBC account can be found at http://news.bbc.co.uk/2/hi/4008731.stm

Oday's journey from the Holy Land: The story of Oday's trip to France is told through interviews with Oday, his parents, Ramzi, Yacine Laghrour, and several other French organizers and musicians.

Chapter 17: Celine

Celine Dagher took her seat: The story of Celine's connection to Ramzi's musical enterprise, and of her family history in Lebanon and France, is told from extensive interviews with her in Ramallah and in the family home in Bethune, France, where I met with her and Ramzi in February 2013. Celine's parents, who generously hosted me during my stay, filled in important details in the family biography. Ramzi also added many details.

Forge a new path: "Forging New Path, Sharon and Abbas Declare Truce," the *New York Times*, February 9, 2005, http://www.nytimes.com/2005/02/09/international/middleeast/09mideast.html

Killed five Israelis: "Suicide Bombing at Tel Aviv Stage Club," Israel Ministry of Foreign Affairs, February 25, 2005, http://mfa.gov.il/MFA/ForeignPolicy/Terrorism/Palestinian/Pages/Suicide-bombing-at-Tel-Aviv-Stage-Club.aspx; and Conal Urquhart, "Tel Aviv Bomb Rocks Peace Process," the *Guardian*, February 26, 2005, http://www.theguardian.com/world/2005/feb/26/israel

Secretly financing a new wave of settlements: Chris McGreal, "Israel Accused of Assisting Illegal Outposts," the *Guardian*, March 10, 2005, http://www.theguardian.com/world/2005/mar/10/israel

Many of whom ended up in the camps in Lebanon: For more information, see "Palestine Refugees in Lebanon," United Nations Department of Public Information, March 2003, http://www.un.org/Depts/dpi/palestine/ch4.pdf

Ramzi's return home: Ramzi's frequent comings and goings between France and Palestine became easier in 2004, after he received a ten-year French residency card. He had submitted the paperwork based on work contracts he had obtained through his band, Dalouna, and later his marriage certificate. The residency card was approved in 2004; this would lead, eventually, to a French passport for Ramzi.

Shin Bet: "Shin Bet: Palestinian Truce Main Case for Reduced Terror," *Haaretz*, January 2, 2006, http://www.haaretz.com/print-edition/news/shin-bet-palestinian-truce-main-cause-for-reduced-terror-1.61607. In addition, it was relatively easy to skirt the barriers, as thousands of Palestinians did on a regular basis, including an estimated fifteen thousand per week as undocumented laborers in Israel. See Ben Hubbard, "Palestinian Worker Killed as He Sneaks into Israel," October 3, 2010, http://www.washingtonpost.com/wp-dyn/content/article/2010/10/03/AR2010100300467.html

Next-door neighbors now had to travel miles: See "Portrait of a Palestinian Family Divided by Israel's Separation Barrier," Associated Press, April 30, 2014, http://www.haaretz.com/news/features/1.588138

Auden citation: See Bryan Magee's 2000 book, *The Tristan Chord: Wagner and Philosophy* (back cover).

Wagner's virulent anti-Semitism: For more on this subject, see the Web site Music and the Holocaust, "Richard Wagner, Music and the Holocaust," http://holocaustmusic.ort.org/politics-and-propaganda/third-reich/wagner-richard; and Magee, *The Tristan Chord*, pp. 343–80. For articles on the informal ban on Wagner's music in Israel, see, for example, "Israeli Orchestra Plays Wagner in Germany," *YNetnews*, July 26, 2011, http://www.ynetnews.com/articles/0,7340,L-4100550,00.html, and "Israel's History of Musical Controversy," the *Telegraph*, July 25, 2011, http://www.telegraph.co.uk/culture/music/classicalmusic/8659676/Israels-history-of-musical-controversy.html

"Descend to the level of those people who persecuted us": Daniel Barenboim and Edward Said, *Parallels and Paradoxes*.

Damascus Opera House: The story of Maria Arnaout and her departure from the Divan Orchestra comes from and is corroborated by multiple sources affiliated now or in the past with the Divan.

Shehada could not shake the memory: The 2002 death of Ali Mohammad Khalil Iqtheir, a sixth grader, was recounted in detail to me in several interviews with Shehada Shalalda. The specifics of Shehada's recollection are corroborated in every relevant detail by the Palestinian human rights group Al Haq, which recorded Ali's death at the time on a "Martyrdom Form." The Al Haq report on the death confirms that Ali was shot from about one hundred meters by three bullets fired from near an Israeli tank in Old Ramallah in April 2002. Other details from the report: "The place of the injury: In the head, mouth and throat . . . a heavy-caliber bullet exploded in the head and [was] fired from the tank in the area." The document was retrieved for me per my communication with Al Haq and translated from the Arabic by my West Bank researchers, Anan Abushanab and Eman Musleh.

"Residents of Ramallah, stay indoors!": Translation taken from the Second Intifada from the documentary film *Soraida: A Woman of Palestine*, https://www.nfb.ca/film/ soraida_a_woman_of_palestine

A ship bearing musical instruments: The story of the opening of Al Kamandjati is told from interviews with Ramzi, Celine, Oday, Jessie, Karim, Alá, the architect Khaldun Bshara, and a half dozen other musicians and supporters, and through the footage of the French documentary *It's Not a Gun*. The interviews with Alá and Oday were translated by Eman Musleh and Anan Abushanab, and in some cases by Nidal Rafa.

THIRD MOVEMENT: PRACTICE

Chapter 18: Beethoven

"The decision to go": This and other quotes from Daniel Barenboim in this chapter are taken largely from his memoir *Music Quickens Time*, pp. 49–71, especially pp. 64–5. The reaction of the musicians is taken from interviews with me, from Elena Cheah's 2009 biography of the Divan, *An Orchestra Beyond Borders*, and from Paul Smaczny's documentary about the Divan, *Knowledge Is the Beginning*.

Across the Allenby Bridge: The musicians were required to carry Spanish passports, because those from Lebanon and Syria would not have been allowed to go back home with an Israeli stamp in their passport.

Beaten by Israeli soldiers at a checkpoint: See http://pamolson.org/Week29.htm, the blog of Pamela Olson, one of Mustafa Barghouti's campaign organizers and author of the memoir *Fast Times in Palestine*.

Boycott, Divestment, and Sanctions: The "BDS Movement Call" was launched on July 9, 2005, about two months before the Divan concert in Ramallah. It stated that "embargoes and sanctions" against Israel "should be maintained until Israel meets its obligation to recognizing the Palestinian people's inalienable right to self-determination and fully complies with the precepts of international law . . ." Similarly, the 2005 Palestinian Civil Society call for BDS calls "upon international civil society organizations and people of conscience all over the world to impose broad boycotts and implement divestment initiatives against Israel similar to those applied to South Africa in the apartheid era ... We also invite conscientious Israelis to support this Call, for the sake of justice and genuine peace." According to www.bdsmovement.net, the Web site of the BDS movement, "Boycotts target products and companies (Israeli and international) that profit from the violation of Palestinian rights, as well as Israeli sporting, cultural and academic institutions." BDS also includes a cultural and academic boycott of Israeli universities and artistic institutions. "Israeli cultural and academic institutions directly contribute to maintaining, defending or whitewashing the oppression of Palestinians, as Israel deliberately tries to boost its image internationally through academic and cultural collaborations." The Divestment part of the BDS movement means "targeting corporations complicit in the violation of Palestinian rights and ensuring that the likes of university investment portfolios and pension funds are not used to finance such companies."

Wasn't normal at all: See, for example, Nicholas Rowe, "An Unfinished Symphony," *This Week in Palestine* 89 (September 2005), http://www.thisweekinpalestine.com/details.php?id=1419&ed=106&edid=106

"Before a Beethoven symphony": Daniel Barenboim, *Everything is Connected*, p. 85.

"A model of equality": Ibid., p. 84.

"Music is the language. It's a humanistic idea. That's exactly what Edward wanted.": This quote from Mariam Said came in an interview with me. See the Fundación Principe de Asturias Web site for more information at http://www.fpa.es/en/prince-of-asturias-awards/

"Chorus of clicking shutters": This and other details of the concert, including its capacity crowd and the quotation from Nabil Shaath, come from "Barenboim's Orchestra Plays for Peace in Ramallah," the *Guardian*, August 21, 2005. Other details come from interviews with Ramzi, Daniel, Mariam, Divan members, Elena Cheah's *An Orchestra Beyond Borders*, Paul Smaczny's documentary *Knowledge Is the Beginning*, and other eyewitness accounts.

Chapter 19: Al Kamandjati

The early days of Al Kamandjati, after its opening in summer 2005, are documented in multiple interviews with Ramzi; Celine; Elsa Ferrari; Samuel Tagardeau; Saed Karzoun; Alá, Rasha, and Shehada Shalalda; and numerous other of the school's teachers, students, and administrators.

Soldier lowered the Israeli flag: CNN, September 11, 2005, http://www.cnn.com/2005/WORLD/meast/09/11/gaza/

Bold move toward peace: See Ariel Sharon's obituary in the *New York Times*, http://www.nytimes.com/2014/01/12/world/middleeast/ariel-sharon-fierce-defender-of-a-strong-israel-dies-at-85.html

"Closed in after that withdrawal": See, for example, "Rice Warns Against Closing Off Gaza," Fox News, July 24, 2005, http://www.foxnews.com/story/2005/07/24/rice-warns-against-closing-off-gaza/

Continued its occupation of the territory: Some analysts saw the Gaza disengagement as part of a broader strategy of, essentially, remote control of the occupied territories. In *Hollow Land: Israel's Architecture of Occupation*, the Israeli architect Eyal Weizman writes: "The process of partial decolonization, which was recently embodied in the evacuation of the ground surface of Gaza and the building of the Wall in the West Bank, is indicative of an attempt to replace one system of domination with another. If the former system of domination relied upon Israeli territorial presence within Palestinian areas and the direct governing of the occupied populations, the latter seeks to control the Palestinians from beyond the envelopes of their walled-off spaces, by selectively opening and shutting the different enclosures, and by relying on the strike capacity of the Air Force over Palestinian areas" (p. 11).

"Open-air prison": See, for example, the BDS Movement's Campaign to End the Occupation, http://electronicintifada.net/content/talking-points-gaza-disengagement/5709

Complained Mahmoud Abbas: Mahmoud Abbas, "Is the Road Map at a Dead End?" the *Wall Street Journal*, October 20, 2005, http://online.wsj.com/news/articles/SB112977056304073951

"Geneva Initiative": See "Summary" at http://www.geneva-accord.org/mainmenu/summary

Soldiers of conscience: See "27 Reserve Pilots Say They Refuse to Bomb Civilians," the *New York Times*, September 25, 2003, http://www.nytimes.com/2003/09/25/world/27-israeli-reserve-pilots-say-they-refuse-to-bomb-civilians.html

Needed to act boldly: See "The Big Freeze," Ari Shavit's interview with top Sharon advisor Dov Weisglass, *Haaretz*, October 7, 2004, http://www.haaretz.com/the-big-freeze-1.136713

Dov Weisglass: See Ari Shavit, "Top PM Aide: Gaza Plan Aims to Freeze the Peace Process," *Haaretz*, October 6, 2004, retrieved from http://www.haaretz.com/print-edition/news/top-pm-aide-gaza-plan-aims-to-freeze-the-peace-process-1.136686

"Formaldehyde" for the peace process: For background on this strategy, see "The Big Freeze," http://www.haaretz.com/the-big-freeze-1.136713. Other analysts close to the situation also concluded that Sharon's pullout from Gaza, far from magnanimous, was part of a long-term strategy to kill the prospect of a Palestinian state. "I don't think the disengagement plan marked in any way the conversion by Sharon to the idea of an independent and viable Palestinian state," wrote outgoing United Nations envoy Alvaro de Soto, in a confidential memo obtained by the *Guardian*. "On the contrary, it was a spectacular move that basically killed and put into 'formaldehyde' the Road Map . . ." See http://image.guardian.co.uk/sys-files/Guardian/documents/2007/06/12/DeSotoReport.pdf

Has been removed indefinitely from our agenda: Weisglass's description of the Sharon vision bore strong resemblance to the "pastrami sandwich plan" Sharon had described in 1973 (Foundation for Middle East Peace, "Sharon's New Map," http://fmep.org/reports/archive/vol.-12/no.-3/sharons-new-map) to journalist Winston Spencer Churchill. In 2005, Sharon reiterated essentially the same strategy in an interview with an ultra-Orthodox Israeli newspaper. "The Americans have often asked us to sketch out the boundaries of the large settlement blocs in Judea and Samaria, and we have refrained from doing so in the hope that by the time the discussion on the settlement blocs comes, these blocs will contain a very large number of settlements and residents." The liberal *Haaretz* newspaper complained, "Building a security fence around those settlements, broadening their jurisdictions without consideration while chopping down olive groves and stealing private property shows that the need to be generous in withdrawal and the future settlement to enable the Palestinians to live honorably on their land has not been fully grasped yet on Israel's side." Rather, the settlements were "scattered throughout the heart of the Palestinian area [so as] to prevent any political agreement." (*Haaretz*, April 20, 2005, http://www.haaretz.com/print-edition/opinion/the-battle-for-the-fingernails-1.156571.) Yet this seemed to be precisely Sharon's "pastrami sandwich" strategy, which he had underscored repeatedly over the years, and which was celebrated by his staunchest supporters. "We break up Arab continuity and their claim to East Jerusalem by putting isolated Islands of Jewish presence in areas of Arab population," a pro-settlement party leader, Uri Bank, told the *Christian Science Monitor*. "Then we definitely try to put these together to form our own continuity. It's just like Legos—you put the piece out there and connect the dots. That is Zionism. That is the way the State of Israel was built." *Christian Science Monitor*, December 12, 2003, http://www.csmonitor.com/2003/1212/p06s01-wome.html/(page)/3.

"Stand up to the challenges of being free": Marie was protective of her privacy, and she turned down numerous requests to sit with me for an interview or to speak by phone. She did agree to answer a few questions via e-mail, and in one response, she said that in the weeks and years after her departure from Al Kamandjati she had "kept in mind all the children's faces, all the smiles, all the stories, all the encounters, all the good and bad times under curfews. That's why I put all my energy into Al Kamandjati."

In the alley near Sido's house: The story of Daniel Barenboim's visit to Ramzi's house in Al Amari was related to me by both men in interviews. Mariam Said also shared insight into the impact the visit had on Daniel.

"I wish . . . Edward were alive to see this": The story of Mariam and Daniel's visit to Al Kamandjati was relayed to me by Mariam and Ramzi. Ramzi told me of Mariam's comment, wishing Edward were alive to see Ramzi's music school; Mariam confirmed it.

Chapter 20: Andalucía

Capture of Gilad Shalit: For more details on Gilad Shalit's capture, see Ben Caspit, "Gilad Schalit's Capture: In His Own Words," *Jerusalem Post*, http://www.jpost.com/Defense/Gilad-Schalits-capture-In-his-own-words-308015

"No-go-zone": The unofficial but deadly restricted area, estimated between one hundred and five hundred meters but often identified as three hundred meters, was confirmed to me in personal communication by Norman H. Olsen, a former U.S. State Department counterterrorism official who served a total of nine years at the U.S. Embassy in Tel Aviv, including four years covering Gaza. In that capacity he made hundreds of trips to the territory, four years as the embassy's senior political officer, and one year as special advisor on the peace process to the American ambassador. See also "Life and Death in Gaza's Border Zone," +972 Magazine, February 19, 2014, http://972mag.com/photos-life-and-death-in-gazas-border-zone/87383/

Strongly pressured Fatah not to join: The refusal to engage Hamas was the politically popular position both within the United States and Israel, but some prominent Israelis, including former Mossad chief Ephraim Halevy, disagreed. "I believe there is a chance that Hamas, the devils of yesterday, could be reasonable people today. Rather than being a problem, we should strive to make them part of the solution," he said. See "Man in the Shadows: An Interview with Efraim Halevy," Opendemocracy.net, http://www.opendemocracy.net/conflict-debate_97/halevy_3490.jsp). See also "What If Israel Talked to Hamas?," the Wall Street Journal, August 1, 2007, http://online.wsj.com/news/articles/SB118593144036684212

"The Quartet": For verification of details and additional background, see the remarkably candid "End of Mission" report, a confidential memo by outgoing United Nations envoy Alvaro de Soto that was leaked to the Guardian. Though the United Nations, as part of the Quartet, supported the sanctions, de Soto strongly disagreed, saying (paragraphs 50 and 51) that the Quartet had been transformed from "a negotiating-promoting foursome guided by a common document (the Road Map) into a body that was all but imposing sanctions on a freely elected government of a people under occupation as well as setting unattainable preconditions for dialogue ... The steps taken by the international community with the presumed purpose of bringing about a Palestinian entity that will live in peace with its neighbour Israel have had precisely the opposite effect." See http://image.guardian.co.uk/sys-files/Guardian/documents/2007/06/12/DeSotoReport.pdf

"Meeting with a dietician": The remark was reported in Haaretz, February 16, 2006, http://www.haaretz.com/print-edition/news/u-s-backs-israel-on-aid-for-human itarian-groups-not-hamas-1.180287. Weisglass denied making the remark, in a meeting with Israel's foreign minister, but its substance was confirmed by several sources in a slightly different variation in various Israeli news media, including Ynet News, http://www.ynetnews.com/articles/0,7340,L-3216790,00.html, and in British media. It is highly unlikely that numerous journalists each with their individual sources would quote essentially the same thing for different news outlets.

[Ismail] Haniyeh sent President Bush an appeal: In the letter, which was sent through Jerome Segal, founder of the Jewish Peace Lobby and a senior research scholar at the Center for International and Strategic Studies at the University of Maryland, and delivered by Segal to officials at the State Department and National Security Council,

Haniyeh states: "We are so concerned about stability and security in the area that we don't mind having a Palestinian state in the 1967 borders and offering a truce for many years . . ." This, as Segal pointed out, could be seen as defacto recognition of Israel. See *Haaretz*, November 4, 2008, http://www.haaretz.com/print-edition/news/in-2006-letter-to-bush-haniyeh-offered-compromise-with-israel-1.257213

Segal corroborated these facts in personal correspondence with me on November 10, 2014. He provided me Haniyeh's original letter and his own cover letter to Secretary of State Rice. In the letter to Bush, Haniyeh wrote, "We are an elected government which came into office through a democratic process, and would like the United States to show respect for our people's choice." In Segal's letter to Rice, he requested a meeting with her or a senior State Department official "about the letter and the larger issues it raises." He faxed the correspondence to Rice's office and to the office of National Security Advisor Stephen Hadley, confirmed receipt, and resent the correspondence to each office. "I never got a reply from either," Segal wrote me.

Bolster Fatah's capabilities against Hamas: See David Rose, "Gaza Bombshell," in *Vanity Fair*, April 2008. In the article, citing original State Department documents, Rose describes "confidential documents, since corroborated by sources in the U.S. and Palestine, which lay bare a covert initiative, approved by Bush and implemented by Secretary of State Condoleezza Rice and Deputy National Security Adviser Elliott Abrams, to provoke a Palestinian civil war." In the article, Rose writes that "Beginning in the latter part of 2006, Rice initiated several rounds of phone calls and personal meetings with leaders of four Arab nations . . . She asked them to bolster Fatah by providing military training and by pledging funds to buy its forces lethal weapons . . . In late December 2006, four Egyptian trucks passed through an Israeli-controlled crossing into Gaza, where their contents were handed over to Fatah. These included 2,000 Egyptian-made automatic rifles, 20,000 ammunition clips, and two million bullets. News of the shipment leaked, and Benjamin Ben-Eliezer, an Israeli Cabinet member, said on Israeli radio that the guns and ammunition would give Abbas 'the ability to cope with those organizations which are trying to ruin everything'—namely, Hamas." Rose's conclusions were largely corroborated in a personal communication I had with a former State Department official with extensive experience in Gaza, who was based at the U.S. Embassy in Tel Aviv during the period in question.

Seven people, including three children, picnicking on a Gaza beach: "Death on the Beach: Seven Palestinians Killed as Israeli Shells Hit Family Picnic," *Guardian*, June 9, 2006, http://www.theguardian.com/world/2006/jun/10/israel

Forty per month: See paragraph 25 of the confidential internal memo sent by United Nations envoy Alvaro de Soto and published by the *Guardian*. Elsewhere in the report (paragraph 22) de Soto cites the targeted killings as a central reason for the rocket attacks. http://image.guardian.co.uk/sys-files/Guardian/documents/2007/06/12/DeSotoReport.pdf

Operation Summer Rains: For a summary of a United Nations investigation on the impact of Operation Summer Rains, see United Nations: "202 Palestinians

Killed Since Operation 'Summer Rain,'" as well as *Haaretz*, August 27, 2006, http://www.haaretz.com/news/un-202-palestinians-killed-since-operation-summer-rain-1.195904

Hamas would not release Shalit . . . for another five years: For more information on Gilad Shalit's release, see the Jewish Virtual Library, http://www.jewishvirtuallibrary.org/jsource/biography/Gilad_Shalit.html, and the article by political analyst Ronen Bergman, "Gilad Shalit and the Rising Price of an Israeli Life," the *New York Times*, November 9, 2011, http://www.nytimes.com/2011/11/13/magazine/gilad-shalit-and-the-cost-of-an-israeli-life.html

Killed three soldiers, and captured two others: According to a Human Rights Watch report on the Second Lebanese War, at around nine in the morning on July 12, 2006, "Hezbollah fighters crossed into Israeli territory and attacked an IDF convoy patrolling the border, killing three IDF soldiers and taking two captured IDF soldiers back into Lebanon." See "Why They Died: Civilian Casualties in Lebanon During the 2006 War," Human Right's Watch 19, no. 5E (September 2007), p. 37, http://www.hrw.org/sites/default/files/reports/lebanon0907.pdf

Israel retaliated with a massive air assault: "IDF warplanes began bombing bridges, roads, and suspected Hezbollah positions . . . Israel soon launched a country-wide offensive against Hezbollah," wrote Peter Bouckeart and Nadim Houry in "Why They Died: Civilian Casualties in Lebanon During the 2006 War," Human Rights Watch 19, p. 39. Israel imposed a total blockage on Lebanon on July 13, 2006, a blockade that continued until September. Israeli warplanes, according to *Why They Died*, "bombed the runways and fuel tanks of Beirut's international airport on the grounds that the 'airport is used as a central hub for the transfer of weapons and supplies to Hezbollah.'" According to a BBC report, Hezbollah launched seven thousand rockets into northern Israel. The death toll in Israel was forty-three civilians and twelve soldiers (HRW, p. 40); the BBC estimated that 915,762 people, or about 25 percent of the Lebanese population, were displaced during the war. See "Middle East Crisis: Facts and Figures, August 31, 2006," BBC News, http://news.bbc.co.uk/2/hi/middle_east/5257128.stm

Israel pledged to crush Hezbollah: "Hezbollah Warns Israel over Raids," BBC, July 12, 2006, http://news.bbc.co.uk/2/hi/middle_east/5173078.stm. See also *U.S. Air Force Magazine*, September 2011, "Behind Israel's 2006 War with Hezbollah," which states: "As Israel's counteroffensive progressed, Prime Minister Ehud Olmert declared his government's main goals as an unconditional return of the two kidnapped soldiers and a permanent removal of Hezbollah as a fighting force in southern Lebanon." See also the summary of Anthony Cordesman's book *Lessons of the 2006 Israeli–Hezbollah War*, which states Israel's goals as ranging "from crippling the Iranian influence in Lebanon, to ending Hezbollah's status as a 'state within a state,' to liberating two captured Israeli soldiers."

"Turn the clock in Lebanon back by twenty years": This was widely quoted. See "Capture of Soldier Was 'Act of War' Says Israel," the *Guardian*, July 12, 2006, http://www.theguardian.com/world/2006/jul/13/israelandthepalestinians.lebanon1

"**Birth pangs of a new Middle East**": For Condoleezza Rice's quote, see: CQ Transcripts Wire, July 21, 2006, http://www.washingtonpost.com/wp-dyn/content/article/2006/07/21/AR2006072100889.html

Beethoven's Ninth Symphony: For further discussion of the Ninth, see Harold C. Schonberg, *The Lives of the Great Composers* (London: Abacus, 1997), p. 122.

She did as she was told: From Elena Cheah, *An Orchestra Beyond Borders*, p. 4: "There were more Israeli than Spanish or Arab cellists in the section that year because of the war. They were deeply offended by the necklace. They insisted she remove it."

The arena held more than fourteen thousand: See Fiona Flores Watson, "Seville City-Plaza de Toros de la Maestranza," Andalucia.com, http://www.andalucia.com/cities/seville/bullring.htm

"**Support a war against one's own colleagues**": Elena Cheah, *An Orchestra Beyond Borders*, p. 5. The quotes from the Israeli musicians supporting the war are also from the Cheah account.

The tiny village of Qana: Details of the Qana bombing are taken from multiple sources, including the late *Washington Post* and *New York Times* correspondent Anthony Shadid's memoir *House of Stone* (pp. 3–4); a 2006 Human Rights Watch report, http://www.hrw.org/en/news/2006/08/01/israellebanon-qana-death-toll-28; and various news accounts, including from the *Telegraph* (UK), http://www.telegraph.co.uk/news/1525271/The-children-went-to-sleep-believing-they-were-safe.-And-then-Israel-targeted-them-as-terrorists.html, and BBC, http://news.bbc.co.uk/2/hi/middle_east/5228554.stm. The pajamas detail also comes from multiple sources, including the McClatchy News Service http://www.mcclatchydc.com/2006/07/30/14328_qana-victims-came-primarily-from.html and the Lebanese newspaper *As Safir*, http://arabist.net/blog/2006/7/30/pictures-from-qana.html

Ramzi went to Daniel: Ramzi's misgivings about staying in the Divan, given what was happening in Gaza and Lebanon, is documented through multiple interviews with Ramzi and with Mariam Said. His attempts to engage the Israeli members of the orchestra were also documented by Rajy Khaznadar, a Palestinian who grew up in Syria and who is a trombonist with the Divan Orchestra.

Cease-fire brokered by the United Nations: By August 13, 2006, both Hezbollah and Israel accepted UN Resolution 1701 and the U.N. call for a cease-fire report. See U.N. Security Council, 5511th Meeting, August 11, 2006, http://www.un.org/News/Press/docs/2006/sc8808.doc.htm, and Steven Erlanger's August 14 account, "Cease-Fire Begins After Day of Fierce Attacks," in the *New York Times*, http://www.nytimes.com/2006/08/14/world/middleeast/14mideast.html

Israel had failed in its central mission to destroy Hezbollah: For more information, see http://www.globalresearch.ca/israel-admits-that-the-justification-for-waging-the-2006-war-on-lebanon-was-fabricated/31884 and *Middle East Forum*, "How Israel Bungled the Second Lebanon War," http://www.meforum.org/1686/how-israel-bungled-the-second-lebanon-war

"We . . . order the said Jews and Jewesses of our kingdom to depart": See "The Edict of Expulsion of the Jews," translated from the Castilian by Edward Peters, Foundation for the Advancement of Sephardic Studies and Culture, http://www.sephardicstudies.org/decree.html.

The Muslims of Spain: See Roger Boase, "The Muslim Expulsion from Spain," *History Today* 52, no. 4 (2002), http://www.historytoday.com/roger-boase/muslim-expulsion-spain

Chapter 21: Palaces

Virtually sealed off by Israeli military order: In April 2007 an IDF commander declared Nablus, as well as sixteen other villages around Nablus, an "area of siege." See "Tightening the Siege on Nablus City and 15 Other Palestinian Villages Surrounding It," *Applied Research Institute-Jerusalem* (ARIJ), June 1, 2008, http://www.poica.org/details.php?Article=1195. See also "OPT: Israeli Lock-Down Cripples Nablus Economy," OCHA, February 5, 2007, retrieved from http://www.irinnews.org/fr/report/69930/opt-israeli-lock-down-cripples-nablus-economy

Bomb-making factories: See "IDF Finds Bomb Lab, Kills Terrorist in Nablus," *Israel Today*, June 29, 2007, http://www.israeltoday.co.il/NewsItem/tabid/178/nid/13272/Default.aspx

The Qasem Palace: Beit Wazan was one of twenty-four "throne villages" where nobility ruled from governates scattered across the central highlands of Palestine, now known as the West Bank. See Kamal Abdulfattah, "Throne Villages of the Highlands: Local Nobility and Their Mansions in Ottoman Palestine," *Near Eastern Archaeology* 70, no. 1 (March 2007), p. 4; and Salim Tamari, "The Last Feudal Lord in Palestine," *Jerusalem Quarterly*, Institute of Jerusalem Studies, November 16, 2002, http://www.jerusalemquarterly.org/images/ArticlesPdf/16_fendallord.pdf

The palaces were being renovated by Riwaq, the same Palestinian historical preservation center that designed Al Kamandjati's headquarters in Ramallah. The renovations were funded by the United Nations Development Program and the Swedish and German governments. They were part of a larger effort by Riwaq to assert Palestinian culture and identity in the face of "the alarming destruction of Palestine's cultural heritage" (http://www.riwaq.org/2010/index.php) owing in large part to the growing presence of Israeli settlers and military personnel in the West Bank.

Now it was time to try an overnight summer music camp: The story of the camp is told through interviews with Ramzi, Celine, Peter Sulski, Rasha, Alá, Shehada, Oday, Muntasser Jebrini, Fany Maselli, French cellist Étienne Cardoze, Riwaq architect Khaldun Bshara, and numerous other musicians. I also made my own visit, with researcher and field guide Eman Musleh, to the Qasem Palace itself, in the summer of 2011. There, architect Ali Shaban Hussein Abdelhamid, director of the Center for Urban and Regional Planning at An-Najah National University, whose office is in the palace courtyard, recalled the camp session and provided geographical and historical context.

Funeral of a hunter: For more on Mahler's First Symphony, see Tom Service, "Symphony Guide: Mahler's First," the *Guardian*, http://www.theguardian.com/music/tomserviceblog/2013/nov/12/symphony-guide-maher-first-tom-service

Dramatic evidence of the fragmentation of Palestine: The West Bank's divisions include Area A, "Palestinian autonomous areas," Area C, under Israel's full military control (and representing 60 percent of the West Bank), and Area B, joint jurisdiction. But even in Area A, Israel retains the right to enter for certain given security reasons. As Joel Beinin, professor of Middle Eastern History at Stanford University, pointed out in a personal communication, "There is no Palestinian sovereignty anywhere in the West Bank or Gaza Strip. Even in Area A, the PA does not exercise many of the most basic elements of sovereignty—control of entry and exit, currency, control of natural resources, et cetera."

The city . . . was ringed by fourteen Israeli settlements: For an overview of the physical obstructions set up by the Israeli government in the West Bank, see "Restriction of Movement: Checkpoints, Physical Obstructions, and Forbidden Roads," B'Tselem, January 16, 2011, http://www.btselem.org/freedom_of_movement/checkpoints_and_forbidden_roads; and the Refugee Review Tribunal (Australia), August 5, 2008, http://www.ecoi.net/file_upload/1997_1300358528_pse33593.pdf

Threats to Mahmoud Abbas: The Bush administration threats to Abbas, according to an American official stationed at the time at the U.S. Embassy in Tel Aviv, centered around their attempts to pressure Abbas to install Fatah strongman Mohammed Dahlan as interior minister, or face severe consequences.

"I like this violence": See paragraph 56, "End of Mission Report," a confidential memo from outgoing United Nations envoy Alvaro de Soto, which was leaked to the *Guardian*: http://image.guardian.co.uk/sys-files/Guardian/documents/2007/06/12/DeSotoReport.pdf. De Soto wrote that his U.S. counterpart "declared twice in an envoys meeting in Washington how much 'I like this violence,' referring to the near-civil war that was erupting in Gaza in which civilians were being regularly killed and injured, because 'it means that other Palestinians are resisting Hamas.'"

Despite American involvement in arranging arms shipments: See David Rose, "Gaza Bombshell," *Vanity Fair*, April 8, 2008. Rose cites confidential documents, including an "Action Plan for the Palestinian Presidency," which included funds for lethal weapons and thousands of additional security personnel. "From Hamas's perspective," Rose wrote, "the Action Plan could amount to only one thing: a blueprint for a U.S-backed Fatah coup." This scenario was essentially confirmed to me by a former U.S. official who was in the American Embassy in Tel Aviv at the time and followed these developments closely.

Israel's director of military intelligence: This conversation is detailed in a classified U.S. government document dated June 13, 2007. It was obtained by Wikileaks and is available at http://www.wikileaks.org/plusd/cables/07TELAVIV1733_a.html. In the document, U.S. Ambassador to Israel Richard Jones recounted his conversation with Amos Yadlin, Israel's director of military intelligence.

"Like a prayer book," "like a lifetime's journey": The violinist Jennifer Koh, quoted in "When Bach Laid Bare His Soul," the *New York Times*, October 21, 2011, http://www.nytimes.com/2011/10/23/arts/music/jennifer-koh-to-play-bachs-partitas-and-sonatas.html

"A whole world of the deepest thoughts and most powerful feelings": Brahms, in a letter to Clara Schumann. Quoted in "When Bach Laid Bare His Soul," the *New York Times*, October 21, 2011, http://www.nytimes.com/2011/10/23/arts/music/jennifer-koh-to-play-bachs-partitas-and-sonatas.html

"The incredible depth and mystery in his music that brings us close to the very nucleus of existence": The violinist Sigiswald Kuijken, quoted in "Titans Talk about the Bach Solo Violin Works," *All Things Strings*, January 2007, http://www.allthingsstrings.com/News/Interviews-Profiles/Titans-Talk-about-the-Bach-Solo-Violin-Works

"Perhaps the greatest example in any art form of a master's ability to move with freedom and assurance, even in chains": From the 1805 review of the sonatas and partitas by Johann Friedrich Reichard, quoted by John Mangum, "Sonata No. 3 for Violin," from the Web site of the Los Angeles Philharmonic, http://www.laphil.com/philpedia/music/sonata-no-3-for-solo-violin-johann-sebastian-bach

"Prevent terrorism against Israelis": Israeli government spokesman David Baker, quoted in "Fatah and Israel Butt Heads in Nablus," Isabel Kershner, the *New York Times*, November 13, 2007, http://www.nytimes.com/2007/11/13/world/europe/13iht-nablus.4.8319974.html

Caught in the middle: See Isabel Kershner, "Fatah and Israel Butt Heads in Nablus," the *New York Times*, November 13, 2007, http://www.nytimes.com/2007/11/13/world/europe/13iht-nablus.4.8319974.html

"I went to the Divan," Ramzi declared, "to make them take a stand.": The tensions between Ramzi and, in particular, Israeli members of the Divan, as well as with Daniel Barenboim and Mariam Said, are documented in interviews with more than a dozen members of the Divan in the summers of 2011 and 2012, in Cologne and London respectively, as well as in numerous conversations with Ramzi, Daniel, and Mariam.

"A six-meter concrete barrier is not a fence": In some areas the barrier reaches up to eight meters (twenty-five feet) high according to B'Tselem: "The Separation Barrier," http://www.btselem.org/separation_barrier

"Courage in the act of music-making": From Daniel Barenboim and Edward Said, *Parallels and Paradoxes.*

"The quality of freedom is not strained": Mark Berry, Boulezian (blog), "Salzburg Festival: West-Eastern Divan Orchestra/Daniel Barenboim, 13 August 2007," http://boulezian.blogspot.com/2007/08/salzburg-festival-west-eastern-divan.html; and the Presto Classical Web site, http://www.prestoclassical.co.uk/r/C%2BMajor/706608

Pathétique: For background on the *Pathétique*, see Thomas May, "About the Piece: Symphony No. 6, Pathétique," on the Web site of the Los Angeles Philharmonic, http://www.laphil.com/philpedia/music/symphony-no-6-pathetique-peter-ilyich-tchaikovsky

The BBC reported that "Israel built the settlement of Gilo on land it captured in 1967. It later annexed the area to the Jerusalem municipality in a move not recognised by the international community." See "Israel Approves 1,100 Settler Homes in Gilo, Jerusalem," BBC News, September 27, 2011, http://www.bbc.co.uk/news/world-middle-east-15080160. For more on the land seized from Palestinian villages, see Ibrahim Mater, "The Quiet War: Land Expropriation in the Occupied Territories," *Palestine-Israel Journal* 4, no. 2 (1997), http://www.pij.org/details.php?id=476, which states: "In August 1970, 13,000 dunums of land were seized for the building of four large fortress-like settlements. These include Ramot on Beit Iksa and Beit Hanina land; Gilo on land belonging to residents of Bethlehem, Beit Jala, Beit Safafa and Sharafat; East Talpiyot on Sur Baher land; and Neve Ya'acov on land owned by Beit Hanina residents."

See also "Gilo—'Jewish Neighbourhood' or Illegal Settlement?," PLO Negotiations Affairs Department, Media Brief, August 2010 (http://www.nad-plo.org/userfiles/file/media%20brief/Gilo%20Settlement%20Final%20II.pdf); Abraham Ashkenasi, ed., *The Future of Jerusalem*, p. 233; and "Impact of the Occupation," Beit Jala Municipality, http://www.vprofile.arij.org/bethlehem/pdfs/VP/Beit%20Jala_cp_en.pdf). For later confiscations from Beit Jala, see Charles Sennott, *The Body and the Blood*, p. 383.

Under international law: Article 49 of the Fourth Geneva Convention states, "The Occupying Power shall not deport or transfer parts of its own civilian population into the territory it occupies." See International Committee for the Red Cross, "Treaties and State Parties to Such Treaties," http://www.icrc.org/ihl/WebART/380-600038

Kyril no longer lived in Gilo: Years later, in London, Daniel grew irritated when asked about Kyril's settler status. "That's simply not true," he told me, riding in the backseat of a sedan after a Beethoven rehearsal at the Albert Hall. "Ramzi unfortunately says things which are not true. The person he's talking about lives in Portugal."

The legendary Jacqueline du Pré: See "Jacqueline du Pré, Noted Cellist, Is Dead at 42," *New York Times*, October 20, 1987, http://www.nytimes.com/1987/10/20/obituaries/jacqueline-du-pre-noted-cellist-is-dead-at-42.html

International marketing survey: "Survey: Israel Worst Brand Name in the World," *Israel Today*, November 22, 2006. The article refers to the National Brand Index, in which Israel placed last in terms of image, http://www.israeltoday.co.il/default.aspx?tabid=178&nid=10395

"We need a strategy" and **"A product undergoing an overhaul"**: Both quotes are from "Marketing a New Image," *Jewish Week*, January 20, 2005. See also "Israel Aims to Improve Its Public Image," *Jewish Daily Forward*, October 14, 2005, http://forward.com/articles/2070/israel-aims-to-improve-its-public-image/

"Refusenik" orchestra: "Refuseniks," in the Israeli context, are Israeli conscientious objectors who refuse on ethical or moral grounds to serve in the Israel Defense Forces, usually because of the IDF's occupation of the Palestinians or its wars in Gaza or elsewhere. In many cases the refuseniks are willing to go to Israeli prison rather than serve in the armed forces. See, for example, "Life of an IDS 'refusenik,'" *Jewish Journal*, January 16, 2013, http://www.jewishjournal.com/israel/article/life_of_an_idf_refusenik

"It is a great honor to be offered a passport": "Israeli Pianist Barenboim Takes Palestinian Passport," *Ynet News*, January 14, 2008, http://www.ynetnews.com/articles/0,7340,L-3493612,00.html

Chapter 22: Luthier

Flying checkpoints: According to B'Tselem, in addition to fixed checkpoints, the "Israeli military erects hundreds of surprise flying checkpoints along West Bank roads. In December 2013 the UN Office for the Coordination of Humanitarian Affairs (OCHA) counted 256 flying checkpoints as compared with . . . 340 in March 2012. OCHA counted a monthly average of . . . 495 surprise checkpoints from January 2011 through September 2011 as compared with a monthly average of 351 surprise checkpoints for the years 2009–2011 and 65 surprise checkpoints from September 2008 through March 2009." See "Restriction of Movement," B'Tselem, http://www.btselem.org/freedom_of_movement/checkpoints_and_forbidden_roads. The story of the flying checkpoints was relayed to me in several interviews with Rasha and Alá Shalalda, and with Muntasser Jebrini.

Ninety per week: Checkpoint and settlement statistics in this paragraph come from "OCHA Closure Update: Occupied Palestinian Territory," United Nations Office for the Coordination of Humanitarian Affairs, April 30–September 11, 2008, http://www.ochaopt.org/documents/ocha_opt_closure_update_2008_09_english.pdf

Protect Israeli lives: For example, Israeli authories said at Huwara they had apprehended a teenager hiding a pipe bomb and a twelve-year-old wearing a suicide belt. See "Myths and Facts: Chapter 16, the Palestinian War (Al Aqsa Intifada)," Jewish Virtual Library, http://www.jewishvirtuallibrary.org/jsource/myths3/MFintifada.html#_edn11

What was once justified: "OCHA Closure Update: Occupied Palestinian Territory," April 30–September 11, 2008.

Infamous Huwara checkpoint: See Gideon Levy, "Twilight Zone/Good Riddance," *Haaretz*, February 18, 2011, http://www.haaretz.com/weekend/magazine/twilight-zone-good-riddance-1.344204; and a short video about the Huwara checkpoint, meant for IDF training, but leaked and published by a group of former Israeli soldiers known as Breaking the Silence (https://www.youtube.com/watch?v=dtTL32Gkb40).

Metastasizing liver cancer: The cancer patient's name was Tayseer Al-Qaisi (sometimes spelled Taysir Kaisi). Multiple accounts of the incident can be found from

Al Jazeera reporter David Chater (http://www.aljazeera.com/news/middleeast/2008/01/20085251343467934.html) and *Haaretz*'s Gideon Levy (http://www.haaretz.com/weekend/magazine/the-twilight-zone-by-the-book-1.211667).

"El Helwadi," or "The Beautiful Girl," a song by Sayed Darwish: For the complete lyrics to "El Helwadi" see http://www.arabiclyrics.net/Sayed-Darwish/El-Helwa-Di.php

Israeli engineers had drawn up plans for tunnels and bridges: During 2007 and 2008, I interviewed several prominent Israelis who were drawing up maps designed to keep most of the West Bank in Israeli hands permanently, or at least for the foreseeable future. One was Knesset member Otniel Schneller, who discussed tunnels and "flyover" ramps and bridges to ferry Palestinians under and around major settlements, which would stay in place. Another was Major-General Uzi Dayan, the hard-line former head of Israel's National Security Council, whose alternative plan would have allowed Israel to keep two thirds of the West Bank, leaving the Palestinians with about 7 percent of historic Palestine. In an interview, Dayan told me the plan would be unilateral and "temporary." When I asked him whether such a plan could ever be acceptable to the Palestinians, the general shrugged. "I say if [the Palestinians] don't want it, [they] can stay in the position of today. That's okay. It's not a dream of the Palestinians, I know, but it's better than the present situation."

"Honest broker": During the negotiations, the United States adopted Israel's position that the right of Palestinians to return to their ancestral lands, as guaranteed by United Nations Resolution 194, was not possible, because it would threaten the Jewishness of Israel. The ethnic-purity argument made Secretary of State Rice, an African American who grew up in Jim Crow Alabama, queasy. "I must admit that though I understood the argument intellectually, it struck me as a harsh defense of the ethnic purity of the Israeli state," Rice recalled in her memoir, *No Higher Honor*, p. 282. "It was one of those conversations that shocked my sensibilities as an American. After all, the very concept of 'American' rejects ethnic or religious definitions of citizenship. Moreover, there were Arab citizens of Israel. Where did they fit in?" Nevertheless, the secretary "took a deep breath and tried to understand, and slowly I came to see [that Israel] was the fulfilment of a long historical and religious journey . . ." Denying the Palestinian right of return, she wrote, "would allow the democratic state of Israel to be 'Jewish.'"

"Then you won't have a state!": Rice's comment echoed Clinton's at Camp David in that both admonished Ahmed Qurei, or Abu Ala, for refusing to accept major Israeli settlements in the midst of a would-be Palestinian state. This and other revelations (including Rice's proposal that Palestinian refugees be moved to Chile and Argentina in a final settlement) can be found in "The Palestine Papers," a trove of more than sixteen thousand leaked official documents contained on the Web sites of the *Guardian* (http://www.theguardian.com/world/palestine-papers) and Al Jazeera (http://www.aljazeera.com/palestinepapers/). Rice's "You won't have a state!" comment is archived at http://www.aljazeera.com/palestinepapers/2011/01/2011122112512844113.html and was

sourced widely, including in the *Jerusalem Post*, January 14, 2011, http://www.
jpost.com/Middle-East/Abbas-We-cant-expect-Israel-to-take-in-a-million-refugees.
For Rice's South America proposal, see "Condoleezza Rice: Send Palestinian Refugees
to South America," the *Guardian*, http://www.theguardian.com/world/2011/jan/24/
condoleezza-rice-palestinian-refugees-south-america

The negotiations, once again, collapsed: See "The Palestine Papers," Al Jazeera (http://
www.aljazeera.com/palestinepapers/) and *Guardian* (http://www.theguardian.com/
world/palestine-papers). As for the collapse of the 2008 talks, a Palestinian spokesmen
cited the proposed solution's lack of "territorial continuity." See *Haaretz*, August 12,
2008, http://www.haaretz.com/news/pa-rejects-olmert-s-offer-to-withdraw-from-93-
of-west-bank-1.251578

Chapter 23: Fire

"You cannot just land blows": The quote from Zakai comes from "Can the First Gaza
War Be Stopped Before It Starts?," *Haaretz*, December 22, 2008, http://www.haaretz.
com/news/can-the-first-gaza-war-be-stopped-before-it-starts-1.260017

Killed six Hamas operatives: Rory McCarthy, "Gaza Truce Broken as Israeli Raid Kills
Six Hamas Gunmen," the *Guardian*, November 5, 2008, http://www.theguardian.
com/world/2008/nov/05/israelandthepalestinians

Israel launched a massive military retaliation: "Israel's technological superiority
and reliance on heavy armor and firepower contributed to a wide disparity in
casualties—approximately 1,440 Palestinians have died (with some organizations
estimating that at least half of the dead are civilians), compared with thirteen
dead (including four civilians) on the Israeli side." See "Israel and Hamas: Conflict
in Gaza (2008–2009)," Congressional Research Service, February 19, 2009, p. 2,
http://www.fas.org/sgp/crs/mideast/R40101.pdf. According to Human Rights
Watch, seven hundred Palestinian civilians died and only three Israelis (http://www.
hrw.org/features/israel-gaza). See also "Palestinians: 1,300 Killed, 22,000 Buildings
Destroyed in Gaza," CNN, January 19, 2009, http://edition.cnn.com/2009/
WORLD/meast/01/19/gaza.war/index.html

Fourteen children taking refuge near a U.N. school: "Cast Lead: 14 Children Killed
in Attack on UNRWA School," Defence for Children International, http://www.
dci-pal.org/english/display.cfm?DocId=928&CategoryId=1

Izzaldeen Abu al-Aish: The loss of the doctor's three daughters and a niece is detailed
in an AP account of January 17, 2009, http://www.haaretz.com/news/israeli-trained-
gaza-doctor-loses-three-daughters-and-niece-to-idf-tank-shell-1.268315. See also
"The Journey of Ezzeldeen Abu al-Aish" in the London-based pan-Arab newspaper
Asharq Al-Awsat, and in Max Blumenthal's *Goliath*, pp. 13–14.

The school, not related to Al Kamandjati, was demolished: "Palestinians: 1,300
killed, 22,000 buildings destroyed in Gaza," CNN, January, 2009, http://edition.cnn.
com/2009/WORLD/meast/01/19/gaza.war/index.html

"Going wild": *Independent*, January 13, 2009, http://www.independent.co.uk/news/world/middle-east/israeli-cabinet-divided-over-fresh-gaza-surge-1332024.html

During a winter tour: According to Clemency Burton-Hill, occasional guest member of the West-Eastern Divan Orchestra: "Between a surreal backstage audition in December, and the day we all converged in early January 2009, Israel launched its Operation Cast Lead offensive against Gaza. The tour was thrown into jeopardy: scheduled concerts in Qatar and Egypt were cancelled after security threats and some Arab members threatened a boycott. Barenboim e-mailed us all on New Year's Eve expressing the heightened importance of meeting during 'this difficult time,' and the tour went ahead." Clemency Burton-Hill, "Sound and Fury," *FT Magazine*, July 1, 2011, http://www.ft.com/cms/s/2/60ab4264-a1f6-11e0-b485-00144feabdc0.html#axzz35AdYF5NU

"We, the members of the West-Eastern Divan Orchestra": The statement was provided by Carsten Siebert, managing director of the Barenboim-Said Foundation in Berlin, via Mariam Said.

Siege of Gaza: For more, see the International Red Cross article on this issue: "Gaza Closure: Not another year!" ICRC, June 14, 2010, http://www.icrc.org/eng/resources/documents/update/palestine-update-140610.htm. According to this article, "Although about 80 types of goods are now allowed into Gaza—twice as many as a year ago—over 4,000 items could be brought in prior to the closure. Generally, the price of goods has increased while their quality has dropped."

Fadi Basha: Julia Katarina's introduction to Fadi Basha, her star student, occurred slightly after the events described in this chapter. For narrative flow, as with a small handful of other instances noted elsewhere here, I have placed their meeting in this chapter.

"There's been a fire": The story of the fire at Al Kamandjati's Jenin center is told through more than a dozen interviews, including with Ramzi, Celine, Iyad Staiti, Alice Howick, Ben Payen, Maddalena Pastorelli, and student Rasha Doulani, and was further corroborated through access to a trove of digital photographs from the day of the fire, and after.

Chapter 24: Birth

Nonviolent protests against the occupation: "Is This Where the Third Intifada Will Start?," *New York Times Magazine*, March 17, 2013, http://www.nytimes.com/2013/03/17/magazine/is-this-where-the-third-intifada-will-start.html

Carter wrote: "In Palestinian villages, non-violent protesters show the way," Jimmy Carter, February 15, 2010, http://theelders.org/article/palestinian-villages-non-violent-protesters-show-way

Policy of good governance: *Financial Times*, April 12, 2010, http://www.ft.com/intl/cms/s/0/715feb10-4643-11df-8769-00144feab49a.html#axzz375BRaPmg

Funds from the United States, the European Union, and the Gulf States: The 2007 "Paris Donors Conference" secured significant funds for the Palestinian Authority. See *Guardian*, December 17, 2007, http://www.theguardian.com/world/2007/dec/17/france.israel

Fayyad worked closely with an American general: Much of Fayyad's actions received attention in 2010 and after, though he was reappointed as Palestinian prime minister in May 2009, shortly before Obama's Cairo speech. For a comprehensive examination of the role played by Keith Dayton, and the steps toward statehood taken by Salam Fayyad, see Nathan Thrall, "Our Man in Palestine," *New York Review of Books*, October 14, 2010, http://www.nybooks.com/articles/archives/2010/oct/14/our-man-palestine/

"Professionalize" the Palestinian Authority's security forces: "International Intervention and the Israeli-Palestinian Peace Process," Chatham House Briefing Paper, February 2010, https://www.chathamhouse.org/sites/files/chathamhouse/public/Research/Middle%20East/bp0210peters.pdf

Ten thousand Palestinians received training: Ten thousand is a figure as of 2013. See "Securing Oslo: The Dynamics of Security Coordination in the West Bank," *Middle East Report* (Middle East Research and Information Project), Winter 2013, p. 269.

The rosy image of the "new men": Dayton speech to the conservative Washington Institute for Near East Policy, May 7, 2009, http://www.washingtoninstitute.org/html/pdf/DaytonKeynote.pdf

Credible reports of torture by PA security forces: See, for example, Human Rights Watch, "West Bank: Reports of Torture in Palestinian Detention," October 2010, http://www.hrw.org/news/2010/10/20/west-bank-reports-torture-palestinian-detention

Targets of stone-throwing shabab: See, for example, "Securing Oslo," p. 269.

The United States had applied financial leverage on Israel: In 1992, U.S. Secretary of State James Baker threatened to withdraw ten billion dollars in loan guarantees to Israel unless "there is a halt or end to settlements activity." See "Baker Bars Israeli Loan Aid Unless Settlements Are Halted," *Washington Post,* February 25, 1992. See also "Israel Must Freeze Settlements to Get Loans, Baker Says," *Los Angeles Times*, February 25, 1992, http://articles.latimes.com/1992-02-25/news/mn-2625_1_loan-guarantees

Cautiously optimistic: See Ghassan Khatib, "Waiting Expectantly," at Bitterlemons.org, http://www.bitterlemons.org/previous/bl080609ed22.html#pal1

"It's normal": Visitors to the West Bank are often surprised to learn of Israeli raids in Ramallah and other semiautonomous parts of Area A, which is nominally under the control of the Palestinian Authority. But such raids are frequent, especially in the early hours of the morning when Israeli forces, who ordinarily notify Palestinian security, enter Ramallah and elsewhere in Area A. This conclusion comes from numerous interviews I've done over the years, especially in Ramallah. See also Radio France Internationale, "Israel Raids West Bank Human Rights Group," December 12, 2012, http://www.english.rfi.fr/middle-east/20121212-israel-raids-offices-human-rights-group-west-bank

Chapter 25: Sebastia

Ramzi slowed as his SUV approached a military kiosk: I accompanied Ramzi, Celine, and baby Hussein on the journey from Ramallah to Sebastia and back in the summer of 2010.

"Effectively push Palestinians off their land and allow the expansion of Israeli sovereignty": *Our Harsh Logic*, p. 3.

Encircled by checkpoints and concrete barriers: The village itself is in Area B, but the historical sites are in Area C, which prevents Palestinians from accessing them and discourages tourists from actually venturing into Sebastia. See Dalia Hatuqa, "Ancient Palestinian Village Threatened by Israeli Settlement," *Al-Monitor*, http://www.al-monitor.com/pulse/originals/2013/03/ancient-sebastia-threatened-israeli-settlement.html. See also "A Happy Id al Fitr in Sebastia," *Jerusalem Post*, April 11, 2005, http://www.jpost.com/Middle-East/A-happy-Id-al-Fitr-in-Sebastia; and "Holy Land Blues," *Al-Ahram Weekly*, January 5–11, 2006, http://weekly.ahram.org.eg/2006/776/feature.htm, which states: "Long before Israel blocked the roads—with mounds, moats or wire—Sabastiya was a busy tourist attraction, drawing in 15–20 coach-loads from across Palestine and numerous private cars from all over the region."

This outpost was illegal: The Israeli government's opinions on Israeli outposts can be seen at http://www.mfa.gov.il/mfa/aboutisrael/state/law/pages/summary%20of%20opinion%20concerning%20unauthorized%20outposts%20-%20talya%20sason%20adv.aspx

His green West Bank identification card: In "Qalandia Checkpoint: The Historical Geography of a Non-Place," *Jerusalem Quarterly* 42 (Summer 2010), Helga Tawil Souri writes: "Behind checkpoints is a suffocating bureaucracy of restriction on movement that is daunting and complicated for a Palestinian to navigate. First, a person needs an identification card, which can only be obtained at the Israeli Civil Administration office of one's region (which usually requires passing a checkpoint). Second, a person needs to obtain a crossing permit to pass (often between two Palestinian towns), which requires that some institution apply on that person's behalf; that the permit gets sent through the proper bureaucratic channels; that it gets approved by the Israeli Civil Administration; and that the person applying go pick it up (which often requires passing a checkpoint with proper documentation already in hand). In the words of Machsomwatch, the Israeli checkpoint watchdog group, 'every movement by Palestinians from place to place, for whatever purpose, is [. . .] in itself [. . .] not a simple action for people whose freedom of movement is restricted . . . At the end of this torturous obstacle race, there is no certainty that the person will actually receive the permits they require.'"

Nearby stood the ruins of a Crusader church: For more on the history of the village of Sebastia, see "Sebaste, Holy Land," Atlas Tour, http://www.atlastours.net/holyland/sebaste.html; and Michael Hamilton Burgoyne and Mahmoud Hawari, "Bayt al-Hawwari, a Hawsh House in Sabastiya," *Levant* 37 (2005), pp. 57–80.

"Price tag attacks": See "Settler Violence: Lack of Accountability," B'Tselem, June 3, 2012. A list of "price tag" attacks appears on Wikipedia at http://en.wikipedia.org/wiki/List_of_Israeli_price_tag_attacks

Zatara checkpoint: The circumstances at Zatara checkpoint came from personal observation and were verified by personal communication from Machsom ("Checkpoint") Watch, an Israeli human rights organization.

Gaza Freedom Flotilla: See "Israeli Attack on Gaza Flotilla Sparks International Outrage," *Guardian*, May 31, 2010, http://www.theguardian.com/world/2010/may/31/israeli-attacks-gaza-flotilla-activists; "Gaza Flotilla," *Haaretz*, http://www.haaretz.com/misc/tags/Gaza%20flotilla-1.476996; and "Gaza Flotilla Incident: Resource Page," Jewish Federations of North America, http://www.jewishfederations.org/page.aspx?id=221602

"Execution-style" killings: A United Nations fact-finding mission concluded (paragraph 170): "The circumstances of the killing of at least six of the passengers were in a manner consistent with an arbitrary, extra-legal and summary execution." United Nations General Assembly, Human Rights Council, Fifteenth Session, September 27, 2010, http://www2.ohchr.org/english/bodies/hrcouncil/docs/15session/A.HRC.15.21_en.pdf. See also "Turkey Flotilla Inquiry: Activists Killed 'Execution Style,'" Tikun Olam (blog of Richard Silverstein), http://www.richardsilverstein.com/2011/02/12/turkey-flotilla-inquiry-activists-killed-execution-style/; and the *Guardian*, February 12, 2011, http://www.theguardian.com/world/2010/jun/04/gaza-flotilla-activists-autopsy-results

Drew widespread international condemnation: For a chronology of these actions, see the BDS timeline, http://www.tiki-toki.com/timeline/entry/28282/BDS-Movement#vars!date=2007-01-07_22:22:30!

"Show Israel's prettier face": See "After Gaza, Israel Grapples with Crisis of Isolation," the *New York Times*, March 18, 2009, which states: "'We will send well-known novelists and writers overseas, theater companies, exhibits,' said Arye Mekel, the ministry's deputy director general for cultural affairs. 'This way you show Israel's prettier face, so we are not thought of purely in the context of war.'"

Caterpillar, makers of the D9 bulldozer: See, for example, the University of Wisconsin's financial circular, "Caterpillar and Human Rights in Israel," http://www.advantagewisconsin.edu/tfunds/Caterpillar2004.htm

Ahava: For background on Ahava, see http://www.stolenbeauty.org, or "West Bank's Ahava Muddies Address as EU Boosts Israel Rules," an economic analysis in Bloomberg News, http://www.bloomberg.com/news/2013-08-14/west-bank-cosmetics-maker-muddies-address-as-eu-boosts-sanctions.html

Threw settlement-made products into a large bonfire: See "Fayyad Helps Burn Settlement Products," *Ynet News*, January 5, 2010, http://www.ynetnews.com/articles/0,7340,L-3830147,00.html

Its tour of South America and the Caribbean: See Daniel Barenboim's Web site for a description of the orchestra's tour in South America, http://www.danielbarenboim.

com/index.php?id=80&tx_ttnews[tt_news]=406&cHash=c6d0ed2583cfd5dbb4bade
ec345134bd

The Palestine National Orchestra: For more on the PNO, see http://ncm.birzeit.edu/
en/page/palestine-national-orchestra

"Today an orchestra, tomorrow, a state": See *Haaretz*, "Today an Orchestra, Tomorrow
a Palestinian State," January 5, 2011, http://www.haaretz.com/print-edition/opinion/
today-an-orchestra-tomorrow-a-palestinian-state-1.335299

Israeli-issued Christmas travel permits: See, for example, Daoud Kuttab, "Palestinian
Christians Surprised to Receive Travel Permits," *Al-Monitor*, June 3, 2013, http://www.
al-monitor.com/pulse/originals/2013/06/palestinian-christians-travel-permits.html

FOURTH MOVEMENT: RESISTANCE

Chapter 26: Fractures

Ramzi rode in the backseat of an orange taxi: I accompanied Ramzi on his journey to
the Jordan Valley, then on to Amman, Beirut, and back, in the summer of 2011.

Shot point-blank in the head: See "Israeli Actor Juliano Mer-Khamis Shot Dead
in Jenin," *Haaretz*, April 4, 2011, http://www.haaretz.com/news/national/israeli-
actor-juliano-mer-khamis-shot-dead-in-jenin-1.354044; "Actor Juliano Mer-Khamis
Gunned Down in Jenin," *Jerusalem Post*, April 4, 2011, http://www.jpost.com/
National-News/Actor-Juliano-Mer-Khamis-gunned-down-in-Jenin; and "Jenin's
Freedom Theatre: From Death and Destruction, a Message of Hope," *Guardian*,
March 3, 2014, http://www.theguardian.com/stage/2014/mar/03/freedom-theatre-
palestinian-refugee-camp-jenin-uk-tour

"Delegitimization challenge": See "The Delegitimization Challenge: Creating a
Political Firewall," Reut Institute, February 14, 2010, http://reut-institute.org/
Publication.aspx?PublicationId=3769

Drawing sharp rebuke from many Israeli critics: The Knesset law is "one of the most
anti-democratic measures in the country's history," according to an article in *+972
Magazine*. See "What Is the Anti-Boycott Law? Who Does It Affect?," http://972mag.
com/anti-boycott-law-to-pass-knesset/

Israel had destroyed twenty-six thousand Palestinian homes: More than half of the
demolitions, according to an Israeli human rights group, have been to facilitate military operations in Gaza and the West Bank, "such as clearing a piece of land to make
way for military vehicles or other such purposes." See "No Home, No Homeland,"
Israeli Committee Against Housing Demolition, December 2011, http://www.icahd.
org/sites/default/files/No%20Home%20No%20Homeland%20V2.0%20(3).pdf

The indigenous Palestinian population of the Jordan Valley had shrunk: See: "Restricted
Access and Its Consequences: Israeli Control of Vital Resources in the Jordan Valley and
Its Impact on the Environment," Ma'an Development Centre, 2011, downloadable at

http://www.badil.org/related-news/3348-8=12=2001 "Humanitarian Fact Sheet on the Jordan Valley and the Dead Sea Area," United Nations, Office for the Coordination of Humanitarian Affairs Occupied Palestinian Territories, February 2012, http://www.europarl.europa.eu/meetdocs/2009_2014/documents/dplc/dv/dead_sea_/dead_sea_en.pdf; and "Parallel Realities: Israeli Settlements and Palestinian Communities in the Jordan Valley," Ma'an Development Center, 2012.

Qalandia offered commercial flights to Lebanon: "'Qalandiya Airport received daily flights from all the capitals of the world.' Muhammad Al-Qutob joyfully remembers these days preceding the fall of Jerusalem during the Six-Day War in the summer of 1967. 'Kings, heads of states, dignitaries, and great actors and singers visited Jerusalem through Qalandiya.'" See Ali Qleibo, "Jerusalem 1948–1967: La Dolce Vita," *This Week in Palestine*, http://archive.thisweekinpalestine.com/details.php?id=4216&ed=228&edid=228, p. 1; and Nahed Awwad's lovely piece, "In Search of Jerusalem Airport," *Jerusalem Quarterly* 35, pp. 51–63, http://www.jerusalemquarterly.org/images/ArticlesPdf/35_airport.pdf

Impossible to travel between Palestine and Lebanon: According to a Lebanese government Web site: "Restricted Entry: The Government of Lebanon refuses entry to holders of Israeli passports, holders of passports containing a visa for Israel, valid or expired, used or unused and passports with entry stamps to Israel." See "Visa Information and Passport Requirements," *Lebanon Tourism*, http://www.lebanontourism.com/TravelerTools/visa.asp.

Slaughtered by a Lebanese Christian militia: For more information on the Phalangists and the Sabra and Shatila massacre, see the notes for Chapter 3: Uprising.

Alice had been working in Shatila camp with an eleven-year-old boy: For more on Abdallah Qasweh's story, see my piece, "Beethoven in Shatila," *Ramallah Café*, http://ramallahcafe.com/?p=297

Chapter 27: Unity

Some audience members fainted or fell ill: "I know of some, and have heard of many, who could not sleep after it, but cried the night away. I feel strongly out of place here," Mark Twain wrote, having just sat through Wagner's *Tristan und Isolde*. See Tim Ashley, "Is This the Most Powerful Music Ever Written?," the *Guardian*, October 13, 2000, http://www.theguardian.com/friday_review/story/0,,381181,00.html

Debussy and Stravinsky similarly stirred up their listeners: Eric Culver and Ben Grow alluded in particular to Stravinsky's pounding, gutteral, and unpredictabale moments of his ballet score *The Rite of Spring*. Hear performances at http://www.youtube.com/watch?v=mb36n034bA0 or http://www.youtube.com/watch?v=kRY7EpxL4mc

Donated a thousand musical instruments: See Roger Butterfield, "Reminiscences of George Eastman; an Introduction," *University of Rochester Library Bulletin* 26, no. 3 (Spring 1971), http://www.lib.rochester.edu/index.cfm?PAGE=3590; and Robert T. Grimm, *Notable American Philanthropists*, p. 90.

Rochester's Eastman School of Music: For more information on the school, see http://www.esm.rochester.edu/

Jalazon camp: For more information on the Jalazon Refugee Camp, see UNRWA camp profile: http://www.ochaopt.org/documents/opt_campprof_unrwa_jalazone_oct_2008.pdf

Chapter 28: Rise, Child

British guerrilla artist Banksy: Banksy, the anonymous yet world-famous artist, made at least two trips to Palestine, in 2005 and 2007. In another image, stenciled onto a wall in downtown Bethlehem, across from the Intercontinental Hotel, a soldier stands with his hands up against the wall, while a girl in pigtails and a pink dress pats him down. For these and other images, see http://www.travelreportage.com/2012/12/09/graffiti-street-art-in-the-west-bank-banksy-separation-wall/

Palestinian village of Al Ezaria: See Chaim Levinson, "Israel Planning to Construct Some 20,000 Housing Units in West Bank," *Haaretz*, November 12, 2013, http://www.haaretz.com/news/diplomacy-defense/.premium-1.557639

Daniel Kurtzer, former American ambassador to Israel, told the *New York Times* that "Since the late 1990s . . . the United States repeatedly has warned Israel not to build in the area abutting East Jerusalem known as E1, because settlements there would effectively bisect the West Bank and could doom plans to create a contiguous Palestinian state." See Mark Landler, "For Obama, Difficult Timing of an Israeli Plan Is Nothing New," the *New York Times*, November 30, 2012, http://www.nytimes.com/2012/12/01/world/middleeast/news-of-israel-settlements-is-bad-timing-for-obama.html

Israeli military bulldozers had plowed them under: According to journalist Jonathan Cook at the Center for Research on Globalization, Israel has uprooted eight hundred thousand olive trees since 1967. "Even the World Bank Understands, Palestine Is Being Disappeared," *Global Research*, October 17, 2013, http://www.globalresearch.ca/even-the-world-bank-understands-palestine-is-being-disappeared/5354591

Hide in the groves: See, for example, "Another Casualty of War: Trees," *Christian Science Monitor*, December 8, 2000, http://www.csmonitor.com/2000/1208/p1s2.html

An estimated eight hundred thousand olive trees: See Oxfam International, http://www.oxfam.org/en/development/opti/what-oxfams-position-israel-palestine-conflict. See also the *Guardian*, October 14, 2013, http://www.theguardian.com/news/datablog/2013/oct/14/palestine-economy-how-does-it-work

Tens of thousands of olive trees were cleared for the path of the separation barrier: Raja Shehadeh, "Plight of the Palestinian Olive Tree," the *New York Times*, November 13, 2012.

Transported and replanted in Tel Aviv: See "Olive Trees Uprooted in Jayyous Apparently to Make Room for Another Settlement," Eccumenical Accompaniment Programme in Palestine and Israel, http://archive-org.com/page/3143278/2013-11-06/http://eappi

.org/de/fotos-videos/photos/59-olive-tress-uprooted-in-jayyyous-appparently-to-make-room-for-another-settlement.html?print=1%253Fprint%253D1. See also "Ancient Olive Trees, Stolen from Palestinian Lands, Now Decorate Israeli Settlement." *Mondoweiss*, August 13, 2012, http://mondoweiss.net/2012/08/ancient-olive-trees-stolen-from-palestinian-lands-now-decorate-israeli-settlement.html; and Pamela Olson, *Fast Times in Palestine*, p. 191.

Close down a literary festival dedicated to Jerusalem as the "Center of Arab Culture": See "Jerusalem: Un centre français encircle," *Le Figaro*, December 17, 2009, http://www.lefigaro.fr/flash-actu/2009/12/17/01011-20091217FILWWW00635-jerusalem-un-centre-francais-encercle.php

British and French cultural attachés hastily arranged receptions on their grounds, and the festival went forward. "British writers who came out for the event were left wondering what threat was posed to Israel by a book fair and readings from children's books, among other things," the British General Consul in East Jerusalem, Richard Makepeace (his actual name), told Mark Thomas. See *Extreme Rambling: Walking Israel's Barrier. For Fun.*, p. 241.

Veto the Palestinian attempt to establish an independent state: The United States had been vocal about its intention to veto the Palestinian bid for statehood. See "With Security Council Report, Palestinian Statehood Bid Stalled at U.N.," CNN, November 11, 2011, http://www.cnn.com/2011/11/11/world/meast/un-palestinians/index.html?_s=PM:MIDDLEEAST. President Obama said the Palestinians' "symbolic actions to isolate Israel at the United Nations in September won't create an independent state." See "Backgrounder on the Palestinians' Bid for Statehood at the United Nations," Center for American Progress, September 21, 2011, http://www.american progress.org/issues/security/report/2011/09/21/10378/backgrounder-on-the-palestinians-bid-for-statehood-at-the-united-nations/

Hundreds of Palestinian refugees living in Syria forced their way over the border: "Israeli Forces Open Fire at Palestinian Protesters," BBC News, May 16, 2011, http://www.bbc.co.uk/news/world-middle-east-13373006. As recounted by Karma Nabulsi, "Slowly, and in spite of the shouted warnings from the villagers from Majdal Shams about the lethal landmines installed by the Israeli military right up to the fence, these remarkable ordinary young people—Palestinian refugees—began to both climb and push at the fence." See Karma Nabulsi, "Nakba Day: We Waited 63 Years for This," *Guardian*, May 19, 2011, http://www.theguardian.com/commentisfree/2011/may/19/nakba-day-palestinian-summer. According to "Unrest on the Borders," *Economist*, May 15, 2011, http://www.economist.com/blogs/newsbook/2011/05/israel, "On Sunday Israel got an unexpected and unpalatable taste of its nightmare scenario: masses of Palestinians marching, unarmed, towards the borders of the Jewish state, demanding the redress of their decades-old national grievance."

"Nakba Law": Jewish Telegraph Agency, http://www.jta.org/2011/03/23/news-opinion/israel-middle-east/knesset-adopts-nakba-law

Tiny Palestinian village islands in the larger Israeli-controlled sea: The villages, including Battir, are confined by settlers-only lands and roads that carve small Palestinian pockets out of the land. Palestinian residents across the West Bank say their lands are becoming isolated ghettos. See "Trampling Onto a Dark Future," Applied Research Institute, Jerusalem, http://www.poica.org/preview.php?Article=795. See also "18,000 Palestinians in W. Bethlehem Villages about to Be Enclosed into a 'Ghetto,'" International Middle East Media Center, http://www.imemc.org/article/18883. This is ongoing across the West Bank. In the Jordan Valley, thirty-seven Jewish settlements in the Jordan Valley represent less than 15 percent of the Valley's population, but they control nearly all access to its land and its water resources. See B'Tselem, "Dispossession and Exploitation: Israel's Policy in the Jordan Valley and Northern Dead Sea," http://www.btselem.org/publications/summaries/dispossession-and-exploitation-israels-policy-jordan-valley-northern-dead-sea. In At-Tuwani, in the South Hebron Hills, roads have become so impassible (improvements are prohibited) that children must walk three miles to their school. On the way, they have often been set upon by the German shepherds of nearby settlers, or pelted with stones and eggs as they pass. See "Palestinian Schoolchildren Attacked by Israeli Settlers, in South Hebron Hills," *Aletho News*, April 9, 2014, http://alethonews.wordpress.com/2014/04/09/palestinian-schoolchildren-attacked-by-israeli-settlers-in-south-hebron-hills/. See also my piece, "The Occupation That Time Forgot," for TomDispatch and posted at *Le Monde Diplomatique, The Nation*, the *American Conservative, Salon*, and at my blog, *Ramallah Café* (http://ramallahcafe.com/?p=538).

Occupying the understory of the West Bank landscape: Tunneling has emerged as the proposed solution to the increasing splintering of Palestinian communities and as a way ostensibly to maintain the possibility of a "viable and contiguous" Palestinian state. In *Hollow Land*, the Israeli architect Eyal Weizman writes: "When bewildered reporters asked [then-Prime Minister Sharon] how the two apparently contradictory terms of continuity and fragmentation could be accommodated within a single territorial reality, Sharon responded . . . [with] 'a combination of tunnels and bridges,'" (p. 179). See also *Haaretz*, December 5, 2002, http://www.haaretz.com/news/right-slams-pm-for-two-state-plan-left-calls-it-electioneering-1.26319. According to the PLO Negotiations Affairs Department, "'The Roads and Tunnels Plan' refers to the series of 24 tunnels and 56 roads for Palestinians. Meanwhile, Israel is constructing a separate highway network to link settlements (colonies) on both sides of the Wall with Israel and each other. Together, both transportation networks serve to facilitate settlement expansion throughout the Israeli-occupied West Bank while limiting any future Palestinian development." ("Israel's Roads and Tunnels Plans," PLO Negotiations Affairs Department, October 23, 2005, http://www.nad-plo.org/print.php?id=154.) This scenario, described a decade before the publication of this book, became steadily more pronounced in the years that followed. In the summer of 2013, Palestinian cartographer Khalil Toufakji, head of the Maps Department at the Jerusalem-based Arab Studies Society, took me on a short drive from Beit Jala to Battir, demonstrating the many ways, horizontally and vertically, that roads, villages, bridges, and tunnels have carved into the landscape in order to separate Palestinians and Israelis in separate and unequal West Bank realities.

Here was one of the few places where no separation barrier carved into the landscape: The open border undermined the claim that the separation barrier had slowed suicide bombers: Anyone could cross here, and it was safe to assume that militants with intent to kill Israelis were not so lazy as to not look for a hole in the line of defense. Even as the barrier grew closer to completion, as many as fifteen thousand Palestinians per week snuck into Israel to work as illegal laborers, some paying smugglers to help them scale the wall. See Ben Hubbard, "Palestinian Worker Killed as He Sneaks into Israel," Associated Press, October 3, 2010. Amon al-Sheikh, "Death and Humiliation: The Journey of Palestinian Workers to Israel," also cites a figure of thousands of illegal crossings of Israel's separation barrier; see *Al Akhbar English*, April 12, 2014, http://english. al-akhbar.com/node/19397. Moshe Arens, Israel's former defense minister, argued that the wall had little or nothing to do with the decline in suicide attacks, and urged Israel to tear it down. See "Tear Down This Wall," *Haaretz*, March 5, 2013, http://www. haaretz.com/opinion/tear-down-this-wall.premium-1.507182. Rather, as security experts and Palestinian militant groups claimed, the sharp decline in suicide bombings appeared more to be the result of a shift of tactics from those groups. See also Haggai Matar, "The Wall, 10 Years On / Part 11: Security for Israel?," *+972 Magazine*, http://972mag.com/the-wall-10-years-on-part-11-security-for-israel/50900

Terraced olive groves, some of the oldest in the Middle East: For more on Battir's terraces, see "In Israel, a Modern Wall Is Halted by Ancient Terraces," *Christian Science Monitor*, May 19, 2013, http://www.csmonitor.com/World/Middle-East/2013/0519/ In-Israel-a-modern-wall-is-halted-by-ancient-terraces

Declare Battir a World Heritage site: According to the UNESCO Web site, "The Committee approved the inscription of the site on the World Heritage List. It also inscribed the property on the List of World Heritage in Danger after finding that the landscape had become vulnerable under the impact of socio-cultural and geo-political transformations that could bring irreversible damage to its authenticity and integrity, citing the start of construction of a separation wall that may isolate farmers from fields they have cultivated for centuries." See "Palestine: Land of Olives and Vines: Cultural Landscape of Southern Jerusalem, Battir, Inscribed on World Heritage List and on List of World Heritage in Danger," UNESCO, June 20, 2014, http://whc.unesco.org/en/ news/1154

Chapter 29: Ode to Joy

A German chorus of 104 filed into the three balcony rows: I was present for many of the orchestra rehearsals and all of the nine Beethoven symphonies performed by the Divan in Cologne in the summer of 2011, and for many such performances and rehearsals the following summer at the Albert Hall in London. It was in London and Cologne that I did many of the interviews with Divan Orchestra members.

"**It has all been likened to the creation of the world**": See "Notes on Beethoven's Ninth Symphony" by Christopher Gibbs of the Philadelphia Orchestra Association, published on the NPR Web site, http://www.npr.org/templates/story/story.php?storyId= 5487727

One of the greatest works of art ever created: For more on Beethoven's Ninth Symphony, see "All About Ludwig van Beethoven," http://www.all-about-beethoven. com/symphony9.html

At the fall of the Berlin wall: "In that Christmas season trip to Berlin, Bernstein would famously conduct two performances of Beethoven's Ninth Symphony with an international orchestra and chorus assembled from the four countries that once shared the city—the U.S., Russia, England and France. And he would change one word so that the 'Ode to Joy' became the 'Ode to Freedom.'" See Greg Mitchell, "When Leonard Bernstein, and Beethoven, Celebrated the Fall of the Berlin Wall," *The Nation*, June 1, 2013, http://www.thenation.com/blog/174610/when-leonard-bernstein-and-beethoven-celebrated-fall-berlin-wall; and Kerry Candaele and Greg Mitchell, *Journeys with Beethoven: Following the Ninth and Beyond.*

"**Rather patchy and underachieved**": See Martin Kettle, "Prom 13: West-Eastern Divan Orchestra/Barenboim: Review," *Guardian*, July 25, 2012, http://www.theguardian. com/music/2012/jul/25/prom-13-west-eastern-divan-review

Chapter 30: A Musical Intifada

Twenty-six thousand Palestinians who worked in the settlements: "Palestinian Workers in Settlements: Who Profits Position Paper," Coalition of Women for Peace, January 2013, http://whoprofits.org/sites/default/files/palestinian_workers_in_settlements_ wp_position_paper.pdf.

The Israeli minimum wage of $6.55 per hour: See *The Situation of Workers in the Occupied Territories*, Boydell and Brewer, p. 15, and "Palestinian Workers in Settlements," Coalition of Women for Peace. For details on the minimum wage, see "One in Eight Israelis Paid Less Than Minimum Wage," *Haaretz*, http://www.haaretz. com/news/national/.premium-1.542225

The conviction rate in such military trials was 99.74 percent: See Ben Ehrenreich, "Is This Where the Third Intifada Will Start?," *New York Times Magazine*, March 15, 2013, http://www.nytimes.com/2013/03/17/magazine/is-this-where-the-third-intifada-will-start.html

Or 40 percent of the adult male population, had spent time in an Israeli prison: "Since 1967, when Israel occupied the West Bank, Gaza Strip and East Jerusalem, more than 650,000 Palestinians have been detained by Israel. This represents approximately 20% of the total population in the Occupied Palestinian Territories (OPT), and 40% of all males. Despite prohibition by international law, Israel detains Palestinians in prisons throughout Israel, far from their families, who almost never obtain the necessary permits to leave the Occupied Palestinian Territories to visit them." See United

Nations General Assembly, "Tenth Emergency Special Session," March 6, 2014, http://unispal.un.org/UNISPAL.NSF/0/CAB3513DB4E2A24685257CA50054B61C

Its last portion would go through Battir: *Al-Monitor*, January 27, 2014, http://www.al-monitor.com/pulse/originals/2014/01/security-fence-israel-palestine-west-bank-rural-region.html

The barrier would destroy the livelihood of most Battir villagers: "Does the World Have Room for Battir Village?" Ma'an News Agency, June 3, 2014, http://www.maannews.net/eng/ViewDetails.aspx?ID=491858

Submit Battir for recognition as a UNESCO World Heritage site: "Battir's Lost Chance to Become a UNESCO Heritage Site Paves Way for Segregation Wall," *Palestine Monitor*, June 22, 2013.

American-backed peace negotiations: "Palestinians Shelve Bid to Have West Bank Village Recognized as UN Heritage Site," Associated Press, June 26, 2013, http://www.haaretz.com/news/diplomacy-defense/1.532183

Even a nearby Israeli settlement: "Palestinians, Settlers Join to Oppose New Security Barrier," *Israel Today*, June 19, 2014.

The World Heritage application . . . would harm talks with Israel: "Palestinians Shelve Bid to Have West Bank Village Recognized as UN Heritage Site," Associated Press, June 26, 2013, http://www.haaretz.com/news/diplomacy-defense/1.532183

Abbas, under pressure from the United States, had also dropped his demand for a freeze on Israeli settlements: "Under Pressure from Kerry, Abbas Softens Preconditions for Peace Talks," *Haaretz*, June 25, 2013, http://www.haaretz.com/news/diplomacy-defense/.premium-1.531999; and "Abbas to Obama: Israel Talks Only in Exchange for Settlement Freeze, Release of Prisoners," *Haaretz*, March 22, 2013, http://www.haaretz.com/news/obama-visits-israel/abbas-to-obama-israel-talks-only-in-exchange-for-settlement-freeze-release-of-prisoners.premium-1.511369

Sixteen hundred new apartments in East Jerusalem: "As Biden Visits, Israel Unveils Plans for New Settlements," *New York Times*, March 9, 2010.

Netanyahu had another demand: The demand that Israel be recognized as a Jewish state was absent from past accords under the Oslo process, as well as from Israel's treaties with Egypt and Jordan. See Christa Case Bryant, "Israel's 'Jewish State' Demand: Why Netanyahu and Abbas can't Agree," the *Christian Science Monitor*, March 17, 2014. http://www.csmonitor.com/World/Security-Watch/2014/0317/Israel-s-Jewish-state-demand-Why-Netanyahu-and-Abbas-can-t-agree-video

Israel does not require such formal diplomatic recognition from other nations, including the United States. The issue emerged in 2007, according to a *Haaretz* commentary, but "Neither the Palestinian nor the American delegations took it seriously, and it seemed to be dropped." *Haaretz*, January 10, 2014, http://www.haaretz.com/opinion/.premium-1.567946

Backed by the United States: The United States sided with the Palestinians at first, agreeing that Jewish-state recognition was unnecessary, then changed its position. See

"John Kerry's Peace Process Is Nearly Dead," *New Republic*, March 25, 2014, http://www.newrepublic.com/article/117141/john-kerrys-peace-process-nearly-dead

Loyalty oaths for non-Jewish citizens: Bloomberg News, May 7, 2014, http://www.bloomberg.com/news/2014-05-07/liberman-condemns-israel-s-arab-citizens-for-espousing-return-.html

Moving the separation barrier to exclude Israeli Arab communities: Ibid.

UNESCO, which approved the bid in April 2014: "UNESCO Names West Bank's Battir a Protected World Heritage Site," Al Jazeera America, June 23, 2014, http://america.aljazeera.com/articles/2014/6/23/unesco-palestinebattir.html

"The era of discord is over": Both sides had been weakened by recent events—Abbas by his failure to deliver a Palestinian state, and Hamas by sharply reduced support from backers Iran, Syria, and Egypt. See Ghassan Khatib, "Who's Calling Whose Bluff?," *Birzeit University Blog*, June 21, 2014, http://www.birzeit.edu/blogs/who%E2%80%98s-calling-whose-bluff

Far more conciliatory than what Hamas had offered: See "How the West Chose War in Gaza" by Nathan Thrall, analyst for the International Crisis Group, the *New York Times*, July 17, 2014: http://www.nytimes.com/2014/07/18/opinion/gaza-and-israel-the-road-to-war-paved-by-the-west.html

"Bent on the destruction of Israel.": See "Israel Suspends Peace Talks with Palestinians After Fatah-Hamas Deal," the *Guardian*, April 24, 2014. http://www.theguardian.com/world/2014/apr/24/middle-east-israel-halts-peace-talks-palestinians

More than two thousand soldiers: "Home Demolitions and Dead Palestinian Teen Follow Netanyahu Call for Revenge," *Mondoweiss*, July 2, 2014, http://mondoweiss.net/2014/07/aftermath-demolitions-palestinian.html

Searching twenty-two hundred homes: "Bodies of Three Israeli Teens Found in West Bank," *Jerusalem Post*, June 30, 2014, http://www.jpost.com/Operation-Brothers-Keeper/Large-number-of-IDF-forces-gather-north-of-Hebron-in-search-for-kidnapped-teens-361048

More than a third of those without charge: "Israel: Serious Violations in West Bank Operations," Human Rights Watch, July 3, 2014, http://www.hrw.org/news/2014/07/03/israel-serious-violations-west-bank-operations%20

A small portion were interrogated about the kidnapping: "Beyond Mission Creep: Why Operation Brother's Keeper Isn't Working," *+972 Magazine*, June 24, 2014, http://972mag.com/beyond-mission-creep-why-operation-brothers-keeper-isnt-working/92471/

Evidence suggested that the Israeli authorities knew within a day: This has been widely reported. See for example "Failure in Gaza," in which the Israeli writer Assaf Sharon states: "Israeli security forces were in possession of evidence strongly indicating the teens were dead, but withheld this information from the public . . . possibly in order to allow time to pursue the campaign against Hamas." *New York Review of*

Books, September 25, 2014, http://www.nybooks.com/articles/archives/2014/sep/25/failure-gaza/?insrc=hpma

"May God avenge their blood": "A Facebook page named 'The People of Israel Demand Revenge' . . . quickly garnered 35,000 'likes.'" Reported by Isabel Kershner, "Arab Boy's Death Escalates Clash over Abductions," the *New York Times*, July 3, 2014, http://www.nytimes.com/2014/07/03/world/middleeast/israel.html

"You're talking about savage actions": "What you have in Palestinian society is a culture of terrorism," added Ron Dermer, Israel's ambassador to the United States. See NPR, *All Things Considered*, July 1, 2014, http://wgbhnews.org/post/addressing-killed-teens-israeli-ambassador-decries-culture-terrorism

1,384 Palestinian children had been killed by Israel's military: B'Tselem collects information on all Palestinian and Israeli casualties and divides them into periods before, during, and after Israel's 2008–09 "Operation Cast Lead" in Gaza. For more, see http://www.btselem.org/statistics. Statistics from the Palestinian Ministry of Social Affairs show the casualty rates among Palestinian children during this period to exceed 1,500. See *Haaretz*, April 5, 2014, http://www.haaretz.com/news/diplomacy-defense/1.583928

"All lives are precious": *Mondoweiss*, July 2, 2014, http://mondoweiss.net/2014/07/narrative-violence-occupation.html

Israel responded with massive airstrikes on Gaza: This is in response to the rocket attacks that began shortly after the murder of Mohammed Abu Khdeir.

Nine men watching the World Cup: "In Rubble of Gaza Seaside Café, Hunt for Victims Who Had Come for Soccer," the *New York Times*, July 10, 2014, http://www.nytimes.com/2014/07/11/world/middleeast/missile-at-beachside-gaza-cafe-finds-patrons-poised-for-world-cup.html

Taking refuge in a U.N. school: See Ben Hubbard and Jodi Rudoren, "Questions of Weapons and Warnings in Past Barrage on a Gaza Shelter," *New York Times*, August 3, 2014, http://www.nytimes.com/2014/08/04/world/middleeast/international-scrutiny-after-israeli-barrage-strike-in-jabaliya-where-united-nations-school-shelters-palestinians-in-gaza.html

Playing hide-and-seek: See Peter Beaumont, "Witness to a Shelling: First-hand Account of Deadly Strike on Gaza Port," *Guardian*, July 16, 2014, http://www.theguardian.com/world/2014/jul/16/witness-gaza-shelling-first-hand-account

Seventy people in the Shejaiya neighborhood: See "More Than 100 Palestinians Dead in Worst Day of Gaza Conflict," *Washington Post*, July 20, 2014, http://www.washingtonpost.com/world/israel-begins-heaviest-bombardment-yet-in-gaza-sending-residents-fleeing/2014/07/20/578ae882-0fe5-11e4-8c9a-923ecc0c7d23_story.html

Less than an hour: See side-by-side images at *Business Insider*: http://www.businessinsider.com/time-lapse-video-shows-israel-flattening-a-gaza-neighborhood-2014-7

More than twenty-one hundred people: For this and other casualty figures, see OCHA, "Gaza Emergency Situation Report," August 28, 2014, http://www.ochaopt. org/documents/ocha_opt_sitrep_28_08_2014.pdf

War crimes investigations: See, for example, "Israel Committed War Crimes in Gaza, Human Rights Watch Investigation Claims," *Haaretz*, September 11, 2014, http:// www.haaretz.com/news/diplomacy-defense/1.615253; and "Israel, Facing Criticism, to Investigate Possible Military Misconduct in Gaza," Isabel Kershner, the *New York Times*, September 10, 2014, http://www.nytimes.com/2014/09/11/world/middleeast/ gaza-strip-israel-criminal-investigation.html

Its attempts to crush Hamas: See David Horowitz, "Netanyahu and the Limits of Military Power," *Times of Israel*, August 28, 2014, http://www.timesofisrael. com/netanyahu-and-the-limits-of-military-power. See also: Maher Abuhakater "In Palestinian Poll, Hamas Emerges as Winner of Gaza War," the *Los Angeles Times*, September 2, 2014, http://www.latimes.com/world/middleeast/la-fg-palestinians-hamas-israel-war-gaza-20140902-story.html; David Rothkopf, "On Israel's Defeat in Gaza," *Foreign Policy*, August 6, 2014, http://www.foreignpolicy.com/articles/ 2014/08/06/on_israel_s_defeat_in_gaza_cease_fire_hamas_public_opinion; and my article, "Israel's Self-defeating 'Victory': How Peace Was Squandered in Gaza," *Salon* (via TomDispatch), August 13, 2014, http://www.salon.com/2014/08/13/ israels_self_defeating_victory_how_peace_was_squandered_in_gaza_partner

Nor had Israel presented compelling evidence: In "Alleged Mastermind of 3 Teens' Killings Indicted," a September 4, 2014 article in the *Times of Israel* quotes a Shin Bet official who "revealed that the terror attack is believed to have been a local initiative rather than a directive from above," see http://www.timesofisrael.com/alleged-mastermind-of-3-teens-killing-indicted

Isabel Kershner of the *New York Times*, on September 4, 2014, cites Israeli official documents that "provide no evidence that the top leaders of Hamas directed or had prior knowledge of the plot to abduct the three Israeli youths." http://www.nytimes. com/2014/09/05/world/middleeast/killing-of-3-israeli-teenagers-loosely-tied-to-hamas-court-documents-show.html

A Hamas official in Turkey and **Other experts were skeptical**: See Orlando Crowcroft, "Hamas Official: We Were Behind the Kidnapping of 3 Israeli Teenagers," the *Guardian*, August 21, 2014, http://www.theguardian.com/world/2014/aug/21/ hamas-kidnapping-three-israeli-teenagers-saleh-al-arouri-qassam-brigades

"WMD of the Gaza onslaught": See Adam Horowitz and Phillip Weiss, "Claim That Hamas Killed 3 Teens Is Turning Out to Be the WMD of the Gaza Onslaught," *Mondoweiss*, July 26, 2014, http://mondoweiss.net/2014/07/killed-turning-onslaught. html

Physically dividing Palestinians from one another: For an analysis and historical overview of Israel's strategy of fragmentation, see the latter part of my August 2014 piece, "Going Wild in the Gaza War," written for TomDispatch and posted on numerous sites, including *Salon*, under the headline, "Israel's Self-defeating 'Victory': How Peace Was Squandered in Gaza," http://www.salon.com/2014/08/13/israels_self_defeating_victory_how_peace_was_squandered_in_gaza_partner

"How will Israel remain democratic . . . ?" The White House, "Remarks as Prepared by White House Coordinator for the Middle East, North Africa, and the Gulf Region Philip Gordon at the Ha'aretz Israel Conference for Peace," July 8, 2014, http://www.whitehouse.gov/the-press-office/2014/07/08/remarks-prepared-white-house-coordinator-middle-east-north-africa-and-gu

"There cannot be a situation . . ." "Netanyahu finally speaks his mind," *Times of Israel*, July 13, 2014, http://www.timesofisrael.com/netanyahu-finally-speaks-his-mind/

"Call into question": "White House: Israel faces estrangement from allies if settlement building proceeds," the *Washington Post*, October 1, 2014, http://www.washingtonpost.com/world/national-security/white-house-israel-faces-estrangement-from-allies-if-settlement-building-proceeds/2014/10/01/cd2680d6-4999-11e4-b72e-d60a9229cc10_story.html

"Chickenshit": Jeffrey Goldberg, the *Atlantic*, "The Crisis in U.S.-Israeli Relations Is Officially Here," October 28, 2014, http://www.theatlantic.com/international/archive/2014/10/the-crisis-in-us-israel-relations-is-officially-here/382031/

Sweden formally recognized: "Sweden Recognizes Palestinian State, Hopes Will Revive Peace Process," Reuters, October 30, 2014, http://www.reuters.com/article/2014/10/30/us-sweden-palestinians-recognition-idUSKBN0IJ1DU20141030

Hunger strike: "Palestinian Prisoners End Hunger Strike," *Today's Zaman* (Turkey), June 25, 2014, http://www.todayszaman.com/world_palestinian-prisoners-in-israel-end-hunger-strike_351260.html

Israel's "administrative detention" policy: B'Tselem, "Administrative Detention," http://www.btselem.org/administrative_detention

His best friend, Mohammad Mahmoud Tarifi, had been killed on the roof: "Two Palestinians, One Israeli Boy Killed in Separate Clashes," the *Los Angeles Times*, June 22, 2014, http://www.latimes.com/world/middleeast/la-fg-palestinians-dead-clashes-west-bank-20140622-story.html. The young man's full name was Mohammad Mahmoud Ismail Tarifi, and various accounts refer to variations of his name. One account put his age at twenty-seven. See "Two Palestinians Shot Dead by Israel," *Gulf News*, June 22, 2014, http://gulfnews.com/news/region/palestine/two-palestinians-shot-dead-by-israel-1.1350602; "Autopsy Proves Slain Palestinian Killed by Israeli Fire in Ramallah," *Ma'an News*, June 23, 2014, http://www.maannews.net/eng/ViewDetails.aspx?ID=706789; and "One Killed in Protests as Israeli Army Takes Control of Ramallah City Center for First Time Since 2007," *Mondoweiss*, June 22, 2014, http://mondoweiss.net/2014/06/ramallah-palestinian-authority.html

He left a wife and a son: A Facebook image of Tarifi's son and widow, taken during his funeral, can be seen at https://www.facebook.com/Arouri.Fadi/photos/a.10150331031338088.372939.16160983087/10152486094028088

Stephen Hawking: "Stephen Hawking Backs Boycott of Israeli Academics," Associated Press, May 8, 2013, http://bigstory.ap.org/article/stephen-hawking-wont-attend-israeli-conference

Scarlett Johansson was forced to resign: Oxfam, the UK-based human rights organization, called Johansson's SodaStream work "incompatible with her role as an Oxfam Global Ambassador . . . Oxfam believes that businesses, such as SodaStream, that operate in settlements further the ongoing poverty and denial of rights of the Palestinian communities that we work to support." See http://www.oxfam.org/en/pressroom/reactions/oxfam-accepts-resignation-scarlett-johansson and http://www.thejc.com/news/uk-news/120297/boycott-row-sodastream-shop-closes

The boycott appeared to threaten the company's financial health: "SodaStream Shop Closes in Brighton after Boycott Row," *Jewish Chronicle*, July 3, 2014, http://www.thejc.com/news/uk-news/120297/boycott-row-sodastream-shop-closes. Bloomberg News cites the 32 percent figure in "Soros No Longer Holds Shares of SodaStream," August 4, 2014, http://www.bloomberg.com/news/2014-08-04/soros-fund-no-longer-holds-shares-of-sodastream.html. See also "Soros Fund Drops Shares in Israel's SodaStream," BDS Movement, August 3, 2014, http://www.bdsmovement.net/2014/soros-fund-drops-shares-in-israels-sodastream-12450

The Presbyterian Church USA: In June 2014, the Presbyterian Church USA voted 310–303 to divest twenty-one million dollars from three companies: Caterpillar, makers of the D9 bulldozer used in the demolition of Palestinian homes (twenty-six thousand of which had been demolished by Israel since 1967); Motorola Solutions, makers of surveillance equipment used in West Bank settlements; and Hewlett-Packard, makers of technology used to enforce Israel's blockade of Gaza. The church said the decision was not connected to the BDS campaign. Nevertheless, BDS cofounder Omar Barghouti called the decision a "sweet victory," while leaders of major Jewish organizations sharply criticized the church. "Presbyterians Dump Companies They Say Are Tied to Palestinian Occupation," CNN, June 22, 2014, http://www.cnn.com/2014/06/21/us/presbyterian-church-palestinians. See also Laurie Goodstein, "Presbyterians Vote to Divest Holdings to Pressure Israel," *New York Times*, June 20, 2014, http://www.nytimes.com/2014/06/21/us/presbyterians-debating-israeli-occupation-vote-to-divest-holdings.html

"Two-state solution" nearly extinguished: See Ian Lustick, "Two-State Illusion," the *New York Times*, September 14, 2013, http://www.nytimes.com/2013/09/15/opinion/sunday/two-state-illusion.html; and my article, "For Arab and Jew, a New Beginning," *Christian Science Monitor*, April 21, 2011, http://www.csmonitor.com/Commentary/Opinion/2011/0421/For-Arab-and-Jew-a-new-beginning

United States' inability or unwillingness to stop Israel's settlement expansion: In his October 14, 2013 article, "What Comes Next: Unlikely, Unrealistic, or Unimaginable," Joel Beinen, professor of Middle East History at Stanford University, sums up the problem succinctly: "By failing to secure Israeli Prime Minister Netanyahu's agreement to a settlement freeze in preparation for restarting direct Palestinian–Israeli negotiations, President Obama most likely put the final nail in the coffin of the two-state solution of the conflict. His willingness to accept public humiliation by the prime minister of a client state further suggests that the president is unlikely to spend the political capital required to resolve the conflict on terms close to the international consensus," http://mondoweiss.net/2013/10/unlikely-unrealistic-unimaginable.html. In the United States' failure to pressure Israel into ceasing its settlement expansion, or even to implement a freeze on construction, domestic American politics become impossible to ignore. M. J. Rosenberg, former director of the Israel Policy Forum and a veteran analyst, wrote that the Gaza war, growing out of Kerry's diplomatic failure, was "a testament to the failure of democracy." He blamed the pro-Israel lobby in the United States. "That is why the Kerry mission failed. It is why every peace initiative going back to Oslo has failed. Every U.S. position has to be cleared by the donors." See "Gaza and Lobby Politics," July 16, 2014, Huffington Post, http://www.huffingtonpost.com/mj-rosenberg/gaza-burns-to-please-fat-_b_5591145.html. See also Connie Bruck's *New Yorker* article about AIPAC, "Friends of Israel," September 1, 2014.

Palestinians themselves, in the Holy Land and the diaspora, debated: Many of these Palestinians were in the global diaspora, and their discourse was sometimes part of a larger debate among Palestinians, activists, and progressive Israelis and American Jews. For a collection of articles, see "What Comes Next? A Forum on the End of the Two-State Paradigm," *Mondoweiss*, http://mondoweiss.net/forum-state-paradigm

A single or binational state: See Omar Barghouti, "A Secular Democratic State in Historic Palestine—A Promising Land," October 21, 2013, *Mondoweiss*, http://mondoweiss.net/2013/10/democratic-palestine-promising.html

"Parallel states": Matthias Mossberg and Mark Levine, "A Solution for Israelis and Palestinians: A Parallel State Structure," *Christian Science Monitor*, April 8, 2010, http://www.csmonitor.com/Commentary/Opinion/2010/0408/The-solution-for-Israelis-and-Palestinians-a-parallel-state-structure

Confederation of states: See Jeff Halper's vision for a binational state, which he envisions could lead to a confederation of states: "What Comes Next: Towards a Bi-national Endgame in Palestine/Israel," *Mondoweiss*, December 3, 2013, http://mondoweiss.net/2013/12/towards-national-palestineisrael.html

The word *apartheid* was spoken . . . by pundits: *New York Times* columnist Thomas L. Friedman wrote on February 11, 2014, that the failure of Kerry's peace mission, would "force Israel onto one of three bad paths: either a unilateral withdrawal from parts of the West Bank or annexation and granting the Palestinians there citizenship, making Israel a binational state. Or failing to do either, Israel by default could become some kind of apartheid-like state in permanent control over the 2.5 million Palestinians. There are no other options." See "Israel's Big Question," http://www.nytimes.com/2014/02/12/opinion/friedman-israels-big-question.html

Israeli and American leaders: Some of the apartheid comparisons have come as warnings of what could transpire (and, it is fair to argue, already has transpired) if a two-state solution is not reached. These include Israeli foreign minister Tzipi Livni (see "Livni

Lambastes Bennett in Facebook Post," *Times of Israel*, January 30, 2014), former prime ministers Ehud Barak and Ehud Olmert, and U.S. Secretary of State John Kerry, all preceded by former president Jimmy Carter, author of *Palestine: Peace Not Apartheid*, in 2006. See "Like Kerry, Senior Israeli Officials Have Warned of Israel Becoming an Apartheid State," Thinkprogress.org, April 30, 2014, http://thinkprogress.org/ world/2014/04/28/3431375/kerry-israel-apartheid. See also "Exclusive: Kerry Warns Israel Could Become Apartheid State," *Daily Beast*, April 27, 2014, http://www. thedailybeast.com/articles/2014/04/27/exclusive-kerry-warns-israel-could-become-an-apartheid-state.html; "PMs Barak and Olmert, Not Hegel, Warned of Israel Becoming an Apartheid State," *Daily Kos*, February 19, 2013, http://www.dailykos.com/ story/2013/02/19/1188347/-PM-s-Barak-and-Olmert-not-Hagel-warned-Israel-becoming-an-apartheid-state#; and "Israel Risks Apartheid-like Struggle if Two-State Solution Fails, Olmert Says," the *Guardian*, November 29, 2007.

Palestinians argued for *sumud*: Sumud, or steadfastness, emerged as a political philosophy by Palestinians following the 1967 war. See, for example, Arthur Neslen, *In Your Eyes a Sandstorm*, p. 10.

"This is a musical intifada": The musical uprising that this chapter is named for took place in June 2011, before some of the other events in the chapter. It is one of the rare cases in which I have changed the chronology in the service of narrative flow. I was present for the trip to Qalandia and for the musical confrontation, through Al Kamandjati's Ramallah Orchestra performances of Mozart and Bizet at the checkpoint.

Selected Bibliography

Archives
Edward Said Archives, Rare Book and Manuscript Library, Columbia University, New York
Israel State Archives, Jerusalem

Electronic Sources (Including Online Media)
+ *972 Magazine*, Israel and the Palestinian Territories
The Age, Melbourne
Al Jazeera, Doha, Qatar
Al-Ahram Weekly, Cairo
Aletho News (blog), Greece
Al-Monitor, Washington, D.C.
American Jewish Yearbook
Asharq Al-Awsat, London
Associated Press, New York City
Atlantic Monthly (theatlantic.com), Washington, D.C.
BBC News, London
Birzeit University Blog, Birzeit, West Bank
Bloomberg News, New York
The Boston Musical Intelligencer, Boston
Boulezian Blog (blog of Mark Berry)
Chicago Tribune, Chicago
Christian Science Monitor, Boston
CNN, Atlanta
Columbia News, New York

Columbia Spectator, New York

Commentary Magazine, New York

Daily Beast, New York

Daily Kos, U.S.-based political blog

Daily Mail, London

Daily Telegraph, London

DP News, Damascus

The Economist, London

Electronic Intifada, Chicago

Financial Times, London

Global Research, Montreal

The Guardian, London

Gulf News, Dubai

Haaretz, Tel Aviv

Haaretz Weekend Magazine, Tel Aviv

Harper's Magazine, New York

Huffington Post, New York

Israel Today, Jerusalem

Jerusalem Post, Jerusalem

Jewish Chronicle, London

Jewish Daily Forward, New York

Jewish Journal, Boston

Jewish Telegraphic Agency (JTA), New York

Jewish Virtual Library, online encyclopedia

Jewish Week, New York

The Independent, London

Le Figaro, Paris

Le Monde Diplomatique, Paris

Los Angeles Times, Los Angeles

Ma'an News Agency, Occupied Palestinian Territories

Magnes Zionist, (Jerusalem-based blog of Jerry Haber)

McClatchy News Service, Sacramento, California.

Mondoweiss, Chicago

New Statesman, London

New Republic, Washington, D.C.

The New York Times, New York

New York Times Magazine, New York

NPR (formerly National Public Radio), Washington, D.C.

Opendemocracy.net, London

A Personal Diary of the Israeli-Palestinian Conflict, Ramallah, West Bank (Nigel Parry blog)

Philly.com, Philadelphia-based news website

RTE News, Dublin

Slate, Washington, D.C.

The Sunday Times, London

Tablet: A New Take on Jewish Life, New York

Telegraph, London

This Week in Palestine, Jerusalem

Time, New York

Times of Israel, Jerusalem

Today's Zaman, Istanbul

US Air Force Magazine, Arlington, Virginia,

Vanity Fair, New York

Voice of America, Washington, D.C.

Wall Street Journal, New York

Washington Post, Washington, D.C.

Ynet News, Tel Aviv

Journals and Journal Articles

Abdulfattah, Kamal. "Throne Villages of the Highlands: Local Nobility and Their Mansions in Ottoman Palestine." *Near Eastern Archaeology* 70, no. 1 (March 2007).

Ali, Tariq. "Remembering Edward Said, 1935–2003." *New Left Review* 24 (November–December 2003).

Andoni, Lamis. "Searching for Answers: Gaza's Suicide Bombers," *Journal of Palestine Studies* 26, no. 4 (Summer 1997): 33–45.

Araj, Bader, and Robert J. Brym. "Opportunity, Culture and Agency: Influences on Fatah and Hamas Strategic Action During the Second Intifada." *International Sociology* 25, no. 6 (November 2010): 842–68. http://projects. chass.utoronto.ca/soc101y/brym/ArajBrymIntSoc.pdf

Awwad, Nahed. "In Search of Jerusalem Airport." *Jerusalem Quarterly* 35: 51–63. http://www.jerusalemquarterly.org/images/ArticlesPdf/35_airport.pdf

Baker, Ahmad A. "The Psychological Impact of the Intifada on Palestinian Children in the Occupied West Bank and Gaza: An Exploratory

Study." *American Journal of Orthopsychiatry* 60, no. 4 (October 1990): 496–505.

Baramki, Gabi. "Palestinian University Education Under Occupation." *The Palestine-Israel Journal of Politics, Economics and Culture* 3, no. 1 (1996). http://www.pij.org/details.php?id=569

Bshara, Khaldun. "Opera Quais wa Yemen." *This Week in Palestine* 90 (October 2005). http://archive.thisweekinpalestine.com/details.php?id=1460&ed=107&edid=107

Boase, Roger. "The Muslim Expulsion from Spain." *History Today* 52, no. 4 (2002). http://www.historytoday.com/roger-boase/muslim-expulsion-spain

Burgoyne, Michael Hamilton, and Mahmoud Hawari. "Bayt al-Hawwari, a *Hawsh* House in Sabastiya." *Levant* 37 (2005): 57–80.

Busailah, Reja-e. "The Fall of Lydda, 1948: Impressions and Reminiscences." *Arab Studies Quarterly* 1981.

Butterfield, Roger. "Reminiscences of George Eastman: An Introduction." *University of Rochester Library Bulletin* 26, no. 3 (Spring 1971). http://www.lib.rochester.edu/index.cfm?PAGE=3590

Imseis, Ardi. "Moderate Torture on Trial: Critical Reflections on the Israeli Supreme Court Judgment Concerning the Legality of General Security Service Interrogation Methods." *Berkeley Journal of International Law* 19, no. 2, article 3 (2001). http://scholarship.law.berkeley.edu/cgi/viewcontent.cgi?article=1202&context=bjil

Krystall, Nathan. "The De-Arabization of West Jerusalem, 1947–50." *Journal of Palestine Studies* 27, no. 2 (Winter 1998): 5–22.

Morris, Benny. "Operation Dani and the Exodus of Palestinians from Lydda and Ramle." *Middle East Journal* 40, no. 1 (Winter 1986): 82–109. https://docs.google.com/file/d/0B-5-JeCa2Z7hZVFmYzdydElxdUU/edit

Munayyer, Spiro. "The Fall of Lydda." *Journal of Palestine Studies* 27, no. 4 (Summer 1998): 80–98.

Pressman, Jeremy. "The Second Intifada: Background and Causes of the Israeli-Palestinian Conflict." *Journal of Conflict Studies* 23, no.2 (Fall 2003). http://journals.hil.unb.ca/index.php/jcs/article/view/220/378

———. "Visions in Collision: What Happened at Camp David and Taba?" *International Security* 28, no. 2 (Fall 2003): 13–14. http://polisci.uconn.edu/people/faculty/doc/Visions_pressman.pdf

Rosen, Steven J. "Kuwait Expels Thousands of Palestinians." *Middle East Quarterly* 19, no. 4 (Fall 2012): 75–83. http://www.meforum.org/3391/kuwait-expels-palestinians

Said, Edward. "The Morning After." *London Review of Books* 15, no. 20 (October 21, 1993): 3–5.

Schweitzer, Yoram. "The Rise and Fall of Suicide Bombings in the Second Intifada." *Strategic Assessment* 13, no. 3 (October 2010).

Souri, Helga Tawil. "Qalandia Checkpoint: The Historical Geography of a Non-Place." *Jerusalem Quarterly* (Summer 2010).

Tamari, Salim. "The Last Feudal Lord in Palestine." *Jerusalem Quarterly*. Institute of Jerusalem Studies (November 16, 2002). http://www.jerusalemquarterly.org/images/ArticlesPdf/16_fendallord.pdf

The Situation of Workers in the Occupied Arab Territories. International Labour Conference, 98th Session. Rochester, NY: Boydell and Brewer, 2009.

Thrall, Nathan. "Our Man in Palestine." *New York Review of Books* (October 14, 2010). http://www.nybooks.com/articles/archives/2010/oct/14/our-man-palestine/

Warner, Marina. "In the Time of Not Yet: Marina Warner on the Imaginary of Edward Said." *London Review of Books* 32, no. 24 (December 16, 2010). http://www.lrb.co.uk/v32/n24/marina-warner/in-the-time-of-not-yet

Non-Governmental Organizations

Alternative Information Center, Jerusalem

Amnesty International, London

Applied Research Institute of Jerusalem, Jerusalem/Bethlehem

Breaking the Silence, Jerusalem

B'Tselem, Jerusalem

Canadians for Justice and Peace in the Middle East, Montreal

Center for American Progress, Washington, D.C.

Christian Peacemaker Teams, Toronto and Chicago

Coalition of Woman for Peace, Israel and Occupied Palestinian Territories

Council on Foreign Relations, Washington, D.C.

Defence for Children International, Geneva

Foundation for Middle East Peace, Washington, D.C.

Human Rights Watch, New York

Institute for Middle East Understanding, Oakland, California

Internal Displacement Monitoring Center, London

International Committee of the Red Cross, Geneva

International Humanitarian Law Research Initiative, Cambridge, Massachusetts

International Middle East Media Center, Occupied Palestinian Territories

Israeli Committee Against Housing Demolition, Jerusalem

Jerusalem Media and Communication Center, Jerusalem

Jewish Federations of North America, Phoenix, Arizona

Jewish United Fund, Chicago

Middle East Forum, Philadelphia

Middle East Research and Information Project, New York

Palestine Human Rights Monitor, Jerusalem

Palestinian Academic Society for the Study of International Affairs, Jerusalem

Palestinian National Initiative, Ramallah, West Bank

Peace Now, Tel Aviv

Reut Institute, Tel Aviv

Riwaq, Ramallah, West Bank

Save the Children, London

Washington Institute for Near East Policy (Washington, D.C.)

Washington Report on Middle East Affairs (Washington, D.C.)

Wolf Foundation, Jerusalem

Government Agencies

Bureau of Democracy, Human Rights, and Labor, U.S. Department of State, Washington, D.C.

Centre for Conflict Resolution Studies, Defense Academy of the United Kingdom, London

Congressional Research Service, Library of Congress, Washington, D.C.

Consulate General of the United States in Jerusalem, Jerusalem

Council for European Palestinian Relations, European Union, Brussels

Geneva International Center for Justice, Geneva, Switzerland

International Court of Justice, The Hague, The Netherlands

Israel Defense Forces, Jerusalem, Israel

Israel Ministry of Foreign Affairs, Jerusalem, Israel

Israeli Central Bureau of Statistics, Jerusalem, Israel

Palestine Liberation Organization Negotiations Affairs Departments, Ramallah, West Bank

Palestinian Central Bureau of Statistics, Ramallah, West Bank

Palestinian Center for Policy and Survey Research, Ramallah, West Bank

Palestinian Initiative for the Promotion of Global Dialogue and Democracy, Jerusalem and Ramallah

United Nations, New York:
Office for the Coordination of Humanitarian Affairs (OCHA)
United Nations Education, Scientific and Cultural Organization (UNESCO)
United Nations Relief and Works Agency (UNRWA)
United Nations Information Center on the Question of Palestine
United States Department of State (Washington, D.C.)

Film and Broadcast Media

All Things Considered. National Public Radio (NPR). July 1, 2014. http:// wgbhnews.org/post/addressing-killed-teens-israeli-ambassador-decries-culture-terrorism

Bernstein, Leonard. *Young People's Concerts with the New York Philharmonic: Special Collector's Edition 9-DVD Set.* Original broadcasts 1958–73. Distributed by Kulture, West Long Branch, New Jersey.

Cotinier, Hélèna, and Pierre-Nicolas Durand. *It's Not a Gun.* France, 2006.

Said, Edward. *In Search of Palestine: Edward Said's Return Home.* BBC Worldwide Ltd., British Broadcasting Corporation. London, 1998. http://www.youtube. com/watch?v=ksTgAL-e9yo

Smaczny, Paul, director. *Knowledge Is the Beginning: Daniel Barenboim and the West-Eastern Divan Orchestra.* Berlin: EuroArts Music International, 2005.

Tolan, Sandy. "From Stones to Songs." NPR, *Weekend Edition*, March 1998.

——. "Ramzi's Story," NPR, *Weekend Edition*, June 2010.

Unpublished Works

Cook, Lindsey Fielder. "A Journey Through Palestine and Israel, 1987–1997."

Coulter, Tracy. "Healing Trauma with Music: A Qualitative Study on How People Have Used Music in Their Personal Healing Journey from Trauma." A thesis submitted in partial fulfillment of the requirements for the degree of Master of Arts in the Department of Educational Psychology and Leadership Studies, University of Victoria, 2010.

Books

Abu-Sharif, Bassam. *Best of Enemies.* (Boston: Little, Brown & Co.), 1995.

Abunimah, Ali. *One Country: A Bold Proposal to End the Israeli-Palestinian Impasse.* (New York: Metropolitan Books), 2006.

Aburish, Said K. *Arafat: From Defender to Dictator.* (New York and London: Bloomsbury), 1995.

Adorno, Theodor W. *In Search of Wagner.* (London: Verso), 2005.

Ahimeir, Ora, and Marshall J. Breger, eds. *Jerusalem: A City and Its Future.* (Syracuse: Syracuse University Press), 2002.

Armstrong, Karen. *Jerusalem: One City, Three Faiths.* (New York: Ballantine Books, Reprint), 1997.

Ashkenasi, Abraham. *The Future of Jerusalem.* (New York: Peter Lang), 1999.

Baramki, Gabi. *Peaceful Resistance: Building a Palestinian University under Occupation.* (London: Pluto Press), 2009.

Barenboim, Daniel. *Everything Is Connected,* ed. Elena Cheah. (London: Orion Books Ltd.), 2008.

Barenboim, Daniel, and Edward Said. *Parallels and Paradoxes: Explorations in Music and Society.* (New York: Vintage), 2004.

Barghouti, Mourid. *I Saw Ramallah.* (London: Bloomsbury), 2005.

Beitler, Ruth Margolies. *The Path to Mass Rebellion: An Analysis of Two Intifadas.* (New York: Lexington Books), 2004.

Benvenisti, Meron. *Sacred Landscape: The Buried History of the Holy Land Since 1948.* (Berkeley: University of California Press), 2002.

Blumenthal, Max. *Goliath: Life and Loathing in Greater Israel.* (New York: Nation Books), 2013.

Breaking the Silence. *Our Harsh Logic: Israeli Soldiers' Testimonies from the Occupied Territories, 2000–2010.* (New York: Metropolitan Books), 2012.

Candaele, Kerry, and Greg Mitchell. *Journeys with Beethoven: Following the Ninth and Beyond.* (New York: Sinclair Books), 2013.

Cheah, Elena. *An Orchestra Beyond Borders.* (London: Verso), 2009.

Cohen, Hillel. *Army of Shadows: Palestinian Collaboration with Zionism, 1917–1948.* (Berkeley: University of California Press), 2009.

Cohen, Michael. "United Nations Discussion on Palestine, 1947." *The Rise of Israel.* Vol. 37. (New York: Garland Publishing, Inc.), 1987.

Cohen, Shaul Ephraim. *The Politics of Planting: Israeli-Palestinian Competition for Control of Land in the Jerusalem Periphery.* (Chicago: University of Chicago Press), 1993.

Collins, John. *Occupied by Memory: The Intifada Generation and the Palestinian State of Emergency.* (New York: NYU Press), 2004.

Cordesman, Anthony. *Lessons of the 2006 Israeli–Hezbollah War.* (Washington, D.C.: Center for Strategic and International Studies), 2007.

Dowty, Alan. *Israel/Palestine*. (Cambridge: Polity Press), 2005.

Friedman, Thomas L. *From Beirut to Jerusalem*. (New York: Doubleday), 1990.

Fuller, Graham E. *A World Without Islam*. (New York: Back Bay Books), 2011.

Gazit, Shlomo. *Trapped Fools: Thirty Years of Israeli Policy in the Territories*. (London: Frank Cass), 2003.

Gelber, Yoav. *Palestine 1948: War, Escape and Emergence of the Palestinian Refugee Problem*. (Brighton: Sussex Academic Press), 2001.

Gendzier, Irene. "The Political Legacy of Edward Said." *The Logos Reader: Rational Radicalism and the Future of Politics*. (Lexington: University Press of Kentucky), 2006.

Glubb, John Bagot. *A Soldier with the Arabs.*(London: Hodder and Stoughton), 1957.

Grimm, Robert T. *Notable American Philanthropists: Bibliographies of Giving and Volunteering*. (Westport, CT: Greenwood Publishing Group), 2002.

Halper, Jeff. *An Israeli in Palestine: Resisting Dispossession, Redeeming Israel*. (London and Ann Arbor: Pluto Press), 2008.

Hammer, Juliane. *Palestinians Born in Exile: Diaspora and the Search for a Homeland*. (Austin: University of Texas Press), 2004.

Hass, Amira. *Reporting from Ramallah: An Israeli Journalist in an Occupied Land*. (Los Angeles and New York: Semiotext(e)), 2003.

Hawthorne, Susan, and Bronwyn Winter. *September 11, 2001: Feminist Perspectives*. (North Melbourne: Spinifex Press), 2002.

Heikal, Mohamed. *Secret Channels: The Inside Story of Arab-Israeli Peace Negotiations*. (London: HarperCollins Publishers), 1996.

Herzog, Chaim. *The Arab-Israeli Wars*. (New York: Random House), 1984.

Hiro, Dilip: *Sharing the Promised Land: A Tale of Israelis and Palestinians*. (Brooklyn, NY and Northampton, MA: Olive Branch Press), 1999.

Hirst, David. *The Gun and the Olive Branch: The Roots of Violence in the Middle East*. (New York: Nation Books), 2003.

Indyk, Martin. *Innocent Abroad: An Intimate Account of American Peace Diplomacy in the Middle East*. (New York: Simon and Schuster), 2009.

Jones, Clive. *Soviet Jewish Aliyah: Impact and Implications for Israel and the Middle East*. (Abingdon, Oxford: Routledge), 2013.

Kabha, M., and N. Sirhan. *Lexicon of Commanders, Rebellions and Volunteers of the Palestinian 1936–1939 Revolt*. (Dar al Huda: Kafr Qari'), 2009.

Kern, Kathleen. *As Resident Aliens: Christian Peacemaker Teams in the West Bank, 1995–2005*. (Eugene, OR: Wipf and Stock Publishers), 2000.

Khalidi, Rashid. *Brokers of Deceit: How the U.S. Has Undermined Peace in the Middle East.* (Boston: Beacon Press), 2013.

———. *Palestinian Identity: The Construction of a Modern National Consciousness.* (New York: Columbia University Press), 1997.

Khalidi, Walid. *All That Remains: The Palestinian Villages Occupied and Depopulated by Israel in 1948.* (Beirut: Institute for Palestine Studies), 2006.

———. *Before Their Diaspora: A Photographic History of the Palestinians.* (Washington, D.C.: Institute for Palestine Studies), 2010.

Kimche, David, and Jon Kimche. *A Clash of Destinies: The Arab-Jewish War and the Founding of the State of Israel.* (New York: Frederick A. Praeger), 1960.

Kretzmer, David. *The Occupation of Justice: The Supreme Court of Israel and the Occupied Territories.* (New York: SUNY), 2002.

Levi, Erik. *Music in the Third Reich.* (New York: St. Martin's Press), 1996.

Magee, Bryan. *Aspects of Wagner.* (Oxford: Oxford University Press), 1988.

Makdisi, Saree. *Palestine Inside Out: An Everyday Occupation.* (New York: W.W. Norton), 2008.

Masalhah, Nur. *Expulsion of the Palestinians: The Concept of "Transfer" in Zionist Political Thought, 1882–1948.* (Washington, D.C.: Institute for Palestine Studies), 1992.

McDonald, David A. *My Voice Is My Weapon: Music, Nationalism, and the Poetics of Palestinian Resistance.* (Durham, NC: Duke University Press), 2013.

Mearsheimer, John, and Stephen Walt. *The Israel Lobby and U.S. Foreign Policy.* (New York: Farrar, Straus and Giroux), 2008.

Morris, Benny. *1948 and After: Israel and the Palestinians.* (Oxford: Clarendon Press), 1994.

———. *Righteous Victims: A History of the Zionist-Arab Conflict, 1881–2001.* (New York: Vintage), 2001.

———. *The Birth of the Palestinian Refugee Problem Revisited.* (Cambridge: Cambridge University Press), 2004.

Mutawi, Samir A. *Jordan in the 1967 War.* (Cambridge: Cambridge University Press), 1987.

Neslen, Arthur. *In Your Eyes a Sandstorm: Ways of Being Palestinian.* (Los Angeles: University of California Press), 2011.

Norman, Julie. *The Second Palestinian Intifada: Civil Resistance.* (Oxford: Taylor & Francis), 2010.

Olson, Pamela. *Fast Times in Palestine: A Love Affair with a Homeless Homeland.* (Berkeley: Seal Press), 2013.

Ophir, Adi, Michal Givoni, and Sari Hanafi. *The Power of Exclusive Inclusion: Anatomy of Israeli Rule in the Occupied Palestinian Territories.* (New York: Zone Books), 2009.

Pappe, Ilan: *A History of Modern Palestine: One Land, Two Peoples.* (Cambridge: Cambridge University Press), 2004.

Pearlman, Wendy. *Occupied Voices: Stories of Everyday Life from the Second Intifada.* (New York: Nation Books), 2003.

Plaw, Avery. *Targeting Terrorists: A License to Kill?.* (Surrey: Ashgate), 2008.

Qabbani, Nizar. *On Entering the Sea: The Erotic and Other Poetry of Nizar Qabbani.* Translated from the Arabic by Lena Jayyuzi and Sharif Elmusa, with Naomi Shihab Nye et al. (New York: Interlink Books), 1996.

Quandt, William. *Peace Process: American Diplomacy and the Arab-Israeli Conflict Since 1967.* (Washington, D.C.: Brookings Institution Press and the University of California Press), 2005.

Raheb, Mitri. *Palestinian Christians in the West Bank: Facts, Figures and Trends.* (Bethlehem: Diyar), 2012.

Rice, Condoleezza. *No Higher Honor: A Memoir of My Years in Washington.* (New York: Broadway Paperbacks), 2012.

Sacco, Joe. *Palestine.* (Seattle: Fantagraphic Books), 2001.

Said, Edward W. *The End of the Peace Process: Oslo and After.* (New York: Random House), 2000.

———. *From Oslo to Iraq and the Road Map: Essays.* (New York: Vintage), 2005.

———. *Out of Place: A Memoir.* (New York: Alfred A. Knopf), 1999.

———. *Peace and Its Discontents: Essays on Palestine in the Middle East Peace Process.* (New York: Vintage), 1996.

———. *The Politics of Dispossession: The Struggle for Palestinian Self-Determination, 1969–1994.* (New York: Vintage), 1995.

———. *Representations of the Intellectual.* (New York: Vintage Books), 1996.

Said, Edward W., and Christopher Hitchens. *Blaming the Victims: Spurious Scholarship and the Palestinian Question.* (London and New York: Verso), 1988.

Saldaña, Stephanie. *Bread of Angels: A Journey to Love and Faith.* (New York: Doubleday), 2010.

Sayigh, Yezid. *Armed Struggle and the Search for State: The Palestinian National Movement, 1949–1993.* (Oxford: Clarendon Press), 1997.

Schiff, Zeev, and Ehud Ya'ari. *Intifada: The Palestinian Uprising.* (New York: Simon and Schuster), 1990.

Schonberg, Harold C. *The Lives of the Great Composers*. (London: Abacus), 1997.

Segev, Tom. *1949: The First Israelis*. (New York: Owl Books), 1998.

——. *1967: Israel, the War, and the Year That Transformed the Middle East*. (New York: Metropolitan Books), 2005.

——. *One Palestine, Complete: Jews and Arabs Under the British Mandate*. (New York: Henry Holt and Company), 1999.

Sennott, Charles M. *The Body and the Blood: The Middle East's Vanishing Christians and the Possibility for Peace*. (New York: Public Affairs), 2002.

Shadid, Anthony. *House of Stone: A Memoir of Home, Family, and a Lost Middle East*. (New York: Houghton Mifflin Harcourt Publishing Company), 2012.

Shehadeh, Raja: *Occupation Diaries*. (London: Profile Books Ltd.), 2012.

——. *Palestinian Walks: Notes on a Vanishing Landscape*. (London: Profile Books Ltd.), 2007.

Shiblak, Abbas. *Reintegration of the Palestinian Returnees*. (Bethlehem: Shaml Publication), 1997.

Shlaim, Avi. *Collusion Across the Jordan: King Abdullah, the Zionist Movement, and the Partition of Palestine*. (New York: Columbia University Press), 1988.

——. *The Iron Wall: Israel and the Arab World*. (New York: Norton Publishers), 2000.

——. "The Rise and Fall of the Oslo Peace Process," in Louise Fawcett, ed. *International Relations of the Middle East*. (Oxford: Oxford University Press), 2005.

Sutton, Julie P. *Music, Music Therapy and Trauma: International Perspectives*. (London: Jessica Kingsley Publishers Ltd.), 2002.

Szepesi, Stefan. *Walking Palestine: 25 Journeys in the West Bank*. (New York: Interlink Pub.), 2012.

Thomas, Mark. *Extreme Rambling: Walking Israel's Separation Barrier. For Fun*. (London: Ebury Press), 2011.

Tolan, Sandy. *The Lemon Tree: An Arab, a Jew, and the Heart of the Middle East*. (New York: Bloomsbury), 2006.

Weizman, Eyal. *Hollow Land: Israel's Architecture of Occupation*. (London: Verso), 2012.

Welchman, Lynn. *Beyond the Code: Muslim Family Law and the Shar'i Judiciary in the Palestinian West Bank*. (Cambridge: Kluwer Law International), 2000.

INDEX

A NOTE ON THE AUTHOR

Sandy Tolan is the author of *Me & Hank* and *The Lemon Tree*. As cofounder of Homelands Productions, Tolan has produced dozens of radio documentaries for NPR and PRI. He has also written for more than forty magazines and newspapers. His work has won numerous awards, and he was a 1993 Nieman Fellow at Harvard University and an I.F. Stone Fellow at the UC Berkeley Graduate School of Journalism. He is associate professor at the Annenberg School for Communication and Journalism at USC in Los Angeles.

The author will donate a portion of the books proceeds to Al Kamandjati, for the musical education of children in Palestine. If you would like to make a tax-deductible contribution, please visit alkamandjati.org. For information about Ramzi Aburedwan's music, and to purchase CDs, please go to ramziaburedwan.com.